The importance of the Mongols' impact on the Rus lands has been recognized by many scholars, but its precise nature and extent is very contentious. While diverse opinions exist on the origins and development of Muscovy, the author argues that no society arises *ex nihilo* and that Muscovy is no exception. Ostrowski considers here the outside origins and influences, as well as the indigenous origins and development, in order that the reader may gain a clearer understanding of Muscovy as a political entity, its political institutions and political culture. During the early period of Muscovy (1304–1448) the dominant outside influences came through Byzantium and through the Qipchaq Khanate. The author shows how these imported institutions and practices were modified by Muscovite ecclesiastical and secular leaders, and, in some cases, combined with already existing institutions and practices to meet specifically Muscovite needs. At the same time, Ostrowski also illustrates the different cultures which influenced ecclesiastical and secular institutions. In considering these outside influences here, Ostrowski does not examine Muscovy in traditional isolation but as an integral and important part of world history. This important and challenging study will be of interest to scholars of medieval and early modern Russian and Eurasian history.

Muscovy and the Mongols

Muscovy and the Mongols

Cross-cultural influences on the steppe frontier, 1304–1589

Donald Ostrowski

Harvard University

PUBLISHED BY THE PRESS SYNDICATE OF THE UNIVERSITY OF CAMBRIDGE
The Pitt Building, Trumpington Street, Cambridge, United Kingdom

CAMBRIDGE UNIVERSITY PRESS
The Edinburgh Building, Cambridge CB2 2RU, UK
40 West 20th Street, New York NY 10011–4211, USA
477 Williamstown Road, Port Melbourne, VIC 3207, Australia
Ruiz de Alarcón 13, 28014 Madrid, Spain
Dock House, The Waterfront, Cape Town 8001, South Africa

http://www.cambridge.org

First published 1998
Reprinted 2000
First paperback edition 2002

Typeface Fahmy 10/12 pt.

A catalogue record for this book is available from the British Library

Library of Congress Cataloguing in Publication data
Ostrowski, Donald, 1945–
Muscovy and the Mongols: cross-cultural influences on the steppe frontier,
1304–1589 / Donald Ostrowski.
        p.   cm.
Includes bibliographical references and index.
ISBN 0 521 59085 X (hardback)
1. Mongols – Russia.   2. Russia – History – 1237–1480.   3. Russia – History
Period of consolidation, 1462–1605.   4. Russia – Foreign Influences.   I. Title.
DK90.086   1998   947'.03–dc21   97-21385   CIP

ISBN 0 521 59085 X hardback
ISBN 0 521 89410 7 paperback

To Wren

Contents

Figures and tables

Figures

Tables

Preface

The catalyst for writing a book on this topic was a discussion that ensued from a chance seating next to Janet Rabinowitch, senior editor for Indiana University Press, in November 1993 on a flight from Honolulu after the AAASS (American Association for the Advancement of Slavic Studies) convention. But the concept of the topic itself has deeper roots. It was in S. V. Utechin's seminar at the Pennsylvania State University in the fall of 1970 that I chose to write my seminar paper on Nil Sorskii, and through that research I embarked on the study of Muscovite Church history, which laid the ground for this study. Perhaps the seed was first planted, however, in the fall of 1973 by Edward L. Keenan in his lecture course at Harvard University on Muscovite history. In that course, he eloquently described the sophistication of nomadic society in general and of the Mongols in particular. Yet, despite his best efforts to awaken the sensibility of all his students to this important point, I did not integrate it into my comprehension of Muscovy. Other influences at Harvard University also prodded me in the direction of looking at both Turkic and Byzantine influences. Omeljan Pritsak impressed me with his vision of interpreting East Slavic history within a Eurasian context. And Ihor Ševčenko did his part in pointing again and again to the Byzantine antecedents of Kievan and Muscovite political culture. Yet, somehow my mind remained obdurate.

By the mid-1980s, I had come to realize that I really did not understand Muscovy, that is, the dynamics and inner workings of its society (some might say I still don't). After studying it intermittently between 1965 (when I took Nicholas Riasanovsky's course on early Russian History at the University of California, Berkeley) and 1973 (when I began focusing on my dissertation topic), and since then as the main focus of my research, I found it unsettling to feel that I knew my chosen field of study only superficially at best. Then in the summer of 1987, two events occurred in juxtaposition. I was teaching early Ukrainian history at the Harvard University Summer School and reading Robert O. Crummey's just published history of Muscovy. In the course, I was trying to debunk the view of Ukrainian nationalist historians that Russian government was despotic and the Russians were servile because of the Mongols, while Ukrainians were not because they had escaped the worst influences of the Tatar Yoke. At the same time, I was trying to understand the exact nature of the impact of the Mongols on Muscovy. If not what the Ukrainian nationalist historians were asserting, then what? At that point, I realized that the sources I was relying on for my understanding of Muscovy were mainly the Church sources – chronicles, narrative tales, saints' lives, and so forth – which often denigrated the Tatars. The non-Church sources had a very different perspective, one that did not treat the Tatars as evil, godless, etc., but simply as another people, sometimes friends, sometimes enemies, but certainly equal in every respect. It was here the idea that Professor Keenan had planted in my mind almost fourteen years earlier coalesced with my own research on Muscovite Church history.

I began undertaking a series of research studies, intending to publish them as separate articles. It was the conversation on the plane that brought them together conceptually. The flower (or weed) of that germination and subsequent conversation is the book you have before you.

Various parts of this book I have given as papers or talks at the AAASS Conventions, the Russian Research (now Davis) Center's Historians' Luncheon series, and the Columbia University Seminar series. I would like to thank the audience at all these gatherings for their questions and comments. Individuals who have read versions and drafts of chapters and sections and provided me constructive criticism and encouragement are David Goldfrank, Ellen Hurwitz, John LeDonne, Janet Martin, and Daniel Rowland. My gratitude also goes to Uli Schamiloglu, who provided me a copy of his unpublished monograph, *The Golden Horde: Economy, Society and Civilization in Western Eurasia, 13th and 14th Centuries*. I thank them for the time they spent and for sharing their expertise with me. Elizabeth Wood had members of her Russian history class at MIT read sections of a draft of the book, and I thank her and them for their advice. Special thanks must go to Richard Fisher and Vicky Cuthill of Cambridge University Press for the professional and reassuring manner in which they shepherded a nervous author and his text through the editorial process.

I have tried to apply the principle of "fair use" to the citing of the works of the many scholars who have preceded me. I could not have written this book without the huge amount of research they did. In two cases, I would like to point out for special citation, the works of Daniel Rowland, whose ideas I have borrowed wholesale, and Craig Kennedy, the footnotes of whose thesis I shamelessly plundered for evidence. Wherever I could I have checked their references and made adjustments accordingly, but there should be no doubt that, in regard to the topics they wrote about, I have merely harvested what they sowed and cultivated.

In transliterating names and terms from Cyrillic, I have followed a modified Library of Congress system. In transliterating from the Arabic alphabet, I have followed the system of the *Encyclopedia of Islam* with certain modifications. In transliterating Mongol and Turkic names and terms, I have followed the practice of David Morgan in his book *The Mongols*. In transcribing Chinese, I have used the Pinyin system, providing the Wade-Giles version in parentheses if there is a significant difference. Certain words that have acquired a standard English-language form, such as *tsar* and *boyar*, I have presented that way rather than presenting the "more correct" transliterated version.

I use the term *Qipchaq Khanate* to refer to the western-most component of the Mongol Empire because that term, along with *Ulus of Jochi*, is what it called itself. The term *Golden Horde* does not appear until the seventeenth century, long after the Khanate itself ceased to exist, and then only in Russian sources. Ekaterina Dashkova invoked a popular understanding for the term when she explained in her *Memoirs* that it was called the *Golden Horde* "because it possessed great quantities of gold and the weapons of its people were decorated with it."[1] Another popular explanation is that the term refers to the golden pavilion of the khan. But we do not know why the term was applied to the Khanate. Contemporary Rus' sources usually refer to the Qipchaq Khanate simply as *Orda*, that is, "the Court."

In the Rus' sources, all the steppe peoples, including the Mongols, were referred to as *Tatars*. William of Rubruck, a papal envoy to the Mongol khan in the 1250s, had pointed out in his report that the Mongols did not like to be called *Tatars*, because the Tatars were a tribe who lived on the border of China next to, and separate from, the Mongols.[2] Besides the traditional hostility between the Tatars and Mongols, the Mongols had another reason for not wanting to be referred to as Tatars. The Tatars had killed Chingiz Khan's father Yisëgu. In European sources, the Mongols and other steppe peoples were called *Tartars*. But as early as the 1240s, according to Salimbene de Parma,

[1] Ekaterina Dashkova, *The Memoirs of Princess Dashkova*, trans. Kyril Fitzlyon, Durham, NC, Duke University Press, 1995, p. 180.

[2] William of Rubruck, "*Itinerarium*," in *Sinica Franciscana*, vol. 1: *Itinera et relationes fratrum minorum saeculi XIII et XIV*, ed. P. Anastasius van den Wyngaert, Florence, 1929 (hereafter Rubruck, *Itinerarium*), ch. 17, paras. 5–6, p. 208; William of Rubruck, *The Journey of William of Rubruck to the Eastern Parts of the World 1253–55*, trans. William Woodville Rockhill, London, Hakluyt Society, 1900 (hereafter Rubruck, *Journey* [Rockhill]), pp. 111–116; William of Rubruck, *The Mission of Friar William of Rubruck: His Journey to the Court of the Great Khan Möngke 1253–1255*, trans. Peter Jackson, London, Hakluyt Society, 1990 (hereafter Rubruck, *Mission* [Jackson]), pp. 124–125.

John of Plano Carpini had mentioned that there should be no medial "r" in Tatar.[3] The instructions of Rubruck and Carpini, however, have had little effect on conventional usage. Insofar as possible I use *Mongols* when I am referring to the Mongols themselves and *Tatars* when referring to steppe peoples in general from the Muscovite, especially Rus' Church, point of view. Otherwise, I have tried to be as specific as I could in referring to particular tribes or people.

I use the term "Eurasia" in the dictionary sense to mean Europe and Asia considered together as one land mass. I do not intend any political meaning thereby, such as that area that was governed by the Russian Empire or the Soviet Union. I maintain a distinction between the term *fictive kinship*, which describes the ruler's relationship to his subjects, and *metaphorical kinship*, which is a diplomatic relationship among sovereign rulers, such as the Byzantine "family of princes." Insofar as possible, given variations in the sources and the inexactitudes of transliteration, I present personal names in a form as close to the original as I can figure them out to be.

Finally, any book needs to be selective to a degree. I have tried to present not only evidence that supports my contentions but also evidence that would seem to refute them. But I am sure others will point out evidence I overlooked or did not understand the significance of. Such "pointings out" are to be welcomed, for that is how scholarship advances. I am well aware that I have not been as exhaustive as some (myself included) would have liked in discussing all aspects of Muscovite life, culture, and politics. Of necessity, I could not be because I wanted to present a conceptualization, an interpretation, of this period of Russian historical development. I could not go into detail, or in some cases even discuss in passing, such phenomena as the early conflicts among the various city-state principalities in northern Rus', Lithuanian–Muscovite relations, the impact of Lithuanian émigrés on the Muscovite court, the dynastic crisis of 1497, etc. I could not do so because the focus of the book is the Mongol impact on the Muscovite polity and the different ways that the ecclesiastical and secular establishments of that polity reacted to it. In the end, however, this book is to be considered merely a work in progress, which has reached but a relative level of completeness. I welcome any comments and suggestions that will improve it and thereby increase our understanding.

Don Ostrowski
don@wjh.harvard.edu

[3] Salimbene de Parma, *The Chronicle of Salimbene de Adam*, trans. Joseph L. Baird, Binghamton, NY, Medieval and Renaissance Texts and Studies, no. 40, 1986, p. 197.

Abbreviations

AAE	*Akty, sobrannye v bibliotekakh i arkhivakh Rossiiskoi imperii Arkheograficheskoi ekspeditsiei imperatorskoi Akademii nauk*
AAASS	American Association for the Advancement of Slavic Studies
AFED	N. A. Kazakova and Ia. S. Lur'e, *Antifeodal'nye ereticheskie dvizheniia na Rusi XIV – nachala XVI veka*
AI	*Akty istoricheskie, sobrannye i izdannye Arkheograficheskoi komissiei*
ChOIDR	*Chteniia v Obshchestve istorii i drevnostei rossiiskikh pri Moskovskom universitete*, Moscow, 1845–1918
CSHB	Corpus scriptorum historiae byzantinae
DDG	*Dukhovnye i dogovornyie gramoty velikikh i udel'nykh kniazei XIV–XVI vv*
GIM	Gosudarstvennyi istoricheskii muzei
MERSH	*Modern Encyclopedia of Russian and Soviet History*
MGH	*Monumenta Germaniae Historica*
NPL	*Novgorodskaia pervaia letopis'. Starshego i mladshego izvodov*
PamSRL	*Pamiatniki starinnoi russkoi literatury*
PDS	*Pamiatniki diplomaticheskikh snoshenii drevnei Rossii s derzhavami inostrannymi*
PFEH	*Papers on Far Eastern History*
PG	*Patrologiae cursus completus. Series Graeca*
PL	*Patrologiae cursus completus. Series Latina*
PLDR	*Pamiatniki literatury drevnei Rusi*
PRP	*Pamiatniki russkogo prava*
PSRL	*Polnoe sobranie russkikh letopisei*
PSZRI	*Polnoe sobranie zakonov Rossiiskoi imperii*
RFA	*Russkii feodal'nyi arkhiv. XIV–pervoi treti XVI veka*
RGB	Russkaia gosudarstvennaia biblioteka
RIB	*Russkaia istoricheskaia biblioteka*
RNB	Russkaia natsional'naia biblioteka
SGGD	*Sobranie gosudarstvennykh gramot i dogovorov khraniashchikhsia v gosudarstvennoi kollegii inostrannykh del*

SRIO	*Sbornik Imperatorskogo Russkogo istoricheskogo obshchestva*
TL	*Troitskaia letopis'*
TODRL	*Trudy Otdela drevnerusskoi literatury*
VMCh	*Velikie minei chetii*

Introduction: understanding Muscovy

Scholars have expressed remarkably diverse opinions on the origins and development of Muscovy. It is fair to say that no consensus exists on the formation of Muscovite institutions, and by extension the development of Muscovite political culture.[1] Nor does it appear likely that there will be a consensus in the near future.

In studying Muscovy, one confronts, in addition to the wide-ranging and often diametrically opposed interpretations of historians, a scarcity of primary source material and often contradictory information in those sources that do exist. If all or most of the interpretations about Muscovy can be supported by evidence, then the diametrically opposed views must result from giving different weight to that evidence, that is, of emphasizing some aspects and dismissing other aspects of the testimony of the primary sources. Therefore, unless we are prepared to continue to deny categorically the contributions of all but a narrow range of studies and evidence that agrees with our own view, we would be well advised to formulate a framework for the study of Muscovite history to cope both with the source problem and with the historiographic problem. By establishing the delimiters of the historiographic tradition, we might better be able to understand that problem, and, thereby, the source problem as well. The following section is not intended to be an exhaustive survey, but one that only characterizes the positions of the different interpretive camps.

I

At one extreme in the historiography are those who believe Muscovite institutions are indigenously "Russian," that in part they were continua-

---

[1] By "political culture" I mean the totality of institutions, attitudes, concepts, and practices connected with the running of a polity. In Muscovy, we have some information about institutions and practices and we have Church writings concerning ideology, but we have to extrapolate from these the attitudes that were operative at any particular time. For a discussion of the concept "political culture," see Keith Michael Baker, "Introduction," in *The French Revolution and the Creation of Modern Political Culture*, 4

tions of Kievan institutions and that in part they were created to meet uniquely Muscovite needs. This interpretation does not admit that "outside" influences, especially that of the Mongols, had any impact. S. M. Solov'ev represented this point of view when he wrote: "we have no reason to assume any great influence [of the Mongols] on [Russia's] internal administration as we do not see any traces of it."[2] S. F. Platonov carried this argument further:

And how could the Tatar influence on Rus' life be considerable when the Tatars lived far off, did not mix with the Rus', and appeared in Russia only to gather tribute or as an army, brought in for the most part by Rus' princes for the princes' own purposes? . . . Therefore, we can proceed to consider the internal life of Rus' society in the thirteenth century without paying attention to the fact of the Tatar yoke.[3]

Both Solov'ev and Platonov were referring specifically to the thirteenth century, but this principle holds for later centuries in their work as well. B. D. Grekov and A. Iu. Iakubovskii also categorically denied any direct influence of the Mongols on Muscovy, but they did see an indirect result: "The Russian state with Moscow at its head was created not with the assistance of the Tatars but in the process of a hard struggle of the Russian people against the yoke of the Golden Horde."[4] We can compare this view with N. M. Karamzin's statement about the Mongol invasion that "the calamity was a blessing in disguise, for the destruction contained the boon of unity. . . Another hundred years of princely feuds. What would have been the result . . . Moscow, in fact, owes its greatness to the khans."[5] The proponents of this interpretation credited the positive result of this struggle to the Russian people. Nicholas Riasanovsky, in his widely used textbook, expressed a negative variant of this interpretation:

It is tempting, thus, to return to the older view and to consider the Mongols as of little significance in Russian history. On the other hand, their destructive impact deserves attention. And they, no doubt, contributed something to the general harshness of the age and to the burdensome and exacting nature of the centralizing Muscovite state which emerged out of this painful background.[6]

vols., ed. Keith Michael Baker and Colin Lucas, Oxford, Pergamon, 1987–1991, vol. 1: *The Political Culture of the Old Regime*, pp. xi–xiii.

[2] S. M. Solov'ev, *Istoriia Rossii s drevneishikh vremen*, 15 vols., Moscow, Sotsialnaia-ekonomicheskaia literatura, 1960–1966, vol. 2, p. 489.

[3] S. F. Platonov, *Lektsii po russkoi istorii*, 3 vols., St. Petersburg, Stolichnaia staropechatnia, 1899, vol. 1, p. 85.

[4] B. D. Grekov and A. Iu. Iakubovskii, *Zolotaia Orda i ee padenie*, Moscow and Leningrad, Akademiia nauk SSSR, 1950, p. 256.

[5] N. M. Karamzin, *Istoriia gosudarstva rossiiskogo*, 5th edn., 12 vols., St. Petersburg, Eduard Prats, 1842–1843, vol. 5, p. 223.

[6] Nicholas Riasanovsky, *A History of Russia*, 4th edn., New York, Oxford University Press, 1984, p. 76.

V. I. Koretskii reiterated this negative assessment of the Mongol impact on Russian development: "The Mongol Yoke and its effects were among the main reasons why Russia became a backward country in comparison with several of the countries of western Europe."[7] The strength of this interpretation is indicated by the fact that it appears even in the work of Eurasian historians, like George Vernadsky, who have done as much as anyone to define positive aspects of Mongol influence on Muscovy. At one point in his volume on the Mongols, Vernadsky wrote: "inner Russian political life was never stifled but only curbed and deformed by Mongol rule."[8] In a variant of this interpretation, the impact of the Mongols is seen not only as destructive of Russian society and political culture but also as detrimental to the development of the Russians themselves. The military historian Christopher Duffy summed up such views this way:

The princes of Muscovy became the most enthusiastic and shameless of the Mongol surrogates and much that was distinctive and unattractive about the Russian character and Russian institutions has been attributed to this experience. Mongol influence has been held variously responsible for the destruction of the urban classes, the brutalisation of the peasantry, a denial of human dignity, and a distorted sense of values which reserved a special admiration for ferocity, tyrannical ways and slyness.[9]

[7] V. I. Koretskii, "Mongol Yoke in Russia," in *Modern Encyclopedia of Russian and Soviet History (MERSH)*, ed. Joseph L. Wieczynski, Gulf Breeze, FL, Academic International Press, 54 vols., 1976–1990, vol. 23, p. 47. For a survey of the Soviet historiographical denial of any positive influence from the Mongols, see Charles J. Halperin, "Soviet Historiography on Russia and the Mongols," *Russian Review*, vol. 41, 1982, pp. 306–322.

[8] George Vernadsky, *A History of Russia*, 5 vols., New Haven, CT, Yale University Press, 1943–1969, vol. 3, *The Mongols and Russia*, p. 344.

[9] Christopher Duffy, *Russia's Military Way to the West: Origins and Nature of Russian Military Power 1700–1800*, London, Routledge & Kegan Paul, 1981, p. 2. The Russians are not the only ones who have been seen as victims of such influence. Recently, John Keegan blamed Mongol influence for the ruthless ferocity of the Spanish *Reconquista* against Islam and for the massacres by the Spanish conquistadores of the Aztecs and Incas. Keegan reasoned that the Mongols brought ruthless ferocity to the Muslims, who in turn introduced it to the Crusaders, who in turn brought it back with them when they returned from the Holy Land, so that it eventually found its way into Spain: "it is not fanciful to suggest that the awful fate of the Incas and Aztecs . . . at the hand of the Spanish conquistadors ultimately harked back to Genghis himself." John Keegan, *A History of Warfare*, New York, Alfred A. Knopf, 1994, p. 214. Not only is it "fanciful," but Keegan's construct is one of the most fanciful I have ever come across in historical study. Ruthless ferocity is one characteristic that individuals within ethnic groups seem quite capable of developing on their own without foreign borrowing or imposition. But if anyone introduced ruthless ferocity to anyone, it is more likely the Crusaders who introduced it to the Muslims rather than vice versa. Contemporary Islamic accounts treat the Crusaders as barbarians not only because of their low cultural attainments but also because of their savage behavior. See Francesco Gabrieli, *Arab Historians of the Crusades*, trans. E. J. Costello, London, Routledge & Kegan Paul, 1969. Eyewitness Christian accounts tend to confirm the Islamic assessment. See, e.g., Raymond of

And the historian and journalist Harrison Salisbury commented in 1969: "It is current history. Russia still struggles against the legacy of backwardness, ignorance, servility, submissiveness, deceit, cruelty, oppression, and lies imposed by the terrible Mongols."[10] Since these historians rarely cite evidence to support their accusations of nefarious Mongol influence, one begins to suspect we are encountering here their own anti-Mongol biases.

It has been somewhat easier to argue that the Mongols had little or no impact than to argue the same for Byzantium. Yet, Edward L. Keenan, who in general accepts the idea that there were outside influences on Muscovy, has categorically denied any specific influence of Byzantium on Muscovite political culture: "To seek evidence of influential links between modern Russia or even Muscovite political culture and that of Kiev or Byzantium is, in my view, futile."[11] Keenan went on to write:

It cannot be demonstrated, for example, that during its formative period (i.e., 1450–1500) Muscovite political culture was significantly influenced either by the form or by the practice of Byzantine political culture or ideology. Nor is there convincing evidence that any powerful Muscovite politician or political group was conversant with Byzantine political culture, except perhaps as the latter was reflected in the ritual and organization of the Orthodox Church, which itself had little practical political importance in early Muscovy and little *formative* impact upon Russian political behavior.[12]

Other scholars have asserted that the overall impact of the Church has been a negative one. Francis Thomson is perhaps the most vociferous of present-day scholars who see a stultifying impact of the Church: "It was not the Mongols who were responsible for Russia's intellectual isolation . . . it was the Church."[13] This view echoes that of Russian liberals of

---

Aguilers' description of the massacre of Muslims and Jews when the Crusaders took Jerusalem in 1099. Raymond D'Aguilers, *Historia Francorum qui ceperunt Jerusalem* in *Recueil des historiens des Croisades. Historiens occidentaux*, 5 vols., Paris, Imprimerie Royale, 1844–1895, vol. 3, p. 300. According to Runciman, "it was this bloodthirsty proof of Christian fanaticism that recreated the fanaticism of Islam." Steven Runciman, *A History of the Crusades*, 3 vols., Cambridge University Press, 1951, vol. 1, p. 287. In a remarkable display of historical oversight, Keegan glosses over this and other outrageous atrocities committed by the Crusaders against Muslims and Jews long before Chingiz Khan was even born. Keegan, *History*, pp. 291–292.

[10] Harrison E. Salisbury, *War Between Russia and China*, New York, W. W. Norton, 1969, p. 31.

[11] Edward L. Keenan, "Muscovite Political Folkways," *Russian Review*, vol. 45, 1986, p. 118.

[12] Keenan, "Muscovite Political Folkways," p. 118.

[13] Francis J. Thomson, "The Nature of the Reception of Christian Byzantine Culture in Russia in the Tenth to Thirteenth Centuries and Its Implications for Russian Culture," *Slavica Gandensia*, vol. 5, 1978, p. 120.

the early twentieth century, like Paul Miliukov,[14] and the writings of
Richard Pipes to the effect that the Church had squandered its ideals,
sold out to the state in return for being allowed to keep its wealth, and
that "[t]he ultimate result of the policies of the Russian Orthodox
Church was not only to discredit it in the eyes of those who cared for
social and political justice, but to create a spiritual vacuum."[15] The next
step in the historiography was to combine the two negative attitudes, the
anti-Mongol and the anti-Church, as Cyril Toumanoff did: "The
Mongol temporal 'Iron Curtain' completed the Byzantine spiritual
one."[16]

The indigenous-origin interpretation is an inherently Manichaean
one. If the proponents of this model allow for any outside influence, that
influence is, by definition, negative or destructive. Everything that is
positive and constructive comes from within Muscovy; everything that is
negative and destructive comes from without. In this interpretation,
social and administrative structures seem to spring up like mushrooms
after a rain, then disappear just as suddenly. They rise and fall, without
any apparent rationale. Furthermore, we then have difficulty in making
structural comparisons of Muscovite society with other traditional
societies in order to gain insights, because Muscovy is presented as
being totally different from any other society.

Numerous examples exist in the historiography to show that concen-
tration on the indigenous-origin model and the concomitant refusal to
look outside Muscovy for possible influence can lead scholars to faulty
interpretations. One small example and one large example should be
sufficient to illustrate this point. First, the small example: grand-princely
seals of the late fifteenth and sixteenth centuries depict a beardless man
in a tunic on horseback slaying a dragon by means of a spear [17] Some
scholars, after pointing out that there is no halo, have asserted that the

[14] See Paul Miliukov, "The Religious Tradition," in *Russia and Its Crisis*, University of
Chicago Press, 1906, pp. 65–130.
[15] Richard Pipes, *Russia Under the Old Regime*, New York, Charles Scribner's Sons, 1974,
p. 245; see also *ibid.*, pp. 233–234.
[16] Cyril Toumanoff, "Moscow the Third Rome: Genesis and Significance of a Politico-
Religious Idea," *Catholic Historical Review*, vol. 40, 1954/55, p. 433. The appeal of this
notion of a dual Byzantine- and Mongol-induced isolation of Russia can be seen in the
fact that it has been used by some textbook writers, along with Russia's geographical
distance from western Europe, to explain the limited European influence during this
period. See, e.g., Anthony Esler, *The Human Venture: a World History from Prehistory to
the Present*, 2nd edn., Englewood Cliffs, NJ, Prentice Hall, 1992, p. 449.
[17] *Snimki drevnikh russkikh pechatei*, 2 vols., Moscow, Komissiia pechataniia gosudarstvennykh gramot i dogorov, 1880, vol. 1, seals nos. 1–7, and 9. These seals date from the
reigns of Ivan III, Vasilii III, and Ivan IV. This same figure appears on Muscovite coins
of the period. From the spear (*kop'e*) that the horseman is carrying we obtain the term
"kopeck" (*kopeika*).

figure is a "tsar on horseback," most likely a representation of the grand prince himself.[18] Yet, as early as 1880, Baron Théodore de Bühler had discussed the improbability of the grand prince's being represented as a half-dressed and beardless youth. Instead, Bühler identified the figure with St. George the Dragonslayer in Byzantine icons.[19] More recently, Robert Croskey pointed out that saints in Byzantine icons were not always shown with halos and that a halo around the head of the rider would have interrupted the inscription on the seal.[20] It is clear that the representation cannot be that of the tsar or grand prince of Muscovy and must be that of St. George in Byzantine icons. Gustave Alef recognized the similarity between the representation of this figure on the seal and that of St. George in a Novgorod icon of the late fourteenth or early fifteenth century.[21] And when we recall that St. George was the name saint of Iurii Dolgorukii, traditionally regarded as the founder of Moscow, and that Iurii built churches dedicated to St. George in Vladimir and Iuriev-Polskii in 1152,[22] it becomes abundantly clear that an attempt to disregard the Byzantine antecedents of Muscovite culture has led some scholars to propose and defend an untenable position.

Now, the large example: a number of historians have been trying for some time to find linkages between Judaism and the Novgorod–Moscow heresy of the late fifteenth and early sixteenth centuries. Yet, all such attempts have failed.[23] The reason these historians are seeking such

[18] E. I. Kamentseva and N. V. Ustiugov, *Russkaia sfragistika i geral'dika*, Moscow, Vysshaia shkola, 1963, pp. 111–113; G. V. Vilinbakhov, "Vsadnik russkogo gerba," *Trudy Gosudarstvennogo Ermitazha*, vol. 21, *Numismatika*, vol. 5, 1981, pp. 117–122.

[19] Fedor Biuler [Baron Théodore de Bühler], "Predislovie," *Snimki drevnikh russkikh pechatei*, vol. 1, p. XVII.

[20] See Robert M. Croskey, *Muscovite Diplomatic Practice in the Reign of Ivan III*, New York, Garland, 1987, pp. 202–204.

[21] Gustave Alef, "The Adoption of the Muscovite Two-Headed Eagle: a Discordant View," *Speculum*, vol. 41, 1966, p. 1; repr. in Gustave Alef, *Rulers and Nobles in Fifteenth-Century Muscovy*, London, Variorum, 1983, item 9. Cf. *Istoriia russkogo iskusstva*, 13 vols., Moscow, Nauka, 1954–1964, vol. 2, illustration facing p. 220 (see also pp. 133 and 235). Cf. Konrad Onasch, *Ikonen*, Berlin, Gütersloher Verlagshaus, 1961, plates 67 and 126.

[22] For his building the church in Vladimir, see *Polnoe sobranie russkikh letopisei* (*PSRL*), 40 vols., St. Petersburg/Petrograd/Leningrad and Moscow, Arkheograficheskaia komissiia, Nauka, and Arkheograficheskii tsentr, 1843–1995, vol. 4, p. 8; vol. 7, p. 57; vol. 9, pp. 196–197; and vol. 24, p. 77. For his building the church in Iuriev-Polskii, see *PSRL*, vol. 4, p. 8; vol. 9, p. 196; vol. 15, pt. 2, cols. 219–220; and vol. 28, pp. 32, 187. For a detailed discussion of the church itself, see N. N. Voronin, *Zodchestva severovostochnoi Rusi XII–XV vekov*, 2 vols., Moscow, Akademiia nauk SSSR, 1962, vol. 2, pp. 68–107. The Compilation of the End of the Fifteenth Centry states that he built a church in Suzdal' dedicated to St. George also in 1152. *PSRL*, vol. 25, p. 56. But this entry may be a mistake on the part of the scribe. See also Voronin, *Zodchestva severovostochnoi Rusi*, vol. 1, pp. 91–100.

[23] See Ia. S. Lur'e [Jakov S. Luria], "Unresolved Issues in the History of the Ideological Movements of the Late Fifteenth Century," in *Medieval Russian Culture*, ed. Henrik

connections is the reference by Archbishop Gennadii and later Church writers to the heretics as Judaizers. But referring to heretics generically as "Jews" and "Judaizers" was commonplace among Byzantine Church writers, even if there was no Jewish influence.[24] It was most likely through the works of John of Damascus that the Byzantine theory of all heresies deriving ultimately from either Judaism or paganism reached Rus'.[25] Not understanding this usage has led many scholars on a wild goose chase to demonstrate a connection between the Novgorod–Moscow heretics and some Hebrew texts that had recently been translated into Ruthenian.

Proponents of the indigenous model have little difficulty in saying they see no influence even when the evidence is overwhelmingly in favor of the influence. A. N. Kirpichnikov, for example, denied any influence of the Mongol army on the Muscovite army.[26] Yet, the Mongol army was the mightiest war machine of its time. To argue that Muscovite military leaders did not borrow from the superior strategies, tactics, and weaponry of the Mongols makes the Muscovites appear not only ignorant but obstinate. Likewise, to argue that Muscovite leaders did not borrow administrative techniques of the largest and most efficiently run empire of the time tends to denigrate their abilities (as though they were incapable of doing so). In short, it is too facile for historians to deny outside influence on Muscovy as long as they continue to succumb to their own mindsets rather than test their beliefs against the evidence.

Likewise, failure to integrate Muscovite history into world history risks keeping the Muscovite field arcane and obsolete. If we maintain Muscovy as completely *sui generis*, then we certainly have a history, but one that no one will be interested in except as a quaint curiosity. As a result, those who write integrative histories[27] will feel free to ignore Muscovy or continue to write the old shibboleths about it and its political culture.

At the other extreme in the historiography are those who believe

Birnbaum and Michael S. Flier, Berkeley, University of California Press, 1984, pp. 150–163.

[24] Steven B. Bowman, *The Jews of Byzantium, 1204–1453*, Birmingham, University of Alabama Press, 1985, pp. 29–30.

[25] Jana Howlett [Ia. R. Khoulett], "Svidetel'stvo arkhiepiskopa Gennadiia o eresi 'novgorodskikh eretikov zhidovskaia mudr''stvuiushchikh'," *Trudy Otdela drevnerusskoi literatury (TODRL)*, vol. 46, 1993, pp. 64–65.

[26] A. N. Kirpichnikov, "Fakty, gipotezy i zabluzhdeniia v izuchenii russkoi voennoi istorii XIII–XV vv.," *Drevneishie gosudarstva na territorii SSSR. Materialy i issledovaniia 1984 god*, Moscow, Nauka, 1985, pp. 233–234 fn. 18 and p. 238 fn. 31.

[27] Joseph Fletcher sketched an outline for such a history in his "Integrative History: Parallels and Interconnections in the Early Modern Period, 1500–1800," *Journal of Turkish Studies*, vol. 9, 1985, pp. 37–57.

Muscovite institutions are all imports. This interpretation tends to see Muscovy as being an imitation of other societies, in particular Byzantine, Mongol, or European. The image of Muscovy as a variant of Byzantine culture was expressed definitively by Dimitri Obolensky:

the attempt to identify and describe the local "recensions" which Byzantine civilisation underwent in medieval Russia is, like the recognition of distinctive styles in art, a worthwhile undertaking, however tentative its outcome may be. In the last resort, however, these local variations may well prove, from the historian's viewpoint, to be less significant than the pattern of values, beliefs, and intellectual and aesthetic experience which, in common with other peoples of Eastern Europe, the Russians of the Middle Ages acquired from Byzantium.[28]

Other scholars also share this viewpoint. John Meyendorff wrote that "nothing in Russian medieval culture and society can be fully explained without reference to the Byzantine inheritance."[29] One of the earliest propagators of this line of interpretation was A. A. Kunik, who asked: "Is it not so, generally speaking, that the greater part of Russian history is the reflection of the history of Byzantium?"[30]

In contrast, the Eurasianists have adopted the Mongol model. Nicholas Trubetskoi, for example, asserted that "the Russian state . . . is the inheritor, the successor, the continuator of the historical work of Chingiz Khan."[31] And George Vernadsky has stated that Muscovy "in a sense, might be considered an offspring of the Mongol Empire."[32] While accepting the destructiveness of the initial Mongol invasions and negative aspects of Tatar hegemony, Vernadsky discussed a number of positive Mongol influences on administration and the army.[33] One of the most visible of those who have argued in favor of the Mongol model has been Karl Wittfogel, who wrote: "Tatar rule alone among the three major Oriental influences affecting Russia was decisive both in destroying the non-Oriental Kievan society and in laying the foundations

[28] Dimitri Obolensky, "The Relations Between Byzantium and Russia (Eleventh to Fifteenth Century)," *XIII International Congress of Historical Sciences. Moscow, August 16–23, 1970*, Moscow, Nauka, 1970, p. 12.
[29] John Meyendorff, "The Byzantine Impact on Russian Civilization," in *Windows on the Russian Past: Essays on Soviet Historiography Since Stalin*, ed. Samuel H. Baron and Nancy W. Heer, Columbus, OH, American Association for the Advancement of Slavic Studies, 1977, p. 45.
[30] A. A. Kunik, "Pochemu Vizantiia donyne ostaetsia zagadkoi vo vsemirnoi istorii?" *Uchenie zapiski Imp. Akademii nauk po pervomu i tret'emu otdeleniiam*, vol. 2, pt. 3, 1853, p. 441.
[31] Nicholas Trubetskoi [I. R.], *Nasledie Chingiskhana. Vzgliad na russkuiu istoriiu ne s Zapada, a s Vostka*, Berlin, Evraziiskoe izdatel'stvo, 1925, p. 9.
[32] George Vernadsky, "The Scope and Content of Chingis Khan's *Yasa*," *Harvard Journal of Asiatic Studies*, vol. 3, 1938, p. 348.
[33] Vernadsky, *Mongols and Russia*, pp. 344–366.

for the despotic state of Muscovite and post-Muscovite Russia."[34] Likewise, Tibor Szamuely, in his reinterpretation of Russian history, wrote: "The Mongols bequeathed to Muscovy not only their conception of society and of the state, but also the system of government and administration that had served them so well, and that was so admirably fitted to the needs of a large, expanding and powerful state."[35] This model is clearly in conflict with other historiographic models that attribute Muscovite development either solely to indigenous causes or predominantly to Byzantine influence.

Some historians, however, have proposed a model that combines the Byzantine and Mongol influences. This model is what B. H. Sumner must have had in mind when he wrote: "In the make-up of tsarism the ideas and ritual traceable to Byzantine influence were fused with the hard fact and practice of the Tatar khans."[36] Michael Cherniavsky and Francis Dvornik explored this road further.[37] One of the first scholars, as far as I know, to have formulated this line of argument was Hedwig Fleischhacker.[38] She, in turn, may have been influenced by the ideas of the Eurasianists. Trubetskoi had formulated the core of the idea when he wrote that the Russians

had to do away with what was unacceptable, what made it [the Tatar state idea] foreign and hostile. In other words, it had to be separated from its Mongolness and connected with Orthodoxy, so it could be declared as one's own, as Russian. In fulfilling this task, Russian national thought turned to Byzantine state ideas and traditions and in it found the material useful in the religious appropriation and Russification of the Mongolian state system. The ideas of Chinghiz Khan, obscured and eroded during the process of their implementation but still glimmering within the Mongolian state system, once again came to life, but in a completely new, unrecognizable form after they had received a Byzantine–Christian foundation.[39]

He suggested that it was because of the Tatar hegemony that "Byzantine state ideologies, which earlier did not have any particular

[34] Karl Wittfogel, *Oriental Despotism: a Comparative Study of Total Power*, New York, Vintage, 1981, p. 225.

[35] Tibor Szamuely, *The Russian Tradition*, London, Secker & Warburg, 1974, p. 20.

[36] B. H. Sumner, *A Short History of Russia*, New York, Harcourt, 1949, p. 82.

[37] Michael Cherniavsky, "Khan or Basileus: an Aspect of Russian Mediaeval Political Theory," *Journal of the History of Ideas*, vol. 20, 1959, pp. 459–476; reprinted in *The Structure of Russian History: Interpretive Essays*, ed. Michael Cherniavsky, New York, Random House, 1970, pp. 65–79. Cherniavsky, however, like the anti-Mongolists, seems to have equated Asiatic with barbaric, a bias that Dvornik did not exhibit. Francis Dvornik, *The Slavs in European History and Civilization*, New Brunswick, NJ, Rutgers University Press, 1962, pp. 378–380.

[38] Hedwig Fleischhacker, *Russland zwischen zwei Dynastien (1598–1613). Ein Untersuching über die Krise in der obersten Gewalt*, Vienna, Rudolf M. Rohrer, 1933, pp. 17–37.

[39] Trubetskoi, *Nasledie Chingiskhana*, p. 19.

popularity, came to occupy a central place in the Russian national consciousness" and that "these ideologies . . . were needed only to link an idea of the state, Mongolian in origin, to Orthodoxy, thereby making it Russian."[40] To reduce and oversimplify this model somewhat: in articulation of theory, Muscovy was Byzantine; in administrative practice, Mongol. I have found this model helpful in understanding much that otherwise is murky about Muscovy, but I am the first to admit that this model is not sufficient by itself to explain the dynamics of Muscovite society adequately.

A fifth model that has been proposed to explain Muscovy uses Europe as an exemplar. A practitioner of this model is Alexander Yanov, who, in his book on autocracy, wrote: "If . . . Russia [of the sixteenth century] was indeed undergoing significant economic expansion, and in particular a building boom, the necessary preconditions which existed in every European country – such as a free labor market, significant free capital, and judicial protection of private property – must have been present there too."[41] The most influential western European model was supplied by Karl Marx with his stages of historical development of societies: tribal, slave, feudal, bourgeois, all based on nineteenth-century conceptions of western European history. How unsuccessful this model has been is particularly clear in the attempts to deny that Muscovy had slavery,[42] or in attempts to find that Muscovy had feudalism the same as in medieval western Europe.[43]

Thus, any variation between the Muscovite form of the institution or practice and its exemplar is dismissed as no more than a local corruption. These import/variant interpretations are slightly more helpful than concentrating solely on indigenous developments because we can at least begin to make structural-functional comparisons of Muscovite institutions and practices with those in other societies. But it can also be faulted as a uni-dimensional approach that all too easily degenerates into superficial schematizations. To be sure, there are those who would like to make sweeping generalizations about which governments were influenced by the Mongols and which were not. Such generalizations show an ignorance of both Muscovy and the Mongols. For example, Boleslaw Szczesniak, in referring to the Mongol hegemony in Rus', calls

---

[40] Trubetskoi, *Nasledie Chingiskhana*, p. 20.

[41] Alexander Yanov, *The Origins of Autocracy: Ivan the Terrible in Russian History*, Berkeley, University of California Press, 1981, p. 4.

[42] For a discussion of this problem, see Richard Hellie, "Recent Soviet Historiography on Medieval and Early Modern Russian Slavery," *Russian Review*, vol. 35, 1976, pp. 1–32.

[43] I discuss this problem in my article "The Military Land Grant Along the Muslim–Christian Frontier," *Russian History*, vol. 19, 1992, pp. 337–343, "Errata," *Russian History*, vol. 21, 1994, pp. 249–250.

it "this sad chapter of history," "this period of national humiliation," "the greatest calamity for the Rus' lands," and "one of the greatest historical evils." Furthermore, he asserts that the "devious traditions" of Mongol rule, which were "embodied in the Muscovite state, are visible even today." Finally, he breathes a sigh of relief that Belarus, Lithuania, and Ukraine were spared "the evil forces created by the Tartar Yoke."[44] After reading such assertions, one finds oneself agreeing more and more with Alan Fisher's assessment: "we still are without sophisticated analyses of the origins of Russian institutions."[45]

One of the problems with the acceptance of the view that the Mongols may have made a positive contribution to Muscovite political culture is the idea that a "pro-Mongol" evaluation must imply an anti-Russian attitude. Richard Pipes pointed out that "[t]he subject of Mongol influence is a very sensitive one for Russians, who are quick to take offence at the suggestion that their cultural heritage has been shaped in any way by the orient, and especially by the oriental power best remembered for its appalling atrocities and the destruction of great centres of civilization."[46] In the Soviet Union, those who attempted to suggest that the Mongol influence may have had some positive results were accused of "idealization of the history of the Turco-Mongol nomads," with the implication they were motivated by nationalist considerations as a result of paying insufficient attention to Marxism.[47]

Over thirty years ago, a telling exchange occurred in the pages of *Slavic Review* among Karl A. Wittfogel, Bertold Spuler, and Nicholas Riasanovsky.[48] Both Wittfogel and Spuler argued in favor of seeing positive Mongol influence on Muscovite and Russian institutional development. Spuler added that "discussion on this issue is today scarcely necessary any longer."[49] Yet, Riasanovsky's position on Mongol

---

[44] Boleslaw Szczesniak, "A Note on the Character of the Tatar Impact upon the Russian State and Church," *Études Slaves et Est-Européens*, vol. 17, 1972, pp. 92, 95, 97.

[45] Alan W. Fisher, "Muscovite–Ottoman Relations in the Sixteenth and Seventeenth Centuries," *Humaniora Islamica*, vol. 1, 1973, p. 213 fn. 11.

[46] Pipes, *Russia Under the Old Regime*, p. 74.

[47] I. P. Petrushevskii, *Zemledelie i agrarnye otnosheniia v Irane XIII–XIV vekov*, Moscow and Leningrad, Akademiia nauk SSSR, 1960, p. 31 fn. 1; pp. 36–37. For a discussion of this point, see Bernard Lewis, "The Mongols, the Turks, and the Muslim Polity," *Transactions of the Royal Historical Society*, 5th ser., vol. 18, 1968, pp. 50–52; reprinted in Bernard Lewis, *Islam in History: Ideas, People, and Events in the Middle East*, 2nd edn., Chicago, Open Court, 1993, pp. 190–191.

[48] *Slavic Review*, vol. 22, 1963: Karl A. Wittfogel, "Russia and the East: a Comparison and Contrast," pp. 627–643; Nicholas Riasanovsky, "'Oriental Despotism' and Russia," pp. 644–649; Bertold Spuler, "Russia and Islam," pp. 650–655; and Karl A. Wittfogel, "Reply," pp. 656–662; reprinted in *The Development of the USSR: an Exchange of Views*, ed. Donald W. Treadgold, Seattle, University of Washington Press, 1964, pp. 323–358.

[49] Spuler, "Russia and Islam," p. 650; *Development*, p. 346.

influence is most clearly represented by his statement: "aspirin is not borrowed from a headache."[50] Riasanovsky was referring here specifically to the fortifications built to repel Tatar intrusions of the sixteenth century, but I think it a not unfair characterization of Riasanovsky's general view on Mongol influence. In response, Wittfogel accused Riasanovsky of a "self-imposed conceptual blackout" that prevented him from seeing the overwhelming influence of the Mongols.[51]

We can explain the vehement difference in opinions, at least partially, by differing perceptual positions. Scholars who deny or minimize outside influence tend to be specialists in Muscovite and Russian studies. Those who see only outside influence tend to be specialists in other historical areas. Likewise, when viewing Muscovy from the inside, one tends to see almost exclusively Muscovite developments; when viewing it from the outside, one tends to see almost exclusively foreign influences. Muscovite political culture thus appears to be both exclusively indigenous and exclusively influenced by outside societies simultaneously, depending upon which frame of reference one is using at the time. Like Schrödinger's Cat, it is in both states of being at the same time until the historian "opens the box" (i.e. makes an arbitrary decision). Benedetto Croce has argued that history is not history until the historian thinks it and remains history only as long as the historian continues to think it.[52] So, too, as each historian thinks it in turn, Muscovy becomes both free from outside influence and influenced from the outside – two states of being at once. The idea is to break down the either/or bifurcation in order to see it as a both/and unity. We can achieve fuller understanding by being aware and having an appreciation of external influences when we focus on internal developments and by being aware and having an appreciation of internal developments when we focus on outside influences. Thus far, however, nationalist intransigence, historical chauvinism, and ideological prefigurations have blocked any attempt at constituting a unified model.

If there had been no Byzantium or Qipchaq Khanate, we might be led to postulate "action at a distance" in relation to influence from western Europe, that is, parallel institutional structures and functions with no direct connections discernible. Although we cannot eliminate western Europe as a possible influence, we can find more direct connections with Byzantium, via the Rus' metropolitans' coming from Constantinople until the mid-fifteenth century, and the Qipchaq Khanate, via the grand princes' frequent trips to Sarai during the fourteenth century. We

---

[50] Riasanovsky, "'Oriental Despotism' and Russia," p. 646; *Development*, p. 342.
[51] Wittfogel, "Reply," p. 662; *Development*, p. 358.
[52] Benedetto Croce, *Teoria e storia della storiografia*, Bari, Laterza, 1917, p. 5.

cannot, nor should we try to, eliminate Europe, the Byzantine Empire, or the Qipchaq Khanate from the historiography, and for that very reason we are not likely to reach any historiographical agreement, since each area of possible influence has its proponents and opponents. I am not optimistic about our moving toward a consensus on the origins and development of Muscovite political culture in part because of the resoluteness with which we historians assert and defend our own particular positions on this issue and our refusal to acknowledge the legitimacy of any interpretation or evidence that runs counter to our own pet theories. We historians of Muscovy, and I include myself in this assessment, often exhibit the characteristic phenomenon that the political scientist Robert Jervis has named "premature cognitive closure" in which "the initial organization of stimuli strongly structures later perceptions."[53] Such a situation is more symptomatic of prefigured views based on metahistorical considerations than of fair-minded interpretations based on a thorough gathering and critical analysis of the evidence. Yet, I know how difficult it is to break through such prefigurations.

II

I would like to propose the following synthesis for the purpose of the further study of Muscovite political culture. This synthesis is necessarily speculative. I do not intend it in any way as definitive, but rather as a proposal for a different approach to the research of early Muscovite institutional development, an approach that may not lead toward building a consensus, but may allow us to disagree in a more fruitful way, with less denigration of the views of those we oppose, and more willingness to accept that their views may have some legitimacy. While I do not see our reaching any consensus, nor even necessarily the desirability of doing so, I do see the way we disagree hindering research, preventing constructive thought, and marginalizing the work of those who have a contribution to make to the study of Muscovy. The examples of scholars whose work has been rejected and denigrated because their views did not happen to coincide with the prevailing paradigm are too numerous to catalog here. Instead of pointing out flaws in the argument or use of evidence, the propagator of such views is often ridiculed for not agreeing with the already existing accepted interpretation.[54] I myself

[53] Robert Jervis, *Perception and Misperception in International Affairs*, Princeton University Press, 1976, p. 187.
[54] A case in point was the reception accorded Antony Grobovsky when he published *The "Chosen Council" of Ivan IV: a Reinterpretation*, Brooklyn, Theo Gaus' Sons, 1969. A

was confronted with this type of attitude not long ago at a conference when I put the question to a distinguished roundtable of Muscovite historians what institutions, structures, or *mentalités* in Muscovy were free of influence from Byzantium or steppe societies. I was told the question was "not helpful." The response brought home to me, in a particularly acute way, the fact that the study of Muscovy is one of the areas in nationalistic historical study where, among a large segment of scholars, the idea of outside influence is treated with scorn and as having no legitimacy.[55]

Yet, no society arises *ex nihilo*. Outside influences contribute to the making of all societies. Such influences become indigenous when a people modify them and make them their own. In literary study, Walter Jackson Bate and Harold Bloom have formulated an entire system of poetry criticism based on the idea of the poet's breaking away from his or her antecedents.[56] We can apply the same concept *mutatis mutandis* to Muscovy to show how Muscovite institutions broke away from (or "misread") their antecedents.

In sum, we have five models with which to investigate Muscovy: Muscovy as spontaneously generated; Muscovy as a variant of Byzantium; Muscovy as a sedentary variant of steppe nomad and/or Mongol society; the combination of Muscovy as a variant of both Byzantium (in theory) and the steppe (in practice); and Muscovy as a variant of the European model. Each of these models tends to exclude the others. Can

number of reviewers dismissed his findings because, as they wrote, he did not really understand Muscovy. See, e.g., Andreyev's comment that "he [Grobovsky] is not as yet fully conversant with this period." Nikolay Andreyev, review of The *"Chosen Council"*, *Slavic Review*, vol. 30, 1971, p. 136. See also Raba's assessment: "it is an example of the danger inherent in a formalistic approach dealing with only one aspect and divorced from the whole picture of the past." Joel Raba, review of The *"Chosen Council"*, *Canadian–American Slavic Studies*, vol. 6, 1972, p. 497.

[55] When one raises arguments and brings in evidence that counters those who have engaged in "premature cognitive closure," such marginalization of that person and his or her views is a common response. For example, in the 1960s, when John Kenneth Galbraith articulated concerns about US policy in Vietnam, his views were characterized as "not useful," that is, not useful for those who wished to reach pre-conceived conclusions. Likewise, the Avvakum scholar N. S. Demkova, who was convinced that the MS. Druzhinin no. 746 contained the autograph copy of Avvakum's *Zhitie* and that it was compiled in 1673, rejected the watermark evidence supplied by T. V. Dianova that some of the paper dates no earlier than 1681 with the statement: "The facts of the paleographic analysis do not help the dating." N. S. Demkova, *Zhitie protopopa Avvakuma*, Izdatel'stvo Leningradskogo universiteta, 1974, p. 21 fn. 19.

[56] Walter Jackson Bate, *The Burden of the Past and the English Poet*, Cambridge, MA, Belknap Press, 1970; Harold Bloom, *The Anxiety of Influence*, New York, Oxford University Press, 1973; Harold Bloom, *A Map of Misreading*, New Haven, CT, Yale University Press, 1975; and Harold Bloom, *Poetry and Repression*, New Haven, CT, Yale University Press, 1976. My thanks to Sue Weaver Schopf for clarifying this point for me.

we combine all five in a non-exclusionary way? Is combining them something we should even try to do?

Some Muscovite institutions may have been totally indigenous. Others may have been based on those of non-Muscovite societies. To ignore non-Muscovite influences on Muscovy is to run the risk of faulty conclusions about institutions and practices. Likewise, to concentrate solely on one antecedent for Muscovite institutions requires ignoring a great deal of evidence and distorting other evidence so as to be able to force it to support a prefigured conclusion. Even the combination of two models, for example, a Byzantine–Mongol combination or an indigenous–European combination, does not explain the origins, and certainly not the development, of all Muscovite institutions. To exclude outside influence altogether is to fall into a trap. To concentrate only on outside influence is to fall into another trap. One can avoid these traps by considering fairly not only indigenous origins and development but also outside origins and influence. To do any less is to manipulate the evidence to fit preconceived notions.

Certain institutions, ways of thinking (*mentalités*), and practices entered Muscovy from outside. During the period of early Muscovy, the dominant outside influences came both through Byzantium *and* through Sarai. These imported institutions and practices were modified by Muscovite ecclesiastical and secular leaders and, in some cases, combined with already existing institutions and practices to meet specifically Muscovite needs. The already existing pre-Muscovite institutions themselves may have been a combination of pre-Mongol steppe nomadic institutions and those that either represent deep structural tribal similarities with European medieval institutions or were brought into Rus' by the Vikings as well as those derived from Kiev. Once established in Muscovy, imported institutions continued to undergo further development and modification to meet changing circumstances. The Church, religion, and articulation of abstract theoretical and philosophical concepts were overwhelmingly influenced by Byzantium with an admixture of Western Church thought. The governmental structure and administration were heavily influenced by Sarai with an admixture from the Islamic world. Subsequently, Byzantine and European influences, as funneled mainly through the Church, had their impact in the transformation of both religious and secular institutions.

Mestnichestvo, the Muscovite system of social status and military rank, provides a typical example. A reading of the extensive literature on *mestnichestvo* and a listening to papers on panels devoted to the topic leaves one with the impression that we do not understand much about how *mestnichestvo* originated, exactly how it worked, and why it ended.

We may have quite a lot of evidence about *mestnichestvo* and the specific instances of its being invoked. Yet, what can we say we understand if we do not understand an institution's origins, operation, or demise – some isolated "facts" unintegrated into any overall conception? To what extent can such "knowledge" provide a satisfactory explanation? It seems to me that we must ask the following kinds of questions to obtain meaning about any particular institution:

1) Where does an institution or practice come from? What were its antecedents both internally and externally?
2) How did it function? What was its structure? What purpose did it serve?
3) Why did it end? Was it ended intentionally by human intervention or did it phase itself out through non-use? Did outside influences replace it with a new institution or practice or amalgamate it with the old institutions or practice to form a hybrid?

In addition, it would be more accurate to stop talking about Muscovy as though it were a homogeneous whole from beginning to end.[57] Just as Hans Georg Beck and Cyril Mango proposed a tripartite periodization of Byzantine history,[58] we can define three periods for Muscovy: Early, Middle, and Late.

Early Muscovy covers the time span from 1304 to 1448. At the beginning of this period, "Muscovy," in terms of territory, constituted little more than the city of Moscow itself, but by the end of this period, its holdings bordered on the Oka River to the south and stretched beyond Lake Beloozero in the north. Moscow was in competition with other northern Rus' principalities, including Novgorod, Riazan', Smolensk, and Tver'. In terms of high culture, especially religion, this period showed heavy Byzantine influence. During this period, the Rus' Church was dependent on the Patriarch of Constantinople and the policies of the Byzantine Church. Politically and militarily, we find heavy Mongol influence with consensus politics, the petition (*chelobit'e*), a system of dual administration, the beginnings of *mestnichestvo*, and the adoption of Mongol techniques of warfare. The legal system, however, was inherited from Kiev with only certain elements, such as collective guilt, gradation of punishment for recidivism, shin beating, etc., showing Mongol influence. The bulk of society was made up of free peasants and slaves. Its economic base was commercial activity and trade controlled by a small ruling class. The land belonged to the grand prince. By 1448, the

---

[57] Kazhdan has addressed this question in relation to Byzantium. Alexander P. Kazhdan and Simon Franklin, *Studies on Byzantine Literature of the Eleventh and Twelfth Centuries*, New York, Cambridge University Press, 1984, pp. 1–22.

[58] Hans Georg Beck, *Das byzantinische Jahrtausend*, Munich, Beck, 1978, pp. 29–32; Cyril Mango, *Byzantium: the Empire of New Rome*, New York, Charles Scribner's Sons, 1980, pp. 1, 4–5.

Rus' Church had taken over from Constantinople the appointment of its own metropolitan. At the beginning of this period, the Muscovite grand prince was completely dependent on the Qipchaq khan for his authority. By 1448, although Muscovy still paid tribute to the khan, the grand prince was virtually independent politically.

Middle Muscovy covers the time span from 1448 to 1589. Territorially, Muscovy continued to expand to include, by the end of this period, almost all of what we consider to be European Russia, parts of northern Ukraine, and a significant thrust across the Ural Mountains into Siberia. Moscow had absorbed into its domains the other northern Rus' principalities that it had previously competed with, as well as the successor khanates of Kazan' and Astrakhan. Intellectually, we find the development of an anti-Tatar ideology within the Church as represented in the chronicles and other Church literature. The Church pushed to make the grand prince the successor to the Byzantine emperor, that is, tsar of all Christians. Socially, we find the beginnings of seclusion of elite women, which also had political implications. Politically, we see the amalgamation of Mongol- and Byzantine-type bureaucracies as Tatar refugees from the successor khanates and Greeks in the entourage of Sofiia (Zoë) Palaeologina converged in Moscow. With the takeover of what was left of the Qipchaq Khanate in 1502 by the Crimean khan, Muscovy was completely independent politically, although the grand prince agreed to continue the payment of tribute to the Crimean khan. Militarily, we see outside influence with the introduction of gunpowder and the formation of the first *strel'tsi* regiments. We also find Italian influence on architecture, particularly in the Moscow kremlin. By the end of this period the free peasants and slaves began to merge into serfdom. Economically, the period was one of mixed commercial and proprietary wealth. The land was still the grand prince's in theory, but, in practice, *de facto*, ownership by service princes, boyars, and the military servitors began to emerge. By 1589, the Patriarchate of Moscow was established, which represented the triumph of the Church-based ideology.

Late Muscovy spans the period from 1589 to 1722. Muscovy expanded across the breadth of Siberia to the Pacific Ocean in the east and acquired all of left-bank Ukraine. During this period we see the culmination of the tendencies emerging in the middle period. We also see an increasing amount of European influence: Dutch and German technological influence, Swedish military and administrative influence, and Polish literary and cultural influence, especially through the Mohyla Collegium in Kiev. In the beginning of this period, as a result of the establishment of the Moscow patriarchate, and in particular the pre-eminence of Patriarchs Filaret and Nikon, the Church enjoyed broad influence. By the end of this period, the Church was subsumed and relegated to being a department of the state. Socially, serfdom became institutionalized. Wealth was predominantly proprietary, but commercial activity was still strong. The gentry acted as *de facto* owners of the land, although the tsar still maintained theoretical ownership. By 1722, a new system of social status and military rank, the Table of Ranks, was established as a replacement for *mestnichestvo*, which had been abolished forty years earlier. The Table of Ranks remained in effect throughout the subsequent imperial period until 1917. It is for this reason that I choose the year 1722 as the divide between Muscovite and Imperial Russia, although Peter's entire reign (1682–1725) effected that transition.

III

In Early and Middle Muscovy, the period discussed in this book, the primary outside influences on Muscovy were Byzantine and Mongol/ Tatar. During the Early Muscovite period, the main conduits for Byzantine and Mongol influence were the metropolitanate and grand princely courts, respectively. During the Middle Muscovite period, the main conduits for Byzantine and Tatar influence were the Eastern Christian book culture and refugees from the various Tatar khanates, respectively. Thus, the mechanism for the transfer of cultural influences changes, but the kinds of cultural influences are similar. A brief overview of these influences and how they interacted will clarify what I mean.

The metropolitan moved from Kiev to Vladimir in 1299, and then to Moscow, where Metropolitan Peter took up residence in 1325. Historians have provided various explanations for the move of the metropolitan see to the northeast, but most historians who have written on the topic attribute the impetus for the move to continued Tatar raids on Kiev. I have argued elsewhere that what the chroniclers refer to as "Tatar violence" in this regard should be understood as the steppe war, just south of Kiev, between Nogai, prince of the Qipchaq, and Toqta, Khan of the Qipchaq Khanate, from 1297 to 1300.[59] The Church was under Mongol protection and had been so since at least the census of 1257, when the Church had been exempted from taxation.[60] In 1261, Khan Berke allowed the establishment of a Rus' episcopal see in Sarai.

---

[59] Donald Ostrowski, "Why Did the Metropolitan Move from Kiev to Vladimir in the Thirteenth Century?" *California Slavic Studies*, vol. 16, 1993, pp. 92–95.

[60] *PSRL*, vol. 1 (1927), col. 475; vol. 10, p. 141; vol. 18, p. 71. See also *PSRL*, vol. 10, p. 152 for the census of 1273–1275.

And in 1267, Khan Möngke-Temür issued a *iarlyk* (*yarlīg*) to Metropolitan Kirill that officially recognized the Orthodox Church, extending his protection over it, exempting it from taxation in return for prayers offered by the Rus' clergy for the well-being of the khan and his family.[61] But the spillover of conflict from the steppe war may have made conditions in Kiev so unstable that the khan could no longer guarantee the safety of the metropolitan.

During the first half of the fourteenth century, at the same time the metropolitan was taking up residence in Moscow, the Muscovite princes established a political administration based primarily on that of the Qipchaq Khanate. This adoption of Mongol political administration resulted from the numerous trips Muscovite princes took to Sarai as subordinates of the khan. As a result, Muscovite princes could see first hand the operations of the Khanate. When they became grand princes of Rus', they adopted the structure and functions of Mongol–Qipchaq institutions. They did so because these institutions worked well for the purpose of collecting taxes and maintaining order over a wide area and because the Moscow city-state had nothing comparable.

During the metropolitanate of Aleksei (1354–1378), that is, at the time of the reign of Ivan II (1351–1359) and the minority of his successor, Dmitrii Donskoi, Byzantine influences asserted themselves anew on the grand princely administration. Aleksei was appointed regent in 1359[62] and was the virtual ruler of Muscovy until his death in 1378.[63] As a member of the politically strong Pleshcheev clan, he

[61] M. D. Priselkov, *Khanskie iarlyki russkim mitropolitam*, St. Petersburg, Nauchnoe delo, 1916, pp. 96–98; and A. I. Pliguzov, "Drevneishii spisok kratkogo sobraniia iarlykov, dannykh ordynskimi khanami russkim mitropolitam," *Russkii feodal'nyi arkhiv. XIV–parvoi troti XVI veka (RFA)*, 5 vols., Moscow, Akademiia nauk SSSR, Institut istorii SSSR, 1986–1992, vol. 3, pp. 588–589.

[62] From 1358 to 1360, Aleksei was in Kiev. The Patriarchal Act of 1380 claims that Grand Duke Ol'gerd of Lithuania had arrested Aleksei when he arrived in Kiev in 1358. *Russkaia istoricheskaia biblioteka (RIB)*, vol. 6, Prilozhenie, col. 167; *Acta patriarchatus Constantinopolitani*, vols. 1–2 of *Acta et diplomata graeca medii aevi sacra et profana*, ed. Fr[anz von Ritter] Miklosich and Ios[if] Müller, 6 vols., Vienna, Carl Gerold, 1860–1890, vol. 2, no. 337, p. 12. This statement, at first glance, may seem incorrect, for the Lithuanians took Kiev only in 1362. A possible explanation, though, is Pelenski's suggestion that Kiev was under a condominium of rule shared by the Lithuanians and Tatars at this time. Jaroslaw Pelenski, "The Contest Between Lithuania-Rus' and the Golden Horde in the Fourteenth Century for Supremacy over Eastern Europe," *Archivum Eurasiae Medii Aevi*, vol. 2, 1982, pp. 307–311. Although Ol'gerd supported Aleksei's rival Roman, Aleksei may have felt it safe to travel to Kiev because it still had a Tatar presence with a resident *bāsqāq*. See, e.g., *Novgorodskaia pervaia letopis'. Starshego i mladshego izvodov (NPL)*, ed. M. N. Tikhomirov, Moscow and Leningrad, Akademiia nauk SSSR, 1950, p. 344; *PSRL*, vol. 4 (1848), p. 52.

[63] But see Henryk Paszkiewicz, *The Rise of Moscow's Power*, trans. P. S. Falla, Boulder, CO, East European Monographs, 1983, p. 352, who stated that by 1364–1366 Dmitrii Donskoi was making his own decisions. The only "evidence" Paszkiewicz cited was

identified the Church with Muscovite political interests. And since he had spent some time in Constantinople, while he was heir to the metropolitan's throne, he had a first hand knowledge of Byzantine practices.[64] Having the head of the Church act as regent during the minority of the prince was an accepted Byzantine practice,[65] so the Patriarch of Constantinople, Philotheus, confirmed his regency[66] and supported his excommunication of Muscovy's enemies.[67] In response, the Prince of Tver', Mikhail, the King of Poland, Casimir, and the Grand Duke of Lithuania, Ol'gerd, complained to Philotheus about Aleksei.[68] Philotheus, then, without removing his support from Aleksei, reproved him for neglecting his spiritual duties toward those areas of his metropolitanate that were not under Muscovite political control, and urged him to heal the breach with Tver'.[69]

This assertion of power by the heads of the Byzantine and Muscovite Churches in the second half of the fourteenth century coincided with weak or cooperative temporal rulers both in Byzantium and in Muscovy, and with the period called "the Great Trouble" in the history of the Qipchaq Khanate. When Tokhtamish gained enough power in the khanate to reassert Mongol hegemony over Rus', his vassal Vasilii I reasserted not only grand princely authority but also Tatar-based practices in Muscovite secular affairs.[70] Thus, after Aleksei's death in 1378 and especially after the sacking of Moscow by Tokhtamish in

---

"the advantages that Moscow secured from the agreement with Dmitry [of Suzdal']." It is difficult to see anyone's personal impact on this agreement, let alone that of someone who was only fifteen at the time. As Kollmann argued, one "can only speculate when the minority [of Dmitrii] ended." She suggested that Dmitrii "grew gradually in power and influence." Nancy Shields Kollmann, "The Boyar Clan and Court Politics: the Founding of the Muscovite Political System," *Cahiers du monde russe et soviétique*, vol. 23, 1982, p. 24 fn. 27. Perhaps, although I doubt Metropolitan Aleksei would have given up real control willingly, even as an octogenerian.

[64] *Acta et diplomata graeca*, vol. 1, pp. 336–337.

[65] See John Meyendorff, *Byzantium and the Rise of Russia: a Study of Byzantino–Russian Relations in the Fourteenth Century*, Cambridge University Press, 1980, p. 185.

[66] *Acta et diplomata graeca*, vol. 1, pp. 520–522; *RIB*, vol. 6, Prilozhenie, no. 18, cols. 109–114; and Meyendorff, *Byzantium and the Rise of Russia*, pp. 283–284.

[67] *Acta et diplomata graeca*, vol. 1, pp. 523–524; *RIB*, vol. 6, Prilozhenie, no. 20, cols. 117–120; and Meyendorff, *Byzantium and the Rise of Russia*, pp. 285–286.

[68] For Casimir's letter, see *Acta et diplomata graeca*, vol. 1, pp. 577–578; *RIB*, vol. 6, Prilozhenie, no. 22, cols. 125–128; and Meyendorff, *Byzantium and the Rise of Russia*, p. 287. For Olgerd's letter, see *Acta et diplomata graeca*, vol. 1, pp. 580–581; *RIB*, vol. 6, Prilozhenie, no. 24, cols. 135–140; and Meyendorff, *Byzantium and the Rise of Russia*, pp. 288–289.

[69] *Acta et diplomata graeca*, vol. 1, pp. 320–322; *RIB*, vol. 6, Prilozhenie, no. 28, cols. 155–160; and Meyendorff, *Byzantium and the Rise of Russia*, pp. 290–291.

[70] See Donald Ostrowski, "The Mongol Origins of Muscovite Political Institutions," *Slavic Review*, vol. 49, 1990, pp. 528–529.

1382, Muscovite secular administration seems to have reverted once more to a predominantly "Mongol" orientation. If such a reassertion occurred the way I am describing it, then the prelates of the Rus' Church might have perceived a loss of ground for their Byzantine tradition. This would have made it all the more important for them to arrange the marriage, in the early fifteenth century, of Vasilii's daughter Anna to the future Byzantine Emperor John VIII.

In the period of Middle Muscovy, that is, from the second half of the fifteenth century to the establishment of the patriarchate, the Muscovite Churchmen pushed for greater influence on political affairs. For example, the Church increasingly required Tatar princes to convert to Christianity before they could enter the service of the grand prince. Muscovite Churchmen based their policies and ceremonial innovations on earlier Byzantine practices. The civil administration continued to view the practices of the steppe khanates as its frame of reference even after 1502 when the Qipchaq Khanate (Great Horde) acknowledged the sovereignty of the Crimean khan. The Oprichnina of Ivan IV, for example, was most likely a throwback to Tatar practices in order to stem the rising tide of Church influence in secular affairs. And the *zemskii sobor* most likely derived from the steppe nomad assembly, the *quriltai*, as Pelenski suggested.[71] Subsequently, during Late Muscovy, that is, after 1589, the Byzantine and Mongol influences recede, to be replaced in part by European influences and in part by further indigenous transformations.

It would be a mistake, however, to see merely two factions, the pro-Byzantine and the pro-Mongol, in Early and Middle Muscovy. Those who operated within a Byzantine frame of reference, such as the metropolitans, could adopt to political realities. The Byzantine Empire itself followed a policy of alliance with the Qipchaq Khanate, which lasted with minor interruptions until 1453. The Patriarch of Constantinople, as head of the Eastern Church, was obliged to support the foreign policy of the Byzantine Emperor. The Rus' Church, as an arm of the Eastern Church, was obliged to follow the policy of the Patriarch and thereby that of the Byzantine Empire as well. Rus' Churchmen in the thirteenth and fourteenth centuries prayed for the well-being of the khan and followed a policy of accommodation with the Mongols to the point of establishing an episcopal see in Sarai, the capital of the Qipchaq

---

[71] Jaroslaw Pelenski, "State and Society in Muscovite Russia and the Mongol–Turkic System in the Sixteenth Century," *The Mutual Effects of the Islamic and Judeo–Christian Worlds: the East European Pattern*, ed. Abraham Ascher, Tibor Halasi-Kun, and Béla K. Király, Brooklyn College Press, 1979, pp. 97–99; reprinted in *Forschungen zur osteuropäischen Geschichte*, vol. 27, 1980, pp. 160–162.

Khanate. The Church declared Aleksandr Nevskii, who was the most prominent of the early "collaborationists" among the Rus' princes, to be a miracle worker and saint. In 1328, Metropolitan Feognost placed an interdiction and curse on the city of Pskov for providing refuge to Prince Aleksandr Mikhailovich of Tver' when the latter fled from a combined Tatar–Muscovite force sent to bring him to Khan Özbeg in Sarai.[72] The metropolitans also traveled to Sarai.[73] According to the chronicles, Metropolitan Aleksei's trip of 1357 was undertaken at the behest of Khatun Taydula, the Khan's wife, in order to cure her of an illness.[74] In addition, before his death in 1431, Metropolitan Fotii, who brokered the agreement between Vasilii II and his uncle Iurii Dmitrievich, acquiesced to the question of succession to the grand-princely throne's being referred to the Qipchaq khan, rather than to the basileus.[75] As late as 1461, Metropolitan Iona wrote favorably to Khan Maḥmud that he "ruled his state (gosudarstvo) by the power of Almighty God."[76] None of these occurrences would have happened if the Church had not acknowledged, at least at some level, the khan's pre-eminence in secular matters.

---

[72] PSRL, vol. 7, p. 201; vol. 10, p. 202; vol. 23, p. 103; vol. 28, pp. 68, 229; Pskovskie letopisi, 2 vols., ed. A. [N.] Nasonov, Moscow and Leningrad, Akademiia nauk SSSR, 1941, 1955, vol. 1, p. 17; vol. 2, p. 91.

[73] For Metropolitan Maksim's trip of 1283, see PSRL, vol. 10, p. 161. For Metropolitan Petr's trip of 1313, see PSRL, vol. 8, p. 186; vol. 10, p. 178; vol. 18, p. 87; vol. 25, p. 160; and vol. 28, pp. 65, 225. For Metropolitan Feognost's trip of 1333, see PSRL, vol. 5, p. 220; vol. 8, p. 204; vol. 10, p. 206; vol. 25, p. 171; vol. 26, p. 112; vol. 28, pp. 69, 229; vol. 39, p. 106; vol. 41, p. 106; and NPL, p. 346. For Metropolitan Feognost's trip of 1342, see PSRL, vol. 5, p. 224; vol. 8, p. 209; vol. 10, p. 215; vol. 18, p. 94; vol. 24, p. 118; vol. 25, p. 174; vol. 28, pp. 70, 231; vol. 39, p. 109; and vol. 41, p. 109. For Metropolitan Aleksei's trip of 1357, see PSRL, vol. 5, p. 228; vol. 10, p. 229; vol. 18, pp. 99–100; vol. 25, p. 180; vol. 26, p. 117; vol. 28, pp. 74, 235; vol. 39, p. 113; and vol. 41, p. 113. For Metropolitan Pimen's trip of 1385, see PSRL, vol. 8, p. 49; vol. 15 (1922), pt. 1, p. 150; vol. 18, p. 135; and vol. 24, p. 156. See also M. D. Poluboiarinova, Russkie liudi v Zolotoi Orde, Moscow, Nauka, 1978, pp. 31–33.

[74] PSRL, vol. 8, p. 10; vol. 10, p. 229; vol. 15 (1922), pt. 1, col. 66; vol. 28, pp. 74, 235; M. D. Priselkov, Troitskaia letopis'. Rekonstruktsiia teksta (hereafter TL), Moscow and Leningrad, Akademiia nauk SSSR, 1950, p. 375.

[75] PSRL, vol. 25, p. 247; vol. 26, p. 184. Fotii had attempted to get Iurii Dmitrievich's submission to Vasilii Vasil'evich as grand prince and had even excommunicated Iurii at one point to obtain his compliance. The compromise that Fotii worked out involved referring the entire matter to Khan Ulug Mehmed. For a description of Fotii's activities in the matter, see John Fennell, A History of the Russian Church to 1448, London, Longman, 1995, pp. 234–236.

[76] Akty istoricheskie, sobrannye i izdannye Arkheograficheskoi komissiei (AI), 5 vols., St. Petersburg, Tipografiia Ekspeditsii zagotovleniia gosudarstvennykh bumag, 1841–1842, vol. 1, no. 67, p. 119. The document, found in the MS. GIM, Sinod. 562, does not mention a name, referring only to the "Волному Царю Казаньскому." The editors of AI added the name "Akhmet" to their title for the document, but Maḥmud was the khan of Kazan' in 1461.

In the second half of the fifteenth century, however, the Church began to articulate an anti-Tatar position. Metropolitan Iona became a symbol not only of religious independence from Byzantium but also of secular independence from the Tatars. And, by the time of Metropolitan Makarii (1542–1563), and in large part due to his efforts, the anti-Tatar ideology was well developed and already well established. Pelenski, for example, delineated seven sets of binary oppositions in the writings of Metropolitan Makarii concerning the differences between the Muscovites and the Tatars: believers vs. non-believers; religious vs. godless; Christian vs. pagan; pious vs. impious; pure vs. unclean; peaceful vs. warlike; and good vs. bad.[77]

Those who operated within a Mongol frame of reference could adapt to the Byzantine cultural presence. Grand Prince Semen displayed curiosity, at least, when he wrote to the Byzantine emperor about the nature of the basileus' power. In 1346 or 1347 (or at least before August 1347), Semen donated money for the repair of Hagia Sophia in Constantinople.[78] In 1347, he supported the request of Metropolitan Feognost to John VI Kantakouzenos for the abolishing of the Metropolitanate of Galicia.[79] Most likely as a result of the influence of Metropolitan Aleksei, the diplomatic communication of the grand prince with other Rus' princes during this period was couched in Byzantine formulaic.[80] In 1398, Vasilii I sent money to help defend Constantinople against the Ottoman Turks.[81] In 1411, Vasilii I sent his daughter Anna to Constantinople to marry the future Emperor John VIII Palaeologus.[82]

[77] Jaroslaw Pelenski, *Russia and Kazan: Conquest and Imperial Ideology (1438–1560s)*, The Hague, Mouton, 1974, pp. 302–303.

[78] Nicephorus Gregoras, *Historiae Byzantinae*, 3 vols., ed. Ludwig Schopen and Immanuel Bekker (*Corpus scriptorum historiae byzantinae* [CSHB], vols. 6–7, 48), Bonn, E. Weber, 1829–1855, vol. 3, bk. 28, §19–21, pp. 198–200. See also Ihor Ševčenko, "Notes on Stephen the Novgorodian Pilgrim to Constantinople in the XIV Century," *Südost-Forschungen*, vol. 12, 1953, pp. 167–168; reprinted in Ihor Ševčenko, *Society and Intellectual Life in Late Byzantium*, London, Variorum, 1981, item 15.

[79] *Acta et diplomata graeca*, vol. 1, p. 267; *RIB*, vol. 6, Prilozhenie, no. 3, cols. 13–19; *Jus graeco-romanum*, ed. K. E. Zachariae von Lingenthal, 4 vols., Leipzig, T. O. Weigel, 1856–1865, vol. 3, p. 701; and Meyendorff, *Byzantium and the Rise of Russia*, p. 281.

[80] See *Dukhovnye i dogovornye gramoty velikikh i udel'nykh kniazei XIV–XVI vv.* (*DDG*), ed. L. V. Cherepnin, Moscow and Leningrad, Akademiia nauk SSSR, 1950, nos. 2, 5, 7, 9, 10, 11, 13, 14, 15, 16, 18, and 19.

[81] *TL*, p. 448; *PSRL*, vol. 8, p. 71; vol. 11, p. 168; vol. 25, p. 228; vol. 28, pp. 88, 253.

[82] *PSRL*, vol. 8, p. 86; vol. 11, p. 217; vol. 18, p. 160; vol. 25, p. 240; vol. 28, pp. 93, 258. On the *sakkos* of Photius, which depicts John VIII and his wife Anna Vasil'evna, see A. V. Bank, *Vizantiiskoe iskusstvo v sobraniiakh Sovetskogo Soiuza*, Sovetskii khudozhnik, 1966, plates 285–288; [A. V.] Alice Bank, *Byzantine Art in the Collections of Soviet Museums*, trans. Inna Sorokina, Leningrad, Aurora Art, 1977, plates 300–304; Dimitri Obolensky, "Some Notes Concerning a Byzantine Portrait of John VIII Palaeologus," *Eastern Churches Review*, vol. 4, 1972, pp. 141–146; Anthony-Emil N. Tachiaos, "The Testament of Photius Monembasiotes, Metropolitan of Russia

Vasilii II imported a Byzantine practice when, in 1436, he ordered that his cousin Vasilii Kosoi be blinded after taking him prisoner.[83] Blinding rival claimants was a practice not unfamiliar in Byzantium,[84] but, as far as we have reliable testimony, had never occurred before in Muscovy and only once in Kievan Rus'.[85] Among the Mongols, by contrast, the shedding of princely blood was considered dishonorable. Marco Polo describes the execution of Nayan, whom Qubilai Khan had wrapped up in a carpet and dragged around until he died "so that the blood of the imperial lineage might not be spilt upon the earth, and that sun and air might not witness it."[86] When Chinghiz Khan ordered his *anda* Jamuqa killed, he specified, in deference to their relationship, that it be done by "not shedding blood."[87] Grigor of Akner reports in his "History" that it was the custom when executing Mongol princes to strangle them with a

(1408–1431): Byzantine Ideology in XVth-Century Muscovy," *Cyrillomethodianum*, vol. 8/9, 1984–1985, p. 98; and Elisabeth Piltz, *Trois sakkoi byzantins. Analyse iconographique*, Stockholm, Almqvist & Wiksell, 1976.

[83] *PSRL*, vol. 5, p. 267; vol. 8, p. 100; vol. 12, p. 22; vol. 18, p. 176; vol. 25, p. 252; vol. 26, p. 192; and vol. 28, pp. 101, 268.

[84] See, e.g., Theophanes, *Chronographia*, ed. Karl de Boor, 2 vols., Leipzig, B. G. Teubner, 1883–1885, vol. 1, p. 151 on Constantine VI's blinding of the Caesar Nikephoros in 792 and p. 472 on Irene's blinding of her son Constantine VI in 797; Anna Komnenē, *Alexiades*, ed. Ludwig Schopen, 2 vols. (CSHB, vols. 37, 49), Bonn, E. Weber, 1839, 1878, vol. 2, p. 21, *PSRL*, vol. 1 (1926), cols. 226–227, and *PSRL*, vol. 2 (1908), col. 217 on the blinding of the pseudo-Diogenes in 1095; Niketas Choniatēs, *Historia*, ed. Immanuel Bekker (CSHB, vol. 23), Bonn, E. Weber, 1835, p. 466 on the blinding of John and Manuel, the sons of Andronikos I in 1185; Choniatēs, *Historia*, p. 595 on the blinding of Isaakios II in 1195; Choniatēs, *Historia*, p. 804, *Novgorodskaia pervaia letopis'. Starshego i mladshego izvodov*, ed. M. N. Tikhomirov, Moscow and Leningrad, Akademiia nauk *SSSR*, 1950, pp. 46, 240 on the blinding of Alexios V Mourtzouphlos in 1204.

[85] See *PSRL*, vol. 1(1926), cols. 260–261 and *PSRL*, vol. 2 (1908), cols. 234–235 on the blinding of Vasilko in 1097 and for Volodimir Monomakh's statement that such a practice had no precedent in Rus': "сего не бывало есть в Руськей земли." The Tver' Chronicle reports that Vasilii II ordered the blinding of the boyar Ivan Dmitrievich in 1434. *PSRL*, vol. 15 (1922), pt. 1, col. 490. But Vernadsky, for one, questioned the accuracy of the report and pointed out that the incident is not confirmed in other chronicles. Vernadsky, *Mongols and Russia*, p. 349 fn. 46. Also, it seems unlikely that blinding would be used on someone who was not a rival for the throne just to punish that person.

[86] Marco Polo, *The Travels*, trans. Ronald Latham, London, Penguin, 1958, p. 118; Marco Polo, *The Books of Ser Marco Polo the Venetian Concerning the Kingdom and Marvels of the East*, 2 vols., trans. and annot. Henry Yule, 3rd edn., rev. Henri Cordier, London, John Murray, 1903, reprinted New York, Dover, 1993, vol. 1, p. 343; see also *ibid.*, p. 344 n. 1. On Nayan, see Paul Pelliot, *Notes on Marco Polo. Ouvrage posthume*, 3 vols., Paris, Imprimerie nationale. Librairie Adrien-Maisonneuve, 1959–1973, vol. 2, pp. 788–789.

[87] *The Secret History of the Mongols*, trans. Francis Woodman Cleaves, Cambridge, MA, Harvard University Press, 1982, § 201, p. 141; "The Secret History of the Mongols," trans. Igor de Rachewiltz, *Papers on Far Eastern History (PFEH)*, vol. 21, 1980, p. 24.

bowstring.[88] Toqta ordered the death of the Rus' soldier who killed Nogai in 1300 because "a commoner is not entitled to kill a prince."[89] But Vernadsky suggests that "Tokhta was indignant that Nogay was not given the privilege of dying without his blood being shed."[90] Toqta had previously, in 1291, ordered Tele-buga and other princes captured with him to be killed by having their backs broken, that is, without the shedding of blood.[91] The prohibition also apparently extended to Mongol treatment of Rus' princes. The *Tale of the Battle on the Kalka* describes the execution of Prince Mstislav Romanovich of Kiev and his two sons-in-law by being suffocated under a platform on which the Mongols held their victory feast.[92] What Vasilii II did, then, was in defiance of Mongol practice and he subsequently paid in kind for his innovation.

In addition, Vasilii II wrote a letter to the Byzantine Emperor Constantine XI in July 1451 reporting the Rus' Church's appointment of its own metropolitan two-and-a-half years earlier.[93] Vasilii's letter of 1451, though presenting the Emperor with a *fait accompli*, is phrased in a submissive tone and acknowledges Constantinople's ecclesiastical jurisdiction over the Rus' Church. In 1468, Ivan III presented a silver tabernacle called the Great Zion to the Assumption Cathedral. The niello-finished vessel is decorated with likenesses of the Twelve Apostles.[94] In 1547, the grand prince, at the behest of the Church, agreed to adopt the title *tsar'* even though he was not a Chingizid, for the only ones in steppe politics eligible to adopt the title of *tsar'* were descendants of Chingiz Khan. In 1557, Ivan wrote to the Patriarch of Constantinople

[88] Grigor of Akner [Akancʻ], "History of the Nation of the Archers (The Mongols)," ed. and trans. Robert P. Blake and Richard N. Frye, *Harvard Journal of Asiatic Studies*, vol. 12, 1949, p. 339.

[89] N. I. Veselovskii, *Khan iz temnikov Zolotoi Ordy Nogai i ego vremia*, Petrograd, Rossiiskaia akademiia nauk, 1922, p. 49.

[90] Vernadsky, *Mongols and Russia*, p. 189.

[91] V. G. Tiesenhausen [Tizengauzen], *Sbornik materialov otnosiashchikhsia k istorii Zolotoi Ordy*, 2 vols., St. Petersburg, S. G. Stroganov, 1884, Moscow and Leningrad, Akademiia nauk SSSR, 1941, vol. 2, pp. 69–70; Veselovskii, *Khan iz temnikov*, pp. 37–38.

[92] *NPL*, pp. 63, 267. Cf. Özbeg's decision in 1325 to execute Grand Prince Dmitrii Mikhailovich for killing Iurii Daniilovich (Iurii III). *PSRL*, vol. 7, p. 200; vol. 10, p. 190; vol. 24, p. 115; vol. 25, p. 168, vol. 28, pp. 67–68, 228; *Novgorodskaia pervaia letopis'*, pp. 97, 340. Cf. *TL*, p. 358. See also Mehmed Fuad Köprülü, "La proibizione di versare il sangue nell'esecuzione d'un membro della dinastia presso i Turchi ed i Mongoli," *Annali dell'Istituto Universitario Orientale di Napoli*, new series, vol. 1, 1940, pp. 15–23.

[93] *AI*, vol. 1, no. 41, pp. 83–85; *RIB*, vol. 6, no. 71, cols. 575–586; *RFA*, vol. 1, no. 13, pp. 88–91.

[94] "Treasures of the Kremlin," *National Geographic*, January 1990, p. 90. Daniel Rowland informs me that the tabernacle was modelled on the cupola of the Church of the Holy Sepulchre in Jerusalem.

to receive his approval for adopting the title.[95] *Tsar'* was also the term the Rus' had used to designate the Byzantine emperor. And in 1589, the representatives of the government conspired with the Church to hold Patriarch Jeremiah captive until he agreed to recognize a Muscovite patriarchate.[96] None of these occurrences would have happened if the grand prince and his administration had not acknowledged the pre-eminence, for the most part, of the Byzantine emperor and patriarch in religious matters.

IV

The forms of civil and military institutions in fourteenth-century Muscovy were overwhelmingly Mongol in origin. The Church found itself in the unusual position of trying to modify and account for Mongol institutions and practices within a Byzantine-based frame of reference. This hypothesis might help to explain why the sources provide such seemingly contradictory information and why historians provide such opposing interpretations. It might also help us to accept as legitimate the contributions of those historians who have such widely divergent views. Part of the rationale for presenting the argument contained herein, while so much of the research remains to be done, has been to encourage others to join in that research either to confirm or to refute specific assertions and speculations made here, to open new lines of investigation, and to reopen some older lines that may have been abandoned prematurely.[97]

Finally, if my argument has any value, it means that we must train future historians of Muscovy not only in Slavic and western European languages and history, as we have been doing, but also in Byzantine, Central Asian, and Chinese languages and cultures. Otherwise, our scholarly descendants will not have the research tools needed for furthering the study of Muscovy, its culture and institutions, and their

---

[95] *Sobornaia gramota dukhovenstva pravoslavnoi vostochnoi tserkvi, utverzhdaiushchaia san tsaria za velikim kniazem Ioannom IV Vasil'evichem, 1561 g.*, ed. M. Obolenskii, Moscow, Sinodal'naia tipografiia, 1850, p. 33. For the letter of Patriarch Josephus II to Ivan IV granting his request, see *RIB*, vol. 22, cols. 68–71. See also *PSRL*, vol. 13, p. 334 and *PSRL*, vol. 29, pp. 292–293.

[96] For a thorough analysis of Patriarch Jeremiah's visit to Moscow, see Boris Gudziak, "Crisis and Reform: The Kievan Metropolitanate, the Patriarchate of Constantinople, and the Genesis of the Union of Brest," Ph.D. Dissertation, Harvard University, 1992, pp. 252–303.

[97] For example, Zimin suggested that the janissaries of the Ottoman Empire may have provided the model for the formation of the *strel'tsy* regiments. A. A. Zimin, *I. S. Peresvetov i ego sovremenniki*, Moscow, Akademiia nauk SSSR, 1958, pp. 354–359. To the best of my knowledge, no one has followed up on this idea.

antecedents. Such training will allow our field to connect as well with the growing realization in the historical profession in general that we need to get beyond teaching and researching only national histories.[98] Otherwise, the study of Muscovy will continue to remain isolated from the study of world history. Over forty years ago the British diplomat and scholar G. B. Sansom made an appeal at the University of Tokyo for the study of Japanese history within a world history context: "I am pleading for the study of Japanese history not as an end in itself, not as a mere record of events occurring in isolation, but as an integral and important part of world history."[99] For too long, we have studied Muscovy "as an end in itself" and "as a mere record of events occurring in isolation," rather than "as an integral and important part of world history." And for too long, we have studied world history without an accurate understanding of a significant area of cross-cultural influences, Muscovite Rus'.

[98] See, e.g., the plea of Sir Herbert Butterfield in his "Universal History and the Comparative Study of Civilization," in *Sir Herbert Butterfield, Cho Yun Hsu, and William H. McNeill on Chinese and World History*, ed. Noah Edward Fehl, Hong Kong, Chinese University of Hong Kong, 1971, pp. 17–29.

[99] G. B. Sansom, *Japan in World History*, Tokyo, Kenkyusha Press, 1951, p. 16.

Part I

Mongol influence: what's what and what's not

1 Setting the scene

In the early fourteenth century, when Muscovy began its rise to prominence, only a few political entities controlled the Eurasian land mass. The Yuan dynasty ruled in China. The Khmer Empire had united most of Southeast Asia. The Delhi Sultanate ruled in what is today Pakistan, India, and Bangladesh. The Chagatáy Khanate, the Ilkhanate, and the Qipchaq Khanate controlled Central Asia. The Mamlūks ruled in Egypt and the Levant. The Byzantine Empire was being threatened by the Ottoman Turks. And Europe, although divided politically, maintained a vital fiction of unity as Christendom under the Holy Roman Emperor, although the Byzantine Emperor also claimed this position.

In terms of core influence, the Eurasian land mass was dominated by three civilizations or organizing cultures: China, Islam, and Christianity.[1] Mongol dynasties ruled in China, Korea, and throughout Central Asia to the Black Sea. Wherever they went they brought with them basic Chinese administrative practices. Where the Mongol rulers came into direct contact with indigenous Muslim populations, as in the Qipchaq Khanate, the Ilkhanate, and the Chagatáy Khanate, they converted to Islam. In the western extremity of this land mass, Christianity provided an underlying idiom of cultural expression, although the Greek (or Eastern) and Latin (or Western) Churches had divided centuries before, and the Western Church was about to be divided further in the Great Schism. The Eastern Orthodox Church held sway in Byzantium and over much of eastern Europe, including Rus' lands.

---

[1] Archibald R. Lewis defined five "civilizations" in Afro-Eurasia: "East Asian, the Indic, the Islamic, the Byzantine-Russian, and the Western European." Archibald R. Lewis, *Nomads and Crusaders AD 1000–1368*, Bloomington, Indiana University Press, 1988, p. 3. I consider the last two to be a single civilization and regard the Indic as being eclipsed during this period by the Islamic and Chinese civilizations, in some areas temporarily, in others more permanently. Lewis also places eastern Turkestan, Tibet, and Mongolia outside the East Asian civilization (*ibid.*, pp. 3–7), but I prefer to treat those areas as frontiers, influenced although not dominated by their neighboring core cultures.

The *Dâr al-Islâm* (Abode of Islam) spanned the southern temperate and northern tropical latitudes from Tangier on the northwest coast of Africa on the Atlantic Ocean across northern and eastern Africa south to Kilwa, through the Levant, Arabia, Mesopotamia, the Iranian plateau, Central Asia, northern India, and into Southeast Asia, with the Muslim kingdom of Arakan and the Sultanate of Malacca.

From the thirteenth through the fifteenth centuries, the cross-cultural influences of the Eurasian land mass can be understood at the deep structural level as the interplay of these three civilizations. These influences had more or less direct interplay in northeastern Rus', as a result both of the Mongol hegemony and of the presence of Byzantine Christianity. The Rus' Church was a major component of the Eastern Church. In respect to religious and cultural influences, Rus' looked to the southwest – to Byzantium. The Rus' princely elite found themselves part of the Mongol Empire, the largest land empire the world had ever seen. In respect of military and political influences, Rus' looked to the southeast. The Mongols brought to northeastern Rus' steppe traditions that were influenced by China and Islam. There they synthesized with the indigenous Slavic and Finnic cultures and the Byzantine Christian culture to help create Muscovy and its religious and political culture. Yet, the carriers of these influences and traditions were only a few among the ruling elite.

Estimates of the total Mongol population in the thirteenth century range widely from 400,000 to 2.5 million. Likewise, the estimates of the numbers in their army vary from a low of 70,000, if one counts only the contingent from Mongolia, to a high of 250,000, if one takes into account all the supplemental troops from other areas.[2] Of these, only about 4,000 genuine Mongols may have found their way as far west as the Qipchaq Khanate and those who did were rapidly assimilated into the host population.[3] For evidence of rapid assimilation of Mongols, David Morgan pointed to the fact that, as early as the 1280s, Turkish replaced Mongol as the language on coinage of the Khanate.[4] A. P. Grigor'ev, however, argued on the basis of four fourteenth-century *paiza*s (*p'ai tsa*) written in Mongol with Uighur script, that the court and state administration continued to conduct matters in the Mongol

---

[2] Leo de Hartog, "The Army of Genghis Khan," *Army Quarterly and Defence Journal*, vol. 109, 1979, p. 484; Dun J. Li, *The Ageless Chinese: a History*, 3rd edn, New York, Charles Scribner's Sons, 1978, pp. 246–247.

[3] Rashīd al-Dīn, *Sbornik letopisei* (Russian trans. of *Jami' al-Tawārīkh*), 3 vols., Moscow and Leningrad, Akedemiia nauk SSSR, 1946–1960, vol. 1, pt. 2, trans. O. I. Smirnova, p. 274; Tiesenhausen, *Sbornik materialov*, vol. 1, p. 235. See also V. L. Egorov, *Istoricheskaia geografiia Zolotoi Ordy v XIII–XIV vv.*, Moscow, Nauka, 1985, pp. 155–156.

[4] David Morgan, *The Mongols*, Oxford, Blackwell, 1986, p. 142.

language until 1380.[5] The maintenance of Mongol for other than diplomatic correspondence seems unlikely. Al-ʿUmarī tells us in the middle of the fourteenth century that the Mongols were completely assimilated by marriage into the Qipchaqs.[6] And, as Ibn Khaldûn declared, a nomadic dynasty on average lasted only about forty years (or three generations of rulers) before it was worn out and succumbed.[7] Ibn Khaldûn's statement would seem to match the experience of the Qipchaq Khanate, because, although the dynasty maintained the semblance of Mongol genealogy, after the 1280s we have no evidence of the use of the Mongol language for internal use.

In theory, the ruling elite of the Qipchaq Khanate were Chingizids, descendants of Chingiz Khan and everyone in society was supposedly related in some way to the ruling khan. These theoretical concepts reflected the early tribal origins of Mongol society, as well as of steppe nomadic society in general. In reality, the claim of most princes to be Chingizids was tenuous at best and very few of the khan's subjects were related to him at all. Rudi Paul Lindner has described the use of "fictional blood ties" to validate the "shared interests" of members of a tribe with those who join it.[8] Lindner argues that political and economic considerations prevailed over kinship ties in defining a tribe. Thus, kinship was predominantly an idiom by which to define relationships once an individual or group of individuals had become part of a tribe. This is an important point, because it allowed Chingiz Khan, and other tribal chiefs, like Attila, before him, rapidly to expand their tribes and tribal confederations for purposes of war. An exclusive reliance on kinship to determine tribal identity would not have allowed such rapid expansion, because it would have excluded so many from the tribe.

The Mongol elite of the Qipchaq Khanate ruled over a mixed sedentary and nomad population, which included the Polovtsi (Cumans, Qipchaq [Kypchak or Kipchak]), Volga Bulgars, Bashkirs, Mordvinians, Qangli, and Alans (Ās), who had lived in the local area for centuries. Besides pastureland for horses, goats, and sheep, the area of the Qipchaq Khanate included grain-growing areas in the northeast and northwest. Rubruck, for example, describes the growing of rye and

[5] A. P. Grigor'ev, "Ofitsial'nyi iazyk Zolotoi Ordy XIII–XIV vv.," *Tiurkologicheskii sbornik 1977*, Moscow, 1981, p. 82.
[6] Ibn Fadl al-ʿUmarī, *Das mongolische Weltreich. Al-ʿUmarī's Darstellung der mongolischen Reiche in seinem Werk Masālik al-abṣār fī mamālik al-amṣār*, Wiesbaden, Otto Harrassowitz, 1968, Arabic text, p. 73; see also paraphrase and commentary by Klaus Lech, pp. 136–147.
[7] Ibn Khaldûn, *The Muqaddimah: an Introduction to History*, trans. Franz Rosenthal, ed. N. J. Dawood, Princeton University Press, Bollingen Series, 1969, pp. 136–138.
[8] Rudi Paul Lindner, "What Was a Nomadic Tribe?" *Comparative Studies in Society and History*, vol. 24, 1982, pp. 696–697.

millet among the Rus' in the area of the Don River when he passed through the area in the 1250s.[9] Once established at Sarai, the ruling class, after a brief period of flirtation with other religions, accepted Islam and adopted Islamic culture and a sedentary way of life.[10] One could have drawn the conclusion that the ruling class was sedentary from studying the archaeological remains of Khanate cities and towns.[11] The remains and building foundations dispel the notion that these were merely tent cities. Yet, although scholars have known about these urban areas for some time, the idea persisted that the ruling class nomadized while governing sedentary people. Uli Schamiloglu's reinterpretation repudiates the idea that the rulers of the Khanate continued to herd sheep and horses moving north to spring pastures and south to winter encampment while at the same time governing a complex polity.

The Mongol elite brought with it Chinese-based methods of administration. Elite relations, line of succession, and military practices were steppe nomadic, some particularly Mongol, in origin. To govern such a vast territory, the Qipchaq Khanate's ruling elite borrowed the institution of *iqṭāʿ* from Islamic society and set up a decentralized system of cavalry maintenance. This *iqṭāʿ* system was added to the already existing system of dual administration derived from China. Thus, the Qipchaq Khanate represented the crossroads of two civilizations, China and Islam, the influences of which interacted and merged with steppe nomadic practices. The Khanate then acted as a conduit for influence from these two civilizations to Muscovy. Our understanding of Muscovy is thus dependent to a great extent on our understanding of the Qipchaq Khanate.

In examining possible influence of one culture upon another, I would like first to discuss some basic principles. To ascertain whether an institution or practice was transferred from one culture to another, either by imposition or borrowing, we can establish at least three criteria: (1) that the institution or practice existed in the source culture; (2) that its existence in the source culture coincided in real time with its appearance in the target culture; and (3) that a mechanism for its transference from the source culture to the target culture was operative.

[9] Rubruck, *Itinerarium*, ch. 13, para. 12, p. 198; Rubruck, *Journey* (Rockhill), p. 98; Rubruck, *Mission* (Jackson), p. 110.
[10] Uli Schamiloglu, "Reinterpreting the Nomad–Sedentary Relationship in the Golden Horde (13th–14th Centuries)," paper presented at the Conference on the Role of the Frontier in Rus'/Russian History, the Eighth Through the Eighteenth Centuries, Chicago, May 29–31, 1992; and Uli Schamiloglu, *The Golden Horde: Economy, Society and Civilization in Western Eurasia, 13th and 14th Centuries* (unpublished).
[11] G. A. Fyodorov-Davydov [Fedorov-Davydov], *The Culture of the Golden Horde Cities*, trans. H. Bartlett Wells, Oxford, BAR International Series, 1984; and Egorov, *Istoricheskaia geografiia Zolotoi Ordy*, pp. 75–150.

Such a mechanism could involve military invasion, governmental administration, trading relations (since ideas follow trade routes), literary or educational access, etc. Without all three of these criteria being present, we should not even consider cross-cultural influence unless we have some other overriding evidence that leads us to think so (for example, a ruling elite's trying to impose its ideas about a defunct culture on to the state it was ruling). Once borrowed, an institution or practice acquires its own integrity and dynamic. To establish connections of institutions and practices between societies does not substitute for understanding their workings within their respective societies. Given the scarcity of evidence for pre-modern history, the workings of an institution or practice in the source society may give us some indication of how it worked in the target society, and vice versa.

Here I will focus on four claims of Mongol influence on Muscovy: (1) administration, political institutions, and the military; (2) seclusion of women; (3) oriental despotism; and (4) economic oppression of the so-called "Tatar yoke." Each of these claims corresponds to a different component of society: political (administration and government), social (status of women), intellectual (theoretical justification of rule), and economic (commercial activity). I will test those claims against the available source evidence and discuss them within the context of their respective societal components. I hope to demonstrate that, of these, only the borrowing of administrative procedures, political institutions, and military matters can be attributed to Mongol influence. For the others, the claims of political, social, and economic oppression do not rest on reliable evidence but more on value-laden presuppositions that the Mongols represented a negative influence on Muscovy because the Mongols themselves were bad.

Evaluations of what is "good" or "bad," in a value-judgment sense, are inescapable because we make them all the time. When we analyze the sources, however, we should try to analyze them on their own bases and in their own contexts. Our value judgments can help us sort out the evidence for what was good or bad for that society or for any society. But we must be prepared to test our value judgments continually during the course of the analysis and to realize that our own ideological commitment toward the society in which we live or study may be interfering with and contaminating our analysis. To allow our value judgments to intrude untested on the analysis inevitably skews that analysis and leads to misrepresentation of the source testimony.[12] We turn now to an analysis of each of these four claims of Mongol influence.

[12] See Donald Ostrowski, "A Metahistorical Analysis: Hayden White and Four Narratives of 'Russian' History," *Clio*, vol. 19, 1990, esp. pp. 234–235.

2   Administration, political institutions,
     and the military

The key to understanding the Muscovite administrative system is the
dual structure that it adopted from the Qipchaq Khanate. This dual-
administrative structure allowed for overlapping jurisdiction and duties
of officials. Its roots were in the Chinese system of local government,
which had been introduced under Shi Huangdi (Shih Huang Ti), the
first emperor of a unified China (221 BC–210 BC) and formalized under
the Han Dynasty.[1] The titles of the provincial governors under the Han
were the *taishou* (*t'ai-shou*, civilian governor) and *duwei* (*tu-wei*, military
governor).[2] Although the titles of the positions subsequently changed,
the principle of a dual civil–military administration remained the
foundation of the Chinese system of local government until the twentieth century.[3] This Chinese system was spread throughout the Mongol
Empire as a result of the Mongols' need to find administrative methods
to govern their burgeoning domains. The Uighur Tata Tonga, keeper of
the seal under the Naiman, could have introduced to the Mongols
certain bureaux of central administration. Yet, the transfer of administrative institutions may have a more pervasive influence behind it.

[1] Derk Bodde, *China's First Unifier: a Study of the Ch'in Dynasty as Seen in the Life of Li Ssŭ
(280?–208 BC)*, Leiden, E. J. Brill, 1938, p. 145; and Michael Loewe, *Records of Han
Administration*, 2 vols., Cambridge University Press, 1967, vol. 1: *Historical Assessment*,
pp. 59, 99–100. For a fuller discussion of the following, see my "The *Tamma* and the
Dual-Administrative Structure of the Mongol Empire," *Bulletin of the School of Oriental
and African Studies*, vol. 61, 1998 (forthcoming).
[2] Rafe de Crespigny, *Official Titles of the Former Han Dynasty*, trans. H. H. Dubs,
Canberra, Australian National University Press, 1967, pp. 24, 30.
[3] E. A. Kracke, Jr., *Civil Service in Early Sung China 960–1067: With Particular Emphasis
on the Development of Controlled Sponsorship to Foster Administrative Responsibility*,
Cambridge, MA, Harvard University Press, 1953, 1968, pp. 54–57; Winston W. Lo, *An
Introduction to the Civil Service of Sung China: With Emphasis on Its Personnel Administra-
tion*, Honolulu, University of Hawaii Press, 1987; Albert Herrmann, *Historical and
Commercial Atlas of China*, Cambridge, MA, Harvard University Press, 1935,
pp. 42–43; Elizabeth Endicott-West, *Mongolian Rule in China: Local Administration in
the Yuan Dynasty*, Cambridge, MA, Harvard University Press, 1989; Paul D. Buell,
"Kalmyk Tanggaci People: Thoughts on the Mechanics and Impact of Mongol
Expansion," *Mongolian Studies*, vol. 6, 1980, pp. 48–49; T'ung-tsu Ch'u, *Local
Government in China Under the Ch'ing*, Stanford University Press, 1969, pp. 1–13, 65.

We often think of Chinese relations with the barbarians in south-to-north terms, divided approximately by the Great Wall and its predecessors. But Owen Lattimore suggested that the "east–west distribution of tribes, and east–west political and military movement, have been as important as this north–south geographical stratification."[4] The eastern Turks, hundreds of years before Chingiz Khan, were borrowing Chinese political and administrative institutions and practices.[5] And the Qara-Khitai Empire in Central Asia may have provided the institutional basis for the Mongol Empire. The Qara-Khitai administrative structure, in Morgan's view, represented a synthesis of Chinese, indigenous steppe (Khitan), and Central Asian–Turkish influences.[6] We have to keep in mind the possibility, as Morgan did, that Khitan influence could have come through other means, for example, Khitans in Jin (Chin) service who preferred to leave for the Mongols or those from the Khitan homeland who were drafted into Mongol service. N. Ts. Munkuev, however, was of the opinion that the Mongols borrowed their political and administrative institutions from the Jurchens.[7] And at least one scholar has expressed the view that the administrative structure of the Mongol Empire "emerged from the guard/household establishment" of Chingiz Khan and, thus, "was not based upon nor inspired by Chinese bureaucratic models."[8] Typical of the problem is the *paiza*s, or tablets of authority, that the Mongols used to convey important information. The *paiza*s are of Chinese origin, but the Mongols adopted them only after contact with the Jurchens and Khitans, among whom they were already in use. Most likely, institutional borrowing corresponded with this adoption either from the Jurchens or from the Khitans. Morgan, nonetheless, concluded that the Mongols must have adopted the administrative structure of the Qara-Khitai Empire after taking it over in 1218. In this sense, he saw the Mongol Empire as "a successor state, on a much grander scale, to the Qara-Khitai empire."[9]

It is important for our purposes to understand the nature of this institutional borrowing because some of the same institutions appear in Rus' in the thirteenth and fourteenth centuries. In particular, the Rus' sources testify to the terms *daruga* and *baskak*, which derive from the

---

[4] Owen Lattimore, "The Geography of Chingis Khan," *Geographical Journal*, vol. 129, 1963, p. 1.

[5] On this point, see Igor de Rachewiltz, "Some Remarks on the Ideological Foundation of Chinggis Khan's Empire," *Papers on Far Eastern History*, vol. 7, 1973, pp. 29–30.

[6] Morgan, *Mongols*, p. 49.

[7] N. Ts. Munkuev [Münküyev], "A New Mongolian P'ai-Tzŭ from Simferopol," *Acta Orientalia Academiae Scientiarium Hungaricae*, vol. 36, 1977, p. 186.

[8] Thomas T. Allsen, "Guard and Government in the Reign of the Grand Qan Möngke, 1251–59," *Harvard Journal of Asiatic Studies*, vol. 46, 1986, p. 521.

[9] Morgan, *Mongols*, p. 50.

equivalent terms *daruɣači* and *bāsqāq* in Mongol and Turkic sources and
which refer to a type of governor (see Glossary). Istvan Vásáry, among
others, argued that these terms, along with the Seljūq *šihna* (Arabic:
shahna) are synonymous and the positions they represent are function-
ally the same. He pointed out that the term *bāsqāq* does not appear in
Mongol sources and that the term *daruɣači* appears in Mongol sources
only after their conquest of the Qara-Khitai Empire. Thus, *daruɣači*
must be the Mongol term for *bāsqāq*.[10]

My own research, however, has led me to agree with those who see
the *daruɣači* and *bāsqāq* as separate though related positions. Although
the term *bāsqāq* does not appear in Mongol sources, the term *tammači*
(plural *tammačin*) does appear in the *Secret History of the Mongols* as a
position that contrasts with the *daruɣači*. Section 274 of the *Secret
History of the Mongols* (*Yuanchao bishi*) states that Khagan Ögödei placed
"*daruɣačin* and *tammačin*" over the conquered peoples whose capitals
were "Asud, Sesüd, Bolar, and Mankerman-Kiwa."[11] References to
tamma appear elsewhere in the *Secret History*[12] and in Rashīd al-Dīn's
world history.[13] The term also appears in Chinese sources: the *Yuanshi*
(the Ming history of the Yuan dynasty), the *Yuan dianzheng* (*Institutions
of the Yuan Dynasty*), and the *Tongchi tiaoge* (*Code of Comprehensive*

[10] Istvan Vásáry, "The Origin of the Institution of *Basqaqs*," *Acta Orientalia Academiae
Scientiarium Hungaricae*, vol. 32, 1978, pp. 203–205.
[11] *Mongɣol-un niuča tobča'an*, in Igor de Rachewiltz, *Index to the Secret History of the
Mongols*, Indiana University Publications, Uralic and Altaic Studies, vol. 121,
Bloomington, Indiana University Press, 1972, § 274, p. 165. Cf. *The Secret History of
the Mongols*, trans. Francis Woodman Cleaves, Cambridge, MA, Harvard University
Press, 1982, p. 215; "The Secret History of the Mongols," trans. Igor de Rachewiltz,
Papers on Far Eastern History (*PFEH*), vol. 31, 1985, p. 31; and "Starinnoe
Mongol'skoe skazanie o Chingiskhane," trans. Archimandrite Palladii, *Trudy chlenov
Rossiiskoi dukhovnoi missii v Pekine*, vol. 4, 1866, p. 155.
[12] *Mongɣol-un niuča tobča'an*, § 273, pp. 165, 166; cf. *Secret History* (Cleaves), pp. 214,
215, 217; "Secret History" (Rachewiltz), vol. 31, 1985, pp. 30, 31, 32; and "Starinnoe
Mongol'skoe skazanie," p. 155.
[13] Rashīd al-Dīn, *Dzhami at-Tavarikh*, vol. 1, pt. 1: *Kriticheskii tekst*, ed. A. A.
Romaskevich, A. A. Khetagurov, and A. A. Ali-zade, Moscow, Nauka, 1965,
pp. 150–151; Rashīd al-Dīn, *Dzhami at-Tavarikh*, vol. 2, pt. 1: *Kriticheskii tekst*, ed.
A. A. Ali-zade, Moscow, Nauka, 1980, p. 26; Rashīd al-Dīn, *Jāmi' al-Tawārīkh*, ed.
Abdul-kerim Ali Ogly Ali-zade, Baku, Akademiia nauk Azerbaidzhanskoi SSR, 1957,
vol. 3, p. 21. Cf. Rashīd al-Dīn, *Djami el-Tevarikh*, ed. Edgar B. Blochet, E. J. W. Gibb
Memorial Series, vol. 18, Leiden, E. J. Brill, 1911, p. 18. Rashīd al-Dīn, *Successors*,
pp. 32–33. Rashīd al-Dīn, *Sbornik letopisei*, vol. 1, pt. 1, trans. L. A. Khetagurov, ed. A.
A. Semenov, pp. 98–99; vol. 1, pt. 2, pp. 54, 279–280. vol. 2, trans. Iu. P. Verkhovskii,
ed. I. P. Petrushevskii, p. 20; vol. 3, trans. A. K. Arends, ed. A. A. Romaskevich, E. È.
Bertel's, and A. Iu. Iakubovskii, p. 23; Rashīd al-Dīn, *Jāmi' al-Tawārīkh*, ed. I. N.
Berezin, *Trudy Vostochnogo otdeleniia Rossiiskogo arkheologicheskogo obshchestva*, vol. 7,
1861, p. 56, vol. 13, 1868, pp. 59, 95, and vol. 15, 1888, pp. 152, 229. My thanks to
Wheeler Thackston for allowing me to consult with him about these passages in Rashīd
al-Dīn's text.

Institutions), all of which use *tanmachi qun* (*tammači* army) when referring to garrison troops.[14]

Almost all these usages are specifically military in nature, as are those of the term *bāsqāq*. By contrast, references to the *daruyači* indicate some functions that we would consider civilian in nature. The *Yuanshi* delineates the following duties for the *daruyači*: conducting the census; recruiting soldiers from the inhabitants of the region; setting up the *yām*; collecting taxes; and sending tribute to the Imperial court.[15] On the basis of the evidence then it seems reasonable to conclude that the *daruyači* was equivalent to the *taishou* or civilian governor, and the *bāsqāq* was equivalent to the *duwei* or military governor. To be sure, they had overlapping and conflicting duties, but that was the beauty of the dual-administrative system. In the words of Roy Mottahedeh: "In a decentralized government, it was desirable to have alternate wires to pull in case any wire (as so easily and frequently happened) disappeared."[16]

When the Mongols first invaded northern China (1211–1215), they captured Jin administrators, among whom was the Khitan Yelü Chucai.[17] After that campaign, Yelü Chucai became one of the chief advisers to Chingiz Khan.[18] And, under Ögödei, Yelü Chucai became the chief administrator of the Mongol Empire. It was in this period of

[14] Ch'i-ch'ing Hsiao, *The Military Establishment of the Yuan Dynasty*, Cambridge, MA, Council on East Asian Studies, 1978, pp. 85 (*Yuanshi*, 98/13b), 89 (*Yuanshi*, 98/16a, 98/16b), 96 (*Yuanshi*, 99/4b), 99 (*Yuanshi*, 99/7a), 102 (*Yuanshi*, 99/10b), 107 (*Yuanshi*, 99/14b), 109 (*Yuanshi*, 99/17a), 112 (*Yuanshi*, 99/20b), 115 (*Yuanshi*, 99/22b), 117 (*Yuanshi*, 99/24a), 120 (*Yuanshi*, 99/26b), 123 (*Yuanshi*, 99/29b); Gunther Mangold, *Das Militärwesen in China unter der Mongolen-Herrschaft*, Bamberg, Foto-druck, 1971, pp. 108–110 (*Yuan dianzheng*, 34/25a–26a), 133 (*Tongchi haoge*, 7/15a), 218 (*Yuan dianzheng*, 35).

[15] *Yuanshi*, 7/16 cited in Palladii, "Starinnoe Mongol'skoe skazanie," p. 256.

[16] Roy P. Mottahedeh, *Loyalty and Leadership in an Early Islamic Society*, Princeton University Press, 1980, p. 182.

[17] On the Mongol campaigns in northern China, see H. Desmond Martin, *The Rise of Chingis Khan and His Conquest of North China*, Baltimore, MD, Johns Hopkins University Press, 1950.

[18] On the career and significance of Yelü Chucai, see Igor de Rachewiltz, "Yeh-lü Ch'u-ts'ai (1189–1243): Buddhist Idealist and Confucian Statesman," in *Confucian Personalities*, ed. A. F. Wright and D. Twitchett, Stanford University Press, 1962, pp. 189–216. For a translation into Russian of the biography of Yelü Chucai that appears in the *Yuanshi*, see N. Ts. Munkuev, *Kitaiskii istochnik o pervykh mongol'skikh khanakh. Nadgrobnaia nadpis' na mogile Eliui Chu-tsaia. Perevod i issledovanie*, Moscow, Nauka, 1965, pp. 185–201. For a paraphrase-cum-translation into French, see Jean Pierre Abel Rémusat, "Yeliu-thsou-tsai, ministre tartare," in *Nouveaux mélanges asiatiques*, 2 vols., Paris, Schubert et Heideloff, 1829 vol. 2, pp. 64–88. For a translation into English of Yelü Chucai's *Siyu lu* ("Account of a Journey to the West"), see Igor de Rachewiltz, "The *Hsi-yu lu* by Yeh-Lü Ch'u Ts'ai," *Monumenta Serica*, vol. 21, 1962, pp. 1–128.

Table 2.1: *Asian dual-administration titles*

	Civilian governor	Military governor
Qin Han	*taishou*	*duwei*
Tang	*cushi* *taishouya*	*duweiya*
Seljūq Persian	*šihna* *shahna*	*bāsqāq*
Mongol	*daruγa(či)*	*tamma(či)*
Turkic	*darūgha*	*bāsqāq*
Yuan	*daluhuachi*	*tanmachi*
Rus'	*daruga, doroga* *doraga*	*baskak*

initial consolidation of the conquests that he was most influential.[19] It may have been specifically through Yelü Chucai that the Mongols adopted the dual-administrative practice that originated with the Chinese. As the table indicates, the dual positions of civilian governor (*taishou*) and military governor (*duwei*) were instituted under the Qin and formalized under the Han. The Chinese term *ya*, meaning "to press," was sometimes suffixed to the names of these positions, and indicated an official who authorized a document by pressing his seal to it. That term followed the export of the idea of the dual positions westward, where the civilian governor emerged as the *shahna* and the military governor emerged as the *bāsqāq* (< Turkic, *bās-* = to press). When the Mongols took the Qara-Khitai Empire, they provided their own terms for the position of the civilian governor, which they called *daruγa* (< Mongol, *daru-* = to press), and for the position of the military governor, which they called *tamma*. The Mongols in the western part of the Empire introduced the Mongol term *daruγa(či)* as the equivalent of the *shahna*. When they adopted Turkic, however, they also substituted the Turkic word *bāsqāq* for the Mongol word *tamma*. During the Yuan dynasty, the Mongols brought into China the name they used for the civilian governor (*daruγači*), which then was transcribed as *daluhuachi*. And they reintroduced the name they used for military governor (*tammači*), which was transcribed *tanmachi*, but with a new meaning that it had not had before in China. The positions themselves, however, were equivalent to those that had initially developed under the Qin and

---

[19] See, *inter alia*, Chuluuny Dalai, *Mongoliia v XIII–XIV vekakh*, Moscow, Nauka, 1983, p. 46.

Han, with the notable exception that ethnic Chinese were not supposed to hold them.

Finally, we find the same two positions appearing in Rus' sources as *daruga* (даруга or some variant) and *baskak* (баскак), which referred specifically to Tatar officials. The Rus' had their own term for a military commander – *voevoda* – which by the sixteenth century came to also mean the governor of a province.[20] This may help to explain the report in a Muscovite source that, after the sack of Kiev in 1240, Batu appointed a *voevoda* there.[21] That *voevoda* would then be the same person that the *Secret History* refers to as the *tammači*. Yet, this information appears only in the Nikon Chronicle, which dates from the sixteenth century and is notorious for manufactured interpolations. It does not appear in any earlier chronicles that I am aware of, so it is unclear how the compiler of the chronicle would have known in the sixteenth century what Batu had done in the thirteenth century. For now, it is a tantalizing bit of testimony, which I cannot use as evidence.

As military commanders in conquered but unpacified areas, both the *bāsqāq* and the *tammači* were, as far as we can determine, the military governors of these regions. The jurisdiction of the military governors (*bāsqāq* or *tammači*) and that of the civilian governors (*daruyači* or *shaḥna*) intentionally overlapped. The category of the area they governed, that is, whether pacified or not, would determine which one had priority in authority.

Some historians have suggested that the *daruyači* "system" replaced the *bāsqāq* "system" in the early fourteenth century in Rus'. They cite as their evidence the disappearance of the word "*baskak*" from Rus' sources in relation to certain areas of northeastern Rus' about that time. Although we still find mention of *bāsqāqs* in Riazan' and Tula well into the late fourteenth century,[22] it is true that it is absent from the sources in relation to the area around Vladimir, Moscow, and Tver' from the early fourteenth century on. Zimin attributed the "replacement" to the Tver' uprising of 1327, that is, to opposition within Rus' to the

---

[20] *Dictionary of Russian Historical Terms from the Eleventh Century to 1917*, comp. Sergei G. Pushkarev, ed. George Vernadsky and Ralph T. Fisher, Jr., New Haven, CT, Yale University Press, 1970, pp. 176–177.

[21] *PSRL*, vol. 10, p. 117.

[22] See *RIB*, vol. 6, no. 18, col. 164 and no. 19, col. 167; *DDG*, no. 10, p. 29 (1382). See also *PSRL*, vol. 28, pp. 69, 229 (1331). Under 1387, the Vologda-Perm' Chronicle version of the *Skazanie o Mamaevom poboishche* reports that Emir Mamai threatened to restore the *baskak* system, which would seem to imply that it had been completely dismantled by then. *PSRL*, vol. 26, p. 157. But the Vologda-Perm' Chronicle is a sixteenth-century text, so we should not rely on it alone for evidence about the fourteenth century.

*bāsqāq*s.[23] Charles Halperin suggested, instead, what he called a "Mongol perspective," that is, a restructuring in the Qipchaq Khanate that brought the *daruyači*s to the fore replacing the *bāsqāq*s during the course of the fourteenth century.[24] Both historians, despite Halperin's claim to the contrary, viewed the issue from the perspective of Rus' sources alone. Instead, the non-Rus' sources indicate that *daruyači*s were prominent in the Mongol Empire from at least the time of Ögödei (1229–1241) and existed wherever there were *bāsqāq*s. There is a better explanation for the absence of the word "*baskak*" in Rus' sources after the fourteenth century and the apparent disappearance of *bāsqāq*s from the areas controlled by Tver' and Moscow in the 1320s. Until that time, the Rus' had dealings mainly with provincial military governors (*bāsqāq*s), who resided in the frontier towns of the Qipchaq Khanate. The Rus' did not have as much contact with the civilian governors, who resided mostly in towns near the center of the Khanate, in particular Sarai. To be sure, Rus' princes, when they visited Sarai, most likely dealt with *daruyači*s as well as the khan himself. But our evidence for Rus' contacts with *bāsqāq*s and *daruyači*s come mostly from the chronicles, written by Churchmen, who had, at best, a vague understanding of the Mongol administrative structure.

In the early fourteenth century, the local Rus' princes, in particular those from Moscow and Tver', took over the duties of the *bāsqāq*s, including the collection of taxes and the use of military force to maintain order.[25] As long as the Qipchaq khan thought Rus' needed pacification, he maintained resident *bāsqāq*s there. When he became convinced the Rus' grand prince could perform the duties of tax and toll collection as well as maintain law and order, he handed over the duties of the *bāsqāq*s to the grand prince. Thus, *bāsqāq*s were withdrawn from most of north-eastern Rus', not because of resistance by the local populace (to suppress such resistance was, after all, one of their functions) but because of acquiescence and acceptance of the Qipchaq khan's hegemony. The khans in Sarai and the *daruyači*s resident in Sarai and other towns of the Khanate maintained contact with the Rus' princes, when they were not at Sarai themselves, through envoys (*posly*).[26] When the

[23] A. A. Zimin, "Narodnye dvizheniia 20-kh godov XIV veka i likvidatsiia sistemy baskachestva v severo-vostochnoi Rusi," *Izvestiia Akademii nauk SSSR. Seriia istorii i filosofii*, vol. 9, 1952, pp. 61–65.

[24] Charles J. Halperin, *Russia and the Golden Horde: the Mongol Impact on Medieval Russian History*, Bloomington, Indiana University Press, 1985, pp. 37–40.

[25] Vásáry, "Origin of the Institution of *Basqaqs*," pp. 201–202. Paszkiewicz put the transfer at "soon after 1313." Paszkiewicz, *Rise of Moscow's Power*, p. 224.

[26] For a partial list of references in the chronicles to envoys sent during the fourteenth and fifteenth centuries, see Halperin, *Russia and the Golden Horde*, pp. 139–140 nn. 37–38.

*bāsqāq*s disappeared from Muscovy and Tver', the next level of administration the chroniclers were aware of was the *daruyači*s and their envoys.

This process was an empire-wide one as two phenomena conjoined to force khans of each *ulus* (see Glossary) to turn over responsibility for maintaining order and collecting taxes to local rulers. First, local rulers became "pacified" in that they, like the grand princes of Moscow, saw that their best interests lay, at least for the time being, in cooperating with the hegemon. Second, each of the *ulus* of the Mongol world empire began to lose the means to maintain armies indefinitely on the frontier areas of their khanates. Having local rulers administer their own territory led to an even more decentralized arrangement within each khanate. This more economical means of maintaining hegemony no doubt facilitated the survival of, at least, the Qipchaq Khanate for over another hundred years. Elimination of *bāsqāq*s from certain areas of Rus' in the early fourteenth century was also a significant development for Rus'. Formerly, Mongol *bāsqāq*s were dependent on Sarai for their power and authority. Now Rus' grand princes could begin to create their own power base, although, until well into the fifteenth century, their authority continued to derive from Sarai. It also helped establish a focal point around which the Rus' Church could eventually unify its own aspirations. Whether that focal point would be the Moscow or Tver' or some other principality was still not clear in the fourteenth century, and would not be ultimately resolved until the middle of the fifteenth century.

Available evidence suggests that there may have been *daruyači*s for different areas of Rus'. For example, in 1431, when Vasilii II and his uncle, Iurii, went to Sarai to have Khan Ulug Meḥmed settle the dispute over succession, they resided in the house of the *daruyači* of Moscow, Amin Bulat.[27] And in 1471, the Simeonov Chronicle refers to Prince Temur of the Great Horde as the "*doroga* of Riazan'."[28] These two references in particular led A. N. Nasonov to propose that there had also been *daruyači*s for Tver' and Suzdal', and possibly other places as well, although there is no direct evidence to support such a proposal.[29] Thus, both *daruyači*s and *bāsqāq*s governed Rus' in the second half of the thirteenth and early fourteenth century. At that point, the Rus' grand prince replaced the foreign *bāsqāq*s and along with the *daruyači*s governed Rus'. This relationship lasted, at least ostensibly, until the end of the Qipchaq Khanate's independence in 1502.

The particulars of Mongol rule in Rus' coincided with those of

---

[27] *PSRL*, vol. 12, p. 15.   [28] *PSRL*, vol. 18, p. 224.
[29] A. N. Nasonov, *Mongoly i Rus' (Istorii politiki na Rusi)*, Moscow and Leningrad, Akademia nauk SSSR, 1940, p. 105.

Mongol rule in other subject areas. Various decrees and ordinances, as well as descriptions in the *Yuanshi*, tell us that the Mongols demanded the following from local ruling elites: (1) provisions for the Mongol army; (2) a census of the local population; (3) support troops; (4) hostages; (5) establishment and maintenance of the *yām* (*iam*) (see Glossary); (6) collection of taxes; (7) acceptance of a *daruyači* as supervisor; and (8) a personal appearance of the local ruler at the khan's court.[30] Rus' sources provide evidence of the fulfillment of each demand with the complete support of the Rus' princes.

Muscovite rulers, notably Ivan Kalita and Semen the Proud, in turn, borrowed the system of dual administration from the Mongols to aid in tax collection, governing, and fulfillment of their new responsibilities. Through frequent visits to Sarai, they had an opportunity to observe first hand the administration of the Khanate of Qipchaq.[31] The sources do not allow us to say which Muscovite prince was the most responsible or who contributed what to the establishment of Muscovite administrative institutions. Iurii III, the older brother of Ivan I, spent two years at Sarai between 1315 and 1317, and married Khan Özbeg's sister, Konchaka (baptized "Agrafa"). Khan Özbeg declared him grand prince in 1319 but deprived him of the grand princely patent in 1322. Iurii seems to have been on campaign continuously between then and his death in 1325,[32] so I doubt he had much to do with institutional borrowing. While subsequent princes of Moscow, like Ivan II and Dmitrii Donskoi, also spent time at the Horde, it seems to me that the formative period of Muscovite political institutions was between 1330 and 1350, the period that roughly coincides with the reigns of Ivan I and Semen as grand princes. These two rulers undertook at least twelve trips to Sarai from 1332 to 1350. And it was precisely because the Muscovite princes were responsible for collecting taxes and maintaining order as grand princes outside their immediate domains that they adopted the administrative structure from Sarai.

While Muscovite rulers functioned as *bāsqāq*s for the Qipchaq khan, they appointed *namestniki*, as the functional equivalent of *daruyačin*, and *volosteli*, as functional equivalent of *bāsqāq*s, within the area under their

---

[30] Thomas T. Allsen, *Mongol Imperialism: the Policies of the Grand Qan Möngke in China, Russia, and the Islamic Lands, 1251–1259*, Berkeley, University of California Press, 1987, p. 114; W. E. Henthorn, *Korea: the Mongol Invasions*, Leiden, E. J. Brill, 1963, p. 194.

[31] Much of the following discussion of Muscovy's administrative setup is based on Ostrowski, "Mongol Origins," pp. 525–542.

[32] *TL*, p. 357; *NPL*, pp. 97, 340; *PSRL*, vol. 4, p. 260; vol. 5, p. 217; vol. 10, p. 189; vol. 15, cols. 42, 415; vol. 25, p. 167.

jurisdiction.[33] By the end of the fourteenth century, according to one estimate, Muscovy had fifteen *namestniki* and around a hundred *volosteli*.[34] Both the *namestniki* and the *volosteli* maintained themselves through *kormlenie* (< *korm* = feeding), that is, through a share of the taxes and court fees collected in each district. *Namestniki* were replaced, in turn, during the course of the sixteenth century by the holders of *pomest'ia* (see Glossary), who were quasi-administrators and tax gatherers of the estates they held. *Volosteli* were replaced during the sixteenth century by *voevody*, military commanders who acted as military governors of their districts.[35] Thus, the original functions of the *bāsqāq* were kept in the position of the *voevoda*, but a radical transformation had taken place in regard to the position that the *daruyači* occupied. Yet, in 1376, Grand Prince Dmitrii appointed a "*doroga* and a *tamozhnik* who resided in Kazan'" over Bulgar when it surrendered to Muscovite forces.[36] The use of the term *doroga* by Rus' chroniclers for an appointment made by the Muscovite grand prince indicates a distinction between internal, Rus' lands, where *namestniki* and *volosteli* governed in the fourteenth and fifteenth centuries, and external, Tatar lands, where *daruyači*s and *bāsqāq*s governed. The *d'iaki* (scribes) of the Muscovite court performed the same functions as the *bitikchi* (Mongol: *bichechi*) of the Uighur chanceries, which often included supervising the chancery as well.[37]

Besides the concept of dual-circuit administration and the de-centralized setup of the Mongol/Chinese administrative apparatus, the

---

[33] Vásáry had suggested that the equivalent of the *daruyači*s of the Qipchaq Khanate were civilian heads (called *putniki*, or, if they were boyars, *putnye boiariny*) of *puti* and that a double transformation occurred in Russian of *darugá*, first, to *doróga* (road), then, to *put'* (path, way). Istvan Vásáry, "The Golden Horde *Daruġa* and Its Survival in Russia," *Acta Orientalia Scientiarum Hungaricae*, vol. 30, 1976, pp. 195–196. Such a double transformation is unlikely because it would also have required a reversal of function, since it was the military governor (the *duwei*) who was in charge of the administrative unit called the circuit (*dao* or *li*), not the civilian governor (*taishou*, later *daluhuachi* [*ta-lu-hua-ch'ih*]).

[34] Nancy Shields Kollmann, *Kinship and Politics: the Making of the Muscovite Political System, 1345–1547*, Stanford University Press, 1987, p. 30.

[35] Kliuchevskii, however, states that *voevody* replaced *namestniki*, as is indicated by the fact that many of the *voevody* of the seventeenth century were the sons and grandsons of *namestniki* of the sixteenth century. V. O. Kluchevsky [Kliuchevskii], *A History of Russia*, trans. C. J. Hogarth, 5 vols., London, J. M. Dent, New York, E. P. Dutton, 1911–1931, vol. 3, pp. 152–153. My conclusion is based more on function than genealogical relationship.

[36] *PSRL*, vol. 8, p. 25; vol. 11, p. 25; vol. 18, p. 192; vol. 28, pp. 78, 241.

[37] On the functions of the *bitikchi*, see Gerhard Doerfer, *Türkische und mongolische Elemente im Neupersischen*, vol. 1: *Mongolische Elemente im Neupersischen*, Wiesbaden, F. Steiner, 1963, p. 266; Igor de Rachewiltz, "Personnel and Personalities in North China in the Early Mongol Period," *Journal of the Economic and Social History of the Orient*, vol. 9, 1966, pp. 137–138 n.; Vernadsky, *Mongols and Russia*, p. 212; and David [O.] Morgan, "The Mongol Armies in Persia," *Der Islam*, vol. 56, 1979, pp. 94–95.

Muscovite princes borrowed the entire interlocking relationship of the Qipchaq Khanate's higher administration, such that the *tysiatskii* (until 1374) and the *bol'shoi namestnik* (after 1374) were equivalent to the *beylaribey* (*beklaribek*). The man who occupied this position was in charge of the judicial high court, the army, and foreign policy. In Muscovy, he was a member of the Boyar Council, which itself was the counterpart to the council of state in the Khanate where the four *qaračï beys* sat.[38]

I have suggested elsewhere that the principle that the Boyar Council should consist of only four members existed in the fourteenth century in Muscovy but ended as the Boyar Council expanded its numbers.[39] As late as 1486, however, a Muscovite diplomat to Milan indicated that "[a]t the court there are four principal lords, who are chosen as his [the grand prince's] councillors, with whom he consults and governs the state, and these four are given lands, jurisdictions, and marks of preeminence by which each maintains an impressive court."[40] Thus, even as the membership of the Boyar Council expanded, the idea that four individuals should be designated to act as a check on the ruler's power, that is, as "defenders of the land," and representatives of the four major clans, continued on into Middle Muscovy. For example, all four had to countersign grand princely documents for those documents to be official in the fourteenth century. Later, when the Boyar Council

---

[38] On the "four-bey system" in the Qipchaq Khanate, see Uli Schamiloglu, "Tribal Politics and Social Organization in the Golden Horde," Ph.D. dissertation, Columbia University, 1986, pp. 127–171; Uli Schamiloglu, "The *Qaračï* Beys of the Later Golden Horde: Notes on the Organization of the Mongol World Empire," *Archivum Eurasiae Medii Aevi*, vol. 4, 1984, pp. 283–297; and Schamiloglu, *Golden Horde*, ch. 5 (unpublished). The term "Boyar Duma," often used to describe this institution is anachronistic, since it does not appear in Muscovite sources. The terms *dumati* and *duma* do appear as verbs in the sense of "to consult." See Kollmann, *Kinship and Politics*, p. 45. It is also misleading because it implies an institution of which only some boyars were members, whereas the grand prince was supposed to consult with all the boyars in council. I am using the term "Boyar Council" as a more inclusive term than "Boyar Duma" for an institution that also included *okol'nichie* and *dumnye dvoriane*.

[39] Ostrowski, "Mongol Origins," p. 533.

[40] "Nota et continentia de la cose et signore de Rossia," in Gino Barbieri, *Milano e Mosca. Nella politica del Rinasciemento. Storia delle relazioni diplomatiche tra la Russia e il Ducato di Milano nell'epoca sforzesca*, Bari, Adriatica editrice, 1957, p. 94. See also "Notes and Information about the Affairs and the Ruler of Russia," in Robert M. Croskey and E. C. Ronquist, "George Trakhaniot's Description of Russia in 1486," *Russian History*, vol. 17, 1990, p. 62. Croskey concluded that these four represent "the most senior membership of the [Boyar] Duma, an inner circle." Croskey and Ronquist, "George Trakhaniot's Description of Russia," pp. 62–63 n. 19. But they should not be confused with the "kitchen cabinet" that I. N. Bersen'-Beklemishev refers to as existing under Vasilii III, who decided policy "alone with three [others] in his bedchamber." *AAE*, vol. 1, no. 172, p. 142. The unofficial status of these later advisers is indicated by their meeting in the quarters of the grand prince rather than in the court, which is precisely Bersen'-Beklemishev's complaint.

expanded in numbers, the *dumnye d'iaki* were designated to perform the service of countersigning the decrees to make them legal. In contrast to the high social status of the boyars, the *dvorskii* of the Muscovite court held no social rank to speak of, although he did exercise a relatively high degree of power. The *dvorskii* was equivalent to the vizier in the Khanate, and controlled both the treasury and the circuit administration.

Besides dual administration, the Mongols adopted from the Chinese the principle that all the land belonged to the ruler. During the Tang Dynasty (618–907), the "nationalization" of the land had culminated in the "equal-lands" reforms.[41] The Mongols, not being a sedentary people, had not developed a principle of land ownership, but borrowed it from the Chinese and brought it westward with them. By the fourteenth century, the principle of all the land belonging to the ruler was adopted by the Muscovite grand princes. Previously, in Kievan Rus', when a boyar left a prince's service, he kept his land. Our earliest extant evidence of the invoking of this principle of ownership by the Muscovite prince was the confiscation by Dmitrii in 1375 of the estates of Ivan Vasil'evich Veliaminov when the latter defected to Tver'.[42] Also the Mongols borrowed from the Chinese the system of post roads (*yām*), which they extended into Rus'.[43] The Muscovite rulers subsequently took over its maintenance and operation.[44] One of the most important of Mongol influences was on the creation of the *mestnichestvo* system, which determined the ordering of the ruling class, at least officially, until 1682. The Muscovite elite had inherited from Kievan Rus' the steppe

---

[41] For a description of the equal-land, or equal-field, system, see *inter alia* Edwin O. Reischauer and John K. Fairbank, *East Asia: the Great Tradition*, Boston, Houghton Mifflin, 1960, pp. 158–161; Etienne Balazs, *Chinese Civilization and Bureaucracy: Variations on a Theme*, trans. H. M. Wright, ed. Arthur F. Wright, New Haven, CT, Yale University Press, 1964, pp. 115–120.

[42] *DDG*, no. 9, p. 27. Earlier, in 1350, Grand Prince Semen had confiscated the possessions of Aleksei Petrovich Khvost, but Khvost remained in grand-princely service. *DDG*, no. 2, p. 13.

[43] On the operation of the *yām* under the Yuan, see Polo, *Travels* (Latham), pp. 150–155; Polo, *Book* (Yule), vol. 1, pp. 435–437; P. Olbricht, *Das Postwesen in China unter der Mongolenherrschaft im 13. und 14. Jahrhundert*, Wiesbaden, Otto Harrassowitz, 1954. On its operation in the Mongol world empire, see Morgan, *Mongols*, pp. 103–107; *The Mongol Hordes: Storm from the East*, produced and directed by Robert Marshall, NHK and BBC, 1992, part 2, *World Conquerors*. On its operation in the Qipchaq Khanate, see Berthold Spuler, *Die goldene Horde. Die Mongolen in Rußland*, Leipzig, Otto Harrassowitz, 1943, pp. 404–415.

[44] On its operation in Muscovite Rus', I. Ia. Gurliand, *Iamskaia gon'ba v Moskovskom gosudarstve do kontsa XVII veka*, Iaroslavl', Tipografiia Gubernskogo pravleniia, 1900; and Gustave Alef, "The Origin and Early Development of the Muscovite Postal Service," *Jahrbücher für Geschichte Osteuropas*, vol. 15, 1967, pp. 1–15; reprinted in Alef, *Rulers and Nobles*, item 8.

practice of lateral succession within families and clans down to the fourth brother. When the fourth brother died, then the eldest son of the eldest brother took his turn as leader. One could succeed to the leadership as long as one's father had been leader. What made *mestnichestvo* distinctive was the addition of clan status relationships, such that one's status also depended upon the status of one's clan, which in turn was determined by genealogical proximity to the ruling family and precedence of service rank. The Daniilovichi themselves had maintained lateral succession until, after a bitter civil war, Vasilii II established the principle of primogeniture, but for succession to the grand-princely throne only. The importance of position based on *mestnichestvo* rank remained for the boyars and gentry through the seventeenth century. It is from this century that we have most of the extant evidence concerning litigation cases involving position, not only in military matters but also in seating position at the tsar's banquet table.[45] Seating arrangements at the khan's banquet was of paramount importance among the Mongols, because that helped determine distribution of the war booty. We can thus obtain a better understanding of the behavior of Muscovite boyars, sometimes kicking and screaming, other times going limp, at such banquets when they felt they were placed in a seat ranked below their status.

In addition, administrative practices from Islamic societies entered Muscovy through the Qipchaq Khanate. Muscovite coinage showed heavy Islamic influence with inscriptions in the Arabic alphabet on them through the reign of Vasilii II, and with more emphasis on the inscription than on the figure.[46] Muscovite coinage in general followed Islamic models as found in the Qipchaq Khanate.

The Qipchaq Khanate was also a conduit for the transmission of Muslim *iqṭāʿ*, which initially formed the basis, first, of the *kormlenie* system, then, when Muscovy began to expand, of the *pomest'e* system in Muscovy.[47] This system of military land grants was meant to maintain a standing cavalry while having the cavalrymen administer newly acquired territories, such as the Novgorodian lands in the late fifteenth and early sixteenth centuries. Most of our extant evidence for *pomest'e* for this period is about the Novgorodian *uezdy*, which has led some scholars to

---

[45] See Robert O. Crummey, *Aristocrats and Servitors: the Boyar Elite in Russia, 1613–1689*, Princeton University Press, 1983, pp. 136–138.

[46] Gustave Alef, "The Political Significance of the Inscriptions on Muscovite Coinage in the Reign of Vasili II," *Speculum*, vol. 34, 1959, p. 5; reprinted in Alef, *Rulers and Nobles*, item 1. On such inscriptions during the reign of Ivan III, see V. A. Kalinin, "Monety Ivana III s russko-tatarskimi legendami," *Trudy Gosudarstvennogo Ermitazha*, vol. 21, *Numismatika*, vol. 5, 1981, pp. 112–116.

[47] See Ostrowski, "Military Land Grant," pp. 358–359.

claim that *pomest'e* was initially isolated to this area. But, the main evidence for *pomest'e* in Novgorodian lands derives from the *pistsovye knigi* (land cadasters), which have not survived from other parts of Muscovite Rus'. It seems more likely that Ivan III instituted *pomest'e* wherever he needed to, not just in one area alone.

Attempts have been made by scholars to attribute to the Prophet Muḥammad the innovation of *iqṭā'* into Islamic societies.[48] But the sources indicate that any land granted by Muḥammad could be sold by the receiver as personal property: this is not our military land grant. Claude Cahen suggested that *iqṭā'* derived from *qaṭ'a*, a type of land grant used to remunerate Arab troops in the early seventh-century conquests.[49] If Cahen is correct, then we might suggest, and the source evidence would seem to support such an idea, that the military land grant that we know as *iqṭā'* was an innovation of 'Umar bin al-Khaṭṭāb (Caliph from 634 to 644), who established the manner in which the newly vanquished territories would be governed, namely to divide them among his military.[50] 'Umar may have derived the idea of *iqṭā'* from the *qaṭ'a*. Bernard Lewis has asserted that *qaṭ'a* was based on Byzantine *emphyteus*.[51] But neither *qaṭ'a* nor *emphyteus* was intended as a measure to support a cavalry or to administer newly vanquished territories.

Furthermore, the various systems of military land grants found in medieval Europe, Byzantium, and the Ottoman Empire may all have been variants of *iqṭā'*, borrowed and modified to fit local needs. Thus, from the hub of the Islamic homeland, *iqṭā'* spread via the Arab conquest of Spain to the Franks and western Europe, where it became the basis of the military fief.[52] In Byzantium, *iqṭā'* was modified into *pronoia*, which was used to replace the military aristocracy with an

---

[48] See, e.g., Frede Løkkegaard, *Islamic Taxation in the Classic Period: With Special Reference to Circumstances in Iraq*, Copenhagen, Brunner and Korch, 1950, pp. 14–17.

[49] Claude Cahen, "L'évolution de l'iqṭā' du IXe au XIIIe siècle: Contribution à une histoire comparée des sociétés médiévales," *Annales: Économies, Sociétés, Civilisations*, vol. 8, 1953, p. 26; Claude Cahen, "Ikṭā'," *Encyclopedia of Islam*, new edn, Leiden, E. J. Brill, 1954–, vol. 3, p. 1088; and Claude Cahen, "Day'a," *Encyclopedia of Islam*, new edn, vol. 2, p. 187. See also Ann K. S. Lambton, "Reflections on the Iqṭā'," in *Arabic and Islamic Studies in Honor of Hamilton A. R. Gibb*, ed. George Makdisi, Cambridge, MA, Harvard University Press, 1965, pp. 360–361.

[50] J. J. Saunders, *A History of Medieval Islam*, London, Routledge & Kegan Paul, 1965, p. 45; Laura Veccia Vaglieri, "The Patriarchal and Umayyad Caliphates," in *The Cambridge History of Islam*, 2 vols., ed. P. M. Holt, Ann K. S. Lambton, and Bernard Lewis, Cambridge University Press, 1970, vol. 1A: *The Central Islamic Lands from Pre-Islamic Times to the First World War*, pp. 64–65; and 'Abd al-'Azīz Dūrī, "Landlord and Peasant in Early Islam: a Critical Study," *Der Islam*, vol. 56, 1979, pp. 99–100.

[51] Bernard Lewis, *The Arabs in History*, rev. edn, New York, Harper, 1966, p. 68.

[52] Ostrowski, "Military Land Grant," pp. 357–358.

aristocracy of civilians and scholars.[53] This strong non-military aspect of *pronoia* would seem to refute the contention of those who assert that Ottoman *timar* was based on it rather than directly on *iqtā'*.[54] North of the Muslim homeland, the Turco-Mongols of the Ilkhanate gave up the nomadic lifestyle in the early fourteenth century for agricultural estates in the form of *iqtā'*.[55] Previously, Mongol soldiers lived off booty. The introduction of the *iqtā'* system in the Ilkhanate by Khan Ghāzān coincided with his conversion to Islam in 1295 and the sedentarization and assimilation of the Mongol horse archers. Indeed, one of the reasons Ghāzān gave in his *iarlyk* for establishing *iqtā'* is the unauthorized raids of horse archer nomads under his command looking for loot to supplement their meager subsistence.[56] Mottahedeh asserts that the Buyids were the first to use *iqtā'* in an extensive way. He suggests that this "system may have had its origins in the monetary crisis" of the tenth century.[57] But *iqtā'* appeared among the Buyids some 300 years after 'Umar bin al-Khaṭṭāb was Caliph. The Buyids may have instituted *iqtā'* because of their money crisis, but they were instituting a practice that already existed in the Islamic world.

Study of various Islamic societies demonstrates that *iqtā'*, as practiced by the Muslims from the eighth through at least the fifteenth century, had certain consistent characteristics, and these same characteristics show up in Muscovite military land-grant practices. One of the outward similarities was the way of fighting of the cavalrymen themselves. From Andalusia in the West across northern Africa, then east of a line that ran north through eastern Europe, cavalry fought using short stirrups. The advantage of short stirrups for shooting with a bow (and, later, a rifle) over long stirrups is that the rider gains enormously in accuracy by having his torso free of the horse's jostlings while the riders' legs act as shock absorbers. The feature film *Dances with Wolves* has footage that allows a comparison of bareback riders trying to aim and shoot bows and arrows with a rider on a long-stirruped saddle trying to shoot a rifle.

---

[53] Ernst H. Kantorowicz, "'Feudalism' in the Byzantine Empire," in *Feudalism in History*, ed. Rushton Coulborn, Princeton University Press, 1956, pp. 160–161.

[54] See, e.g., Speros Vryonis, Jr., *The Decline of Medieval Hellenism in Asia Minor and the Process of Islamization from the Eleventh Through the Fifteenth Century*, Berkeley, University of California Press, 1971, pp. 469–470. For references to other proponents of this view, see *ibid.*, p. 470 n. 94.

[55] Morgan, "Mongol Armies in Persia," pp. 94–96. See also David Nicolle, *The Mongol Warlords: Genghis Khan, Kublai Khan, Hülegü, Tamerlane*, Poole, Dorset, Firebird Books, 1990, p. 123.

[56] Rashīd al-Dīn, *Sbornik letopisei*, vol. 3, pp. 280–285; cf. A. P. Martinez, "The Third Portion of the History of Ğāzān Xān in Rašidu 'd-Dīn's Ta'rīx-e Mobārak-e Ğāzānī," *Archivum Eurasiae Medii Aevi*, vol. 6, 1986[1988], pp. 84–108.

[57] Mottahedeh, *Loyalty and Leadership*, pp. 36–37.

The bareback riders must lean over low and close to the target to obtain accuracy. The cavalry-saddle rider is able to keep his upper body erect, but must gauge the pulling of the trigger to correspond with the downward motion of his body while he is bouncing in the saddle.[58] Neither method allows for as much accuracy in shooting gun or bow as standing in the stirrups does.

In the thirteenth century, the Song general Peng Daya described the Mongols' method of riding a horse: "It is their custom when they gallop to stand semi-erect in the stirrup rather than to sit down. Thus, the main weight of the body is upon the calves or lower part of the leg with some weight upon the feet and ankles."[59] Even today, Mongol nomads teach their children (both boys and girls) how to ride while standing in the saddle. Tim Severin reported that the Mongol horsemen he encountered usually stand in the stirrups while riding, even as much as fifty miles a day.[60] Members of the modern-day Mongolian army can be seen shooting rifles from horseback while standing in the stirrups. Although the horses are at full gallop, the riders' upper bodies are completely steady.[61]

Richard Chancellor, an English traveler to Muscovy in 1553, testified that the main part of the Muscovite army fought "not on foot but altogether on horseback" and that they use "a short stirrup after the manner of the Turks."[62] Chancellor also described the arrows and the reflex, or composite, bows of the Muscovite horse archers as similar to that of the Tatars.[63] Likewise, Giles Fletcher, who was in Muscovy in the late 1580s, described the weapons and methods of fighting of the Muscovite and Tatar forces as being alike.[64] Gravures that accompany the 1556 Basel edition of Herberstein's *Notes upon Russia* show

[58] *Dances with Wolves*, dir. Kevin Costner, with Kevin Costner, Mary McDonnell, Graham Greene, Rodney A. Grant, Floyd Red Crow Westerman, Tantoo Cardinal et al., Panavision, 1990. My thanks to Morris Schopf for bringing this to my attention.

[59] Quoted in Sechim Jagchid and Paul Hyer, *Mongolia's Culture and Society*, Boulder, CO, Westview Press, 1979, p. 35.

[60] Tim Severin, *In Search of Genghis Khan*, London, Hutchinson, 1991, p. 50.

[61] See, e.g., *The Mongol Onslaught 850–1500*, "World TV History," BBC Production, 1985.

[62] Richard Chancellor, "The First Voyage to Russia," in *Rude & Barbarous Kingdom: Russia in the Accounts of Sixteenth-Century English Voyagers*, ed. Lloyd E. Berry and Robert O. Crummey, Madison, University of Wisconsin Press, 1968, p. 28. By the *Turks*, Chancellor means the *Tatars*.

[63] On the reflex bow, see W. F. Paterson, "The Archers of Islam," *Journal of the Economic and Social History of the Orient*, vol. 9, 1966, pp. 69–87. On the contemporary evidence concerning Mongol use of archery in warfare, see G. D. Gaunt and Ann M. Gaunt, "Mongol Archers of the Thirteenth Century," *Journal of the Society of Archer-Antiquaries*, vol. 16, 1973, pp. 18–22. See also Robert W. Reid, "Mongolian Weaponry in *The Secret History of the Mongols*," *Mongolian Studies*, vol. 15, 1992, pp. 85–95.

[64] Giles Fletcher, "Of the Russe Commonwealth," in *Rude & Barbarous Kingdom*, p. 193.

Muscovite horse archers with reflex bows and short stirrups.[65] The short stirrup, while it allowed for accuracy in shooting arrows, left the rider more vulnerable to being unhorsed, as Herberstein pointed out.[66]

Chancellor also remarked on another aspect of the Muscovite horse archers that is unusual from a European perspective. In describing their armor, Chancellor pointed out they used silk with their coat of mail. Chancellor seemed to think that this had something to do with their desire to display their wealth.[67] But the Muscovite horse archers probably knew about the defensive use that silk had in steppe warfare. When an arrow penetrates the outer armor and enters the body, the most damage it does is when it is taken out. The barbed tip of the arrow pulls flesh and tissue with it. Silk is not pierced by an arrow, but wraps around the head of the arrow as it enters the body. Thus, one can remove the arrow more easily without doing so much damage to the body.[68] Evidence from archaeological digs in the field at Kulikovo from the end of the fourteenth century indicates that the Rus' and Tatar horse archers were similarly equipped.[69] Since the Muscovite and Tatar tactics and matériel of warfare were so similar, it is not unreasonable to conclude that their respective method of treating their cavalrymen would be similar.

One of the main reasons for the success of Mongol campaigns was their long-range planning, down to exact details of timing and food procurement. Denis Sinor has described this exactness of strategy in regard to the invasion of eastern Europe.[70] It is not easy to determine

---

[65] These gravures are widely reproduced. See, e.g., Sigismund von Herberstein, *Notes upon Russia*, 2 vols., trans. R. H. Major, New York, Burt Franklin, 1851–1852, between pp. 96 and 97, and the cover of *Rude & Barbarous Kingdom*.

[66] Herberstein, *Notes upon Russia*, vol. 1, p. 96.

[67] Chancellor, "First Voyage to Russia," p. 28. Cf. Herberstein, *Notes upon Russia*, vol. 1, p. 96. The German editions (Vienna 1557, Basel 1563, 1567) of Herberstein's work add that the garment of silk stuffed with wool was meant as a defense against arrows. See Sigismund von Herberstein [Sigizmund Gerbershtein], *Zapiski o Moskovii*, ed. V. L. Ianin, A. V. Nazarenko, A. I. Pliguzov, and A. L. Khovoshkevich, Moscow, Izdatel'stvo Moskovskogo universiteta, 1988, p. 114 fn. H.

[68] See *Mongol Hordes: Storm from the East*, part 3, *Tartar Crusaders*.

[69] M. V. Gorelik, "Oruzhie i dospekh russkikh i mongolo-tatarskikh voinov kontsa XIV v.," *Vestnik Akademii nauk SSSR*, 1980, no. 8, pp. 102–103. Also compare the evidence provided in the article of I. Ia. Abramzon and M. V. Gorelik, "Nauchnaia rekonstruktsiia kompleksa vooruzheniia russkogo voina XIV v. i ego ispol'zovanie v muzeinykh ekspositsiiakh," in *Kulikovskaia bitva. V istorii i kul'ture nashei Rodiny*, ed. B. A. Rybakov et al., Moscow, Izdatel'stvo Moskovskogo universiteta, 1983, pp. 238–244, with the article by M. V. Gorelik, "Mongolo-tatarskoe oboronitel'noe vooruzhenie vtoroi poloviny XIV–nachala XV v.," in *Kulikovskaia bitva. V istorii i kul'ture nashei Rodiny*, pp. 244–269.

[70] Denis Sinor, "On Mongol Strategy," *Proceedings of the Fourth East Asian Altaistic Conference*, December 26–31, 1971, Taipei, China, ed. Ch'en Chieh-hsien, Department of History, National Ch'engkung University, Tainan, Taiwan, ROC, n.d.,

from the existing sources whether the Muscovite Rus' adopted the Mongols' strategy of long-range planning. But the choice by Dmitrii Donskoi of Kulikovo Pole for the battle against the troops of Mamai may be an indication of such influence of preparation. Dmitrii arranged his army in such a way, bounded by rivers, that he did not have to fear envelopment, a favorite Mongol battle maneuver.

Finally, Schamiloglu's argument that the ruling class of the Qipchaq Khanate developed a sedentary lifestyle makes sense when we consider that the ruling class in the Ilkhanate underwent an evolution from nomad to sedentary lifestyle during approximately the same time. In other words, the Qipchaq Khanate followed the same nomad-to-sedentary line of development that the Ilkhanate followed. Members of the lower classes would often move back and forth between an agricultural and a nomadic lifestyle in response to economic conditions.[71] It stands to reason, however, that the Mongol ruling elite would have had to give up the nomadic lifestyle, such as tending flocks, living off the land, and so forth, in order to govern the various *ulus* of the Empire.

Even before the Mongols introduced *iqṭā'* into the Ilkhanate and Khanate of Qipchaq, they had introduced it into northern China, sometime after 1234.[72] Until that time, Mongol warriors, in keeping with steppe practice, were given jurisdiction over people not land. Significantly, the change to jurisdiction over land came after Muslims entered Mongol service in order to help administer the vast new territories conquered by the Mongols.[73] It may have been these Muslims who brought the idea of *iqṭā'* along with them to be instituted in northern China either under Ögödei or when Maḥmūd Ali Khwajah, known as Yalavach (the envoy), a Muslim merchant from Bukhara, who had been the minister of Mawarannahr under Ögödei, was appointed minister of north China by Güyük.[74] Maḥmūd had restored financial

pp. 238–249; see also John Fennell, *The Cases of Medieval Russia 1200–1304*, London, Longman, 1983, p. 84.

[71] For descriptions of this tendency among quasi-peasant-nomads, see Philip Carl Salzman, "Introduction: Process of Sedentarization as Adaptation and Response," in *When Nomads Settle: Processes of Sedentarization as Adaptation and Response*, ed. Philip Carl Salzman, New York, Praeger, 1980, pp. 13–14.

[72] On the "appanages" in northern China see Endicott-West, *Mongolian Rule in China*, pp. 89–103.

[73] Morris Rossabi, "The Muslims in the Early Yüan Dynasty," in *China Under Mongol Rule*, ed. J. D. Langlois, Jr., Princeton University Press, 1981, pp. 263–266.

[74] Rashīd al-Dīn, *The Successors of Genghis Khan*, trans. John Andrew Boyle, New York, Columbia University Press, 1971, pp. 183, 218; and Ala-ad-Din 'Ata-Malik Juvaini [Juvaynī], *The History of the World-Conqueror*, trans. John Andrew Boyle, 2 vols., Cambridge, MA, Harvard University Press, 1958, p. 257. His appointment was confirmed by Möngke (1251–1258). Rashīd al-Dīn, *Successors*, p. 218; and Juvaini, *History*, p. 597.

stability to Mawarannahr and the Transoxiana area by basing the tax system on *iqtā'*, whereby the inhabitants paid for the upkeep of their soldier-administrators. Such a system also contributed to the decentralization of power, although not authority, since the local agents, in order to carry out their responsibilities, could claim that their authority derived from the ruler.

Pomest'ia replaced the *kormlenie* system in sixteenth-century Muscovy in large part to accommodate the influx of Tatar princes and nobility from the steppe khanates. One of the clearest indications of this influx is the large number of Russian gentry families of Tatar descent.[75] The Nikon Chronicle reports that, as early as the winter of 1444–45, Vasilii II had two Tatar tsarevichi in his service whom he sent on a campaign against towns in Lithuanian territory.[76] John Fennell identified the two tsarevichi as the sons of Ulug Meḥmed, Kasim and Iagub.[77] But the chronicles report that Iagub was still fighting on the side of his father at the Battle of Suzdal' in the summer of 1445, and that both Kasim and Iagub came into Muscovite service two years later, in 1447.[78] Ivan III gave Kasim the town of Gorodets on the Oka River, which became the basis of the Kasimov Khanate, as a reward for his service in fighting against Dmitrii Shemiaka and the Kazan' Khanate.[79] One of the tsarevichi mentioned in the Nikon Chronicle may have been Berdedat, who was unable to join Vasilii II in time for the Battle of Suzdal',[80] but as yet we have no name for the other. In 1471, Ivan III invited Prince Murtaza, son of the Kazan' khan Mustafa, into his service.[81] When Murtaza entered Muscovite service in 1473, Ivan III granted him the town of Novogorodok on the Oka River along with a number of *volosts*.[82] In a decree dated July 31, 1485, Ivan III sent his *"oghlan*s

[75] For a list of some Tatar princes who served Muscovy, see *RIB*, vol. 22, cols. 60–64. See also George Vernadsky, *History of Russia*, vol. 5, *The Tsardom of Muscovy 1547–1682*, New Haven, CT, Yale University Press, 1969, pp. 92–93, 142.

[76] *PSRL*, vol. 12, p. 63. Although this information appears only in the Nikon Chronicle, I tentatively accept it as reliable evidence for two reasons. In contrast to other interpolations of the Nikon Chronicle, it is not anti-Tatar in intent; and the editor of the Nikon Chronicle wrote that he had obtained this information from another chronicle, something he does not ordinarily indicate that he has done.

[77] J. L. I. Fennell, *Ivan the Great of Moscow*, London, Macmillan, 1961, p. 14.

[78] *PSRL*, vol. 12, pp. 64, 72–73; *Ioasafovskaia letopis'*, ed. A. A. Zimin, Moscow, Akademiia nauk SSSR, 1957, pp. 32, 40–41.

[79] *PSRL*, vol. 12, pp. 72, 73, 75, 118, 122. See also Fennell, *Ivan the Great*, p. 14.

[80] *PSRL*, vol. 6, p. 170; vol. 12, p. 65; vol. 25, p. 262; vol. 26, p. 197; vol. 27, p. 109; vol. 28, pp. 103, 270; *Ioasafovskaia letopis'*, p. 32. For an analysis of the diplomacy surrounding the battle, see Gustave Alef, "The Battle of Suzdal' in 1445: an Episode in the Muscovite War of Succession," *Forschungen zur osteuropäischen Geschichte*, vol. 25, 1978, pp. 11–20; reprinted in Alef, *Rulers and Nobles*, item 2.

[81] *PSRL*, vol. 12, p. 141; *Ioasafovskaia letopis'*, p. 73.

[82] *PSRL*, vol. 12, p. 154; *Ioasafovskaia letopis'*, p. 86.

[*ulany*, i.e. members of Tatar princely families] and princes and all [their] cossacks" to fight the Qipchaq Khanate.[83] The Vologda-Perm' Chronicle reports that Vasilii III invited Tatars from Astrakhan' to Muscovy and gave them prominent court positions.[84] All this evidence from Church chronicles, which are generally not favorably disposed toward Tatars during this period, renders only a small part of the Tatar émigrés in Muscovite service.

One of the more extraordinary stories of crossover concerns the tsarevich Kudai Kul (Kaidakal), who was captured in the attack on Kazan' by the forces of Ivan III in 1487. After eighteen years of "captivity," Kudai Kul converted to Christianity, being baptized "Petr Ibraimov" (Abreimov, Obreimovich) by Metropolitan Simon on December 21, 1505. One week later, he pledged his loyalty to Vasilii III.[85] Within a month (January 25, 1506), he married Evdokiia Ivanovna, the grand prince's sister. Vasilii assigned him Goroden, Klin, and five villages close to Moscow for his maintenance.[86] Kudai Kul/Peter became one of the closest advisers to Vasilii III, and Zimin even argued that Vasilii tapped him as his heir in the first version of his Testament (1509).[87] In 1521 he was *namestnik* of Moscow and organized its defense against the Crimean Tatar attack of that year.[88] When Kaida Kul/Peter died in 1523, after a distinguished career in Muscovite service, his body was buried in the Cathedral of the Archangel in Moscow. Evdokiia and Kudai Kul/Peter had two daughters, both named Anastasiia, one of whom married Prince Fedor Mikhailovich Mstislavskii and was the mother of Ivan Fedorovich Mstislavskii, the second of whom married Prince Vasilii Vasil'evich Shuiskii and was the mother of Marfa Vasil'evna Shuiskaia, who married Prince Ivan Dmitrievich

---

[83] *Sbornik Imperatorskogo Russkogo istoricheskogo obshchestva* (*SRIO*), 148 vols., St. Petersburg, 1867–1916, vol. 41, no. 12, p. 44.

[84] *PSRL*, vol. 26, p. 296.

[85] *Sobranie gosudarstvennykh gramot i dogovorov khraniashchikhsia v gosudarstvennoi kollegii inostrannykh del* (*SGGD*), 5 vols., St. Petersburg, N. S. Vsevolozhskii, 1813–1894, vol. 1, no. 145, pp. 401–403.

[86] *PSRL*, vol. 4, pp. 468, 536; vol. 6, pp. 244–245; vol. 13, pp. 1–2; vol. 20, p. 376; vol. 21, p. 583; vol. 22, p. 516; vol. 24, p. 215; vol. 26, p. 297; vol. 28, p. 339; vol. 39, p. 177; *Ioasafovskaia letopis'*, p. 148. *Razriadnaia kniga 1475–1605 gg.*, 3 vols., Moscow, Akademiia nauk SSSR, 1977–1985, ed. N. G. Savich and L. F. Kuz'mina, vol. 1, p. 91; V. I. Buganov, *Razriadnye knigi. Poslednei chetverti XV–nachala XVII v.*, Moscow, Akademiia nauk SSSR, 1962, pp. 76, 175. Cf. Herberstein, *Zapiski o Moskovii*, pp. 171, 216; Herberstein, *Notes*, vol. 2, p. 59.

[87] A. A. Zimin, "Ivan Groznyi i Simeon Bekbulatovich v 1575 g.," *Uchenye zapiski Kazanskogo gosudarstvennogo pedagogicheskogo universiteta*, vyp. 80: *Iz istorii Tatarii*, vol. 4, 1970, pp. 146–147.

[88] *PSRL*, vol. 6, p. 263; *Razriadnaia kniga 1475–1605 gg.*, vol. 1, p. 183; *Razriadnaia kniga 1475–1598 gg.*, ed. V. I. Buganov, Moscow, Nauka, 1966, p. 69.

Bel'skii.[89] The Mstislavskiis, Shuiskiis, and Bel'skiis were three of the most prominent and powerful families in Muscovy during this time.

The career of Kudai Kul/Peter is just one more, although rather sensational, example of how, once Tatar émigrés met the Church's requirement and converted to Christianity, they were accepted with full honors and without any apparent prejudice or penalty into the Muscovite service system. Even when they did not convert to Christianity, steppe nobility who paid allegiance to the tsar were accorded the respect due their rank. The seventeenth-century official Grigorii Kotoshikhin tells us that Siberian and Kasimov tsarevichi, that is descendants of Chingiz Khan, had a higher place of honor (*chest'*) than boyars in the Muscovite court.[90] And, as exemplified by Kudai Kul/Peter's burial in the Archangel Cathedral, converted Tatar émigrés were accepted without prejudice by the Church. Tales of Church provenance also speak favorably of such converts. Peter Ordynskii, who converted in Rostov in the late thirteenth century and was canonized in Moscow by 1610, is described in *The Life of Peter, Tsarevich of the Horde* as ethically and spiritually superior to the local Rus' prince.[91] And in the late sixteenth century, monks of the Kostroma Monastery compiled a tale demonstrating the genealogical linkage of their patron Boris Godunov with a Tatar emir, Chet-Murza (Zakhariia), who converted in the early fourteenth century.[92] Even if the ancestral connection is a legend, it nonetheless demonstrates the legitimacy that Tatar ancestry continued to hold in Muscovite political culture.

It has been estimated that, by 1600, at least sixty Jochid princes along with their families and retainers, numbering several thousand, had been accepted into Muscovite service.[93] Estimates of the total number of gentry families of Tatar origin in the service of the Muscovite tsar in the seventeenth century run as high as 17 percent.[94] But other scholars

---

[89] For the determination that there were two daughters with the same name, see Kollmann, *Kinship and Politics*, p. 282 n. 113.

[90] Grigorii Kotoshikhin, *O Rossii v tsarstvovanii Alekseia Mikhailovicha*, 4th edn, St. Petersburg, Glavnoe upravlenie udelov, 1906, p. 27.

[91] *Russkie povesti XV–XVI vekov*, ed. M. O. Skripil', Moscow and Leningrad, Akademiia nauk SSSR, 1958, pp. 98–105.

[92] Veselovskii expressed doubts of the authenticity of the genealogical connection and of Chet-Murza himself. S. B. Veselovskii, *Issledovaniia po istorii klassa sluzhilykh zemlevladel'tsev*, Moscow, Nauka, 1969, pp. 162–165. See also R. G. Skrynnikov, *Boris Godunov*, Moscow, Nauka, 1978, p. 5.

[93] Craig Gayen Kennedy, "The Juchids of Muscovy: a Study of Personal Ties Between Émigré Tatar Dynasts and the Muscovite Grand Princes in the Fifteenth and Sixteenth Centuries," Ph.D. Dissertation, Harvard University, 1994, abstract.

[94] M. F. Vladimirskii-Budanov, *Obzor istorii russkogo prava*, 3rd edn, Kiev, N. Ia. Ogloblin, 1900, p. 135 fn. 1 cites figures of N. P. Zagoskin that 156 of 915 gentry families of the seventeenth century were of Tatar and "other eastern peoples" origin, or 17.05 percent.

have questioned such a high percentage. They argue that conclusions based on Tatar surnames like Baskakov, Iarlikov, or Iasak are risky because they may not be evidence of Tatar ancestry. Likewise, heraldic devices with crescents (interpreted as an allusion to Islam) or bow and arrows (interpreted as an allusion to the steppe) may not support these interpretations at all. Instead, these scholars argue that the vast majority of gentry families were indigenous Russians and that, for some reason, it became fashionable for them to compile false genealogies showing non-Russian origins.[95] Alef went so far as to claim that "[n]o one wanted to be known as being originally Russian. Even the tsar claimed descent from the imperial pagan Roman line."[96] This is simply not the case. The false genealogy for the grand prince that the Church manufactured in the sixteenth century to show a connection with Prus', the brother/kinsman of Augustus Caesar, did not replace the "Russian" genealogy of the grand princes through the Riurikid line, but only extended it further back.

Certainly, falsification of genealogies was not an uncommon practice either in Muscovy or in other polities for those trying to establish aristocratic status.[97] And families will often invoke a famous personage as ancestor, even if it is a foreigner. Yet, as Nancy Kollmann pointed out, such legends carried little weight in the Muscovite *mestnichestvo* conflicts.[98] Instead, the direct genealogies that could be confirmed, especially claims of Chingizid descent, generally prevailed. Thus, Muscovy exhibited less flexibility in recognizing "fictional blood ties" than nomadic societies and confederations, in part because in Muscovy genealogical relationships were written down. In addition, it was not beneficial for an aristocratic family already in the indigenous ruling class to invoke a foreign genealogy, because they might lose some of their hard-won status thereby. But, as we know from the next large influx of non-Russians into the Russian aristocracy, that is, when the Hetmanate

---

Zagoskin's numbers are based on his statistical analysis of family names in the *Barkhatnaia kniga* (*Velvet Book*) of Muscovite ruling class families compiled during the regency of Sophia (1682–1689).

[95] Halperin, *Russia and the Golden Horde*, pp. 111–112; Veselovskii, *Issledovaniia po istorii klassa sluzhilykh*, pp. 466–469; N. A. Baskakov, "Russkie familii tiurskogo proiskhozhdeniia," *Onomastika*, Moscow, Nauka, 1969, pp. 5–26; V. N. Bochkov, "'Legenda' o vyezde dvorianskikh rodov," *Arkheograficheskii ezhegodnik za 1969 g.*, Moscow, Nauka, 1971, pp. 73–93; M. E. Bychkova, *Rodoslovnye knigi XVI–XVII vv. kak istoricheskii istochnik*, Moscow, Nauka, 1975, pp. 124–144.

[96] Gustave Alef, "Aristocratic Politics and Royal Policy in Muscovy in the Late Fifteenth and Early Sixteenth Centuries," *Forschungen zur osteuropäischen Geschichte*, vol. 27, 1980, p. 96 n. 110; reprinted in Alef, *Rulers and Nobles*, item 10.

[97] For the "craze" of forging genealogies in Tudor England, see Lawrence Stone, *The Crisis of the Aristocracy, 1558–1641*, Oxford, Clarendon Press, 1965, p. 23.

[98] Kollmann, *Kinship and Politics*, p. 57.

and left-bank Ukraine was absorbed into the Russian Empire in the eighteenth and nineteenth centuries, it was potentially beneficial for those entering the aristocratic pecking order to attempt to gain leverage by invoking the privileges they had formerly held.

Although some "Russians" may have claimed a Tatar ancestry and some names of apparent Tatar provenance may not represent Tatar ancestry, it is likely that the percentage of families of Tatar origin in Muscovite service is higher than the numbers based on such evidence indicate. One reason for this is that a number of Tatars adopted Russian names, such as Serkizov and Miachkov, when they Christianized, thus obscuring their Tatar ancestry.[99] The number doing so had to have been higher than Russians adopting Tatar names. Another reason for this may have been that, although the secular court maintained the legitimacy of the Tatar frame of reference well into the sixteenth century, the Church was already discouraging such connections from the second half of the fifteenth century. Churchmen would have put pressure on Tatar émigrés to "Russify" themselves and their names, much in the way that American immigration officers encouraged immigrants to the United States to take "American" names upon entering the country. The pressure may have been subtle at times, overt at others, but pervasive nonetheless. For a Tatar émigré to withstand that pressure and maintain a visible sign of Tatar ancestry would have required an active decision, more difficult than a passive acquiescence.[100] If my reasoning is correct, then the number of Tatar aristocrats entering Muscovite service was larger than we have direct evidence for and the need to fit such numbers into the Muscovite system was correspondingly greater. In addition, the numbers of those entering Muscovite service from the fifteenth through seventeenth centuries from areas west of Muscovite Rus' was apparently even larger. Zagoskin calculated the families with Polish-Lithuanian and "western European" origins at 452 of 915, or 49.4 percent. This means that those families whose names indicated an indigenous Rus' origin were in a definite minority – 210 of 915, or 22.95 percent,[101] and even

[99] Veselovskii, *Issledovaniia po istorii klassa sluzhilykh*, pp. 397–411, 412–417.

[100] Recently, Carol Stevens has pointed that in the second half of the seventeenth century in towns on Muscovy's southern frontier, where large numbers of Tatars resided, less than 10 percent of the given names of all servitors were other than Christian. Carol Stevens, "The Naming of Warriors: Name and Usage on Muscovy's Southern Frontier, 1650–1700," unpublished paper, reported in Daniel Kaiser, "Naming Cultures in Early Modern Russia," in *Kamen" Kraeug"l'n": Rhetoric of the Medieval Slavic World. Essays Presented to Edward L. Keenan on His Sixtieth Birthday by His Colleagues and Students*, ed. Nancy Shields Kollman, Donald Ostrowski, Andrei Pliguzov and Daniel Rowland, Cambridge, MA, *Harvard Ukrainian Studies*, vol. 19, 1995, p. 277.

[101] For Zagoskin's numbers, see Vladimirskii-Budanov, *Obzor istorii russkogo prava*, p. 135

that percentage may be artificially high. *Pomest'e* solved both the problem of administering the vast newly acquired territories and the influx of service men at the same time.

By the seventeenth century, *pomest'e* landholding became the standard administrative method in the countryside, and in 1714 officially replaced *votchina* (see Glossary).[102] *Pomest'e* shared a number of characteristics with *votchina*, both in being inheritable and in granting the gentry full administrative powers over their estates because they were members of the ruling class. *Pomest'e* could be exchanged for other *pomest'e* but not for *votchina* before 1649. According to the *Ulozhenie of 1649*, one could be exchanged for the other, provided that the *pomest'e* then became *votchina* and vice versa.[103] The reason for this was to prevent any loss in the total *pomest'e* land fund, not because of any scarcity of land but more likely because of sparseness of population. Land without farmers to till the soil would not contribute to the support of a cavalryman. Although both *pomest'e* and *votchina* were heritable, they were usually maintained in the family only with a male heir who could provide military service, or its equivalent if the heir was a non-servitor. An exception to this practice was the government's allowing the widows and mothers of deceased *pomeshchiki* to hold a share of the *pomest'e* estate for their support.[104] Otherwise, both *pomest'e* and *votchina* reverted to the grand prince.

The *pistsovye knigi* tell us that in the Novgorodian *uezdy*, the sons of *pomeshchiki* inherited the same lands their fathers held from the very beginning of the introduction of the *pomes'te* system. By the 1560s, however, the tsarist administration was beginning to exercise more control over this practice by granting sons *pomest'ia* elsewhere. Even those scholars who believe that *pomest'e* evolved from being a conditional land grant acknowledge that it was heritable from the very beginning.[105]

---

fn. 1. Kliuchevskii's percentages for families of indigenous Russian origin (33 percent) and for families of unknown origin (1 percent), if they are based on Zagoskin's numbers, are incorrect. For Kliuchevskii's percentages, see Kliuchevskii, *History of Russia*, vol. 2, p. 110. The more accurate percentage for families of unknown origin is 10.6 percent.

[102] *Pamiatniki russkogo prava (PRP)*, 8 vols., Moscow, Gosudarstvennoe izdatel'stvo iuridicheskoi literatury, 1952–1961, vol. 8: *Zakonodatel'nye akty Petra I. Pervaia chetvert' XVIII v.*, ed. K. A. Sofronenko, pp. 246–251.

[103] *Sobornoe ulozhenie 1649 goda. Tekst. Kommentarii*, ed. L. I. Ivina, commentary by G. V. Abramovich, A. G. Man'kov, B. N. Mironov, and V. M. Paneiakh, Leningrad, Nauka, Leningradskoe otdelenie, 1987, ch. 16, art. 5, p. 74.

[104] On this point, see Janet Martin, "Widows, Welfare, and the *Pomest'e* System in the Sixteenth Century," in *Kamen" Kraeug"l'n"*, pp. 376–377.

[105] Iu. G. Alekseev and A. I Kopanev, "Razvitie pomestnoi sistemy v XVI v.," in *Dvorianstvo i krepostnoi stroi Rossii XVI–XVIII vv. Sbornik statei, posviashchennyi pamiati Alekseia Andreevicha Novosel'skogo*, ed. N. I. Pavlenko, I. A. Bulygin, E. I. Indova, A. A. Preobrazhenskii, and S. M. Troitskii, Moscow, Nauka, 1975, p. 59;

Thus, a son was entitled to an equivalent *pomest'e* estate but not necessarily the one that his father held. This indicates that the tsarist regime maintained its privilege over the land as part of a *pomest'e* land fund and thereby maintained the distinction from familial lands. The *votchinnik*, by contrast, could claim his particular land as familial. None of this, of course, prevented the tsarist regime from confiscating *votchina* when the necessity arose. Finally, both *pomest'e* and *votchina* could be donated to monasteries.

Pomest'e was not, as is often asserted, a land-for-service exchange. Members of the gentry were expected to provide service to the grand prince whether they held *pomest'e* or not. Many *pomeshchiki* avoided service when they could with little or no loss of land. According to figures compiled by R. G. Skrynnikov, a decreasing number of service people, many of them *pomeshchiki*, took part in military campaigns during the 1560s and 1570s, from 18,105 in 1563 to 11,972 in 1572, and then only 7,279 in 1577 and 10,532 in 1579.[106] Although this period overlaps with the Oprichnina, we cannot account for the difference in numbers solely on the basis of Oprichnik killing of *pomeshchiki*. This tendency of non-compliance continued well into the seventeenth century, as indicated by the Zamoskovskii region in 1625, where of 555 gentry called to service only 324 (or 58 percent) mustered.[107] The Military Service Decree of 1556 allows for reduction of the size of the *pomest'e* for unsatisfactory service but does not stipulate confiscation for non-service. Instead, it requires the *pomeshchik* to provide enough money to support the equivalent number of fully equipped men and horses.[108] In other words, the *pomeshchik* could avoid service by paying a fee.

The *Ulozhenie of 1649* prescribes three levels of punishment for *pomeshchiki* who provide neither service nor this non-service fee: for the first occasion, beating with the knout; for the second occasion, beating with the knout and the deduction of a ruble per *chetvert*[109] of his *pomest'e*

A. Ia. Degtiarev, "O mobilizatsii pomestnykh zemel' v XVI v," in *Iz istorii feodal'noi Rossii. Stat'i i ocherki k 70-letiiu so dnia rozhdeniia prof. V. V. Mavrodina*, ed. A. Ia. Degtiarev, V. A. Ezlov, V. A. Petrova, I. Ia. Froianov, and A. L. Shapiro, Izdatel'stvo Leningradskogo universitete, 1978, pp. 85–89; V. B. Kobrin, "Stanovlenie pomestnoi sistemy," *Istoricheskie zapiski*, no. 105, 1980, p. 180.

[106] R. G. Skrynnikov, *Rossiia posle oprichniny*, Izdatel'stvo Leningradskogo universiteta, 1975, p. 46; cf. R. G. Skrynnikov, "Obzor pravleniia Ivana IV," *Russian History*, vol. 14, 1987, p. 369.

[107] Iu. V. Got'e, "Zamoskovnyi krai v XVII veke. Opyt issledovanie po istorii ekonomicheskogo byta Moskovskoi Rusi," *Uchenye zapiski Imperatorskogo Moskovskogo universiteta. Otdel istoriko-filologicheskii*, vol. 36, 1906, p. 312.

[108] *PSRL*, vol. 13, pp. 267–269; vol. 20, pt. 2, pp. 569–571.

[109] A *chetvert'* or *chet*, literally "one-quarter," had various meanings, depending on context. In land measure it could mean either 1.35 acres or 4.1 acres. See *Dictionary of Russian Historical Terms*, pp. 7–8.

compensation scale; for the third occasion, beating with the knout and confiscation of his *pomest'e*.[110] The point is that confiscation came only as a punishment for recidivism; otherwise it would have occurred on the first occasion for non-fulfillment of contract. Nor would the knout have been used to punish someone considered an independent contractor who was providing service in exchange for land. It is clear from the loyalty oaths that service princes made to the grand prince during the fifteenth and sixteenth centuries that their commitment to him was unconditional for life, and that there was no reciprocal obligation on the part of the grand prince.[111] Indeed, Horace Dewey pointed out in his study of these documents that they explicitly exclude any limitations on the grand prince in invoking punishments and retributions if it was discovered a service prince was not abiding by his obligations.[112] If service princes could expect no reciprocal obligations on the part of the grand prince then it is highly unlikely a *pomeshchik* would be granted them. The ruler could take away the land for any reason at any time or leave it with servitors who did not provide military service. Thus, the term "conditional" applied to these lands seems a misnomer, unless we mean "conditional" on the will of the ruler and the ruling elite, not on whether the recipient provides military service.

In contrast to northern China, however, where the agricultural population was sedentary, northern and northeastern Rus', during the fourteenth through sixteenth centuries, had agriculturalists who were mobile, constantly moving every few years to clear new lands in the forest. The techniques of slash-and-burn agriculture used in these areas would exhaust the soil of any given location within seven years, sometimes less. Then, some of those, probably the young adults, would move deeper into the forest to locate a new homestead. Depending on the degree of exhaustion of the soil around the old homestead and other factors, the older adults might pick up stakes and join them in a year or two. These mobile agriculturalists had to be tied to the land to make *pomest'e* work the same way *iqṭā'* did in Islamic countries and in northern China with their non-mobile agriculturalists. In any case, *pomest'e* most likely derived from Islamic practice, and it was the basis for the ruling elite's power in Russia until the nineteenth century.

Ironically, the steppe-nomadic practice of granting jurisdiction over people rather than land might have suited sixteenth-century Muscovite

---

[110] *Sobornoe ulozhenie 1649 goda*, ch. 6, art. 8, p. 25.

[111] See, e.g., *SGGD*, vol. 1, no. 103, pp. 249–250 (1474); no. 145, pp. 401–403 (1505); no. 146, pp. 403–404 (1506); no. 155, pp. 428–430 (1527); no. 196, pp. 561–565 (1571).

[112] Horace W. Dewey, "Political *Poruka* in Muscovite Rus'," *Russian Review*, vol. 46, 1987, p. 131.

conditions better and would not have necessitated enserfment. Some historians have expressed a different view on the matter. J. J. Saunders, for one, has asserted that Muscovite serfdom originated with the Qipchaq Khanate.[113] Not only does he not demonstrate that serfdom existed in the Qipchaq Khanate, but also he does not indicate how, even if it had existed there, it could have been implemented in Muscovy from the late sixteenth century on, long after the Khanate disappeared as an independent entity. Likewise, Vernadsky stated that serfdom in Muscovy derived from "the principle of universal obligatory service" reported by Juvaini and Bar Hebraeus as appearing in the so-called Great *Yāsā* (Law Code) of Chingiz Khan.[114]

Much speculation has taken place concerning what regulations were in the *Yāsā*. Yet, no reconstruction of the *Yāsā* includes any articles or stipulations regarding serfdom *per se*. Indeed, Morgan has concluded that there is "very little convincing evidence that a written legal code ever did exist."[115] Morgan pointed out that there is no reliable evidence that anyone actually saw such a code. Furthermore, he credited David Ayalon with showing that all the supposed fragments of the Great *Yāsā* derive from one secondary source – Juvaini,[116] who, Morgan concluded, was not referring to a code of laws at all.[117] One can add that the manner in which the Great *Yāsā* is often referred to makes it unlikely a written law code is being secretly kept by the Mongol ruling elite. For example, Rashīd al-Dīn reports the following speech by Batu when he recognized the legitimacy of Möngke's claim to be Great Khan: "Of the princes the only one who has seen with his eyes and heard with his ears the *yasaq* and *yarligh* of Chingiz Khan is Möngke Qa'an."[118] Clearly an abstraction is meant here, not a physical document that other princes would also have had access to.

Morgan's analysis is perceptive and representative of scholarship at its finest. Having said that, perhaps I might be allowed to quibble about one point. Morgan stated that it is unlikely the contents of a legal code

[113] J. J. Saunders, *History of the Mongol Conquests*, London, Routledge & Kegan Paul, 1971, p. 161.

[114] Vernadsky, "Scope and Contents of Chingiz Khan's Yasa," pp. 347–348. See also Halperin's critique of Vernadsky's views on this matter. Charles J. Halperin, "Russia and the Steppe: George Vernadsky and Eurasianism," *Forschungen zur Osteuropäischen Geschichte*, vol. 36, 1985, p. 132.

[115] Morgan, *Mongols*, p. 98.

[116] David Ayalon, "The Great *Yāsā* of Chingiz Khān: a Reexamination," *Studia Islamica*, vol. 33, 1971, pp. 97–140.

[117] For his reasoning, see David [D. O.] Morgan, "The 'Great Yāsā of Chingiz Khān' and Mongol Law in the Ilkhanate," *Bulletin of the School of Oriental and African Studies*, vol. 49, 1986, pp. 166–168; and Morgan, *Mongols*, pp. 96–99.

[118] Rashīd al-Dīn, *Successors*, p. 202.

would be kept secret from those who were expected to obey it.[119] Yet, there are numerous historical examples, from pre-Draco Athens to the Soviet Union, of governments keeping their laws secret, all the better to keep the populace enthralled. Also, I know from personal experience that, even within an administrative structure, it is often difficult to find out what the rules and procedures are because those who know them treat them as tokens of power. And I have encountered the invoking of non-existent rules given authority by the citation of closed reports in order to block or promote whatever it is the invoker wanted to block or promote. I think this may be what occurred with the Great *Yāsā*. Those who were in power invoked a non-existent law code in order to give added authority to their own decrees. It may have been similar in certain respects to early Islamic invocation of the *Sunna*, that is, the oral legal tradition before it was written down. The *Sunna* invoked the example of the Prophet as authoritative precedent in all matters. Thus, not only must one be cautious in attributing any influence to the Great *Yāsā* as such, but one must also be aware that no such work may have ever existed.

Thus, for Muscovite borrowing of administrative procedures from the Qipchaq Khanate, all three of our criteria are filled: (1) the administrative setup was present in the source culture – the Qipchaq Khanate; (2) it coincided in time with its appearance in the target culture – the fourteenth century; and (3) a mechanism for its transference was operational – the frequent, long visits of the Muscovite princes to Sarai. In the late fifteenth and early sixteenth centuries, the influx of Tatar princes and dynasts into Muscovite service may have provoked the transformation to *pomest'e* administration.

---

[119] Morgan, *Mongols*, p. 98

3   Seclusion of women

One of the practices that has been most often associated with Mongol influence is the seclusion of women among the Muscovite elite (see Glossary). We do not know at what point seclusion of women was introduced into Muscovy. Our first evidence of it comes from the early sixteenth century. Herberstein reported that "they consider no woman virtuous unless she live shut up at home, and so closely guarded that she go out nowhere."[1] How long it had been practiced before that is difficult to determine. Halperin, among others, argued against the notion that the Muscovites borrowed seclusion from the Mongols because the Mongols did not seclude their women.[2] F. I. Leontovich, in discussing the possible origins of seclusion in Muscovy, rejected the idea that it originated with the Mongols. Leontovich pointed out the "huge significance in Mongol society of women as the chief laborer and producing force, who took on their shoulders all the cares and labor of the nomad economy."[3] Both William of Rubruck and Marco Polo testify in the second half of the thirteenth century to the prominent place women occupied in the activities of the Mongol encampment.[4] Carpini testifies likewise in the 1240s to the integral participation of women in Mongol society:

Young girls and women ride and gallop on horseback with agility like the men. We even saw them carrying bows and arrows. Both the men and the women are able to endure long stretches of riding. They have very short stirrups. They look

---

[1] Herberstein, *Notes upon Russia*, vol. 1, p. 93. He does mention, however, that they are allowed to go out to "pleasant meadows" on certain holidays (*ibid.*, p. 94).

[2] Halperin, *Russia and the Golden Horde*, p. 116.

[3] F. I. Leontovich, "K istorii prava russkikh inorodtsev drevnii mongolo-kalmytskii ili oiratskii ustav vzyskanii (Tsaadzhin-Bichik)," *Zapiski Imperatorskogo Novorossiiskogo universiteta*, vol. 28, Odessa, 1879, p. 273. See also Paul Ratchnevsky, "La condition de la femme mongole au 12e/13e siècle," in *Tractata Altaica Denis Sinor*, ed. Walther Heissig, John R. Krueger, Felix J. Oinas, and Edmond Schültz, Wiesbaden, Otto Harrassowitz, 1976, p. 509.

[4] Cf. Rubruck, *Itinerarium*, ch. 7, paras. 1–2, pp. 183–184; Rubruck, *Journey* (Rockhill), pp. 75–76; Rubruck, *Mission* (Jackson), pp. 90–91; Polo, *Travels* (Latham), p. 98; Polo, *Book* (Yule), vol. 1, p. 252.

after their horses. Indeed, they take the greatest care of all their possessions. Their women make everything, garments, tunics, shoes, and leggings that are made of leather. They also drive the carts and repair them. They load the camels, and in all tasks they are very swift and energetic. They all wear breeches and some of them shoot like the men.[5]

Within the Mongol ruling elite itself, we also have no evidence that women were secluded. Nor is there evidence they were excluded from the political process. Indeed, it is just the opposite, as the *Secret History* tells us of the concern that Chingiz Khan had for the opinions of his primary wife, Börte, and his mother, Ho'elun.[6] Qubilai Khan's wife, Chabi, played an important role as adviser to her husband.[7] And women of the ruling family on occasion served as regents. Töregene, the widow of Ögödei, Oghul-Qaimish, the widow of Güyük, Sorqoqtani Beki, the widow of Tolui, and Orgina, the widow of Qara-Hülegü, acted as regents after the deaths of their husbands until a new khan or khagan was chosen.[8] These women regents did not give up power easily. Töregene continued to issue decrees during the first few months of her son Güyük's reign until she died. Sorqoqtani worked with Batu to get her son Möngke declared grand khan. And Möngke executed Oghul-Qaimish when he became grand khan for continuing to oppose him. In the fourteenth century, the Mamlūk writer al-'Umarī expressed some amazement at the relative power of women in the Mongol aristocracy: "Indeed, I have not seen any women among us that have as much power as they have there."[9] He also remarked that wives "take part in ruling on equal terms with their husbands, the decisions being taken in common."[10]

---

[5] John of [Iohannes de] Plano Carpini, "Ystoria Mongalorum," in *Sinica Franciscana*, vol. 1 (hereafter Carpini, *Ystoria*), ch. 4, para. 11, pp. 50–51; John of Plano Carpini, "History of the Mongols," in *The Mongol Mission: Narratives and Letters of the Franciscan Missionaries in Mongolia and China in the Thirteenth and Fourteenth Centuries*, ed. Christopher Dawson, London, Sheed and Ward, 1955 (reprinted as *Mission to Asia*, New York, Harper Torchbooks, 1966), p. 18.

[6] *Secret History* (Cleaves), § 118–119, pp. 50–51; § 245, pp. 180–181; § 244, pp. 177–178. "Secret History" (Rachewiltz), *PFEH*, vol. 5, pp. 160–161; vol. 26, pp. 50–51; vol. 26, pp. 48–49.

[7] Morris Rossabi, "Khubilai Khan and the Women in His Family," in *Studia Sino–Mongolica: Festschrift für Herbert Franke*, ed. Wolfgang Bauer, Wiesbaden, Franz Steiner Verlag, 1979, pp. 153–180.

[8] Rashīd al-Dīn, *Successors*, pp. 176–179 (Töregene), pp. 185–186 (Oghul-Qaimish), pp. 199–200 (Sorqoqtani); Juvaini, *History*, pp. 240–244 (Töregene), pp. 262–266 (Oghul-Qaimish), 550, 552, 562 (Sorqoqtani); p. 274 (Origina); Carpini, *Mongol Mission*, p. 26. For more on Sorqoqtani, see Rossabi, "Khubilai Khan and the Women," pp. 158–166. For more on Origina, see Barthold, *Turkestan*, pp. 480, 483, 487–491.

[9] Tiesenhausen, *Sbornik materialov*, vol. 1, p. 208.

[10] Tiesenhausen, *Sbornik materialov*, vol. 1, p. 288.

To be sure, this was still a patriarchal society and women, therefore, did not have equal social status with men. But, as is common with most traditional societies before they become "civilized" and thus more highly stratified, women, both common and elite, participated fully and openly in almost all social activities. This is an important point because, although those few Mongols who came to the Qipchaq Khanate were rapidly assimilated, they were assimilated into a steppe-nomadic culture that likewise eschewed seclusion of women.

Yet, while this may be true of the Mongols and of the steppe nomads of the Qipchaq Khanate, the argument can be made that, when the rulers of the Khanate became sedentary and converted to Islam, they might also have adopted the practice of seclusion from the Muslims. To counter that argument we have the direct eyewitness testimony of Ibn Baṭṭūṭa from the middle of the fourteenth century about his seeing the "respect shown to women" in the Khanate, to the point that "they are higher in dignity than the men."[11] He testifies that the *khatuns* (princesses) were neither veiled nor secluded.[12] And in describing the wives of merchants and commoners, he wrote that the women are not veiled and frequently appear in the marketplace. He was further astonished that, when a wife appeared in public with her husband, "anyone seeing him would take him to be one of her servants."[13] Ibn Baṭṭūṭa's remarks about the respect shown for women in the Khanate could have been in the context of seclusion and veiling, which were limited in Islamic society to those who were considered to be respectable women. He shared this prevailing notion of respectability and was offended whenever it was not followed.[14] So, his remarks directly juxtaposing respect, on the one hand, with non-veiling and non-seclusion, on the other, are particularly significant. In the sixteenth century, Sigismund von Herberstein also reported that the Tatars did not seclude their women, although he does mention veiling: "The men use a similar dress to that of the women, except that the latter cover the

---

[11] Ibn Baṭṭūṭa, *The Travels of Ibn Baṭṭūṭa AD 1325–1354*, 4 vols., vols. 1–3, trans. H. A. R. Gibb, vol. 4, trans. C. F. Beckingham, Cambridge University Press, 1958–1994, vol. 2, p. 480.

[12] Ibn Baṭṭūṭa, *Travels*, vol. 2, p. 483.   [13] Ibn Baṭṭūṭa, *Travels*, vol. 2, p. 481.

[14] For example, Ibn Baṭṭūṭa was astounded when, in Walata in West Africa, he found the local *qāḍī* in casual conversation with a woman companion in his house. Ibn Baṭṭūṭa, *Ibn Battuta in Black Africa*, trans. Said Hamdun and Noël King, Princeton, NJ, Markus Wiener, 1994, p. 38; see also Ross E. Dunn, *The Adventures of Ibn Battuta*, Berkeley, University of California Press, 1986, pp. 299–300. He was again astounded in Walata when he found a Muslim man, with whom he had traveled, sitting on a mat while his wife sat on the bed engaged in conversation with her male companion. Ibn Baṭṭūṭa refused to visit the man's house again. Hamdun and King, *Ibn Battuta in Black Africa*, pp. 38–39.

head with a linen veil, and wear linen breeches like those of sailors. When their queens go into public they are accustomed to cover their faces."[15] Thus, the first direct evidence we have among the Muslim Tatars of veiling is after the collapse of the Qipchaq Khanate's power. The Khanate may have acted as a barrier to the spread of this practice to the north from Muslim territories to the south. Even if we wanted to designate the Tatars as the source of veiling in Muscovy on the basis of concomitance of practice, we could not designate them as the source of seclusion according to any of our criteria for establishing influence.

Other historians have rejected any outside influence for the practice of seclusion in Muscovy. While acknowledging the possible influence of similar practices in other societies, Kollmann pointed out that the chronicles and other Muscovite sources tend to depict women in the same way from the fourteenth through seventeenth centuries, and suggested "that it [seclusion] either existed throughout Muscovite times or developed gradually in the fourteenth or fifteenth century."[16] Halperin also argued that seclusion of women was an indigenous Muscovite innovation, but of the sixteenth century.[17]

The claim that seclusion of women in Muscovy derives from the Mongols has a long tradition and was seen to be one of the bad things the Russians obtained from Asia. For example, Vissarion Belinskii wrote in 1841:

The seclusion of women, the habit of burying money in the ground and of wearing rags from the fear of revealing one's wealth, usury, Asiaticism in the way of life, a laziness of the mind, ignorance, contempt for oneself – in a word, all that Peter the Great was uprooting, everything that was in Russia directly opposed to Europeanism, everything that was not native to us but *had been grafted* on to us by the Tatars.[18]

More recently, there has been a tendency in the historiography to look at seclusion as an indication of an increased misogynist attitude and of its implementation in a particularly oppressive way. Yet, in those societies where seclusion and veiling of women were practiced, it applied only to "respectable" women. In ancient Assyria, for example, the law prohibited women who were not respectable (slaves and harlots)

---

[15] Herberstein, *Notes upon Russia*, vol. 2, p. 56.
[16] Nancy Shields Kollmann, "The Seclusion of Elite Muscovite Women," *Russian History*, vol. 10, 1983, p. 176. Later in the same article, she suggests more strongly that it developed from the fourteenth century on (*ibid.*, p. 182).
[17] Halperin, *Russia and the Golden Horde*, p. 116.
[18] V. G. Belinskii, *Polnoe sobranie sochinenii*, ed. S. A. Vengerov, 12 vols., St. Petersburg, Tipografiia Tovarishchestva "Obshchestvennaia pol'za," 1903, vol. 6, p. 187 (emphasis in original).

from veiling themselves.[19] There would not seem to be a need for such a law if veiling and seclusion were perceived by the women in these societies as being more oppressive. One consequence of the development of civilization was the subordination of women within the patriarchal society. Seclusion and veiling, as restrictive as these practices might seem to us, were perceived in the Middle East as signs of status and of gentility both by men and by women in those societies. For the husband and father, it showed he had sufficient wealth to maintain separate quarters and servants for his wife and daughters. For the wife and daughter, it showed they had a strong protector.[20] In addition, in societies where most marriages were prearranged by the parents and where abuse by husbands of their wives was not only tolerated but recommended, some women may have welcomed the physical separation from their husbands. This is not meant as a defense of seclusion and veiling, just a suggestion that it might not necessarily represent an increase in the degree of oppression of women but only a different form of their continued subordination within the patriarchal structure. Some women may have found this form of oppression less repulsive than the sexual taunts and confrontations of the marketplace or continued physical proximity with abusive husbands.

One prominent scholar, Dorothy Atkinson, in asserting Mongol influence on the seclusion of women, referred to "the brutalization of life in" Muscovy. Although she cited V. A. Riasanovsky's claim that the Mongols did not seclude their women, she also pointed to his statement that there was a "general crudening of moral standards" and the effects of being exposed to the practice of "unconditional obedience" as a result of the Mongol presence. Her claim does not meet the first of our three criteria for considering cross-cultural influences, that is, the existence of the institution in the source culture. Yet, she asserted that life in Rus' was made harsher by the Mongols and that the importation of "'Asiatic' attitudes denigrating women" may have led to seclusion.[21] One should mention that Riasanovsky, in the same article Atkinson cited, explicitly denied Mongol influence on seclusion: "The seclusion of women might have been the result of the influence of the settled people of the Moslem East (Persia, Turkey) or more probably of

---

[19] "The Middle Assyrian Laws," trans. Theophile J. Meek, in *Ancient Near Eastern Texts*, ed. James B. Pritchard, Princeton University Press, 1950, p. 183.

[20] Nikki Keddie and Lois Beck, "Introduction," in *Women in the Muslim World*, ed. Nikki Keddie and Lois Beck, Cambridge, MA, Harvard University Press, 1978, p. 8.

[21] Dorothy Atkinson, "Society and the Sexes in the Russian Past," in *Women in Russia*, ed. Dorothy Atkinson, Alexander Dallin, and Gail Warshofsky Lapidus, Stanford University Press, 1977, pp. 13–14.

Byzantium; but by no means of the Mongol-Tartars."[22] We need to explain how the idea of Mongol influence on seclusion persists despite the outright rejection of it by a number of specialists.

Let us examine the idea that life was harsher in Rus' as a result of the Mongol hegemony and that it led to seclusion. To support her claim, Atkinson cited two phenomena as evidence: (1) "devastating attacks" of the Tatars that continued into the sixteenth century; and (2) internal legal changes, such as "flogging, torture, and capital punishment [that] appeared now as penalties for the first time in Russian law."[23] She argued that "seclusion of women could have been simply an outgrowth of the general insecurity of the times."[24] The unsupported assumption that insecure times leads to the seclusion of women implies that Muscovite aristocratic men were trying to protect their women from Mongol male intruders. Yet, if Mongols could overrun cities, it is difficult to see how having Muscovite women stay in separate rooms would help protect them from Tatar attack. Riasanovsky did refer to the "roughening of manners" as a "direct consequence of the invasion,"[25] but he was probably referring to the manners of the Russians themselves, not to those of the Mongols. One does not expect conquerors to be polite or to avoid entering a room because it was part of the "women's quarters." Seclusion does not protect women in a rough society. Rather, it can only occur in a society that considers itself to have a civil elite and as an indication of the civility of its elite, in contrast to the non-civility of the marketplace. Besides, our sources indicate that seclusion was regularly practiced in Muscovy in the seventeenth century, when Tatar attacks on Moscow were a thing of the distant past. Atkinson's reference to "'Asiatic' attitudes denigrating women" can be supported by the evidence of traditional Chinese society, especially in regard to such customs as immobilization through foot binding. Although the Mongols adopted many of the Chinese administrative practices, they did not, as far as we can tell, adopt any such Chinese customs toward their own women. And we have no evidence that any of these customs were transferred to Rus'. During the time that the Yuan Dynasty ruled in China, Mongol women enjoyed much greater freedom

[22] V. A. Riasanovsky, "The Influence of Ancient Mongol Culture and Law on Russian Culture and Law," *Chinese Social and Political Science Review*, vol. 20, 1937, p. 509.
[23] Atkinson, "Society and the Sexes in the Russian Past," p. 14. In fairness to Atkinson, one should point out that even prominent specialists like Francis Dvornik claimed that "[c]orporal and capital punishment, unknown in Kiev but practiced by the Mongols, was introduced into Muscovy, also probably torture." Dvornik, *Slavs in European History*, p. 380.
[24] Atkinson, "Society and the Sexes in the Russian Past," p. 14.
[25] Riasanovsky, "Influence of Ancient Mongol Culture," p. 506.

than their Chinese counterparts. They, for example, maintained their property rights and did not engage in footbinding.

Atkinson's other point about the changes in legal penalties resulting from harsher conditions, especially those introduced by the Mongols, is also difficult to accept, although it too has a long tradition in the historiography.[26] First, it is incorrect to say that capital punishment first appeared in Rus' under the Mongols. The Treaty of 912 between the Rus' and the Byzantine Empire explicitly calls for capital punishment for murder.[27] Later, the *Pravosudie Mitropolich'e*, which derives from Byzantine law, specifies decapitation for dishonoring the grand prince and possible hanging for a thief, but mutilation and slavery for a murderer.[28] It is true that the *Russkaia pravda* does not prescribe capital punishment as such and mentions flogging only in regard to slaves.[29] It does, however, allow thieves caught in the act to be killed on the spot, certainly a form of capital punishment.[30]

The evidence about capital punishment among the Mongols and Tatars is ambiguous. Herberstein reports that the Tatars he encountered did not practice capital punishment for murder: "If in any quarrel among themselves a man be killed, they are simply deprived of their horses, arms, and clothing, and are then set free. Even a murderer, after giving up his horse and his bow, is dismissed by the judge, merely with the charge to go and mind his own business."[31] According to Rashīd al-Dīn, the Mongols did practice capital punishment, but it was reserved for other crimes, like adultery, sodomy, lying, etc.[32] And Al-Maqrīzī reports that a murderer could get off by paying a fine.[33] By contrast,

[26] For a discussion of the historiography up to that point of the relationship of the Tatar hegemony to physical punishment in Rus', see A. G. Timofeev, *Istoriia telesnykh nakazanii v russkom prave*, 2nd edn., St. Petersburg, V. Bezobrazov, 1904, pp. 63–79, 85-87.

[27] *PSRL*, vol. 1 (1926), col. 34; vol. 2 (1908), col. 25.

[28] *PRP*, vol. 3, arts. 1, 13, and 12, respectively, pp. 426–427, The reference to *gradskii zakon* in article 12 means the Procheiros Nomos and thus indicates a Byzantine law origin. On this point, see Daniel Kaiser, *The Growth of the Law in Medieval Russia*, Princeton University Press, 1980, p. 222 n. 71.

[29] *Pravda Russkaia*, ed. B. D. Grekov, 3 vols., Moscow and Leningrad, Akademiia nauk SSSR, 1940–1963, vol. 1, p. 398, art. 17 (short version), and vol. 1, pp. 430–433, art. 65 (long version).

[30] *Pravda Russkaia*, vol. 1, p. 399, art. 38 (short version), p. 419, art. 40 (long version). This stipulation also appears in the Treaty of 912. *PSRL*, vol. 1 (1926), col. 34; vol. 2 (1908), col. 25. Apparently it was still the practice in Muscovy in the early sixteenth century. See Herberstein, *Notes upon Russia*, vol. 1, p. 101. Most likely, the intent of this law, as Keenan pointed out to me, was to discourage the thief's kin from seeking retribution or recompense.

[31] Herberstein, *Notes upon Russia*, vol. 2, p. 57.   [32] Rashīd al-Dīn, *Successors*, p. 74.

[33] Cited in V. A. Riasanovsky, *Fundamental Principles of Mongol Law*, Tientsin, 1937, p. 85, art. 28.

both Rubruck and Xiao Daheng (Hsiao Ta-heng) report that the Mongols executed murderers.[34] The contradiction in our sources is only apparent because those found guilty of murder most likely were executed unless they could make a substantial payment. Both Marco Polo and Ibn Baṭṭūṭa report that thieves could get away without further punishment if they could pay nine times the worth of what they stole.[35]

Significant aspects of Muscovite law most likely did derive from the Mongols, but these are of a specific not pervasive nature.[36] Shin beating may have been conveyed to Rus' from China by the Mongols.[37] Mongol laws may have been the source for some forms of capital punishment. For example, in regard to recidivism for thievery, on the third conviction, the thief was executed.[38] Similarly, Herberstein tells us that in Muscovy "[t]hefts, and even murders, unless they have been committed for the sake of gain, are seldom visited with capital punishment."[39] The *Sudebnik of 1497* more or less confirms Herberstein's statement, for only felonies committed by hard-core criminals or those murders occurring during the act of committing another crime were punishable by death.[40]

[34] Rubruck, *Itinerarium* ch. 8, para. 2, pp. 185–186; *Journey* (Rockhill), p. 79; *Mission* (Jackson) p. 93. Henry Serruys, "*Pei-lou fong-sou.* Les coutumes des esclaves septertrionaux de Hsiao Ta-heng," *Monumenta Serica*, vol. 10, 1945, p. 134, reprinted in Henry Serruys, *The Mongols and Ming China: Customs and History*, ed. Françoise Aubin, London, Variorum, 1987, item 1. One of the Latin MSS of Marco Polo's *Travels* implies that execution is the punishment for homicide, but this appears to be a *lectio singula*. Polo, *Travels* (Latham), p. 101n.
[35] Polo, *Travels* (Latham), p. 101; Polo, *Book* (Yule), p. 266; Ibn Baṭṭūṭa, *Travels*, vol. 2, p. 474.
[36] Kaiser, in his *The Growth of the Law in Medieval Russia*, provided no indication he sees any Mongol influence on Russian law. V. A. Riasanovsky saw influence of a general pervasive nature, but very little specific influence. Harold Berman claimed a pervasive imposition of Mongol law on Muscovite public, as opposed to civil, law. Harold Berman, *Justice in Russia*, Cambridge, MA, Harvard University Press, 1950, pp. 128–130; repeated in Harold Berman, *Justice in the USSR*, Cambridge, MA, Harvard University Press, 1963, pp. 193–196. Although Berman based his conclusions on Vernadsky, they are of the anti-Mongol variety, for Berman was trying to argue that the Russians have no concept of law as a result of the Mongols. Dewey saw Mongol influence but not a pervasive one, only in specific cases and in specific laws, for example, in regard to collective guilt. Horace W. Dewey, "Russia's Debt to the Mongols in Suretyship and Collective Responsibility," *Comparative Studies in Society and History*, vol. 30, 1988, pp. 249–270.
[37] Horace W. Dewey and Ann M. Kleimola, "Coercion by Righter (*Pravezh*) in Old Russian Administration," *Canadian–American Slavic Studies*, vol. 9, 1975, p. 157 n. 6; cf. Halperin, *Russian and the Golden Horde*, p. 93.
[38] Cf. *The Charter of the Dvina Land* (1397), art. 5 in *PRP*, vol. 3, pp. 162–163; and the *Pskov Judicial Charter* (1397), art. 8 in *PRP*, vol. 2, p. 303. We might call this punishment, "three strikes and you're dead." Cf. the *Sudebnik of 1497*, art. 11 in *Sudebniki XV–XVI vekov*, p. 20, where вьдругие (second) replaces третьие (third).
[39] Herberstein, *Notes upon Russia*, vol. 1, p. 101.
[40] *Sudebniki XV–XVI vekov*, ed. B. D. Grekov, Moscow and Leningrad, Akademiia nauk SSSR, 1952, p. 20, arts. 8 and 9.

Presumably, other individuals found guilty of murder were not, as a matter of course, executed. Muscovite practice in those situations involved the payment of wergild or bloodwite as stipulated in the *Russkaia pravda*.[41] And, as the seventeenth-century traveler Samuel Collins observes, murder could "be bought off with money."[42] Capital punishment in these prescribed circumstances may have derived from Mongol, Tatar, or steppe laws, but our evidence about those laws regarding capital punishment is too scanty for us to make any definite correlations. Not all Mongol capital crimes were designated as such in Muscovy. This indicates a selective adoption on the part of the Muscovite rulers of specific laws, not a passive assimilation of harshness in general. Finally, with the exception of the Oprichnina period, capital punishment seems to be a less frequent occurrence in Muscovy than in western Europe of the time.

Second, harsh legal penalties do not necessarily imply a harsh society. Both the Tang and Song dynasties, for example, had a methodically prescribed system of punishments from flogging (ranging from ten to one hundred strokes) through forced labor, deportation, and execution by means of strangulation or decapitation.[43] Societies that have cruel punishments are not necessarily more brutal societies than those that do not.[44] Harsh punishments could reflect the harsh customs of a society or, as in the case of the Song, they could reflect the determination with which such societies defend their civility. This may also be true in regard to severe punishments for particular crimes. For example, among the Franks, an abductor could be deprived of his life (or exiled if he managed to claim sanctuary in a church).[45] In eleventh-century Norman England the designated punishment for rape was castration. In fourteenth-century Venice, by contrast, the designated punishment, as long as there were no complicating factors such as the low age or high social status of the victim, was a fine or six months in jail.[46] Which

---

[41] *Pravda Russkaia*, vol. 1, pp. 397–399, arts. 1, 19–27, 38 (short version), pp. 402–409, arts. 1, 3–20, (long version).

[42] Samuel Collins, *The Present State of Russia*, London, John Winter, 1671, p. 71.

[43] Kracke, *Civil Service in Early Sung China*, p. 171 (table 7). Marco Polo reports that, under the Yuan, the number of strokes increased by tens from 7 to 107 depending on the severity of the crime and degree of recidivism. Polo, *Travels* (Latham), p. 101; Polo, *Book* (Yule), pp. 266, 267–268. The Mongols preferred to inflict an odd, rather than even, number of strokes.

[44] The eighteenth-century Italian *philosophe* Cesare Beccaria made the correlation between cruel punishments and brutalization of society. Cesare Beccaria, *On Crimes and Punishments*, trans. David Young, Indianapolis, Hackett, 1986, pp. 51–52. The Song, however, did not have the advantage that we do of being able to read Beccaria.

[45] *The Laws of the Salian Franks*, trans. Katherine Fischer Drew, Philadelphia, University of Pennsylvania Press, 1991, ch. 6, pt. 2, no. 2, p. 157.

[46] John P. McKay, Bennett D. Hill, and John Buckler, *A History of World Societies*, 3rd

society would we consider to be more civil? Into the category of harsh punishments reflecting the determination of a civil society to protect its values, I would place the punishments of the Byzantine Empire. Although Byzantine law did not usually prescribe capital punishment, it did designate mutilation as a punishment.[47] And the practices of legal torture and mutilation most likely entered Muscovite jurisprudence from Byzantium via the Church.

Scholars who attribute Muscovite seclusion of women to Mongol influence usually make no mention that Byzantine women were secluded as early as the tenth century. I think that what has happened in the historiography is the association of institutions and practices historians find odious with outside influences they consider nefarious, in this case, the Mongols. This type of thinking carries over into discussions of seclusion of women in other societies as well. In discussing the origins of the ḥarēm in the Ottoman Empire, Alev Lytle Croutier pointed to the combination of Turkish polygamy with the Byzantine practice of sequestering royalty as the basis on which Sultan Meḥmet II set up this institution. But Croutier focused on patriarchal society as the cause of inequality in general.[48] Yet, inequality does not necessarily lead to seclusion, for there are any number of patriarchal societies where seclusion has not been practiced.

Certainly, one of the faults with a patriarchal society is that it is unable to find ways of involving the majority of its population in contributing to that society in meaningful and productive ways other than as sex providers and childbearers (women), and as domestics and servants (women in general, and women and men who are members of suppressed groups). With that in mind, we have to ask: why did patriarchal societies win out over non-patriarchal societies contemporary to them? How was this possible, since patriarchality would seem to be an inefficient way to draw on the talents and merits of the entire population within any given society? The rise of the state may have been a contributing influence to suppression. In archaeological terms, states exist as the result of hierarchy. An egalitarian community has no

edn, Boston, Houghton Mifflin, 1992, p. 523; Guido Ruggiero, *The Boundaries of Eros: Sex Crime and Sexuality in Renaissance Venice*, Oxford University Press, 1985, pp. 93, 95–96.

[47] Wilhelm Ensslin, "The Emperor and the Imperial Administration," in *Byzantium: an Introduction to East Roman Civilization*, ed. N. H. Baynes and H. St. L. B. Moss, Oxford, Clarendon Press, 1949, p. 292. See also Angeliki E. Laiou, "Sex, Consent, and Coercion in Byzantium," in *Consent and Coercion to Sex and Marriage in Ancient and Medieval Societies*, ed. Angeliki E. Laiou, Washington, DC, Dumbarton Oaks Research Library and Collection, 1993, pp. 122, 124, on nose-slitting for illicit sexual behavior.

[48] Alev Lytle Croutier, *Harem: the World Behind the Veil*, New York, Abbeville Press, 1989, p. 24 (origins of the ḥarēm) and pp. 17–18 (cause of inequality).

hierarchy and constitutes a one-level structure. A tribal society with a chief has a first-order hierarchy and constitutes a two-level structure. The state with a king or other head of state over the chiefs has at least a second-order hierarchy, and constitutes a three-level structure or more.[49] A standard archaeological classification recognizes a tri-partite division for the evolutionary development of human societies: (1) egalitarian, (2) tribal, and (3) state. Each represents, in the words of the authors of a standard textbook, a "greater formalization of political and social structure."[50] One of the results of this "greater formalization" was the cultural, political, social, and economic suppression of women.

But hierarchy in itself does not necessitate that women be suppressed. Instead, agriculture has been proposed as an answer. According to this theory, women's labor was not as valuable as it had been in hunter-gatherer societies. As the idea of property grew in importance, to ensure ownership of agricultural land, women were subordinated in the same way as land, because they fulfilled the function of providing a male heir. Thus, law codes prescribe absolute fidelity on the part of a wife, on pain of death if transgressed, while men received lesser punishment. Although agriculture may have contributed to patriarchy, in itself it is not enough to account for the intensity of oppression and exploitation of women. An intensifier of this subordination of women to lower rungs in the social hierarchy most likely was warfare. Men would arrange their wars for times of the year when agricultural needs, such as plowing, planting, and harvesting, were low.

The earliest city-states in the Near East, places like Uruk, Nippur, and Ur, seem to have been theocracies centered on the temple of the god or goddess of the city. An *ensi*, or steward, interpreted the orders, demands, and requests of the reigning deity, and thereby controlled everyone and everything within that society.[51] From about 2800 BC, we begin to have evidence of the glorification of war-making capabilities and the building of empires. The characteristic of the Akkadians and the Assyrians to depict their exploits in battle in massive stone reliefs is merely one of the more visible examples of this glorification. As a result, warriors, most notably at the time of the establishment of the Sumerian empire (ca. 2800 BC) attained high social status. Most, if not all, of the warriors were men, which in part derived from the division of labor in

---

[49] Brian Hayden, *Archaeology: the Science of Once and Future Things*, New York, W. H. Freeman, 1993, pp. 361–367.

[50] C. C. Lamberg-Karlovsky and Jeremy A. Sabloff, *Ancient Civilizations: the Near East and Mesoamerica*, Menlo Park, CA, Benjamin/Cummings, 1979, p. 104.

[51] The techniques Jim Jones used to begin his cult and move it to Jonestown must have been similar to those the *ensi* used in the early Mesopotamian city to mobilize the society.

hunter-gatherer societies, where men tended to be the hunters and women the gatherers. We can attribute this tendency for gender differentiation of tasks to several considerations, including that males are more prone to violence on the whole than women are, probably as the result of hormonal differences, and males on average are larger and stronger than women. A third consideration is that women can be immobilized for a time by childbirth and caring for the infant. Armies made up exclusively of men would, as Gerda Lerner pointed out, look to capture and enslave their enemy's women as symbols of their power and prestige.[52] Lerner uses the term "reification" to describe this process of marginalization and suppression of women's status. From Sumeria, Akkadia, and Assyria through ancient Greece and Rome (rape of the Sabines) to present-day Sri Lanka and Bosnia, reification of women by soldiers through rape and enslavement has been a practice not only accepted but also encouraged.

There can be no question that the Mongols had a patriarchal society that often engaged in warfare, with one of its goals to "reify" the women of the vanquished enemy. For example, according to *The Secret History of the Mongols*, when Temujin was proclaimed "Universal Ruler" (Chingiz Khan), three Mongol tribal leaders, Altan, Quchar, and Sacha Beki, declared: "When you are khan, we as vanguard will hasten after many foes. We will bring fine-looking maidens and ladies of rank, palatial tents from foreign people, ladies and maidens with beautiful cheeks, and geldings with fine rumps at the trot. We will bring them and we will give them to you."[53] It was then a sign of generosity, a highly regarded quality in the steppe, for the ruler to distribute the captured women, horses, and booty among his generals. Likewise, Rashīd al-Dīn attributes to Chingiz Khan a lurid description of the goals of warfare.[54] Nonetheless, Mongol women held a relatively higher status within their own society than women did in many other patriarchal societies, mainly because Mongol women were responsible for doing so much of the work. We can explain this phenomenon as a result of men's being absent from the homestead a large part of the time to engage in herding and war. Women then took up the activities in which men were the primary

---

[52] Gerda Lerner, *The Creation of Patriarchy*, New York, Oxford University Press, 1986, esp. pp. 76–100: "The Woman Slave."

[53] *Secret History* (Cleaves), § 123, p. 54; "Secret History" (Rachewiltz), *PFEH*, vol. 5, p. 163. Cf. *Secret History* (Waley), p. 245. See also *Secret History* (Cleaves), § 179, p. 107; and "Secret History" (Rachewiltz), *PFEH*, vol. 16, p. 39.

[54] Rashīd al-Dīn, *Sbornik letopisei*, vol. 1, pt. 2, p. 265. For another example, see *Secret History* (Cleaves), § 112–113, pp. 47–48; "Secret History" (Rachewiltz), *PFEH*, vol. 5, pp. 157–158.

participants, such as hunting and, when the men were away at war, herding too.

But men, either as hunters or as warriors, were not always engaged in martial activities in patriarchal societies. When they became members of civil society, they brought their warrior prestige and female slaves back with them. The ruler, in turn, in order to maintain his army's good will had to ensure the warriors would receive comparable prestige in a civil setting. To do this, the government reserved the top positions in society for men/warriors by excluding women from these positions and relegating them to the domestic sphere. Men, in turn, would have used their exclusive access to the civil sphere as a rationale for establishing their dominance over that domestic sphere. A similar displacement of women has occurred any number of times when returning male soldiers have demanded their jobs back, as in Russia after the Civil War or in the United States and England after the Second World War. The crucial difference in this respect between nomadic and sedentary societies is that, when men in nomadic societies return from war, they resume activities that can continue to keep them absent from the homestead for extended periods of time, whereas men in agricultural societies return to homestead-based work.

Thus, those societies that cultivated the warrior were more aggressive and could conquer those societies that may have been more efficient in terms of utilizing the talents of all its citizens. In fact, the more efficient an egalitarian society was and the more prosperous it became, the more it would have been a target for attack by less efficient but more aggressive societies that had a male-dominated internal structure.[55] Eventually, these male-warrior societies overwhelmed whatever more egalitarian, less patriarchal societies there were. Then, in those societies with slaves to do the work, the respectable women were kept home and secluded to show their husbands were well off enough that their wives did not have to work. In ancient Greece, however, where women were not secluded in separate quarters but only from public areas, they performed industry in the home as part of the *oeconomicus*. Ancient Egypt, as Herodotus pointed out, and Sparta were somewhat anomalous among ancient Mediterranean societies in that women maintained a relatively higher status. It may be significant then that Greek males from other city-states considered both Sparta and Egypt to have limited freedom.

Elsewhere in the ancient world, however, women found themselves increasingly subjugated to male-dominated social structures. The Athenians prohibited their women from appearing in public except on

---

[55] This relationship would, in effect, have been the so-called "sexual contract." See, e.g., Carole Pateman, *The Sexual Contract*, Stanford University Press, 1988.

specified occasions: weddings, funerals, and religious festivals. For a time, there was even a woman's police (*gynaikonomoi*) to arrest women if they ventured into town and to return them to their homes.[56] But, again, this applied only to "respectable" women. The hetaerae, as well as female small traders, retailers, and slaves, were allowed to move about relatively freely.[57] Likewise, in Muslim societies, married women have veiled themselves, among other reasons, to show that they are not available for male interest. The veiling of married women and the seclusion of elite women, both before and after marriage, fulfills several social functions. For one, it prevents conflicts arising between males in the societies over women. Also, in societies where rape is not considered a serious crime, one way for a male to protect his wife and daughters is to keep them at home.

It has been asserted that rape was considered a serious crime among the Orthodox Slavs.[58] But this was in Church law, which considered rape serious in the same sense that it considered adultery serious (the punishments were the same), and for the same reasons. Secular law is conspicuously silent on this matter. *The Statute of Iaroslav*, which (despite the title) delineates Church law, assigned jurisdiction over rape, fornication, adultery, abduction, and so forth to the Church. The first thirty-one articles of the Expanded Redaction of the *Statute* (which has fifty-nine overall in its longest form) discuss punishments for these crimes. The fact that over half of the entire *Statute* is devoted to such transgressions is probably an accurate reflection of the Church's social concerns. Yet the punishment for abduction or violation of a boyar's wife or daughter is the same as for calling her a whore – 10 grivnas of gold, 5 of which went to the woman and 5 to the metropolitan.[59] A gold grivna, according to Vernadsky, was equivalent to half a troy pound (six ounces) of gold.[60] At

---

[56] Eva C. Keuls, *The Reign of the Phallus: Sexual Politics in Ancient Athens*, New York, Harper & Row, 1985, p. 209. See also Sarah B. Pomeroy, *Goddesses, Whores, Wives and Slaves*, New York, Schoken Books, 1975, p. 131.

[57] Roger Just, *Women in Athenian Law and Life*, London, Routledge, 1989, pp. 105–125.

[58] Eve Levin, *Sex and Society in the World of the Orthodox Slavs, 900–1700*, Ithaca, NY, Cornell University Press, 1989, pp. 212–246.

[59] Ia. N. Shchapov, *Drevnerusskie kniazheskie ustavy XI–XV vv.*, Moscow, Nauka, 1976, on abduction and violation, see arts. 2 and 3: pp. 86, 91–92, 94, 100; arts. 4 and 5: p. 104 (Expanded Redaction); pp. 110, 116, 121–122, 126, 128, 133 (Short Redaction); on whore calling, see art. 30: p. 88; art. 31: p. 96; art. 29: p. 101; art. 28: p. 105 (Expanded Redaction); art. 25: pp. 113, 118–119, 123, 134; art. 31: p. 130 (Short Redaction). See also *Rossiiskoe zakonodatel'stvo X–XX vekov*, 9 vols., ed. O. I. Chistiakov, Moscow, Iuridicheskaia literatura, 1984, vol. 1: *Zakonodatel'stvo Drevnei Rusi*, ed. V. L. Ianin, p. 168 (Short Redaction) with commentary on pp. 173–175; and p. 189 (Expanded Redaction) with commentary on pp. 194–195.

[60] George Vernadsky, *History of Russia*, vol. 2, *Kievan Russia*, New Haven, CT, Yale University Press, 1948, p. 122.

the present (1997) rate for gold ($350/oz.), the total payment was equivalent to $21,000, of which the woman received the equivalent of $10,500. In some societies, as Lerner pointed out, the wife, daughter, or slave who was raped was also guilty, because "they are dishonored by being dishonorable."[61] The fact that in the *Statute of Iaroslav* the victim received a monetary compensation and that no penance was prescribed for her indicates that, at least in legal terms, the woman was not considered dishonorable although she had been dishonored.

As we might expect, monetary compensation for the victim accords with Byzantine Church law, in particular, the *Ecloga* and the *Procheiros Nomos*.[62] We find, however, two significant differences of Rus' laws from Byzantine laws in regard to the punishment: (1) a fixed amount was stipulated as payment rather than, as in Byzantine law, a percentage of the offender's wealth; and (2) no mutilation of the offender, such as having his nose slit, was prescribed. In other words, the perpetrator of abduction or rape in Rus' law was liable for civil damages only, not subject to any exemplary or retributive punishment. Why the metropolitan should receive 5 grivnas when a boyar's wife or daughter was abducted, raped, or called a whore is not made clear in the *Statute*. V. L. Ianin suggested that both the woman and the metropolitan were paid in the case of abduction in order to unite women with the Church in the struggle against this pagan custom associated with marriage. But he provides no explanation for the identical stipulations in regard to rape and whore calling.[63] We can suppose the justification is that the Church considered these crimes to be just as much an offense to God and to the social order that the Church defended as to the woman.

Helpful for studying the laws and court cases in Muscovy are the distinctions that Mary Lefkowitz found in ancient Greek law and mythology between seduction, abduction, and rape. Within seduction the Greeks distinguished between off-premises and on-premises seduction (that is, within the house or on the property of the father, husband, or brother), in which case it was a serious crime. Within abduction, the Greeks distinguished between abduction that resulted in sexual intercourse and that which did not. In the latter case, the abductor could be absolved if all agreed to a marriage between him and the abductee. The consent of the woman is crucial as mitigating circumstance in both seduction off premises and abduction. Rape, on the other hand, was clearly a crime with no mitigating circumstances, because force was

---

[61] Lerner, *Creation of Patriarchy*, p. 98.
[62] Laiou, "Sex, Consent, and Coercion in Byzantium," pp. 122–123.
[63] *Zakonodatel'stvo Drevnei Rusi*, p. 173.

applied and the woman did not provide consent.[64] Other societies may have treated the circumstances differently, but these distinctions seem to hold up to a certain extent in Muscovite law.

A common misconception in the historiography is the view that Muscovy was a society where the dishonor and crime of rape could be rectified through marriage. Kollmann, for example, cites articles from the law code *Zakon sudnyi liudem* to this effect.[65] But the articles in question distinguish between seduction, that is, with the maiden's consent but without that of her parents (article 10, short redaction, article 11, expanded redaction), and rape, that is, without the maiden's consent (article 11, short redaction, not in expanded redaction).[66] In the former circumstance, marriage was allowed; in the latter, it was not. Not only do we not have evidence in Rus'ian law of marriage absolving rape, but also, as Eve Levin pointed out, we have examples where the Rus'ians changed the laws they inherited from the South Slavs, such as in *Kormchie knigi* and *trebniki*, to eliminate any such possible interpretation.[67] Women in Muscovy, although second-class citizens, were not abject slaves. Detailed research on the sources has shown that they had property and legal rights, much more than we might have assumed.[68]

On the other hand, the societies we are discussing here did not usually have a police force or the concept of equality before the law. When a rape occurred and the perpetrator of the crime was of higher social rank

[64] Mary R. Lefkowitz, "Seduction and Rape in Greek Myth," in *Consent and Coercion*, pp. 18–21.

[65] Nancy Shields Kollmann, "Women's Honor in Early Modern Russia," in *Russia's Women: Accommodation, Resistance, Transformation*, ed. Barbara Evans Clements, Barbara Alpern Engel, and Christine D. Worobec, Berkeley, University of California Press, 1991, p. 65.

[66] *Zakon sudnyj ljudem (Court Law for the People)*, trans. H[orace] W. Dewey and A[nn] M. Kleimola, Michigan Slavic Materials, no. 14, Ann Arbor, MI, Department of Slavic Languages and Literatures, 1977, pp. 12–13, 34–35.

[67] Levin, *Sex and Society*, pp. 220–221. Halperin recounted a story that supposedly appears in the sixteenth-century *Life of Pafnutii Borovskii*. According to Halperin's account, the saint's grandfather, a Tatar *baskak*, rapes an unmarried Christian woman. He saves his soul from perdition when he converts to Christianity, baptized with the name Martin, and rights the moral wrong by marrying the woman. Halperin, *Russian and the Golden Horde*, p. 36. Levin repeated Halperin's story. Levin, *Sex and Society*, p. 213. But such a story does not appear in the published version of Pafnutii's *Life*. For the baptism of Martin, see A. P. Kadlubovskii, "Zhitie Pafnutiia Borovskogo, pisannoe Vassianom Saninym," *Sbornik Istoriko-filologicheskogo obshchestva pri Institute kniazia Bezborodko v Nezhine*, vol. 2, Nezhin, M. V. Glezer, 1899, p. 118; and the Volokolamsk Patericon, GIM, Sinod. 927, fols. 4v–5, published in Arkhiepiskop Pitirim, "O Volokolamskom paterike," *Bogoslovskie trudy*, vol. 10, 1973, p. 178. See also Zimin, "Narodnye dvizheniia," p. 63.

[68] See, e.g., Sandra Levy, "Women and the Control of Property in Sixteenth-Century Muscovy," *Russian History*, vol. 10, 1983, pp. 201–212; and Kollmann, "Women's Honor in Early Modern Russia," pp. 60–73.

than the victim's husband or father, then a woman had very few options for justice to be served. Besides, if women in such societies wanted to develop identities of their own, basically they had three alternatives: (1) suppress that ambition in deference to men; (2) try to find their identity, as best they could, while facilitating men's culture; or (3) form their own separate culture, even if unequal. Again, this is not meant as a defense of seclusion or veiling, but only as an attempt to understand why women in these societies would be willing to accept and even actively support such practices. When women in a society that practices seclusion and veiling have a better alternative, they then challenge those customs.[69]

It is difficult to see how societies like India, where seclusion seems to have been a reaction to Muslim in-migration, or the Ottoman Empire could have influenced Muscovy to seclude its elite women. Kollmann has suggested that "[t]reatment of women in the Near Eastern Islamic royal courts with which Muscovy traded . . . may perhaps have been an inspiration" for similar practice in Muscovy.[70] This is unlikely in the case of the Ottoman Empire, because of the lack of an intermediate mechanism to effect the transference. Although, as Fisher wrote, "[i]nstead of hostility, trade and ordinary diplomacy characterized Muscovite–Ottoman relations in these two centuries,"[71] Muscovite merchants would not have had access to the royal court, nor would they have had the influence back home to get the Muscovite ruling class to imitate such practices. Diplomats would, presumably, have had access to these royal courts and the earliest mentions of official relations between Muscovy and the Ottoman Empire date to the mid-1490s.[72] But these contacts were minimal and sporadic. Besides, the ḥarēm at the Ottoman Court was an entirely different institution from what appeared in Muscovy.[73]

---

[69] Even today, women are, at times, killed by Muslim extremists for opposition to veiling. Associated Press, "Algerians Say 2 Women Who Shunned Veils Killed," *Boston Globe*, March 31, 1994, p. 14. Meanwhile, in Israel, a rabbi declared that an orthodox Jewish husband may divorce his wife if she bares her arms in public. Reuters, "Where Bare Elbow Might Be Grounds for a Broken Home," *Boston Globe*, August 25, 1994, p. 2. And the rabbinical court in Bnei Brak, a town near Tel Aviv, declared that women should sit, separately from men, in the back of public buses for the sake of "modesty and purity." *Boston Globe*, July 4, 1995, p. 2.

[70] Kollmann, "Seclusion of Muscovite Elite Women," p. 177.

[71] Fisher, "Muscovite–Ottoman Relations," p. 211.

[72] *SRIO*, vol. 41, no. 48, p. 221 (1495); no. 49, p. 224 (1496); no. 50, pp. 231–236 (1496); *PSRL*, vol. 6, p. 42 (1497); vol. 24, p. 243; vol. 26, p. 291; vol. 28, p. 329. See also B. M. Dantsig, "Iz istorii russkikh puteshestvii i izucheniia blizhnego Vostoka v dopetrovskoi Rusi," *Ocherki po istorii russkogo vostokovedeniia*, 6 vols., Moscow, Akademiia nauk SSSR, 1953, vol. 1, p. 210; Vernadsky, *Russia at the Dawn of the Modern Age*, pp. 90–91; and Croskey, *Muscovite Diplomatic Practice*, pp. 59–60.

[73] See N. M. Penzer, *The Harēm: an Account of the Institution as It Existed in the Palace of the Turkish Sultan*, London, Spring Books, 1965.

A likely source of seclusion in Muscovy is the Byzantine Empire, where we have evidence that the seclusion and veiling of elite women were practiced.[74] Angeliki Laiou, however, argued that in Byzantium "[t]he confinement of [aristocratic] women to women's quarters was not a functional reality after the eleventh century."[75] She supports her argument with two assertions: (1) the sources after the eleventh century that speak of seclusion present it "merely as an ideal" that "does not really describe the contemporary situation"; and (2) Palaeologian aristocratic women freely interacted with men. Yet interaction could occur with veiling. Veiling was an institution that allowed aristocratic women mobility and that allowed them to interact with males who were not relatives.[76] Laiou seems to assume that Byzantine women had to be unveiled in order to be active. But veiling often meant that only certain male relatives were allowed to see their faces. Indeed, the veiled Begums ruled India's Bhopal state from 1844 to 1926. And seclusion, that is, separate quarters, does not necessarily mean total confinement. Otherwise, there would be no need for veiling. In fact, veiling, it could be argued, was an improvement over complete seclusion in that it allowed women to leave their rooms and houses and to interact (cautiously and

[74] The Byzantine jurist and historian Attaleiates, after an earthquake in 1063, expressed indignation that women who usually were secluded inside their house "forgot their innate shame" in running out into the street. Michael Attaleiates, *Historia*, ed. Immanuel Bekker, Bonn, 1853, p. 88, lines 13–15. Anna Comnena mentions a woman who "drew aside the veil that covered her face" as though it were common practice for women to be veiled when they went into public. Anna Comnena [Komnenē], *Alexiade*, ed. Bernard Leib and P. Gautier, 4 vols., Paris, Les belles lettres, 1967–1976, vol. 1, p. 78, lines 29–30 (2.V.8). Moschus tells us of a virtuous maiden who never revealed her face to men who were strangers. John Moschus, *Patrum spirituale*, ch. 78, in *Patrologiae cursus completus. Series Graeca* (PG), ed. Jacques-Paul Migne, 161 vols., Paris, J. P. Migne, 1857–1866, vol. 87, pt. 3, cols. 2933–2934. A tenth-century aristocrat writes that he allowed his daughter out for a once-a-week trip to the segregated public baths, but only veiled and chaperoned. Eduard Kurz, "Zwei griechische Texte über die Hl. Theophano, die Gemahlin Kaisers Leo VI," *Zapiski Imperatorskoi Akademii nauk*, series 8, *Po istoriko-filologicheskomu otdeleniiu*, vol. 3, no. 2, 1898, p. 3. See also Evelyne Patlagean, "Byzantium in the Tenth and Eleventh Centuries," in *A History of Private Life*, 5 vols., eds. Philippe Ariès and Georges Duby, Cambridge, MA, Belknap Press, 1987–1991, vol. 1: *From Pagan Rome to Byzantium*, p. 573; José Grosdidier de Matons, "La Femme dans l'empire byzantin," in *Histoire mondiale de la femme*, 4 vols., ed. Pierre Grimal, Paris, Nouvelle Librairie de France, 1965–1967, vol. 3, pp. 28–30; Judith Herrin, "In Search of Byzantine Women: Three Avenues of Approach," in *Images of Women in Antiquity*, eds. Averil Cameron and Amélie Kuhrt, Detroit, Wayne State University Press, 1983, pp. 171–172; Leila Ahmed, *Women and Gender in Islam: Historical Roots of a Modern Debate*, New Haven, CT, Yale University Press, 1992, pp. 26–28.

[75] Angeliki E. Laiou, "The Role of Women in Byzantine Society," *Jahrbuch der österreichischen Byzantinistik*, vol. 31, 1981, p. 249.

[76] Lady Mary Wortley Montagu made this point in a letter to her sister dated April 1, 1717, about veiled women she saw in Istanbul. *The Letters and Works of Lady Mary Wortley Montagu*, ed. Lord Wharncliffe, London, Henry G. Bohn, 1861, pp. 298–300.

with many restrictions, to be sure) with males who were not relatives. In Muscovy, as Kollmann has concluded, "[w]omen, however secluded, were integrated into the life of the elite."[77] Runciman made the point that seclusion of women in Byzantium was different from the ḥarēm in that, although men were not allowed in the women's quarters, the women could leave their quarters.[78] Although he distanced Byzantine seclusion from its counterpart in Muscovy as well, the similarities between the two may be more significant than their differences.

If Laiou is right that Byzantine women were not secluded after the eleventh century, that still would not exclude the possibility that Muscovite Churchmen derived the practice from Byzantium. As Laiou herself pointed out, seclusion was praised in Byzantine sources as the ideal even if it was not widely practiced. That praise of an ideal could have carried over into Muscovy via the Church book culture or via Greek clergy assigned duties in Rus'. And while one can condemn "'Asiatic' denigration of women" all one wants, the Christian Church and Western societies were second to none in articulating misogynist attitudes.[79] Karen Armstrong pointed out that the "position [of women] was particularly poor in [ancient] Greece, for example – a fact that Western people should remember when they decry the patriarchal attitudes of the Orient."[80] In addition, one cannot forget the impact that reading the misogynist book *Lamentationum Matheoluli* had on Christine de Pizan.[81] If Meḥmet II organized his ḥarēm, at least in part, in imitation of Byzantine practice, then seclusion must have been more prevalent than Laiou is willing to admit. If, on the other hand, Meḥmet II organized his ḥarēm according to traditional Muslim practice, that still does not absolve Christianity from any complicity, since there is general agreement among historians that the Muslims adopted the ideas of seclusion and veiling from Syrian Christians in the middle of the seventh century.[82]

In the end, we must admit that not only do we not know when

---

[77] Kollmann, "Seclusion of Elite Muscovite Women," p. 186.

[78] Steven Runciman, "Some Notes on the Role of the Empress," *Eastern Churches Review*, vol. 4, 1972, p. 121.

[79] See, e.g., G. P. Fedotov, *the Russian Religious Mind*, 2 vols., Cambridge, MA, Harvard University Press, 1946, 1966, vol. 2, ed. John Meyendorff, pp. 75–78; Herrin, "In Search of Byzantine Women," p. 182; and Mango, *Byzantium: the Empire of New Rome*, pp. 225–227.

[80] Karen Armstrong, *A History of God: the 4000-Year Quest of Judaism, Christianity and Islam*, New York, Alfred A. Knopf, 1993, p. 50.

[81] See her *The Book of the City of Ladies*, trans. Earl Jeffrey Richards, New York, Persea, 1982, pp. 3–5.

[82] Mark Kishlansky, Patrick Geary, and Patricia O'Brien, *Civilization in the West*, New York, HarperCollins, 1991, p. 207.

seclusion was introduced into Muscovy but we also do not have definite answers for why and how. We might give some consideration to the possibility that diaspora Greeks in the entourage of Sofiia (Zoë) Palaeologina were responsible for bringing the innovation to Muscovy in the late fifteenth century. Since the Church conducted marriage ceremonies, the arrangement of marriages would also seem to be their bailiwick. As Keenan has discussed, seclusion of elite women in Muscovy was part of marriage politics, so that families and clans could more easily arrange nuptials. Arranged marriages precluded the young from choosing their own marriage partners in a haphazard way.[83]

The marriages of Ivan IV after the death of his second wife, Mariia Temriukovna, seem to fall outside these politically scripted arrangements. One problem was that the Church frowned upon third and later marriages in general as uncanonical.[84] The bride-show of 1571, in which Ivan chose Marfa Sobakina for his third wife, did have precedent in Byzantium.[85] Between 768 and 882, six imperial bride-shows are recorded; but as Runciman suggested, these may have had a steppe model. The wife of Constantine V was a Khazarian princess and the first bride-show was for her son Leo IV.[86] The bride-show may have developed from the steppe practice of presenting women captured in battle to the khan. Thus, the direct antecedent for the bride-show of 1571 could have been either Byzantium or the steppe. All this, however, is complete speculation.

One might wonder why the Rus' prelates would be willing to advance Byzantine political practices in Muscovy. After all, from their point of view, Constantinople had dishonored itself by seeking union with the Latins and then had been punished by God with the Ottoman conquest. And, since the late 1440s, the Rus' Church was virtually autonomous, having declared its own metropolitan independently. Yet, from those same Rus' prelates' point of view, Constantinople was the source of the true religion – Orthodoxy. Although the Byzantine Empire had fallen

[83] Edward L. Keenan, "Ivan the Terrible and His Women: the Grammar of Politics in the Kremlin" and "Ivan the Terrible and His Women II: Dowagers, Nannies, and Brides," both unpublished papers given as lectures at Wellesley College, Newton, Massachusetts, February 1981.
[84] See, e.g., the chiding remarks of Theophanes concerning Constantine V, "the trigamist." Theophanes, *Chronographia*, vol. 1, pp. 442–443.
[85] For Ivan's bride-show, see "Poslanie Ioganna Taube i Elerta Kruze," ed. Iu. V. Got'e, in *Russkii istoricheskii zhurnal*, vol. 8, 1922, p. 55; and *AAE*, vol. 1, no. 284, p. 329. See also Karamzin, *Istoriia gosudarstva rossiiskogo*, vol. 9, col. 110; A. A. Zimin, *Oprichnina Ivan Groznogo*, Moscow, Mysl', 1964, p. 466; and Ruslan G. Skrynnikov, *Ivan the Terrible*, ed. and trans. Hugh F. Graham, Gulf Breeze, FL, Academic International Press, 1981, pp. 173–174.
[86] Runciman, "Some Notes on the Role of the Empress," pp. 120–121.

because of its sins, it was still the archetypal model of the universal empire for the ecclesiastical elite, just as the Mongol Empire was the archetypal model of the universal empire for the secular elite. If seclusion was introduced into Muscovy during the late fifteenth or early sixteenth century, which is our earliest evidence of it, then that does not coincide in time with the existence of our proposed source culture (Byzantium). Instead, we then have to resort to explaining it as a book-based innovation and represented what Muscovite Churchmen thought had been the case in Byzantium, whether or not it was extensively practiced there after the eleventh century. I have no better explanation at the moment.

4   Oriental despotism

The historiographical tradition of attributing Russian autocracy to Mongol despotism is a long one. Ukrainian nationalist historians, for example, have used this theory to "explain" why the Ukrainian people are "freedom loving" and the Russian people are "servile." Dmytro Doroshenko, whom one can consider a moderate among Ukrainian historians, nonetheless claimed that it is due to close contact "with the Tatars and centuries of submission to their control that the Russians owe their autocratic form of their own government. From this experience all the Asiatic or Eastern features of their character and philosophy, features that were entirely foreign to the Eastern Slavs, distinguish the Russians from the Ukrainians and from other Slavs."[1] My own view is that (1) all people are freedom loving, and (2) assertions that the Russian people are not are based more on anti-Russian sentiments of the person making the assertion than on any historical evidence. Nonetheless, we must come to grips with the continued claims about the origins of Russian autocracy.

First, we should acknowledge that the terms "autocracy" and "despotism" have similar connotations but different denotations. Both "despotism" and "autocracy" have the sense of the ruler's having unrestricted power within his or her realm. Subsequently, these terms came to connote someone who exercised unfair and arbitrary power. The denotation of an *auto-crat* (literally, "self-ruler") is someone who is not in a subordinate relationship to another ruler. Likewise, despotism derives from the Greek *despotēs*, which meant a lord or master. But a *despotēs* could be appointed by someone else and derive their authority from that person. For purposes of this discussion, I will use "autocrat" in the denotative sense, as a self-ruler, unbeholding to anyone else for authority. I will use "despotism" in the connotative sense as the ruler's unrestricted power in a society, with the implication of an unfair and arbitrary exercise of that power. This means that I am using "des-

---

[1] Dmytro Doroshenko, *A Survey of Ukrainian History*, ed. and updated by Oleh W. Gerus, Winnipeg, Trident Press, 1975, p. 72.

potism" more in a structural than a functional sense, because any government, no matter what its structure, can potentially act in a despotic way. Even the government of the United States, with its elaborate system of checks and balances, can act despotically, that is, with unrestricted power, if all three branches of the federal government are in agreement. It is just more difficult, one hopes, for it to do so. Now we can proceed with our analysis.

Karl Wittfogel theorized that Muscovy acquired "oriental despotism" from China via the Mongols.[2] One can reject that idea out of hand, for the simple reason that the Mongols had no tradition of despotism as such, even when they ruled in China. According to Elizabeth Endicott-West, "[t]he Mongolian *qan* or *qayan* was *primus inter pares*, and decisions were rendered in a conciliar, not an autocratic, fashion."[3] The major characteristic of the Mongol rule throughout Asia and into Muscovy was decentralization – what Beatrice Forbes Manz has called "division and confusion of responsibilities."[4] In addition, the various Tatar khans had limitations on their power within their own realms. The role of the *qaračï beys* was to act as a check on and balance to the rule of the khan in the various *ulus* of the Mongol Empire.[5]

Even beyond that, one can question the term "oriental despotism" itself. Wittfogel's definition of the term seems to derive from its use by certain French writers, in particular Bodin and Montesquieu, in relation to the governments of Safavid Persia and the Ottoman Empire,[6] but these writers' understanding of these governments was meager at best. Instead, Bodin and Montesquieu were holding up a mirror to European rulers, showing the worst aspects of their own rule and attributing the totality of these worst aspects to "oriental" society.[7]

Other writers, Wittfogel included, applied the French writers'

---

[2] Wittfogel, *Oriental Despotism*, pp. 191–192.

[3] Endicott-West, *Mongolian Rule in China*, p. 44.

[4] Beatrice Forbes Manz, "The Office of *Darugha* under Tamerlane," *Journal of Turkish Studies* (= *An Anniversary Volume in Honor of Francis Woodman Cleaves*), vol. 9, 1985, p. 64.

[5] Schamiloglu, "Tribal Politics and Social Organization," pp. 25–32; Schamiloglu, *Golden Horde*, ch. 5: "Socio-Political Organization of the Golden Horde and the Later Golden Horde." See also Edward L. Keenan, "Muscovy and Kazan: Some Introductory Remarks on the Patterns of Steppe Diplomacy," *Slavic Review*, vol. 26, 1967, p. 551.

[6] Jean Bodin, *Les six livres de la République*, Paris, 1576; and Charles-Louis de Secondat de Montesquieu, *The Persian Letters*, originally published in 1721, nos. 103–105.

[7] See, e.g., Lawrence Meyer Levin, *The Political Doctrine of Montesquieu's* Esprit des lois: *Its Classical Background*, New York, Columbia University Press, 1936, p. 112: "If Montesquieu devotes so much attention in the *Esprit* to a polity that he detests as heartily as he does despotism, the reason seems to be that it is an 'épouvantail qu'il présente aux gouvernements modérés', and particularly to the French monarchy which according to Montesquieu's account in the *Esprit* offers certain alarming absolutist tendencies." Levin goes on to say that Montesquieu's version of despotism based on

concept of "oriental despotism" to Chinese government. There may be some justification to seeing centralizing tendencies during the Zhou, Qin, and Han dynasties. And there certainly seems to have been a continuity of institutional development in China from ancient times to the twentieth century. For example, the thirteenth-century historian Ma Duan-Lin asserted that the "[l]aws and institutions . . . [of Chinese dynasties until his own time] are actually interrelated." In addition, he pointed out that

from the Qin and the Han down to the Tang and the Song, the regulations concerning rites, music, warfare, and punishments, the system of taxation and selection of officials, even the changes and elaborations in bureaucratic titles or the developments and alternations in geography, although in the end not necessarily the same for all dynasties, yet did not suddenly spring into being as something unique for each period.[8]

Ma Duan-Lin also warned against seeing any relationship between the ways dynasties come to power or lose power. This means that we should not confuse political unification in China over the course of centuries with administrative centralization. A civil service developed during the Han dynasty, and the rules became codified under the Song. The Chinese civil service of scholar-administrators governed an enormously prosperous China for centuries.

The success of the Chinese system of government "dwarfed" all other empires in history, and as Caroline Blunden and Mark Elvin have suggested, "possibly even all of them put together."[9] During that period, China was the fountainhead of innovation for half the world, exporting invention after invention to the rest of Eurasia as well as northern and eastern Africa. Lynn White pointed out that medieval Europe imported so many innovations from China that "the whole of the Middle Ages seems to shrivel into a mere appendix to China!"[10] White did suggest that in the future perhaps some of these borrowings may be seen to have been from the West to China. Since White made that suggestion, however, even more innovations than he mentions have been attributed to China. Robert Temple has declared that "[o]ne of the greatest secrets

"oriental prototypes, specifically Turkey and Persia" is "a grossly exaggerated version" (*ibid.*).

[8] Ma Duan-Lin, "Preface to the General Study of Literary Remains," in *Sources of Chinese Tradition*, 2 vols., comp. Wm. Theodore de Bary, Wing-tsit Chan, Chester Tan, and Burton Watson, New York, Columbia University Press, 1964, vol. 1, p. 446.

[9] Caroline Blunden and Mark Elvin, *The Cultural Atlas of the World: China*, Alexandra, VA, Stonehenge, 1991, p. 90.

[10] Lynn White [Jr.], "Technology and Invention in the Middle Ages," *Speculum*, vol. 15, 1940, p. 148; reprinted in Lynn White, Jr., *Medieval Religion and Technology*, Berkeley, University of California Press, 1978, p. 11.

is that the 'modern world' in which we live is a unique synthesis of Chinese and Western ingredients."[11] Under the Ming, however, the Chinese government reined in this innovative spirit and exploratory curiosity. The Manchu (Qing) Dynasty continued this closed-China policy after it came to power in 1644. As a result, the Jesuit missionaries of the late sixteenth and seventeenth centuries, as well as the British diplomats of the eighteenth century, were sending reports that created the image of a society quite different from what the evidence tells us of China just a few centuries earlier. As Robert Hartwell has documented, from the middle of the eighth century through the middle of the sixteenth century, that is, during most of this innovative period, the trend in Chinese government was toward greater power for regional and local levels of government.[12] Thus, the period when the Mongols acquired methods of Chinese government was a period of decentralization, not despotism, and of technological innovation, not stultification.

"Despotism," as Melvin Richter has pointed out, has been a term of denigration for governmental practices the user dislikes: "most often despotism has been a label applied, not only in a polemical spirit, but with a set of practical purposes in view: to identify and discredit arrangements antithetical to or incompatible with those regarded by the analyst as making for political freedom."[13] Richter goes on to indicate that its use has more than a hint of racism about it: "The concept of despotism began as a distinctively European perception of Asian governments and practices: Europeans as such were considered to be free by nature, in contrast to the servile nature of Orientals."[14] We should be very careful about trying to use it as a scholarly tool to explain how a particular government functioned, especially governments in Asia.

In Muscovy, as elsewhere, no matter what the theoretical justification for the power of the ruler was, that person ruled only with the permission of the ruling class of which he was a part.[15] The role of the Boyar Council is paramount here. Not only could no laws or decrees be issued without the approval of the boyars but also no foreign affairs were

[11] Robert Temple, *The Genius of China: 3,000 Years of Science, Discovery and Invention*, New York, Simon & Schuster, 1986, p. 9. See also Joseph Needham et al., *Science and Civilisation in China*, 6 vols. in 16 pts., Cambridge University Press, 1954–1988.

[12] Robert M. Hartwell, "Demographic, Political, and Social Transformations of China, 750–1550," *Harvard Journal of Asiatic Studies*, vol. 42, 1982, pp. 365–442.

[13] Melvin Richter, "Despotism," *Dictionary of the History of Ideas: Studies of Selected Pivotal Ideas*, 5 vols., ed. Philip P. Wiener, New York, Charles Scribner's Sons, 1973, vol. 2, p. 1.

[14] Richter, "Despotism," p. 1.

[15] On this point, for later Russian history, see John P. LeDonne, *Absolutism and the Ruling Class: the Formation of the Russian Political Order, 1700–1825*, Oxford University Press, 1991, pp. 3–9, 311–312.

to be conducted without their being present. When, for example, in 1489, the Imperial ambassador Nicholaus Poppel requested a private audience with Ivan III, he was turned down on the basis that the Boyar Council had to be in attendance.[16]

Historians who support the contention that Muscovite government was despotic or patrimonial generally cite one or more of the following: (1) subjects of the Muscovite ruler called themselves his *kholopy* ("slaves"); (2) they declared their obeisance to the ruler with the *bit' chelom* (literally "hit the forehead [on the ground]"); and (3) they referred to the Muscovite sovereign as *gosudar* ("lord"). All three components appear in the courtiers' formal address to the ruler: "Господину государю великому князю . . . холопъ, господине, твой . . . челомъ бьетъ" ("To the lord, sovereign, and grand prince . . . , your slave makes obeisance").[17] Yet, Marshall Poe has challenged the notion that any of these can be considered evidence for despotism or patrimonialism as such.[18] Poe's argument is that none of these components should be taken literally as indicating the abject subservience of a slave to his lord and owner. Instead, its usage indicates a formal commitment as a royal servant, a tsar's man, with the corresponding increase in social and political status that that position brought.

The formal address itself contains components that show both Byzantine and Mongol influence as well as the indigenous Slavic tradition. The concept of the rulers' men being slaves in terms of obedience derives from the Byzantine concept of "the *doulos* of the majesty," which carried with it a sense both of proximity to the ruler and of being an honorific title.[19] The obeisance (*bit' chelom*), from which derives the term *chelombitie* (petition), itself derives from Turkic *baš ur-*

---

[16] *Pamiatniki diplomaticheskikh snoshenii drevnei Rossii s derzhavami inostrannymi (PDS)*, 10 vols., St. Petersburg, 1851–1871, *PDS*, vol. 1, col. 1. Poppel did eventually meet with Ivan III alone but with no apparent agreement resulting. See Fennell, *Ivan the Great*, pp. 120–121; and Alef, "Adoption of the Muscovite Two-Headed Eagle," p. 6.

[17] *SRIO*, vol. 35, no. 20, p. 87 (address of Iakov Zahar'ich Koshkin to Ivan III). Cf. *PDS*, vol. 1, col. 125 (namestniks of Novgorod Daniil Vasil'evich and Vasilii Shuiskii to Ivan III, 1505): "Государю, великому княю . . . всеа Руси холопи твои, Государь . . . челом бьють"

[18] Marshall Poe, "What Did Muscovites Mean When They Called Themselves 'Slaves of the Tsar'?" *Slavic Review* (forthcoming).

[19] "Doulos," *Oxford Dictionary of Byzantium*, 3 vols., ed. Alexander P. Kazhdan, New York, Oxford University Press, 1991, vol. 1, p. 659; J. B. Bury, *History of the Later Roman Empire from the Death of Theodosius I to the Death of Justinian (AD 395 to AD 565)*, 2 vols., New York, Macmillan, 1923, vol. 1, p. 16; Helga Köpstein, *Zur Slaverei im ausgehenden Byzanz. Philologisch-historische Untersuchung*, Berlin, Akademie-Verlag, 1966, pp. 31–42. Alexander P. Kazhdan, "The Concept of Freedom (*eleutheria*) and Slavery (*duleia*) in Byzantium," in *La notion de liberté au Moyen Age. Islam, Byzance, Occident*, eds. George Makdisi, Dominique Sourdel, and Janine Sourdel-Thomine, Paris, Société d'Édition Les Belles Lettres, 1985, pp. 219–222.

and ultimately from Chinese *kou tou*.[20] The *kou tou* was a sign of voluntary obedience and love within the Chinese family, for one's parents, ancestors, and the deities. The American envoy to China in 1859 John E. Ward had the idea of it when he said that he would kowtow only before God and women.[21] Servants did not kowtow because that would be considered demeaning to them. Instead, they performed the *semba*, a gesture of respect, which involved bowing, clasping the hands, and raising them to the face. As Madame Wellington Koo expressed it: "In a Chinese household, no outsider offers obedience to the family; respect is sufficient."[22] The Imperial *kou tou* was an extension of the family *kou tou*. This perhaps explains why the Qianlong Emperor allowed George Macartney and other British envoys to genuflect as they would for George III rather than kowtow.[23] Likewise, in Muscovy, foreign diplomats did not *bit' chelom* before the grand prince or tsar. Finally, the term *gosudar* derives from common Slavic *gospodin*, *hospodar*.[24]

These components of the formal address to the ruler are symbolic of three of the main influences on Muscovy during the period we are examining here: (1) Byzantine, (2) Tatar, and (3) Slavic. The combination of these elements was uniquely Muscovite. Nonetheless, it is clear that neither the practice of centralized authority nor the theory of autocratic rule came to Muscovy from the Qipchaq Khanate, since neither that practice nor that theory existed in the Khanate. Instead, autocratic theories entered Muscovy from Byzantium through the written culture of the Church.[25] From the late fifteenth century on, the theoretical justification of the Muscovite ruler's authority over society derived from Byzantium.

This combination of decentralized implementation of power along with an appeal to a centralized authority to legitimize that implementation is an extremely significant point. Since the fourteenth century,

---

[20] Peter B. Golden, "Turkic Calques in Medieval Eastern Slavic," *Journal of Turkish Studies*, vol. 8, 1984, p. 109.

[21] Li, *Ageless Chinese*, p. 390 n. 1.

[22] Madame Wellington Koo, with Isabella Tares, *No Feast Lasts Forever*, New York, Quadrangle, 1975, p. 25.

[23] See his initial reaction to Macartney's request, as reported in Alain Peyrefitte, *The Collision of Two Civilizations: the British Expedition to China, 1792–4*, trans. Jon Rothschild, London, Harvill, 1992, p. 85.

[24] Max Vasmer [Fasmer], *Etimologicheskii slovar' russkogo iazyka*, 2nd edn., 4 vols., trans. O. N. Trubachev, Moscow, Progress, 1986, vol. 1, p. 446.

[25] Ihor Ševčenko, "A Neglected Byzantine Source of Muscovite Political Ideology," *Harvard Slavic Studies*, vol. 2, 1954, pp. 141–179; reprinted in *The Structure of Russian History: Interpretive Essays*, ed. Michael Cherniavsky, New York, Random House, 1970, pp. 80–105; also reprinted in Ihor Ševčenko, *Byzantium and the Slavs: In Letters and Culture*, Cambridge, MA, Harvard Ukrainian Research Institute, 1991, pp. 49–87.

Muscovy (and then Russia) has been an astoundingly successful political entity.[26] There were setbacks to be sure, but each time Muscovy/Russia overcame them. An important reason for this success was the ability to change models of governing when the needs changed. Looking for and following successful models, instead of trying to reinvent the wheel each time, is one of the successful strategies of any organization.[27] Following a successful model may work for a time if it is the right model for that time. When the needs change, then a new "right" model needs to be found, although the tendency is for the elite within an organization to hold onto the model that worked in the first place no matter how inappropriate it may have become.[28] People in countries that gain ascendancy over their neighbors because of technological superiority have a habit of attributing that ascendancy to the superiority of their culture, religion, political system, economic system, and themselves as human beings. This mindset hinders them from changing their system or themselves to meet changing circumstances.

What Muscovite leaders were able to do was modify their approach and change governing models when needed. During the fourteenth and fifteenth centuries, Muscovy prospered as a commercial power taxing trade along the rivers and portages. At that time, the loose administrative structures borrowed from the Qipchaq Khanate were sufficient.[29]

[26] For the typology of historical bureaucratic empires oriented toward collective-executive goals, into which Russia fits, as opposed to those oriented toward maintenance of cultural patterns, see S. N. Eisenstadt, *The Political Systems of Empires*, Glencoe, IL, Free Press, 1963, pp. 223–253.

[27] For example, between 1984 and 1992 the National Basketball Association achieved what has been called "unprecedented global success." Commissioner David Stern attributed this success to borrowing from successful models: "A lot of what we did over the years was to find out what others were doing and decide what models we might follow, if we ever had the time or luxury to deal with something other than a series of crises that afflicted us . . . . In those days, we were looking around to see whose success we could copy. It took over a decade." Quoted in Larry Whiteside, "Stern the Point Man in NBA's Team Effort," *Boston Globe*, December 20, 1992, p. 84.

[28] In analyzing the problems IBM faced in 1992, Mark Stahlman, president of New Media Associates, described the tendency this way: "Once a team has achieved success with one approach (and, remember, most teams never get this far because they fail), it will inevitably try to replicate the winning style over and over again. Once a team has struggled to win and ultimately traveled the road to power and riches, just try to tell it that its approach is obsolete. Just try to tell it that the grass-is-greener market on the other side of the fence requires a completely different business model. Just try to tell it to forget what it has accomplished and start over again. Good luck." Mark Stahlman, " 'Big Blue' Sees Red," *Boston Globe*, December 20, 1992, p. A22.

[29] On the efficiency of the pre-Petrine bureaucracy, see Borivoj Plavsic, "Seventeenth-Century Chanceries and Their Staffs," in *Russian Officialdom: the Bureaucratization of Russian Society from the Seventeenth to the Twentieth Century*, eds. Walter McKenzie Pintner and Don Karl Rowney, Chapel Hill, University of North Carolina Press, 1980, pp. 19–45; reprinted in *Major Problems in Early Modern Russian History*, ed. Nancy Shields Kollmann, New York, Garland, 1992, pp. 155–181. For a general survey of the

In the late fifteenth century, Muscovy's territorial acquisitions began to exceed the present-day boundaries of Moscow province. The administrative structures were modified and, significantly, the Church introduced a theoretical justification of the ruler's power. While the Muscovite elite had borrowed its administrative procedures and political institutions from Sarai, no ideological justification was needed earlier for the grand prince's authority, since he obtained his authority from the khan in Sarai. The Mongols, in turn, had obtained their justification for conquest from the Chinese concept of the Mandate of Heaven (*tian ming*).

China had a well-developed ideology in place for centuries with political, social, and virtual past components. The political component was the Mandate of Heaven, which legitimated the emperor's rule. Confucianism provided the social component by extolling the importance of individual relationships with others and the duties contained therein. Individuals accepted their positions in society and were supposed to perform the required social duties of that position based on the four personal relationships – between friends, older and younger siblings, husband and wife, and parents and children. These relationships within the family, especially the last, filiopiety, were easily extended into the political sphere as the relationship between subject and ruler.[30] The virtual past component was provided by the official history of Chinese dynasties (such as the *Songshi*, *Yuanshi*, and so forth).

In regard to the political component of Mongol rule, the Chinese Mandate of Heaven emerged in Mongol political doctrine as decrees from Eternal Heaven (*möngke tengri* [or *tenggeri*]).[31] Both Rashīd al-Dīn and Jūzjānī report that, before the beginning of the campaign against the Jin (Jürched) Dynasty in 1211, Chingiz Khan withdrew from the *quriltai* for a time to commune with and call on the assistance of Eternal Heaven.[32] When he returned to the *quriltai*, Chingiz declared: "Heaven

pre-Petrine bureaucracy, see Peter Brown, "Early Modern Russian Bureaucracy: the Evolution of the Chancery System from Ivan III to Peter the Great, 1478–1717," Ph.D. Dissertation, University of Chicago, 1978.

[30] Herrlee G. Creel, *Chinese Thought: From Confucius to Mao Tse-Tung*, University of Chicago Press, 1953, pp. 41–43; see the remarks of Wang Gungwu, Vice Chancellor of Hong Kong University, in *The Genius That Was China*, PBS, 1990, part 1: *The Rise of the Dragon*.

[31] But Khazanov has argued that "supposed influence could vary" and "the concept could originate independently in the Eurasian nomadic societies." Anatoly M. Khazanov, "Muhammad and Jenghiz Khan Compared: the Religious Factor in World Empire Building," *Comparative Studies in Society and History*, vol. 35, 1993, p. 465.

[32] Rashīd al-Dīn, *Sbornik letopisei*, vol. 1, pt. 2, p. 263; and Minhāj al-Dīn Jūzjānī, *Tabakāt-i-Nāṣirī: a General History of the Muhammadan Dynasties of Asia*, trans. M. G. Raverty, 2 vols., London, Gilbert and Rivington, 1881, vol. 2, p. 954. Juvaini also describes the episode but does not explicitly say that Chingiz Khan prayed to Heaven.

has promised me victory." Invoking Heaven was particularly important for Chingiz in order for him to be able to challenge the legitimacy of the Chinese Emperor's claim to carry the Mandate of Heaven. Thus, if anyone resisted the agent of Eternal Heaven, the agent in this case being the Mongol khan, then that person who resisted, even if he was the Chinese Emperor, was a rebel against heavenly decree.[33] This idea provided a justification for Mongols to deal harshly with peoples and towns that refused to submit to them. It was also the basis of the reply of Khan Güyük (1246–1248) to Pope Innocent IV, who had complained about Mongol treatment of conquered Christian peoples. Güyük wrote: "We do not understand these words of yours. The Eternal Heaven (tengri) has slain and annihilated these lands and peoples, because they have heeded neither Chingiz Khan nor the Khagan [Ögödei], both of whom have been sent to make known God's command. Nor [have these lands and people heeded] the command of God."[34] As Eric Vogelin pointed out, the wording on such documents indicates the khan saw himself as much subject to the orders of Eternal Heaven as everyone else, and that it was his duty to carry out these orders.[35] While it might be argued that Rashīd al-Dīn and Jūzjānī were presenting a post-facto

Juvaini, *History of the World Conqueror*, pp. 80–81. Rashīd al-Dīn tells us that Chingiz Khan similarly prayed to Heaven before the campaign against Khwarezm. Rashīd al-Dīn, *Sbornik letopisei*, vol. 1, pt. 2, p. 189.

[33] Rachewiltz, "Some Remarks on the Ideological Foundations," pp. 23–25; Herbert Franke, *From Tribal Chieftain to Universal Emperor and God: the Legitimation of the Yüan Dynasty*, Munich, Bayerische Akademie der Wissenschaften, 1978, pp. 18–19. See also *Secret History* (Cleaves), § 203, p. 143; "Secret History" (Rachewiltz), *PFEH*, vol. 21, p. 27. For an analysis of the references to Heaven in the *Secret History*, see Rachewiltz, "Some Remarks on the Ideological Foundations," pp. 26–28. Rachewiltz pointed out that in the *Secret History* the Earth-goddess is also invoked (*ibid.*, p. 27).

[34] For the Persian translation (now in the Vatican archives) made by Güyük's chancery, see Paul Pelliot, "Les Mongols et la Papauté," *Revue de l'Orient chrétien*, vol. 23, 1923, pp. 17–18. For a French translation made from the Persian, see Pelliot, "Les Mongols et la Papauté," vol. 23, 1922, pp. 18–23; reprinted in Eric Vogelin, "The Mongol Orders of Submission to European Powers, 1245–1255," *Byzantion*, vol. 15, 1941, pp. 386–387. For an English translation from the Persian, see Igor de Rachewiltz, *Papal Envoys to the Great Khans*, Stanford University Press, 1971, pp. 213–214. For the Latin translation made from the Mongol original (now lost), see *Cronica fratris Salimbene de Adam Ordinis minorum*, ed. Oswald Holder-Egger, *Monumenta Germaniae historica. Scriptorum*, vol. 32, Hanover, Impensis Bibliopolii Hahniani, 1905–1913, p. 208; reprinted in Vogelin, "Mongol Orders," p. 388. For an English translation of the Latin (although the editor says it is from the Persian), see *Mongol Mission*, pp. 85–86.

[35] Vogelin, "Mongol Orders," p. 405. See also Vernadsky, *Mongols and Russia*, pp. 92–99; Saunders, *History of the Mongol Conquests*, pp. 94–95; and Morgan, *Mongols*, pp. 179–183. Prawdin reported that, at the *quriltai* of 1206, Chingiz Khan declared: "Heaven has appointed me to rule all the nations, for hitherto there has been no order upon the steppe." Michael Prawdin, *The Mongol Empire: Its Rise and Legacy*, London, George Allen and Unwin, 1940, p. 89. Such a statement would have been out of place as early as 1206, and I have been unable to find Prawdin's source.

justification for Mongol world conquest, the same cannot be said for the author of the *Secret History*, who seems uninterested in such an undertaking. The *Secret History* focuses primarily on internal tribal matters and then on the conquest of China; and it discusses the other conquests only in a superficial way.[36] Its invoking of Eternal Heaven to justify only limited and specific conquest, therefore, provides particularly strong confirmation for how the Mongols thought at the time. Thus, the Mongols do not seem to have developed the idea and justification for world conquest until after they conquered Turkic peoples who had a developed tradition of such a concept.[37]

Turkic tribes on the borders of the Chinese Empire had been exposed to Chinese ideas long before Chingiz Khan. For example, Tonyuquq, the chief minister of the eastern Turks in the seventh century had been educated in China.[38] The Khitans, especially, had acted as the agents for the transfer of political ideas and administration to the eastern Turks, and it is well known that Chingiz Khan's father, Yisügei, had dealings with the Jin Dynasty (1115–1234).[39] There may also have been an Islamic component to Mongol political doctrine. John Keegan has suggested that Mongol contact with the *ghazis*, Muslim frontier warriors who proselytized with the sword, may have given Chingiz Khan the idea of combining traditional war-making with the abstract notion of doing so in the service of a higher cause.[40] Instead of the *ghazis'* appeal to Allah, Chingiz appealed to Eternal Heaven and gave it an aggressive expansionary aspect the Mandate of Heaven lacked under the Chinese.

By 1219, in a letter to the Daoist Qang-qun, Chingiz Khan, or at least his advisers writing for him, provided a rationale for his supremacy over the Jurchens: "Heaven has abandoned China owing to its haughtiness and extravagant luxury. But I, living in the northern wilderness, have not inordinate passions."[41] Although Chingiz Khan's passions for

---

[36] On this focus of the *Secret History*, see Morgan, *Mongols*, p. 14. Elsewhere, Morgan states that the Mongols did not begin with the idea of world conquest but acquired the idea as they conquered more of it. David O. Morgan, "The Mongols and the Eastern Mediterranean," *Mediterranean Historical Review*, vol. 4, 1989, p. 200.

[37] Osman Turan, "The Ideal of World Domination Among the Medieval Turks," *Studia Islamica*, vol. 4, 1955, pp. 77–90; Peter Jackson and David Morgan, "Introduction," in Rubruck, *Mission*, p. 25.

[38] Rachewiltz, "Some Remarks on the Ideological Foundations," p. 30; and René Grousset, *The Empire of the Steppes: a History of Central Asia*, trans. Naomi Walford, New Brunswick, NJ, Rutgers University Press, 1970, p. 106.

[39] Rachewiltz, "Some Remarks on the Ideological Foundations," pp. 31–32.

[40] Keegan, *History of Warfare*, p. 207.

[41] E. Bretschneider, *Medieval Researches from Eastern Asiatic Sources*, 2 vols., London, Trübner, 1888; repr. Kegan Paul, Trench, Trübner, 1919, vol. 1, p. 37. Bretschneider suggested that Yelü Chucai was the author of the letter. See also Rachewiltz, "Yeh-lü Ch'u-ts'ai," p. 196.

hunting, warfare, and women were nothing if not inordinate from our point of view, and even though it is unlikely those phrases and concepts are Chingiz Khan's own, the letter is nonetheless revealing. It represents an articulation by those who had gathered around him by this time, including Yelü Chucai, of the ideological justification for his authority – the simplicity of his lifestyle in contrast to the luxury and decadence of the Chinese court.

Through the Mongols and the Qipchaq Khanate, Muscovite rulers became familiar with the concept of the Mandate of Heaven. They could not, however, adopt this concept as their own in the fourteenth or fifteenth centuries, even if they wanted to, for it was the specific prerogative of the Mongols. Muscovite princes had borrowed from Byzantium via the Church another concept, that is, the Grace of God. By claiming, in the late fourteenth and fifteenth centuries, that they ruled by the Grace of God, Muscovite princes thereby avoided coming into conflict with the justification for authority that the Mongol khans claimed. The earliest extant evidence of the grand prince's use of the phrase "by the Grace of God" (Божьею милостью) is in the agreement between Vasilii I and Prince Mikhail Aleksandrovich of Tver' from *c.* 1396.[42] But the use of the phrase here is anomalous, since it refers not to the source of the grand prince's authority but to God's approval of this agreement. During this period, extant Muscovite documents indicate the importance of the metropolitan, who had to approve such diplomatic documents. From *c.* 1367 (our earliest extant diplomatic document) until at least 1428, the phrase "with the blessing" (по благословению) of the metropolitan appears in the heading of agreements.[43] It would appear that such practice began during the regency of Metropolitan Aleksei and continued through the metropolitanates of Kiprian, Pimen, and Fotii, although these metropolitans were no longer regents. Such a policy of having a non-regent metropolitan approve diplomatic agreements appears to be a Muscovite innovation. What is significant from the viewpoint of diplomatics is that none of these documents makes reference to the Khan in Sarai as the source of the grand prince's authority, nor do they follow the formulas of the Tatar *iarlyki*. This absence of reference would seem to indicate that the individuals who created the formulas for these documents were Byzantine trained, because they followed the Byzantine diplomatic formulas.

[42] *DDG*, no. 15, p. 40.
[43] *DDG*, no. 5 (*c.* 1367), p. 19; no. 9 (1375), p. 25; no. 10 (1382), p. 29; no. 11 (1389), p. 30; no. 14 (*c.* 1390), p. 39; no. 15 (*c.* 1396), p. 40 [here "with the blessing of Metropolitan Kiprian" is used in conjunction with "by the Grace of God"]; no. 16 (*c.* 1401–1402), p. 43; no. 18 (*c.* 1401–1402), p. 51; no. 19 (1402), p. 52; no. 24a (1428), p. 63; no. 246 (1428), p. 65.

It is also possible, though less likely, that (with the exception of the *iarlyki* to the Church) all other documents indicating a Tatar authority were destroyed.

The phrase "by the Grace of God" began to be used regularly, starting with the Agreement of 1433 between Vasilii II and Prince Vasilii Iaroslavich of Serpukhov and Borovsk, and replaced the phrase "with the blessing" of the metropolitan.[44] The formula became part of the grand prince's title in 1449 in a treaty with the King of Poland, Casimir IV.[45] Inalcik has asserted that Vasilii II's claim that he ruled by the Grace of God "was clearly a notion in conflict with the khan's suzerainty."[46] But it is doubtful the khan would have been concerned with the use of this phrase by the grand prince of Muscovy. Instead, the challenge, if there was one, was to the Byzantine Church, since "by the Grace of God" was the phrase the Byzantine Emperor used to justify his authority. The timing of its adoption in the grand-princely title (1449) is significant because it occurred within a year of Muscovy's formal decision to choose its own metropolitan in defiance of the Byzantine Church. The use of this phrase also brought Muscovy within the orbit of other countries of Christian Europe, in which this phrase was used by their respective rulers as well. Such a consideration may have been behind Ivan III's sharply worded retort to the Imperial ambassador Nicholaus Poppel in 1489. When Poppel suggested that Frederick III could grant him the crown of king, Ivan III responded:

By the Grace of God, we have been sovereigns in our own land since the beginning, since our earliest ancestors. Our appointment comes from God, as did that of our ancestors, and we beg God to grant us and our children to abide forever in the same state, namely as sovereigns in our own land. And as before we did not desire to be appointed by anyone, so now too we do not desire it.[47]

One must consider this a rather pretentious response in light of the fact that the phrase "Grace of God" in the title of the grand prince had been in use for only forty years, and only two years previous to that the khan

---

[44] *DDG*, no. 27, p. 69; see also *DDG*, no. 31 (1434), p. 80; no. 32 (1434), p. 82; no. 33 (1434), pp. 83–84; no. 34 (1434), p. 87; no. 35 (1436), pp. 89, 92, 95, 97; no. 36 (1439), pp. 100, 103; no. 37 (c. 1439), p. 105; no. 38 (1441–1442), pp. 107, 109, 112, 115; no. 40 (1445), p. 119; no. 41 (1445), p. 121; no. 42 (c. 1445), p. 123; no. 43 (c. 1445), p. 125; no. 44 (1447), p. 126; no. 45 (c. 1447), pp. 129, 131, 134, 137; no. 48 (1447), p. 146; no. 51 (1448), pp. 150, 152, 153; and no. 52 (1448–1449), pp. 155, 157.

[45] *DDG*, p. 160, no. 53.

[46] Halil Inalcik, "Power Relationships Between Russia, the Crimea and the Ottoman Empire as Reflected in Titulature," in *Turco–Tatar Past Soviet Present: Studies Presented to Alexandre Bennigsen*, ed. Ch. Lemercier-Quelquejay, G. Veinstein, and S. E. Wimbush, Paris, Éditions de l'École des Hautes Etudes en Sciences Sociales, 1986, p. 177.

[47] *PDS*, vol. 1, col. 12.

of the Qipchaq Khanate, Ulug Mehmed, had in effect appointed Ivan's father, Vasilii II, as grand prince. And before that, the grand princes had clearly been appointed by the Qipchaq khan. So, if Ivan III did say these words, he was being a bit disingenuous. But the wording of the response to the representative of the Holy Roman Emperor placed Muscovy within the context of Christendom.

When Muscovy acquired Kazan' and Astrakhan', successor states to the Qipchaq Khanate in the steppe along the middle and lower Volga River, Muscovy also adopted the concepts, although not the specific terminology, of the Mongol khans, in dealing with Tatars, Cossacks, Kalmyks, and other peoples who had been part of the Mongol empire.[48] In regard to people of the steppe and Central Asia, the tsar was acting as khan in diplomatic dealings with societies as though they were under his jurisdiction. He was, in effect, laying claim to being the successor of the Mongol khan who ruled by divine right and therefore did not need to enter into agreements with the leaders of implicitly subject societies. When dealing with Christian princes, such as those from Tver' in the fourteenth century, the Muscovite grand princes used the Byzantine diplomatic practice of other rulers' being part of a family, of which the Byzantine Emperor was the head.[49] As late as the entry for 1439, the

---

[48] See, e.g., the wording of the report of Buturlin concerning the so-called Treaty of Pereiaslavl' of 1654 with the Zaporozhian Cossacks, in particular the assertion that the Muscovite tsar does not enter into agreements. *Polnoe sobranie zakonov Rossiiskoi Imperii, s 1649 (PSZRI)*, 1st series, 46 vols., St Petersburg: Tip. II Otdeleniia Sobstvennoi Ego Imperatorskogo Velichestva Kantseliarii, 1830, vol. 1, pp. 315–321. We know the tsar did enter into agreements with rulers of non-steppe societies, that is those who were not previously under the jurisdiction of the Mongol Empire. The wording of the charter that Tsar Aleksei granted Khmel'nyts'kyj is revealing: "By the Grace of God, we, the great sovereign, tsar, and grand prince Aleksei Mikhailovich, autocrat of all Great and Little Rus', have bestowed (пожаловали) upon Our Tsariot Majesty's subjects," *Akty, otnosiashchiesia k istorii iuzhnoi i zapadnoi Rossii*, 15 vols., St. Petersburg, Tipografiia brat. Panteleevykh, 1863–1892, vol. 10, cols. 489–491 (italics added). Compare the similar wording in the report of a Muscovite embassy to the Kalmyks in 1650, where the phrase "bestowed favors" (*zhaloval*) is used in regard to Tsar Mikhail's relationship with the Kalmyks. "A Kalmyk–Muscovite Diplomatic Confrontation, 1650: a Translation," in Michael Khodarkovsky, *Where Two Worlds Met: the Russian State and the Kalmyk Nomads, 1600–1771*, Ithaca, NY, Cornell University Press, 1992, p. 245.

[49] See, e.g., (1) the Agreements of *c.* 1367, *c.* 1374–75, 1389, and 1390, in which Grand Prince Dmitrii Ivanovich refers to Prince Vladimir Andreevich of Serpukhov and Borovsk as "my younger brother." *DDG*, no. 5, pp. 19–21; no. 7, pp. 23–24; no. 11, p. 30; no. 13, pp. 37–39; (2) the Agreement of *c.* 1375 in which Grand Prince Dmitrii Ivanovich refers to Prince Mikhail Aleksandrovich of Tver' as "my younger brother." *DDG*, no. 9, pp. 25–28; (3) the Agreement of *c.* 1382 in which Prince Oleg Ivanovich of Riazan' refers to Dmitrii as "elder brother." *DDG*, no. 10, p. 29; and (4) the Agreement of 1445 between the Galich prince Dmitrii Iur'evich, on one side, and the Suzdal' princes Vasilii Iur'evich and Fedor Iur'evich, on the other, in which the Suzdal' princely brothers establish themselves as "son" and "nephew" respectively of Dmitrii

Rus' chronicles report that the Byzantine Emperor John VIII called Grand Prince Vasilii II "my great brother."[50] We find that this type of diplomatic relationship, which we are calling "metaphorical" kinship, shows up in Muscovite dealings with the steppe in the late fifteenth and sixteenth centuries.[51] When one looks at the earliest dates of the use of

and "equal brother" and "younger brother" respectively of Dmitrii's son Ivan. *DDG*, no. 40, p. 119. For further examples, see *DDG*, no. 16, p. 42; no. 18, p. 51; no. 19, p. 52; and no. 24, p. 63. For the Byzantine emperor's diplomatic practice of referring to other rulers as "friend," "brother," or "son," see Georg Ostrogorsky, "Die byzantinische Staatenhierarchie," *Seminarium Kondakovianum*, vol. 8, 1936, pp. 41–61; reprinted in Georg Ostrogorsky, *Zur byzantinischen Geschichte. Ausgewählte kleine Schriften*, Darmstadt, Wissenschaftliche Buchgesellschaft, 1973, pp. 119–141. See also Georg Ostrogorsky, "The Byzantine Emperor and the Hierarchical World Order," *Slavonic and East European Review*, vol. 35, 1956–57, pp. 11–13; and Franz Dölger, "Die 'Familie der Könige' im Mitteralter," *Historisches Jahrbuch*, vol. 60, 1940, pp. 397–420; reprinted in Franz Dölger, *Byzanz und die europäische Statenwelt*, Ettal, Buch-Kunstverlag, 1953, pp. 70–115, and Darmstadt, Wissenschaftliche Buchgesellschaft, 1976, pp. 34–69.

[50] *PSRL*, vol. 6, p. 151; vol. 12, p. 26.

[51] In 1474, Ivan III refers to Mengli Girei as "brother and friend." *SRIO*, vol. 41, no. 1, p. 1. In March 1474, Ivan III cites "brotherhood and friendship" when addressing a Muscovite agent of Mengli Girei. *SRIO*, vol. 41, no. 1, p. 6. Nur Sultan, Mengli Girei's wife, refers to Ivan III, by extension, as her "brother." *SRIO*, vol. 91, no. 194 (1493), p. 176; vol. 41, no. 58 (1498), pp. 272–273. And she refers to the Turkish sultan as her "father." *SRIO*, vol. 41, no. 28 (1491), p. 109. In 1487, Ivan III refers to "brotherhood and friendship" with Mengli Girei. *SRIO*, vol. 41, no. 16, p. 59. In the same document, Ivan III refers to Mehmet Amin, who he set up as khan of Kazan', as "son." *SRIO*, vol. 41, no. 16, p. 59. Later, in *c.* 1489, Ivan III refers to that same Mehmet Amin as "my brother and son." *SRIO*, vol. 41, no. 23, p. 83. Also in *c.* 1489, the Nogai noble Talach referred to himself as "younger brother and son" in relation to Ivan III. *SRIO*, vol. 41, no. 23, p. 83. In *c.* 1490, the Nogai leader Musa refers to "friendship and brotherhood" in addressing Ivan III. *SRIO*, vol. 41, no. 25, pp. 89–91. In 1490, in a letter of safe passage to Devlesh, the nephew of Mengli Girei, Ivan III refers to his "friendship" with Hadji Girei, his "friendship and brotherhood" with Mengli Girei and Nur Devlet khan, and his "friendship" for Devlesh. *SRIO*, vol. 41, no. 27, p. 100. In 1495, Ivan III refers to Mengli Girei as "my brother." *SRIO*, vol. 41, no. 48, p. 220. In 1508, Mengli Girei refers to Vasilii III as "my brother." *SRIO*, vol. 95, no. 2, p. 25. In *c.* 1508–1509, *tsarevich* Bogatyr refers to himself as "your younger brother" in a letter to Vasilii III. *SRIO*, vol. 95, no. 2, p. 37. In 1517, Sigismund I of Poland-Lithuania attempted to coopt this terminology by urging Khan Mehmet Girei to be his "brother and friend" rather than with Vasilii III. *SRIO*, vol. 95, no. 21, p. 360. In 1517, while informing Nur Sultan of the death of her son, Abdullatif, the former khan of Kazan', Vasilii III refers to him as "my brother," *SRIO*, vol. 95, p. 488. In 1533, Vasilii III in a gramota to Islam Girei of the Crimean Khanate referred to him as "brother and son." The text of the gramota is published in Russell E. Martin, "Royal Weddings and Crimean Diplomacy: New Sources on Muscovite Chancellory Practice During the Reign of Vasili III," in *Kamen" Kraeug"l'n"*, pp. 412–413. Under Ivan IV, the mother of a Nogai ally stated that Ivan IV was her "brother." *Prodolzhenie Drevnei Rossiiskoi vivliofiki*, 11 vols., St. Petersburg, 1786–1801, vol. 8, p. 144. For a discussion of these cases, see Kennedy, "The Juchids of Muscovy," pp. 199–201, 213–215; and Craig Kennedy, "Fathers, Sons and Brothers: Ties of Metaphorical Kinship Between the Muscovite Grand Princes and the Tatar Elite," in *Kamen" kraeug"l'n"*, pp. 292–301. In the Rogozhskii and Simeonov chronicles, the entry for 1409 states that Edigei called

metaphorical kinship in diplomatic relations, one sees a chronological progression, with its first occurrence being in Byzantine diplomatic documents,[52] then in Muscovite grand-princely documents with other Rus' princes by the 1370s. By the 1440s, other Rus' princes are using it among themselves. At this point, however, the grand prince began to use the term "sovereign" (*gospodar'/gosudar'*) in his dealings with other Rus' princes. Around 1447, Vasilii II started to inscribe his coins with the words "*Ospodar' vseia Rusi*" ("Sovereign of All Rus'") or "*Ospodar' vseia russkoi zemli*" ("Sovereign of All the Rus' Land").[53] We see this change graphically in a letter dated 1454 that Metropolitan Iona wrote to Misail, Bishop of Smolensk, concerning the activities of Prince Ivan of Mozhaisk: "Know, my son, . . . what has occurred because of what Prince Ivan Andreevich [has done] to . . . his eldest brother, but should I say not to his brother but to his sovereign [осподаремъ], Grand Prince Vasilii Vasilievich."[54] In dealings with non-Rus' princes, the term *gosudar'* first appears in the report concerning the Nicholaus Poppel embassy cited above.

Our first evidence of the use of metaphorical kinship in documents between Muscovy and the Tatars dates to the 1470s. By the 1510s, such use occurs in a document between two non-Rus' rulers, King Sigismund I and Khan Mehmet Girei (although to be sure in discussing the khan's previous alliance with Muscovy).

I was unable to find much evidence of a standard metaphorical kinship in diplomatic relations among steppe rulers outside of documents dealing with Muscovy. One finds an early thirteenth-century reference to "sons" in a Mongol diplomatic dealing, but this occurrence does not fit our case. The Khwarezm Shah took offense, according to Nasawī, at being referred to as "on a level with the dearest of his sons"

himself the "father" of Vasilii I. *PSRL*, vol. 15, pt. 1, col. 182; vol. 18, p. 157; cf. *PSRL*, vol. 11, p. 208. But this formulation may be an anachronistic one from the second half of the fifteenth century. It would also have been out of place for Edigei, who was only an emir (although a powerful one), to claim this relationship to the Muscovite ruler.

[52] See the letter (*c*. 581) from Childebert of the Franks and the Duke of Istria requesting to be accepted as sons of the Byzantine Emperor Tiberius II Constantine. *Epistolae Austrasicae, MGH*, vol. 3, no. 48, pp. 152–153.

[53] A. Oreshnikov, *Russkie monety do 1547 g.*, Moscow, Tipografiia A. I. Mamontova, 1896, no. 545, pp. 102–103 (illus. 394); no. 579, pp. 107–108 (illus. 425); no. 586, p. 108 (illus. 431); no. 602, p. 111 (illus. 447); no. 611, p. 112 (illus. 457); no. 613, p. 113 (illus. 459 and 460); no. 615, p. 113 (illus. 462); no. 617, p. 113 (illus. 464); no. 618, p. 114 (illus. 465); no. 619, p. 114 (illus. 466); no. 625, p. 115 (illus. 471); no. 627, p. 115 (illus. 474); no. 628, p. 115 (illus. 475); no. 629, pp. 115–116 (illus. 476); no. 632, p. 116 (illus. 480); no. 634, pp. 116–117 (illus. 482); no. 646, p. 119 (illus. 492 and 493).

[54] *AI*, vol. 1, no. 56, pp. 103–104.

by the envoys of Chingiz Khan in 1218.[55] But this appears to be an
isolated incident, not one that appears in an official document, and it is
not clear, in any case, that Chingiz Khan was calling the Khwarezm
Shah his "son" as such. A clearer example of metaphorical kinship
occurs in regard to the *iduq qut* (leader) of the Uighurs, Barchuq, to
whom Chingiz Khan assigned the title of "fifth son."[56] In the Altaic
system of lateral succession, only the first four sons could inherit
property and be in line to succeed the ruler. The rank of "fifth son" was,
thus, an honorific one bestowed on Barchuq for bringing the Uighurs
under Mongol control. Presumably, this honorific status did not
impinge on the family status of Chingiz Khan's own fifth and sixth
biological sons. One also finds an ambiguous mid-thirteenth-century
reference to "son" in the Ilkhan ruler Aljigidai's letter to King Louis IX
of France.[57] The *Yuan kao-li chi shi*, which Yu Chi compiled in 1329,
reports that the Mongol general Ĵara and the Korean general Zhuo
Chong agreed in 1218 to be older and younger brothers.[58] But this was
most likely an *anda* (blood brother) relationship, not an explicitly
diplomatic one.

Until evidence of a standard diplomatic practice of metaphorical
kinship among the Mongols is found, I have to conclude that what
shows up in Tatar usage in the fifteenth century derives from Muscovy.
This conclusion is exactly opposite from the one I expected to make and
certainly counter-intuitive. I had begun my research looking for evidence that Mongol *anda* was the origin of metaphorical kinship terms in
Muscovite documents. Instead, the chronological progression of its
appearance first in Byzantine then in Muscovite documents implies a
geographical progression of the idea from Byzantium to Muscovy, then
to the Tatars, and finally to Poland's dealings with the Tatars. The idea
of using it in formal diplomatic practice most likely was adopted by
these various societies because the relations of friends, brothers, and

[55] Sikhab ad-Din: Muḥammad an-Nasawī, *Histoire du sultan Djelal ed-din Mankobirti*, 2 vols., trans. O. Houdas (= *Publications de l'école des langues orientales vivantes*, 3rd series, vols. IX–X), Paris, 1891–1895, vol. 2, p. 58; Sikhab ad-Din: Muhammad an-Nasawī, *Zhizneopisanie sultana Dzhalal ad-Dina Mankburny*, ed. and trans. Z. M. Buniiatov, Baku, Elm, 1973, p. 78.
[56] On Barchuq as "fifth son," see Thomas T. Allsen, "The Yüan Dynasty and the Uighurs of Turfan in the 13th Century," in *China Among Equals: the Middle Kingdom and Its Neighbors, 10th–14th Centuries*, ed. Morris Rossabi, Berkeley, University of California Press, 1983, pp. 246–248, 271 n. 31.
[57] Pelliot, "Les Mongols et la Papauté," vol. 28, 1931–1932, p. 30.
[58] *Yuan kao-li chi shi*, 2a, as reported in Gari Ledyard, "The Establishment of Mongolian Military Governors in Korea in 1231," *Phi Theta Papers*, vol. 6, May 1961, p. 2.

fathers and sons coincided with the internal importance of kinship relations within these societies.

Foreign rulers were also given metaphorical ranks at the Byzantine court.[59] But in each case the ruler was in a subordinate alliance with the Byzantine Emperor, so the Muscovite ruler was not part of that system. Some scholars have claimed the Muscovite princes of the fourteenth century had a Byzantine metaphorical rank of "table attendant" (ἐπὶ τῆς τραπέζης) (стольник).[60]

Such claims that Rus' (possibly Muscovite) princes were designated "table attendant" have been based on three Greek sources. One source is a statement by the Byzantine writer and historian Nicephorus Gregoras in his *History* to the effect that the Emperor Constantine the Great bestowed the title "table attendant" on the "ruler of the Rus'."[61] Despite the obvious anachronism, scholars have accepted the reliability of Gregoras on this point. A second source of the claim is a statement that has been attributed to Maximus Planudes.[62] This source states that the Emperor Augustus bestowed the title "table attendant" on "the prince of the Rus'" and, furthermore, that Andronicus II Palaeologus (1282–1328) received the following words from a Rus' envoy: "ὁ αὐθέντης μου ὁ βασιλεύς τῶν ῥῶς ὁ ἐπὶ τῆς τραπέζης τῆς ἁγίας βασιλείας σου προσκυνεῖ δουλικῶς τὴν ἁγίαν βασιλείαν σου" ("My master, king of the Ros, table attendant of your holy majesty, prostrates himself obsequiously before your holy majesty").[63] A. A. Vasiliev opined that "king of the Ros" had to be a reference to the Muscovite grand prince, but he provided no evidence or argument to support this contention.[64] Platon Sokolov speculated, also

---

[59] E.g., Clovis, king of the Franks was named a consul. Gregory of Tours, *History of the Franks*, trans. E. Bréhaut, New York, W. W. Norton, 1969, p. 47. The king of the Armenians was named keeper of the palace (κουροπαλάτης). Deno John Geanakoplos, *Byzantium: Church, Society, and Civilization Seen Through Contemporary Eyes*, University of Chicago Press, 1984, p. 32. The Georgian princes in the tenth century also received the metaphorical rank of κουροπαλάτης. Constantine Porphyrogenitus, *De Administrando Imperio*, 2 vols., ed. Gy. Moravcsik and R. J. H. Jenkins, Budapest, Pazmany Peter Tudomamyegyetemi Gorog Filologiai Intezet, 1949–1962, vol. 1, chs. 45–46, pp. 204–223. Philotheus in his *Kleitorologion*, a ninth-century court ceremony manual, provides the proper rank at the court for foreign ambassadors. J. B. Bury, *The Imperial Administrative System in the Ninth Century*, London, H. Frowde, 1911, pp. 155–157.

[60] See, e.g., R. G. Skrynnikov, *Ivan Groznyi*, Moscow, Nauka, 1975, p. 22. Skrynnikov adds that, by that time, the term had no political significance, since the Muscovite princes were subordinate to the Mongols.

[61] Gregoras, *Historiae Byzantinae*, vol. 1, bk. 7, § 5, p. 239.

[62] Dimitri Obolensky, "Byzantium, Kiev and Moscow: a Study in Ecclesiastical Relations," *Dumbarton Oaks Papers*, vol. 11, 1957, p. 30 n. 32.

[63] Herman Haupt, "Neue Beiträge zu den Fragmenten des Dio Cassius," *Hermes*, vol. 14, 1879, p. 445; *RIB*, vol. 6, *Prilozhenie*, cols. 273–274.

[64] Cf. A. A. Vasiliev, "Was Old Russia a Vassal State of Byzantium?" *Speculum*, vol. 7, 1932, p. 354 fn. 1.

without evidence or argument, that the title alludes to all Rus' princes back to Vladimir I.[65] A. V. Soloviev proposed that the embassy being described may have been the one that came from Grand Prince Mikhail Iaroslavich of Tver' in 1305.[66]

A third source of the claim is a letter that Nicephorus Gregoras addressed to ἐπὶ τῆς τραπέζης "one who serves at the table."[67] In 1805, Xavier Berger decided that this epithet was a reference to a Rus' prince, since Gregoras had referred to the Rus' prince this way in his *History*.[68] Guilland went further and concluded that this statement referred specifically to Gregoras' contemporary Ivan I Kalita.[69] Yet, the addressee of Gregoras' letter, to whom the epithet "table attendant" is applied, as Ševčenko pointed out, was a Byzantine, not a Rus', dignitary.[70] Thus, it should not be used to support the contention of a metaphorical rank for the Muscovite prince at the Byzantine court. Ševčenko examined the manuscript that contains the so-called Planudean excerpts and identified the handwriting of the passages in question as being that of Gregoras himself.[71] He argued that these excerpts were parts of a notebook that Gregoras kept and from which he wrote his *History*. Ševčenko rejected the idea that this metaphorical rank could have been a long-standing one on the basis that one would expect such a designation applied to Rus' princes over the course of centuries to be better attested in the sources. Since we cannot accept the attribution of the excerpts to Maximus Planudes, they cannot be used as independent confirmation of the statement in Gregoras' *History*.[72] Ševčenko sug-

---

[65] Platon Sokolov, *Russkii arkhierei iz Vizantii i pravo ego naznacheniia do nachala XV veka*, Kiev, 1913, p. 36.

[66] A. V. Soloviev, "Zu den Metropolitensiegeln des kiewer Rußlands," in *Byzantinische Zeitschrift*, vol. 56, 1963, pp. 318–319; reprinted in A. V. Soloviev, *Byzance et la formation de l'etat russe*, London, Variorum, 1979, item IXb.

[67] For a recent edition of this letter, see *Nicephori Gregorae epistulae*, ed. Pietro Luigi [Petrus Aloisius] Leone, 2 vols., Matino, Tipografia di matino, 1983, vol. 2, no. 73, pp. 210–212.

[68] "Nicephori Gregorae epistola ad Praefectum mensae seu Russiae principem," edited and annotated by Fr. Xavier [Xav.] Berger, in *Beyträge zur Geschichte und Literatur*, ed. Johann Christoph von Aretin, 9 vols., Munich, Kommission der Schererschen Kunst- und Buchhandlung, 1803–1807, vol. 4, 1805, pp. 611–615.

[69] R. Guilland, *Correspondance de Nicéphore Grégoras*, Paris, Société Française d'Imprimerie d'Angers, 1927, pp. 16, 378–379. On that basis, Guilland redated the composition of the letter from 1325–1330 to around 1340, the year Ivan I died (*ibid.*, p. 378).

[70] Ihor Ševčenko, "Some Autographs of Nicephorus Gregoras," *Mélanges Georges Ostrogorsky II. Zbornik Radova Vizantoloshkog Instituta*, vol. 8, 1964, p. 450; reprinted in Ševčenko, *Society and Intellectual Life*, item XII. Obolensky had previously expressed doubts about Guilland's assertion. Obolensky, "Byzantium, Kiev and Moscow," p. 31 fn. 41.

[71] Ševčenko, "Some Autographs," p. 448. The MS is Heidelberg, Universitätsbibliothek, Palat. Gr. 129, with the reference to cupbearer on fol. 37ᵛ.

[72] Ševčenko, "Some Autographs," p. 449.

gested instead that we understand Gregoras' statement in the excerpts, which should be accepted as primary in relation to the *History*, as being based on a mistranslation applied to the Rus' word for "throne" (пръстолъ). The locative пръстолъ ("at the throne") could have been heard as при столъ ("at the table") and then mistranslated as ἐπὶ τραπέζης ("one who serves at the table").[73] Thus, we should understand the unmistranslated words as: "My master, king of the Ros, at the throne of your holy majesty, prostrates himself obsequiously before your holy majesty." In the end, we have no reliable source evidence that any Rus' prince was referred to as "table attendant" at the Byzantine court. Ševčenko's conjecture, therefore, stands as the most likely explanation for its appearance in Gregoras' writings.

Finally, I might add the observation that it would have been highly unlikely for the Byzantine emperor to have given the Rus' grand prince, whether Muscovite or Tverite, a metaphorical Byzantine court rank. To do so would have been interpreted as a political act and would have conflicted with the alliance the Byzantines had with the Qipchaq Khanate. In effect, the Byzantine emperor would then have been sending a message to the khan that the Rus' grand prince is "my man not yours," and this would have been a serious breach of fourteenth-century diplomatic etiquette. Surely, whatever reference is being made in Gregoras' texts was to the King of Galicia, not the prince of Moscow. The princes of Galicia, who were not under direct Mongol suzerainty, had a much closer relationship to the basileus at that time than the northeastern Rus' princes did.

It also seems unlikely in terms of metaphorical kinship in diplomatic practice that Confucianism's four personal relations – friends, siblings, parents–children, and spouses – had any impact. Confucianism had little influence on the Yuan Dynasty. The three Confucian family relationships may have influenced Chingiz Khan, for Rashīd al-Dīn reported that he deplored societies where "sons do not heed the admonitions of their fathers; younger brothers pay no attention to the words of their elder brothers; a husband cannot trust his wife and a wife will not follow her husband's orders."[74] Nonetheless, Confucianism was not enacted into either Mongol practice or theory. The Yuan dynasty did revive some Confucian ritials that had fallen into abeyance, but

---

[73] Ševčenko, "Some Autographs," p. 450 and fn. 55.
[74] Rashīd al-Dīn, *Sbornik letopisei*, vol. 1, pt. 2, p. 259. See also B. Ia. Vladimirtsov, *Obshchestvennyi stroi Mongolov. Mongol'skii kochevoi feodalizm*, Leningrad, Akademiia nauk SSSR, 1934, p. 62. If Chingiz Khan did express these sentiments, there may have have been a degree of self-reproach, either intentional or unintentional, involved. He had killed his half-brother Begter and had suspected his future wife Qulan of having an affair with his general Naya. *Secret History* (Cleaves), § 77, p. 23; § 197, pp. 130–131. "Secret History" (Rachewiltz), *PFEH*, vol. 4, pp. 136–137; vol. 18, pp. 57–58.

mainly for the sake of public relations. Confucianism made no impact on the Qipchaq Khanate, where, instead of scholar administrators who passed exams based on the Confucian classics, kinship prevailed as the idiom that defined political relations.[75]

We can discern three main kinship units within Mongol society: the family, the encampment (*ordo*), and the clan lineage (*oboγ*). With an increase in the complexity of clan lineage came division into sub-lineages (*yasun*).[76] The status of one's clan became the basis for relationships among members of the ruling class. The Mongol clan-status relationship was borrowed by the Muscovite ruling class and, along with the steppe nomadic principle of lateral succession, became the basis of *mestni-chestvo*. To be sure, Kievan Rus' had its clans, but they were arranged differently, that is, primarily in a struggle for the princely throne of Kiev. By the twelfth century, they had arranged themselves into four major clans or houses – the Ol'govichi (of Chernigov), the Rostislavichi (of Smolensk), the Vsevolodovichi (of Rostov-Suzdal'), and the Iziaslavichi (of Galicia and Volynia).[77] Each of these clans was "white bone" in steppe terms, because each had a claim to the grand-princely throne of Kiev. The arrangement of "black-bone" clans being ranked in relationship to one "white-bone" ruling family distinguishes Muscovy from Kievan Rus'. Even after the Muscovites formally did away with *mestni-chestvo* in the late seventeenth century, clan and family relations continued to dominate Russian politics until the Revolution of 1917.[78] While "clanship" was sufficient for the Qipchaq Khanate to hold together a highly decentralized trade empire for a time, it eventually broke down completely in the fifteenth century.

[75] Vladimirtsov, in interpreting the use of the term *ongu bogol* by Rashīd al-Dīn, wrote that it referred to these kinship relations, and called it *unagan bogol*. Rashīd al-Dīn, *Sbornik letopisei*, vol. 1, pt. 1, pp. 107, 177. Vladimirtsov, *Obshchestvennyi stroi Mongolov*, pp. 63–64; see also Lawrence Krader, "Feudalism and the Tatar Polity of the Middle Ages," *Comparative Studies in Society and History*, vol. 1, 1958, pp. 82–87. But Fedorov-Davydov, after earlier accepting Vladimirtsov's interpretation, rejected it for a number of reasons. G. A. Fedorov-Davydov, *Obshchestvennyi stroi Zolotoi Ordy*, Izdatel'stvo Moskovskogo universiteta, 1973, pp. 36–39. One reason for the rejection is that the term does not appear in Mongol sources of the time. E. R. Rygdylon, "O mongol'skom termine *ongu-bogol*," *Filologiia i istoriia mongol'skikh narodov. Pamiati Akademika Borisa Iakovlevicha Vladimirtsova*, Moscow, Vostochnaia literatura, 1958, p. 167. According to Jagchid and Hyer, *unaghan bo'ol* refers specifically to a type of slave, that is one "born into the household." Sechin Jagchid and Paul Hyer, *Mongolia's Culture and Society*, Boulder, CO, Westview Press, 1979, p. 284.

[76] Jagchid and Hyer, *Mongolia's Culture and Society*, pp. 245–247.

[77] Martin Dimnik, *Mikhail, Prince of Chernigov and Grand Prince of Kiev, 1224–1246*, Toronto, Pontifical Institute of Medieval Studies, 1981, pp. 2–7, 12–13, 158–161.

[78] John P. LeDonne, "Ruling Families in the Russian Political Order 1689–1825," *Cahiers du Monde russe et soviétique*, vol. 28, 1987, pp. 233–322; LeDonne, *Absolutism and the Ruling Class*.

Table 4.1 *Ideological components*

	political	social	virtual past
Muscovy	Grace of God	*mestnichestvo*	monastic chronicles
Mongols	Eternal Heaven	*oboγ*	dynastic histories e.g. *Altan debter*
China	Mandate of Heaven	Confucianism	dynastic histories
Byzantium	Grace of God	Christ's Kingdom	secular elite's historical narratives
Islamic	Will of Allah	*Shari'ah*	narratives of Muslim historians

At the same time as they borrowed internal clan rankings, Muscovite rulers began to adopt, if begrudgingly and incrementally and for internal consumption only, the ideological justification of authority provided by the Church on the basis of Byzantine political theory. Thus, instead of Confucianism or kinship, Byzantine ideas of the ruler's authority and limitations on it came to form the ideological basis of the Muscovite ruler's legitimacy, especially after 1547 when Ivan IV was crowned tsar. But these ideas were not explicitly despotic either. Table 4.1 sums up three of the ideological components of Muscovy, the Mongols, China, Byzantium, and Islamic societies, of which the Qipchaq Khanate became one after the conversion of its ruling class to Islam.

Both the Rus' chronicles and the *Secret History of the Mongols*, just as the Old Testament and Icelandic sagas do, focus on genealogy. What all these sources indicate are the tribal origins of their respective societies based on the clan as a fundamental social unit. Clan relationships in such societies were normative means of organizing social relations but were often not followed strictly and could be modified to reflect new political relationships within and among clans.[79] In Muscovy, clanship relations could not be so easily modified in steppe societies because these relationships were written down in the *mestnichestvo* books. To be sure, enterprising scribes could falsify the books to make their own and others' genealogies appear better than they were. For example, in the

[79] See, e.g., Emrys Peters who pointed out that, although the Bedouin of Cyrenaica claimed that they followed the model of segmentary lineage, as defined by Marshall Sahlins, in fact they often did not. Emrys Peters, "The Proliferation of Segments in the Lineage of the Bedouin of Cyrenaica," *Journal of the Royal Anthropological Institute*, vol. 90, 1960, pp. 29–53; and Emrys Peters, "Some Structural Aspects of the Feud Among the Camel-Herding Bedouin of Cyrenaica," *Africa*, vol. 37, 1967, pp. 261–282. On this point and an explanation for it, see Lindner, "What Was a Nomadic Tribe?" pp. 694–710.

early sixteenth century, the Kikin family managed to create a forged genealogy to indicate that their ancestor Loggin Mikhailovich was an adviser to Dmitrii Donskoi and that his son was a member of the Boyar Council.[80] In the late sixteenth century, the Shchelkalov brothers, Andrei and Vasilii, are known to have altered *mestnichestvo* records and other documents to enhance the status of Boris Godunov as well as the Dolgorukov and Golitsyn princes.[81] This adherence to the letter of clanship created a monumental nuisance in Muscovy, and finally led to its abandonment in 1682 and the burning of the *mestnichestvo* books. In addition, the Muscovite Church provided a fictional genealogy for the descent of the ruler that counteracted that of the steppe. In this regard, as in so much else, the Church's virtual past won out in Muscovy over competing virtual pasts.

The decentralized administrative structure of Muscovy remained intact in a modified form until Peter I successfully used the Swedish model to replace that administrative structure in the early eighteenth century.[82] And the possible influence of the Mughal administrative structure on the Table of Ranks requires further exploration. In particular, in 1716, in Riga, Peter met with two merchants, Andrei Semenov and Semen Malenkii, who had been to India, including Agra and Delhi in 1696.[83] It was only after meeting with them that plans, which had been stalled, for a new hierarchical system to replace *mestnichestvo* resumed.

Despotism, as such, did not exist in Muscovy, either in theory or in practice. Nor did despotism (or at least what is usually described as such) exist in the Byzantine or Mongol Empires: in both empires, there were well-established limitations on the power and authority of the ruler.

[80] Gustave Alef, "The Crisis of the Muscovite Autocracy: a Factor in the Growth of Monarchical Power," *Forschungen zur osteuropäischen Geschichte*, vol. 15, 1970, p. 20 fn. 7; reprinted in Alef, *Rulers and Nobles*, item 5.

[81] Ann M. Kleimola, "Justice in Medieval Russia: Muscovite Judgment Charters (*Pravye gramoty*) of the Fifteenth and Sixteenth Centuries," *Transactions of the American Philosophical Society*, n.s. vol. 65, pt. 6, 1975, pp. 19–20; Ann M. Kleimola, "Boris Godunov and the Politics of Mestnichestvo," *Slavonic and East European Review*, vol. 53, 1975, pp. 361–362; Daniel Rowland, "Shchelkalov, Vasilii Yakovlevich," in *MERSH*, vol. 34, p. 181. The Shchelkalov brothers' great grandfather was a horse trader, their grandfather a priest, and their father a d'iak in the Razboinyi Prikaz. Indicative of the upward social mobility that the Shchelkalovs experienced was their marrying their daughters into princely and boyar families. Andrei's daughter married a Dolgorukov and Vasilii's daughter married a Morozov.

[82] For the influence of the Swedish administrative system on Peter's reforms, see Claes Peterson, *Peter the Great's Administrative and Judicial Reforms: Swedish Antecedents and the Process of Reception*, trans. Michael F. Metcalf, Stockholm, A.-B. Nordska, 1979.

[83] Eugene Schuyler, *Peter the Great Emperor of Russia: a Study of Historical Biography*, 2 vols., New York, Charles Scribner's Sons, 1884, vol. 2, p. 462.

The entire issue of "oriental despotism" is a false one, concocted initially in the eighteenth century by critics of the French monarchy as a means of criticizing that government. The French critics used the Ottoman Empire and Safavid Persia as their means of pointing out what they disliked about the French monarchy. Later historians adopted the term and concept as a means of criticizing other governments they did not like. It was then one short step to connect "oriental despotism" with earlier foreigners' claims that Muscovy was despotic.[84] Those earlier claims were driven by similar motives to those that drove the later French political writers.

---

[84] The most extensive analysis of sixteenth-century foreign descriptions of Muscovite "despotism" can be found in Marshall Poe, "'Russian Despotism': the Origins and Dissemination of an Early Modern Commonplace," Ph.D. dissertation, University of California, Berkeley, 1993. See also Samuel Baron, "Marx and Herberstein: Notes on a Possible Affinity," in *Kamen" kraeug"l'n"*, pp. 66–79.

5   Economic oppression

The consensus view in the historiography is that Rus' suffered long-term economic devastation as a result not only of the Mongol conquest but also of the oppressive taxation policies during the so-called "Tatar Yoke." In this view, the Muscovite economy was basically agricultural in nature and did not develop a trade or commercial sphere to any significant degree. For example, the economic historian P. I. Liashchenko, although acknowledging the role of Novgorod as a commercial power in the thirteenth and fourteenth centuries and the introduction of money under the Tatars, nonetheless cautioned that "we must not overrate the social and economic significance of commercial capital accumulation during this age. In the thirteenth and fourteenth centuries the basic social-economic force was still landownership and agricultural economy – in other words, the feudal lord."[1] Nicholas Riasanovsky, after pointing out that the role of trade "needs further study," concluded that, "although the inhabitants of northeastern Russia in the appanage period did retain some important commercial connections with the outside world and establish others, and although trade did grow in the area with the rise of Moscow, agricultural economy for local consumption remained dominant."[2] Likewise, A. M. Sakharov described "the Mongol-Tatar ravages" as destroying the towns and their commerce but allowing the relative recovery of agriculture.[3] This view of economic destruction by the Mongols and their reducing of Rus' to an almost purely agricultural economy has a metahistorical appeal both to Russian nationalists and to Marxist historians. For the Russian nationalists, Mongol destruction and the oppressiveness of the "Tatar Yoke" explain the backwardness of Russia vis-à-vis "the West." For Marxist historians,

---

[1] P. I. Liashchenko [Peter I. Lyashchenko], *History of the National Economy of Russia to the 1917 Revolution*, trans. L. M. Herman, New York, Macmillan, 1949, p. 165.
[2] Riasanovsky, *A History of Russia*, 4th edn, p. 115.
[3] A. M. Sakharov, "Rus' and Its Culture, Thirteenth to Fifteenth Centuries," *Soviet Studies in History*, vol. 18, no. 3, 1979–1980, pp. 26–32.

it fits into the conceptual structure of Russia as a feudal regime based on an agricultural and manorial economy.

A few historians have challenged this view of extensive economic decline, but lack of statistical evidence has hindered these challenges. For example, R. H. Hilton and R. E. F. Smith have pointed out that there is "little evidence for any overall decline in European Russia in the twelfth to fifteenth centuries."[4] And Walther Kirchner asserted that "[i]n the thirteenth and following centuries, just when the Tartars ruled in Russia, the curve of Russian Western trade climbs steadily."[5] He concluded from this that the Tatar presence "was of little importance as far as commercial relations with the West were concerned."[6] Kirchner, however, provided no statistical evidence to support this claim. I agree with Kirchner that trade in northern Rus' increased significantly under Tatar hegemony, but, in contrast to Kirchner, I think that it was precisely because of Mongol protection and sponsorship that trade, both western and eastern, increased. This increased trade benefited not only Novgorod but also northeastern Rus', in particular Moscow. As rulers of an economic empire, the Mongols profited from encouraging the commercial development of each area of their empire, including Rus'.

We have narrative accounts telling us that Rus' territory, especially the northeast around Muscovy, suffered severe devastation. Yet, the more florid accounts, such as the *Tale of the Destruction of Riazan'*, can be dated no earlier than the late fifteenth century. These contrast sharply with the straight-forward narratives of the time, like the *Tale of the Battle on the Kalka* and the Hypatian Chronicle's account of the taking of Kiev. John Fennell, for one, questioned the reliability of that later evidence.[7] Nasonov pointed out that a number of major towns, such as Iaroslavl', Novgorod, Rostov, and Tver', were not destroyed.[8] And Gumilev questioned how "ruined" Rus' could have been when only 14 out of 300 known Rus' towns were sacked.[9] Even though the Mongol invasion was assuredly destructive, we need to put that destruction into some

---

[4] R. H. Hilton and R. E. F. Smith, "Introduction," in R. E. F. Smith, *The Enserfment of the Russian Peasantry*, Cambridge University Press, 1968, p. 15.
[5] Walther Kirchner, *Commercial Relations Between Russia and Europe 1400–1800*, Bloomington, Indiana University Press, 1966, p. 5.
[6] Kirchner, *Commercial Relations*, pp. 4–5.
[7] See John Fennell, *The Crises of Medieval Russia 1200–1304*, London, Longman, 1983, pp. 88–89; and Morgan, *Mongols*, pp. 137–138. Cf. A. L. Khoroshkevich and A. I. Pliguzov, "Rus' XIII stoletiia v knige Dzh. Fennela," in Dzhon Fennel [John Fennell], *Krizis srednevekovoi Rusi 1200–1304*, ed. and trans. A. L. Khoroshkevich and A. I. Pliguzov, Moscow, Progress, 1989, pp. 20–22.
[8] Nasonov, *Mongoly i Rus'*, p. 37.
[9] L. N. Gumilev, *Drevniaia Rus' i velikaia step'*, Moscow, Mysl', 1989, p. 466. See also Janet Martin, *Medieval Russia, 980–1584*, Cambridge University Press, 1995, pp. 145–147.

perspective. As Bernard Lewis suggested, we can compare the Mongol conquest of Islamic lands with other areas devastated by conquest, such as central Europe in the twentieth century, where the area ravaged by warfare revitalized itself rather quickly.[10] To be sure, other considerations, like the Marshall Plan, assisted in the reinvigoration of economic life in this latter instance, but that does not negate the point. While Mongol destruction of cities in Central Asia and the Middle East was unprecedented, some cities, like Khwarezm,[11] Samarqand,[12] and Tabriz recovered rapidly. Bukhara also recovered from the Mongol sack of 1220, but was destroyed in wars with the Ilkhans in 1273 and again in 1316.[13] New cities, like Sarai, Krym,[14] and Kaffa, flourished, while other cities, like Baghdad, Balkh,[15] Ghazna,[16] Kiev, and Merv,[17] recovered much more slowly.[18] The common denominators of these differences are commercial activity and trade.

The Qipchaq Khanate and the Ilkhanate, as two supposedly "friendly" parts of the same Mongol Empire, were engaged in competition and at times open warfare to control the best trade routes at least through the 1360s.[19] A major part of the silk route from China divided into two branches at Bukhara. The Qipchaq Khanate controlled the northern branch, which went through Urgendj, south of the Aral Sea to Khiva, north of the Caspian Sea to Sarai, across the steppe then either down the Don River to Tana, whence one could embark across the Sea

[10] Lewis, "The Mongols, the Turks and the Muslim Polity," pp. 52–55; reprinted in Lewis, *Islam in History*, pp. 191–195. Morgan disputed this claim in regard to the agriculture of Persia, although in general he accepted Lewis' point. Morgan, *Mongols*, pp. 79–82.

[11] See, e.g., Ibn Baṭṭūṭa, *Travels*, vol. 3, p. 541.

[12] See, e.g., Ibn Baṭṭūṭa, *Travels*, vol. 3, pp. 567–568.

[13] W. Barthold, "Bukhara," *Encyclopedia of Islam*, 1st edn, vol. 2, p. 781; W. Barthold and Richard N. Frye, "Bukhara," *Encyclopedia of Islam*, new edn, vol. 1, pt. 2, p. 1295.

[14] See, e.g., Ibn Baṭṭūṭa, *Travels*, vol. 2, p. 471.

[15] Balkh initially surrendered to the Mongols and was spared. But then the inhabitants revolted (or the Mongols suspected a revolt) and it was destroyed. Juvaini, *History*, pp. 130–131; Ibn Baṭṭūṭa, *Travels*, vol. 3, p. 571. See also W. Barthold, *Turkestan down to the Mongol Invasion*, 3rd edn, London, Luzac, 1968, pp. 438, 453; R. Hartmann, "Balkh," *Encyclopedia of Islam*, 1st edn, vol. 2, p. 623. It recovered somewhat under the Timurids. Richard N. Frye, "Balkh," *Encyclopedia of Islam*, new edn, vol. 1, pt. 2, p. 1001.

[16] See Ibn Baṭṭūṭa, *Travels*, vol. 3, p. 590. *Encyclopedia of Islam*, new edn, vol. 2, p. 153; vol. 4, p. 130.

[17] Juvaini, *History*, pp. 159–168. See also Barthold, *Turkestan*, pp. 447–449; W. Barthold, *An Historical Geography of Iran*, trans. Svat Souchek, ed. C. E. Bosworth, Princeton University Press, 1984, pp. 42–45; A. Iu. Iakubovskii and C. E. Bosworth, "Marw al-Shāhidjān," *Encyclopedia of Islam*, new edn, vol. 6, pp. 620–621.

[18] A list of destroyed cities, including Baghdad, Balkh, Merv, and Isfahan, can be found in Rashīd al-Dīn, *Sbornik letopisei*, vol. 3, p. 308.

[19] See, e.g., George Mellinger, "The Mongols' Main Interest – Trade," transcript of remarks at the AAASS Convention in Miami, Florida, November 1991.

of Azov, or further overland through the Crimean Peninsula to Kaffa and across the Black Sea to Constantinople. Marco Polo's father and uncle followed this northern route more or less on their journey to China in the early 1260s,[20] as did Pegolotti almost a hundred years later.[21] A variant of this northern route connected Sarai north of the Aral Sea with the Bukhara–Samarqand–Tashkent main road at Otrar. This was the route that John of Plano Carpini followed on his way to and from Qaraqorum. William of Rubruck, in general, followed this same route but made two "short cuts," one going to Qaraqorum by the way south of Lake Balkash joining the main road at Balasaghun, the other, north of Lake Balkash (returning).[22] The Ilkhanate controlled the southern branch, which went through Merv, Nishapur, Rayy, Tabriz, and Trebizond across the Black Sea along the northern coast of Anatolia to Constantinople.[23] The spice route through the Indian Ocean was diverted by the Ilkhanate northward through Hormuz to Tabriz away from the Basra–Baghdad entrepôts.[24]

After the battle of 'Ayn-Jālūt in 1260, Hülegü closed off trade with Syria and Mamlūk Egypt, which he viewed as a hostile power.[25] Hülegü's successors continued his policy of political and military confrontation and economic boycott toward the Mamlūks. It was not until 1322 that an Ilkhan, Abū Saʿīd (1316–1335), concluded a peace agreement with them. In addition, the Ilkhans made Tabriz their capital and ruled Iraq as a province from Persia. When, in 1291, the Mamlūks evicted the Crusaders from Syria, they razed the port cities on the Mediterranean coast.[26] They were apparently more interested in

---

[20] Polo, *Book* (Yule), vol. 1, pp. 2–10.
[21] "Itinerary of Pegoletti Between Asof and China, in 1355," in *General History and Collection of Voyages and Travels*, 10 vols., ed. Robert Kerr and F. A. S. Edin, vol. 1, Edinburgh, George Ramsay, 1811, pp. 435–437.
[22] See "Route Map of John of Pian de Carpine and William of Rubruck. 1246–1255," in Rubruck, *Journey* (Rockhill), following p. 304. Cf. Irene M. Franck and David M. Brownstone, *The Silk Road: a History*, New York, Facts on File, 1986, p. 218.
[23] Clavijo followed this southern branch of the silk route when he journeyed to Samarqand from Constantinople and back in the 1400s. *Clavijo: Embassy to Tamerlane 1403–1406*, trans. Guy Le Strange, ed. E. Denison Ross and Eileen Power, London, George Routledge and Sons, 1928, pp. 94–236. For another description of the northern and southern routes, see Grousset, *Empire of the Steppes*, p. 312.
[24] The Tver' merchant Afanasii Nikitin traveled the Hormuz–Tabriz–Trebizond route on his way back from India, c. 1473–1474. " 'Khozhdenie za tri moria' Afanasiia Nikitina," *Pamiatniki literatury drevnei Rusi (PLDR)*, 11 vols., Moscow, Khudozhestvennaia literatura, 1978–1987, *Vtoraia polovina XV veka*, pp. 474–477 (see also the map on p. 656).
[25] Eliahu [E.] Ashtor, *A Social and Economic History of the Near East in the Middle Ages*, Berkeley, University of California Press, 1976, p. 263.
[26] Janet L. Abu-Lughod, *Before European Hegemony: the World System AD 1250–1350*, New York, Oxford University Press, 1989, pp. 146, 150–151.

keeping the Crusaders from returning from the west than in reopening trade connections toward the east. All these events effectively precluded the reestablishment of Baghdad as a major trading center for some time to come. Similarly, the Qipchaq Khanate directed its northern trade up the Volga toward Novgorod, thus bypassing the Kiev–Kraków–Breslau overland route. It was this northern shift of trade in Rus' that benefited Muscovy and northeastern Rus' economically, and was so detrimental to Kiev as a center of trade.

The Qipchaq Khanate's protection of trade in the steppe also allowed the existence of three trade routes to the east of Kiev that connected northeastern Rus' with the Black Sea. As V. E. Syroechkovskii described these, the most easterly one was along the Don River to Tana. The second (middle) one cut straight across the steppe through Perekop to the Crimean Peninsula. A third route, just to the east of Kiev, ran from Moscow to the Crimean Peninsula thorough Kaluga, Bryn, Briansk, Novgorod-Seversk, and Putivl'.[27] A variant of this third route did, however, lead through Kiev.[28] Most of our evidence concerning these trade routes derives only from the second half of the fifteenth century, when the Muscovite government began taking over protection of Rus' merchants on these routes. But, we can postulate, as Syroechkovskii did, that these routes existed for some time before our extant evidence tells us they were there. The use of these trade routes, which bypassed Kiev, as well as merchants' avoidance of the area of conflict between Lithuania and the Qipchaq Khanate, contributed to Kiev's slow recovery.

The meager evidence about commercial activity in northeastern Rus' before the late fourteenth and fifteenth centuries would seem to support the contentions of those who claim extensive economic devastation. But we do have evidence of continued handicraft production[29] and material culture during the latter half of the thirteenth century, although of a reduced quality and amount. During the fourteenth century, handicraft production returns to and then exceeds pre-invasion standards in both quality and quantity.[30] The temporary reduction in production of crafts

[27] V. E. Syroechkovskii, "Puti i usloviia snoshenii Moskvy s Krymom na rubezhe XVI veka," *Izvestiia Akademii nauk SSSR. Otdelenie obshchestvennykh nauk*, 1932, no. 3, pp. 200–202 and map; Janet Martin, "Muscovite Relations with the Khanate of Kazan' and the Crimea (1460s to 1521)," *Canadian–American Slavic Studies*, vol. 17, 1983, p. 442.

[28] Syroechkovskii, "Puti i usloviia," p. 217. Janet Martin, "Muscovite Travelling Merchants: the Trade with the Muslim East (15th and 16th Centuries)," *Central Asian Survey*, vol. 4, no. 3, 1985, p. 23.

[29] B. A. Rybakov, *Remeslo drevnei Rusi*, Moscow, Akademiia nauk SSSR, 1948, pp. 525–538.

[30] B. A. Kolchin, "Remeslo," in *Ocherki russkoi kul'tury XIII–XV vekov*, ed. A. V. Artsikhovskii, A. D. Gorskii, B. A. Kolchin, A. K. Leont'ev, A. M. Sakharov, and V. L.

immediately after the Mongol invasion can be attributed to the reduction in the number of craftsmen and artisans. No doubt some were
killed and many fled to Galicia. In describing the rebuilding of the city
of Kholm by Daniil in 1259, the Galician chronicler writes: "They came
day after day, both apprentices [уноты] and artisans [мастеръ] of every
kind, saddle, bow, and quiver craftsmen and iron-, copper-, and silver-
smiths who had fled from the Tatars."[31] Still others, like their counterparts from Central Asia, were transported to Qaraqorum and capitals of
the various *ulus*. William of Rubruck, for example, describes his
encounter with a Rus' goldsmith at the court of Güyük Khan.[32] And
finally, some were sent to handicraft colonies, such as Chinkhai Balaγasun by the Argun Mountains[33] and Tuva on the upper Yenisei River.[34]
Ariγ Böke used the Tuva region in 1260–1261 as a staging and
economic-resource area for his conflict with Qubilai.[35] John W. Dardess
has proposed the idea that the Mongol capital at Qaraqorum was
situated within 500–900 miles of four economic-resource areas
stretching in an arc from northwest to southeast – upper Yenisei (500
miles), Uighur kingdom (700 miles), former Tangut Empire (650
miles), and northern China (750–900) miles.[36] It was Qubilai's control
of three of these four areas that helped him defeat Ariγ Böke in 1261.[37]
Dardess also proposed that the Qipchaq Khanate also had its "economic
dependencies" within similar distances, including Moscow (700 miles),
Kiev (600 miles), and Khwarezm (800 miles).[38] With the substitution of
Kaffa for Kiev by the fourteenth century, one can accept Dardess'
formulation. In the thirteenth century, the economic zones had their
capitals at Saksin, Bulgar, Tana (Azov), and Kiev.

After the conquest of Rus', the Mongols continued the policy of

Ianlli, Izdatel'stvo Moskovskogo univershteta, 1969, part 1. *Material'nala kul'tura*, pp.
156–230; A. L. Shapiro, *Problemy sotsial'no-ekonomicheskoi istorii Rusi XIV–XVI vv.*
Izdatel'stvo Leningradskogo universiteta, 1977, pp. 94–103.
[31] *PSRL*, vol. 2 (1908), col. 843.
[32] Rubruck, *Journey* (Rockhill), p. 26.
[33] Chinkai Balaγasun was a settlement of artisans and craftsmen founded on the orders of
Chingiz Khan and near which passed the Daoist monk Chang-chun in 1220. *Travels of
an Alchemist*, trans. Arthur Waley, London, George Routledge and Sons, 1931, pp.
72–73.
[34] L. R. Kyzlasov, "Pamiatnik musul'manskogo srednevekov'ia v Tuve," *Sovetskaia
arkheologiia*, 1963, no. 2, pp. 208–210; L. R. Kyzlasov, *Istoriia Tuvy v srednie veka*,
Izdatel'stvo Moskovskogo universiteta, 1969, pp. 138–159.
[35] Rashīd al-Dīn, *Successors*, pp. 253–256; Rashīd al-Dīn, *Sbornik letopisei*, vol. 2, pp.
161–164. See also John W. Dardess, "From Mongol Empire to Yüan Dynasty:
Changing Forms of Imperial Rule in Mongolia and Central Asia," *Monumenta Serica*,
vol. 30, 1972–1973, p. 129.
[36] Dardess, "From Mongol Empire," p. 122.
[37] Dardess, "From Mongol Empire," pp. 128–129.
[38] Dardess, "From Mongol Empire," p. 125.

conscripting craftsmen and artisans, this time for work in the cities of the Qipchaq Khanate.[39] Archaeological evidence indicates a thriving material culture and crafts industry in cities of the Khanate.[40] In addition, Ibn Baṭṭūṭa reports seeing thirteen Friday mosques and numerous smaller mosques in New Sarai in the early fourteenth century.[41] The historian Luc Kwanten has argued that it was after the reigns of Ögödei and Güyük that craftsmen and artisans began to be returned to their own regions. By then, an administration for the empire was being elaborated and a tax-gathering system set up.[42] But, as pointed out above, extensive administrative organization had already taken place during the reign of Ögödei under the direction of Yelü Chucai. Of more consequence was Qubilai's decision in 1260 to establish his capital at Dadu (Khan-beliq; Beijing) rather than Qaraqorum. Since there were great numbers of artisans and craftsmen in China,[43]

[39] See, e.g., Vernadsky, *Mongols and Russia*, pp. 213, 338.

[40] Fyodorov-Davydov [Fedorov-Davydov], *Culture of the Golden Horde Cities*, pp. 63–193.

[41] Ibn Baṭṭūṭa, *Travels*, vol. 2, pp. 515–516. Fedorov-Davydov argued that Ibn Baṭṭūṭa visited Old Sarai on the basis that Ibn 'Arabshah wrote that [New] Sarai had been built sixty-three years before the "destruction of the customs houses." Tiesenhausen, *Sbornik materialov*, vol. 1, p. 463. Fedorov-Davydov associated this destruction with Timur's sack of Sarai in 1395. That would place the city's construction in 1332. Fyodorov-Davydov, *Culture*, pp. 16–17. Yet, New Sarai is called Sarai-Berke because it was supposedly built in the reign of Khan Berke (1257–1267). The "destruction of the customs houses" might not necessarily refer to the sack of 1395 but to another event in the early fourteenth century not yet identified. Besides, Ibn Baṭṭūṭa visited the Qipchaq Khanate in 1332–1333 (or 1334–1335 in an alternate chronology) and would most likely have known of the construction of a new capital if it were going on then. Dunn suggested that Özbeg had constructed New Sarai in 1330, a date he based on J. M Rogers' unpublished review of numismatic evidence. Dunn, *Adventures*, p. 180 n. 21. If the city had been so recently constructed, we might expect that Ibn Baṭṭūṭa would have made mention of this fact. The simplest explanation that accounts for the evidence is that New Sarai existed since the time of Berke, and that Özbeg simply moved to it as his capital after a period during which Old Sarai had once again been used as the capital following Berke's death. See Spuler, *Die Goldene Horde*, pp. 266–269; and Frances Balodis, "Alt-Serai und Neu-Serai, die Hauptstädte der Goldenen Horde," *Latvijas Universitates Raksti. Acta Universitatis Latviensis*, vol. 13, 1926, pp. 3–82.

[42] Kwanten writes: "[t]he reigns of Ogodei and Guyuk were characterized by maladministration: for all practical purposes, the empire was not administered at all. Their reigns were strictly within the steppe tradition. The Mongols lived off their loot and the tribute they exacted, without regard for the possible consequences – depletion of resources, economic collapse, and so on." Luc Kwanten, *Imperial Nomads: a History of Central Asia, 500–1500*, Philadelphia, University of Pennsylvania Press, 1979, pp. 198–199. Kwanten goes on to suggest that the empire survived only because the reign of Güyük was so brief. For critical remarks about Kwanten's book, see Chin-fu Hung, "China and the Nomads: Misconceptions in Western Historiography on Inner Asia," *Harvard Journal of Asiatic Studies*, vol. 41, 1981, pp. 597–628.

[43] Jacques Genet, *Daily Life in China: On the Eve of the Mongol Invasion 1250–1276*, New York, Macmillan, 1962, p. 87. Chü Ch'ing-yüan, "Government Artisans of the Yüan Dynasty," in *Chinese Social History: Translations of Selected Studies*, trans. and ed. E-tu Zen Sun and John De Frances, New York, Octagon Books, 1966, pp. 234–246.

the Mongol khan did not have to draw so heavily on the talents of the rest of the empire. Thus, the Mongol leadership sent non-Chinese artisans and craftsmen back to their home districts, where they could contribute more to the economic well-being of the empire than they did being under-utilized in Qaraqorum. The same thing may have happened to those who had been commandeered into the artisan and craftsmen settlements, which apparently did not pan out. We have evidence in early chronicles that, in the 1280s, the *bāsqāq* of Kursk, Aḥmed, established two settlements (*slobody*) for artisans and craftsmen.[44] How widespread this practice was in Rus' territory, we are unable to say.

Some scholars have not given much consideration to control of trade routes as a reason for the establishment of the Mongol Empire. Lattimore, for example, argued that the direction of Mongol conquests had mainly geopolitical motivations. In his view, Chingiz Khan avoided the "classical mistake" of attacking the frontier with China before securing his rear by subduing the Turkic tribes to the west. The traditional Chinese policy, "to use barbarians to control the barbarians," would not work against Chingiz Khan if there were no "barbarians" to use against him.[45] Lattimore's purely geopolitical hypothesis does not account, however, for why Chingiz Khan took northern China before heading west or for why he attacked Khwarezm, Tashkent, and Samarqand, all non-nomadic centers, before sending Subedei further west to subdue the Polovtsi. Morgan has suggested that Chingiz Khan wanted to neutralize northern China and Hsi Hsia first in order to have a free hand to subdue the Turkic tribes to the west.[46] But that corollary to Lattimore's theory renders it virtually meaningless, since any conquest that Chingiz Khan made can be explained as neutralizing somebody or other in order to get on with the next conquest. Indeed, the initial raid

Wassaf, e.g., reports that in Kinsai alone there were 32,000 craft dyers. *Geschichte Wassaf's*, ed. and trans. [Joseph von] Hammer-Purgstall, Vienna, Kaiserlich-königlichen Hof- und Staatsdruckerei, 1856, pp. 42–43. Wassaf, which means "panegyrist," was a Persian official who picked up the narrative of Juvaini's *History* from 1257 and carried it through to 1328. See Saunders, *History of the Mongol Conquests*, p. 257. Needham finds the craftsmen and artisans of China comparable with those of the European Renaissance in terms of "skill and ingenuity." Joseph Needham, *Clerks and Craftsmen in China and the West: Lectures and Addresses on the History of Science and Technology*, Cambridge University Press, 1970, p. 237. One should note that Matteo Ricci did not have as high an opinion as this of Chinese artisanship. Matteo Ricci, *China in the Sixteenth Century: the Journals of Matthew Ricci, 1583–1610*, trans. Louis J. Gallagher, New York, Random House, 1953, p. 19.

[44] *PSRL*, vol. 1, cols. 481–482; vol. 18, pp. 79–81; *TL*, pp. 340–342. On *slobody*, see Robert Craig Howes, "Survey of the Testaments," in *The Testaments of the Grand Princes of Moscow*, trans. and ed., with commentary, Robert Craig Howes, Ithaca, NY, Cornell University Press, 1967, pp. 60–61.

[45] Lattimore, "Geography of Chingis Khan," pp. 1–7.

[46] Morgan, *Mongols*, p. 73.

through Polovtsian territory in 1223 was little more than an incidental result of chasing after the Khwarezm Shah. Thus, Chingiz Khan and his successors certainly used and consolidated the Turkic nomadic tribes, but with the primary goal of subduing settled areas along the entire silk route. To suggest that the Mongols subdued the Polovtsi and invaded Rus' and eastern Europe *in order to* be able to attack Song China 4,500 miles to the east at some later time is too much of a stretch, both geographically and conceptually.

A simpler and better explanation is that the Mongols followed the trade routes in their conquests and took what they did when they could. Trade centers were their primary strategic objectives, although they certainly would have followed the tactical measure of subduing or neutralizing particular tribes along the way that may have posed a threat to the successful completion of their campaigns. The scholarly literature is coming more and more to reflect the realization that nomads in general have depended for their very existence on commercial relations with sedentary areas.[47] These commercial relations could take various forms including trade, raids, and collection of tribute. Specific studies have discussed the importance of commercial relations as a necessity for those nomadic tribes to the north and west of China, such as the Hsiung-nu and the Mongols themselves.[48] The nomads, if allowed, usually traded peacefully for the grain, cloth, and commodities they needed. But, when trade was blocked, they resorted to raids and war to acquire these commodities necessary for their way of life. The point is that sedentary societies could survive quite well without trade with the nomads, but the nomads could not survive without trade with sedentary societies. Since nomadic tribes depended on commercial relations with sedentary populations for their existence, then the logical next step is to conclude that nomadic empires expanded by securing military and political control of long-distance trade networks in order to maintain their way of life.[49] And the Mongol Empire, looked at in this context,

---

[47] Anatoly [A.] M. Khazanov, *Nomads and the Outside World*, Cambridge Studies in Social Anthropology, no. 44, Cambridge University Press, 1984, pp. 202–212.

[48] Barthold, *Turkestan*, pp. 394–395; Robert P. Blake, "The Circulation of Silver in the Moslem East down to the Mongol Epoch," *Harvard Journal of Asiatic Studies*, vol. 2, 1937, p. 312; Thomas J. Barfield, "The Hsiung-nu Imperial Confederation: Organization and Foreign Policy," *Journal of Asiatic Studies*, vol. 41, 1981, pp. 45–61; Sechin Jagchid, "Patterns of Trade and Conflict Between China and the Nomads of Mongolia," *Zentralasiatische Studien*, vol. 11, 1977, pp. 177–204; Jagchid and Hyer, *Mongolia's Culture and Society*, pp. 297–310; Sechin Jagchid and Van Jay Symons, *Peace, War and Trade Along the Great Wall: Nomadic–Chinese Interaction Through Ten Millennia*, Bloomington, Indiana University Press, 1989, pp. 24–51.

[49] Peter A. Boodberg, "Turk, Aryan and Chinese in Ancient Asia," in *Selected Works of Peter A. Boodberg*, comp. Alvin P. Cohen, Berkeley, University of California Press,

can be seen to be only the most successful of all nomadic confederations in gaining dominance over the Eurasian trade routes.[50]

In this way, the conquest of the Eurasian landmass evolved not as some kind of grand strategy from the beginning but simply as a means of optimizing control over the next commercial entrepôt. Our sources tell us that Chingiz Khan, when he first received envoys from the Khwarezm Shah in 1215, sincerely sought peace and friendship as long as trade could be maintained. According to Juvaini, when relations began to deteriorate, Chingiz Khan sent envoys to the Khwarezm Shah in a last-ditch effort to maintain peace by offering the restoration of trade "on which the welfare of the world depends."[51] Jūzānī, Rashīd al-Dīn, and Nasawī each report a different wording for this message, but the importance of commercial relations to Chingiz is clear in every one of them.[52] Although the event that triggered the war was the killing of Mongol envoys, ultimately it was the Khwarezm Shah's decision to disrupt commercial relations that led to the Mongol attack and conquest of Khwarezm.[53]

W. E. Henthorn, in his study of the Mongol conquest of Koryŏ (Korea), concluded that the underlying purpose of the various decrees and ordinances issued by the Mongol rulers was "economic exploitation" of the area.[54] As Saunders pointed out, "trade was the life-blood of the [Mongol] State . . .; the ruins of Sarai contain traces of caravanserais and workshops as well as of palaces, and a steady stream of glass, pottery and human merchandise flowed across the Black Sea and the eastern Mediterranean to Mamluk Egypt."[55] In excavations at Sarai Berke archaeologists found fragments of bricks, pottery, and plates, as well as evidence of manufacturing such as tanned skins, textile products, tiles, weapons and tools, copper chandeliers and goblets, horse-trappings, and nails and needles.[56] Both the archaeological and the contemporary written evidence indicates wide commercial contacts on the part of the Qipchaq Khanate[57] as well as throughout the Mongol

1979, pp. 10–11; Omeljan Pritsak, *The Origin of Rus'*, vol. 1: *Old Scandinavian Sources Other than the Sagas*, Cambridge, MA, Harvard University Press, 1981, pp. 10–20.
[50] Thomas T. Allsen, "Mongolian Princes and Their Merchant Partners, 1200–1260," *Asia Major*, 3rd series, vol. 2, 1989, pp. 83–126.
[51] Juvaini, *History of the World-Conqueror*, p. 79.
[52] Juzjani, *General History*, vol. 2, p. 966; Rashīd al-Dīn, *Sbornik letopisei*, vol. 1, pt. 2, p. 188; Nasawī, *Histoire*, vol. 2, pp. 57–58; Nasawī, *Zhizneopisanie*, p. 78.
[53] For a discussion of these events, see Barthold, *Turkestan*, pp. 396–400.
[54] Henthorn, *Korea*, p. 194.
[55] Saunders, *History of the Mongol Conquest*, pp. 158–159. See also Schamiloglu, *Golden Horde*, ch. 2: "The Rise of the Golden Horde."
[56] E. D. Phillips, *The Mongols*, London, Thames & Hudson, 1969, p. 138.
[57] Fyodorov-Davydov, *Culture*, pp. 213–220.

imperium. Contrary to the misrepresentations of Ming Dynasty historians, the Yuan Dynasty, as Schurmann pointed out, encouraged economic development in China with all the resources at its command.[58]

Early in the consolidation of their gains in Rus', the Mongols
emphasized the importance of trade. The Khan of Qipchaq, Möngke-
Temür, sent the following message to Grand Prince Iaroslav Iaroslavich,
around the year 1270, guaranteeing protection of trade throughout the
area controlled by the Qipchaq Khanate: "give passage to foreign
merchants in your domain. From Prince Iaroslav to the people of Riga,
and to the great and the small, and to those who trade, and to everyone:
your passage is unhindered through my domain. Whoever comes to me
with arms, them I will deal with myself; but the merchant has unhindered passage through my domain."[59] Articles that stipulate the khan's
protection of merchants appear in Novgorod's treaties with the Tver'
grand princes in the fourteenth century.[60] We can also see the importance of trade for the Mongols in the *tamyā*, which was a kind of value-
added tax (VAT) of 5 percent on all commercial transactions except
those involving grain. As Morgan indicated: "Its very existence testifies
to the importance attached by the Mongols to trade and its profits."[61]

The system of taxation that the Mongols established in the various
ulus of their empire was also put into place in the Rus' principalities.
H. F. Schurmann, who made a study of the Mongol tax system, asserted
that only in China and Persia was a "unified fiscal system" established,
while in the Qipchaq Khanate "no rationalization ever took place" and
in Rus' "only the confused multiplicity of obligations remained."[62] Yet,
Schurmann's assertion about the Qipchaq Khanate is based on argument from silence as a result of paucity of sources. And his assertion
concerning the obligations in Rus' is based on the misunderstanding of
that system on the part of later historians, who did not have the
advantage, as we do, of knowing the tax system in the Mongol Empire,
in great part thanks to Schurmann's own work.

Basing his conclusions, then, primarily on a study of taxation in
northern China under the Mongols and in the Ilkhanate, although
expanding it to other parts of the Mongol Empire, Schurmann classified

---

[58] Herbert Franz Schurmann, *Economic Structure of the Yüan Dynasty*, Harvard Yenching
Institute Studies, no. 16, Cambridge, MA, Harvard University Press, 1967, p. 116.

[59] *Gramoty velikogo Novgoroda i Pskova*, ed. S. N. Valk, Moscow, Akademiia nauk SSSR,
1949, no. 30, p. 57.

[60] *Gramoty Velikogo Novgoroda i Pskova*, no. 6, p. 16 (1304–1305); no. 14, p. 28
(1326–1327); no. 15, p. 30 (1371).

[61] Morgan, *Mongols*, p. 101.

[62] H. F. Schurmann, "Mongolian Tributary Practices of the Thirteenth Century,"
Harvard Journal of Asiatic Studies, vol. 19, 1956, p. 309.

the revenue gathering into three categories. The first category included the fiscal obligations that were the traditional methods of exploitation within Mongol nomadic society: the tribute and service, both regular and extraordinary, owed to the ruler by his subjects. The second category included fiscal obligations that resulted from Mongol control of commerce and production in sedentary areas: the *tamyā* (customs duty) and the *myt* (transportation toll). In Rus' sources, we also encounter the term *kostki*, which was also a customs duty. It may have been a different type of customs duty or merely another word for the *tamyā* (Rus'ian: *tamga*). The third category included traditional fiscal obligations of conquered sedentary societies: the land taxes, tolls, and work service, including construction of walls and fortifications, maintenance of the *yām*, feeding of officials, and so forth.

Schurmann, by drawing on a northern Chinese source, the *Heida shilue*, written in 1236 by Peng Daya and Xu Ting, also postulated that categories two and three of revenue gathering by the Mongols over conquered peoples evolved from category one. More specifically, Mongol taxes on commerce and production were merely extraordinary tribute and service carried over to sedentary societies. And traditional obligations within a sedentary society under Mongol control matched up with regular tribute and service within Mongol nomadic society. Schurmann noted, furthermore, that the Mongol tax system in northern China was called *chaifa*, of which there were two types: of the steppe and of the land of the Han. Schurmann identified these two types of *chaifa* with categories two and three of revenue collection in other parts of the Mongol Empire, that is, with Mongol-imposed taxes and traditional, non-Mongol, taxes, respectively. And he equated the two meanings of the term *chaifa* with the Turkic *yasāq qalān*, such that the Qipchaq Khanate term *yasāq* was equivalent to the Mongol term *qubčiri(n)*, the Ilkhanate term *qubchūr* and the Rus' term *poshlina* and indicated the traditional non-Mongol taxes of the given area, while *qalān* was equivalent to the Mongol *alba(n)*, the Ilkhanate *qalān*, and the Rus' *dan'* and indicated the Mongol-imposed taxes.

John Masson Smith, Jr., suggested an improvement on Schurmann's equivalences by pointing out that one should not reverse the Persian phrase *qubchūr qalān* and the Turkic phrase *yasāq qalān* as Schurmann did. Instead, one should leave them as they appear in the sources, which matches the same order as *dan' i poshlina* found in Rus' sources.[63] Since the Rus' phrase is a translation from the Turkic, we would expect it to maintain the same word order. I. N. Berezin and Spuler had previously

[63] John Masson Smith, Jr., "Mongol and Nomadic Taxation," *Harvard Journal of Asiatic Studies*, vol. 30, 1970, p. 49.

equated *poshlina* with *qalān* by other means and Vernadsky had tentatively accepted their identification.[64] So, Schurmann's equating *poshlina* with *qubčiri(n)* was difficult to resolve with their findings. And, according to Smith, the two components of the Chinese term *chai-fa* can be seen to have the same meaning as *alba qubčār*, although, in contrast to the latter phrase as well as *yasāq qalān* and *dan' i poshlina*, they are not found independently of one another. Thus, with Smith's modifications of Schurmann's framework, we obtain the equivalences shown in Table 5.1 for revenue gathering throughout the various *ulus* of the Mongol Empire.

Schurmann also pointed out that the title *darqan* (*tarkhan*), which designated an individual who was exempt from obligations, "appears in every *ulus* from China to Russia."[65] In Rus', the document granting the exemption was called a *tarkhannaia gramota* and was the equivalent of the edicts (*iarlyki*) the Church received from the khans exempting it from fiscal obligations. From the extant versions of these edicts we can see that the Mongols carried their empire-wide tax categories over into the Rus' principalities. These categories became the basis of early and middle Muscovite taxation policies. Furthermore, we can better understand the importance for the Muscovite princes to take over the duties of the Tatar *bāsqāq*s during the first half of the fourteenth century. Once that occurred, all the monetary *poshlina*, Schurmann's third category of revenue, would remain in Rus' lands, to be sure passing through the hands of the Muscovite grand princes and their court first. Only part of

Table 5.1. *Tax-gathering equivalences*[66]

	Traditional, non-Mongol taxes	Mongol-imposed taxes and tributes
Mongol	*alba(n)*	*qubčiri(n)*
Northern Chinese	*chaifa (Han)*	*chaifa (steppe)*
Uighur	*qalan*	*qubchir*
Ilkhanate Persian	*qalān/mal*	*qubchūr*
Qipchaq Turkic	*qalān*	*yasāq*
Rus'ian	*poshlina*	*dan'*

[64] I. N. Berezin, *Vnutrennoe ustroistvo Zolotoi Ordy*, St. Petersburg, 1850, p. 19; Berezin, "Ocherk vnutrennogo ustroistva Ulusa Dzhuchieva," *Trudy Vostochnogo otdeleniia Russkogo arkheologicheskogo obshchestva*, vol. 8, 1864, p. 475; and Spuler, *Die Goldene Horde*, p. 335; Vernadsky, *Mongols and Russia*, p. 222.

[65] Schurmann, "Mongolian Tributory Practices," p. 323.

[66] Adapted from Schurmann, "Mongolian Tributary Practices," p. 358; Smith, "Mongol and Nomadic Taxation," pp. 49, 60; and Allsen, *Mongol Imperialism*, p. 154. Allsen accepted Smith's identification of *qalān* with *mal* in the Ilkhanate.

Schurmann's second-category revenues made up the *dan'*, or tribute, from Rus' in the early fourteenth century. From Mozhaisk, Kolomna, Serpukhov, and Zvenigorod, the *tamyā* was sent to Sarai, while the *myt* remained with the Rus' princes. But from Moscow, it was just the reverse, as the *myt* was sent to Sarai and the *tamyā* stayed with the Muscovite prince. S. M. Kashtanov concluded from this evidence that the distribution of proceeds "between Rus' princes and the Mongol-Tatars could involve various compromises and combinations."[67]

By the time of Dmitrii Donskoi, the revenues from both the *myt* and *tamyā* were kept by the grand prince, and the *dan'* was paid separately. Such an arrangement would seem to indicate that, by the first half of the fourteenth century, the proceeds from *tamyā* in principalities outside Moscow and from the *myt* within Moscow matched the required amount of the *dan'* for these principalities. The local princes could keep the rest. But by the second half of the fourteenth century, the *tamyā* and the *myt* each separately exceeded the amount of the *dan'*, so the grand prince kept the proceeds from both and merely paid the required amount of the *dan'* out of his pocket, so to speak.[68] As long as the *dan'* continued to be sent out (*vykhod*) to Sarai, the Tatar khan allowed Muscovy to gain wealth and power until it was able to eclipse its former suzerain.

We have evidence, beginning in the fourteenth century, that Moscow was benefitting economically from this Mongol protection and encouragement of trade as well as from Muscovite princes' use of the Mongol taxation system. The Muscovite prince Ivan I was nicknamed *Kalita* ("money-bag"), evidence that at least the grand prince was getting rich at this time. In addition, the Simeonov and Nikon chronicles report that in 1388, Theognostus, Metropolitan of Trebizond, came to Moscow for donations for the Byzantine Church.[69] In 1398, at the request of Emperor Manuel II Palaeologus and Patriarch Matthew, Vasilii I contributed money (*srebro*) to the defense of Constantinople.[70] A letter (*pittakion*) from the Byzantine patriarch Matthew I to Metropolitan Kiprian from *c*. 1400 tells us that the patriarch and emperor sent another embassy with a request for additional money even before the

---

[67] S. M. Kashtanov, "Finansovye ustroistvo moskovskogo khiazhestva v seredine XIV v. po dannym dukhovnykh gramot," in *Issledovaniia po istorii i istoriografii feodalizma. K 100-letiiu so dnia rozhdeniia akademika B. D. Grekova*, Moscow, Nauka, 1982, p. 178. My thanks to Larry Langer for bringing Kashtanov's article to my attention and for supplying me with a copy of his own unpublished article "The End of Mongol Rule in Medieval Rus'," part of which he presented as a paper at the 28th AAASS Convention in Boston, Massachusetts, November 15, 1996.

[68] *DDG*, no. 4, p. 15; no. 12, p. 33.   [69] *PSRL*, vol. 11, p. 94; vol. 18, p. 138.

[70] *TL*, p. 448; *PSRL*, vol. 8, p. 71; vol. 11, p. 168; vol. 25, p. 228; vol. 28, pp. 88, 253.

previous embassy had returned.[71] The Novgorod I Chronicle reports that Vasilii II was able to pay a ransom of 200,000 rubles for his release after being captured by Ulug Mehmed at the Battle of Suzdal' in 1445.[72]

Prelates were wealthy too. In the opinion of Anthony-Emil Tachiaos, in the early fifteenth century, Metropolitan of Moscow "Photius [Monembasiotes] had at his disposal much more money than the Patriarch of Constantinople, and possibly more than the emperor himself."[73] Tachiaos pointed out that Photius frequently supported the patriarchate with financial donations, gave "a great deal of money to [the] Pantocratoros Monastery," and was counted on for financial assistance by Patriarch Joseph in order to hold a council in Constantinople between the Greeks and Latins.[74] The donation of money to Constantinople would seem to indicate that Muscovy may have been fairly wealthy and that the "Tatar yoke" did not involve economic oppression, at least not of the grand princes and metropolitans. In addition, we have evidence from the late fifteenth century that other prelates of the Church were also well off financially. A recently discovered document recounts the gifts that Archbishop Tikhon brought with him to Moscow when he was elevated to the archiepiscopal see of Rostov and Iaroslavl' in 1489. These gifts to the grand prince and his family as well as to the metropolitan, the Archbishop of Novgorod, bishops, and lesser Church officials amounted to over 60 rubles in cash and 400 sables, as well as other furs.[75]

There is little question that both the Church prelates and the grand prince and his court were wealthy, but the question is: how did they obtain their wealth? It had to come from tariffs and tolls on trade. Although peasants constituted the overwhelming majority of the population, such wealth could not have come from squeezing them economically. The peasants were engaged in subsistence slash-and-burn

[71] *Acta patriarchatus Constantinopolitani*, vol. 2, pp. 359–361; *RIB*, vol. 6, cols. 311–316; J. W. Barker, *Manuel II Palaeologus (1391–1425): a Study in Late Byzantine Statesmanship*, New Brunswick, NJ, Rutgers University Press, 1969, pp. 202–204. See also Dimitri Obolensky, "A Byzantine Grand Embassy to Russia in 1400," *Byzantine and Modern Greek Studies*, vol. 4, 1978, pp. 123–132.

[72] *NPL*, p. 426.   [73] Tachiaos, "Testament of Photius Monembasiotes," p. 89.

[74] Tachiaos, "Testament of Photius Monembasiotes," p. 89 n. 52; see also V. Laurent, *Les "Mémoires" du Grand Ecclésiarque de l'Église de Constantinople Sylvestre Syropoulos sur le concile de Florence (1438–1439)*, Rome, Pontificium institutum orientalium studiorum, 1971 (= *Concilium Florentinum documenta et scriptores*, Series B, vol. 9), § 19, pp. 120–121; § 28, pp. 188–191.

[75] Published according to the MS. GIM, Zabelin 419, fols. 54–56 in Andrei Pliguzov, "Tikhon of Rostov, or Russian Political Games in 1489," *Russian History*, vol. 22, 1995, pp. 319–320.

agriculture in a non-fertile soil area.[76] To be sure, some historians have attempted to explain the rise of Muscovy on the basis of its being an agricultural power. P. P. Smirnov suggested that the invention of a new type of plow (*sokha*) during the time of Ivan I gave impetus to Muscovite agriculture and was one of the main reasons for the rise of the Muscovite state.[77] The idea that the *sokha* was invented in the fourteenth century derives from the mistaken conclusions of D. K. Zelenin.[78] Not only is there ample evidence of the *sokha* before the fourteenth century, but also a scratch plow, like the *sokha*, could not support an agricultural revolution and large surpluses for export.[79] Smirnov's suggestion seems to have been a desperate effort to find some kind of evidence of new technology to support the Marxist theory of an agriculturally based rise of "feudal" Muscovy.

It is clear that, in the early fourteenth century, a large amount of silver was coming through Novgorod. In 1315, for example, Novgorod sent 50,000 grivna of silver to Grand Prince Mikhail.[80] Most likely, the products that brought prosperity to northern Rus' in the early fourteenth century were exports of furs, honey, wax, and potash – all high-unit-value goods – which continued through the seventeenth century. In return, the northern Rus' trading network transshipped spices, wine, and fabrics from Catholic Europe down the Volga toward the Caspian Sea. Grain exports from Baltic ports began to increase only during the late fourteenth century. This increase resulted not only from Dutch entrepreneurship but also from technological advances in ship construction, which allowed for larger tonnage to transport the low-unit-value bulky grains and timber, and the circumvention of the Lübeck–Hamburg portage by use of The Sound between Skåne and Zealand, thus avoiding costly unloading and loading expenses.[81] Although there is evidence of abundant grain in Muscovy in the fifteenth century,[82] this grain may not have been for export and it is unlikely that it was a major

---

[76] G. E. Kolchin, *Sel'skoe khoziaistvo na Rusi v period obrazovaniia Russkogo tsentralizovannogo gosudarstva: kontsa XIII–nachala XVI v.*, Moscow and Leningrad, Nauka, 1965, pp. 129–143; R. E. F. Smith, *Peasant Farming in Muscovy*, Cambridge University Press, 1977, plates 4 and 5; and Robert O. Crummey, *The Formation of Muscovy, 1304–1613*, London, Longman, 1987, p. 4.

[77] P. P. Smirnov, "Obrazovanie russkogo tsentralizovannogo gosudarstva v XIV–XVI vv.," *Voprosy istorii*, 1946, pts. 2–3, pp. 78–79.

[78] D. K. Zelenin, *Russkaia sokha. Ee istoriia i vidy*, Viatka, 1907, p. 121.

[79] See Smith, *Peasant Farming*, pp. 17–21.

[80] *NPL*, pp. 95, 336; *PSRL*, vol. 10, p. 179.

[81] Carlo M. Cipolla, *Between Two Cultures: an Introduction to Economic History*, trans. Christopher Woodall, New York, W. W. Norton, 1991, p. 106.

[82] Contarini testified to the abundance of grain when he visited Moscow in 1476. Ambrogio Contarini, "Viaggio in Persia," in *Barbaro i Kontarini o Rossii. K istorii italo-russkikh sviazei v XV v.*, ed. E. Ch. Skrzhinskaia, Leningrad, Nauka, 1971, p. 204; see

basis of wealth. Grain was not a big enough cash crop at this time to sustain the import of so much bullion from Catholic Europe into the area.[83]

Evidence from the second half of the fifteenth century points to Muscovy as a prominent commercial power. The Rus' chronicles report that in 1474, an entourage of 3,200 merchants and 600 envoys traveled from Sarai to Moscow, where they sold 40,000 horses to the Muscovites.[84] Under 1534, the Voskresenie and Nikon chronicles report a trade contingent from the Nogai Tatars of 4,700 merchants, 70 *murzy* (gentry), 70 envoys, and 8,000 horses.[85] Although such economic information in the chronicles is rare and, therefore, subject to question, we can find some confirmation of the numbers of horses the Tatars sold annually in Moscow in the account of Giles Fletcher from the late sixteenth century: "there are brought yearly to the Moscow to be exchanged for other commodities thirty or forty thousand Tatar horse which they call *koni*."[86] George Trakhaniot (Percamota), a Greek in the employ of the Muscovite grand prince, when he was sent as a diplomat to the court of the Duke of Milan,[87] reported that the income of the Muscovite state "exceeds each year over a million gold ducats, this ducat being of the value and weight of those of Turkey and Venice."[88] Trakhaniot goes on to report that

also Josafa Barbaro and Ambrogio Contarini, *Travels to Tana and Persia*, London, Hakluyt Society, 1873, p. 161.

[83] On the import of bullion from Catholic Europe into Rus', see Artur Attman, *The Russian and Polish Markets in International Trade 1500–1650*, trans. Eva Green and Allan Green, Göteborg, Kungsbacka, 1973, p. 110.

[84] *Ioasafovskaia letopis'*, p. 88; *PSRL*, vol. 8, p. 180; vol. 12, p. 156; vol. 18, p. 249; vol. 26, p. 254; vol. 28, p. 308.

[85] *PSRL*, vol. 8, p. 287; vol. 13, p. 80. Cf. *PSRL*, vol. 20, p. 425.

[86] Fletcher, "Of the Russe Commonwealth," p. 197.

[87] For introduction, notes, and translation, see Croskey and Ronquist, "George Trakhaniot's Description of Russia in 1486," pp. 55–64. The name "Percamota," which appears in the document itself, is most likely a distortion of "Trakhaniot" (*ibid.*, p. 55). We have no evidence that anyone named Percamota was connected with Muscovy, but George Trakhaniot was a prominent ambassador to western Europe. The Russian version of the name may itself be a mild distortion of Tarchaniotes. See also A. L. Khoroshkevich, *Russkoe gosudarstvo v sisteme mezhdunarodnykh otnoshenii kontsa XV–nachala XVI v.*, Moscow, Nauka, 1980, p. 189; [Evgenii Shmurlo], *Rossiia i Italiia. Sbornik istoricheskikh materialov i issledovanii*, 4 vols., St. Petersburg, Tipografiia Imperatorskoi Akademii nauk, 1907–1911, Leningrad, Akademiia nauk SSSR, 1927, vol. 3, pt. 1, pp. 22–27; and Gustave Alef, "The Origins of Muscovite Autocracy: the Age of Ivan III," *Forschungen zur osteuropäischen Geschichte*, vol. 39, 1986, p. 260. Gukovskii, on the other hand, does not accept this view. M. A. Gukovskii, "Soobshchenie o Rossii moskovskogo posla v Milane (1486 g.)," *Voprosy istoriografii i istochnikovedeniia istorii SSSR. Sbornik statei*, ed. S. N. Valk, "Trudy Leningradskogo otdeleniia Instituta istorii," vol. 5, 1963, p. 651.

[88] "Nota et continentia de la cose et signore de Rossia," p. 92; and "Notes and Information about the Affairs and the Ruler of Russia," p. 61. Croskey took this

[c]ertain provinces . . . give in tribute each year great quantities of sables, ermines, and squirrel skins. Certain others bring cloth and other necessaries for the use and maintenance of the court. Even the meats, honey, beer, fodder, and hay used by the Lord and others of the court are brought by communities and provinces according to certain quantities imposed by ordinance.[89]

These statements of Trakhaniot confirm the earlier report of Contarini concerning the importance of Moscow as a fur-trading center:

Many merchants from Germany and Poland gather in the city throughout the winter. They buy furs exclusively – sables, foxes, ermines, squirrels, and sometimes wolves. And although these furs are procured at places many days' journey from the city of Moscow, mostly in the areas toward the northeast, and even maybe the northwest, all are brought to this place and the merchants buy the furs here.[90]

Thus, the wealth reported in these sources could only have derived from commercial activity along the Volga, Oka, and Moskva rivers. This commerce included trade between Novgorod and Sarai, and reached into the northern forests. Forest products, including furs, honey, and wax, as well as customs duties (tamga, kostki) and tolls (myt) on trade passing through their territory were the basis of Muscovite prosperity during the fourteenth and fifteenth centuries. Muscovy extended its tribute collection to the north and northeast and, in doing so, came into conflict with Novgorod and Rostov. The Vychegodsko-Vymsk Chronicle claims that, as early as 1333, the people of Vychegoda and Pechora began giving tribute to the Muscovite grand prince, whereas formerly Novgorod had collected it.[91] According to this same chronicle, after a conflict with Konstantin, Prince of Rostov, Muscovy acquired rights of collecting tribute from Rostov, Ustiug, and Ustiug's possessions in Velikaia Perm' in 1364. After another conflict with Novgorod in 1367, Muscovy acquired the rest of Velikaia Perm', Pechora (again), as well as

reference to ducats as an inaccurate statement that gold coins circulated in Muscovy. Croskey and Ronquist, "George Trakhaniot's Description of Russia in 1486," p. 58. Instead, Trakhaniot's statement more likely refers to the equivalent amount of wealth. He was merely indicating what kind of ducat he was estimating that wealth in.
[89] "Nota et continentia de la cose et signore de Rossia," p. 92; and "Notes and Information," p. 61. Croskey suggested that da Vinci's portrait Lady with an Ermine may have resulted from the gifts of furs and live sables that Trakhaniot brought to Milan. Croskey and Ronquist, "George Trakhaniot's Description of Russia," pp. 58–59. This event may have been the beginning of the fur trade with Italy that Castiglione writes so amusingly about. Baldesar Castiglione, The Book of the Courtier, trans. George Bull, London, Penguin, rev. edn, 1974, pp. 164–165.
[90] Contarini, "Viaggio in Persia," p. 205; see also Barbaro and Contarini, Travels to Tana, p. 162.
[91] P. Doronin, "Dokumenty po istorii Komi," Istoriko-filologicheskii sbornik Komi filiala AN SSSR (Syktyvkar), vol. 4, 1958, p. 257.

Mezen' and Kegrola.[92] In other words, Muscovite expansion followed trade routes too. As late as 1572, Ivan IV confided to Anthony Jenkinson: "We know that merchant matters are to be heard, for that they are the stay of our princely treasures." This is not to say that commercial activities superseded other concerns, for as Ivan continued: "But first prince's affairs are to be established and then merchants."[93]

Very little is known about economic activity in Rus' during the early Mongol hegemony. The assumption has been that Rus' in general, and northeastern Rus' in particular, continued to undergo economic oppression throughout that period. Historians have tended not to look for evidence that would indicate otherwise. Yet, even if they had wanted to, evaluation of economic activity during this period is hindered by a scarcity of evidence, especially of a statistical nature. There are, however, exceptions. One of these is the research of Artur Attman, who in the chapter "Russia and the Asian markets," provides evidence that "during the 15th century Moscow became a commercial centre of ever increasing importance."[94] Another significant contribution to the study of the Muscovite economic success during the centuries of Mongol hegemony has been made by Janet Martin.[95] She concluded that "[t]he fur trade was an economic factor that certainly and significantly influenced the political development and growth of the Rus' and mid-Volga principalities between the tenth and mid-sixteenth centuries."[96]

The little economic evidence we do have provides a basis to question further the bleak accounts of devastation in the narrative sources. Coin finds in Rus' indicate that there was no diminishing of trade with Asian markets from the twelfth through the fourteenth centuries.[97] The "boat-shaped" ingots from the fourteenth century found along the Volga River are similar to Chinese ingots of the period. This similarity shows that

[92] Doronin, "Dokumenty po istorii Komi," pp. 257–258.

[93] *Pervyia sorok snoshenii mezhdu Rossieiu i Angleeiu 1553–1593*, ed. Iurii Tolstoi, St. Petersburg, A. Transhel', 1875, p. 129.

[94] Artur Attman, *The Bullion Flow Between Europe and the East 1000–1750*, trans. Eva Green and Allan Green, Göteborg, Kungl. Vetenskaps- och Vitterhets-Samhället, 1981, p. 104.

[95] Janet Martin, "The Land of Darkness and the Golden Horde: the Fur Trade Under the Mongols XIII–XIVth Centuries," *Cahiers du monde russe et soviétique*, vol. 19, 1978, pp. 401–421; Janet Martin, "Muscovy's Northeastern Expansion: the Context and a Cause," *Cahiers du monde russe et soviétique*, vol. 24, 1983, pp. 459–470; Janet Martin, *Treasures of the Land of Darkness: the Fur Trade and Its Significance for Medieval Russia*, Cambridge University Press, 1986.

[96] Martin, *Treasures of the Land of Darkness*, p. 169.

[97] See Th[omas] S. Noonan, "Russia's Eastern Trade, 1150–1350: the Archaeological Evidence," *Archivum Eurasiae Medii Aevi*, vol. 3, 1983, pp. 201–264. See also the list of gold and silver bars from the fourteenth century found in eastern Rus' territory in N. Bauer, "Die Silber- und Goldbarren des russischen Mittalters," *Numismatische Zeitschrift*, n.s., vol. 24, 1931, pp. 91–94 [75–78].

the Mongols had adopted Chinese methods of casting ingots.[98] Other evidence indicates that northeastern Rus' towns maintained their contact with the Baltic trade and, through that trade, with Catholic Europe.[99] It has been estimated that, during the course of the fourteenth century, forty new towns made their appearance in northeastern Rus', mostly along river routes. These include Serpukhov (1328), Peremyshl' (1339), Kaluga (1372), Elat'ma (1381), and Perevitsk (1381) on the Oka River and Borovsk (1356), Novgorod (1358), Obolensk (1369), and Vereia (1381) on the Protva River.[100] The towns of the Tver' principate saw a resurgence of growth during the late fourteenth and early fifteenth centuries, in spite of the hostile pressures from Moscow to the east and Novgorod to the west.[101]

Recent studies of masonry construction in Rus' have been particularly revealing. The evidence includes accounts in chronicles and other written sources, as well as archaeological finds. Such evidence may not be accurate in terms of the number of actual brick or stone buildings, walls, fortifications, etc., that were built. There could have been more construction than we have written or archaeological evidence for. In addition, it does not account for differences in quality of construction. For example, the mention of a "stone wall" could indicate a relatively simple architectural feat, such as the many stone walls or fences built in New England during colonial times[102] or in Castile during the Middle Ages. Or it could indicate an astounding architectural achievement, like the stone walls of Great Zimbabwe[103] or those of medieval towns and fortresses of Catholic Europe, many of which are still standing. Likewise, reference to a "stone church" could encompass almost anything from a simple stone chapel, such as the crudely constructed Baptistry at Poitiers, to a cathedral, like at Chartres. For Rus', our evidence indicates construction that falls somewhere in the middle of the spectrum in terms of architectural achievement.

---

[98] I. G. Spassky, *The Russian Monetary System: a Historico-Numismatic Survey*, trans. Z. I. Gorishina and L. S. Forrer, rev. edn, Amsterdam, Jacques Schuman N. V., 1967, pp. 72–73.

[99] Lawrence N. Langer, "The Medieval Russian Town," in *The City in Russian History*, ed. Michael F. Hamm, Lexington, KY, University Press of Kentucky, 1976, p. 19.

[100] R. A. French, "The Urban Network of Later Medieval Russia," *Geographical Studies on the Soviet Union: Essays in Honor of Chauncey D. Harris*, ed. George J. Demko and Roland J. Fuchs, University of Chicago Department of Geography, 1984, p. 42.

[101] E. A. Rikman, "Obsledovanie gorodov Tverskogo kniazhestva," *Kratkie soobshcheniia o dokladakh i polevykh issledovaniiakh Instituta istorii material'noi kul'tury AN SSSR*, vol. 41, 1951, pp. 71–84.

[102] See, e.g., Susan Allport, *Sermons in Stone: the Stone Walls of New England and New York*, New York, W. W. Norton, 1990.

[103] See, e.g., Peter S. Garlake, *Great Zimbabwe*, London, Thames & Hudson, 1973.

Another risk in drawing conclusions from this type of evidence is that the abundance of trees in northern Rus' often made construction in wood preferable to construction in stone even when stone construction was possible.[104] We have the testimony of Josef Barbaro, who in (or shortly after) 1436 reported that "both towns [Riazan' and Kolomna] have wooden fortifications and all the houses are wooden because there is not sufficient stone in these places."[105] We know that sufficient stone does exist in these places, but Barbaro was seeking an explanation for why the people of Riazan' and Kolomna would use wood when he expected to find stone instead.

The loss of skilled craftsmen who fled, or were taken, where they could better demonstrate their skills most likely retarded the stone-construction revival even when the economic resources were available. Yet, Dvornik has written that "the traditions of [earlier] Suzdal'-Vladimir architecture were not forgotten during the Mongol period." As examples of this he pointed to the earliest stone churches in Moscow, the Danilov Monastery church (1272) and the Savior in the Forest church (1330). As further indications of the survival of this type of architecture in northeastern Rus' in general, Dvornik mentioned the churches of the Assumption (1399) and Our Lady's Nativity (1404) in Zvenigorod, as well as the churches of the Trinity-St. Sergius Monastery (1422) and the church of Aleksandrovo. Besides construction in stone, Dvornik acknowledged that "Russian native architects were more daring in the Mongol period in their wooden architecture."[106] Dvornik concluded that Rus' construction of the Mongol period continued to improve on the architectural models from Kiev and Byzantium. And Riasanovsky, who provides an informed discussion of wooden church architecture of the period, also concluded: "The Russians not only translated Byzantine stone church architecture into another medium, wood, but they also developed it further in a creative and varied

---

[104] For an analysis of wooden architecture in Russia as a parallel development to and "mutual inspiration" with masonry architecture, see William Craft Brumfield, "Russian Wooden Architecture," in his *A History of Russian Architecture*, Cambridge University Press, 1993, pp. 501–520.

[105] Iosaphat Barbaro, "Viaggio alla Tana," in *Barbaro i Kontarini o Rossii. K istorii italo-russkikh sviazei v XV v.*, ed. E. Ch. Skrzhinskaia, Leningrad, Nauka, 1971, p. 132. Cf. "Travels of Josaphat Barbaro, Ambassador from Venice to Tanna, now called Asof, in 1436," in *General History and Collection of Voyages*, vol. 1, ed. Robert Kerr and F. A. S. Edin, Edinburgh, George Ramsay, 1811, p. 509. The Hakluyt translators have, instead: "bicause there is small quantitie of stone to be founde thereabouts." Barbaro and Contarini, *Travels to Tana*, pp. 31–32.

[106] Dvornik, *Slavs in European History*, p. 317. See, e.g., the fourteenth-century wooden church on display in the Ipatiev Monastery in Kostroma, as well as the fourteenth-century wooden Church of Lazarus on display in Kizhi.

manner."[107] This last statement, coming as it does from a historian who has decried the pernicious impact of the Mongol hegemony upon all aspects of life in Rus', must be given suitable consideration.

Construction in the Moscow kremlin provides illustrations of what was occurring architecturally during this period. The Church of the Archangel Michael in the Moscow kremlin was originally built in wood in the year 1250. Ivan I had this structure replaced with a stone one between 1328 and 1333. Subsequently, Ivan III, at the end of his reign in 1505, had that structure replaced with a new stone one designed by an Italian architect. Two other stone churches were also built in the kremlin during the reign of Ivan I: the Church of the Assumption and the Church of Ivan Lestvichnik.[108] The Church of the Assumption was rebuilt in 1474 using stone cutters from Pskov and Italy.[109] The original Church of the Annunciation was built in the Moscow kremlin between 1396 and 1416, and may have been decorated by the icon painter Andrei Rublev around 1405. It was subsequently rebuilt by Pskovian architects between 1482 and 1490. In addition, between 1359 and 1374, the wooden walls of the Moscow kremlin were replaced with white stone brought from Miachkov, fifteen miles away. Tver' already had stone walls around its kremlin by that time.

Since construction in stone or brick was a significant event, however, and since much of it was in terms of stone churches (something the chroniclers would be interested in), we can take this type of evidence as a starting point. The research of David B. Miller has been a step forward in providing statistical data for masonry construction in Rus' from 900 to 1462. Miller's research should help to focus attention on finding more evidence of masonry construction during the Mongol period, since the common notion thus far has been that there was none or very little.[110] Insofar as the present evidence provides an accurate reflection of the masonry construction in northern Rus' from the twelfth through the fifteenth centuries, we have a rough indication of a pattern of economic growth.

According to Miller's research, from the time of the Mongol invasion

---

[107] See Riasanovsky, *History of Russia*, 4th edn, pp. 126–128, quotation on p. 127.

[108] *PSRL*, vol. 7, p. 202; vol. 18, p. 91. For a further description of construction in the Moscow Kremlin from the thirteenth through the fifteenth centuries, see N. Ia. Tikhomirov and V. I. Ivanov, *Moskovskii kreml'. Istoriia arkhitektury*, Moscow, Stroiizdat, 1966, pp. 6–31.

[109] *Ioasafovskaia letopis'*, p. 88; *PSRL*, vol. 8, p. 180; vol. 12, pp. 155–156; vol. 18, p. 249; vol. 26, p. 254; vol. 28, p. 308.

[110] See, e.g., Zenkovsky's comment that "during more than two centuries of the Tatar Yoke, no large edifices were built and Russians forgot how to build them." Serge A. Zenkovsky, ed., *The Nikonian Chronicle*, 5 vols., Princeton, NJ, Kingston Press, Darwin Press, 1984–1989, vol. 5: *From the Year 1425 to the Year 1520*, p. 163 fn. 180.

of northeastern Rus' (1238) until the 1280s (a period of forty-five to
fifty years), there is almost no evidence of masonry construction in all of
northern Rus'. We have evidence in the 1280s of a few masonry
constructions. Then the twenty-five-year period of 1288–1312 matches
in terms of numbers of masonry constructions the last twenty-five-year
period (1213–1237) before the Mongol conquest, i.e. eighteen and
seventeen, respectively. For the next twenty-five-year period
(1313–1337) the evidence is the same – seventeen masonry constructions. Then, from 1338 on, we have much more evidence of
masonry construction: thirty-one (1338–1362); sixty-two (1363–1387);
seventy-three (1388–1412); sixty-two (1413–1437; and fifty-two
(1438–1462).[111] Each of the three twenty-five-year periods between
1363 and 1437 shows more masonry building in northern Rus' alone
than in *all* of Rus' during any twenty-five-year period before the Mongol
conquest. The most masonry building in all of Rus' for any twenty-five-
year period before 1238 is for the years 1188–1212, when the evidence
testifies to fifty-six cases.[112] In short, insofar as our evidence for masonry
building correlates with economic prosperity, by the latter half of the
fourteenth century, when it was supposed to be in the throes of economic
depression and political oppression as a result of the "Tatar yoke,"
northern Rus' alone may have been more prosperous than the whole of
Rus' at any time before the Mongol hegemony was established.

Finally, we have to acknowledge that the majority of this type of
construction was in Novgorod and Pskov, towns that did not experience
any destruction during the Mongol conquest. Yet we have evidence of
substantial masonry construction going on in northeastern Rus' (i.e.
excluding Novgorod and Pskov) from the early fourteenth century on:
seven (1313–1337); seven (1338–1362); sixteen (1363–1387); twenty-
one (1388–1412); eight (1413–1437); and thirteen (1438–1462). By
1363–1387, the number of masonry constructions in northeastern Rus'
is comparable with the number of masonry constructions in all of

---

[111] David B. Miller, "Monumental Building as an Indicator of Economic Trends in
Northern Rus' in the Late Kievan and Mongol Periods, 1138–1462," *American
Historical Review*, vol. 94, 1989, pp. 367–374. Miller uses the term "monumental
building" in a general sense to apply to any construction in stone or brick. The
archaeologist Bruce G. Trigger, however, has suggested that we reserve the term
"monumental" to those constructions that in "scale and elaboration exceed the
requirements of any practical function." Bruce G. Trigger, "Monumental Architecture: a Thermodynamic Explanation of Symbolic Behavior," *World Archaeology*, vol.
22, 1990, p. 119. Thus, I will use the neutral terms "masonry construction" or
"masonry building" here.

[112] David B. Miller, "Monumental Building and Its Patrons as Indicators of Economic
and Political Trends in Rus', 900–1262," *Jahrbücher für Geschichte Osteuropas*, vol. 38,
1990, p. 350. In the article cited in the previous footnote, Miller indicates fifty-five
cases for the period 1188–1212. I take here the higher figure in the later article.

northern Rus' in the twenty-five-year period (1213–1237) immediately preceding the Mongol conquest (sixteen and seventeen, respectively). Thus, it had already exceeded the amount of masonry construction in northeastern Rus' during any previous period.[113] In other words, the evidence seems to indicate that, by the second half of the fourteenth century, northeastern Rus' was more prosperous than it had ever been before. One would like to see a follow-up study to determine the quality of construction and differences in that quality. But we can say this on the basis of Miller's findings: the Mongol conquest of Rus' had an immediate negative impact, but the destructiveness and duration of the resulting economic depression is open to reevaluation. By the early fourteenth century, northeastern Rus' was participating in the economic revival that resulted from the *Pax Mongolica*. That economic revival had an enormous impact on the rise of Muscovy.

To sum up the findings of Part I: we can speak of Mongol influence on the military and on the civil administration of Muscovy. Military influence in regard to weapons, strategy, and tactics is primary and direct. Administrative influence is secondary but still direct: dual civil and military administration from China and *iqtā'* from Islamic countries came through the conduit of the Qipchaq Khanate. We cannot speak of Mongol influence in either a primary or a secondary way, either direct or indirect, on the Muscovite practice of seclusion of elite women, or on theories of despotism or autocracy. No doubt the Mongol invasion of 1237–1240 brought death and destruction. But the long-term economic devastation of northern Rus' has been exaggerated. Following the apparent economic stagnation of the second half of the thirteenth century, northern Rus' in general, and northeastern Rus' in particular, displayed vital signs of recovery in the early fourteenth century, followed by a flourishing economy from the mid-fourteenth century on. This economic revival was based primarily on commercial activity, and resulted in the acquisition of wealth not only by the grand princely court and the Church but also by merchants, craftsmen, and artisans.

We cannot say that the Mongol conquest cut Muscovy or north-eastern Rus' off from Catholic Europe because that area had no direct contact with Catholic Europe anyway. Novgorod and Pskov maintained their contact with the rest of Europe, but mainly for commercial reasons. Little cultural influence from Catholic Europe penetrated through to northeastern Rus' even before the Mongols. Instead, the Mongol conquest, which included Rus' in the Mongol world Empire, opened up northeastern Rus' to influences from China and the *Dâr al-*

---

[113] Miller, "Monumental Building . . . 1138–1462," pp. 366, 373; Miller, "Monumental Building . . . 900–1262," p. 355.

Islâm that it would not have known otherwise. The Muscovite secular elite chose to accept specific aspects of administration, law, trade, and the military from these core cultures. They did not borrow other aspects of Chinese and Islamic culture, either because those aspects did not make it through to the Khanate of Qipchaq or because the Muscovite secular elite did not see any need for them. Thus, Chinese and Muslim religion, philosophy, and science had no appreciable impact. Social attitudes toward women developed indigenously and specific practices, like seclusion and veiling, may have been borrowed from Byzantine society through the Church. Early and Middle Muscovite diplomatic practices were flexible: Byzantine-based in general, especially, when dealing with other Rus' princes, but adjustable to Mongol-based practices when dealing with Tatars. Muscovite political theory, which was autocratic but not despotic, derived from Byzantium. And the *Pax Mongolica*, which followed the initial devastation of conquest, helped northeastern Rus' recover economically into a prosperous commercial zone during the fourteenth and fifteenth centuries.

Part II

Development of an anti-Tatar ideology
in the Muscovite Church

6   Defining ideology

Religious establishments have traditionally created sacred justifications for the activities of the governments under which they operate. As long ago as the fourteenth century, Ibn Khaldûn pointed out that religious doctrine gives the ruling dynasty additional power. Supporters, imbued with the teachings of religion, are fearlessly willing to die to advance the objectives of the dynasty, which are seen thereby as divinely sanctioned and morally just.[1] The Rus' Church was no exception to this general practice, but, during the fifteenth and sixteenth centuries, the political views expressed by Muscovite Churchmen underwent significant changes. These views evolved from being merely an adjunct of Byzantine political thought to the formulation of an independent ideology that supported the Muscovite state.

Those who invoke the term "ideology" have tended to use it in referring to any politically related pattern of ideas. But, as Robert Putnam has pointed out, the scholarly literature in this regard is daunting: "a dip in the cold and murky waters of the literature on 'ideology' is a shocking and disillusioning experience. Few concepts in social analysis have inspired such a mass of commentary, yet few have stimulated the production of so little cumulative knowledge about society and politics."[2] Putnam's assessment of the present vague use of "ideology" is clear-minded, but his own definition of ideology is laden with negative values. For example, he calls a "political actor" ideological when that actor, among other things, is "[h]ostile and intolerant toward political opponents"; "[o]pposed to compromise, bargaining, incrementalism and other aspect of 'pluralist' politics"; and an "[e]xtremist."[3] While these characteristics could be filled by someone who is merely stubborn, pigheaded, or intractable, without its being due to any

[1] Ibn Khaldûn, *Muqaddimah*, pp. 126–128.
[2] Robert D. Putnam, "Studying Elite Political Culture: the Case of 'Ideology,'" *American Political Science Review*, vol. 65, 1971, p. 651. For evidence of the confusion Putnam is referring to, see *L'Analyse de l'ideologie*, 2 vols., ed. Gérard Duprat, Paris, Galilée, 1980–1983.
[3] Putnam, "Studying Elite Political Culture," p. 655.

ideological commitment, it could also define someone who is firm in upholding their principles, such as devotion to truth or justice. Besides, a pluralist, non-extremist, compromiser may be doing so on the basis of an ideological commitment of their own, that is to pluralism, non-extremism, and compromise.

I will try to use the term "ideology" more precisely.[4] First, it might be helpful to draw a distinction between ideology in a pre-modern society and ideology in a modern society. After all, the term *ideology* itself has a rather recent (late eighteenth-century) origin. In any pre-modern society that develops an ideology (as I define it below), a notable and significant absence is the lack of a specific economic component in the articulation of that ideology. To be sure, economics may underpin the ideology itself, but that underpinning is not made visible by those who give expression to their ideological commitments. For example, mercantilism, a policy that a number of western European states followed in the late medieval and early modern period, was provided a systematic formulation only many centuries after it had been put into practice. Additionally, I would like to maintain a distinction between, on the one hand, *ideology*, that is, a tightly coherent and consciously purposeful network of ideas, and, on the other, *mentalité*, which I take to be a pattern of ideas people in a society subscribe to, but without a particularly conscious design or purpose to it. Thus, I would put the archaeologist Brian Hayden's definition of ideology as "a layer of community values"[5] in the category of *mentalité*. I would also put a people's religion in that category as well, because it represents a shared set of beliefs, which involve (1) agreement on symbols to represent those beliefs, and (2) agreement on behavior that conforms to those beliefs. An ideology purports to have, or strives for, all those components, but it also consciously presents itself as a means of mobilizing society in a particular direction, that is, to achieve a specific goal or set of goals.

Finally, I would like to distinguish between previous approaches to defining an ideology, almost all of which have been based on structural identification, and my approach, which is based on a functional identification. For the purpose of this investigation, we can say an ideology exists when a belief system fulfills all three of the following functions:

---

[4] For other views on what constitutes ideology, see Clifford Geertz, "Ideology as a Cultural System," in *Ideology and Discontent*, ed. David Apteher, New York, Free Press, 1964, p. 64 (reprinted in Clifford Geertz, *The Interpretation of Culture*, New York, Basic Books, 1973, pp. 193–229); and Nigel Harris, *Beliefs in Society: the Problem of Ideology*, Harmondsworth, Penguin, 1971, p. 43; Raymond Boudon, *The Analysis of Ideology*, trans. Malcolm Slater, Cambridge, Polity, 1989; Fred Weinstein, *History and Theory After the Fall*, University of Chicago Press, 1990, p. 35.

[5] Hayden, *Archaeology: the Science of Once and Future Things*, p. 103.

(1) interprets social experience; (2) provides a guide for political action; and (3) creates a collective consciousness through, among other things, the formulation of a commonly agreed upon virtual past. Thus, a pre-modern ideology has social, political, and intellectual components. The social component describes what the social hierarchy should be and how the various groups in society should interact. The political component delineates a program of political struggle, especially in terms of battling designated enemies, both internal and external. The intellectual com-ponent justifies the existence of the present social hierarchy and political actions by placing them within the context of an artificial construct, the virtual past, which is then designated the historical past, or "what really happened." This artificial construct provides the narrative basis for the "lessons of the past," which interpreters build into their formulations about the historical past (i.e. the mythistory that explains why the interpreter's people are different from and better than other people).[6] Plato's "noble lie," as expressed by Socrates in *The Republic*, is a form of mythistory by means of which the populace can be attuned to a central ideology that mobilizes them. Similarly, Ibn Khaldûn describes the concept of 'aṣabiyya, or group feeling, as a unifying influence on a tribe, dynasty, ruling elite, or state. The absence of a mythistory, "noble lie," or 'aṣabiyya leads a nation to what Emile Durkheim called "anomie" – a sense of loss of meaning and direction – and what Bill Clinton called being "in a funk."

   The religious virtual past, in early Muscovy, was supplied to the Rus' Church by the Byzantine Church, and involved the unfolding of God's will (theophany). The secular virtual past was supplied to the Rus' princes by the Qipchaq Khanate, and involved more mundane matters of administration and tax collection as subordinate tributaries to the "world-ruling" Chingizid dynasty. By the second half of the sixteenth century, the Muscovite ruling elite had adopted the Church's virtual past. It was not until Peter secularized that ideology by turning to Europe for inspiration that a new synthesis developed. Of course, a virtual past need not be a myth or noble lie; it can simply represent an interpretation of the source testimony, that is, of how the sources came to be the way they are. In this source-oriented sense, scholarly interpret-ation transcends ideology because it is not meant as a way of mobilizing the populace in an intellectual, political, or social sense. In the period

---

[6] For a general discussion of the concept of a virtual past, see Donald Ostrowski, "The Historian and the Virtual Past," *The Historian: a Journal of History*, vol. 51, 1989, pp. 201–220. For the concept of "mythistory," see William McNeill, "Mythistory, or Truth, Myth, History, and Historians," and "The Care and Repair of Public Myth," in his *Mythistory and Other Essays*, University of Chicago Press, 1986, pp. 3–42.

we are dealing with, such a source-oriented virtual past was subsumed to ideological commitments on the part of the interpreters.

A pre-modern thought system, to be considered an ideology, then should have social, intellectual, and political components, and have the intention of mobilizing the people by creation of a unified view of the world. The Muscovite Church developed systematic views that fulfilled all three of these criteria, and thus had a fully articulated pre-modern ideology by the middle of the sixteenth century. While the Church tacitly accepted the secular social relationships of *mestnichestvo*, it did require that all members of the ruling class be baptized. The development of an ideology among Churchmen in Muscovy had a number of specific time and place components to it. One of the most important of these was the changing attitude toward the Tatars (Mongols) as represented both in the chronicles and in hagiographical and other Church literature.

The policy of Rus' ecclesiastical acquiesence to Mongol rule had its roots in Byzantine policy. After the defeat of his ally, the Seljuks, in 1243, the Nicaean Emperor John III Vatatzes chose to follow a friendly policy toward the Mongols. Alliances and marriages between the Byzantine and Chingizid dynasties ensued as his successor continued that policy. Maria, the daughter of Michael VIII Palaeologus married Abaqa, the son of Hülegü in 1265. The daughter of Adronicus II, also named Maria, married Toqta, khan of the Qipchaq Khanate, at the end of the thirteenth century. The daughter of Adronicus III married another khan of the Qipchaq Khanate, Özbeg, in the early fourteenth century.[7] This policy of acquiesence on the part of the Rus' Church in Muscovy ended in the 1440s, when that Church rejected the agreement of collaboration with the Latin Church that Byzantium had adopted at the Council of Florence. It thereby also divorced itself from the policy of collaboration with the Qipchaq Khanate, or what remained of it. Metropolitan Isidor, a Greek appointee, had accepted the Council of Florence, which, in 1438, called for a union of the Eastern Orthodox and Roman Catholic Churches. When the prelates of the Rus' Church in Muscovy realized what this meant in practice, they and Grand Prince Vasilii II ousted Isidor in 1441.

---

[7] For the background of relations between the Qipchaq Khanate and the Court of Nicaea when this alliance was made, see M. A. Andreeva, "Priem tatarskikh poslov pri Nikeiskom dvore," in *Sbornik statei, posviashchennykh pamiati N. P. Kondakova. Arkheologiia. Istoriia iskusstva. Vizantinovedenie*, Prague, Seminarium Kondakovianum, 1926, pp. 187–200. For subsequent exceptions to this general alliance, see Ostrowski, "Why Did the Metropolitan Move?" p. 101 n. 74. See also Meyendorff, *Byzantium and the Rise of Russia*, p. 44; and Omeljan Pritsak and Anthony Cutter, "Mongols," in *Oxford Dictionary of Byzantium*, p. 1395.

On December 15, 1448, a council of Rus' bishops chose one of their own, Iona, as metropolitan without the official approval of the Patriarch of Constantinople. In July 1451, Vasilii II wrote a letter to the Emperor Constantine XI to inform him what had been done, to request the "blessing" of the Byzantine Church, and to ask for the Emperor's "good will" toward Iona.[8] This letter contrasts with another letter that Vasilii supposedly wrote to Patriarch Mitrophanes in 1441 advancing the candidacy of Iona to be appointed metropolitan.[9] During the 1440s, Vasilii II and Dmitrii Shemiaka were engaged in a bitter civil war for control of the Muscovite polity. At the time, Iona, as archbishop of Riazan', may have supported Shemiaka. Zimin and Ia. S. Lur'e suggested that it was Shemiaka who elevated Iona to the position of metropolitan in 1446 in return for Iona's help in retrieving Vasilii's sons from hiding.[10] I prefer, however, to accept the December 15, 1448, document as representing the official decision to elevate Iona to that position.

Decisive, I think, is the letter the council of bishops wrote just one year earlier, December 29, 1447, in which they make a number of accusations against Shemiaka. Besides those faults we might expect, such as his refusal to defend Moscow against the attack of the Khan Ulug Mehmed, to assist Vasilii II at the battle of Suzdal' in 1445, to return the grand-princely testaments and treasury, or to recognize Sadi Ahmed as khan of the Qipchaq Khanate, the letter charges Shemiaka with pro-Tatar activity, namely, bringing Tatars into the land of Rus' and unauthorized negotiations with the khan of Kazan'.[11] It is doubtful whether these accusations were in response to charges of an anti-Tatar nature that Shemiaka supposedly made against Vasilii II, because the charges attributed to Shemiaka first appear in our sources only at a much later date, in chronicles of the last quarter of the fifteenth century.[12] The fact that this later chronicle account claims that She-miaka was motivated by the devil to make his charges suggests it is a post-facto concoction intended to discredit further the losing side in the civil war. Among these pseudo-charges are that Vasilii had made a deal to gain his freedom after being captured at the battle of Suzdal' whereby he would give Moscow and other cities to Ulug Mehmed to rule while

---

[8] *AI*, vol. 1, no. 41, pp. 83–85; *RIB*, vol. 6, no. 71, cols. 575–586; *RFA*, vol. 1, no. 13, pp. 88–91. I am accepting here Pliguzov's dating of the letter in *RFA*, vol. 4, 1988, p. 913.

[9] *AI*, vol. 1, no. 39, pp. 71–75; *RIB*, vol. 6, no. 62, cols. 525–536.

[10] A. A. Zimin, "V bor'be za Moskvu (vtoraia chetvert' XV stoletiia)," *Voprosy istorii*, 1982, no. 12, p. 89; Ia. S. Lur'e, "Iz nabliudenii nad letopisaniem pervoi poloviny XV v.," *TODRL*, vol. 39, 1985, p. 302.

[11] *AI*, vol. 1, no. 40, pp. 75–83.

[12] *PSRL*, vol. 8, p. 115; vol. 18, p. 196; vol. 25, p. 263; cf. vol. 33, pp. 51–52.

Vasilii took over Tver'. Such charges would have made no sense in the political atmosphere of the 1440s and were obviously intended to be understood as bogus. A diatribe containing more severe charges of an anti-Tatar flavor against Vasilii can be dated to the time of the civil war. This earlier indictment is attributed to the Mozhaisk Prince Ivan and appears in the Novgorod IV Chronicle.[13] Prince Ivan accuses Vasilii of bringing Tatars to Rus'; assigning them towns and districts as *kormlenie*; loving Tatars; loving their language; and of giving them "gold, silver, and possessions." The early date associated with the appearance of Prince Ivan's list of grievances as well as the council of bishops' accusation against Shemiaka of pro-Tatar activity dating from the same time indicates that in the Muscovite civil war of the late 1440s lies the first open manifestation of the anti-Tatar rhetoric that was to lead, by the sixteenth century, to the full-blown anti-Tatar ideology of the Rus' Church.[14]

If any deals were made with ecclesiastical prelates, it seems likely that it was Vasilii who reached agreement with the council of bishops in 1447. In return for their support against Shemiaka, Vasilii agreed to support their independent choosing of a metropolitan for Rus' whether or not the Patriarch of Constantinople approved. The letter dated 1441, therefore, is most likely a forgery, composed later in the century to bolster the claim that the Rus' Church reluctantly, and of necessity, chose a metropolitan on its own and that Vasilii has supported Iona earlier. Muscovite chronicles of the end of the fifteenth century and sixteenth century contain the statement that Iona had gone to Constantinople, where the patriarch had given Iona his blessing to become metropolitan after Isidor.[15] But, as Lur'e pointed out, this entry must be considered a later interpolation entered into the Muscovite chronicles to provide legitimacy for Iona's usurpation of the metropolitanate.[16] Iona's testament, for example, does not mention any such trip to Constantinople, although we can expect that it would if such a trip had

---

[13] *PSRL*, vol. 4, p. 125; cf. *PSRL*, vol. 13, pp. 66–68, 72; vol. 16, p. 189.

[14] Halperin perceptively realized the sharp contrast between these anti-Tatar charges of 1447–48 and the neutral language of the account of the Qipchaq khan's arbitration of the succession dispute between Vasilii and his uncle Iurii in 1432. Halperin, *Tatar Yoke*, p. 147. He discusses these same documents and chronicle entries but presents a somewhat different interpretation of them.

[15] *PSRL*, vol. 8, p. 122; vol. 12, p. 74; vol. 18, p. 204; vol. 25, p. 270; vol. 26, p. 208; vol. 28, pp. 110, 277; *Ioasafovskaia letopis'*, p. 42.

[16] Ia. S. Lur'e [Iakov S. Luria], "Fifteenth-Century Chronicles as a Source for the History of the Formation of the Muscovite State," *Medieval Russian Culture*, vol. 2, ed. Daniel Rowland and Michael Flier, Berkeley, University of California Press, 1994, pp. 52–53. Ia. S. Lur'e, *Dve istorii Rusi XV veka. Rannie i pozdnie, nezavisimye i ofitsial'nye letopisi ob obrazovanii Moskovskogo gosudarstva*, St. Petersburg, Dmitrii Bulanin, 1994, pp. 100–104.

occurred.[17] Despite the likelihood that the letter of 1451 is authentic, it is not clear that it was sent either.

Vasilii did not, significantly enough, ask permission in the letter of 1451 to appoint Iona, which had already been done anyway. The Emperor was in no position to do anything about that appointment, even if he had wanted to, since Constantinople was surrounded by the Ottoman Turks at the time; in any event, there was no emperor after 1453. To counter, however, what he may have perceived as a move toward autocephalization, the patriarch excommunicated the Muscovite metropolitanate and appointed another metropolitan in Kiev in 1458.[18] The Muscovite Church's choosing its own metropolitan in 1448, along with Grand Prince Vasilii's letter addressed to the Byzantine Emperor in 1451 informing him of the *fait accompli* (even if not sent), constituted not so much a break as a rearrangement of relations between the Rus' Church in Muscovy and the parent Church in Constantinople.[19] The year 1448 is a somewhat arbitrary date for a process that must have taken some years to come to fruition.[20] Once the Muscovite Church had chosen its own metropolitan without confirmation from Constantinople, it was then in a position to formulate and follow its own policy. Yet, the Muscovite Church still acknowledged the ecclesiastical jurisdiction of Constantinople, as was clearly stated in Vasilii's letter to Constantine XI: "our Rus' Church, the holy Rus' metropolitanate . . . seeks and requires blessing" from the Byzantine Church.[21]

After 1448, an ambivalence culminating in outright animosity toward the Tatars resulted in Muscovite Churchmen's attempts to vilify the Tatars and portray them as "the enemy." Political differences between those who favored anti-Tatar and pro-Tatar positions could be more easily expressed and understood in religious terms because no idiom of political debate or political philosophy had yet been developed to express such differences in Muscovy. This religious terminology was of

[17] *RFA*, vol. 3, pp. 649–654.

[18] Ia. N. Shchapov, *Vostochnoslavianskie i iuzhnoslavianskie rukopisnye knigi v sobraniiakh Polskoi narodnoi respubliki*, 2 vols., Moscow, Institut istorii SSSR, 1976, vol. 2, Appendix, no. 52, pp. 145–147. See also E. V. Beliakova, "K istorii uchrezhdeniia avtokefalii russkoi tserkvi," in *Rossiia na putiakh tsentralizatsii*, ed. V. T. Pashuto et al., Moscow, Nauka, 1982, pp. 152–156.

[19] For a discussion of these issues, see Ia. S. Lur'e, "Kak ustanovilas' avtokefaliia russkoi tserkvi v XV v.," *Vspomogatel'nye istoricheskie distsipliny*, vol. 23, 1991, pp. 181–198. Lur'e, *Dve istorii Rusi*, pp. 93–108.

[20] Pliguzov has suggested that the process began as early as 1392 with the change of the metropolitan's title to include Kiev. Andrei Pliguzov, "On the Title 'Metropolitan of Kiev and All Rus'," *Harvard Ukrainian Studies*, vol. 15, 1991, pp. 340–353; see also A. I. Pliguzov, "O titule 'Mitropolit Kievskii i vseia Rusi,'" *RFA*, vol. 5, 1992, pp. 1034–1042.

[21] *AI*, vol. 1, no. 41, p. 84; *RIB*, vol. 6, no. 71, col. 584; *RFA*, vol. 1, pp. 90–91.

Byzantine provenance, but was given new meaning because of a different political context. Thus, the Patriarch of Constantinople in his prayer at the coronation of the Byzantine Emperor would ask God to "subdue unto him all barbarian nations."[22] Metropolitan Makarii used the same prayer, translated into Russian, at the coronation of Ivan IV.[23] When Patriarch Antonios IV used the phrase at the coronation of Manuel II in Constantinople in 1392, the allusion could be understood as referring specifically to the Ottoman Turks. When Makarii used the same phrase in Moscow in 1547, it could be understood as referring specifically to the Tatars.

One indication of the new anti-Tatar policy was to recall officially the Bishop of the Don and Sarai from Sarai around this time and to set him up in Krutitsk, a suburb of Moscow.[24] The bishop of that eparchy, while in residence in Sarai, had three main functions: (1) to deal diplomatically with the government of the Qipchaq Khanate; (2) to act as a liaison between Sarai and Constantinople;[25] and (3) to attend to the religious needs of Christian merchants, as well as those of the grand prince, and his entourage, when the grand prince attended his sovereign, the Qipchaq khan, in Sarai. With the decline in importance of the Qipchaq Khanate, the growing independence of the Rus' Church vis-à-vis the Greek Church, and the fall of Constantinople in 1453, any need for the Rus' Church to maintain a bishop in Sarai for diplomatic purposes had vanished. The decision may have only confirmed a reality, that the bishop no longer resided in Sarai, but in Moscow, where by this time he had become the metropolitan's chief foreign policy adviser.

Important aspects of this new ideology were the replacement of the Byzantine basileus as the protector of the Church by the Muscovite ruler and the defining of the Muscovite ruler's authority in terms that had been applied to the Byzantine basileus. Another important aspect was the creation of a virtual past that designated Muscovy as the true inheritor of Kievan Rus', as well as of Byzantium. This new virtual past

---

[22] R. P. Jacobi Goar, *Euchologion sive rituale Græcorum*, 2nd edn, Venice, Ex Typographia Bartholomæi Javarina, 1730, p. 726; P. Schreiner, "Hochzeit und Krönung Kaiser Manuels II im Jahre 1392," *Byzantinische Zeitschrift*, vol. 60, 1967, p. 77, lines 14–15.

[23] E. V. Barsov, "Drevne-russkie pamiatniki sviashchennogo venchaniia tsarei na tsarstvo," *ChOIDR*, 1883, bk. 1, pp. 27–28, 34, 51; see also Pelenski, "Muscovite Imperial Claims," p. 575 and fn. 70. For identification of Makarii's prayer with that of the Byzantine Patriarch, see Ševčenko, "Muscovy's Conquest of Kazan," p. 542 fn. 1.

[24] Pavel Stroev, *Spiski ierarkhov i nastoiatelei rossiiskie tserkvi*, St. Petersburg, V. S. Balashev, 1877, col. 1033; Karamzin, *Istoriia gosudarstva Rossiiskogo*, vol. 6, *Primechaniia*, p. 38 n. 219.

[25] In 1279, e.g., Metropolitan Kirill and Khan Möngke Temür sent Bishop Feognost of Sarai to the Emperor Michael Palaeologus in Constantinople with an official document and gifts. *TL*, pp. 336–337; *PSRL*, vol. 7, p. 174; vol. 10, p. 157; vol. 18, p. 77; vol. 20, p. 168; vol. 28, pp. 61, 220.

also worked to deny Muscovy's status as the inheritor of the Tatar Khanate of Qipchaq. In discussing the changing attitudes toward the Tatars as represented in Church sources, I will attempt to demonstrate how these changes contributed to a Church ideology, specifically in regard to the formation of a collective consciousness through the creation of an agreed-upon virtual past, and the setting up of an interpretive framework by which to "explain" Muscovite–Tatar relations.

7   Anti-Tatar interpolations in the Rus' chronicles

No chronicle entry that has an anti-Tatar bias can be dated to the period between 1252 and 1448. Instead, passages with anti-Tatar content were entered into the Rus' chronicles only before 1252 and after 1448. It was during the intervening period of 196 years between these two dates that the Rus' Church followed the policy of the Byzantine Church and accommodated itself to the Qipchaq Khanate. Insofar as one can trust the reporting in the chronicles, one would have to say that the Rus' Church at first (between 1237 and 1252) encouraged opposition to the Mongols among the Iziaslavichi of Galicia-Volynia. Admittedly, the evidence for this conjecture is meager. Even so, the source testimony is provocative. The Church does not tar with the brush of "evil" the activities of the Mongols within lands under their direct control. Galicia, an area in some dispute, is another matter. The Church's method of encouraging opposition to the Tatars there merely continued Church practice toward the Pechenegi and Polovtsi.[1] For example, the Galician-Volynian Chronicle refers to the Mongols when they first appear in 1224 as "the godless Moabites called Tatars . . ."[2] and when they reappear in 1237 as "the godless descendants of Ishmael."[3] The Galician-Volynian Chronicle's account of Prince Daniil's visit to Batu in 1245 is particularly revealing, as it contains such phrases as: "they were ruled by the Devil"; "their foul pagan acts of fornication and Chingiz Khan's flights of fancy, his disgusting bloodsucking and endless sorcery"; "Oh, how repugnant was their false faith"; "Oh, the greatest disgrace is to be honored by the Tatars," and so forth.[4]

Even then, there was an acknowledgment of the secular authority of the khan.[5] When Prince Mikhail of Chernigov refuses to bow to a pagan idol at the court of Batu in 1246, Mikhail is reported to have said:

---

[1] See, e.g., Leonid S. Chekin, "The Godless Ishmaelites: the Image of the Steppe in Eleventh–Thirteenth-Century Rus'," *Russian History*, vol. 19, 1992, pp. 9–28.
[2] *PSRL*, vol. 2 (1908), col. 740.   [3] *PSRL*, vol. 2 (1908), col. 778.
[4] *PSRL*, vol. 2 (1908), cols. 806–807.
[5] See Michael B. Zdan, "The Dependence of Halych-Volyn' Rus' on the Golden Horde," *Slavonic and East European Review*, vol. 35, 1956/57, pp. 505–522.

"Since God has delivered us and our lands into your hands because of our sins, we bow down to you and pay honor to you."[6] Likewise, the Hypatian Chronicle reports that Prince Daniil of Galicia went to Batu in 1245 "to pay him homage" and was welcomed by Batu as "already one of us – a Tatar."[7]

From 1252 to 1448, the Rus' Church took a position of accepting the overlordship of the khans as the will of God in accordance with the fact that the Byzantine Empire was then in alliance with the Qipchaq Khanate. Anti-Tatar propaganda, which appears earlier in the Rus' chronicles, is absent after 1252. Fennell noticed that "[f]rom the early fourteenth-century chronicles one gets the impression that the Tatars were a benevolent rather than an oppressive force"[8] and remarks that the accounts of the Mongol's crushing of the Tver' rebellion of 1327 "reveal an astonishingly neutral attitude towards the Tatars."[9] He goes on to point out that, although one can "find the Tatars described as vile, evil, pagan, lecherous, etc., and aggressively anti-Christian," such descriptions "are rarely, if at all, contemporary" to the early fourteenth century.[10] Throughout the fourteenth century, the Church continued the policy initiated by Metropolitan Kirill in the 1250s when he and Aleksandr Nevskii agreed on a policy of cooperation with the Mongols.[11] This policy accorded with that of the Byzantine Church, which supported the diplomatic alliance between the Byzantine Empire and the Qipchaq Khanate. This long-term Byzantine–Qipchaq alliance also helps to explain why no specifically anti-Tatar ideology developed in Byzantium.

[6] *PSRL*, vol. 2, col. 795; see also *PSRL*, vol. 25, p. 138. The idol was supposedly an image of Chingiz Khan. For a discussion of this event and the dating of it, see Dimnik, *Mikhail, Prince of Chernigov*, pp. 130–135.
[7] *PSRL*, vol. 2, col. 807. Chingiz Khan had made a similar statement about Xiedu, the son of the Khitan leader Ila Liuge: "But Xiedu has now become a Mongol. He accompanied me on the western campaign and has rendered great services." *Yuanshi*, 149: 4a, quoted in Paul Ratchnevsky, *Genghis Khan: His Life and Legacy*, trans. and ed. Thomas Nivison Haining, Oxford, Blackwell, 1991, p. 138.
[8] See J. L. I. Fennell, "The Ideological Role of the Russian Church in the First Half of the Fourteenth Century," *Gorski vijen: a Garland of Essays Offered to Professor Elizabeth Hill*, ed. by R. Auty, L. R. Lewitter, and A. P. Vlasto, Cambridge, Modern Humanities Research Association, 1970, p. 106.
[9] Fennell, "Ideological Role," p. 110.
[10] Fennell, "Ideological Role," pp. 110–111. Cf. the critical remarks of Michael Stanton, "The Things That Are God's: the Rus' Church in the Fourteenth Century," unpublished paper; and Charles J. Halperin, "The Russian Land and the Russian Tsar: the Emergence of Muscovite Ideology, 1380–1408," *Forschungen zur osteuropäischen Geschichte*, vol. 23, 1976, p. 38 fn. 118.
[11] *PSRL*, vol. 1, col. 473. Joseph T. Fuhrmann, "Metropolitan Cyril II (1242–1281) and the Politics of Accommodation," *Jahrbücher für Geschichte Osteuropas*, vol. 24, 1976, pp. 165–168.

During this period, Rus' ecclesiastical writers and chroniclers describe Mongol raids as though those raids were motivated by God with the Mongols' acting as divine agents. In the *Life of Aleksandr Nevskii* Khan Batu is reported as saying "O Aleksandr, know you that God has subjected many peoples to me."[12] The Novgorod I Chronicle's description of the battle of 1223 on the river Kalka begins with "for our sins, unknown tribes came."[13] The phrase "favored by God and the tsar" (i.e. the Mongol khan) appears frequently in the chronicles.[14] Although the thirteenth-century writer Serapion, Bishop of Vladimir, decried the devastation wrought by the Mongol invasion, he cited the rectitude of the Mongols as superior, specifically in regard to the Christians' not treating each other as well as the Mongols treat their own kind.[15]

Other scholars have noted this absence of literary attack on the Tatars in the early sources. A. E. Presniakov suggested that Rus' chroniclers were reticent about recording the discord among Rus' princes that their dependency on Tatar domination engendered because it was too painful and humiliating.[16] Charles Halperin saw Rus' chronicle treatment of the Qipchaq Khanate as fitting a "common pattern . . . an ubiquitous method of mitigating the conflict between theoretical hatred and practicing tolerance, between open warfare and institutional borrowing, between prejudice and pragmatism" of Christian–Muslim relations during the Middle Ages.[17] Halperin calls this pattern "the ideology of silence" because sources contain no articulation of "an ideology for coexistence with the Tatars."[18] What Halperin is describing might more properly be called a "conspiracy of silence" rather than an ideology.

Yet, there are at least three significant ways in which Rus' does not conform to this pattern that Halperin identifies elsewhere. First, pejorative terms toward the Tatars are absent from the chronicles even before the khans of the Qipchaq Khanate finally converted to Islam in the early fourteenth century. The first Islamic khan of the Khanate had been Berke (1257–1266), who succeeded the brief reign of Sartak (1255), a

[12] *PLDR. XIII vek*, p. 435.
[13] *NPL*, pp. 61, 264.
[14] See, e.g., *PSRL*, vol. 13, p. 92 (1339); *PSRL*, vol. 15 (1922), pt. 2, col. 56 (1344); *PSRL*, vol. 18, p. 92 (1344); and cf. *PSRL*, vol. 10, p. 206 (1334); *PSRL*, vol. 15 (1922), pt. 2, col. 92 (1336).
[15] E. V. Petukhov, *Serapion Vladimirskii. Russkii propovednik XIII veka*, Pribavlenie, St. Petersburg, Imperatorskaia Akademiia nauk, 1888, pp. 25, 14.
[16] A. E. Presniakov, *The Formation of the Great Russian State*, trans. A. E. Moorhouse, Chicago, Quadrangle Books, 1970, p. 74; A. E. Presniakov, *Obrazovanie velikorusskogo gosudarstva. Ocherki po istorii XII–XV stoletii*, Petrograd, Ia. Bashmakov, 1918, p. 64.
[17] Charles Halperin, "The Ideology of Silence: Prejudice and Pragmatism on the Medieval Religious Frontier," *Comparative Studies in Society and History*, vol. 26, 1984, p. 443.
[18] Halperin, "The Ideology of Silence," p. 464.

Nestorian Christian. The next four successors of Berke were all sky worshippers, until Özbeg (1313–1341), who established Islam as the religion of choice of the khans.[19] Thus, the presumed Christian hatred of Islam that Halperin sees as underlying the Rus' Church's silence post-dates by some sixty years the Church's adoption of the policy of accommodation with the Khanate. To be sure, once Özbeg established Islam as the religion of the Qipchaq Khanate, one might expect to find some hesitancy in Church writings toward an Islamic ally of their own government. Even so, anti-Islamic remarks almost completely disappear from Rus' Church literature between the early fourteenth century and the mid-fifteenth century. Second, underlying Halperin's hypothesis is an assumption that the Qipchaq Khanate was considered the "enemy" before the mid-fifteenth century.[20] Instead, the reliable evidence that dates to before 1448 tends to support the contention that the Muscovite princes and the Rus' Churchmen considered the Mongols of the Qipchaq Khanate to be the legitimate sovereigns of Rus' and allies of Byzantium. The Muscovite princes and Churchmen readily acknowledged the suzerainty of the Qipchaq khans. In other words, before the taking over of the appointment of its own metropolitan, the Rus' Church in general exhibited no signs of ambivalence toward the Mongol rulers of Rus'. Third, we would not expect to find "an ideology of coexistence" articulated in the sources for someone who is not an enemy.

One point, however, that Halperin made about the Rus' chronicles is undeniable: we find no general articulation of the Qipchaq Khanate's suzerainty over Rus'.[21] This absence is odd because the Qipchaq khan was the effective sovereign of northeastern Rus', where most of the chronicles were being written, well into the fifteenth century. Instead, the Tatars are usually presented as interlopers into the area of Rus'.

---

[19] István Vásáry, "History and Legend in Berke Khan's Conversion to Islam," *Aspects of Altaic Civilization III. Proceedings of the XXX PIAC, Bloomington,* ed. Denis Sinor, Bloomington, Asian Studies Research Institute, Indiana University, 1990, pp. 230–252. See also J. Richard, "La conversion de Berke et les débuts de l'islamisation de la Horde d'Or," *Revue des études islamiques,* 1967, pp. 173–184. On the conversion in general, see M. A. Usmanov, "Etapy islamizatsii Dzuchieva ulusa i musul'manskoe dukho-venstvo v tatarskikh khanstvakh XIII–XVI vekov," in *Dukhovenstvo i politicheskaia zhizn' na Blizhnem i Srednem Vostoke v period feodalisma,* ed. G. F. Kim, G. F. Girs, and E. A. Davidovich, Moscow, Nauka, 1985, pp. 177–185; and Devin DeWeese, *Islamization and Native Religion in the Golden Horde: Baba Tükles and Conversion to Islam in Historical and Epic Tradition,* University Park, Pennsylvania State University Press, 1994, pp. 67–158.

[20] See, e.g., Charles Halperin, "'Know Thy Enemy': Medieval Russian Familiarity with the Mongols of the Golden Horde," *Jahrbücher für Geschichte Osteuropas,* vol. 30, 1982, pp. 161–175.

[21] Halperin, *Russia and the Golden Horde,* p. 63.

There is no explanation of the Tatar involvement, such as a statement that "because the Tatars had conquered Rus'." So, even in the period when the chroniclers presented the Tatars in a matter-of-fact way, we find no political role explicitly defined for the Qipchaq khan. Possibly this was because, in the Byzantine worldview, there was a place for Christian rulers but not for non-Christian rulers. The Rus' grand prince could be a member of the Byzantine family of Christian princes but the Qipchaq khan could not. The chroniclers never resolved, or seemed to have attempted to resolve, this anomaly. Not only is there no ideology or conspiracy in this regard, there is no political formulation at all.

The compilation of the Nikon Chronicle represents an important stage in the revision of the Muscovite virtual past. It contains information not found in earlier chronicle accounts. A typical argument that has been advanced to justify our accepting this information as reliable is that the sixteenth-century editors had access to earlier sources that are not extant. B. A. Rybakov made such an argument in regard to the reliability of information provided by the Nikon Chronicle not found in the Primary Chronicle.[22] Zenkovsky agreed with this line of argument and went further to suggest that even the folkloristic elements in the Nikon Chronicle can be accepted as reliable because "such folkloristic recollections in many lands, including Russia and Scandinavia (its sagas), often actually did reflect historical facts."[23] Furthermore, Zenkovsky argued that, because of the oppressiveness of the Tatar yoke, chronicle writing of the thirteenth and fourteenth centuries "becomes very dry and the annual entries are often reduced to the mere enumeration of deaths of princes, plagues, Tatar inroads and extremely short reports of political events." By contrast, the Nikon Chronicle takes "the form of a historical-literary anthology" based not only on various local chronicles but also on literary works that "often contain . . . more interesting details about the life and psyche of the Russian people than do the materials which record strictly historical events."[24] Underlying Zenkovsky's reasoning seems to be a presumption that folklore performed a function similar to that of *samizdat'* in the Soviet Union – one of providing the true views of the people at a time when such views could not be expressed officially.

Just how extensive the destructiveness of the Mongol invasions of 1237–1240 was, however, remains to be demonstrated. As I have

[22] B. A. Rybakov, *Drevniaia Rus'. Skazaniia. Byliny. Letopisi*, Moscow, Akademiia nauk SSSR, 1963, pp. 162–173, 182–187.
[23] Serge A. Zenkovsky, "Introduction," *The Nikon Chronicle*, vol. 1: *From the Beginning to the Year 1132*, p. xxxvi.
[24] Zenkovsky, "Introduction," *Nikonian Chronicle*, vol. 3: *From the Year 1241 to the Year 1381*, p. xxi.

argued above, northeastern Rus' soon benefited economically from Mongol suzerainty. In addition, "the mere enumeration of deaths of princes, plagues, Tatar inroads, and extremely short reports of political events" seems not much different from the kinds of information reported in the chronicles before the Mongol conquest. There was just less of it, which might be an indication of more peaceful conditions – a *Pax Mongolica* – rather than of the oppressive nature of the Tatar rule. In the end, I find it difficult to accept the notion that Tatar officials somehow censored Christian monks writing in a Slavic language in their own monasteries.

Lur'e has described the tendency of historians to rely heavily on the Nikon Chronicle, which reflects a "Muscovite political bias" of the sixteenth century, and, as a result, to produced skewed histories. He pointed out that M. D. Priselkov warned against the "consumer approach" to historical study, that is, picking indiscriminately from any information found in the chronicles without understanding the relationship of the chronicles to each other.[25] Some historians have now begun taking Priselkov's warning to heart and have incorporated the work of A. A. Shakhmatov and Lur'e on chronicle relationships into their own studies. Jaroslaw Pelenski, for example, took a skeptical stance toward sixteenth-century chronicle interpolations and urged that the "Nikon Chronicle's 'additions' . . . must be treated with caution, because they are representations of sixteenth-century Russian political thought."[26] Pelenski was referring here specifically to the Nikon Chronicle's account of Bogoliubskii's destruction of Kiev in 1169, but it is a fair assessment of the skeptical approach to sixteenth-century interpolations in general.

We can see three types of interpolations by the editor of the Nikon Chronicle of earlier chronicle entries. The first type is the simple revision, which modifies an earlier entry that is neutral toward the Tatars in order to put an anti-Tatar spin on it. The entry for 1262 exemplifies this type. In the pre-Nikonian chronicles, this entry describes the calling of the *veches* (assemblies) of certain towns to dispose of some Muslims or pagans, depending on the chronicle. According to the earliest extant account, in the Suzdal' Chronicle, from which all

---

[25] Ia. S. Lur'e [J. Luria], "Problems of Source Criticism (with Reference to Medieval Russian Documents)," *Slavic Review*, vol. 27, 1968, pp. 3–7; Ia. S. Lur'e, "O nekotorykh printsipakh kritiki istochnikov," *Istochnikovedenie otechestvennoi istorii. Sbornik statei*, vol. 1, ed. N. I. Pavlenko et al., Moscow, Nauka, 1973, pp. 81–84; Lur'e, "Fifteenth-Century Chronicles," pp. 47–49; Lur'e, *Dve istorii Rusi*, pp. 9–13.

[26] Jaroslaw Pelenski, "The Sack of Kiev of 1169: Its Significance for the Succession to Kievan Rus'," *Harvard Ukrainian Studies*, vol. 11, 1987, p. 313 fn. 31. See also Donald Ostrowski, "What Makes a Translation Bad? Gripes of an End User," *Harvard Ukrainian Studies*, vol. 14, 1990, pp. 443–445.

other chronicle accounts of this event derive, the people of the Rostov land called a *veche* and drove the Muslims/pagans from Rostov, Vladimir, Suzdal', and Iaroslavl'. These Muslims/pagans were apparently tax collectors, agents of the Mongols, who were requiring forced labor on the part of people not able to pay their taxes. Morris Rossabi has suggested that in China the Yuan Dynasty sent in Muslims to collect taxes in order to deflect the antagonism of the populace from their Mongol overlords.[27] Instead, it is more likely the Mongols, in China as in Rus', employed Muslims in this capacity because they had the skills and administrative experience. The pre-Nikonian versions of this story make no mention of any involvement either by the Mongols themselves or by the Rus' princes.[28]

In the Nikon Chronicle, by contrast, we find a prominent role reserved for the leadership of the Rus' princes. These Rus' princes first reach an agreement among themselves, then "they drove the Tatars (изгнаша Татаръ) [not just their Muslim agents] from their towns." Not only did they drive them away, but they killed some and converted others to Christianity.[29] The forcible conversion of Tatars to Christianity and of Russians to Islam is a *topos* (or cliché) that we can associate with post-1448 chronicle writing. In another sixteenth-century version of this story, that of the Ustiug Chronicle, Aleksandr Nevskii appeals to the people of Ustiug to rise up against the Tatars. An Ustiug woman, who had been forced to become the mistress of the Tatar tax collector Buga, convinces him to convert to Christianity because Nevskii had ordered that all Tatars be killed.[30] Clearly, this is a romantic fable and should not be made to bear the weight of historical reliability concerning the uprising of 1262. Nonetheless, Nasonov found the account sufficient to argue that Nevskii planned and directed the entire uprising.[31] This demonstrates that sixteenth-century chronicle editors and interpolators still have a gullible audience among us historians.

Another example of this type of simple revision occurs under the entry for 1293. All the pre-Nikonian Chronicle accounts present, more or less, the same story. Prince Andrei Aleksandrovich with other Rus' princes goes to the khan to complain about Andrei's brother, the grand

[27] Rossabi, "Muslims in the Early Yüan Dynasty," p. 277.
[28] *TL*, pp. 327–328; *PSRL*, vol. 1(1927), cols. 476, 524; vol. 4, p. 39; vol. 5, p. 190; vol. 7, pp. 162–163; vol. 15 (1922), pt. 1, col. 32, pt. 2, col. 402; vol. 16, col. 53; vol. 18, p. 72; vol. 20, p. 164; vol. 23, p. 85; and vol. 24, p. 98.
[29] *PSRL*, vol. 10, p. 143.
[30] *PSRL*, vol. 37, pp. 30, 70, 104–105, and 110. Cf. *PSRL*, vol. 37, p. 129 (Chronicle of Lev Vologdin). In the second redaction of the Ustiug Chronicle and in the Chronicle of Vologdin, the Ustiug woman is given the name Mariia.
[31] Nasonov, *Mongoly i Rus'*, pp. 52–53.

prince Dmitrii Aleksandrovich. The khan (Toqta) sends a Tatar army under the command of Diuden (Tudan?) his brother. They chase Dmitrii to Pskov and take fourteen towns, including Vladimir, Pereiaslavl', Moscow, and Volok, and do much harm to the land.[32] The younger redaction of the Novgorod I Chronicle adds as a lament that they did much harm to Christians as well.[33] Later chronicles pick up this phrase in various forms.[34] The Chronicle of Avraamka not only includes this *topos* (in the form: много христианъ посѣкоша), but adds that other Christians were imprisoned (а иныхъ плѣниша).[35] The compiler of the Nikon Chronicle adds narrative details not found in previous chronicle accounts (e.g. Toqta at first wanted to send for Dmitrii to come to Sarai but then changed his mind). The compiler does not include the phrase about harm to Christians but does depict the Tatar army as being particularly destructive of the church in Vladimir: "The Tatar army . . . took Vladimir and robbed the Vladimir church. They tore up [выдраша] the wondrous upper floor and took all the sacred vessels."[36] The compiler also adds that, "thanks to God's intercession," the Tatar army did not reach Tver'. This simple interpolation places God in the role of protecting Christian Rus' rather than punishing it through the agency of the Tatars.

The second type of interpolation is the double-layered revision, where a post-1448 but pre-Nikon Chronicle revision puts an anti-Tatar spin on an earlier entry, and then is further revised and enhanced in the Nikon Chronicle. The entry for 1327 about Chol-khan (Shchelkan, Shevkal) exemplifies this type. According to Fennell's analysis of the passage, the original form of the story begins with Chol-khan's going to Tver', where he drives Grand Prince Aleksandr Mikhailovich from the throne. The people of Tver' rise up and kill Chol-khan and all the Tatars, except for a few who escape back to the khanate via Moscow.[37] In the subsequent

---

[32] *PSRL*, vol. 1 (1928), col. 527; vol. 18, p. 82; vol. 30, p. 98.

[33] *NPL*, p. 327: О, много бяше пакости крестияномъ. The older redaction has missing folios here, so we do not know what it said.

[34] *PSRL*, vol. 5 (Sofiiskaia I), p. 201: Они же много пакости учиниша християномъ; *PSRL*, vol. 6 (Voskresenskaia), p. 180: Они же пришедше много пакости учиниша християномъ; *PSRL*, vol. 20 (L'vovskaia), p. 171: и шеше, много пакости учиниша крестьяномъ; *PSRL*, vol. 24 (Tipografskaia), p. 105: Они же, пришедше, много пакости учиниша хрестьяномъ; *PSRL*, vol. 28, pt. 1 (Compilation of 1497), p. 63: много пакости починиша християном; *PSRL*, vol. 28, pt. 2 (Compilation of 1518), p. 223: много пакости сътвори християном; *PSRL*, vol. 33 (Kholmogory), p. 76: много пакости учиниша.

[35] *PSRL*, vol. 16, col. 56.   [36] *PSRL*, vol. 10, p. 169.

[37] John L. I. Fennell, "The Tver' Uprising of 1327: a Study of the Sources," *Jahrbücher für Geschichte Osteuropas*, vol. 15, 1967, pp. 161–179. One should point out that the original version of this story as Fennell describes it is not extant in any chronicle; it is a hypothetical reconstruction. If one does not accept Fennell's reconstruction, then one

reworking of this story in the Tver' Compilation of 1455, a number of literary *topoi* are added that signal more of an anti-Tatar interpretation. The Tver' Compilation describes how, because of the sins of the Tverites, "God allowed the Devil to put evil things in the hearts of the godless Tatars." The Devil instructs Chol-khan, "the destroyer of Christians and wicked instigator of all evil," to convince the khan to allow him to go to Rus' to destroy Christianity, to kill their princes, and bring their princesses and children back to the khan. Once on the throne, Chol-khan "raises up a great persecution against the Christians with great violence and plunder and beating and desecration."[38] Neither the earlier version, as reconstructed by Fennell, nor the Tver' Compilation version has Grand Prince Aleksandr Mikhailovich taking an active part in the uprising. In both versions, the grand prince merely advises the people of Tver' to be patient.

The Moscow Compilation of 1479 does not include the drama-like discourse of Chol-khan to the khan that the Tver' Compilation begins with, nor does it include the *topos* of God's punishing the people of Tver' for their sins. It does include Chol-khan's intention to slay Aleksandr Mikhailovich and his brothers, to place himself on the throne, to place Tatar princes in other Rus' towns, and to convert Christians to Islam. It also adds a further elaboration. Unable to accomplish these things, Chol-khan tries to kill all the people, but Grand Prince Aleksandr, having perceived Chol-khan's plan, summons the people of Tver'. An all-day battle between the forces of Aleksandr and those of Chol-khan ensues. It ends with Chol-khan's fleeing to the anteroom (на съни) of the palace, which the people of Tver' set afire, burning up Chol-khan and all the remaining Tatars.[39]

Note that this reworking by the editor of the Moscow Compilation of 1479, like the Nikon Chronicle's reworking of the entry for 1262, introduces, and places emphasis on, the Rus' princes' opposition to the Tatars, whereas the earliest versions of these entries do not include any conflict between the Tatars and the Rus' princes. The idea behind such interpolations is to create a virtual past that provides a precedent and justification for grand-princely opposition to the Tatars.

The Nikon Chronicle version of the Tver' uprising of 1327 derives from the version in the Moscow Compilation of 1479, but includes

can argue either of two ways: (1) the version that appears in the Tver' Compilation (svod) of 1455 is an accurate representation of the original version of the story that must have appeared in pre-1448 versions or (2) the compiler of the Tver' Compilation made up the story out of whole cloth where no previous entry exists. He would have done so to provide a plausible explanation for the replacing of Aleksandr Mikhailovich as grand prince by Ivan Daniilovich.

[38] *PSRL*, vol. 15, pt. 2, cols. 415–416.   [39] *PSRL*, vol. 25, p. 168.

further embellishments. Chol-khan (Щелхан) is now a tsarevich and cousin of Khan Özbeg. As a Chingizid, he is of significantly higher rank than an envoy (посоль), as he is described in the Compilation of 1479 (the Tver' Compilation does not provide a rank for Chol-khan). In addition, he is given the patronymic Diudenevich, which may be an allusion to the Diuden who led the Tatar expedition of 1293, and is clearly related to the historical song of Shchelkan Dudent'evich.[40] Furthermore, the Nikon Chronicle describes how, because of the actions of Prince Ivan Daniilovich, God spared Moscow the destruction that the Tatars visited upon the rest of Rus' in retaliation.[41] The compiler of the Nikon Chronicle seems to have felt the need to "explain" the collaboration of a Muscovite prince with the Tatars on one of their inroads into Rus'. The chroniclers were spokesmen for the Church, while the actions of the grand princes, as is demonstrable from the documentary evidence, often appear to be contradictory to the views that the chroniclers express.[42]

In contrast to the way later chroniclers describe them, officially sanctioned Tatar military actions of the fourteenth century in Rus' territory were most likely undertaken to recover revenue from those towns that were reluctant to pay their taxes. Raiding by horse archers no doubt continued to occur, but those who perpetrated such renegade actions were potentially subject to punishment by the khan. Conflicts between Lithuania and the Qipchaq Khanate dominated diplomacy in the western steppe of the late thirteenth and fourteenth centuries. For the Muscovite princes this meant acting as vassals of the Qipchaq khans against Lithuania and, at times, other Rus' princes, who might be recalcitrant in fulfilling their obligations or who were allied with the

---

[40] *Istoricheskia pesni XIII–XVI vekov*, ed. B. N. Putilov and B. M. Dobrovol'skii, Moscow and Leningrad, Akademiia nauk SSSR, 1960, pp. 76–78. Presniakov wrote that "the chronicle compilations reflect certain legends and folk songs." While he seemed to reject the more "fantastic goals" that are attributed to the Tatars, such as wanting to destroy Christianity and kill all the Rus' princes, Presniakov accepted the contention that Chol-khan occupied the grand-princely throne with pride and began a persecution of Christians. He asserted that these events provided the factual basis for the elaborations in the legends and songs. Presniakov, *Obrazovanie russkogo gosudarstva*, p. 137.

[41] *PSRL*, vol. 10, p. 194.

[42] Fisher made the same point about the relationship of Ottoman chroniclers to actions of their government. Fisher, "Muscovite–Ottoman Relations," p. 210. I do not accept the prevailing consensus that some Rus' chronicles were "grand princely" and others "metropolitanate." All were "metropolitanate" or "eparchial" in that all were written, compiled, and edited by monks or prelates, and all received the approval of the reigning prelate in a diocese. No chronicle writing can be traced to any grand-princely scriptorium. But, see Ia. S. Lur'e, *Obshcherusskie letopisi XIV–XV vv.*, Leningrad, Nauka, 1976, pp. 160, 166–167, 244–254, for the contention that such a phenomenon as "grand-princely" chronicles existed.

Lithuanian Grand Duke.[43] Even the Nikon Chronicle maintains the report that, in 1279, Rus' princes joined with the Tatars against the Lithuanians.[44] In the fifteenth and sixteenth centuries, Muscovite princes engaged in alliances with one or more of the successor khanates, the Crimean, Kazan', Kasimov, or Nogai against the others or against Lithuania.[45] By then, Tatar military activities in Rus' were undertaken mostly as part of alliance systems.

The third type of interpolation is inclusion of anti-Tatar material where no previous entry exists in the earlier chronicles. The Nikon Chronicle's account of the "accursed" Temur in 1348 exemplifies this third type of interpolation:

That same year Temur, a prince of the Horde, came with an army to the town of Aleksin, [the town] of holy miracleworker Petr, Metropolitan of Kiev and all Rus'. They burned the suburbs and returned to the Horde with a great number of captives. But God delivered His servants from those who offended them and avenged them with His true judgment: his [Temur's] own Tatar servants killed him in the Horde the same year, and in such a way the accursed one perished with his children.[46]

We can compare this interpolation with another interpolation in the entry for 1273. In that passage, which again appears only in the Nikon Chronicle, the combined forces of Iargaman, the *bāsqāq* of Vladimir, a khan called Aidar, and Vasilii Iaroslavich, one of the brothers of Aleksandr Nevskii, attack Novgorodian lands. As with the interpolated passage under 1348, the attackers returned "with many captives."[47] But there is no coda in the 1273 interpolation, as there is in the 1348 one about anyone's being accursed or being killed by their own servants. Fennell, who is skeptical of any information that appears only in the Nikon Chronicle, argued for acceptance of this passage under 1273 as reliable: "The entry . . . is detailed, bears little trace of padding or invention and probably reflects a non-extant Novgorod or Tver' source."[48] We can reject the 1348 interpolation out of hand because it is implicitly anti-Tatar, but we cannot reject the 1273 interpolation on the same basis.

By contrast, an anti-Tatar interpolation that occurs in the entry for 1252 in the Nikon Chronicle has Andrei Iaroslavich say: "O Lord, why do we quarrel amongst ourselves and lead the Tatars against one another! It would be better for me to flee to a foreign land than to be

---

[43] Pelenski, "The Contest Between Lithuania-Rus' and the Golden Horde," pp. 303–320.
[44] *PSRL*, vol. 10, p. 157.
[45] Keenan, "Muscovy and Kazan: Some Introductory Remarks," pp. 552–557.
[46] *PSRL*, vol. 10, p. 220.   [47] *PSRL*, vol. 10, p. 151.
[48] Fennell, *Crisis*, p. 158 n. 10.

friends with, and serve, the Tatars."[49] This passage is yet another indication that the chroniclers were aware that Rus' princes had often allied with the Tatars, although after 1448 the chroniclers openly deplore such alliances. We have no evidence that any of these passages existed in earlier chronicles. One should also mention in this regard that the compilers of the Nikon Chronicle would, on occasion, promote Muscovite princes after the fact. The entry for 1282 in the Nikon Chronicle, for example, calls Daniil "Grand Prince" although he never occupied that position.[50]

With this understanding of the post-1448 interpolative nature of anti-Tatar remarks in the Rus' chronicles, we can now begin to resolve one of the major controversies in fifteenth-century literary studies, that is, the dating of the tales and chronicle accounts of the Kulikovo cycle. In 1380, Grand Prince Dmitrii Ivanovich (Donskoi) led a mixed Rus' and Tatar army against a mixed Tatar and Rus' army led by an emir of the Qipchaq Khanate Mamai at Kulikovo Pole (field). The ensuing battle elicited a wide range of interpretations, not only in chronicle accounts and tales written about this event but also in the scholarly literature. One point they are all agreed upon is that it was a great victory for the forces of Dmitrii. Yet, one can question the nature of this "victory."

The description of the battle itself occurs only in Rus' sources and archaeologists seem intent on finding evidence to support that description. But even the Rus' sources acknowledge that Dmitrii lost most of his army in the battle. Mamai, by contrast, had enough forces to encounter and then lose to Tokhtamish shortly afterward. If Mamai was defeated, it is difficult to explain how he still had an army to face Tokhtamish. Both the Short and Long Chronicle Tales (discussed below) explain that Mamai went to raise another army. In the meantime, he received word that Tokhtamish was advancing against him from the Blue Horde and went to encounter him, with disastrous results. Some commentators have suggested that this second battle must have occurred in 1381 to allow time for Mamai to raise another army, but there is no evidence to support this conjecture. Indeed, if Mamai disengaged in the battle with Dmitrii in order to meet the threat of Tokhtamish's forces, it seems unlikely he would have had enough time to raise another army.

The Rus' sources go on to state that Dmitrii and what remained of his army spent up to a week on the battlefield, looting and burying the dead. If this was the case, then it was a fatal delay. German chroniclers of the time, Johann von Posilge and Detmar of Lübeck, the only other

---

[49] *PSRL*, vol. 10, p. 138.   [50] *PSRL*, vol. 10, p. 160.

contemporaries who make reference to the battle, describe how Dmitrii and his army were overtaken on the way back to Moscow by the Lithuanian army under Jagiełło (Jagailo) and cut to ribbons.[51] The Chronicle Tales tell a different story: Jagiełło and the Lithuanian army arrived a day late, were terrified, and fled. We have indirect confirmation, however, of the German chroniclers' report that Dmitrii's forces were annihilated. Two years later, when Tokhtamish attacked Moscow, Dmitrii was unable to raise a force in defense. Finally, it may seem odd that, if Dmitrii had defeated Tokhtamish's enemy Mamai, Tokhtamish would need to attack Dmitrii in Moscow. Yet, we know from Dmitrii's *Testament* that he was looking to the day when the grand prince would no longer have to send tribute to the Tatar khan: "And should God change the Orda [so that] my children do not have to pay the *vykhod* to the Orda, then the *dan'* that each of my sons collects in his own *udel* will be his."[52] Dmitrii may have taken his campaign against Mamai as a reason to end tribute paying, but Tokhtamish would not let him get away with it. In the end, the "victory" of Dmitrii changed nothing in terms of Muscovy's relationship to the Qipchaq Khanate.

Nonetheless, the battle on the Don River is considered a major event in Russian history and literature. Among the chronicle accounts are (1) the Suzdal' Chronicle account,[53] (2) the Novgorod I Chronicle account,[54] (3) the *Kratkaia letopisnaia povest'* (Short Chronicle Tale) (hereafter, *KLP*) as maintained in the Rogozhskii and Simeonov Chronicles,[55] and (4) the *Prostrannaia letopisnaia povest'* (Expanded Chronicle Tale) (hereafter, *PLP*), as maintained in the Novgorod IV and Sofiiskii I Chronicles.[56] Among the tales are (1) *Skazanie o Mamaevom poboishche* (*Narrative of the Battle with Mamai*) in four redactions,[57] (2) *Zadonshchina* (*Events Beyond the Don*) in two redactions,[58] and (3) *Slovo o zhitii i prestavlenii velikogo kniazia Dmitriia Ivanovicha* (*Oration Con-*

---

[51] *Scriptores rerum Prussicarum: die Geschichtsquellen der Preussischen Vorzeit bis zum Untergange der Ordensherrschaft*, 6 vols., ed. Theodor Hirsch, Max Toppen, and Ernst Strehlke, Leipzig, S. Hirzel (Breitkopf & Hartel), 1861–1874; reprinted Frankfurt, Minerva, 1965, vol. 3, pp. 114–115.

[52] *DDG*, no. 12, p. 36.   [53] *PSRL*, vol. 1 (1928), col. 536.

[54] *NPL*, pp. 376–377 (Komissionnyi spisok).

[55] *PSRL*, vol. 15 (1922), pt. 1, cols. 139–141; vol. 18, pp. 129–131; *Skazaniia i povesti o Kulikovskoi bitve*, ed. L. A. Dmitriev and O. P. Likhacheva, Leningrad, Nauka, 1982, pp. 14–15 with variants on p. 374.

[56] *PSRL*, vol. 4, pt. 1 (1853), pp. 90–91, 95; vol. 4, pt. 1, fasc. 1 (1915), pp. 311–320; vol. 4, pt. 1, fasc. 2 (1925), pp. 321–325; vol. 8, pp. 34–39; *Skazaniia i povesti*, pp. 16–24 with variants on pp. 374–375.

[57] *Skazaniia i povesti*, pp. 25–127 with variants on pp. 375–378.

[58] *Skazaniia i povesti*, pp. 7–13 with variants on pp. 369–374. For an English translation, see Basil Dmytryshyn, *Medieval Russia: a Source Book, 850–1700*, 3rd edn, Fort Worth, TX, Holt, Rinehart, & Winston, 1990, pp. 202–209.

cerning the Life and Passing Away of Grand Prince Dmitrii Ivanovich).[59]
Significant fontological issues include dating the various accounts and
narratives, the relationship of these works to each other, and how far one
can backdate the various chronicle accounts by creating hypothetical
svody (compilations).

The generally accepted view is that the *Skazanie* derives from *PLP.*
S. K. Shambinago, among others, concluded that *KLP* also derived
from *PLP* and represented an abbreviated version of it.[60] Accordingly,
PLP was composed shortly after the battle, around 1381–1382, and
appeared first in the Compilation of 1448, while *KLP* was composed
later but included in the Compilation (*svod*) of 1408. The difficulty was
to explain how the earlier work showed up first in the later compilation,
and the later work in the earlier compilation. One way to resolve the
difficulty was to reverse the order of relationship between *PLP* and *KLP.*
Although Shakhmatov concluded that the Novgorod I Chronicle
account was composed between 1453 and 1462, that is, after the *svod* of
1448, he argued that it derived from an earlier *svod*, the hypothetical
Polichron of 1423.[61] *KLP*, which represented the *svod* of 1425, in turn,
derived from it and was expanded into the *PLP* in 1448.[62] Lur'e, after
an intensive study of fifteenth-century chronicle writing in Rus', proposed that we would do better to disregard the notion of intermediate
Muscovite *svody* between 1412 and 1448.[63] Thus, in Lur'e's scheme,
KLP derives from the *svod* of 1412 (effectively the *svod* of 1408), while
PLP derives from the *svod* of 1448. His contention has met with
opposition,[64] but his conclusions lent support to the textual studies of
those, like M. A. Salmina, who also argued that *KLP* is primary in

[59] *PSRL*, vol. 6, pp. 104–111, *PLDR. XIV–seredina XV veka*, pp. 208–229. For an
English translation, see *Medieval Russia's Epics, Chronicles and Tales*, rev. and enlarged,
ed. Serge A. Zenkovsky, New York, E. P. Dutton, 1974, pp. 316–322. Kloss has argued
that Epifanii Primudryi should be considered the compiler of the Troitskaia letopis'
(Trinity Chronicle). B. M. Kloss, "Determining the Authorship of the Trinity
Chronicle," *Medieval Russian Culture*, vol. 2, pp. 57–72. Kloss also asserted that
Epifanii wrote *Tale About the Battle of Kulikovo Field, Oration About the Life of Grand
Prince Dmitrii Ivanovich*, and others (*ibid.*, p. 72).

[60] S. K. Shambinago, "Povesti o Mamaevom poboishche," in *Sbornik Otdeleniia russkogo
iazyka i slovesnosti*, vol. 81, 1906, no. 7, pp. 81–83.

[61] A. A. Shakhmatov, *Obozrenie russkikh letopisnykh svodov XIV–XVI vv.*, Moscow and
Leningrad, Akademiia nauk SSSR, 1938, p. 171.

[62] A. A. Shakhmatov, *Otzyv o sochinenii S. K. Shambinago "Povesti o Mamaevom
poboishche"*, St. Petersburg, 1910, pp. 122–123, 132–137.

[63] Of the several times Lur'e has addressed this issue, see in particular Ia. S. Lur'e, "K
probleme svoda 1448 g.," *TODRL*, vol. 24, 1969, pp. 142–146; and Lur'e, *Obshcherusskoi letopisi*, pp. 36–121. For a fuller list, see Charles J. Halperin, *The Tatar Yoke*,
Columbus, OH, Slavica, 1986, p. 201 n. 15.

[64] For bibliography, see Halperin, *Tatar Yoke*, p. 202 n. 19.

relation to *PLP*.[65] Salmina has argued that these narratives of the Kulikovo cycle, which include the Expanded Chronicle Tale, the *Life of Dmitrii Donskoi*, the *Zadonshchina*, and the *Skazanie o Mamaevom poboishche*, must be dated no earlier than the 1440s.[66] I agree with her conclusions, for reasons both of textual criticism and of the anti-Tatar expressions in these texts.

I find no compelling reason to associate *KLP* with the *svod* of 1412 and thereby the *svod* of 1408, as Lur'e proposed. We have no indication from Priselkov's reconstruction of the Trinity Chronicle what its account contained, because his source, Karamzin, was silent about its account of the 1380 battle.[67] A possible explanation for Karamzin's silence is the Trinity Chronicle's containing no more information than is contained in the Suzdal' Chronicle. The latter account has nothing of an anti-Tatar bias about it, only a straightforward, brief description. Indeed, there is no compelling reason to associate *PLP* with the *svod* of 1448, or even conclude there was a *svod* of 1448. Few rules apply in hypothesizing *svody*. One can assign a hypothetical *svod* to the last entry date of a particular chronicle or even before that last entry date, but in no case after the date of the chronicle itself. Other than that, textologists pretty much make up the rules as they go along. For example, after arguing for the existence of the *svod* of 1448, Shakhmatov changed his mind on the basis of a personal letter he received from A. V. Markov.[68]

[65] M. A. Salmina, "Letopisnaia povest' o Kulikovskoi bitve i 'Zadonshchina,'" in *Slovo o polku Igoreve i pamiatniki Kulikovskogo tsikla. K voprosu o vremeni napisaniia 'Slova'*, ed. D. S. Likhachev and L. A. Dmitriev, Moscow and Leningrad, Nauka, 1966, pp. 360–363; M. A. Salmina, "Eshche raz o datirovke 'Letopisnoi povesti' o Kulikovskoi bitve," *TODRL*, vol. 32, 1977, pp. 3–39. At first, Salmina accepted the idea that *PLP* could have been composed in the 1430s, but later she opted for a date no earlier than the late 1440s. Halperin accepted Salmina's textual arguments in regard to the relationship of *KLP* to *PLP* but still held to the view that all these texts derive from the late fourteenth and early fifteenth centuries. Halperin, *Tatar Yoke*, pp. 97–103.

[66] M. A. Salmina, "'Slovo o zhitii i o prestavlenii velikogo kniaza Dmitriia Ivanovicha, tsaria Rus'skago,'" *TODRL*, vol. 25, 1970, pp. 81–104; Salmina, "K voprosu o datirovke 'Skazanie o Mamaevom poboishche,'" pp. 98–124; Salmina, "Eshche raz o datirovke 'Letopisnoi povesti'," pp. 3–39. See also Jaroslaw Pelenski, "The Origins of the Official Muscovite Claims to the 'Kievan Inheritance,'" *Harvard Ukrainian Studies*, vol. 1, 1977, p. 51; Jaroslaw Pelenski, "The Emergence of the Muscovite Claims to the Byzantine–Kievan 'Imperial Inheritance,'" *Harvard Ukrainian Studies* (= *Okeanos: Essays Presented to Ihor Ševčenko on his Sixtieth Birthday by His Colleagues and Students*), vol. 7, 1983, p. 521; V. A. Kuchkin "Pobeda na Kulikovom pole," *Voprosy istorii*, 1980, no. 8, p. 7; Halperin, "Russian Land," pp. 7–103; Ia. S. Lur'e, "O putiiakh dokazatel'stva pri analize istochnikov," *Voprosy istorii*, 1985, no. 5, pp. 64–65. Lur'e, *Dve istorii*, pp. 23–31.

[67] *TL*, p. 419 fn. 1.

[68] A. A. Shakhmatov, "Kievskii Nachal'nyi svod 1095 g.," Arkhiv Akademii nauk, fond 134, op. 1, no. 227 (unpublished article), cited in D. S. Likhachev, *Russkie letopisi i ikh kul'turno-istoricheskoe znachenie*, Moscow and Leningrad, Akademiia nauk SSSR, 1947, pp. 313, 448–449.

Shakhmatov then argued that the *svod* of 1448 was really a *svod* of the 1430s. And, as pointed out above, Shakhmatov was able to backdate the description of the Kulikovo battle in the Novgorod I Chronicle to 1423 by creating a hypothetical *svod* for that date. Lur'e attempted to reestablish the validity of the *svod* of 1448, but then treated this hypothetical construct as equivalent to an extant chronicle.

Instead, let us begin with the extant chronicles themselves. Those chronicles that testify to *KLP* and *PLP* can be dated no earlier than the end of the fifteenth century. By the time of the composition of *KLP*, when the Rus' Church was formalizing its autonomous status in relationship to the Byzantine Church, anti-Tatar remarks, such as references to the Tatars as "pagan," "godless," "Hagarenes," and so forth, begin to pepper narrative accounts. Then the *Skazanie*, written most likely in the late fifteenth century or later,[69] expands on these anti-Tatar sentiments. I would like to propose that *KLP* was not composed before 1449 for four reasons. First, its anti-Tatar epithets, like those of *PLP*, are out of place in the pre-1448 period of Byzantium-induced accommodation with the Tatars. Second, my text-critical analysis of the texts, which I could not present here, supports Shakhmatov's and Salmina's contention of a *KLP* → *PLP* progression. Third, the battle at Kulikovo Field was not given the huge importance at the time that it was given later. The catalyst, in my opinon, for revisiting the battle of 1380 and seeing it in a different light were the campaigns of the 1440s, in which Vasilii II faced a similar situation: battle with a Tatar army on one side and concern about an approaching Lithuanian army on the other. And fourth, we find no anti-Lithuanian or anti-Jagiełło sentiment expressed in *KLP* as there is in *PLP* and the *Skazanie*. Indeed, we also find none in the *The Life of Sergii Radonezhskii* (*Zhitiia Sergiia*), the Novgorod I Chronicle, the *Slovo o zhitii Dmitriia*, and *Zadonshchina*.

Thus, we have a sharp dichotomy in the works of the Kulikovo cycle: (1) those that condemn Jagiełło for his alliance with Mamai and (2) those that do not. The difference is not regionally marked, for both the *KLP* and the *PLP* are found in Novgorod-based chronicles. Instead, we must conclude that a change in relations among Muscovy, Novgorod, Poland-

---

[69] Zimin argues that the *Skazanie* borrowed from the short redaction of *Zadonshchina*, while the long redaction of *Zadonshchina*, which also derives from the short redaction, borrowed from the *Skazanie*. A. A. Zimin, "'Skazanie o Mamaevom poboishche' i 'Zadonshchina'," *Arkheograficheskii ezhegodnik za 1967 g.*, Moscow, Nauka, 1969, pp. 41–58; M. A. Salmina, "K voprosu o datirovke 'Skazaniia o Mamaevom poboishche,'" *TODRL*, vol. 29, 1974, pp. 98–124; A. I. Pliguzov, "Bitva na Kulikovom pole v svidetel'stvakh sovremennikov i v pamiati potomkov," in *Zhivaia voda Nepriadvy*, Moscow, Molodaia gvardiia, 1988, pp. 625–626. Shakhmatov proposed a date of composition for the *Skazanie* in the early sixteenth century. Shakhmatov, *Otzyv o sochinenii S. K. Shambinago "Povesti o Mamaevom poboishche"*, p. 177 (cf. p. 204).

Lithuania, and Tver' determined whether Jagiełło would be presented in a negative light. In 1449, Casimir IV, Polish king and Lithuanian grand duke, signed a treaty with Vasilii II.[70] He also signed one with Boris Aleksandrovich of Tver'.[71] As a result, from 1449 until the 1470s, exactly the period that *Slovo o zhitii Dmitriia* and the short redaction of *Zadonshchina* may have been written (and covering the period in which I think *KLP* was written), Muscovy and Poland-Lithuania enjoyed friendly relations. After Muscovite–Lithuanian relations deteriorated, around 1480, the authors of *PLP* and the *Skazanie* not only expanded on the anti-Tatar sentiment of the earlier round of texts but also began to invoke an anti-Lithuanian sentiment that was absent from these earlier texts. The catalyst for the second round of Kulikovo texts may have been the encounter with the Tatar Khan Aḥmed on the Ugra River. At that time Ivan III had to be concerned with a Lithuanian army approaching from the west, a situation reminiscent of Dmitrii in 1380 and of Vasilii II in the 1440s. Finally, the time of composition of the full version of *Zadonshchina* suggested by Zimin, the 1520s, coincides with the period of peaceful relations following the truce subsequently concluded between Vasilii III and the Polish king (and Lithuanian grand duke) Sigismund I.[72] Figure 7.1 "Relationship of texts of the Kulikovo cycle," depicts my understanding of the relationship and dates of these works.[73]

Comparison of the types of narratives about the Tatars that appear in the pre-1448 chronicles with those that appear in the chronicles that were compiled after 1448 demonstrates the determination of the later chroniclers to create a virtual past, in which the Tatars are presented as being intolerant of Christianity, as committing sacrileges against the Rus' Church, wantonly destroying life and property, and as being directly opposed in their excesses by the Rus' princes with military force.

An apparent exception to this general rule is the *Life* of the thirteenth-century prince of Iaroslavl', Fedor Rostislavich. The earliest form of the text is thought to date from the second half of the fifteenth century, because of the discovery of the relics of Fedor in 1463.[74] But, as Nikolai

---

[70] *DDG*, no. 53, pp. 160–163.   [71] *DDG*, no. 54, pp. 163–164.

[72] *SRIO*, vol. 35, pp. 642–672 (1523).

[73] For another diagram that depicts these texts in a similar relationship, but with a different dating based on accepting the existence of earlier *svody*, see Pliguzov, "Bitva na Kulikovom pole," p. 401. Both Pliguzov and I accept Zimin's conclusions concerning the relationship of the Short Redaction of *Zadonshchina*, as represented by the Kirillo–Belozersk (K–B) copy of the 1470s, and the Expanded Redaction of that same work with the *Skazanie o Mamaevom poboishche*.

[74] See e.g., V. O. Kliuchevskii, *Drevnerusskie zhitiia sviatykh kak istoricheskii istochnik*, Moscow, K. Soldatenkov, 1871, pp. 171–174; L. A. Dmitriev, "Zhitie Feodora Iaroslavskogo," *Slovar' knizhnikov i knizhnosti drevnei Rusi. XI–pervaia polovina XIV v.*, ed. D. S. Likhachev, Leningrad, Nauka, 1987, pp. 179–181.

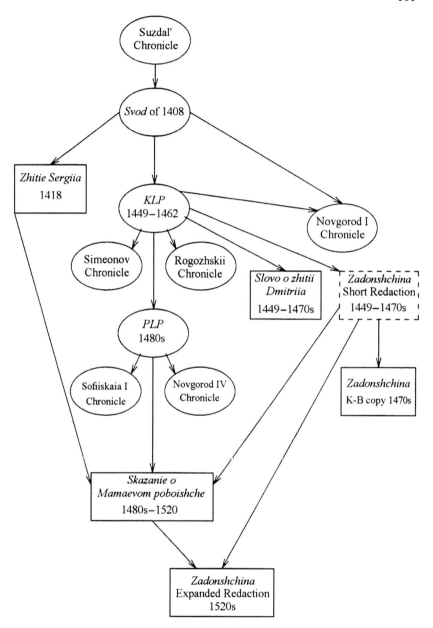

Fig. 7.1 *Relationship of texts of the Kulikovo cycle*

Serebrianskii suggested, it must have been based on an earlier narrative, perhaps from the fourteenth century.[75] It exhibits a positive if not benevolent attitude toward the Qipchaq khan and to the Tatars in general.[76] Fedor is requested by the khan to remain in Sarai because he likes him. There Fedor marries the khan's daughter and they have two sons – David and Konstantin. The khan then helps Fedor regain his principality of Iaroslavl', which in the meantime had been taken over by his son Mikhail. The description of such an attitude of humaneness on the part of a Tatar khan is definitely out of place in post-1448 ecclesiastical narrative literature. Either it represents a pro-Tatar faction in the Church in the second half of the fifteenth century, which is doubtful, or its basic version derives from an earlier time. Gail Lenhoff noted a difference in style in the *Zhitie* between the part dealing with Fedor's activities in the Horde and the rest of the text. She analyzed the various possible explanations for this difference and concluded that the part discussing Fedor's relationship with the khan and his marriage derives from local Iaroslavl' oral tradition from which the author, the monk Antonii, drew his evidence.[77] This part of the *Life of Fedor Rostislavich*, like pre-1448 chronicle accounts, indicates a Tatar regime that was tolerant of Christianity and protective of the Rus' Church.

As early as the entry for 1257, the Suzdal' Chronicle states that "hegumens, monks, priests, members of the clergy, and those who vow loyalty to the Holy Mother of God and the Lord" were not counted in the census. This means they were not subject to taxation.[78] When Rus' princes took over the duties of tax collection from Mongol *bāsqāq*s and their agents, they modified this Mongol policy of non-taxation. Churches and monasteries were now assessed for the general tax for

---

[75] N[ikolai] Serebrianskii, *Drevne-russkie kniazheskie zhitiia. (Obzor redaktsii i teksty)*, Moscow, Sinodal'naia tipografiia, 1915, pp. 227–229.

[76] *PSRL*, vol. 21, pt. 1, pp. 306–314; vol. 33, pp. 74–75; *VMCh*, vol. 2, cols. 1261–1282; Serebrianskii, *Drevne-russkie kniazheskie zhitiia*, Prilozhenie, pp. 90–92.

[77] Gail Lenhoff, *Early Russian Hagiography: the Lives of Prince Fedor the Black*, Berlin, Veroffentlichungen der Abteilung für slavische Sprachen und Literaturen des Osteurop-Instituts (Slavisches Seminar) an der Freien Universitat Berlin, 1997, pp. 112–120. My thanks to Professor Lenhoff for sending me a copy of the page proofs of her book before publication.

[78] *PSRL*, vol. 1 (1927), col. 475. This entry also appears in the Simeonov Chronicle, *PSRL*, vol. 18, p. 71 and the Nikon Chronicle, *PSRL*, vol. 10, p. 141. On the Tatar protection of the Church, see Vladimir Miliutin, "O nedvizhimykh imushchestvakh dukhovenstva v Rossii," *ChOIDR*, 1859, bk. 4, pp. 33–42. See also Sergei Hackel, "Under Pressure from the Pagans? – The Mongols and the Russian Church," in *The Legacy of St. Vladimir: Byzantium, Russia, America*, ed. J. Breck, J. Meyendorff, and E. Silk, Crestwood, NY, St. Vladimir's Seminary Press, 1990, pp. 47–56.

tribute to be sent to the Tatars, but were still exempt from other kinds of taxes.[79] The Church may, thus, have had an added financial reason why it would want Rus' princes to end tribute paying to the Qipchaq Khanate after 1448, although it is not possible to determine whether the amount of money involved was enough to have been a significant factor in influencing Church policy. Pre-1448 chronicle entries describe Tatar punitive raids against towns only in order to collect taxes, and as never being opposed by the Rus' princes either politically or with military force. A Rus' prince might find himself fighting Tatars as the result of conflict with another Rus' prince (often one of his brothers, uncles, or cousins) when the Tatar khan would support one Rus' prince against another. Or a Rus' prince might side with one Tatar faction against another in the Qipchaq Khanate.

Nonetheless, the Church, after 1448, would often attempt to have it both ways. Churchmen would invoke previous Mongol tolerance of the Rus' Church to their advantage when arguing against grand princely taxation or confiscation of Church lands. For example, the L'vov chronicler upbraided Muscovite princes and boyars by citing this Mongol protection: "But alack and alas, my tears flow greatly, for the holy churches received such favor [милость] from these faithless pagans. As for you, Orthodox princes and boyars, strive to show beneficence [благотворение показати] to the holy churches, lest on the day of judgment you be shamed by those barbarians."[80] The compiler of the Short Collection of Iarlyki from the Tatar khans expressed the same sentiment in his Afterword to the collection.[81] And the Church was not above forging documents to support its position, as in the case of the false iarlyk of Khan Özbeg to Metropolitan Peter.[82] Sections of this false iarlyk were used in the Council Answer of 1503 and in the Reply of Makarii in regard to grand-princely confiscation of church and monastic lands.[83] But the Church-concocted virtual past of Rus' princes trying to free the Rus' land from the Tatars is a post-1448 invention. In the chronicles, such a view appears only in interpolative passages of the late fifteenth and sixteenth centuries.

[79] See, e.g., "Ustavnaia dogovornaia gramota velikogo kniazia Vasiliia Dimitrievicha i mitropolita Kipriana," Pamiatniki russkogo prava, vol. 3, pp. 421–422, arts. 1 and 9.
[80] PSRL, vol. 20, p. 189.   [81] RFA, vol. 3, p. 594.
[82] P. P. Sokolov, "Podlozhnyi iarlyk khana Uzbeka mitropolitu Petru," Russkii istoricheskii zhurnal, no. 5, 1918, pp. 70–85. For an English translation of this forgery, see Reinterpreting Russian History: Readings 860–1860s, ed. Daniel H. Kaiser and Gary Marker, New York, Oxford University Press, 1994, pp. 101–102.
[83] Donald Ostrowski, "A 'Fontological' Investigation of the Church Council of 1503," Ph.D. Dissertation, Pennsylvania State University, 1977, pp. 174–176.

8   Fashioning the khan into a basileus

After 1448, an elaborate anti-Tatar ideology developed not only in the chronicles but also in Muscovite Church literature in general. From the mid-fifteenth century on, the Muscovite Church began to create an anti-Tatar propaganda that had been entirely absent earlier when the Byzantine Church supervised the policies of the Rus' Church. During that period Byzantium considered the Qipchaq Khanate to be an ally and trading partner, and the Rus' Church was obliged to act in accord with those considerations.

The earliest post-1448 literary works, such as the narratives of the Kulikovo cycle, are cautious in challenging Mongol legitimacy. In describing the events surrounding the battle at Kulikovo Pole on the Don River, they depict Emir Mamai as a usurper who wanted to kill Rus' princes, loot churches and monasteries, and in general destroy Rus'.[1] Halperin has pointed out that, in these narratives, Muscovy defends Chingizid legitimacy (and, by implication, Daniilovich legitimacy) against the usurper.[2]

Subsequently, after 1480, a letter, the *Poslanie na Ugru*, addressed to Ivan III and attributed to Vassian Rylo, the Archbishop of Rostov, turns up the anti-Tatar rhetoric a notch.[3] In the letter, Rylo criticizes Ivan's tactics and apparent vacillation in his confrontation in 1480 on the Ugra River with Ahmed, Khan of the Great Horde. The archbishop pleads with Ivan not to listen to "evil men" (злым человекам), who are advising peaceful negotiation with the Tatars. Rylo condemns the Tatar khan as "this godless and evil one who calls himself a tsar." Instead, Ivan, the "great Christian tsar of the Rus' lands" should lead the "sons

---

[1] *PSRL*, vol. 4, p. 75; *Povesti o Kulikovskoi bitvy*, pp. 44–47.
[2] Halperin, "Russian Land," p. 38.
[3] *PLDR. Vtoraia polovina XV veka*, pp. 522–537; *PSRL*, vol. 4, fasc. 2, pp. 517–523; vol. 6, pp. 225–230; vol. 8, pp. 207–213; vol. 12, pp. 203–212 (Shumilovskii copy); vol. 20, pt. 1, pp. 339–347; vol. 26, pp. 266–275. For a discussion of the fontological issues surrounding the *Poslanie na Ugru* and the *Stoianie na Ugru*, in particular the "vacillation" of Ivan III, see Lur'e, *Dve istorii Rusi*, pp. 168–195.

of Israel" in battle against the "godless Hagarenes."[4] As Cherniavsky pointed out, Rylo is promoting the Muscovite grand prince to the now vacant position of true tsar in order to combat the false tsar, the Tatar khan.[5] David Miller detected caution in Rylo's letter: "Vassian consciously refrained from delineating the qualities of a true Christian tsar with reference to Ivan III for fear that these qualities might have mistakenly been attributed to the Tatar khan who was also a tsar."[6] But Rylo's letter appears cautious only in retrospect when compared with the nature of the anti-Tatar rhetoric that was yet to come. One can, in this respect, contrast the rhetoric of Rylo's letter, on the one hand, with that of the historical tales about the "Stand on the Ugra" as well as the *Iarlyk of Aḥmed Khan*, on the other. The historical tales date from no earlier than the early sixteenth century.[7] The *Iarlyk* must be dated to the early seventeenth century, *pace* Keenan, who declared it to be "a historical ballad, in epistolary form" and connected it with other literary compositions on Turkic themes that emanated from the *Posol'skii prikaz* about that time.[8]

If the confrontation between Ivan III and Khan Aḥmed represented the overthrow of the Tatar yoke, then it seems odd that Rylo would criticize Ivan for his lack of action. The point is that the "Stand on the Ugra" of 1480, while significant enough in terms of steppe diplomacy of the time, was a non-event in terms of so-called "Muscovite independence" from Tatar rule.[9] By 1480, the Muscovite grand prince, Ivan III, had established himself more or less as an autonomous ruler. He still rendered tribute to the various khans, as a token of nominal subservience. That tribute continued to be sent to the khan of the

---

[4] *PSRL*, vol. 8, pp. 207–213.

[5] Cherniavsky, "Khan or Basileus," pp. 472–473.

[6] David B. Miller, "The Velikie Minei Cheti and the Stepennaia Kniga of Metropolitan Makarii and the Origins of Russian National Consciousness," *Forschungen zur Osteuropäischen Geschichte*, vol. 26, 1979, p. 335.

[7] Ia. S. Lur'e, "Novonaidennyi rasskaz o 'stoianii na Ugre,'" *TODRL*, vol. 18, 1962, pp. 289–293.

[8] Edward L. Keenan, "The *Jarlyk* of Axmed-Xan to Ivan III: a New Reading," *International Journal of Slavic Linguistics and Poetics*, vol. 12, 1969, pp. 44–47. On the literary works of the seventeenth-century *Posol'skii prikaz*, see M. D. Kagan, "'Povest' o dvukh posol'stvakh' – legendarno-politicheskoe proizvedenie nachala XVII veka," *TODRL*, vol. 11, 1955, pp. 218–254; M. D. Kagan, "Legendarnaia perepiska Ivana IV s turetskim sultanom kak literaturnyi pamiatnik pervoi chetverti XVII v.," *TODRL*, vol. 13, 1957, pp. 247–272; M. D. Kagan, "Legendarnyi tsikl gramot turetskogo sultana k evropeiskim gosudariam – publitsisticheskoe proizvedenie vtoroi poloviny XVII v.," *TODRL*, vol. 15, 1958, pp. 225–250; and Daniel Clarke Waugh, *The Great Turkes' Defiance: On the History of the Apocryphal Correspondence of the Ottoman Sultan in Its Muscovite and Russian Variants*, Columbus, OH, Slavica, 1978.

[9] This point has been made before. See, e.g., Keenan, "Muscovy and Kazan': Some Introductory Remarks," p. 549; Martin, *Medieval Russia*, p. 318.

Great Horde both before and after 1480 until its loss of independence in 1502. It was then sent to the Crimean Khan Mengli Girei.[10] The main result of the encounter on the Ugra was to set the annual tribute that Moscow paid at 1,000 rubles, in contrast to the 7,000 rubles it had previously paid. One other result may have been the disappearance of Arabic inscriptions on the coins Moscow minted; from about that time on, all such coins had inscriptions completely in Cyrillic.[11] The event on the Ugra River in 1480 was no more and no less than the same type of normal steppe diplomacy that had occurred a number of times earlier in the century across that and other rivers in the northeast, when, amidst much bluff and bluster, rival leaders met to negotiate a settlement.[12]

Crummey expressed surprise that the so-called "grand-princely" chronicles are critical of the actions of Ivan III at the Ugra River for failing to fight the Muslims.[13] He suggested that the "compilers took the story directly from a non-Muscovite source, possibly a Rostov ecclesiastical compilation, and failed, for some reason, to revise it." Instead, if we eliminate the notion that there were such things as grand-princely chronicles, in contrast to Church chronicles, a simpler explanation offers itself. That is, the Church intentionally maintained the criticism in the chronicles as a continued warning to reigning grand princes that reaching agreements with, or even hesitating to fight, the Muslim Tatars was not a good thing. The genius of Vassian Rylo was to turn a normal diplomatic event into a grand confrontation between Tatar (read: Muslim) oppression and Muscovite (read: Christian) independence. By the second half of the sixteenth century, however, Muscovite Church sources memorialize the "Stand on the Ugra" as one of the most significant events in the history of the world.[14] And in the seventeenth century, the author of the *Kazanskaia istoriia* enshrined the "overthrow of the Tatar yoke" into historical certitude by adding numerous fictional

---

[10] For the *vykhod* (tribute) of 1389, see *DDG*, no. 11, p. 31; no. 12, p. 35; no. 13, p. 38. For 1401–1402, see *DDG*, no. 16, p. 44; no. 17, p. 49. For 1433, see *DDG*, no. 29, p. 74. For 1481, see *DDG*, no. 72, p. 254; no. 73, p. 270. For 1486, see *DDG*, no. 81, p. 318; no. 82, p. 325. And for 1504, see *DDG*, no. 89, p. 362.

[11] G. B. Fedorov, "Moskovskie den'gi Ivana III i Vasiliia III," *Kratkie soobshcheniia o dokladakh i polevykh issledovaniiakh Instituta istorii material'noi kul'tury AN SSSR*, vol. 30, 1949, pp. 71–72.

[12] See, e.g., the confrontation of Vasilii I in 1409 with his father-in-law, Vytautas (Vitovt), Grand Duke of Lithuania. *PSRL*, vol. 11, p. 207; vol. 15 (1922), pt. 2, col. 474; vol. 18, p. 155.

[13] Crummey, *Formation of Muscovy*, p. 195.

[14] See the letter addressed to Ivan IV and variously attributed to Metropolitan Makarii or the priest Sil'vestr. D. P. Golokhvastov and Archimandrite Leonid, "Blagoveshchenskii ierei Sil'vestr i ego poslaniia," *ChOIDR*, 1874, bk. 1, pp. 71–72.

details.[15] Thus, the criticism that Rylo leveled against Ivan III now seems out of place because of the Church's subsequent reinterpretation of the significance of the event.

Other works from the late fifteenth century, especially the *Life of Merkurii of Smolensk*, the *Tale of Timur the Lame*,[16] and the *Tale of the Death of Batu*, pound hard on the anti-Tatar drum. In the *Life of Merkurii*, the phrase "yoke of slavery" (*rabotno igo*), applied to Tatar domination of Rus', first appears.[17] Narratives of the sixteenth century, like the *Tale of the Destruction of Riazan' by Batu*, intensify the rhetorical attacks.[18] Descriptions of Batu, as Halperin pointed out, are a particularly good indicator of this transformation.[19] Yet, I cannot completely agree with Halperin that "the image of Batu is a legitimate barometer of Russian attitudes toward the Tatars during the period of the 'Tatar yoke.'"[20] What ecclesiastical propagandists and ideologues articulated as the Church's position did not necessarily coincide with the general attitudes of the secular rulers or even of the population as a whole. It may, however, be seen as an accurate gauge of the Church's position. The secular elite of the Muscovite state was not necessarily in accord with the Church's political viewpoint.

The tendency in the historiography has been to equate pronouncements of Muscovite Churchmen with what "the Russians" believed. For

[15] *Kazanskaia istoriia*, ed. G. N. Moiseeva, Moscow and Leningrad, Akademiia nauk SSSR, 1954, p. 55–57; *PSRL*, vol. 19, cols. 6–8, 200–203.
[16] For the ordering and dating of the various redactions of the *Tale*, see David B. Miller, "How the Mother of God Saved Moscow from Timur the Lame's Invasion in 1395: the Development of a Legend and the Invention of a National Identity," *Forschungen zur osteuropäischen Geschichte*, vol. 50, 1995, pp. 247–265. For translation into English of two of the redactions, see *ibid.*, pp. 265–272.
[17] *PSRL*, vol. 21, pp. 262–263; L. T. Beletskii, "Literaturnaia istoriia povesti o Merkurii Smolenskom. Issledovaniia i teksty," *Sbornik Otdelenua russkogo iazyka i slovesnosti*, vol. 99, 1922, pp. 61–62. See *VMCh*, November 23–25, cols. 3297–3306.
[18] An edition of the text published according to the MS. RGB, Volokolamsk Collection, no. 526, can be found in *PLDR. XIII vek*, pp. 184–199. Although the *Tale* is extant only in copies from the sixteenth century, scholars have tried to find evidence that it was composed earlier. See, e.g., N. V. Vodovozov, "Povest' o razorenii Riazanii Batyem," *Uchenye zapiski Moskovskogo gorodskogo pedagogicheskogo instituta imeni V. P. Potemkina. Kafedra russkoi literatury*, vol. 18, no. 5, 1956, pp. 3–37; D. S. Likhachev, "Literaturnaia sud'ba 'Povesti o razorenii Riazani Batyem' v pervoi chetverti XV veka," in *Issledovaniia i materialy po drevnerusskoi literatury*, 6 vols., Moscow, Akademiia nauk SSSR, 1961–1980, vol. 1, ed. V. D. Kuz'mina, pp. 9–22; D. S. Likhachev, "K istorii slozheniia 'Povesti o razorenii Riazani Batyem,'" *Arkheograficheskii ezhegodnik za 1962 god*, Moscow, 1963, pp. 48–51; D. S. Likhachev, "'Zadonshchina' i 'Povest' o razorenii Riazani Batyem,'" in *Drevniaia Rus' i slaviane*, ed. T. V. Nikolaeva, Moscow, Nauka, 1978, pp. 366–370. Even if it drew on earlier works, the anti-Tatar rhetoric in it places its composition closer to the time of the extant copies.
[19] See Charles J. Halperin, "The Defeat and Death of Batu," *Russian History*, vol. 10, 1983, pp. 50–65.
[20] Halperin, "Defeat and Death of Batu," p. 50.

example, Vernadsky wrote: "The grim political situation required unity of the nation's effort; without it the task of freeing Russia from Mongol rule could not be achieved. This was well understood not only by many princes but by most of the people – boyars and commoners alike. They intuitively felt that only a strong ruler could lead them to victory."[21] While Vernadsky was an outstanding historian, one must question on what basis he asserts that he knew what the princes, boyars, and commoners "well understood" and "instinctively felt." One finds such views as freeing Rus' lands from the Tatars and supporting a strong ruler expressed only in ecclesiastical sources, not in secular sources of the time.

The Church did have some impact to be sure on political thought and actions in the secular sphere, but this impact, while significant, was limited. Secular figures through the sixteenth century may have held in common an unarticulated political thought system (or ideology) that was Mongol based and that contrasted with the Byzantine-based theories of the Church. Periods of open hostility in the Church sources toward the Tatars can be seen to represent implicit criticism of the Mongol principle in Muscovite government, for example, in the Boyar Council's ability to limit the power of the ruler. A council of state, such as the Boyar Council, did not exist formally in Byzantium, which Church bookmen were using as the model for their ideal secular government. But it did exist in the Qipchaq Khanate in the divan of the four *qaračï beys*. The Church's opposition to the Boyar Council diminished, however, as the Church leaders found the boyars more in agreement with their own position.

Along with anti-Tatar propaganda, we also find that, during the second half of the fifteenth century, ecclesiastical writers began touting Muscovy as the inheritor of Kievan Rus'. The *Oration Concerning the Life of Dmitrii Donskoi*, for example, made the Kievan connection by, among other things, indicating that Vladimir I as well as Boris and Gleb were Dmitrii's ancestors, and comparing Dmitrii Donskoi's battle with Mamai to Iaroslav's battle with his half-brother Sviatopolk.[22] *Zadonshchina*, likewise, makes explicit the genealogical connection between Dmitrii and the Kievan princes, including Vladimir I, Iaroslav, and Igor'.[23] And the author of the Rogozhskii Chronicle account of Edigei's invasion of 1408 alludes to the "lesson" of Sil'vestr, the compiler of the *Povest' vremennykh let*, against trusting individuals like Edigei.[24] The Muscovite Church at this time also showed a particular interest in the

[21] Vernadsky, *Mongols and Russia*, p. 350.
[22] *PLDR. XIV–seredina XV veka*, pp. 208, 212.   [23] *Skazaniia i povesti*, pp. 7–8.
[24] *PSRL*, vol. 15 (1922), pt. 1, col. 185; vol. 18, p. 159.

Life of Constantine (St. Cyril, Apostle of the Slavs). It is from late fifteenth-century Muscovy that the earliest extant copies date.[25] This fact has led Harvey Goldblatt to look again at the phrase "роусьскыми писмены" ("Rus'ian writing") that appears in every copy of the *Life of Constantine*, but which has been thought by a number of scholars to represent a metathesis of the primary form "соурьскыми" (Syrian). Goldblatt suggested "роусьскыми" be accepted as the primary reading but stopped short of arguing that the *Life of Constantine* was composed in the late fifteenth century.[26] Even if we accept the traditional date of composition of the *Life of Constantine*, that is, the ninth century, the fact that none of the sixty or so extant copies date earlier than the late fifteenth century from East Slavic territory is indicative of some kind of literary revival. And the practitioners of that literary revival began looking to the ecclesiastical antecedents of the Muscovite Church, not only to Kiev but to Byzantium as well.

Keenan has argued against the notion that there was any revival of Muscovite interest in Kiev during this period. He pointed out, for example, that in V. B. Kobrin's list of almost 3000 names in the court rolls of the sixteenth century, we find no one with the "Kievan" names Igor', Sviatoslav, or Mstislav, and relatively few Vladimirs and Glebs. Keenan then stated: "A Muscovite courtier of Ivan's time was more likely to be called Temir or Bulgak than Vladimir or Gleb or Vsevolod."[27] Yet on Kobrin's lists, Vladimir seems to be a much more popular name than either Bulgak or Temir, as there are twenty-eight people named Vladimir, while only seven are named Bulgak and five named Temir.[28] Keenan does not account for the relative popularity of the "Kievan" name Boris (fifty-three times, tied for fifteenth on the list), nor for the relative unpopularity of the "Muscovite" name Sergei (four times, tied for forty-fourth on the list). It seems to me that it is mainly

[25] Kliment Ohridski, *S"brani s"chineniia*, Sofiia, ed. B. St. Angelov, K. M. Kuev, and Kh. Kodov, 3 vols., Sofia, Bulgarska akademiia na naukite, 1970–1973, vol. 3, pp. 34–45.

[26] Harvey Goldblatt, "On 'rusьskymi pismeny' in the *Vita Constantini* and Rus'ian Religious Patriotism," *Studia Slavica Mediaevalia et Humanistica Riccardo Picchio dicata*, ed. M. Colucci, G. Dell'Agata, and H. Goldblatt, Rome, Edizioni Dell'ateneo, 1986, pp. 311–328; and Harvey Goldblatt, "History and Hagiography: Recent Studies on the Text and Textual Tradition of the *Vita Constantini*," in *Kamen" kraeug"l'n"*, pp. 158–179.

[27] Edward L. Keenan, "On Certain Mythical Beliefs and Russian Behaviors," in *The Legacy of History in Russia and the New States of Eurasia*, ed. S. Frederick Starr, Armonk, NY, M. E. Sharpe, 1994, p. 23.

[28] V. B. Kobrin, "Genealogiia i antroponimika (po russkim materialam XV–XVI vv.)," in *Istoriia i genealogiia. S. B. Veselovskii i problemy istoriko-genealogicheskikh issledovanii*, ed. N. I. Pavlenko et al., Moscow, Nauka, 1977, pp. 87, 89–90.

Church writers, not the secular elite, who are exhibiting an interest in Kiev during this period. What the secular elite named their children had little to do with politics in high Church circles. Although Keenan does not make the connection here, this difference could be evidence in support of his "two cultures" theory, that is, the "rather sharp contrast between secular and religous cultures" in the sixteenth century.[29] Finally, Kobrin's lists indicate that the fourteen most popular names, from Ivan, Vasilii, and Andrei to Danila, Timofei, and Afanasii, are all derivatives of Byzantine names or Byzantine forms of biblical names. Only at number fifteen/sixteen on the list (fifty-two examples) do we find a name with a Slavic provenance, Boris. The next name with a Slavic provenance occurs at number eighteen on the list (forty-five examples), Bogdan, followed by Vladimir, number twenty-one (twenty-eight examples). Although it is risky to use the names of sixteenth-century courtiers as a reflection of interest or lack of interest in Kiev among the secular elite, the naming of children in that elite demonstrates the strong Church influence on popular culture.

It is from this period that the Church begins to formulate the concept of the oppressiveness of Tatar rule over the Rus' land (Русская земля), defined as including Kiev, Novgorod, Moscow, and other towns that made up the territory under the jurisdiction of the Rus' metropolitan. Pelenski attributed the newly found interest in Kiev to the Muscovite reaction against the Council of Florence, which the Muscovites saw as a betrayal of Orthodoxy, and to the fall of Constantinople itself. But it could also be seen as the Church's harking back to a pre-Mongol age before the Rus' ruler owed allegiance to the Qipchaq khan. It may be indicative of the Church's newly found interest in Kiev that when the Crimean Tatar khan, Mengli Gerei, sacked Kiev in 1482, he sent the chalices of the St. Sophia Cathedral to Ivan III, which Ivan may have requested at the behest of the Church.[30] Otherwise, he would have kept them for himself. By contrast, it is unlikely Ivan III would have encouraged Mengli Girei to attack Kiev if, at that time, he had had any interest in Kiev as a precursor to the Muscovite polity. The Church's newly found interest in Kiev was not shared by the secular authorities.

---

[29] Edward L. Keenan, *The Kurbskii-Groznyi Apocrypha: the Seventeenth-Century Genesis of the "Correspondence" Attributed to Prince A. M. Kurbskii and Tsar Ivan IV*, Cambridge, MA, Harvard University Press, 1971, pp. 53–54.

[30] *PSRL*, vol. 6, p. 234; vol. 20, pt. 1, p. 349; vol. 26, pp. 274–275; Jaroslaw Pelenski, "The Sack of Kiev of 1482 in Contemporary Muscovite Chronicle Writing," *Harvard Ukrainian Studies*, vol. 3/4, 1979–80, pp. 638–649. The Nikon Chronicle places the sack of Kiev under 1484, but says nothing about the chalices. *PSRL*, vol. 12, p. 215.

The reassertion of the Kievan antecedents of the Muscovite grand princes came to fruition in the Monomakh legend. By the first half of the sixteenth century, the Byzantium–Kiev–Moscow connection found formal exposition in the complex of texts associated with the *Skazanie o kniaz'iakh vladimirskikh* (*Story About the Vladimir Princes*).[31] R. P. Dmitrieva dated the composition of the *Skazanie* to the period between the late 1520s and 1533.[32] She argued that the *Skazanie* derives from another work, the *Poslanie Spiridona-Savvy* (*Letter of Spiridon-Savva*), the composition of which she placed slightly earlier than that of the *Skazanie*, that is, 1511–1521.[33] Zimin took issue with R. P. Dmitrieva's argument concerning the relationship of the *Skazanie* to the *Poslanie*. He argued that both works derived from a common source, called the Chudov *Povest'* (because it is contained in a manuscript in the Chudov Collection of the State Historical Museum in Moscow).[34] Zimin placed the composition of the *Povest'* around 1498, the year when Dmitrii Ivanovich was crowned co-ruler, because the first mention of the crown as the Cap of Monomakh is in the chronicle accounts of that investiture.[35] Lur'e questioned Zimin's dating of the Chudov *Povest'* to 1498. He suggested, instead, that a no-longer-extant "Tver' variant" of the Monomakh legend dating to 1498 was the source of the *Povest'*.[36]

A. L. Gol'dberg differed with Dmitrieva, Zimin, and Lur'e concerning the relationship of texts and the dating of them. Gol'dberg pointed out that, although the *Poslanie* contains some primary readings in relation to the *Skazanie*, the *Skazanie* also contains some primary readings in

[31] The best edition of the *Skazanie* is in R. P. Dmitrieva, *Skazanie o kniaz'iakh vladimirskikh*, Moscow and Leningrad, Akademiia nauk SSSR, 1955, pp. 171–181.

[32] Dmitrieva, *Skazanie*, pp. 91–109; R. P. Dmitrieva, "K istorii sozdaniia 'Skazaniia o kniaz'iakh vladimirskikh,'" *TODRL*, vol. 17, 1961, pp. 342–347; R. P. Dmitrieva, "O tekstologicheskikh zavisimosti mezhdu raznymi vidami rasskaza o potomkakh Avgusta i o darakh Monomakha," *TODRL*, vol. 30, 1976, pp. 217–230.

[33] For the text of the *Poslanie*, see Dmitrieva, *Skazanie*, pp. 159–170. For a summary of the arguments favoring the primacy of the *Poslanie*, see Jack V. A. Haney, "Moscow – Second Constantinople, Third Rome, or Second Kiev? (The Tale of the Princes of Vladimir)," *Canadian Slavic Studies*, vol. 3, 1968, p. 356.

[34] A. A. Zimin, review of R. P. Dmitrieva, *Skazanie o kniaz'iakh vladimirskikh*, in *Istoricheskii arkhiv*, 1956, no. 3, pp. 236–237; A. A. Zimin, "Antichnye motivy v russkoi publitsistike kontsa XV v.," *Feodal'naia Rossiia vo vsemirno-istoricheskom protsesse. Sbornik statei, posviashchennyi L'vy Vladimirovichu Cherepninu*, ed. V. T Pashuto et al., Moscow, Nauka, 1972, pp. 128–138; parts reprinted in A. A. Zimin, *Rossiia na rubezhe XV–XVI stoletii (Ocherk sotsial'no-politicheskoi istorii)*, Moscow, Nauka, 1982, pp. 152–159. Zimin listed twenty-three significant differences among the three texts. Zimin, "Antichnye motivy," pp. 130–131. The text of the Chudov *Povest'* can be found in two MSS: GIM, Chudov no. 264 (1540s) and RGB, Rumiantsev no. 253, and was published in Dmitrieva, *Skazanie o kniaz'iakh vladimirskikh*, pp. 196–200.

[35] *PSRL*, vol. 6, pp. 241–243; vol. 8, pp. 234–236; vol. 12, pp. 246–248; vol. 20, pt. 1, pp. 366–368; vol. 28, pp. 330–331; and *Ioasafovskaia letopis'*, pp. 134–137.

[36] Lur'e, *Ideologicheskaia bor'ba*, pp. 386–390.

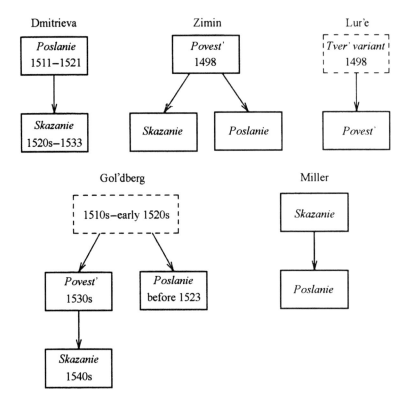

Fig. 8.1: *Proposed relationship of texts associated with* Skazanie o kniaz'iakh
vladimirskikh

relation to the *Poslanie*.[37] He agreed with Zimin and Lur'e to the extent
that the *Skazanie* derives from the Chudov *Povest'*, but he concluded
that both the *Povest'* and the *Poslanie* derive from a common source, a
no-longer-extant protograph, which he dated no earlier than the 1510s
or early 1520s. He dated the composition of the *Poslanie* to before 1523,
the composition of the Chudov *Povest'* to the 1530s, and the composition of the *Skazanie* itself to the end of the 1540s.[38] Miller rejected all

[37] A. L. Gol'dberg, "K istorii rasskaza o potomkakh Avgusta i o darakh Monomakha,"
TODRL, vol. 30, 1976, p. 211. For example, the *Poslanie* clears up some murky
passages in the *Skazanie*. It is more likely a scribe would clear up murky passages than
that another scribe would take clear passages and make them murky. The *Poslanie* has
more information about certain individuals, and it is more likely this information was
added in the *Poslanie* than that it was eliminated in the *Skazanie*.

[38] Gol'dberg, "K istorii rasskaza o potomkakh Avgusta i o darakh Monomakha," pp.
211–215.

these previous conclusions as unconvincing and reversed Dmitrieva's conjectured relationship between the *Poslanie* and the *Skazanie*.[39] Although we find no scholarly consensus about the relationship of these texts, we can tentatively accept Gol'dberg's view concerning the earliest appearance of the Monomakh legend. The drawback to Gol'dberg's dating of its first appearance was his not addressing the issue of the reference to the Cap of Monomakh in the crowning of Dmitrii in 1498. As both Zimin and Lur'e pointed out, one would expect a written justification for the use of the Monomakh cap and regalia at the time they were being used, not some twelve to twenty years later. That drawback to Gol'dberg's dating was eliminated, however, some years later. I. A. Tikhoniuk described and dated four redactions of the *Chin venchaniia* (*Ceremony of Crowning*): (1) *Prostrannaia* (before February 4, 1498); (2) *Formuliarnaia* (1511–1518); (3) *Chudovskaia* (1510s–early 1540s); and (4) *Letopisnaia* (1518–early 1520s). Both the *Prostrannaia* redaction and the *Formuliarnaia* redaction refer to the crown merely as a *shapka*. In the *Chudovskaia* redaction and the *Letopisnaia* redaction, the phrase *shapka Monomakha* is introduced. But, according to Tikhoniuk, both these redactions derive from the *Formuliarnaia* redaction, and the *Letopisnaia* redaction appears no earlier than the *svod* of 1518. Tikhoniuk attributed the introduction of "*shapka Monomakha*" to their redactors' familiarity with the early version of the Monomakh legend.[40] Thus, all the evidence points to the appearance of the Monomakh legend in Muscovite sources no earlier than the 1510s.

The complex of texts associated with the *Skazanie* has five major components to it: (1) a genealogy of the descendants of Noah; (2) a "creative" story about Augustus Caesar, with the message that the Riurikids are descendants of Augustus' kinsman Prus';[41] (3) the legend about the dispatch by the Byzantine Emperor Constantine Monomachos (1042–1055) of the crown and other items to the Grand Prince of Kiev Vladimir Vsevolodovich Monomakh (1113–1125); (4) an account of the excommunication of the Western Church by the Eastern Church in 1054; and (5) a genealogy of the Lithuanian princes. The author of

[39] David B. Miller, "Creating Legitimacy: Ritual, Ideology, and Power in Sixteenth-Century Russia," *Russian History*, vol. 21, 1994, pp. 302–303 fn. 21.

[40] I. A. Tikhoniuk, "Chin postavleniia Dmitriia-vnuka," *RFA*, vol. 3, pp. 604–607. Cf. Herberstein, *Zapiski o Moskovii*, pp. 302–303 n. 183–183 (by Pliguzov and Tikhoniuk). Published versions of the first three redactions can be found in *RFA*, vol. 3, pp. 608–625. My thanks to Pliguzov for bringing Tikhoniuk's article to my attention.

[41] The epithet "kinsman" (сродник) appears only in the *Skazanie*, not in the *Poslanie*, where it is left unclear at that point what relationship Prus' had to Augustus although Spiridon-Savva does clarify that relationship later in his letter. Dmitrieva, *Skazanie o kniaz'iakh vladimirskikh*, pp. 162, 175.

this complex of texts plays fast and loose with historical accuracy and is unconcerned with chronological impossibilities.[42] The third component of the complex of texts, the Legend of Monomakh, recounted how the Muscovite grand princes received their authority from the Byzantine emperors, in this case Constantine Monomachos, and how they were descended from the family of Augustus Caesar. It provides an ancient genealogical lineage for the Muscovite ruler and a Byzantine provenance for the grand-princely crown, as well as a justification for the Muscovite grand prince to designate himself *tsar'*. The genealogical connection with Augustus Caesar may have had an appeal to those entering Muscovite service from the Polish-Lithuanian Commonwealth, where the Roman Empire was held in high esteem.[43] In the legend of Monomakh section of the *Skazanie* complex, Constantine Monomachos' message to Vladimir Monomakh is:

we seek peace and love from your Highness so that the Church of God may be untroubled and all Orthodoxy may be peaceful under the existing power of our tsardom and of your independent autocracy [вольнаго самодержавъства] of Great Rus', for you may be called from now on God-crowned tsar', coronated with the imperial crown by the hand of the Most Holy Metropolitan Lord Neophytos and the bishops. And from this time Grand Prince Vladimir Vsevolodovich was known as Monomakh, tsar of Great Rus' . . . And thus even to the present day the Grand Princes of Vladimir are crowned with the imperial crown that the Greek tsar Constantine Monomakh sent.[44]

Likewise, the *Skazanie* complex provided a Byzantine provenance for the grand-princely crown, but the author manages to overlook the fact that Vladimir Monomakh was grand prince of Kiev, not of Vladimir, when he was supposed to have received the crown. His son, Iurii Dolgorukii, the traditional founder of Moscow, was Prince of Vladimir and head of the most junior branch of the Monomachi. Members of that branch were almost shut out from being in line to succeed to the Kievan grand-princely throne. This consideration led Iurii to take Kiev by force

---

[42] For example, the *Skazanie* has Julius Caesar send his "brother" Augustus to battle Antony in Egypt. But Octavian (Augustus) was Julius Caesar's nephew and adopted son, and when Octavian went to battle Antony, Julius Caesar was no longer alive. It lists among the slayers of Julius Caesar both Pompey and Crassius. But both Pompey and Crassius were dead in 44 BC; the author may have confused Crassius with Cassius, who was indeed among the slayers. The Emperor Constantine Monomachos could not have sent crown and regalia to Vladimir Vsevolodovich when he was grand prince, since Constantine died when Vladimir was two years old, fifty-eight years before he became grand prince. Neither was Hilarion patriarch of Constantinople nor was Formosus pope in 1054, as the author states.

[43] M. E. Bychkova, "Obshchie traditsii rodoslovnykh legend praviashchikh domov Vostochnoi Evropy," in *Kul'turnye sviazi narodov Vostochnoi Evropy v XVI v.*, Moscow, Nauka, 1976, pp. 292–303.

[44] Dmitrieva, *Skazanie o kniaz'iakh vladimirskikh*, pp. 165, 177.

in 1149 and again in 1151, and finally to become Grand Prince of Kiev in 1154 after the death of Iziaslav, the reigning grand prince. Thus, the crown would accordingly belong to the grand princes of Kiev, not of Vladimir. Yet, the crown in question, the so-called *shapka Monomakha* ("Cap of Monomakh"), was of Central Asian manufacture and most likely had no connection with Constantine Monomachos, Vladimir Monomakh, or Iurii Dolgorukii. The earliest mention of it is from 1341, in the Testament of Ivan Kalita, where it is called the *shapka zolotaia* ("Golden Cap").[45] It continues to be mentioned as the "Golden Cap" in the Testaments of Ivan II, Dmitrii, Vasilii I, and Vasilii II, but not in Ivan III's Testament (presumably because the crown had already been passed on to his co-ruler, Vasilii III).[46] Anthony Jenkinson, who saw Ivan IV wear it during the Epiphany Ritual of January 1558, referred to it as "a crown . . . of the Tatarian fashion."[47] It appears in the Testament of Ivan IV as the "Cap of Monomakh."[48] This cooptation by the Church of the crown's origin, Byzantine rather than Mongol, provides an apt symbol of the entire process of the Church's cooptation of Muscovy's virtual past.

From its inception in the 1510s, the Monomakh legend received widespread and official acceptance. Heberstein's reference to "certain insignia which are used at the present day at the inauguration of princes" that was bequeathed by Vladimir Monomakh may be an allusion to the Monomakh legend contained in the *Skazanie* complex.[49] If so, it is independent confirmation that the Monomakh legend was known in Moscow in either the 1510s or 1520s when Herberstein was there. More likely, it was the earlier decade, since the Patriarch of Constantinople Theoleptos referred to Vasilii III as *tsar'* when he sent a delegation to Muscovy in 1516–17 to request donations.[50] By the mid-1550s, the murals on the ceiling of the Throne Room in the kremlin's

---

[45] For an analysis of its provenance, see A. A. Spitsyn, "K voprosu o Monomakhovoi shapke," *Zapiski Russkogo arkheologicheskogo obshchestva. Otdelenie russkoi i slavianskoi arkheologii*, vol. 7, pt. 1, 1906, pp. 152–163. For the Testament of Ivan I, see *DDG*, no. 1, pp. 8, 10.

[46] *DDG*, no. 4, pp. 16, 18; no. 8, p. 25; no. 12, p. 36; no. 20, p. 57; no. 21, p. 59; no. 22, p. 61; and no. 61, p. 197. The Testament of Vasilii III is no longer extant.

[47] Anthony Jenkinson, "The Voyage to Russia in 1557," in *Rude & Barbarous Kingdom*, p. 55.

[48] *DDG*, no. 104, p. 433.

[49] Herberstein, *Notes upon Russia*, vol. 1, p. 17. Likewise, his statement that "The Russians boast that these brothers [Riurik, Sineus, and Truvor] derived their origin from the Romans, from whom even the present prince of Russia asserts that he is sprung," appears to be a reference to the Augustus' story. Herberstein, *Notes upon Russia*, vol. 1, p. 9.

[50] The document called Vasilii "the most exalted and benevolent tsar and great king of the whole Orthodox land of Great Rus'." *AI*, vol. 1, no. 121, p. 175.

Zolotaia palata (Golden Palace) depicted, among other things, the transfer of the regalia to Monomakh.[51] The throne of the tsar in the kremlin's Uspenskii Cathedral portrays sixteen reliefs concerning the life of Vladimir Monomakh and the transfer of the regalia.[52] Visual imagery was a particularly effective medium for getting the Church's political message across to illiterate and semi-literate boyars. In 1556, an embassy from Ivan IV to the Polish king, Sigismund II, justified Ivan's adoption of the title *tsar'* by referring not only to the legends of Prus' and Monomakh but also to Ivan's recent acquisition of the Tatar khanates of Kazan' and Astrakhan'.[53] And when he made his request to the patriarch of Constantinople in 1557 to recognize the title *tsar'*, Ivan IV again cited his conquests of Kazan' and Astrakhan' as justification.[54] These references in court documents indicate that, to Ivan IV and his chancery, his conquests of Kazan' and Astrakhan' were at least as important as the Monomakh legend in claiming the title *tsar'*. By contrast, the Church sources do not mention these conquests as justification for adoption of the title. And in 1561, the Patriarch of Constantinople, Josephus II, accepted the Monomakh legend as a basis on which formally to recognize Ivan IV as tsar.[55]

While the head of the Rus' Church was no longer appointed by the Patriarch of Constantinople after 1448 and the grand prince of Rus' was

[51] O. A. Pobedova, *Moskovskaia shkola zhivopisi pri Ivane IV raboty v Moskovskom kremle 40-kh–70-kh godov XVI v.*, Moscow, Nauka, 1972, appendix by K. K. Lopialo, pp. 193–198; Frank Kämpfer, "Russland an der Schwelle zur Neuzeit Kunst, Ideologie und historisches Bewusstein unter Ivan Groznyj," *Jahrbücher für Geschichte Osteuropas*, vol. 23, 1975, pp. 505–514; Miller, "Creating Legitimacy," pp. 304–305. Daniel Rowland reported on the significance of the murals in his paper "The Political Messages of the Golden Palace," delivered at the 27th AAASS Convention in Washington, DC, October 29, 1995.

[52] I. Zabelin and V. Shchepkin, *Tron ili Tsarskoe mesto Groznogo v Moskovskom Uspenskom sobore*, Moscow, Sinodal'naia tipografiia, 1909. Michael Flier reported on the significance of the throne in his paper "The Throne of Monomakh: Cathedra Ex Cathedra," delivered at the 27th AAASS Convention in Washington, DC, October 29, 1995.

[53] *SRIO*, vol. 59, no. 33, p. 519. According to Dvornik, this shows that Ivan IV was not "fully conscious of a Byzantine heritage." Dvornik, *Slavs in European History*, p. 377.

[54] *Sobornaia gramota dukhovenstva pravoslavnoi vostochnoi tserkvi, utverzhdaiushchaia san tsaria za velikim kniazem Ioannom IV Vasil'evichem, 1561 goda*, ed. M. A. Obolenskii, Moscow, Sinodal'naia tipografiia, 1850, p. 33. Contrary to the assertion of Chaev, there is no reference or allusion to Third Rome in Ivan's request. Nor is there any attempt to justify adoption of the title *tsar'* by appeal to Third Rome. N. S. Chaev, "'Moskva – tretii Rim' v politicheskoi praktike moskovskogo pravitel'stva XVI veka," *Istoricheskie zapiski*, 1945, no. 17, pp. 18–19. This is a typical example of the extravagant claims made by some nineteenth- and twentieth-century historians for the importance of Third Rome, completely unsupported by the evidence.

[55] *RIB*, vol. 22, cols. 68–69; *Sobornaia gramota*, pp. 17–18, 23.

no longer appointed by the Qipchaq khan after 1462, Church bookmen, nonetheless, had to work hard to establish an ideological legitimacy for an independent, sovereign Rus' monarchy. The secular ruling elite seems not to have been eager to fill the role that the Church was fashioning for it because it still held on to a residual Mongol/steppe orientation, according to which only Chingizids could be tsars. As late as the 1660s, Grigorii Kotoshikhin, who had been an official in the Posol'skii prikaz for at least nineteen years, wrote that Ivan IV acquired the title *tsar'* as a result of conquering the Kazan', Astrakhan', and Siberian khanates, that is, the successor states of the Qipchaq Khanate.[56] Notably, he mentions neither the Monomakh legend nor the supposed genealogical connection with Augustus Caesar as a reason, and we can suppose his views on this matter conform to those within the Posol'skii prikaz at the time.

What we find in the Church sources after 1448, by contrast, are concerted and persistent attempts on the part of Churchmen to modify certain aspects of this Mongol-based political practice of the Muscovite secular authorities,[57] or at least to provide a Byzantine-based theoretical justification as a substitute. The metropolitan, as head of the Church, pushed for the Muscovite grand prince to adopt the words *samoderzhets* (autocrat) and *tsar'* (emperor), which would accord with *autokrator* and *basileus*, respectively, in the title given to the Byzantine emperor. In 1492, Metropolitan Zosima began to use *samoderzhets* when referring to the grand prince.[58] Marc Szeftel pointed out that, significantly, the Muscovite rulers did not use *samoderzhets* as part of their official title: "[o]nly the spokesman of the church consistently used this term when addressing the monarch or speaking about him, from 1492 on."[59] It was not until 1591 that the term *samoderzhets* was officially added by the

---

[56] Kotoshikhin, *O Rossii*, p. 1.
[57] See, e.g., the abolishing of *tarkhannye gramoty* (fiscal immunity charters) in the *Sudebnik of 1550*. *Sudebniki XV–XVI vekov*, p. 153, art. 43, and the commentary on pp. 223–232, esp. pp. 227–228, where Metropolitan Makarii's opposition to *tarkhan* is described. See also I. I. Smirnov, "Sudebnik 1550 goda," *Istoricheskie zapiski*, vol. 24, 1947, pp. 322–330. According to Kashtanov, however, *tarkhannye gramoty* may have been abolished because the *sokha* was only then being defined in terms of a specific number of *chetverti*. This precise definition of land area, thus, made it easier for immunity-holders themselves to deliver the taxes to the central authorities. S. M. Kashtanov, "The Centralised State and Feudal Immunities in Russia," *Slavonic and East European Review*, vol. 49, 1971, p. 251.
[58] "Mitropolita Zosimy izveshchenie o paskhalii na os'muiu tysiachu let," *RIB*, vol. 6, no. 118, col. 799. See Marc Szeftel, "The Title of the Muscovite Monarch Up to the End of the Seventeenth Century," *Canadian–American Slavic Studies*, vol. 13, 1979, p. 65.
[59] Szeftel, "Title of the Muscovite Monarch," p. 66.

chanceries to the ruler's title, and then, at first, only for foreign affairs.[60] The term was adopted for domestic usage in 1598.[61]

A parallel development occurs in relation to the use of *tsar'* in that others applied it to the Muscovite ruler long before he adopted it for himself. In Church literature from the second half of the fifteenth century on, the term *tsar'* was used not only in relation to the current grand prince, but retroactively to grand princes as far back as Dmitrii Donskoi. The *Oration Concerning the Life of Dmitrii*, incorporated into the chronicles in the 1470s, refers to Dmitrii as *tsar'* nine times.[62] This was part of the Church's attempt to mythlogize Dmitrii as the implacable foe of the Tatars, much the same way the Spanish Church mythlogized El Cid as the implacable foe of the Muslims.[63] And as we saw, in the early sixteenth century, the author of the *Skazanie o kniaz'iakh vladimirskikh* pushes the appellation *tsar'* back to the twelfth century to Vladimir Monomach.

The secular administration seems to have been reluctant to accept the addition of *tsar'* to the title of the grand prince, since its formal adoption does not take place until 1547. The term *tsar'* was used from time to time before then in documents sent both to and from the grand prince. While a number of historians have pointed out this practice, none has provided an adequate explanation for the seemingly sporadic and random usage.[64] Skrynnikov, for example, has suggested that Ivan III "confined its use to relations with the Livonian Order and a few German princes" because he "[a]ssum[ed] that adjacent states would refuse to recognize it."[65] But this is an incorrect statement, for Ivan III did use the title *tsar'* on other occasions, for example, in 1484 and 1488, in his letters to Zakhariia, a Genoese merchant in Kiev, and in 1485, in a letter to another merchant, Khodja Asan.[66] And leaders of "adjacent" states,

---

[60] George Ostrogorsky, "Avtokrator i Samodržac," *Glas Srpska Kral'jevski Akademije*, no. 164, Belgrad, 1935, pp. 173–174.

[61] Ostrogorsky, "Avtokrator i Samodržac," pp. 176–177.

[62] *PSRL*, vol. 4, pt. 1 (1925), pp. 351–366; vol. 6, pp. 104–111; vol. 25, pp. 215–218; and vol. 27, pp. 82–87.

[63] On the myth of El Cid, see Richard Fletcher, *The Quest for El Cid*, New York, Alfred A. Knopf, 1990, pp. 196–200.

[64] See, e.g., Iskra I. Ilieva, "Vladetel'skii titul Moskovskikh velikikh kniazei (s serediny XV–do pervoi chetverti XVI veka)," *Bulgarian Historical Review*, vol. 12, 1984, pp. 75–87; Wladimir Vodoff, "Remarques sur la valeur du term 'tsar' appliqué aux princes Russes avant le milieu du XVe siècle," *Oxford Slavonic Papers*, vol. 11, 1978, pp. 1–41; Wladimir Vodoff, "La titulature princière en Russie du XIe au début du XVe siècle," *Jahrbücher für Geschichte Osteuropas*, vol. 35, 1987, pp. 1–35; Wladimir Vodoff, "Le titre *tsar'* dans la Russie du nord-est vers 1440–1460 et la tradition littéraire vieux-russe," *Studia Slavic-Byzantina et Mediaevalia Europensia*, vol. 1, 1989, pp. 54–60; and Szeftel, "Title of the Muscovite Monarch."

[65] Skrynnikov, *Ivan the Terrible*, p. 15.

[66] For the letters to Zakhariia, see *SRIO*, vol. 41, no. 10, p. 41 and no. 20, pp. 72–73. For

most notably the Polish prince Conrad Mazoretski and the Crimean khans, did use it in diplomatic correspondence with the grand prince.[67] We can expect that the use of *tsar'* before 1547 had an underlying rationale to it, for diplomacy depends on order and consistency of formalities, especially in the use of titles. The notion that the grand prince put forth *tsar'* as a counterpart to the German *Kaiser*, used by the Holy Roman Emperor, is defeated by at least two considerations. First, the Muscovite chancery did not use *tsar'* to apply to the grand prince in any of its dealings with the Habsburg emperors before 1514, although dealings with the Habsburgs began in the fifteenth century.[68] In the treaty of 1514 between Vasilii III and the Holy Roman Emperor, Maximilian I, the German version of the treaty uses *Kayser* and the Latin version uses *Cæsar* to apply to both rulers. But the Russian version distinguishes between *tsar*, which is applied only to Vasilii, and *tsesar'*, which is applied solely to Maximilian.[69] Second, as Daniel Prinz, the ambassador of the Holy Roman Emperor to Muscovy in 1575, pointed out, the terms *tsar'* and *Kaiser* were understood to denote different things.[70] In other words, sixteenth-century Muscovites did not see *tsar'* and *Kaiser* as Russian and German counterparts of the same term,

the letter to Khodja Asan, see *SRIO*, vol. 41, no. 12, p. 45. This Zakhariia should not be confused with the Jewish writer Zakhariia ben Aharon, who was in Kiev in the 1450s, but by the 1480s was living in Jerusalem. Lur'e, "Unresolved Issues," p. 162; Moshe Taube, "The Kievan Jew Zacharia and the Astronomical Work of the Judaizers," in *Jews and Slavs*, ed. Wolf Moskovich, Samuel Schwarzband, and Anatoly Alekseev, 3 vols., Jerusalem, Israel Academy of Sciences and Humanities; Hebrew University of Jerusalem, Department of Russian and Slavic Studies, Center for the Study of Slavic Languages and Literature; St. Petersburg, Slavonic Bible Foundation, Russian Academy of Sciences, 1993–1995, vol. 3: *Ioudaikh arxaiologia: In Honour of Professor Moshe Altbauer*, pp. 169–173.

[67] *SRIO*, vol. 35, p. 91.

[68] The kings of Spain did use *tsar'* in two speeches, Ferdinand in 1492 and Philip in 1505, to refer to the grand prince, at least in the Russian translation. When Maximilian was king of the Romans in 1492, his envoy, von Thurn, greeted Ivan III as "Tsar' of all Rus'" and as "sole (единъ) Tsar' of all Rus'." *PDS*, vol. 1, cols. 73, 77; see also *PDS*, vol. 1, col. 129, where Philip, the son of Maximilian, calls Ivan "Tsar' of all Rus'" in 1505.

[69] German, Latin, and Russian versions of the Treaty of 1514 can be found in Joseph Fiedler, "Die Allianz zwischen Kaiser Maximilian I. and Vasilji Ivanovič, Grossfürsten von Russland, von dem jahre 1514," *Sitzungsberichte der Kaiserlichen Akademie der Wissenschaften. Philosophisch-historische Classe*, vol. 43, no. 2, 1863, pp. 247–250 (Russian version), 250–252 (Latin version), and 253–256 (German version). Another publication of the Treaty of 1514 is by G. Stökl in *1100 Jahre österreichische und europäische Geschichte*, ed. Leo Santifaller, Vienna, Druck und Kommissionsverlag der Österreichischen Staatsdruckerei, 1949, pp. 53–54 (Russian version), 54–56 (German version).

[70] Daniel Prinz [Printz], *Moscoviae ortus, et progressus*, Gubenae, Christophor Gruber, 1681, p. 203 as reprinted in *Scriptores Rerum Livonicarum*, 2 vols., Riga and Leipzig, Eduard Franken, 1853, vol. 2, p. 721. Daniel Prinz [Daniil Prints], "Nachalo i vozvyshenie Moskovii," trans. I. A. Tikhomirov, *ChOIDR*, 1876, no. 3, p. 60.

deriving from the Latin *Caesar*, but as distinct terms that designate different types of rulers. Usually, in diplomatic correspondence, the term *tsesar'* was used to translate *Kaiser*.[71] Likewise, Herberstein describes the difference this way: "Czar in the Russian language signifies king, but in the common Slavonic dialect among the Poles, Bohemians, and all the rest, through a certain resemblance of sound in the last, which is the most important syllable, czar [or czeszar] would be understood as emperor or kaiser."[72] It is possible that *tsar'/tsesar'* is being used as a parallel construction to khan/khagan (*qan/qaɣan*). A khagan, in steppe terms, is a "super" khan, that is, one who has khans owing him allegiance. Not all khans owe allegiance to a khagan, but a khagan requires subordinate khans to be considered such.[73] In maintaining the distinction between *tsesar'* and *tsar'*, the Muscovite chancery may be acknowledging the higher status of the Holy Roman Emperor (*tsesar'*) in relationship to the Muscovite ruler without specifying a subordinate position on Vasilii's part. Thus, the *tsesar'* (Emperor) has subordinate tsars (understood in this sense as "kings"), while the Muscovite tsar does not.

From at least the thirteenth century on, the chroniclers use *tsar'* to apply both to the khan and to the basileus,[74] as also is the case in diplomatic treaties from at least the end of the fourteenth century.[75] This usage indicates that, rather early, the word *tsesar'* had been conflated with *tsar'*, but the difference in meanings was still understood and maintained through the sixteenth century. A survey of the documents from 1474 to 1505 that use *tsar'* to refer to Ivan III does show a common denominator.[76] Each of these documents concerns, in one form or another, the

---

[71] See, e.g., the letter from Ivan IV to the Holy Roman Emperor Maximilian II in 1572. *RIB*, vol. 22, cols. 75–76. See also Croskey, *Muscovite Diplomatic Practice*, p. 219. Khoroshkevich pointed out what may be exceptions to this practice in the treaties between Pskov and the Livonian order from as early as 1417. A. L. Khoroshkevich, "Ob odnom iz epizodov dinasticheskoi bor'by v Rossii v kontse XV veka," *Istoriia SSSR*, 1974, no. 5, p. 134. But the Russian versions of the earlier treaties are not extant, so it is open to speculation which word they contained. See also Croskey, *Muscovite Diplomatic Practice*, p. 216.

[72] Herberstein, *Notes upon Russia*, p. 33. See also Major's footnote 7, pp. 33–34. In the German edition, Herberstein went to even greater lengths to explain the distinction. See Gerbershtein, *Zapiski o Moskovii*, pp. 74–75. Vernadsky tried to make a similar point, although his historical linguistics may be weak, when he suggested that *tsar'* derives from Iranian *sar* ("head," "chief") while *tsesar'* derives from *Caesar*. George Vernadsky, *History of Russia*, vol. 1: *Ancient Russia*, New Haven, CT, Yale University Press, 1943, p. 254.

[73] See, e.g., Lawrence Krader, "Qan-Qaɣan and the Beginnings of Mongol Kingship," *Central Asiatic Journal*, vol. 1, 1955, pp. 17–35.

[74] See, e.g., *PSRL*, vol. 2, col. 806 (1250); vol. 25, pp. 180, 249, 332, 333.

[75] *DDG*, no. 15, p. 41 (ca. 1396); *DDG*, no. 37, p. 106 (ca. 1439).

[76] For a list of these documents, see Croskey, *Muscovite Diplomatic Practice*, pp. 299–300.

guarantee of safe passage across Rus' territory. During the time of the Mongol hegemony, the khan at Sarai was the one who had the power and authority to guarantee safe passage.[77] With the decline of the Qipchaq Khanate in the fifteenth century, the khan still maintained the authority but no longer had the power to guarantee that safe passage. By 1474, the grand prince of Moscow had the power to do so, but not the authority, unless he claimed for himself the authority of the tsar (= khan). Most likely, then, the grand prince and his foreign office decided, for practical reasons, to usurp the authority of the Qipchaq khan but only in this particular type of case. Without such usurpation, the guarantee would not have carried the necessary weight of authority. Yet, this particular usurpation of the term *tsar'* remained a discrete type throughout the forty-five years from the demise of the independent Qipchaq Khanate in 1502 until its formal adoption in 1547.[78] The reason for the delay in full usurpation of the title is the problem of genealogy. The Muscovite princes were not Chingizids and, therefore, could not legitimately claim the title *tsar'* in all its manifestations.

The reluctance on the part of the Muscovite government to designate their ruler as *tsar'* does not seem to have been shared by the Tatars themselves or others. The term *belyi tsar'* ("white tsar") was used by Tatar khans in addressing the grand prince.[79] The term *belyi tsar'* in referring to the grand prince also appears in the *Tale of Isidore's Council* by Simeon of Suzdal' (thought to have been written around 1460).[80] In the 1550s, the monks of Hilandar Monastery on Mt. Athos wrote letters to Ivan IV addressing him as *belyi tsar'*.[81] As late as the seventeenth century, Kotoshikhin tells us that the Kalmyks addressed Aleksii Mikhailovich as *belyi tsar'*.[82] So the term enjoyed a wide distribution as

See also Metropolitan Simon's letter to Perm' in 1501. *AI*, vol. 1, no. 112, pp. 166, 168. In the Uvarov copy of Metropolitan Iona's letter to Pskov in 1461 (RGB, Uvarov 512, fols. 179ᵛ–183) the word *tsar'* is interpolated into the grand prince's title. *RIB*, vol. 6, col. 673. But this word was not in the original. See *AI*, vol. 1, no. 60, pp. 107–108, published according to the MS. GIM, Sinod. 562, fols. 128–130.

[77] See, e.g., *Gramoty velikogo Novgoroda i Pskova*, p. 57.

[78] For a list of those documents that use *tsar'* to refer to the grand prince during the time of Vasilii III, see V. Savva, *Moskovskie tsari i vizantiiskie vasilevsy k voprosu o vliianii Vizantii na obrazovanie idei tsarskoi vlasti moskovskikh gosudarei*, Khar'kov, M. Zil'berberg, 1901, pp. 278–284.

[79] Edward L. Keenan, "Muscovy and Kazan, 1445–1552: a Study in Steppe Politics," Ph.D. Dissertation, Harvard University, 1965, p. 385; Szeftel, "Title of the Muscovite Monarch," pp. 70–71. Croskey, *Muscovite Diplomatic Practice*, pp. 235–236.

[80] V. Malinin, *Starets Eleazarova monastyria Filofei i ego poslanie. Istoriko-literaturnoe issledovanie*, Kiev, Tipografiia Kievo-Pecherskoi Uspenskoi Lavry, 1901, Appendix, p. 98.

[81] "Dokumenti koji se tichu odnosa izmeću srpske tsrkve i Rusije u XVI veku," ed. M. Dimitrijević, in *Spomenik*, vol. 39, 1903, no. 14, p. 22; no. 21, p. 28.

[82] Kotoshikhin, *O Rossii*, p. 38.

being understood to apply to the Muscovite grand prince, but it does not appear in documents emanating from the Muscovite chanceries.

Pipes asserted that "white tsar" derives from "white bone," that is, the term used for the Chingizid ruling family.[83] It is doubtful that "white tsar" derives from "white bone," for the simple reason that all tsars/ khans had to be white bone, by definition. The adjective "white" would not distinguish the Muscovite prince from the others. More likely, the term "white tsar" had a directional meaning (that is, white = west) and may refer to Muscovy's growing importance in steppe political matters.[84] Marco Polo, for example, refers to the khans of Qipchaq as "Lords of the West" (*Ponent*), in contrast to the khans of the Ilkhanate, whom he called "Lords of the East" (*Levant*).[85] The reference to *belyi tsar'* may be merely an acknowledgment that the Muscovite tsar was being seen by some as the legitimate successor to the Qipchaq (= western) khans.

Prinz reports that the Muscovites, apparently with the collusion of at least some boyars, at one point plotted to drive Ivan IV from the throne and replace him with the Crimean khan.[86] If Prinz's information is correct, then this would be evidence that these boyars realized the importance of having a Chingizid on the throne of Muscovy, in order (a) to be able to keep the title *tsar'* for their ruler, and (b) to reinforce legitimacy to Muscovy's takeover of the successor states of the Qipchaq Khanate. A letter to Ivan IV in 1554 from Khan Bekbulat makes it clear that, after the adoption of the title *tsar'*, the ruler of Muscovy could be referred to as a Chingizid.[87] Thus, the problem was resolved in steppe terms by the reversal of the equation that only a Chingizid could be a khan (= tsar). Since the Muscovite grand prince, as of 1547, claimed to be a tsar (= khan), then he must, by definition, be a Chingizid. The deception in claiming a Daniilovich to be a Chingizid was made easier

[83] Pipes, *Russia Under the Old Regime*, p. 76.
[84] On this point, see Keenan, "Muscovy and Kazan: Some Introductory Remarks," p. 558; and Croskey, *Muscovite Diplomatic Practice*, pp. 235–236. For a discussion of the use of color in cosmography, geographical names, and ethnonymy, see Jacques Bačić, *Red Sea – Black Russia: Prolegomena to the History of North Central Eurasia in Antiquity and the Middle Ages*, New York, East European Monographs, no. 171, 1995, pp. 112–273.
[85] *Book* (Yule), vol. 1, pp. 5, 8 n. 3, and 490–491.
[86] Prinz [Printz], *Moscoviae ortus, et progressus*, p. 76 as reprinted in *Scriptores Rerum Livonicarum*, vol. 2, p. 702. Prinz [Prints], "Nachalo i vozvyshenie Moskovii," p. 22. Plots such as this may have been the reason Ivan sought the possibility of asylum in England in 1570 from Elizabeth I.
[87] *Prodolzhenie Drevnei Rossiiskoi vivliofeki*, vol. 8, 1793, pp. 316–317. My thanks to Craig Kennedy for bringing this reference to my attention. Khan Bekbulat was the grandson of the khan of the Qipchaq Khanate, Aḥmed, and the father of Simeon Bekbulatovich (Sayin Bulat).

by the fact that the documents of the Qipchaq Khanate had been destroyed when Sarai was razed by Tamerlane in 1395, and by the fact that there was no one with sufficient power to deny the Muscovite grand princes this claim. It also was in keeping with the fluidity of nomadic tribal identification.[88] Ibn Khaldûn had pointed out that common interests and common experiences can supplant the common ancestry that originally created 'aṣabiyya. Then a fictitious ancestry is adopted to affirm an 'aṣabiyya created by these other considerations.[89]

The grand princes could not have resolved the problem simply by marrying a Chingizid princess. Their sons could then have had a claim to being Chingizids, but not an undisputed one. In steppe genealogy, inheritance passed from father to son not from mother to son. But the issue never came up. In 1317, Iurii III had married Konchaka, the sister of the Qipchaq khan Özbeg, but she died in Tver' before they had any children.[90] The khans may have been reluctant to provide the Muscovite rulers with the possibility of that kind of legitimacy. After Özbeg converted to Islam, the issue was moot, for the khans would not have allowed their sisters or daughters to convert to Christianity, which was a requirement of the Church for any marriage to an Eastern Orthodox Rus' prince.[91] And a Rus' prince who converted to Islam would lose his status in the Christian Rus' ruling class. After 1448, the Church was pushing for the other meaning of tsar', i.e. tsesar' or basileus. This meaning the Church covered by another deception, the imaginary genealogy that detailed the grand prince's descent from the brother of Augustus Caesar.[92] This fictional genealogy, which was the second component of the Skazanie complex of texts, served to counteract any fictional steppe genealogy that attempted to depict the Muscovite ruler as a Chingizid.

Fisher pointed out that the concepts "sultan" in the Ottoman Empire, "khan" in the Mongol Empire, and "basileus" in the Byzantine Empire have more in common with each other conceptually than they do with the concepts "king" as used in Europe, "caliph" among the Arabs, or

---

[88] See, e.g., Lindner, "What Was a Nomadic Tribe?" pp. 696–697; Kennedy "Juchid," pp. 123–125.

[89] Ibn Khaldûn, Muqadimmah, pp. 100–101. See also Muhsin Mahdi, Ibn Khaldûn's Philosophy of History: a Study in the Philosophic Foundation of the Science of Culture, University of Chicago Press, 1964, pp. 196–197.

[90] NPL, pp. 96, 338; TL, p. 356; PSRL, vol. 5, p. 207; vol. 10, pp. 180–181; vol. 23, p. 98; vol. 25, p. 161. The chronicle accounts are divided over whether she was killed in Tver' or died of natural causes there.

[91] Cf. Halperin, Russian and the Golden Horde, p. 111.

[92] Prinz [Printz], Moscoviae ortus, et progressus, p. 204 as reprinted in Scriptores Rerum Livonicarum, vol. 2, p. 721. Prinz [Prints], "Nachalo i vozvyshenie Moskovii," p. 58. See also Haney, "Princes of Vladimir."

"sultan" among the Mamlūks. In principle, Ottoman Turks, Mongols, and Byzantine Greeks could claim that the secular ruler also had religious authority.[93] Thus, it would seem to have been fairly easy for the Church to refurbish the "khan" into a "basileus."[94] With the fall of Constantinople in 1453, the position of the basileus (tsar) lay vacant from the Church's point of view, and with the capture of the Qipchaq Khanate in 1502, the position of khan (tsar) was up for grabs from the secular administration's point of view.

Nonetheless, it took ninety-six years after Constantinople's fall and forty-five years after the Crimean khan Mengli Girei took over the remnants of the Qipchaq Khanate for the Muscovite religious and secular leaders to agree on a formulation. In part, this delay may be traced to certain noteworthy differences between the concept "khan" and the concept "basileus." For one, the khan was chosen by the *quriltai*, whereas the basileus was, in theory, chosen by the people. Until the end of the twelfth century in Byzantium, the army or senate had held the formal right to choose the emperor with the acclamation of the people. Then, according to the *History* of Choniatēs, the people claimed the right by custom to acclaim the emperor more or less directly.[95] At about the same time, the emperor began convoking an assembly made up of senators, clergy, and representatives of commercial trade and the craft industry.[96] Until the end of the Empire, the principle of popular acclamation was maintained, although in practice the son of a reigning emperor, more often than not, was seen as the legitimate successor.

We have evidence that, by the end of the sixteenth century, at least some Muscovites considered election by the "whole land" to be Byzantine practice. A sixteenth-century *Rodoslovnaia kniga* (genealogy book) traces the genealogy of the Lascaris family back to one of four brothers who had been brought to Constantinople by Constantine the Great in the early fourth century. According to the legend, Constantine directed that the basileus be chosen from the four families that constituted the respective descendants of these four brothers by the whole land (*vsia zemlia*) if the imperial line should die out.[97] The "four families" idea of this legend may represent an echo of the four *qaračï*

---

[93] Fisher, "Muscovite–Ottoman Relations," p. 213.

[94] See Cherniavsky, "Khan or Basileus," pp. 459–476; see also Szeftel, "Title of the Muscovite Monarch," p. 71.

[95] Choniatēs, *Historia*, p. 600.

[96] In 1197, Alexios III convoked such an assembly to raise funds. Choniatēs, *Historia*, p. 631. In 1347, John Kantakouzenos convoked an assembly to deal with the Empire's financial problems. John Kantakouzenos, *Historiae*, 3 vols., ed. Ludwig Schopen (CSHB, vols. 2–4), Bonn, 1828–1832, vol. 3, p. 34.

[97] "Rodoslovnaia kniga . . ." *Vremennik imp. Moskovskogo obshchestva istorii i drevnostei rossiiskikh*, vol. 10, 1851, pp. 176–181.

beys of the Qipchaq council of state. The *qaraçï* beys, however, were not white bone and, therefore, could not become rulers in their own right.

After 1549, when it was first called in Moscow, the *zemskii sobor* acted to choose and advise the tsar. Coming up with explanations for the origins of the *zemskii sobor* has taxed historians' ingenuity. Perhaps the most widely accepted view is the one expressed by L. V. Cherepnin, who asserted that its origins were entirely indigenous to Rus' and reflected the centralization of the Muscovite state. In this view, the *zemskii sobor* merely rubber-stamped tsarist policy and acted as a means for the tsar to circumvent the Boyar Council.[98] If the *zemskii sobor* was entirely indigenous or based on Kievan precedent, then that does not explain why no *zemskii sobor*s were called earlier. Cherepnin argued that the *zemskii sobor* replaced the town assembly, the *veche*, but there was no *veche* in Moscow itself, so there was no need to wait to replace it. In addition, centralized monarchy developed elsewhere by eliminating or refusing to call representative institutions. It would be an unusual case if Muscovy developed centralized monarchy by creating a representative institution that could potentially limit the power of the ruler. In any event, the *zemskii sobor* does not seem to have circumvented any policies of the Boyar Council. By contrast, Pelenski argued that the *zemskii sobor* was a copy of the *quriltai* in Kazan', which in turn reflected the *quriltai* of the Qipchaq Khanate.[99] Elsewhere, I have provided objections to Pelenski's argument that Muscovy borrowed its political and administrative institutions from Kazan' in the middle of the sixteenth century.[100] The basis of my objections was the question of timing, in particular, why the Muscovite ruling class would wait to borrow extraneous institutions, and then from a conquered state at that. As I have tried to show, the primary borrowing of steppe institutions and practices came in the fourteenth century. The timing, however, of the calling of the first *zemskii sobor* is significant in determining its origin.[101] In the steppe, the *quriltai* was linked with the khan, both in terms of advising the reigning khan and in choosing a new khan. The *zemskii sobor* performed both these functions in Muscovy for the position of tsar. Thus, no *quriltai*-like *zemskii sobor*s were called before 1549 in Muscovy, because it was only in 1547 that the grand prince laid claim to being a tsar/khan. The institutional form of the *zemskii sobor* may have borrowed

---

[98] L. V. Cherepnin, *Zemskie sobory Russkogo gosudarstva v XVI–XVII vv.*, Moscow, Nauka, 1978, pp. 61–62. Cf. Richard Hellie, "Zemskii sobor," *MERSH*, vol. 45, pp. 224–234.

[99] Pelenski, "State and Society," p. 98.

[100] Ostrowski, "Mongol Origins," pp. 526–527.

[101] My thanks to Leslie McGann, who, in a paper on the origin of the *zemskii sobor* for my course at Boston University, formulated a distinction between "institutional origins" and "situational origins," which helped me clarify my thinking on the issue.

from previous councils called in Rus' territory, but the functions were specifically steppe in origin and may thus have been influenced by the form of the *quriltai* in Kazan' as Pelenski suggested. The difference in functions between the *quriltai* and western European parliaments may have led historians to the conclusion that the *zemskii sobor* merely rubber-stamped tsarist policy, but this again is to view a Muscovite institution through the wrong lens. Thus, the establishment of the *zemskii sobor* as an institution most likely was the result of steppe influence. Its similarity to Byzantine assemblies may have made it more palatable to Church authorities.

For another difference between the khan and the basileus, although neither of them was absolutist in the historiographical sense often applied to seventeenth- and eighteenth-century western Europe, the type of restrictions imposed on their power was different. The khan's power could be restricted by the council of state, whereas the basileus' power was limited, to a certain extent, by the Church.[102] Wilhelm Ensslin argued that in the patriarch's right of excommunication of the emperor "we may see an indication that arbitrary despotism was kept within limits."[103] Invoking that tactic was a rare occurrence. The usual interaction between patriarch and basileus seems to have depended more on how much influence the basileus would allow the patriarch. Ultimately, however, when irreconcilable differences arose, the basileus, through influencing the Holy Synod, would have the patriarch deposed. By contrast, we have no record of any patriarch's deposing of a basileus, although a patriarch could lend his support to his opponent.

The ceremony proclaiming the grand prince to be the tsar was clearly based on Byzantine precedent, or, rather, Muscovite religious leaders' perception of the Byzantine ceremony.[104] Yet, the fact that the Musco-

---

[102] See, e.g., Leo Diakonos' description of the struggle between Patriarch Polyeuktos (956–970) and Emperor John Tzimiskes (969–976). Leo Diakonos, *Historia*, ed. Karl Benedict Hase (CSHB, vol. 5), Bonn, E. Weber, 1828, pp. 100–102.

[103] Ensslin, "Emperor and the Imperial Administration," p. 276.

[104] See George P. Majeska, "The Moscow Coronation of 1498 Reconsidered," *Jahrbücher für Geschichte Osteuropas*, vol. 26, 1978, pp. 356–357, and George P. Majeska, *Russian Travelers to Constantinople in the Fourteenth and Fifteenth Centuries* (Dumbarton Oaks Studies, vol. 19), Washington, DC, Dumbarton Oaks Research Library and Collection, 1984, pp. 435–436, where he describes the pouring of the gold coins over the head of Dmitrii in 1498 and of Ivan IV in 1547 as the result of Ignatii of Smolensk's "peculiar word choice" in describing the largesse thrown to the crowds by the recently crowned Byzantine Emperor Manuel II in 1392. The fault may not have been Ignatii's, but that of a scribe. See the text of Ignatii's *Journey* in Majeska, *Russian Travelers*, pp. 111–113, where the Trinity copy could be read: *osypasha i stovratami* [they showered them with silver] rather than *osypasha ego stavratami* [they showered him with silver] as in the Nikon Chronicle copies (see also *PSRL*, vol. 11, p. 104). Perhaps the change was a conscious one, since coins thrown over the head of the new ruler could be recovered while coins thrown as largesse to the crowd could not. For

vite government during the 1550s and 1560s attempted to revive for itself the power and authority of the Qipchaq Khanate in taking one by one the successor states, that is, the Kasimov Khanate, the Kazan' Khanate, and the Astrakhan' Khanate, demonstrates that, as late as the reign of Ivan IV, the secular authority was seeing Muscovy as the successor to the Qipchaq Khanate, not as the successor to the Byzantine Empire or Kievan Rus'.[105]

There is a prevailing historiographical notion that Ivan IV turned his attention to the east only after he was blocked going west in the Livonian War. Such a view overlooks the fact that Ivan's earliest conquest was Kazan', in the east. Other historians claim that the conquest of Kazan' was an attempt to neutralize an enemy in the east before proceeding against the primary target in the west.[106] But Janet Martin has argued that "Muscovy's methods of pursuing its goals vis-à-vis Kazan' were influenced by its relations with the other Tatar khanates."[107] That is, it was to Muscovy's benefit to maintain an independent but friendly Kazan'. Only under Ivan IV, when Kazan' allied with the Crimean khan against Moscow, was the conquest of Kazan' undertaken. A case could be made that Muscovite policy was predicated on neutralizing hostile powers in the west, such as Poland-Lithuania, before continuing the conquest of the successor khanates to the east. Instead, we might profitably apply here John LeDonne's model for Imperial Russian foreign policy based on geopolitical considerations.[108] That is, by the time of Ivan IV, Muscovy was combatting two hostile core areas: Poland-Lithuania to the west and the Crimean Khanate to the south. Kazan' to the east was a frontier area that acted as a buffer against an attack up the Volga. Once the Kazan' khan allied himself with the Crimean khan, however, the buffer that served to protect Moscow could then be turned into an advanced position for attack from the steppe. Precursing a pattern that was to repeat itself many times over in

the showering of coins over Dmitrii, see *RFA*, vol. 3, pp. 613, 620, 624; *PSRL*, vol. 12, p. 248. For the showering of coins over Ivan IV, see *PSRL*, vol. 13, pp. 151, 453.

[105] See Jaroslaw Pelenski, "Muscovite Imperial Claims to the Kazan' Khanate," *Slavic Review*, vol. 26, 1967, pp. 559–576.

[106] For references, see Martin, "Muscovite Relations with the Khānates of Kazan'," p. 435 fn. 2. See also K. V. Bazilevich, *Vneshnaia politika russkogo tsentralizovannogo gosudarstva. Vtoraia polovina XV veka*, Izdatel'stvo Moskovskogo universiteta, 1952, pp. 61–62; and I. I. Smirnov, "Vostochnaia politika Vasiliia III," *Istoricheskie zapiski*, vol. 27, 1948, p. 18.

[107] Martin, "Muscovite Relations with the Khanates of Kazan' and the Crimea," p. 435.

[108] John P. LeDonne, *The Russian Empire and the World 1700–1917: the Geopolitics of Expansion and Containment*, New York, Oxford University Press, 1997, pp. 1–8; John LeDonne, "The Geopolitical Context of Russian Foreign Policy, 1700–1917," *Acta Slavica Iaponica*, vol. 12, 1994, pp. 1–23.

subsequent centuries, Muscovy simply took over the frontier area to protect itself. In support of this view that Poland-Lithuania was not the most important concern of Muscovite foreign policy, we can cite the research of Knud Rasmussen, who concluded, after a study of the sixteenth-century Posol'skii prikaz instructions (*nakazy*) to envoys, that the highest level of interest of the Muscovite foreign office was reserved for the Crimean Khanate and Wallachia, followed closely by the Ottoman Empire.[109]

Furthermore, the bizarre "abdication" of Ivan IV in favor of the Chingizid and former khan of the Kasimov Khanate, Simeon Bekbulatovich, in 1575 can best be understood in terms of the secular authority's residual Mongol orientation.[110] Ivan was replicating the actions of powerful non-Chingizid emirs (*bek*s), such as Nogai, Tamerlane, Edige, and Mamai, who set up Chingizid puppet khans on the throne. These emirs could not claim the title or authority of a khan (tsar) but could exercise the power of one nonetheless. Ivan's acceptance of the Church's claim that he was descended from a brother of Augustus Caesar, not from Chingiz Khan, may have led Ivan to feel an affinity with the powerful non-Chingizid emirs. Not surprisingly, the term *tsar'* does not appear in the title given to Bekbulatovich as head of the Muscovite state.[111] At the same time as Ivan was declaring himself only a prince of Moscow, he and his chancery were issuing *zhalovannye gramoty* (immunity charters) for landholdings in the Kazan' Khanate, reaffirming himself as tsar of that khanate.[112] Ultimately, however, the entire episode was a parody of Muscovite–steppe relations.

A number of historians have pointed to Ivan's "split personality" as an explanation for his apparently contradictory actions. As long ago as the eighteenth century, M. M. Shcherbatov remarked about the representation of Ivan "in such a variety of forms that he does not appear to be one person."[113] More recently James Billington saw Ivan IV's behavior as "the product . . . of a kind of schizophrenia. Ivan was, in effect, two

[109] Knud Rasmussen, "On the Information Level of the Muscovite Posol'skij Prikaz in the Sixteenth Century," *Forschungen für osteuropaische Geschichte*, vol. 24, 1978, pp. 91, 94.

[110] Omeljan Pritsak, "Moscow, the Golden Horde, and the Kazan Khanate from a Polycultural Point of View," *Slavic Review*, vol. 26, 1967, pp. 577–583.

[111] See, e.g., Ivan's letter to Simeon Bekbulatovich dated October 30, 1575, in *RIB*, vol. 22, cols. 76–77, where Semen is referred to only as "Grand Prince of All Rus'."

[112] S. M. Kashtanov, "O vnutrennei politike Ivana Groznogo v period 'velikogo kniazheniia' Simeona Bekbulatovicha," *Trudy Moskovskogo gosudarstvennogo istoriko-arkhivnogo instituta*, vol. 16, 1961, pp. 456–457; S. M. Kashtanov, "Finansovaia problema v period provedeniia Ivanom Groznym politiki 'udela'," *Istoricheskie zapiski*, no. 82, 1968, pp. 244–245.

[113] M. M. Shcherbatov, *Istoriia Rossiiskaia*, 7 vols., St. Petersburg, M. M. Stasiulevich, 1901–1904 (originally published 1770–1791), vol. 5, col. 825.

people; a true believer in an exclusivist, traditional ideology [Byzantium] and a successful practitioner of experimental modern statecraft."[114] Billington asserted that Ivan derived this "experimental modern statecraft" from European Protestantism; but there is no evidence that Protestantism influenced Ivan in any way. John Meyendorff claimed that Muscovite rulers of the sixteenth and seventeenth centuries were "inspired largely by Western Renaissance models and ideas."[115] He further claimed that Ivan IV "was an avid reader of Machiavelli" and that "[t]he focus of his cultural and political interests was Europe."[116] Despite Cherniavsky's article typing Ivan IV as a Renaissance prince,[117] there is no evidence that any Muscovite ruler was inspired in any way, let alone "largely," by any Renaissance model or idea. Likewise, there is no evidence Ivan IV read Machiavelli (and it is doubtful that he was literate at all). Nor is there any evidence that Ivan IV focused his political and cultural interests on Europe. Andrei Shchelkalov's characterization to Jerome Bowes of Ivan IV as "your English tsar" was probably meant to convey nothing more than that Ivan was friendly to English merchants and envoys.[118]

Cherniavsky, likewise, suggested a dialectical conflict influencing the behavior of Ivan IV: "The two images [of khan and basileus] were not really synthesized; both existed separately, if in a state of tension which the first Russian Tsar, Ivan IV, exemplified so tragically: killing by day and praying by night."[119] One may ask, however, which of these behaviors represented the khan and which represented the basileus. The idea of the Church's pulling in one direction, along with a faction of the boyar elite that it had by this time managed to convince, and others in the secular elite pulling in the opposite direction is a better explanation, in my opinion, for Ivan's erratic behavior as he tried to improvise a consistent synthesis of Byzantine and Mongol.

Thus, the discrepancy between the secular administration's Mongol-based political practice and the Church's Byzantine-based theoretical outlook helps provide a rational understanding of the seemingly irrational and "crazy" actions that Ivan IV is described as having taken. The Oprichnina, Ivan's setting up of a separate state within a state, is

---

[114] James H. Billington, *The Icon and the Axe: an Interpretive History of Russian Culture*, New York, Vintage, 1970, p. 99.
[115] John Meyendorff, "Was There Ever a 'Third Rome'? Remarks on the Byzantine Legacy in Russia," in *The Byzantine Tradition After the Fall of Constantinople*, ed. John J. Yiannias, Charlottesville, University Press of Virginia, 1991, p. 49.
[116] Meyendorff, "Was There Ever a 'Third Rome'?" p. 51.
[117] See Michael Cherniavsky, "Ivan the Terrible as Renaissance Prince," *Slavic Review*, vol. 27, 1968, pp. 195–211.
[118] Quoted in S. M. Platonov, *Moskva i zapad*, Berlin, Obelisk, 1926, p. 26.
[119] Cherniavsky, "Khan or Basileus," p. 476.

perhaps the most frequently cited example of Ivan's irrationality. Yet, historians have found no consensus, even in this, to explain the motives of Ivan in originating the Oprichnina or in its subsequent actions. Three main interpretive camps have developed. The historians who have a completely negative interpretation of the Oprichnina see it as a personal and capricious vendetta on Ivan's part against particular individuals, without any discernible pattern. In this interpretation, the Oprichnina led to destruction, confusion, and chaos in the realm. Historians whose interpretation fits into this camp include Shcherbatov, Kostomarov, Sheviakov, Veselovskii, Koretskii, and Hellie, as well as most popular biographers, including Robert Payne and Nikita Romanoff, Ian Grey, and Benson Bobrick, to mention only a few of the more recent ones.[120] A second interpretive camp has a completely positive evaluation of the Oprichnina. These historians see it as an attempt to limit the disruptive power of the boyars, who they consider to be representative of the powers of "feudal fragmentation," and to strengthen the centralized autocratic state by an alliance with the gentry or merchants. Proponents of this interpretation see Ivan as having achieved some success in pursuit of his goal. Historians whose interpretation fits into this camp include Tatishchev, Boltin, Kavelin, Vipper, Sadikov, Bakhrushin, I. I. Smirnov, and Pipes, as well as the popular biographer Henri Troyat and the Institute of History's official history in 1955.[121] A third interpretive

[120] See Shcherbatov, *Istoriia rossiiskaia*, vol. 5, pt. 2, cols. 483–484; N. I. Kostomarov, *Russkaia istoriia v zhizneopisaniiakh ee glavneishikh deiatelei*, 4th edn, 2 vols., St. Petersburg, M. M. Stasiulevich, 1895–1896, vol. 1, pp. 459–488; V. N. Sheviakov, "K voprosu ob oprichnine pri Ivan IV," *Voprosy istorii*, 1956, no. 9, pp. 74–76; S. B. Veselovskii, *Issledovaniia po istorii oprichniny*, Moscow, Akademiia nauk SSSR, 1963, pp. 29–36, 478–479; V. I. Koretskii, "Oprichnina," *Sovetskaia istoricheskaia entsiklopediia*, vol. 10, 1967, cols. 564–567; Richard Hellie, *Enserfment and Military Change in Muscovy*, University of Chicago Press, 1971, pp. 282–283; Richard Hellie, "In Search of Ivan the Terrible," in S. F. Platonov, *Ivan the Terrible*, ed. and trans. Joseph L. Wieczynski, Gulf Breeze, FL, Academic International Press, 1974, pp. x–xxxiv; Richard Hellie, "What Happened? How Did He Get Away with It?: Ivan Groznyi's Paranoia and the Problem of Institutional Restraints," *Russian History*, vol. 14, 1987, p. 199; Robert Payne and Nikita Romanov, *Ivan the Terrible*, New York, Thomas Y. Crowell, 1975, pp. 338–339; Ian Grey, *Ivan the Terrible*, London, Hodder & Stoughton, 1964, p. 167; Benson Bobrick, *Fearful Majesty: the Life and Reign of Ivan the Terrible*, New York, G. P. Putnam's Sons, 1987, p. 221.

[121] See V. N. Tatishchev, *Istoriia Rossiiskaia*, 7 vols., Moscow and Leningrad, Akademiia nauk SSSR, 1962–1968, vol. 6, pp. 170, 184; I. N. Boltin, *Primechaniia na istoriiu gospodina Leklerka*, 2 vols., St. Petersburg, Gornoe uchilishche, 1788, vol. 1, pp. 309–311; I. N. Boltin, *Otvet General–Maiora Boltina na pis'mo Kniazia Shcherbatova*, 2nd edn, St. Petersburg, Imperatorskaia tipografiia, 1793, pp. 98–102; K. D. Kavelin, *Sobranie sochineniia*, 4 vols., St. Petersburg, M. M. Stasinlevich, 1897, vol. 1, p. 639; R. Iu. Vipper [Wipper], *Ivan Groznyi*, trans. J. Fineberg, Moscow, Foreign Languages Publishing House, 1947, pp. 157–166, see also *ibid.*, pp. 230–246: "A Posthumous Judgment of Ivan Grozny"; P. A. Sadikov, *Ocherki po istorii oprichniny*, Moscow and Leningrad, Akademiia nauk SSSR, 1950, pp. 63–64; S. V. Bakhrushin,

camp presents a mixed evaluation. These historians see the intention of the Oprichnina as a positive one (as those historians who hold a completely positive view do), that is, as the strengthening of the centralized autocratic state. But they condemn the carrying out of the plan and attribute its excesses, cruelties, and ultimately its failure to problems of Ivan's personality. Historians whose interpretation fits into this camp include Karamzin, Solov'ev, Kliuchevskii, Platonov, Zimin, Skrynnikov, Shapiro, Vernadsky, and Kobrin.[122] A fourth, idiosyncratic, view was outlined by M. N. Pokrovskii. He sees the Oprichnina as having no significant impact on Muscovite historical development. For Pokrovskii, Ivan's personality is irrelevant, since "the tsar's personal authority was only a tool, of the ruling class."[123]

None of these interpretations explains the evidence satisfactorily. The evidence compiled by Kobrin and Veselovskii, for example, indicates that there was no difference in the social composition between the

Ivan Groznyi, Moscow, OGIZ, 1945, pp. 52–70, reprinted in S. V. Bakhrushin, *Nauchnye trudy*, 4 vols. in 5 pts., Moscow, Akademiia nauk SSSR, 1952–1959, vol. 2, pp. 300–304; I. I. Smirnov, *Ocherki politicheskoi istorii russkogo gosudarstva 30–50kh godov XVI veka*, Moscow and Leningrad, Akademiia nauk SSSR, 1958, pp. 5–15; Pipes, *Russia Under the Old Regime*, pp. 94–95; Henri Troyat, *Ivan the Terrible*, trans. Joan Pinkham, New York, E. P. Dutton, 1984, pp. 106–118; *Ocherki istorii SSSR*, 9 vols., Moscow, Akademii nauk SSSR, 1953–1958, *Period feodalizma konets XV v.–nachalo XVII v.*, ed. A. N. Nasonov, L. V. Cherepnin, and A. A. Zimin, pp. 301–321.

122 See Karamzin, *Istoriia gosudarstva rossiiskogo*, vol. 8, cols. 187–188 (but cf. N. M. Karamzin, *Zapiska o drevnei i novoi Rossii*, ed. V. V. Sipovskii, St. Petersburg, M. N. Tolstoi, 1914, p. 13); S. M. Solov'ev, *Istoriia otnoshenii mezhdu kniaz'iami Riurika domu*, Moscow, 1847, pp. 546–547; Solov'ev, *Istoriia Rossii s drevneishikh vremen*, vol. 3, p. 553 and vol. 5, p. 258; Kliuchevskii, *History of Russia*, vol. 2, pp. 74–90; S. F. Platonov, *History of Russia*, trans. E. Aronsberg, New York, Macmillan, 1925, pp. 130–133; S. F. Platonov, *Ocherki po istorii smuty v Moskovskom gosudarstve XVI–XVII vv.*, Moscow, Sotsekgiz, 1937, p. 119; Zimin, *Oprichnina Ivan Groznogo*, pp. 477–480; R. G. Skrynnikov, *Nachalo oprichniny*, Izdatel'stvo Leningradskogo universiteta, 1966, pp. 3–4, 315–317, 411–412; R. G. Skrynnikov, *Oprichnyi terror*, Izdatel'stvo Leningradskogo universiteta, 1969, pp. 3–96; A. L. Shapiro, "Ob absoliutizme v Rossii," *Istorii SSSR*, 1968, no. 5, pp. 73, 79; Vernadsky, *Tsardom of Muscovy*, pp. 107–109, 138–139; V. B. Kobrin, *Vlast' i sobstvennost' v srednevekovoi Rossii (XV–XVI vv.)*, Moscow, Mysl', 1985, pp. 134–135.

123 M. N. Pokrovskii, *History of Russia: From the Earliest Times to the Rise of Commercial Capitalism*, trans. and ed. Jesse D. Clarkson and M. R. M. Griffiths, Bloomington, IN, University Prints and Reprints, 1966 [1928], pp. 132, 149. To a certain extent, and without the class struggle aspect, Keenan would most likely agree with Pokrovskii's view that the Oprichnina resulted only in futile flailings by an impotent monarch who could be dangerous to individuals but who had no real impact one way or the other on political or economic developments. Edward L. Keenan, "Ivan Vasil'evich, Terrible Czar: 1530–1584," *Harvard Magazine*, January–February, 1978, pp. 48–49; Edward L. Keenan, "Ivan the Terrible: The Man," lecture given at Harvard University, November 16, 1981, typescript notes by Jack E. Kollmann, pp. 111–112.

Oprichnina and the Zemshchina.[124] This shows that Ivan was not trying to crush the boyars as a class or to engage in class warfare by favoring the gentry over the boyars. Also, we do have to take into account Ivan's mental outlook, insofar as we can discern it, for understanding the form that the Oprichnina took.

The Oprichnina is better explained in terms of representing a "Tatar" principle, or at least Ivan IV's conception and invoking of it, as opposed to the "Byzantine" principle of the Church hierarchy. I have in mind, in particular, Ivan's complaint of interference in his letter to Metropolitan Afanasii in 1565 after he left Moscow for Aleksandrova Sloboda. Ivan accused the prelates of interfering in state matters, especially in regard to interceding to prevent certain people from being punished:

> whenever he, the sovereign, wanted to investigate and punish his boyars and all the bureaucrats as well as the serving princes and *deti boiarskie* for their misdeeds, the archbishops, bishops, archimandrites, and hegumens, colluding with the boyars, the courtiers, *d'iaki*, and all the bureaucrats would begin to protect them from the sovereign tsar and grand prince.[125]

In steppe societies, religious leaders represented no institutional limitation on the power and authority of the ruler.[126] But in Muscovy the religious leaders were claiming that they did represent such an institutional limitation. And they were expanding their influence over a faction of the Boyar Council.

Ivan obtained from the Church prelates and those boyars allied with them the promise of non-interference in his separate realm – the Oprichnina – as a condition for returning to Moscow. While remaining religious and committed to Orthodox Christianity, Ivan tried to set up the equivalent of a steppe khanate within Muscovy in which the Church had no political power to speak of. Thus, those he considered to be loyal to him as tsar (khan), he welcomed into the Oprichnina, while those who supported the Byzantine orientation of the Church ideologists, he excluded and attacked. In this way, he was dividing the boyars' patronage networks, not trying to destroy them. It would also explain his allowing foreigners, such as Germans, into the Oprichnina; they owed no allegiance to the Rus' Church.

---

[124] Veselovskii, *Issledovanie po istorii Oprichniny*; V. B. Kobrin, "Sostav oprichnogo dvora Ivan Groznogo," *Arkheologicheskii ezhegodnik za 1959 god*, Moscow, 1960, pp. 16–91.

[125] *PSRL*, vol. 13, p. 392; *PSRL*, vol. 29, p. 342.

[126] Individual shamans, however, could and, on occasion, did challenge the tribal leaders. Even Chingiz Khan decided he had to deal in a high-handed manner with his shaman Kököchu (Teb-tengri) by having his back broken. *Secret History* (Cleaves), § 245, pp. 178–182; "Secret History" (Rachewiltz), *PFEH*, vol. 26, pp. 49–52. Cf. Juvaini, *History*, p. 39. See also the discussions in Grousset, *Empire of the Steppes*, pp. 217–218 and in Ratchnevsky, *Genghis Khan*, pp. 96–101.

Ivan's appointment of Prince Mikhail Temriukovich (see Figure 8.2), a recently baptized boyar of Tatar descent, as head of the Oprichnina Council was indicative of this reinvoking of the "Tatar" principle. Mikhail was the brother of Ivan's second wife, Mariia Temriukovna (a.k.a. Kochenei), and the son of Prince Temriuk, the non-Chingizid leader of the Kabardians, a Muslim Circassian people who lived on the north slopes of the Caucasus Mountains. Payne and Romanoff refer to Prince Afanasii Viazemskii, Peter Zaitsev, Aleksei Basmanov, and his son Fedor as a "Council of Four" that ran the daily activities of the Oprichnina.[127] Yet, Fedor Basmanov, as junior to his father, would have had no independent status in such a council. Instead, one can suggest that Mikhail Temriukovich was the fourth official member of this council of state, which, in effect, was a reinstitution of the divan of the *qaračï beys* of the Tatar khanates.

The role of Mariia Temriukovna, who married Ivan in 1561, should not be overlooked. Heinrich von Staden, a German mercenary in the employ of the Oprichnina, claims it was Mariia's advice that led Ivan to set up the Oprichnina.[128] Not only was Mariia the daughter of Temriuk and sister of Mikhail but she was also the aunt of Simeon Bekbulatovich, by virtue of the marriage of her sister Altynchach to Khan Bekbulat. According to contemporary accounts, many in the Muscovite court disliked her because of her preference for Tatars.[129] The very concept that the term *oprichnina* denotes, that is, a grant for widows and orphans, was a common Mongol practice.[130] Its adoption by Ivan to indicate his orientation goes far to explain the Church's opposition to it in principle. In the *Stepennaia kniga*, composed in the 1580s, for example, we find the formulation of the concept of the Tatar ruler as robber. Miller described it this way: "the author [of the *Stepennaia kniga*] proceeded to demonstrate the difference between the Christian tsar of Moscow and 'pagan' Tatar tsars. To allow the Tatar tsar to be confused with a Christian tsar would have made the later tsars of Moscow to appear as successors of Tatar rulers."[131] The model for the

---

[127] Payne and Romanoff, *Ivan the Terrible*, p. 232.
[128] Heinrich von Staden, *Aufzeichnungen über den Moskauer Staat*, ed. Fritz T. Epstein, Hamburg, Cram, de Gruyter, 1964, pp. 19–20; Heinrich von Staden, *The Land and Government of Muscovy*, trans. Thomas Esper, Stanford University Press, 1967, pp. 17–18.
[129] Zimin, *Oprichnina Ivan Groznogo*, p. 90. She met her end in September 1569, it was claimed, from poison.
[130] See e.g. *Secret History* (Cleaves), § 185, p. 113, § 217–218, p. 158; "Secret History" (Rachewiltz), vol. 16, 1977, p. 44, vol. 23, 1981, p. 117.
[131] See Miller, "Velikie Minei Cheti," p. 335. See also Cherniavsky, "Khan or Basileus," pp. 459–476, and Vernadsky, *Mongols and Russia*, pp. 385–387.

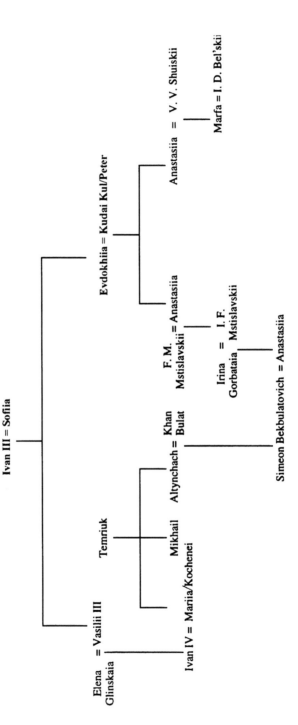

Fig. 8.2: *Genealogical relationships of Simeon Bekbulatovich*

robber tsar in the *Stepennaia kniga* may well have been Ivan IV's activities in the Oprichnina.

Ivan left the Boyar Council in charge of the *Zemshchina*, that is, "the land" (*zemlia*). In the Qipchaq Khanate, the council of state (represented by the four *qarači beys*) was supposed to represent "the land" in dealings with the khan. In turn, the khan was not allowed to attack members of the council of state. By creating a thing apart (the Oprichnina), Ivan established for himself the privilege of attacking those who, in his view, were not true representatives of the interests of the land. Indeed, the Oprichnina terror was carried out on the basis of steppe principles of collective guilt. This explains why the male relatives, retainers, and servants of individuals charged with disloyalty were sometimes also executed. Crummey has written about this phenomenon: "When the tsar turned on a prominent noble like [I. P. Cheliadnin-] Fedorov, he systematically annihilated his entire family and all his retainers who, in some mysterious way, must have shared in his guilt."[132] Yet, there is nothing mysterious about it.

The principle of collective guilt entered Russian law from the Mongols and was carried on at least through the late nineteenth century. J. N. Westwood considered collective guilt to be a form of police abuse, because the entire village from which a murderer came would be punished when the criminal could not be found.[133] Westwood exhibits here a modern-day distinction between public and private that is anachronistic for steppe societies and those societies influenced by the steppe. In such societies, no one was a "private" person; instead, everyone owed an obligation to the maintenance of social law and order. Failing that obligation, they were responsible for making compensation to society. That compensation could affect all those associated with the guilty individual, beginning with the immediate family, then expanding in ever-wider concentric circles to include the extended family or clan, the village or town, and even at times entire ethnic populations. As was also the case in steppe societies, the vertical patronage network that a "guilty" party headed, including retainers and servants, was fair game for punishment. When Möngke became grand khan, according to Rashīd al-Dīn, he had seventy-seven conspirators, the followers and

---

[132] Crummey, *Formation of Muscovy*, p. 167. Ivan Petrovich Cheliadnin had served as governor of Moscow and Master of Horse. As such, he would run the government when the tsar was absent. Cheliadnin was implicated as one of the boyars who was to receive a letter from King Sigismund Augustus of Poland inviting him to come over to the Polish side. For further information and discussion on him, see Zimin, *Oprichnina Ivana Groznogo*, pp. 273–283; and Skrynnikov, *Nachalo Oprichniny*, pp. 353–410.

[133] J. N. Westwood, *Endurance and Endeavor: Russian History 1812–1980*, 2nd edn, Oxford University Press, 1981, p. 89.

family of his predecessor Ögödei, executed.[134] When Qubilai defeated Ariɣ Böke, he had his followers, many of whom had been supporters of Möngke, executed.[135] Like much else in Mongol and steppe practice, the principle of collective guilt may have had its origins in China, where it was frequently applied. For example, when Zhudi (Chu Ti), the Yongle (Yung-lo) Emperor, ascended to the throne in 1402, he sentenced to death not only the civil and military officials who had opposed him but also their relatives to the ninth and tenth degrees, as well as their friends, neighbors, servants, students, and teachers.[136] It has been estimated that "thousands had perished" as a result.[137]

Thus, Ivan adopted a "Tatar" solution to the resistance he was encountering with the Church. Ironically, a devastating raid on Moscow in 1571 by the Crimean khan Devlet Girei and genuine Tatars contributed to Ivan's decision to dissolve the pseudo-Tatar Oprichnina.[138] Ivan ostensibly blamed the Zemshchina for the debacle, demoting its head, Prince Ivan Fedorovich Mstislavskii (see Figure 8.2), to namestnik of Novgorod after he "confessed" to collusion with Devlet Girei.[139] I. F. Mstislavskii was the grandson of Kudai Kul/Peter and Evdokiia Ivanovna, and therefore one-quarter Tatar. He could not claim Chingizid (white bone) descent, however, because the connection with Kudai Kul was through his mother, Anastasiia. Mstislavskii married Irina Gorbataia, whose father Aleksandr and brother Peter were subsequently killed by the Oprichnina in 1565. Their daughter, also named Anastasiia, married Simeon Bekbulatovich.

[134] Rashīd al-Dīn, *Successors*, pp. 212–213; see also Juvaini, *History of the World Conqueror*, pp. 579–583.

[135] Rashīd al-Dīn, *Successors*, pp. 262–264.

[136] F. W. Mote and L. Carrington Goodrich, "Chu Ti," *Dictionary of Ming Biography 1368–1644*, ed. L. Carrington Goodrich and Chaoying Fang, New York, Columbia University Press, 1976, p. 360. Louise Levathes, *When China Ruled the Seas: the Treasure Fleet of the Dragon Throne 1405–1433*, New York, Simon & Schuster, 1994, p. 72.

[137] Charles O. Hucker, "Yung-lo," *The New Encyclopaedia Britannica*, 30 vols., 15th edn, Chicago, Encyclopaedia Britannica, 1974, vol. 12, p. 876. Dreyer asserted that, although "some fifty" civil officials who had been designated the "evil ministers" were executed, the Yongle Emperor, nonetheless, on the whole followed a conciliatory policy toward the old guard. Edward L. Dreyer, *Early Ming China: a Political History 1355–1435*, Stanford University Press, 1982, pp. 169, 173. Notions of collective guilt still show up in the twentieth-century China. See, e.g., Liang Heng and Judith Shapiro, *Son of the Revolution*, New York, Vintage, 1984, p. 11, where they point out that during the Cultural Revolution "the whole family could be considered as guilty as the single member who had committed the crime."

[138] Karamzin, Solov'ev, Kliuchevskii, and Platonov all believed that Ivan only abolished the name "Oprichnina" and continued its policies until his death. But see S. B. Veselovskii, "Uchrezhdenie oprichnogo dvora v 1565 g. i otmena ego v 1572 godu," *Voprosy istorii*, 1946, no. 1, pp. 86–104.

[139] *SGGD*, vol. 1, no. 196, pp. 561–565.

But Ivan's harshest punishment was reserved for those in the Oprichnina. He had Prince Mikhail Temriukovich executed among others. Although Ivan abolished the Oprichnina, he did not give up his Tatar orientation. In 1572, he appointed the recently baptized Astrakhan' tsarevich Mikhail Kaibulich to head the newly recombined Boyar Council.[140] In 1575, he declared Simeon Bekbulatovich to be the grand prince of all Rus'. One can also understand Ivan's marriage (his seventh) to Mariia Nagaia in 1581 as signifying a further defiance of the Church, since, like his previous two marriages, it was considered uncanonical.[141] The fact that Mariia Nagaia was of Tatar descent no doubt added to the defiant aspects of it.

There remains the question of the impact of the Oprichnina on the Muscovite state and economy. Skrynnikov has written that "[b]y 1572, the *oprichnina* had brought the country to a standstill."[142] He then estimated the number killed during Ivan's reign as "up to three or four thousand persons."[143] Although this is not a small number, it is about 1/25 of 1 percent of the population under Muscovite control at the time, and it pales in comparison with the hundreds of thousands of deaths from famine and plague during the same period. In comparison, those executed in Paris during the Terror of 1793–1794 amounted to 14,140 people, or approximately 1/20 of 1 percent of the total population of France at that time.[144] It had the desired political effect of stopping anti-government demonstrations, but it is difficult to determine any economic impact. The Stalinist purges of the 1930s resulted in the deaths of what may have been as much as 10 percent of the total population of the Soviet Union, yet the economy continued to expand during that decade. Whether or not Muscovy was brought to a standstill politically is an open question. But whatever economic detriment the country may have endured at that time was more likely the result of plagues and famines than of Ivan's reign of terror.

Thus, while the Muscovite grand-princely administration was continuing to follow Tatar governing practices, the Church was formulating

---

[140] *SRIO*, vol. 129, pp. 219, 221, 224–226, 228.

[141] Horsey claims that Ivan married again to allay suspicion among the boyars that he was planning to flee to England. Jerome Horsey, "Travels," in *Rude & Barbarous Kingdom*, p. 286. Given Ivan's previous insouciance to marriage and the fact that the Church did not even recognize the union, it is difficult to see how such concerns, if they existed, would be diminished.

[142] R. G. Skrynnikov, "An Overview of the Reign of Ivan IV: What Was the *Oprichnina?*" *Soviet Studies in History*, vol. 24, 1985, p. 81.

[143] Skrynnikov, "Overview," p. 81; see also Hugh F. Graham, "Oprichnina," *MERSH*, vol. 26, 1982, p. 53.

[144] J. M. Thompson, *The French Revolution*, New York, Oxford University Press, 1945, p. 93.

a Byzantine-based ideology. As the Church began having more influence within the secular government, Ivan IV reacted strongly by castigating the Church leaders, by leaving Moscow (returning only when certain conditions were met), and by forming the Oprichnina. Subsequently, Ivan played out the position he found himself in by appointing the Chingizid Simeon Bekbulatovich as puppet ruler of Muscovy. But the Oprichnina was a last-ditch and futile effort on the part of Ivan to stem the political tide. Although it was brutal and terroristic, the Oprichnina had no significant impact on economic or political development. The Church had gained the ascendancy in political theory by coopting the symbols of secular authority and by redefining the very nature of the authority of the tsar himself.

9   Byzantine political thought and Muscovy

In redefining the authority of the ruler, so as to make him appear to be the inheritor of the basileus' authority, not that of the Mongol khan, the Muscovite Churchmen had an already articulated, ready-made political theory from Byzantium to draw upon. Adapting and applying that political theory to Muscovite realities, however, were not such easy processes. In Muscovy, while the authority of the temporal ruler's position was in principle unlimited, in practice the power of the individual who occupied the throne could be influenced, modified, and even restricted by both the Church and the Boyar Council. Although recognizing it is risky to apply western European political concepts to Muscovite government, we can say that Muscovy was closer to being a constitutional monarchy than an absolutist monarchy, unless we understand the term "absolutist monarchy" to include exactly those kinds of institutional restraints that existed in Muscovy. For, as B. Lyon pointed out in regard to Edward I of England and Philip the Fair of France: "It was not theory, not professed belief in tradition and established institutions and law, not admiration of a saintly king, and not counsel from a council, but political pressure become constant and institutionalized that made medieval kings constitutional. To understand medieval constitutionalism otherwise is to misunderstand medieval politics."[1] Individual Muscovite secular rulers at times limited their power, owing to pressure from the metropolitan (e.g. Gerontii, Makarii, or Filipp) or the patriarch (e.g. Filaret or Nikon). Likewise, in Byzantium, the basileus at times found it prudent to back off on particular policies in the face of opposition from the patriarch and public opinion. This was far different from how Runciman characterized Eastern Church theory as the "exact reversal of the Hildebrandine theory of the Western Church."[2] Theore-

---

[1] B. Lyon, "What Made a Medieval King Constitutional?" in *Essays in Medieval History Presented to Bertie Wilson*, ed. T. A. Sandquist and M. R. Powicke, University of Toronto Press, 1969, p. 175.
[2] Steven Runciman, *The Emperor Romanus Lecapenus and His Reign*, Cambridge University Press, 1929, p. 25.

tically, both the basileus and the patriarch were the viceroys of God and were supposed to act in harmony. For example, Title 2, Article 8 of the *Epanagōgē* states:

The polity (πολῑτεἰας), like man, consists of parts and members, [among these] the most important and the necessary parts are the Emperor and the Patriarch. Wherefore the peace and happiness of subjects, in body and soul, consist in the full agreement and concord of the kingship and the priesthood.[3]

Practice was another matter, for disharmony, i.e. disagreement between the basileus and patriarch, could and did occur. Nor did the basileus always win out whenever there was conflict with the head of the Church. Byzantine emperors could be forced to rescind orders at the behest of the patriarch and public opinion. In the thirteenth century, as the result of patriarchal and popular opposition, Emperor Michael VIII had to give up the Church union he had agreed to at the second Council of Lyon in 1274.[4] The Emperor John VIII had to change his position concerning Church union in the 1440s also as the result of the pressure of public opinion.[5] Sixteenth- and seventeenth-century Muscovy also had examples of the impact of public opinion that affected the government. The inhabitants of the city would, on occasion, storm the kremlin, with sometimes fatal results for members of the ruling elite but without much impact on policy.[6]

During the second half of the fourteenth century in Byzantium, when the basileus was weak, Patriarchs Philotheus Coccinus and Antonios IV made claims of power and authority in regard to themselves of which any Hildebrandine theorist would have approved. In his letter of June 1370 to Metropolitan Aleksei supporting his regency, Patriarch Philotheus not only indicates that God appointed him ("Our Humility") as patriarch and as the "leader of all Christians found anywhere on the inhabited earth," but also promises that those who are favorably disposed toward Metropolitan Aleksei will "receive your reward in this

[3] *Jus graeco-romanum*, vol. 4, p. 183; *Jus graecoromanum*, ed. J Zepos and P. Zepos, 8 vols., Darmstadt, Scientia Aalen, 1962 (reprint of 1931 edn), vol. 6, pp. 59–60.
[4] J. M. Hussey, *The Orthodox Church in the Byzantine Empire*, Oxford, Clarendon Press, 1986, pp. 229–242.
[5] Markos Eugenikos, Metropolitan of Ephesus, "Marci Ephesii epistola ad Theophanem Sacardotem in Euboea insula," ed. Louis Petit, *Patrologia orientalis*, vol. 17, fasc. 2, 1923, p. 481.
[6] On the Moscow uprising of 1547, see *PSRL*, vol. 13, pp. 455–457. For sources on the uprisings in Moscow, Kozlov, Kursk, and Ustiug Velikii in 1648, see K. V. Bazilevich, *Gorodski vosstaniia v Moskovskom gosudarstve XVII v. Sbornik dokumentov*, Moscow and Leningrad, Gosudarstvennoe Sotsial'no-ekonomicheskoe izdatel'stvo, 1936. See also Valerie Kivelson, "The Devil Stole His Mind: the Tsar and the 1648 Moscow Uprising," *American Historical Review*, vol. 98, 1993, pp. 733–756. On the 1682 storming of the kremlin, see Schuyler, *Peter the Great*, vol. 1, pp. 49–70.

present life having acquired God as your ally and helper in whatever [you] need." Philotheus goes on to promise that God "will grant you increase of power, long life, abundance of riches, success in all good things, untroubled, painless existence and bodily health."[7] By claiming that God appointed the Patriarch of Constantinople the leader of all Christians everywhere, Philotheus was claiming for himself the same power that the Pope and the Byzantine Emperor also claimed. By promising reward in the present life, Philotheus was articulating a concept that differed from the traditional message of Christianity, that is, that pain and suffering in this life will be rewarded with joy in the next. It is, nonetheless, in keeping with the concept of Byzantium's being the incarnation of the kingdom of Christ on earth. Antonios, likewise, emphasized that he sat on the throne of Christ and was acting in his behalf when he wrote to Vasilii I, c. 1393.[8] Yet, when the secular rulers in both Byzantium and Muscovy decided to exert their power over the Church, they could do so by having the Holy Synod depose the head of the Church. For example, the compiler of the *Life of Filipp* has Metropolitan Filipp indicating to Ivan Groznyi that the tsar could not depose the head of the Church, for only the Synod could do so. Paul Bushkovitch has argued that Filipp's statement indicated an implicit Church-based challenge to the secular authority.[9] Bushkovitch can draw such a conclusion only by ignoring the Byzantine heritage of relations between the patriarch and basileus. What the hagiographer has Filipp describing to Ivan IV was the same policy as had existed in Byzantium and continued to exist in the Eastern Church under the Ottoman sultans.[10] Instead of representing a religious challenge to secular authority, it represented one of the bases of harmony between Church and State. On the other side, Runciman used the story of Ivan's having Filipp killed as evidence that Ivan IV "claimed an authority over it [the

---

[7] *Acta et diplomata graeca*, vol. 1, no. 266, pp. 521–522; *RIB*, vol. 6, Prilozhenie, no. 18, cols. 109–114; and Meyendorff, *Byzantium and the Rise of Russia*, pp. 283–284.

[8] *Acta et diplomata graeca*, vol. 2, no. 447, p. 189; *RIB*, vol. 6, Prilozhenie, no. 40, col. 271; Barker, *Manuel II Palaeologus*, p. 106. On dating this letter to 1393, see *Les regestes des actes du Patriarcat de Constantinople*, vol. 1: *Les actes des patriarches*, 7 fascs., ed. J. Darrouzès, Paris, Institut Français d'études byzantines, 1972–1979, fasc. 6: *Les regestes de 1377 à 1410*, pp. 211–212, 217. Ostrogorsky dated it to the years 1394–1397. George Ostrogorsky, *History of the Byzantine State*, trans. Joan Hussey, New Brunswick, NJ, Rutgers University Press, 1969, p. 554. Meyendorff specified 1397 as its year of composition. Meyendorff, *Byzantium and the Rise of Russia*, pp. 12, 103. Antonios was patriarch from 1389 to 1390 and again from 1391 to 1397. Any of these dates are possible.

[9] Paul Bushkovitch, "The Life of Saint Filipp: Tsar and Metropolitan in the Late Sixteenth Century," in *Medieval Russian Culture*, vol. 2, p. 42.

[10] For a description of this policy, see Steven Runciman, "The Greek Church Under the Ottoman Turks," *Studies in Church History*, vol. 2, 1957, p. 41.

Church] that no Emperor in Constantinople would have dared to claim."[11] But Runciman neglected to mention that, in the meantime, Ivan prevailed upon the Holy Synod to depose Filipp, who was exiled from the court as a common monk, first to the Bogoiavlenskii Monastery, then to the Nikol'skii Monastery, and finally to the Otroch' Monastery in Tver'.[12] Maliuta Skuratov, an agent of the tsar, and one of the chief enforcers in the Oprichnina, murdered Filipp in his cell, but it is not clear in the *Life of Filipp* whether the tsar ordered him to do so.[13] Even if Ivan ordered Skuratov to kill Filipp when he was a monk, it is significant that he did not do so when Filipp was metropolitan.[14] Ivan could claim that he was merely exercising his duty as tsar in regard to the external Church by punishing a monk, but he could not punish or discipline a metropolitan.

One may well ask how and when Byzantine political theory entered Muscovy. According to Dvornik, Byzantine political literature was known in Muscovy after the mid-fifteenth century.[15] These works included Agapetus' treatise on kingship, the Instruction of Basil I to his son Leo, writings of Simeon of Saloniki (in a Russian manuscript of the seventeenth century), Patriarch Photios' letter to Boris of Bulgaria on kingship, and the treatise on kingship by Theophylakt of Bulgaria (from the twelfth century). The *Pchela*, translated from one of the four recensions of the Greek *Melissa* (Μέλισσα), contained numerous political maxims. Vassian Rylo, for example, for his admonition to Ivan III, used the *Pchela* to obtain the words of Democritus: "It is becoming to a prince to show wisdom whenever the moment requires it, display

[11] Steven Runciman, "Patriarch Jeremias II and the Patriarchate of Moscow," *Aksum Thyateira: a Festschrift for Archbishop Methodios of Thyateira and Great Britain*, ed. George Dion. Dragos, London, Thyateira House, 1985, p. 236.

[12] George P. Fedotov, *St. Filipp Metropolitan of Moscow: Encounter with Ivan the Terrible*, trans. Richard Haugh and Nickolas Lupinin (= vol. 1 of *The Collected Works* of George P. Fedotov), Belmont, MA, Nordland, 1978, pp. 126–133.

[13] Fedotov, *St. Filipp Metropolitan of Moscow*, pp. 135–136. Olearius, in his account, is specific in writing that Ivan IV "sent one of his servants to the monastery to strangle him with a rope." *The Travels of Olearius in Seventeenth-Century Russia*, trans. and ed. Samuel H. Baron, Stanford University Press, 1967, p. 258. Pseudo-Kurbskii is unsure about the specific means by which Filipp met his demise, but definitely attributes the cause to a "tsar's command." *Prince A. M. Kurbsky's History of Ivan IV*, ed. and trans. J. L. I. Fennell, Cambridge University Press, 1965, pp. 240–241.

[14] See Taube and Kruse's description of the refusal of the Synod to condemn Metropolitan Filipp to death. "Poslanie Ioganna Taube i Elerta Kruze," pp. 43–44. See also Fedotov, *St. Filipp Metropolitan of Moscow*, p. 133.

[15] Francis Dvornik, "Byzantium, Muscovite Autocracy and the Church," in *Re-Discovering Eastern Christendom: Essays in Commemoration of Dom Bede Winslow*, ed. A. H. Armstrong and E. J. B. Fry, London, Darton Longman & Todd, 1963, p. 113. See also Francis Dvornik, "Byzantine Political Ideas in Kievan Russia," *Dumbarton Oaks Papers*, vol. 9/10, 1956, p. 102.

strength, manliness, and courage when facing the enemy."[16] In addition, John Meyendorff has suggested hymns as a means by which political theory could be conveyed:

Innumerable heroes of the faith were constantly exalted precisely because they had opposed heretical emperors; hymns sung in church praised Basil for having disobeyed Valens, Maximus for his martyrdom under Constans, and numerous monks for having opposed the iconoclastic emperors in the eighth century. These liturgical praises alone were sufficient to safeguard the principle that the emperor was to preserve, not to define, the Christian faith.[17]

Finally, iconography was a standard means of communicating information in a semi-literate society. In the *Zolotaia palata* of the Moscow kremlin, the ceilings of the vestibule and throne room were covered with images of Old Testament kingship and scenes from Russia's virtual past, respectively.[18] As Daniel Rowland has pointed out, the organizing motif of the throne-room iconography was the Muscovite ruler's receiving his legitimacy directly from God.[19] Although the throne-room iconography is Russian, the vestibule iconography depicts Old Testament events through the filter of Byzantine political thought.

Yet, Byzantine influence on Muscovite political thought was not such a simple matter to implement. As S. V. Utechin has pointed out, the Muscovite Churchmen were not able simply to follow the Byzantine teachings on defining the power of the monarch, because we find two apparently contradictory points of view represented in Byzantine political thought: (1) the ostensibly unlimited power of the emperor, and (2) the limitation of that "power by the law of God to which he was subject."[20] Here the research of Daniel Rowland helps us to understand how the apparent contradiction was resolved in Muscovite political thought. We can then extrapolate to see how it must also have been resolved in Byzantium in the same way.

The ruler was absolute in both power and authority, and was, therefore, to be obeyed without question, but only as long as he followed the

[16] *PSRL*, vol. 21, pt. 2, p. 559; Viktor Semenov, "Drevniaia russkaia Pchela po pergamennomu spisku," *Sbornik Otdeleniia russkogo iazyka i slovesnosti Imperatorskoi Akademii nauk*, vol. 54, no. 4, 1893, p. 103. On the point, see Ševčenko, "Neglected Byzantine Source," pp. 153–154.

[17] John Meyendorff, *Byzantine Theology: Historical Trends and Doctrinal Themes*, 2nd edn, New York, Fordham University Press, 1979, p. 17.

[18] O. I. Pobedova, *Moskovskaia shkola zhivopisi pri Ivane IV. Raboty v Moskovskoi kremle 40-kh–70-kh godov XVI v.*, Moscow, Nauka, 1972, appendix.

[19] Daniel Rowland, "The Political Messages of the Golden Palace," AAASS, Washington, DC, October 28, 1995.

[20] S. V. Utechin, *Russian Political Thought: a Concise History*, New York, Frederick A. Praeger, 1963, p. 7.

Table 9.1 *Relations between temporal ruler and his advisers*

case	Harmony	Disharmony	Conflict	Breakdown
type	Legitimate ruler abides by God's Law	Legitimate ruler transgresses God's law	Legitimate ruler orders subjects to transgress God's law	False ruler identified as a tyrant
action	Concord and harmony	Wise advisers speak up	Wise advisers recommend disobedience	Wise advisers actively oppose tyrant
result	Silent obedience	Non-silent obedience	Vocal + passive disobedience	Vocal + active opposition

law of God. This situation was the usual one in which concord and harmony prevailed between the temporal ruler and his spiritual and temporal advisers. And the people were to follow and obey "as voiceless as fish."[21] But if the temporal ruler transgressed that law, then it was the duty of the wise advisers, both temporal and spiritual, that is, "the strong in Israel" (sil'nye bo Izraili), to speak up.[22] This situation constituted one of disharmony but was not a reason to disobey the temporal ruler, because he still received his legitimation from God. Instead, the ruler's "evil advisers" (злые советники), the flatterers, are blamed as the source of the problem. The ruler's responsibility lies primarily in having listened to them and not to the good advisers. All the elements of this second position appear in the *Poslanie na Ugru* (described above). A third situation arises when a legitimate ruler orders subjects to transgress God's law, which would threaten the salvation of their souls. Then it is their duty to refuse to obey, even unto death. In his *Reply* to Ivan IV, Metropolitan Makarii writes: "Even if I am constrained by the tsar himself or by his grandees, if they order me to do (сътворити) something contrary to divine rules, I will not obey them – even if they threaten me with death, I will not obey them in any way."[23] This disobedience is a passive one.

[21] The phrase is Ivan Timofeev's. See *Vremennik Ivana Timofeeva*, ed. O. A. Derzhavina, Moscow and Leningrad, Akademiia nauk SSSR, 1951, p. 109.

[22] Daniel Rowland, "Did Muscovite Literary Ideology Place Limits on the Power of the Tsar (1540s–1660s)?" *Russian Review*, vol. 49, 1990, pp. 141–142. The phrase appears twice in pseudo-Kurbskii's First Letter (KI). *Perepiska Ivana Groznogo s Andreem Kurbskim*, ed. Ia. S. Lur'e and Iu. D. Rykov, Moscow, Nauka, 1981, pp. 7, 9. In the second redaction of KI, the words "and noble" (*i blagorodnye*) were added between *sil'nye* and *vo Izraili* (*ibid.*, p. 11).

[23] Ostrowski, "A 'Fontological' Investigation," p. 489; *RFA*, vol. 4, 1988, p. 743. Two MSS – RGB, Volok. 522 and RGB, Muz. 1257 – instead of сътворити (to do) have говорити (to speak). But this is a secondary reading. Pliguzov and I independently

There was, however, a fourth situation that could develop, when the harmony between the head of the Church and the temporal ruler broke down completely. Then the head of the Church could declare the temporal ruler heretical and non-legitimate, which meant that the people had the duty not only to disobey but also actively to oppose that ruler. In this case, the ruler is then declared a tyrant and tormentor.[24] Both Byzantine and Muscovite political theory as espoused by Church bookmen prescribed these four positions for wise advisers: (1) non-critical and silent obedience; (2) vocal criticism but obedience nonetheless; (3) vocal criticism with passive disobedience; and (4) vocal and active opposition. These four options for the wise advisers depended upon whether a legitimate ruler was following or not following God's law, ordering others to transgress God's law, or simply lacked legitimacy.

We find expression of this quadrapartite political thought formulated in sixteenth-century Muscovy in the writings of Iosif Volotskii. The complexity of Iosif's thought has elicited confusion in the historiography. Some historians have focused on Discourse no. 16 of his *Prosvetitel'*, where Iosif recommends silent obedience to the ruler who obeys God's law[25] and, thus, saw Iosif as a proponent of grand-princely power.[26] Other historians have focused on Discourse no. 7 of the same work, where Iosif describes the tyrant who transgresses God's laws as a "tormentor" (muchitel') who should not be obeyed.[27] Val'denberg, for

reached almost identical conclusions about the relationship of the MS copies. Ostrowski, "A 'Fontological' Investigation," pp. 131–145; A. I. Pliguzov, "'Otvet' Mitropolita Makariia Tsariu Ivanu IV," *RFA*, vol. 4, 1988, pp. 719–722.

[24] Rowland, "Muscovite Literary Ideology," pp. 136–137. An interesting parallel to this progression from Harmony to Breakdown occurred in the relationship of the English colonists in North America with King George III. In the Olive Branch Petition of July 1775, the members of the Continental Congress blamed the king's advisers as the cause of the problems between England and the colonies. By July 1776, the Declaration of Independence accuses George himself of being a tyrant and of being the cause of the breakdown of relations. See *Primary Sources Supplement to Accompany World History*, ed. Donald Ostrowski, Minneapolis/St. Paul, West, 1995, pp. 60–67.

[25] Iosif Volotskii, *Prosvetitel'*, ili oblichenie eresi zhidovstvuiushchikh, 3rd edn, Kazan', Tipografia Imperatorskogo universiteta, 1896, p. 547.

[26] See, e.g., Marc Raeff, "An Early Theorist of Absolutism: Joseph of Volokolamsk," *American Slavic and East European Review*, vol. 8, 1949, pp. 77–89, reprinted without footnotes in *Readings in Russian History*, ed. Sidney Harcave, 2 vols., New York, Thomas Y. Crowell, 1962, vol. 1, pp. 177–187; William-Kenneth Medlin, *Moscow and East Rome: a Political Study of the Relations of Church and State in Muscovite Russia*, Geneva, E. Droz, 1952, pp. 87–91; Igor Smolitsch, *Russisches Mönchtum. Entstehung, Entwicklung und Wesen, 988–1917* (Das Östliche Christentum, N.S. nos. 10–11), Wurtzburg, Augustinus, 1953, pp. 119–126; and Pipes, *Russia Under the Old Regime*, p. 232.

[27] Volotskii, *Prosvetitel'*, p. 287; see also p. 549; cf. N. A. Kazakova and Ia. S. Lur'e, *Antifeodal'nye ereticheskie dvizheniia na Rusi XIV–nachala XVI veka (AFED)*, Moscow and Leningrad, Akademiia nauk SSSR, 1955, p. 346.

example, has described it as the "most original and extraordinary part of his political system."[28] Still others have pointed out the seeming paradox between advising silent obedience and opposing a tyrant. They have sought the resolution of this apparently contradictory advice in Iosif's involvement in the politics of the time: that is, when Iosif needed the ruler's favor, he wrote about silent obedience; when he was in opposition to the ruler on some issue, he wrote about disobeying the "tsar-tyrant."[29]

Instead, we should incorporate all aspects of Iosif's analysis and, as Rowland has argued, see it as a consistent whole.[30] Otherwise, we are put in the rather untenable position of arguing that Iosif was a hypocrite and crass opportunist who made up contradictory views depending on his relations with the grand prince at any particular time without any concern for consistency in his writings. If this were so, then we would have to say the same about Ivan Timofeev, who, subsequently, articulated further the significance of this quadrapartite formulation.[31] What is more, by seeing Iosif's images of the ruler as part of a consistent whole, shared by other writers of the sixteenth and seventeenth centuries in Muscovy, we can also see that it is part of a larger systematic outlook that more or less accurately reflects the views expressed by Byzantine Church political writers of an earlier time.

The concept of the head of the Church speaking out in opposition to policies of the temporal ruler was articulated in Byzantium in the ninth century by Patriarch Photios in the *Epanagōgē* (at least in the parts

---

[28] V. E. [Vladimir] Val'denberg, *Drevnerusskie uchenie o predelakh tsarskoi vlasti. Ocherki russkoi politicheskoi literatury ot Vladimira Sviatogo do kontsa XVII veka*, Petrograd, A. Benke, 1916, pp. 201–222 (the quotation is on p. 219). Elsewhere, Val'denberg terms Iosif's teaching "revolutionary." V. E. Val'denberg, "Poniatie o tiranne v drevnerusskoi literature v sravnenii s zapadnoi," *Izvestiia po russkomu iazyku i slovesnosti*, vol. 2, bk. 1, 1929, p. 219. Utechin pointed out a similarity between Iosif's formulation of the tyrant and the views of Thomas Aquinas, but adds that there is no evidence that Iosif knew of Aquinas' views. Utechin, *Russian Political Thought*, p. 24.

[29] M. A. D'iakonov, *Vlast' moskovskikh gosudarei. Ocherk iz istorii politicheskikh idei drevnei Rusi do kontsa XVI veka*, St. Petersburg, I. N. Skorokhodov, 1889, pp. 92–96; A. A. Zimin, "O politicheskoi doktrine Iosifa Volotskogo," *TODRL*, vol. 9, 1953, pp. 159–177; Lur'e, *Ideologicheskaia bor'ba*, pp. 204–284 and 426–481; Marc Szeftel, "Joseph Volotsky's Political Ideas in a New Political Perspective," *Jahrbücher für Geschichte Osteuropas*, vol. 13, 1965, pp. 19–29, reprinted in Marc Szeftel, *Russian Institutions and Culture Up to Peter the Great*, London, Variorum, 1975, item 7.

[30] Rowland, "Muscovite Literary Ideology," p. 127.

[31] On Timofeev, see Daniel Rowland, "Towards an Understanding of the Political Ideas in Ivan Timofeev's *Vremennik*," *Slavonic and East European Review*, vol. 62, 1984, pp. 371–399. Keenan has expressed doubts about Timofeev's authorship of the *Vremennik* and suggested instead Artemii Elasonskii, a Greek prelate who came to Russia in 1589 and stayed many years, helping to set up the patriarchate. Keenan's argument is based on the mistakes and grammatical infelicities in the *Vremennik* that no Novgorodian (as Timofeev was supposed to be) would have made.

attributed to him).[32] Title 2 of the *Epanagōgē*, for example, delineates the duties of the patriarch, especially Article 4, which makes the point that the patriarch should "raise his voice on behalf of the truth and the vindication of doctrines before kings, and not to be reticent."[33] Those parts that defined the respective duties of the basileus and patriarch were translated into Serbian in the *Syntagma* of Matthew Blastares in the fourteenth century,[34] and were known in Muscovy by the middle of the sixteenth century at the latest.[35]

Still, an additional wrinkle needed to be ironed out. Here the work of Deno Geanakoplos on the relation between the temporal and spiritual rulers in Byzantium can help us understand the parallel relationship in Muscovy. The emperor and patriarch in Byzantium were to act together in close harmony for the good of their subjects and both were God's

[32] J. Scharf, "Photius und die Epanagoge," *Byzantinische Zeitschrift*, vol. 49, 1956, pp. 385–400; see also Ernest Barker, *Social and Political Thought in Byzantium: From Justinian I to the Last Palaeologus*, Oxford, Clarendon Press, 1957, p. 89.

[33] *Jus graeco-romanum*, vol. 4, p. 183; *Jus graecoromanum*, vol. 6, p. 59.

[34] Ostrogorsky has noted that, although the *Epanagōgē* "was never completely translated into Slavonic," parts of it, in particular the pronouncements on the roles of the Emperor and Patriarch were "known in the Slav world through the *Syntagma* of Matthew Blastares . . . translated into Slavonic in 1335 by order of Stephen Dušan." Ostrogorsky, *History of the Byzantine State*, p. 240 fn. 2.

[35] According to Sobolevskii, a number of Serbian copies of the Slavonic translation of the *Syntagma* reached Muscovy ("до нас") in the fourteenth and fifteenth centuries. For this information he cited T. D. Florinskii. Sobolevskii further asserted, without citation of source, that a copy of the *Syntagma* was transferred from Moldavia to Moscow in 1556. A. I. Sobolevskii, *Perevodnaia literatura Moskovskoi Rusi XIV–XVII vekov. Bibliograficheskie materialy*, in *Sbornik Otdeleniia russkogo iazyka i slovesnosti Imperatorskoi Akademii nauk*, vol. 74, no. 1, St. Petersburg, 1903, p. 11 n. 3, pp. 13–14 n. 3. Žužek declared that the *Syntagma* came to Muscovy in the sixteenth century, and cited Stojan Novaković, *Matije Vlastara Sintagmat, azbuchni zbornik vizantijskikh crkvenikh drzhavnikh zakona i pravila*, Belgrad, Stampano u Državnoj štampariji, 1907, p. xxxii (who in turn cited Florinskii), and N. Il'inskii, *Sobranie po alfavitnomu poriadku vsekh predmetov, sovderzhashchikhsia v sviashchennykh i bozhestvennykh kanonakh, sostavlennoe i obrabotannoe smirenneishim ieromonakhom Matfeem, ili Alfavitnaia sintagma M. Vlastaria*, Simferopol', 1892, p. v. See P. Ivan Žužek, *Kormčaja kniga: Studies on the Chief Code of Russian Canon Law*, in *Orientalia Christiana Analecta*, no. 168, Rome, 1964, p. 201 fn. 14. Furthermore, Žužek pointed out that, although Metropolitan Fotii cited a Greek MS of the *Syntagma* in the early fifteenth century in composing his letters, there is no evidence Fotii brought a copy with him from Constantinople. Žužek, *Kormčaja kniga*, pp. 139–140. Florinskii cited copies of the *Syntagma* in Russian collections. Some of these copies dated to before the middle of the sixteenth century, while others were of indeterminate date. Timofei [Dmitrievich] Florinskii, *Pamiatniki zakonodatel'noi deiatel'nosti Dushana Tsaria Serbov i Grekov. Khrisovuly. Serbskii Zakonnik. Sborniki vizantiiskikh zakonov*, Kiev, Tipografiia Imperatorskogo universiteta Sv. Vladimira, 1888, pp. 308, 316–318. But Florinskii made no indication of when he thought these MSS may have arrived in northeastern Rus'. Val'denberg cited Il'inskii that traces of the *Syntagma* began to appear in Rus' in MSS of the fifteenth century, and that it was translated in its entirety in the beginning of the sixteenth century. Val'denberg, *Drevnerusskie uchenie*, p. 58.

representatives on earth. They had distinctive yet overlapping responsibilities. The emperor clearly was responsible for the matters that were of
a purely temporal nature, such as running the state, conducting foreign
affairs, and commanding the military. In this sphere, the emperor made
the laws and he had complete direct authority. A second sphere existed,
that of administrative, organizational, and disciplinary matters of the
Church, regarded as the external Church, where the temporal and
spiritual spheres interfaced. Here the emperor and patriarch shared the
responsibilities and were to function in agreement with each other. The
Byzantine emperor could convoke Church councils to discuss these
matters.[36] The emperor could also, with the accord of the patriarch,
modify the boundaries of particular dioceses, reestablish the relative
ranks of episcopal sees, and transfer prelates from one diocese to
another. In addition, the Byzantine emperor had the benefit of certain
liturgical privileges. He was the only lay person who was allowed to
preach. He could bless the congregation as a bishop would with the
trikyra and incense the icons. He was the only non-ecclesiastic who was
allowed to enter the sanctuary. During the coronation service, the
emperor, although not ordained, was anointed. It was from this
anointing that the emperor derived his theoretical authority as representative of God on earth.[37]

The third sphere was purely spiritual and was made up of dogmas of
faith and holy sacraments, regarded as the internal Church. In this
sphere, the patriarch was to have complete and direct authority. Just as
the emperor was not to participate in matters dealing with the internal
Church, which was exclusively the jurisdiction of the patriarch, so the
patriarch was not to participate in the temporal sphere, the exclusive
jurisdiction of the emperor.[38]

Muscovite sources tell us that these distinctions were maintained
between secular and ecclesiastical rulers, and that the second sphere,
that of dual authority, was more or less fully operative. We can see this

---

[36] In his responses to the sixty-one questions that Tsar Aleksii Mikhailovich had posed to
the Metropolitan of Gaza, Paisios Ligarides, in the winter of 1662–1663, Ligarides
indicated that the emperor could indeed convoke a local council. See Ihor Ševčenko,
"Byzantium and the Eastern Slavs After 1453," *Harvard Ukrainian Studies*, vol. 2,
1978, p. 15; Ihor Ševčenko, "A New Greek Source Concerning the Nikon Affair:
Sixty-One Answers by Paisios Ligarides Given to Tsar Aleksej Mikhajlovič," unpublished paper read at Early Slavicists Luncheon, Russian Research Center, March 19,
1996. The source Ševčenko cites is the MS. Sinaiticus gr. 1915, fols. 29–60.

[37] For a fuller discussion, see Deno J. Geanakoplos, *Byzantine East and Latin West: Two
Worlds of Christendom in Middle Ages and Renaissance. Studies in Ecclesiastical and Church
History*, Oxford, Basil Blackwell, 1966, pp. 67, 69–73. See also Gudziak, "Crisis and
Reform," p. 290 fn. 84.

[38] Geanakoplos, *Byzantine East and Latin West*, p. 64. See also Ostrogorsky, *History of the
Byzantine State*, pp. 240–241.

Table 9.2 *Spheres of responsibility of temporal and spiritual rulers*

Sphere of temporal ruler	Sphere of shared responsibilities	Sphere of spiritual ruler
state and military institutions and practices	external Church (administrative and organizational hierarchy, disciplinary measures)	internal Church (doctrines, dogmas, tenets, teachings, and precepts of faith)

especially in the Decisions of the Church Councils that dealt with matters concerning the external Church, wherein both the grand prince and the metropolitan are listed as presiding.[39] By contrast, Church councils that dealt with internal Church matters only, such as the 1490 Council, which was an inquiry into the Novgorod heresy, convened and reached their decisions without the participation of the grand prince.[40] But councils that decided punishment for the heretics, such as the 1504 Council, were in the dual-authority sphere and, therefore, deliberated under the supervision of the grand prince. The gathering of prelates to investigate the views of Maksim Grek provide further evidence of this distinction. The grand prince presided over the trial of Maksim Grek in 1525, after which Maksim was punished by being imprisoned in the Volokolamsk Monastery.[41] But he did not preside over the inquiries of 1531 and 1549, neither of which resulted in further punishment of Maksim.[42] After the inquiry of 1531, Maksim was merely moved to the Otroch' Monastery in Tver', presumably to make room for Vassian Patrikeev, who was being incarcerated in the Volokolamsk Monastery. The grand prince did not personally preside over the trial of Vassian

[39] For the 1447 council, see *AI*, vol. 1, no. 40, pp. 75–83; for the 1448 council, see *RIB*, vol. 6 (1908) cols. 555–564 and *AI*, vol. 1, no. 43, p. 86; for the 1459 council, see *RIB*, vol. 6 (1908), cols. 627–632; for the 1503 council, see *AAE*, vol. 1, nos. 382 and 383a, pp. 484–487, Ostrowski, "A 'Fontological' Investigation, pp. 517–547, and *RFA*, vol. 3, pp. 658–662; for the 1547 council, see *AAE*, vol. 1, no. 213, pp. 203–204; for the 1551 council, see *Stoglav*, ed. I. M. Dobrotvorskii, 2nd edn, Kazan', Tipografiia Imperatorskogo universiteta, 1887, pp. 13–14; for the 1553 council, see *AAE*, vol. 1, no. 238, pp. 246–249; for the 1554 council, see *AAE*, vol. 1, no. 239, pp. 249–256; for the 1564 council, see *AI*, vol. 1, no. 173, pp. 331–333; for the 1572 council, see *AAE*, vol. 1, no. 284, pp. 329–332; for the 1580 council, see *SGGD*, vol. 1, no. 200, pp. 583–587; for the 1584 council, see *SGGD*, vol. 1, no. 202, pp. 592–593; for the 1589 council, see *SGGD*, vol. 2, no. 59, pp. 93–105; and for the 1598 council, see *AAE*, vol. 2, no. 6, pp. 13–16.
[40] For the 1490 Church Council, see *AFED*, no. 20, pp. 382–386.
[41] *Sudnye spiski Maksima Greka i Isaka Sobaki*, ed. N. N. Pokrovskii, Moscow, Glavnoe arkhivnoe upravlenie pri Sovete ministrov SSSR, 1971, pp. 90, 140, 160.
[42] *Sudnye spiski Maksima Greka*, pp. 138–139.

Patrikeev for heresy (also in 1531), but Mikhail Iur'evich Zakhar'in, a senior boyar, acted in his place.[43] Iosif Volotskii makes it clear in his letter to Bishop Nifont that the secular ruler is the one to punish and put to death heretics: "the bishop is not required to execute or imprison [heretics], but the pious tsars put to death many of the unrepentant among the Jews and heretics."[44] And in his *Prosvetitel'*, Iosif affirms that the Churchmen are not the ones to do the physical punishment: "The venerable . . . Fathers, the hierarchs, and the pastors condemned heretics and apostates to death and fierce punishments, not by a weapon but by prayer and the strength given to them by God."[45] Such a distinction corresponds with the practice in the Byzantine Empire, where the basileus might take an interest in the theology of heretical disputes but actively participated only when punishment of the heretic became an issue.[46]

Notions that a deal was crafted at the 1503 Church Council whereby Grand Prince Ivan III gave his support for continued church and monastic landowning in return for Iosif Volotskii's allowing the grand prince jurisdiction over the external Church can be seen in this context to be nonsensical. First, the secular ruler already had that jurisdiction within the Eastern Church. The duties of the basileus were known to the Muscovite grand princes not only through the advice of Rus' Church prelates but also through Patriarch of Constantinople Antonios' letter to Vasilii I:

They [the emperors] convoked the ecumenical councils; they confirmed and ordered acceptance of the pronouncements of the divine and holy canons concerning true doctrines and the government of Christian people; they struggled hard against heresies; and it was imperial decrees that, along with the councils, fixed the metropolitan sees of the hierarchs, the division of dioceses, and the lines of their boundaries.[47]

And since there was no longer a basileus, and because the Rus' Church

---

[43] "Sudnoe delo Vassiana Patrikeeva (1531 god, 11 maia)," in N. A. Kazakova, *Vassian Patrikeev i ego sochineniia*, Moscow and Leningrad, Akademiia nauk SSSR, 1960, p. 285. On the career of M. I. Zakhar'in, see Kollmann, *Kinship and Politics*, pp. 93, 102. Zakhar'in's father, Iurii, and his uncle, Iakov, had been *namestniks* in Novgorod and had aided Gennadii in his campaigns against heretics there. *AFED*, pp. 314–317, 375. See also David Goldfrank, "Theocratic Imperatives, the Transcendent, the Worldly, and Political Justice in Russia's Early Inquisitions," in *Religious and Secular Forces in Late Tsarist Russia: Essays in Honor of Donald W. Treadgold*, ed. Charles E. Timberlake, Seattle, University of Washington Press, 1992, p. 33.

[44] *Poslanie Iosifa Volotskogo*, ed. A. A. Zimin and Ia. S. Lur'e, Moscow and Leningrad, Akademiia nauk SSSR, 1959, p. 165; cf. *Prosvetitel'*, p. 533.

[45] Iosif Volotskii, *Prosvetitel'*, p. 497; *AFED*, p. 496.

[46] Hussey, *Orthodox Church*, p. 305.

[47] *Acta et diplomata graeca*, vol. 2, no. 447, p. 190; *RIB*, vol. 6, Prilozhenie, no. 40, cols. 271–272; Barker, *Manuel II Palaeologus*, p. 107.

had adopted a semi-autonomous position in 1448, the duties of the basileus would logically be taken over by the grand prince in regard to the Rus' Church. Second, Iosif, although hegumen of a prominent monastery, was not in a position to make deals for the Rus' Church. Only the metropolitan, with agreement of the bishops, could do that.

The liturgical privileges that the Byzantine emperor enjoyed carried over to the Muscovite tsar. In 1547, for instance, when Ivan IV was crowned tsar, not only was he anointed as the Byzantine emperor had been after the late twelfth century, but he was also allowed to communicate in the sanctuary with the clergy.[48]

It is difficult to find any evidence of interference by the Muscovite grand prince or tsar directly in matters of Church dogma and the internal Church. On the contrary, we have specific evidence that the tsars respected this distinction. In his discussions with the Italian Jesuit Antonio Possevino in 1582, Ivan IV, for example, gave as one of the reasons he would not discuss theology was that he had not received the "blessing and consecration" to do so by the metropolitan and the Holy Synod. Furthermore, Ivan states that "it is not appropriate for me to discuss the faith in their absence."[49] Possevino, in his account to the Pope, states that Ivan's reasons for not discussing theological issues were (1) "fear that I might touch upon matters that could give offense to you," and (2) "because my duty is to attend to temporal affairs, for which I have received the blessing of my metropolitan, not spiritual ones."[50] Ivan's demurral was not just an "excuse" to avoid being bested by a Jesuit in theological discussion. He was abiding by the prescribed relationship between spiritual and temporal leaders in the Eastern Church.

Such recognition on Ivan's part of this distinction tends to refute the contention that he wrote the *Reply to Jan Rokyta*.[51] The historiographical views on this issue are divided between those who think Rokyta, a chaplain of the Czech Brethren, undertook his trip to Moscow to convert Ivan IV and those who think Ivan organized the debate to exhibit his erudition. The latter scenario is unlikely for Rokyta's report of the encounter, like Possevino's, shows no attempt at eloquence on the tsar's part, merely straightforward questions as prepared by the Po-

---

[48] David B. Miller, "The Coronation of Ivan IV of Moscow," *Jahrbücher für Geschichte Osteuropas*, vol. 15, 1967, p. 565.

[49] PDS, vol. 10, col. 300; *The Muscovia of Antonio Possevino, S. J.*, trans. Hugh F. Graham, Pittsburgh, University Center for International Studies, University of Pittsburgh, 1977, p. 173

[50] *Muscovia of Antonio Possevino*, p. 69.

[51] For a summary of the historiography on this issue, see Valerie A. Tumins, *Tsar Ivan IV's Reply to Jan Rokyta*, The Hague, Mouton, 1971, pp. 28–31.

sol'skii prikaz.[52] The formal questioning by Ivan IV and response by Rokyta occurred on May 10, 1570. Some historians claim that in June or July Ivan handed Rokyta his formal answer, that is the extant *Reply*. But problems of attribution make this unlikely. First, neither Rokyta nor Paul Oderborn, who in 1585 wrote about the encounter, mentions a reply from Ivan IV.[53] Second, a seventeenth-century copy of the *Reply* has the name of Parfenii Iurodivii as author. Ludolf Müller accepted this attribution and accused Ivan IV of having borrowed Parfenii's composition wholesale, only making some awkward changes for the *Reply* he handed Rokyta.[54] But D. S. Likhachev claimed that "Parfenii Iurodivii" was a pseudonym that Ivan IV used to write the *Reply* and another work, *Canon and Prayer to the Angel the Wrathful Warrior*.[55] Either case would tend to refute those who argue that Ivan would try to display his erudition to foreigners. In the end, any such response by the tsar, even if written under a pseudonym or plagiarized, would have been prohibited and, therefore, extremely unlikely.

In the middle of the seventeenth century, Patriarch Nikon confirmed this relationship between the temporal and ecclesiastical establishments in Muscovy based on the *Epanagōgē*:

the tsar doubtless has power within his proper bounds set him by God to give power to secular people, but not to bishops and archimandrites and the other ecclesiastical authorities; but as thou thyself also writest: "the things which are heavenly belong to the judgment of God, but the things which are of earth, belong to the judgment of the Tsar." . . . The tsar neither is nor can be the head of the Church, but is one of the members. And on this account he can do nothing whatever in the Church, not even what belongs to the order of the lowest reader or cleric . . . The Tsar has committed to him the things of this earth, but I have committed to me the things of heaven. The tsar has committed to him the bodies, but the priest the souls of men.[56]

---

[52] Jan [Johannis] Rokyta, "Odpowiedź na pytanie u wielkiego hospodara moskiewskiego na pismie podana pythanie hospodarskie," in Tumins, *Tsar Ivan IV's Reply*, pp. 453–468 (facsimile), 471–477 (transcription), and 479–485 (translation into English).

[53] Paul Oderborn, *Ioannis Basilidi Magni Moscoviae Ducis vita*, Görlitz, Heinrich Räteln zu Sagan, 1589.

[54] Ludolf Müller, *Die Kritik des Protestantismus in der russischen Theologie vom 16. bis zum 18. Jahrhundert*, Wiesbaden, Akademie der Wissenschaften und der Literatur in Mainz, in Komm. bei F. Steiner Verlag, 1951, pp. 23–31.

[55] D. S. Likhachev, "'Kanon' i 'Molitva' Angelu Groznomu voevode Parfeniia Urodivogo (Ivana Groznogo)," in *Rukopisnoe nasledie drevnei Rusi. Po materialam Pushkinskogo doma*, ed. A. M. Panchenko, Leningrad, Nauka, 1972, pp. 10–27; D. S. Likhachev, "Sochineniia Tsaria Ivana Vasil'evicha Groznogo," in D. S. Likhachev, *Velikoe nasledie*, Moscow, Sovremennik, 1975, pp. 284–286.

[56] William Palmer, *The Patriarch and the Tsar*, 6 vols., London, Trübner, 1871–1876, vol. 1, pp. 555, 129–130. Cf. M. V. Zyzykin, *Patriarch Nikon. Ego gosudarstvennye i*

Although Matthew Spinka acknowledged that Nikon "only repeated
... the provisions of the *Epanagōgē*, and at no time went beyond them,"
he nonetheless thought "the real cause of the overthrow of Nikon" was
his trying to defend the independence of the Church against an attempt
by Tsar Aleksei's boyars to subsume it to the State.[57] Such an interpretation bespeaks a Western Church model of Church–State conflict.
Instead, "the real cause" of Nikon's downfall was his arrogant personality, which led him to challenge the traditional prerogatives of the
temporal ruler, such as appointing prelates.[58]

The duty of the head of the Church was to speak up on all matters,
whether temporal or spiritual, that affected the internal Church. He
could probably also do so on the basis that such matters affected the
external Church, that is, the sphere of shared responsibility. But the
question is: did the head of the Church in Muscovy have the duty to
speak up in matters that were purely temporal, the exclusive domain of
the grand prince/tsar? As discussed above, Ivan IV complained about
ecclesiastical interference in temporal matters and justified the origin of
the Oprichnina in this way. But was the Church supported by Byzantine
political theory in doing so?

The Church articulated criteria for evaluating the ruler's activities and
for judging whether the ruler was a true ruler or a tormentor. Rowland
pointed out that, according to the ideology articulated in seventeenth-
century ecclesiastical and secular sources, the tsar had three basic
obligations: (1) to act as a "mediator between God's will and the
people's actions"; (2) to preserve the Orthodox faith; and (3) to
maintain "the general order" of the realm.[59] The "wise subjects" in turn
had a duty to indicate to the tsar when he had violated any of these
obligations and, in order to restore his piety, they had to remind him of
his need to obey the will of God.[60] Vassian Rylo's letter to Ivan III on
the Ugra River must be seen within this context. Metropolitan Filipp
spoke up against the Oprichnina policies of Ivan IV. And the *Chrono-
graph of 1617* testifies that the Patriarch of Moscow, Germogen, tried to
warn Tsar Vasilii Shuiskii that, by listening to evil advisers, he was

kanonicheskie idei, 3 vols., Warsaw, Sinodal'naia tipografiia, 1931–1938, vol. 2, pp. 15,
17.

[57] Matthew Spinka, "Patriarch Nikon and the Subjection of the Russian Church to the
State," *Church History*, vol. 10, 1941, pp. 359–360.

[58] Palmer, *The Patriarch and the Tsar*, vol. 1, p. 554. Cf. Zyzykin, *Patriarch Nikon*, vol. 2,
p. 19.

[59] Rowland, "Muscovite Literary Ideology," pp. 132–139. See also Daniel Rowland,
"The Problem of Advice in Muscovite Tales about the Time of Troubles," *Russian
History*, vol. 6, 1979, pp. 264–270.

[60] Rowland, "Muscovite Literary Ideology," p. 141; Rowland, "Problem of Advice,"
pp. 270–283.

falling into sin.[61] Such a political role for the Church was articulated also later, in post-Petrine Russia, for example in the writings of Karamzin: "Its [the clergy's] function had been to serve the latter [secular authority] as a useful tool in affairs of state, and as a conscience at times when it occasionally left the path of virtue. Our primate had one right: not to act, not to rebel, but to preach the truth to the sovereign."[62]

When we examine Byzantine sources, we find similar principles described for evaluating and judging the actions of the basileus. The *Epanagōgē*, in particular, specifies that the "Emperor's duty is to enforce and maintain, first and foremost, all that is set out in the Holy Scriptures, thereafter the doctrines established by the Seven Holy Councils, and finally the laws established by the Romans." Furthermore, "if anything is proposed contrary to the canons [of the Church] it is not to be followed."[63]

Besides the *Epanagōgē* of Photios, we also have the letter of the Patriarch of Constantinople Antonios where he wrote to Vasilii I in the late fourteenth century "that Christians reject only those emperors who were heretical, who were raging against the Church and were introducing dogmas corrupt and alien to the teachings of the Apostles and of the Fathers,"[64] that is, those who interfere in the internal Church. Yet, in the letter of Theophylakt, Archbishop of Bulgaria, to the crown prince Constantine where he distinguishes between a tyrant and king, he also writes that the "true king . . . does not yield [his] primacy even to the clergy."[65] As with Muscovite Church writings, most commentators have interpreted such expressions either as ecclesiastical challenges to the authority of the basileus or as evidence of Caesaropapism, yet it should be seen as neither.[66] Geanakoplos, on the other hand, explained that Byzantine political theory must be seen as beginning with Eusebius' description of the authority of Constantine the Great. Eusebius drew on the traditions of the Roman Empire in which the Emperor was perceived as *Pontifex Maximus*, chief priest. But, as Geanakoplos pointed out,

---

[61] This passage may be an emendation from later in the seventeenth century. Even so, this would not negate its value for determining what the theoretical justifications for questioning the ruler's actions may have been. Rowland, "Problem of Advice," pp. 269–270.

[62] Nikolai Karamzin, *Notes on Ancient and Modern Russia*, ed. and trans. Richard Pipes, Cambridge, MA, Harvard University Press, 1959, p. 125.

[63] *Jus graecoromanum*, vol. 4, pp. 181, 182; *Jus graecoromanum*, vol. 6, p. 58.

[64] *Acta et diplomata graeca*, vol. 2, p. 191; *RIB*, vol. 6, Prilozhenie, no. 40, cols. 275–276; Barker, *Manuel II Palaeologus*, p. 108.

[65] *PG*, vol. 126, cols. 269–270.

[66] One can find a brief survey of the secondary literature on the issue of the basileus' relationship to the Church in Geanakoplos, *Byzantine East and Latin West*, pp. 195–196.

Roman civil officials performed the pagan religious services and rituals because there was no separate priesthood as such. As the Christian Church extended its power, it took over the religious duties of civil officials. It, thus, was able to stake out two areas: one that overlapped with the ruler's power and another that was beyond the Emperor's control.[67]

The political attitudes and actions as described by Muscovite bookmen and taken by Muscovite prelates derived from, and were a further development of, Byzantine political theory of the harmony and sharing of powers between the temporal and spiritual rulers. By contrast, there was no written secular articulation of limitations on the ruler's power in Muscovy. Yet, the Boyar Council's participation in the decision-making process was established by tradition,[68] and its legislative function was formalized in the *Sudebnik of 1550*. Article 98 of the *Sudebnik* states: "And whatever new matters there will be, but [such that] are not written in the *Sudebnik*, and however these matters are resolved with the report of the sovereign and verdict of all the boyars, those matters are to be appended to this *Sudebnik*."[69] In other words, no laws could be issued by the tsar without the approval of the Boyar Council, meaning all the boyars in consultation with the sovereign. Through the seventeenth century, government edicts began with the formula: "the tsar has decreed and the boyars have assented." And the Boyar Council could be influenced by the Church. So a neat parallelism presented itself. While the grand prince or tsar was not to interfere in the internal matters of the Church, he could determine who was metropolitan by influencing the Holy Synod. Likewise, the metropolitan was not to interfere in the internal matters of the state, but he could determine which laws were passed by influencing the Boyar Council. The Church could also have a say when the temporal power of the state affected the external Church, such as regulation of monastic land acquisition. In these ways, the Church could limit the secular power in Muscovy. The Church's exercise of this influence is what seems to have driven Ivan IV to establish the Oprichnina, that is, to escape what he perceived as ecclesiastical attempts to limit his secular power.

One historiographical view holds that Catholic influence on the circle of Gennadii, Archbishop of Novgorod, introduced the concept of limitations on secular power into Muscovy. In particular, so this

---

[67] Geanakoplos, *Byzantine East and Latin West*, pp. 60–63.
[68] See, e.g., *SRIO*, vol. 35, p. 503: "И князь великий приговорил з братьею своею и з бояры . . ."; and *ibid.*, p. 630: "И приговорил князь великий з бояры . . ." See also Martin, *Medieval Russia*, pp. 289–293.
[69] *Sudebniki XV–XVI vekov*, p. 176, and "Commentary," pp. 334–337.

argument goes, such influence affected the ideological views of Iosif Volotskii.[70] Instead, one finds the concepts that Iosif expressed completely in accord with, and derivable from, Eastern Church writing and traditions. Goldfrank has made the same point about Iosif's monastic doctrines and their sources.[71] It may have been important for reasons of ideological purity for the Church bookmen to base their articulations of political theory and monastic doctrines solely on Eastern Church sources.[72]

It is somewhat ironic, then, that the relationship of the tsar to those he rules over is reformulated in the late seventeenth century through the influence of Western political theories of absolutism on the author or authors of *Pravda voli monarshei*.[73] By articulating the formulation that God acted through the people, the author(s) were able to combine Hobbes' view, which was that in the natural state the people chose the ruler, with Bossuet's view, which was that God chose the ruler.[74] Like Hobbes and Bossuet, *Pravda voli monarshei* argues that once a legitimate choice is made, the people cannot withdraw their support.[75] This synthesis corresponds with both the

[70] See, e.g., Joseph L. Wieczynski, "Archbishop Gennadius and the West: the Impact of Catholic Ideas upon the Church of Novgorod," *Canadian–American Slavic Studies*, vol. 6, 1972, p. 386: "The Catholic cast of the Josephite mind is a credit to the work of Gennadius." For a discussion and rejection of such a view, see Lur'e, *Ideologicheskaia bor'ba*, pp. 266–284.

[71] David Goldfrank, "Old and New Perspectives on Iosif Volotsky's Monastic Rules," *Slavic Review*, vol. 24, 1975, p. 283; David Goldfrank, *The Monastic Rule of Iosif Volotsky*, Kalamazoo, Cistercian, 1983, pp. 25–29. See also Tomaś Špidlík, *Joseph de Volokolamsk: Un chapitre de la spiritualité russe*, in *Orientalia Christiana Analecta*, vol. 146, 1956.

[72] Ševčenko has gone furthest in tracing this influence in regard to political theory. Ševčenko, "A Neglected Byzantine Source," pp. 141–179; Ihor Ševčenko, "Muscovy's Conquest of Kazan: Two Views Reconciled," *Slavic Review*, vol. 26, 1967, pp. 542–543 fn. 1; Ihor Ševčenko, "Agapetus East and West: Fate of a Byzantine 'Mirror of Princes,'" *Revue des études sud-est Européennes*, vol. 16, 1978, pp. 1–44.

[73] For a discussion of the authorship of *Pravda voli monarshei* see James Cracraft, "Did Feofan Prokopovich Really Write *Pravda Voli Monarshei*?" *Slavic Review*, vol. 40, 1981, pp. 173–193. Cracraft argues that "the attribution to Feofan Prokopovich of . . . *Pravda voli monarshei* . . . rests on sand," and furthermore "that nearly every other major work traditionally and for the most part unquestioningly ascribed to Prokopovich is similarly open to doubt" (p. 173). Cracraft concludes, however, that the *Pravda voli monarshei* was "probably written by him [Prokopovich] in collaboration with one or more persons" (p. 192).

[74] "Pravda voli monarshei," *PSZRI*, vol. 7, p. 625: "It must be understood that the will of the people, either in an elective or in a hereditary monarchy, as in other forms of government, exists not without the personal supervision [смотрънія] of God"; and p. 624: "every form of government, including hereditary monarch, has its inception from the original agreement of the people, always and in all places according to their will, wisely acting under the supervision [смотрънію] of God."

[75] "Pravda voli monarshei," *PSZRI*, vol. 7, p. 625: "The people must, without contradiction or murmur, do everything that is ordered by the autocrat."

Byzantine and the Muscovite ideological definition of the tsar's authority. Karamzin makes reference in his *Notes on Ancient and Modern Russia* to the concept *vox populi, vox dei* "the voice of the people is the voice of God."[76] But Karamzin also believed that once the choice of government was made, the people "were not free to withdraw their support." He even urges Alexander I "to act rashly, to give the people no time to come to their senses"[77] and advises that his "ministers speak frankly only to the monarch, never to the people."[78] In this sense, Karamzin pre-answered Marc Szeftel's question, posed in 1963: "where was the guarantee that the Monarch would consistently observe this ideal of self-limitation?"[79]

That ideal was the principle of *zakonnost'* by which the rulers of Russia were obliged to limit their own power in accordance with precedent established by the actions of their predecessors and themselves. This same principle is described in Articles 6 and 7 of Title 1 of the *Epanagōgē*: "The Emperor must interpret the laws laid down by the men of old; and he must as they did decide the matters on which there is no law. In interpreting the laws, he must pay attention to the custom of the *polis*."[80] Thus, the duty of self-restraint on the part of the ruler was articulated similarly not only in Byzantium and Muscovy but also in Imperial Russia. And Karamzin's answer concerning who should speak up when the ruler failed to do his duty in this regard was the same answer that applied in sixteenth- and seventeenth-century Muscovy as well as in Byzantium. That is, it was the tsar's good advisers (like Karamzin himself), the "strong in Israel," and the clergy who had the duty to speak the truth to the sovereign, even at risk to themselves.

Since the Emperor was to use the Holy Scriptures as a guide to conducting state business, we might also consider the idea that, as has been suggested for Byzantium, the Gospels served in Muscovy a function similar to that of a constitution in a modern democratic state, that is, as the ultimate written authority of the land. This would be true only insofar as the head of the Church could convince the temporal authorities that Muscovy, like Byzantium formerly, was the kingdom of Christ on earth. But in Muscovy, the Gospels were not placed open on a

---

[76] Karamzin, *Notes on Ancient and Modern Russia*, p. 147.
[77] Karamzin, *Notes on Ancient and Modern Russia*, p. 157.
[78] Karamzin, *Notes on Ancient and Modern Russia*, p. 173.
[79] Marc Szeftel, "The Form of Government of the Russian Empire Prior to the Constitutional Reforms of 1905–06," in *Essays in Russian and Soviet History: In Honor of Geroid Tanquary Robinson*, ed. John Shelton Curtiss, Leiden, E. J. Brill, 1963, p. 106.
[80] *Jus graeco-romanum*, vol. 4, pp. 181–182. *Jus graecoromanum*, vol. 6, p. 58.

throne beside the ruler as they were in Byzantium.[81] Instead, the iconography of the throne room of the *Zolotaia palata* may be taken as Muscovy's physical manifestation of a constitution, especially adopted for illiterate and semi-literate boyars.

We can say, then, that in regard to political theory, the Muscovite Church selectively adapted significant aspects of Byzantine political theory. This selective adaptation influenced and was influenced by Muscovite political realities. Ultimately, however, the ideals of both Byzantine and Muscovite Church political theory were the same – harmony between secular and ecclesiastical rulers, separate spheres of responsibility that also overlapped, and means for resolving conflicts. The mechanism by which Byzantine political theory was transferred to Muscovy after 1448 was through the Rus' Churchmen's translation of Byzantine political texts and the *Melissa*, reproducing Byzantine iconography, and possibly also the singing of hymns.

If the history of the Third Rome concept is any indication, certain Church bookmen were not always so successful in getting acceptance of their formulations either by the secular authorities or within the Church itself. Instead, Muscovite literary culture focused on the Old Testament and adopted the concept of Muscovy's being the "New Jerusalem" or the "New Israel."[82] While the concept of Rus' as the Third Rome does appear in some sixteenth- and seventeenth-century sources, it is too strong to say, as Crummey does, that it "entered the mainstream of Russian ecclesiastical thinking."[83] For example, there is no iconographical representation of Moscow or the Rus' state as the Third Rome. And to say that the "Third Rome" influenced governmental policy in any way is simply incorrect, because we have no evidence whatever that it became operative in any policy, foreign or domestic, of the secular government.

---

[81] René Guerdan, *Byzantium: Its Triumphs and Tragedy*, trans. D. L. B. Hartley, New York, Capricorn, 1962, p. 29. See the illumination of the Emperor Theodosius I at the Council of Constantinople in 381 found in a ninth-century MS in the Bibliothèque Nationale, Parisinus Graecus 510, fol. 355. My thanks to George Majeska for providing me the information about this illumination.

[82] For a discussion of the exorbitant influence historians have given the Third Rome concept, see Daniel Rowland, "Moscow – The Third Rome or the New Israel?" *Russian Review*, vol. 55, 1996, pp. 591–614. Rowland pointed out that the Church bookmen, in general, were committed to the New Israel model for Muscovy rather than a Third Rome model.

[83] Crummey, *Formation of Muscovy*, p. 137.

10 Third Rome: delimiting the ruler's power and authority

The popular view of Third Rome theory is that: (1) it derived from Western Church sources; (2) it was an unabashed propaganda piece extolling the unlimited power and authority of the Muscovite ruler; (3) it was the dominant political theory of Muscovite grand princes and tsars; and (4) it became the dominant imperial ideology of Russia as it expanded during subsequent centuries. Specialists have questioned how dominant and pervasive Third Rome theory was in political decision making at any time in Russian history.[1] Yet, the view that it had great importance persists, while at the same time most specialists have pretty much accepted the refutation of such a notion.[2] At least one scholar has questioned the Western basis of its formulation; but, until recently, few have questioned its intent to enhance the power and authority of the Muscovite ruler.[3] Yet delimiting the duties of the sovereign may have been the original intent of the formulators of Third Rome theory before 1589. Let us look again at the source question and then at our understanding of the intent of the formulation. In the process, we will find out more about the Church's development of an anti-Tatar ideology in the course of the sixteenth century.

The formulation of the Third Rome theory was the result of the reworking of concepts from several sources. In general, scholars have accepted the Western Church's Apocalypse of Ezra, included in the

---

[1] Donald Ostrowski, "Moscow the Third Rome as Historiographical Ghost," unpublished (and probably unpublishable) paper, an early version of which I presented at the New England Slavic Conference, Cambridge, MA, April 10, 1992.

[2] This difference does not prevent specialists from occasionally taking advantage of popular notions. For example, a popular version of R. G. Skrynnikov's scholarly monograph *Gosudarstvo i tserkov' na Rusi XIV–XVI vv. Podvizhniki russkoi tserkvi*, Novosibirsk, Nauka Sibirskoe otdelenie, 1991, came out as *Tretii Rim*, St. Petersburg, "Dmitrii Bulanin," 1994, although there is no real discussion of the Third Rome formulation in either book.

[3] Among the exceptions, we might include David Goldfrank, "Third Rome," in *MERSH*, vol. 23, p. 119; Rowland, "Muscovite Literary Ideology," pp. 152–153; and Rowland, "Moscow – The Third Rome or the New Israel?" p. 595.

Gennadii Bible from the Latin Vulgate, as one of those sources.[4] The Book of Daniel (7:1–23) describes four beasts, which have been traditionally associated with the Babylonian, Persian, Macedonian, and Roman empires, respectively. Daniel remarks that his third beast has four heads and his fourth beast has ten horns. The Apocalypse of Ezra (12:33) attributes three heads to Daniel's fourth beast, which have traditionally been associated with the Emperor Vespasian and his two sons Titus and Domitian.[5] This is not to say that they could not have been interpreted differently in the religious world of the early sixteenth century. But Richard Pope has questioned Ezra as a possible source of Third Rome on the basis of the following arguments.[6] First, the three heads exist on the fourth beast together simultaneously, which does not fit the image of successive kingdoms.[7] Second, the three heads represent three wicked kings in Ezra, whereas the three Romes are protectors and saviors of Christianity. Finally, Ezra describes the third head as dying by the sword, hardly a propitious model for the Third Rome, which is not to fall. I might also point out that if the fourth beast represents Rome then it is unlikely that any of the three heads would also represent Rome. Instead, Pope suggested the main, but by no means the only, source may be a Bulgarian apocryphal work, which he called *Razumnik-Ukaz*.[8] Among the reasons why the *Razumnik-Ukaz* could not stand alone as a source of the Third Rome formulation is that it explicitly eliminates Rome as one of the tsarstvos ("The first is the Greek tsarstvo, the second is the German, the third is the Bulgarian tsarstvo"). Although the progression through three tsarstvos fits Third Rome theory, this particular progression does not.

---

[4] For the view that the Third Rome concept derives from the Ezra-Apocalypse, see Dmitri Strémooukhoff, "Moscow the Third Rome: Sources of the Doctrine," *Speculum*, vol. 28, 1953, pp. 91–101; reprinted in *Structure of Russian History*, pp. 108–125. Schaeder had previously mentioned the Ezra-Apocalypse as one of the possible sources. Hildegard Schaeder, *Moskau das dritte Rom. Studien zur Geschichte der politischen Theorien in der slavischen Welt* (= *Osteuropäische Studien*, vol. 1), Hamburg, Friederichsen, de Gruyter, 1929, p. 41; 2nd edn, Darmstadt, 1957, p. 56. Lur'e supported Strémooukhoff's contention. Lur'e, *Ideologicheskaia bor'ba*, pp. 486–487; and Ia. S. Lur'e, "Zametki k istorii publitsisticheskoi literatury kontsa XV–pervoi poloviny XVI v.," *TODRL*, vol. 16, 1960, p. 458.

[5] W. O. E. Oesterly, *The Books of the Apocrypha: Their Origin, Teaching, and Contents*, London, Robert Scott, 1914, p. 520.

[6] Richard W. F. Pope, "A Possible South Slavic Source for the Doctrine: Moscow the Third Rome," *Slavia*, vol. 44, 1975, pp. 247–248.

[7] See also the comment of G. H. Box, in *The Ezra-Apocalypse: Being Chapters 3–14 of the Book Commonly Known as 4 Ezra (or II Esdras)*, trans. G. H. Box, London, Sir Isaac Pitman, 1912, p. 249.

[8] For the text of the *Razumnik-Ukaz* passage itself, along with MS descriptions, see Richard W. F. Pope, "Bulgaria: the Third Christian Kingdom in the *Razumnik-Ukaz*," *Slavia*, vol. 43, 1974, pp. 141–153.

We have a commentary on the paschal canon dating to 1492 by Metropolitan Zosima, which, it has been suggested, indicates a progression that begins with Rome. In the published version, edited by A. S. Pavlov, the commentary states: "And by the will of God, he [Constantine] created a city in his own name that is Constantinople, which is Tsar'grad, that is to say the New Rome [Новый Рим]."[9] Zosima's commentary goes on to refer to Ivan III as "the new Emperor Constantine of the new Constantinople – Moscow and of all the Rus' land and many other lands."[10] The phrase "that is to say the New Rome" led Pavlov and, more recently Lur'e, to conclude that the Rome → Constantinople → Moscow progression of Zosima's commentary was a basis for the formulation of Moscow the Third Rome.[11] But, in his publication of Zosima's commentary, Pavlov had pointed out and dismissed a variant to the reading "Rome." Pavlov wrote: "In other copies *Jerusalem* is mistaken."[12] In the 1980s, I. A. Tikhoniuk, after a text-critical analysis of the copies of Zosima's commentary, noted that the reading "Rome" appears only in the Trinity copy, which, although early (1493), is countered by the reading "Jerusalem" in three other copies of the commentary also from the 1490s. He realized that these three copies are more accurate overall in representing the archetype than the Trinity copy. Tikhoniuk concluded that the reading "Jerusalem" is primary and, therefore, the most likely word used in the author's protograph.[13] In addition, Pliguzov pointed out that the unnamed town referred to in the beginning of the commentary, where "the apostles convened as one and testifying affirmed the faith" could only be Jerusalem.[14]

Indeed, there is no reference or allusion to Rome elsewhere in the entire commentary. We can only conclude that the copyist of the Trinity manuscript telescoped "*иерусалимъ*" into "*римъ*" either intentionally or unintentionally. If this was done unintentionally, then Zosima's commentary cannot be designated a source of the progression from Rome, since Constantinople was being referred to as "New Jerusalem" and Moscow as "New Constantinople." Thus, Moscow could only be

[9] "Mitropolita Zosimy izveshchenie o paskhalii na os'muiu tysiachu let," *RIB*, vol. 6, no. 118, col. 798.

[10] "Mitropolita Zosimy izveshchenie o paskhalii," col. 799.

[11] A. S. Pavlov, "Vopros o eresi zhidovstvuiushchikh na VI Arkheologicheskom s"ezde," *Sovremennye izvestiia*, Odessa, September 29, 1884, no. 266; Lur'e, *Ideologicheskaia bor'ba*, pp. 377–378.

[12] "Mitropolita Zosimy izveshchenie o paskhalii," col. 798 n. 7.

[13] I. A. Tikhoniuk, "'Izlozhenie paskhalii' Moskovskogo mitropolita Zosimy," *Issledovaniia po istochnikovedeniiu istorii SSSR XIII–XVIII vv. Sbornik statei*, ed. V. I. Buganov, V. A. Kuchkin, and V. G. Litvak, Moscow, Akademiia nauk SSSR, 1986, pp. 53–54.

[14] Tikhoniuk, "Izlozhenie paskhalii," pp. 54–55.

the "Third Jerusalem" in this sequence. Even if the copyist of the
Trinity manuscript intentionally changed "Jerusalem" to "Rome," this
still may not have significance in the formulation of the progression from
Rome, since the copyist may have honestly thought he was merely
correcting an error in the text. Constantinople had been referred to as
"new Rome" at least since the second ecumenical council at Constantinople in 381.[15] The fourth ecumenical council at Chalcedon in 451
incorporated this decision.[16]

It would have been sufficient, as Pope argued, for someone in Rus' in
the early sixteenth century to come up with the Third Rome formulation
based solely on a combination of these Eastern Church sources and
tradition.[17] The initiator of Third Rome theory could have taken from
the *Razumnik-Ukaz* the ideas that there are three tsarstvos and that a
progression occurred from one to the other. These ideas along with the
pre-existing concept of Constantinople as the "New Rome" and Zosima's declaration of Moscow and the Rus' land as the "New Constantinople" would have provided all the necessary components of the basic
theory. Thus, it seems to me that the Third Rome formulation coincides
with the idea that concepts of the ruler's authority and the nature of the
state, as articulated by Church writers in Rus', derived solely from
within the Eastern Church tradition. But, as I will now argue, Third
Rome was initially an idea that sought to define and to make explicit the
restrictions on the grand prince's authority, especially in regard to two
cities, Novgorod and Pskov, over which Moscow had recently extended
its control.

The first formulation of Third Rome occurs in three letters that have
been attributed to Filofei, a monk in Pskov. These letters have been
given various titles in the historiography, but I will continue the
convention followed by A. L. Gol'dberg: (1) *Letter Against Astrologers*

[15] John Meyendorff, *Imperial Unity and Christian Divisions: the Church 450–680 AD*,
   Crestwood, NY, St. Vladimir's Seminary Press, 1989, p. 61. Canon 3 of this council
   grants to the bishop of Constantinople "an honorary seniority after the bishop of
   Rome, because that city is the New Rome."
[16] *Syntagma ton Theion kai hieron xanonon ton te hagion kai paneuphemon Apostolon*, ed.
   G. A. Rhalles and M. Potles, 6 vols., Athens, G. Chartophylakos, 1852–1859, vol. 1,
   pp. 280–281. Canon 28 of Chalcedon confirms Constantinople as second or "equal"
   after Rome. On this point, see Ihor Ševčenko, review of *Podil iedynoi Khrystovoi tserkvy*
   by Mytropolyt Ilarion, in *Südost-Forschungen*, vol. 13, 1954, p. 388; review reprinted in
   Ševčenko, *Byzantium and the Slavs*, pp. 89–91. For the concept of Constantinople as
   "New Rome" in Byzantine thought, see Franz Dölger, "Rom in der Gedankenwelt der
   Byzantiner," *Zeitschrift für Kirchengeschichte*, vol. 56, 1937, pp. 1–42; reprinted in
   Dölger, *Byzanz und die europäische Staatenwelt*, pp. 70–115. For the time when
   Constantinople began to be called "New Jerusalem," see Mango, *Byzantium, the Empire
   of New Rome*, p. 208.
[17] Pope, "Possible South Slavic Source," p. 249.

("Послание на звездочетцев") to Mikhail Grigor'evich Misiur' Munekhin, the grand-princely d'iak in Pskov;[18] (2) *Letter About the Sign of the Cross* ("Послание о крестном знамении") to Vasilii III;[19] and (3) *Work About the Offenses to the Church* ("Соченение об обидах церкви") to Ivan Vasil'evich.[20]

Questions concerning the dating and sequence of composition of these letters have found no definitive answers in the historiography. V. Malinin dated the *Letter About the Sign of the Cross* to 1510 and, thus, considered it to be Filofei's original expression of Third Rome theory. Malinin dated the letter to Munekhin to 1524. For the letter to Ivan Vasil'evich, Malinin did not provide a specific date but argued that it was sent to Ivan IV sometime between 1533 and 1546.[21] Andreyev argued that the *Work About the Offenses* was addressed not to Ivan IV but to his grandfather, Ivan III (both were referred to as Ivan Vasil'evich). According to Andreyev, that would place the most likely time of its composition to around 1499–1500. Andreyev accepted the 1510–1511 date for the *Letter About the Sign of the Cross* and assigned a date of 1528 for the *Letter Against Astrologers*.[22] Frank Kämpfer proposed that the *Work About the Offenses* was the earliest of the three compositions.[23]

Gol'dberg concluded, after an extensive text-critical analysis, that only the *Letter Against Astrologers*, addressed to Munekhin, is Filofei's composition and was the first of the three letters. Gol'dberg placed the time of its composition to around 1523–24.[24] The other two compositions were written later, according to Gol'dberg, but he did not suggest a

[18] Malinin, *Starets Eleazarova monastyria Filofei i ego poslanie*, Appendix, pp. 37–47; also published as *Letter About Unpropitious Days and Hours* ("Послание о неблагоприятных днях и часах") by V. V. Kolesov in *PLDR. Konets XV–pervaia polovina XVI veka*, pp. 442–455.

[19] Malinin, *Starets Eleazarova monastyria Filofei*, appendix, pp. 49–56, also published by Kolesov in *PLDR. Konets XV–pervaia polovina XVI veka*, pp. 436–441.

[20] V. Zhmakin, "Odin iz literaturnykh pamiatnikov XVI veka," *Zhurnal Ministerstva narodnogo prosveshcheniia*, part 221, 1882, June, Otdel nauk, pp. 242–248; Malinin, *Starets Eleazarova monastyria Filofei*, Appendix, pp. 57–66.

[21] Malinin, *Starets Eleazarova monastyria Filofei*, pp. 373, 269, 374–382, 440–491, and 645–658. N. N. Maslennikova agreed that the *Letter About the Sign of the Cross* preceded the other two and she put the time of Filofei's writing this letter at around the same time that Malinin did, that is, 1510–1511. N. N. Maslennikova, "K istorii sozdaniia teorii 'Moskva – tretii Rim,'" *TODRL*, vol. 18, 1962, p. 575.

[22] N. E. Andreyev, "Filofey and His Epistle to Ivan Vasil'yevich," *Slavonic and East European Review*, vol. 38, 1959, p. 28–29; reprinted in Nikolay Andreyev, *Studies in Muscovy: Western Influences and Byzantine Inheritance*, London, Variorum, 1970, item 2.

[23] Frank Kämpfer, "Beobachtungen zu den Sendschreiben Filofejs," *Jahrbücher für Geschichte Osteuropas*, vol. 18, 1970, p. 138.

[24] A. L. Gol'dberg, "Tri 'poslaniia Filofeia' (Opyt tekstologicheskogo analiza)," *TODRL*, vol. 29, 1974, pp. 79, 85. According to Gol'dberg, the *Letter Against Astrologers* is extant in over eighty MS copies (p. 69).

likely author or authors for them. He initially placed the *Letter About the Sign of the Cross* in the late 1520s or even early 1530s (Vasilii III died in 1533) and the *Work About the Offenses* he placed in the 1540s.[25] Later, he dated both works to the end of the 1540s or beginning of the 1550s, around the time of the Stoglav Council (1551).[26] The arguments of Malinin and Gol'dberg in favor of the *Work About the Offenses* having been sent to the young Ivan IV are stronger than Andreyev's arguments that it was sent to Ivan III.

Andreyev tried to argue that the issues raised in the *Work About the Offenses* fit the concerns of the period around 1499–1500 better than they do the period of Ivan IV's minority. But his arguments are contrived and weak. For one, it is highly unlikely that an unknown monk, as Filofei was in 1499, would have circumvented the hegumen of his monastery as well as the archbishop of Novgorod, to whom he and his hegumen were answerable, to write directly to the grand prince on such serious matters as church discipline and confiscation of church and monastic lands. At the time, as Andreyev admitted, Filofei "did not occupy any outstanding position in the monastic hierarchy."[27] Andreyev speculated that Gennadii, who was archbishop of Novgorod at the time, was too busy preparing a campaign against the Novgorod–Moscow heretics to write such a letter and that Pamfil, the hegumen of the Eleazarov Monastery, where Filofei was a monk, would "not take it upon himself to try to call the grand duke of Moscow to order or deliver him a lecture on the rules of behavior" because the confiscation of church lands in Novgorod "had no direct bearing on Pskov itself."[28] But Gennadii apparently had time to write letters to other people while he was campaigning against the heretics.[29] And if the confiscation of church lands did not affect Pskov, then it is doubtful a monk in a Pskovian monastery would be writing about it at all.

In addition, Malinin had made the point that, if this letter to Ivan Vasil'evich was to Ivan III, then there should have been mention in it of the heretics, in light of Gennadii's campaign against them at the time.[30] Andreyev tried to counter that point by arguing that "it would . . . have been inexpedient to introduce the delicate topic of heresy."[31] Yet, the author of the letter does not feel it inexpedient to discuss the issue of

[25] Gol'dberg, "Tri 'poslaniia Filofeia,'" pp. 84–85, 92.

[26] A. L. Gol'dberg, "Ideia 'Moskva – Tretii Rim' v sochineniiakh pervoi poloviny XVI v.," *TODRL*, vol. 37, 1983, pp. 142–143.

[27] Andreyev, "Filofey and His Epistle," p. 23 fn. 102.

[28] Andreyev, "Filofey and His Epistle," p. 19.

[29] See, e.g., *AFED*, pp. 309–313, 315–320, 373–382, and 388–391.

[30] Malinin, *Starets Eleazarova monastyria Filofei*, pp. 377–381.

[31] Andreyev, "Filofey and His Epistle," p. 24.

simony, an issue that proved to be Archbishop Gennadii's undoing in 1504, in addition to being one of the damaging accusations that Iosif Volotskii hurled at Metropolitan Zosima. These would seem to be issues much more sensitive for the author to raise than "safely" affirming his opposition to heresy. On the other hand, the issues of determining who was guilty of heresy was outside the grand-princely sphere of responsibility, whereas punishing heretics was in his sphere. Both Malinin and Gol'dberg made a convincing case that the pattern of issues discussed in the letter to Ivan Vasil'evich fits better with the pre-Stoglav concerns of the late 1530s and 1540s, including the continued confiscation of church and monastic lands.[32] Finally, Gol'dberg's argument that the letter to Ivan Vasil'evich and the letter to Vasilii III are secondary in relation to the letter to Munekhin is based on an internal textual comparison of the three works and is stronger than the arguments of Andreyev, which are based almost solely on external, contextual considerations.[33] In such cases, where the two appear to be in conflict, we must prefer the internal textual evidence.

When one reads each of these works closely, one finds no basis to draw the conclusion that whoever wrote them was formulating an imperial ideology for the Muscovite ruler or for expansion of the Muscovite state. Instead, one finds a very different intent, that is, a delineation of the power and authority of the ruler and reminders to the ruler to perform his duty specifically in regard to the Church. The only way these compositions could have been misread and misused was by taking the passages that refer to Third Rome out of the context of the entire letter in which they appear.

Let us take a look at the *Letter About the Sign of the Cross* written to Grand Prince Vasilii III to illustrate this point. A number of commentators have considered it to be the earliest formulation of the Third Rome theory and it is certainly the one most often cited in the scholarly literature. The author opens the letter with a bit of extravagant stereotype flattery[34] of the kind found in Byzantine letters to the basileus, all the more to sweeten the bitter pills that are about to follow:

To you who have been selected to rule, by the highest, the all-powerful and almighty hand of God, by Whose will all rulers on earth govern and Whom all great people praise and about Whom the powerful write the truth, to you, the illustrious sovereign, Grand Prince, occupier of the high throne, the Orthodox Christian Tsar and lord of all, the administrator of all Holy Churches of God

[32] Malinin, *Starets Eleazarova monastyria Filofei*, pp. 644–646; Gol'dberg, "Tri 'poslaniia Filofeia,'" pp. 90–91.

[33] Gol'dberg, "Tri 'poslaniia Filofeia,'" pp. 82–83, 87.

[34] But see Andreyev who wrote that "Filofey was a stranger to flattery." Andreyev, "Filofey and His Epistle," p. 13 fn. 56.

and of the Holy Universal and Apostolic Church and of the Church of the Holy Mother of God, that has made such honest and illustrious progress that it has been enabled to triumph over the Church of Rome as well as over the Church of Constantinople.

There now follows the classic formulation of the Third Rome doctrine:

For the Church of old Rome fell through the skepticism [невѣрием] of the Apollinarian heresy. The grandsons of Hagar used their scimitars [секирами] and axes to cleave the church doors of the second Rome, the city of Constantine. And here now, in the new, third Rome, your mighty [дръжавнаго] tsarstvo, is the Holy Synodal Apostolic Church, which to the ends of the universe in the Orthodox Christian faith, shines brighter than the sun over the firmament. Pious Tsar! Let your state know that all Orthodox tsarstvos of the Christian faith have now merged into one, your tsarstvo. You are the only tsar in all the Christian firmament.[35]

A number of surprising ideas are then expressed, that is, surprising in the context of a document that is supposed to provide the basis of Russian messianic expansion down to the present. First, there is the rather mild admonition: "Do not hope for gold and wealth and glory," followed by the appropriate biblical quotations. But then the author of the *Letter* begins to list some fairly biting complaints. He points out that "people in your tsarstvo do not make the sign of the holy cross correctly." As co-authorities of the external Church, the grand prince and the metropolitan had the duty to make sure that people were performing the rituals appropriately. For the author to declare to the grand prince that people were not making the sign of the cross properly was to imply that the grand prince and the metropolitan were not fulfilling their duties.

Furthermore, the author of the *Letter* urges the ruler to "fill the Holy Synodal churches with bishops. Do not allow the holy divine Church to

---

[35] Malinin, *Starets Eleazarova monastyria Filofei*, Appendix, p. 50; *PLDR. Konets XV–pervaia polovina XVI veka*, p. 436. The Apollinarian heresy derives from Apollinaris of Laodicea (c. 315–c. 390), who taught that Christ possessed divine Logos rather than a human mind. This teaching anticipated Eutyches and Monophysitism, but it certainly was not the cause of the fall of Rome. Indeed, Monophysite ideas were more prominent in the eastern part of the Roman Empire, especially Syria, Egypt, and Armenia. It was from encounters with the Armenian Church, after Byzantium took Armenia in the tenth century, that Byzantine theology developed arguments against the unleavened bread the Armenians used in the church service. The Byzantine theologians asserted that the dead azymes used to make the bread indicated a denial of the soul of Christ as man. They then drew a parallel between the unleavened bread of the Armenians and the unleavened bread of the Western Church. So, in a rather round about way, Apollinarianism was associated with the downfall of old Rome. These notions most likely entered Rus' via the Christological controversies that hesychasts were engaged in during the fourteenth century. See, *inter alia*, Meyendorff, *Byzantine Theology*, pp. 95–96, 204–205.

be widowed during your reign." As a number of investigators have pointed out, this is most likely a reference to the fact that there was no archbishop of Novgorod between 1509 and 1526.[36] It was the duty of Vasilii III to appoint that archbishop, and his failure to do so left the Church, in the words of the author, "widowed." Gol'dberg rejected this conjecture as a means of dating the *Letter About the Sign of the Cross*, because it could not have been written before the *Letter Against Astrologers* to Munekhin.[37] But Gol'dberg's objection does not eliminate the possibility that the *Letter About the Sign of the Cross* was written after 1523–1524, when Gol'dberg says Filofei wrote his letter to Munekhin, and before 1526, when the archiepiscopal see of Novgorod was filled with the appointment of Makarii. The author of the *Letter* then expresses a concern that the ruler may be a threat to the traditional relationships within society: "Do not violate the order that was chosen by your great predecessor Constantine." This is followed immediately by an explicit expression of concern that the ruler may act in a way that is detrimental to the external Church: "Do not harm the Holy churches of God and honest monasteries, that which has been given to God in return for eternal blessing of the memory of a family." Andreyev took this passage to mean that Filofei was writing the letter to save the monastic and church lands of Novgorod and Pskov from further confiscation.[38] During the first half of the sixteenth century, *votchiny* were being donated to monasteries in ever-increasing amounts for repose of the soul of deceased family members. These donations, however, were not being registered with the government and were thus subject to confiscation by the local agents of the grand prince, and either returned to their former owners or kept by the state. This issue emerged as a potential Church–State confrontation in the 1530s.[39]

Next, there is a plea for the tsar to enforce the rules against sodomy in the monasteries, which again implies that the ruler has not been doing his job in this respect. Although the author of the *Letter* acknowledges the Muscovite ruler's temporal power, there is strong implicit criticism that the tsar is miserly and truculent and that he needs to do something about it: "Change your stinginess to generosity and your inclemency to kindness. Comfort those who cry and moan day and night. Protect the innocent from their tormentors." Andreyev saw in this last admonition a reference to the abuses that the compiler of the Pskov Chronicle alleges

---

[36] For example, see A. A. Shakhmatov, "Puteshestvie M. G. Misiuria Munekhina na Vostok i Khronograf redaktsii 1512 g.," *Izvestiia Otdeleniia russkogo iazyka i slovesnosti*, vol. 4, 1899, p. 209 fn. 1.

[37] See Gol'dberg, "Tri 'poslaniia Filofeia,'" p. 84.

[38] Andreyev, "Filofey and His Epistle," pp. 15–20.

[39] Ostrowski, "Church Polemics," pp. 370–375.

the grand-princely *namestniki* were perpetrating against the people of Pskov.[40] The author closes the *Letter* with a return to overblown flattery: "Pious Tsar! Listen and remember that all Christian tsarstvos have now merged into one, yours. Two Romes have fallen and the third stands. A fourth will not be. Another will not replace your Christian tsarstvo." Even here in the midst of the flattery, there may be a hidden sting. The tsar must respect the Church and do no harm to it, do his duty in regard to enforcing discipline within the Church, and be generous to the Church, for there is and will be no one else to protect the Christian Church and community of Christian believers. As Andreyev pointed out, "[t]he moral was clear: fidelity to Orthodoxy was essential for political well-being and if the state was to prosper."[41] The author is telling the tsar that his is the last chance. If the tsar does not do these things, then we can not expect history to continue or a Fourth Rome to be established. Instead, disaster will ensue for the Christian faith. But the author of the *Letter* forbears from making explicit the innuendo in this regard. Throughout the *Letter*, there is no mention of Moscow as the Third Rome, only "your tsardom" and "your Christian tsardom." Commentators have dismissed the significance of this absence, because they assume that Moscow was meant. But was it?

The *Letter Against Astrologers* is generally accepted as having been written to the grand-princely d'iak Munekhin, who Shakhmatov argued is the same person as Mikhail Gureev, *kaznachei* (treasurer) to the grand prince. If so, then this means that the recipient of the *Letter* was of Tatar descent.[42] Andreyev, while accepting Shakhmatov's identification, nonetheless assures us that "Munekhin was profoundly Orthodox in his outlook and his origin distinguished him from his purely Russian contemporaries only insofar as it may have been a contributory reason for the remarkable impartiality which he showed during his term of office in Pskovia."[43] That may well be, for the Pskov Chronicle attributes to Munekhin and his assistant Ortiusha (Artemii) founding of the Pskov-Pecherskii Monastery.[44] But it adds a certain poignancy to the writing of the letter if we accept Gol'dberg's arguments that the

---

[40] Andreyev, "Filofey and His Epistle," p. 26. Cf. *PSRL*, vol. 5, p. 288. See also the anonymous letter describing Filofei's intervention with the grand prince against the boyars and *namestniki* on behalf of the people of Pskov. Malinin, *Starets Eleazarova monastyria Filofei*, Appendix, p. 25.

[41] Andreyev, "Filofey and His Epistle," p. 21.

[42] See Shakhmatov, "Puteshestvie M. G. Misiuria Munekhina," pp. 206–207; Malinin, *Starets Eleazarova monastyria Filofei*, pp. 159–161 and "Primechaniia," pp. 16–17 n. 587.

[43] Andreyev, "Filofey and His Epistle," p. 6 fn. 22.

[44] *Pskovskie letopisi*, ed. A. N. Nasonov, 2 vols., Moscow and Leningrad, Akademiia nauk SSSR, 1941, 1955, vol. 1, p. 101; *PSRL*, vol. 4, p. 293.

letter to Munekhin represents the first formulation of the Third Rome theory and the only one of the letters that can reliably be assigned to Filofei. We then have a Pskovian ecclesiastic with Byzantine literary roots expositing on the Byzantine heritage of Rus' to a government official of Tatar descent, who symbolically and actionably represented the Mongol heritage in Rus'.

Some scholars have proposed that Filofei's letter was written to counter the pro-Catholic and pro-Union writings of Nicholas Bulev, a doctor and practitioner of astrology.[45] In this view, Filofei was rejecting the claim that the Holy Roman Empire was the Third Rome. In his letter, Filofei does condemn astrology as being atheistic and also criticizes the Latin Church for using unleavened bread in the church service.

What is surprising about the letter to Munekhin is that not only does Filofei not refer to Moscow as the Third Rome but there is also no mention of Rus' or even the "Christian tsarstvo" as the Third Rome. As near as we can reconstruct the archetype of the *Letter* based on Gol'dberg's textual analysis, Filofei indicates that the "Roman [po-мейское] tsarstvo" is the Third Rome.[46] Thus, the archetype of Filofei's letter most likely reads: "all the Christian tsarstvos came to an end and gathered in one tsarstvo of our sovereign, according to the books of the prophets, and this is the Roman tsarstvo: for two Romes have fallen, a third stands, and a fourth will not be."[47] In this context, "Roman tsarstvo" could mistakenly be understood to refer to the Holy Roman Empire of Charles V. It seems that copyists of what Gol'dberg calls "fragments" of the *Letter Against Astrologers*, for inclusion in various codices, were concerned that their readers would misunderstand what was meant, because a number of them add some kind of explanatory phrase to the effect that the Roman tsarstvo means the Russian tsarstvo.[48] Copyists of one variant branch of the main text merely changed *me* to *cи*, and thereby transformed ромеиское царство, the "Roman tsarstvo," directly into росииское царство, the Russian tsarstvo.[49] Clearly some copyists were uncomfortable with the original form of Filofei's expression of Third Rome.

I am not suggesting that Filofei meant to indicate the Holy Roman Empire was the Third Rome. What it does indicate is that Filofei was understanding the concept of "Rome" on a purely abstract and non-

[45] Goldfrank, "Moscow, the Third Rome," p. 119.
[46] Gol'dberg, "Tri 'poslaniia Filofeia,'" pp. 73, 75, 78.
[47] Malinin, *Starets Eleazarova monastyria Filofei*, Appendix, p. 45; *PLDR. Konets XV–pervaia polovina XVI veka*, p. 452.
[48] Gol'dberg, "Tri 'poslaniia Filofeia,'" p. 78.
[49] Gol'dberg, "Tri 'poslaniia Filofeia,'" pp. 73, 75, 77–78.

temporal plane: "although the grandchildren of Hagar conquered the Greek tsarstvo, they did not harm the faith and did not force the Greeks to renounce their faith, for the Roman tsarstvo is indestructible, because our Lord settled in a Roman province."[50] When Filofei refers to "the Holy Apostolic Church, which is in the place of the Roman and the Constantinopolitan and which is situated in the divinely protected town of Moscow, the Church of the Dormition of the Most Pure Mother of God," he means to indicate that the Christian realm in the ideal sense has not moved. It cannot move because it is universal and eternal. Only the capital of its secular protector, which is connected with the physical world, has moved within the eternal abstraction called "the Church." This is not a political but a religious doctrine, in which the Moscow grand prince is the protector of the non-temporal "Rome," that is, "the Christian realm," which knows no geographical or chronological limitations or boundaries. As the only sovereign Christian emperor, it is the Muscovite ruler's duty to protect Christianity throughout the world. This duty had previously been performed by the Emperor in Rome and then by the Emperor in Constantinople, but, because they were part of the temporal world, they no longer existed. In short, the Third Rome theory as formulated by Filofei had nothing to do with *translatio imperii*, and had everything to do with establishing what the grand prince's duties were in regard to the Church. Thus, we can accept Gol'dberg's date of composition for the *Letter Against Astrologers* as 1523–1524. We can modify his date for the *Letter About the Sign of the Cross* to 1524–1526. And we can accept the date for the *Work About the Offenses* as the 1540s (or late 1530s). And while each of them refers to the Third Rome, none of them refers specifically to Moscow as that Third Rome.

Another apparent early occurrence of the "Third Rome" formulation

---

[50] Malinin, *Starets Eleazarova monastyria Filofei*, Appendix, p. 43; *PLDR. Konets XV–pervaia polovina XVI veka*, p. 448. The idea that Rome ruled the world extended as far back as the second century BC when Polybius wrote: "the Romans succeeded in less than fifty-three years [220–167 BC] in bringing under their rule almost the whole of the inhabited world, an achievement that is without parallel in human history." Polybius, *The Rise of the Roman Empire*, trans. Ian Scott-Kilvert, Harmondsworth, Penguin, 1979, p. 41; see also p. 42. Polybius made this statement when Rome controlled at most some scattered areas around the Mediterranean Sea: the Italian peninsula, the Iberian peninsula, some islands, the coastal areas of Greece, the northern part of Tunisia, and the western part of Asia Minor. This left "almost the whole of the inhabited world" still outside Roman rule. At around the same time, Shi Huangdi had brought a larger area under his control as first emperor of China. Historians of Shi Huangdi's time were making the same claims of world rule for the Chinese empire that Polybius was making for Rome. See, e.g., chapter 88 of the *Shih chi*: "After Ch'in had unified the world (in 221 BC) . . ." Derk Bodde, trans., *Statesman, Patriot, and General in Ancient China: Three Shih Chi Biographies of the Ch'in Dynasty (255–206 BC)*, New Haven, CT, American Oriental Society, 1940, p. 54.

is in the *Tale About the Novgorodian White Cowl*. Accompanying many copies of the *Tale* is a letter addressed to Gennadii, Archbishop of Novgorod. The title of the letter reports that it is from "Dmitrii Grek, the Translator." In the text, however, this person is referred to only as "Mitia the Small." It has been asserted that this Dmitrii is Dmitrii Gerasimov, and it is to him that the authorship of the *Tale* has usually been attributed. There are other prominent Dmitrii's of Greek descent of the late fifteenth to early sixteenth century. Dmitrii Vladimirovich Ovtsa-Khovrin was treasurer and became a boyar under Ivan III, but his family most likely came to Muscovy in the embassy of 1402.[51] It is unlikely that someone who was born and raised in Rus' would have been called "the Greek." The same is true for Dmitrii Ralev (or Larev). Dmitrii Trachaniotes, by contrast, came with the entourage of Ivan III's second wife, Sofiia, when she came to Moscow in 1472. And we have a letter that Dmitrii Trachaniotes wrote to Archbishop Gennadii, so we know there was contact between them.[52] We can also surmise that he held Gennadii in high esteem. In the 1520s, Dmitrii Trachaniotes' son Iurii was shorn a monk in the Chudov Monastery, where Gennadii had been archimandrite before he became Archbishop of Novgorod. What is more, Iurii took the spiritual name "Gennadii" apparently in honor of the by-then disgraced former archbishop.[53] But Dmitrii Trachaniotes was known as "Dmitrii Staroi" (Dmitrii the Elder) whereas the nickname "Mitia Malyi" would have been considered inappropriate. And none of them was known as a translator, as Gerasimov was thought to be one of the translators of the Latin Vulgate for the Gennadii Bible. If the author of the *Tale* is Dmitrii Gerasimov, then that would provide an indication when the *Tale* was written. In the letter to Gennadii, the author explains that he was given a copy of the *Tale* by someone in the Vatican when he visited Rome. Gerasimov visited Rome in 1525–1526 with a letter from Vasilii III to the Pope, returning in July 1526. But, in the letter to Gennadii, the author writes as though Gennadii were still alive and still the Archbishop of Novgorod: "Because of your episcopal blessing and prayers, I was able to reach the City of Rome in [good] health. I followed your orders concerning the White Cowl." The problem is that Gennadii was deposed as archbishop in 1504 and died

---

[51] For the sources on Dmitrii Khovrin, see Kollmann, *Kinship and Politics*, p. 256 n. 129.

[52] A. I. Pliguzov and I. A. Tikhoniuk, "Poslanie Dmitriia Trakhaniota novgorodskomu arkhiepiskopu Gennadiiu Gonzovu o sedmerichnosti schisleniia let," in *Estestvenno-nauchnye predstavleniia Drevnei Rusi*, ed. R. A. Simonov, Moscow, Nauka, 1988, pp. 51–71.

[53] GIM, Sinod. 667, fols. 92–92ᵛ, according to A. A. Zimin as reported in Pliguzov and Tikhoniuk, "Poslanie Dmitriia Trakhaniota," p. 57.

in 1506, twenty years before Gerasimov's journey to Rome. How do we resolve this discrepancy?

If we speculate that Gerasimov wanted to hide his complicity in writing the *Tale* by referring to himself as Dmitrii Grek or Mitia the Small, rather than as Dmitrii Gerasimov, and he addressed his accompanying letter to a person who was no longer archbishop to make it appear that it had been written over twenty years earlier, then we encounter another problem. That is, if Gerasimov is trying to hide his identity, he did not do a good job of it, for the simple reason that there were very few Dmitrii's from Muscovy who visited Rome in those days. Any Dmitrii who said he had visited Rome could be tracked down fairly easily. It is more likely that the author was not Dmitrii Gerasimov but was someone who was trying to hide his own identity by framing Dmitrii Gerasimov as the author of the letter. The author furthermore stated that the *Tale* was given to him in Rome rather than his having composed it himself, with the implication that he had only translated it. In any event, discrepancies in chronology were of little concern to the author of the letter "to Gennadii," just as they were of little concern for the author of the *Tale* (more about this below). This suggests that the author of the letter to Gennadii was indeed the author of the *Tale*, but it virtually eliminates Dmitrii Gerasimov as the author of either work. I am also rejecting here the testimony of the *Writing (Napisanie) of Gennadii*, a brief work found frequently attached as an epilogue to various redactions of the *Tale*.[54] In the *Writing*, pseudo-Gennadii states that he sent Dmitrii Gerasimov to Rome. While it is possible that Gerasimov went to Rome during the time when Gennadii was archbishop, we have no record of it in any other source. Therefore, I think that the *Writing*, just like the letter "to Gennadii," was written later in the sixteenth century to obfuscate the true identity of the author of the *Tale*.

The *Tale*, itself, is extant in over 250 manuscripts copies from the sixteenth through the nineteenth centuries, so it has had a fairly wide distribution. But the dating of the sixteenth-century manuscript copies is not precise enough to help us determine when in the sixteenth century it was written.[55] A late sixteenth-century date for the composition of the *Tale* would fit the pattern of extant manuscripts, that is, a few from the sixteenth century and late sixteenth to early seventeenth centuries. Such a date would tend to support those scholars who have argued that the

---

[54] For the publication of the text, see N. N. Rozov, "Povest' o novgorodskom belom klobuke kak pamiatnik obshcherusskoi publitsistiki XV veka," *TODRL*, vol. 9, 1953, pp. 218–219.

[55] Rozov, "Povest'," pp. 207, 211, 215, and 216.

Tale was written in the wake of Ivan IV's execution of over 2,000 Novgorodians suspected of conspiracy in 1570. In addition, N. N. Rozov has argued that the letter accompanying the *Tale* was written "not earlier than the middle of the sixteenth century" as an attempt to provide the *Tale* with an "older 'Roman' origin."[56] If so, then these considerations would also preclude Gerasimov as the author both of the *Tale* and the letter "to Gennadii," since he was born in the 1460s and was no longer alive at the time of the mass executions in Novgorod.

Rozov has divided the extant copies of the *Tale* into five redactions: (1) Shortest, (2) Short, (3) First Long, (4) Second Long, and (5) Special.[57] No consensus has been reached on the relationship of the redactions to one another. N. Subbotin suggested that the Short Redaction, which does not contain the Third Rome formulation, is primary in relation to the others.[58] O. Nazarevs'kyi, by contrast, argued that the Short Redaction derived from, and therefore was secondary to, the Second Long Redaction, which does contain the Third Rome formulation.[59] Rozov has proposed that the First Long Redaction, which also contains the Third Rome formulation, is primary.[60] Miroslav Labunka tried to find a middle ground between the conclusions of Subbotin and Rozov by arguing that the Short Redaction "represents an early draft . . . destined for inclusion in a chronicle," while the First Long Redaction "represents a final form of a tract which was to stand out as an independent and separate work."[61] In other words, they both derive from a common protograph. The Short Redaction does have a year (6845 = 1337) attached to the beginning of it as though it were meant for a chronicle entry.

[56] Rozov, "Povest'," p. 182.
[57] Rozov, "Povest'," pp. 183, 209–217. The Short Redaction was published by O. Nazarevs'kyj [A. A. Nazarevskii] in "Otchet o zaniatii v Voronezhskom gubernskom muzee," *Universitetskie izvestiia*, Kiev, 1912, no. 8, pp. 36–40. The First Long Redaction was published by N. I. Kostomarov from a text prepared from the MS. RNB, Q.I.262: "Povest' o Novgorodskom belom klobuke," *Pamiatniki starinnoi russkoi literatury* (*PamSRL*), ed. N. I. Kostomarov, compl. Grigorii Kushelev-Bezborodko, vol. I: *Skazaniia, legendy, povesti, skazki i pritchi*, St. Petersburg, 1860, pp. 287–303. In 1985, N. N. Rozov published another edition of the text of the First Long Redaction, this time based on the MS. RNB, Q.I.1409: *PLDR. Seredina XVI veka*, pp. 200–231 and commentary on pp. 588–591.
[58] N. Subbotin [S – n], "Kak izdaiutsia u nas knizhki o raskole," *Russkii vestnik*, vol. 10, 1862, pp. 363–365.
[59] O. Nazarevs'kyi, "Znadoby do istorii davn'oi povisty," *Zapysky Istorychno-filolohichnoho viddilu Vseukrains'koi akademii nauk*, vol. 25, 1929, p. 324.
[60] Rozov, "Povest'," p. 183.
[61] Miroslav Labunka, "The Legend of the Novgorodian White Cowl: the Study of Its 'Prologue' and 'Epilogue,'" Ph.D. dissertation, Columbia University, 1978, pp. 41–42.

Labunka's suggestion, while ingenious in trying to reconcile two apparently mutually exclusive views, becomes more complicated when we realize that no redaction of the *Tale* appears in any chronicle. That is, not only do we need to provide an explanation for why an early draft version was intended for a chronicle but also another explanation for why it never made it into a chronicle. On the other hand, Rozov's reasoning for his preference for the First Long Redaction is also unsatisfactory. He argues that it presents an "all-Russian" point of view, as opposed to the Short Redaction, which seems more parochial, specifically, Novgorodian, in outlook. But Rozov provides no argument for why he thinks an "all-Russian" point of view would be primary. Instead, there are good reasons to believe that the earliest form of the *Tale* would indeed have focused on Novgorod, and that later someone tried to modify the focus of that outlook to a more general point of view perhaps more relevant to the Church as a whole. Thus, I tend to agree with Subbotin that the primary version of the *Tale* is the Short Redaction, in which Third Rome is not mentioned. The First Long Redaction was compiled using it, at which point, the Third Rome formulation was added. Filofei's letter to Munekhin had already appeared in the *Velikie chet'i-minei* (Great Menology) of Makarii, so the reviser of the *Tale* may have thought it safe enough to include it in his revision.

In the First Long Redaction, the *Tale* tells how Constantine the Great gave a white cowl to Pope Sylvester in gratitude for curing him of an illness. A subsequent pope, Formosus, sends the white cowl to Patriarch Philotheus of Constantinople, who is told in a dream to send it to Archbishop Vasilii of Novgorod. Throughout the *Tale*, the author plays fast and loose with chronology, none more so than here. Formosus was pope from 891 to 896, while Philotheus Coccinus was patriarch from 1353 to 1354 and from 1364 to 1376. Apparently it took over four-and-a-half centuries for the white cowl to travel from Rome to Constantinople. In addition, Vasilii became Archbishop of Novgorod in 1330 and ceased being archbishop in 1342, some eleven years before Philotheus became patriarch.[62] In any event, when the white cowl does finally reach Constantinople, Philotheus balks at sending it to Vasilii in Novgorod

---

[62] The patriarchs of Constantinople during the reign of Formosus as pope were Stephen I (886–893) and Antonios II Cauleas (893–901). The popes during the reign of Philotheus as patriarch were Innocent VI (1352–1362), Urban V (1362–1370), and Gregory XI (1370–1378). The patriarchs of Constantinople at the time Vasilii was archbishop of Novgorod were Isaias (1323–1332) and John XIV Calecas (1334–1347). Whoever wrote the Short Redaction would have had the correct date (1337), for Vasilii's being archbishop. But the author of the Short Redaction names the patriarch to whom the cowl was sent as a certain "Uvenalii" (Juvenal?). There was no such patriarch with that name. See Hussey, *Orthodox Church*, pp. xxv–xxvii.

because he wants to wear it himself. Then he has another dream in which Constantine and Sylvester appear to him. Sylvester tells him the reason he should send the white cowl to Novgorod:

for ancient Rome fell from glory and from the faith of Christ through pride and willfulness. In the new Rome, that is in Constantinople, the Christian faith will also perish through the violence of Hagar's sons. In the Third Rome, which is in the Rus' land, the grace of the Holy Spirit will be revealed [возсия]. Know then, Philotheus, that all Christians will come in the end and unite in one Rus' tsardom for the sake of Orthodoxy.[63]

Subsequently, Sylvester tells Philotheus that "radiant Russia" (свѣтлая Росия) will be "made more honorable than the first two" (паче первыхъ сихъ).

Nowhere in the *Tale* does the phrase "Moscow the Third Rome" appear. Like the author of the *Story About the Vladimir Princes*, the author of the *Tale About the White Cowl* is unconcerned with historical accuracy. Both works can be classified as historical fiction. But unlike the *Story About the Vladimir Princes*, which is pro-Muscovite and pro-princely in orientation, the *Tale About the White Cowl*, in fact, is explicitly pro-Novgorodian and implicitly anti-Muscovite in both secular and ecclesiastical terms. Significantly, the white cowl was not sent to the head of the Rus' Church, the metropolitan, who resided in Moscow. It was sent to the second-ranked prelate, the Archbishop of Novgorod, whom the *Tale* thus designates as the spiritual leader of Rus'. But before the author of the *Tale* has Patriarch Philotheus send the white cowl to Archbishop Vasilii, he offers an explanation that provides an implicit anti-Muscovite significance. After Constantine the Great gives Sylvester the white cowl, he decides that it is not appropriate for the temporal ruler to reside in the same city as the spiritual ruler. Since Sylvester, as pope, is ruler in Rome, Constantine repairs to Byzantium, where he founds the city of Constantinople.[64] In drawing the parallel with Rus', we find the Archbishop of Novgorod, as the spiritual ruler, is in a city separate from the temporal ruler in Moscow. And by Constantine's injunction the temporal ruler in Constantinople (read: Moscow) should leave the spiritual ruler in Rome (read: Novgorod) alone, not only in regard to spiritual matters but also in regard to temporal matters affecting that city. This interpretation provides a marked counterpoint to the Muscovite rulers' treatment of the Novgorodian Church, specifically: Ivan III's confiscation of Novgorodian church and monastic lands

---

[63] *PamSRL*, vol. 1, p. 296; *PLDR. Seredina XVI veka*, p. 224.
[64] *PamSRL*, vol. 1, p. 292; *PLDR. Seredina XVI veka*, p. 212.

in 1478–1479[65] and in 1499;[66] Vasilii III's refusal to appoint an archbishop to the Novgorodian eparchy from 1509 until 1526; as well as Ivan IV's banishment of Archbishop Pimen in 1570.[67]

The *Tale* does not appear in the *Velikie chet'i-minei*, but one of the letters of the Third Rome cycle attributed to Filofei, the *Letter Against Astrologers*, does. While we would ordinarily not expect letters of an ordinary monk to appear in the *Great Menology*, we could think an exception was made for this exceptional letter, one that defended the religious rights of Novgorod and Pskov, demanded that the grand prince abide his duty, and delineated the power and authority of the ruler. While we can thus explain the presence of at least one of the letters of the Third Rome cycle, we have to go further afield to explain why the *Tale About the White Cowl* was not included in the *Velikie chet'i-minei*. Its absence seems particularly odd in light of the fact that Makarii began compiling the *Velikie chet'i-minei* while he was Archbishop of Novgorod. Surely he would have known of this extraordinary text had it existed and surely he would have included it had he known of it. Ultimately, all these problems are resolved by the simplest and most likely explanation, that is, the *Tale* was simply not written by the time the *Velikie chet'i-minei* was compiled (*c.* 1550). Issues concerning a white cowl do, however, appear in official Church documents in the second half of the sixteenth century.

A Church Council in February 1564 decreed that Metropolitan Afanasii could wear the white cowl when he was appointed head of the Rus' Church. His predecessor, Makarii, had done so as a former Archbishop of Novgorod. The council decree pointed out that "there was nothing written explaining why the Archbishops of Novgorod wore the white cowl."[68] The *Tale About the White Cowl* may well have been written in response to this assertion so as to keep the white cowl in Novgorod for use of the archbishop there. The author of the *Tale* would then have attempted to pre-date the "discovery" of the *Tale* to the time of Archbishop Gennadii. If that was the case, then the *Tale About the White Cowl* could not have been written before 1564. Later redactions of the *Tale* were then composed possibly after 1570, as propaganda to keep the Muscovite secular and religious authorities from continuing what

---

[65] *PSRL*, vol. 25, p. 319; *PSRL*, vol. 12, pp. 182–184; *Ioasafovskaia letopis'*, ed. A. A. Zimin, Moscow, Akademiia nauk SSSR, 1957, p. 111.

[66] *PSRL*, vol. 4, p. 271; *PSRL*, vol. 12, p. 249; *Ioasafovskaia letopis'*, p. 138.

[67] The Solovetskii Chronicle reports that Pimen died September 29, 1572, at the Venev-Nikolaevskii Monastery in Tula. M. N. Tikhomirov, "Maloizvestnye letopisnye pamiatniki XVI v.," *Istoricheskii arkhiv*, vol. 7, 1951, pp. 225–226.

[68] *PSRL*, vol. 13, p. 379; *AI*, vol. 1, no. 173, p. 332. Cf. *PSRL*, vol. 24, pp. 80–82 (1169): "О Феодорцѣ бѣломъ клобуцкѣ," which concerns Rostov.

the Novgorodians' perceived as interference in their internal affairs. The author of the First Long Redaction borrowed the Third Rome formulation and gave it an added twist in suggesting that it meant the Muscovite ruler had specific limitations in regard to the exercise of his duty toward the center of spiritual authority in Rus', that is, Novgorod. Basically, the *Tale* is telling the Muscovite authorities, both temporal and ecclesiastical, to keep their hands off Novgorod, as well as off the white cowl.

The two earliest manifestations of the Third Rome formula occur in an area with a tradition of opposition to Muscovy. While the Archbishop of Novgorod had to accept the Grand Prince of Moscow as the secular authority, as the result of force of arms, he did not have to accept the intrusion of the Muscovite grand prince into matters concerning the external Church in Novgorod and Pskov. The fact that the ostensible ecclesiastical head of the Rus' Church, the metropolitan, resided in Moscow lent weight to the activities of the Muscovite grand prince in Novgorod and Pskov. But the relationship between the metropolitan, in Moscow, and archbishop, in Novgorod, was not always such a clear-cut one of hierarchical obedience. The Archbishop of Novgorod had an enormous amount of political power and authority within his diocese. This power and authority was now in danger of being curtailed, probably with the full concurrence of the metropolitan. For example, Archbishop Feofil was arrested January 19, 1480, and sent to Moscow, where he was imprisoned in the Chudov Monastery.[69] Archbishop Gennadii was ousted in 1504 as the result of a Church Council decision. In 1507, Iosif Volotskii appealed over the head of his ecclesiastical superior, the Novgorodian Archbishop Serapion, to the grand prince in Moscow, who intervened on Iosif's behalf. From 1509 to 1526, the metropolitan apparently concurred in Vasilii III's decision to leave the Novgorodian archiepiscopal see vacant. And, as pointed out above, in January 1570, Ivan IV ousted the Novgorodian Archbishop Pimen from his position and imprisoned him in a monastery. The formulation of Third Rome, both in the *Tale About the White Cowl* and in the letters attributed to Filofei, was clearly meant to define the limits of the Muscovite grand prince's relationship to the Novgorodian archiepiscopal see.

A significant amount of evidence indicates that adoption of the Third Rome idea by Muscovite religious and secular leaders would have been out of place in the sixteenth century. First, it is explicitly anti-Byzantine.

[69] *PSRL*, vol. 8, p. 204; vol. 12, p. 197; vol. 18, p. 266; vol. 21, pt. 1, p. 551; vol. 24, p. 198; vol. 25, p. 326; vol.28, pp. 148, 313; and *Ioasafovskaia letopis'*, p. 119. See also Vernadsky, *Russia at the Dawn of the Modern Age*, pp. 61–62.

Polemics against Byzantium might have appealed to the Muscovite Church in the middle of the fifteenth century, when the Byzantine Church was proposing union with Rome. As late as 1470, Ivan III declared to Archbishop Iona of Novgorod that Greek "Orthodoxy had fallen" and that the Patriarch was "alien and renounced."[70] But the capture of Constantinople in 1453 by the Ottoman Turks effectively negated union. The patriarch in Constantinople remained head of the Eastern Church. And the Muscovite Church began once again slowly and cautiously to recognize the patriarch's authority, at least nominally. In 1472, Ivan married Sofiia (Zoë) Palaeologina, the niece of the last Byzantine emperor. Although this marriage was brokered by the papacy because it still had hopes of union, the nuptials merely signaled, from the Muscovite viewpoint, a more benign attitude toward the Church in Constantinople. I am not intending to suggest that the marriage to Sofiia represented a wholesale adoption by the Muscovite court of Byzantine theory and practice.[71] But one can detect in the sources of the time a softening of attitudes toward the Greek patriarch, and then a tacit recognition of the patriarch's authority in ecclesiastical matters (although not his power, since he effectively had none). Monks, like Nil Sorskii, ostensibly under the jurisdiction of the Moscow metropolitan, continued to travel to Mount Athos for religious edification. Patriarch Theoleptos I sent Maksim Grek to Muscovy in 1518 to help with translation of books at Moscow's request. Ivan IV requested the patriarch's approval for adopting the title *tsar'* in 1547, which Patriarch Josephus II conditionally granted in September 1561.[72] These would not have happened if either the metropolitan or the grand prince had accepted the notion that Rus' had replaced Constantinople in the scheme of things and was now the Third Rome.

Indeed, the Moscow patriarchate could only be established when the Patriarch of Constantinople, Jeremiah II, gave his imprimatur in 1589. The establishment of the patriarchate represented the high watermark of Church influence on the Muscovite government in the sixteenth century. Indicative of the strength of this influence is the fact that Metropolitan Iov did not meet with Jeremiah until he was ordained and

---

[70] "Poslanie velikogo kniazia Ivana Vasil'evicha k novgorodskomu arkhiepiskopu Ione, o tom, chtob on ne imel obshcheniia s kievskom izhe mitropolit Grigoriem," *RIB*, vol. 6, no. 100, col. 711.

[71] George Majeska refuted such notions that have been expressed in the historiography. Majeska, "Moscow Coronation of 1498 Reconsidered," pp. 353–361.

[72] *RIB*, vol. 22, no. 2, cols. 67–75. Although Josephus' approval was technically contingent on the performance of a new ordination, his request was ignored and the patriarchate apparently did not press the issue.

installed.[73] As a subordinate to the patriarch, Iov was not in a position to coerce Jeremiah into declaring the patriarchate and him patriarch. But he could influence government representatives like Boris Godunov and Andrei Shchelkalov who conducted the negotiations. The tsar at the time, Fedor, nicknamed "the Bellringer" for his propensity to ring church bells, was not a strong proponent of a pro-Tatar focus of opposition to the Church. Finally, the goal of convincing the patriarch united the various factions within the Muscovite Church, as is evident from the reappearance of the extremist element's Third Rome theory. The document that established the patriarchate of Moscow contains the following invocation of Third Rome:

For the old Rome fell through the Apollinarian heresy. The second Rome, which is Constantinople, is held by the grandsons of Hagar – the godless Turks. Pious Tsar! Your great Russian [Росїйское] tsarstvo, the third Rome, has surpassed them all in piety, and all pious people have been united as one in your tsarstvo. And you alone in the firmament are called Christian tsar in the whole universe among all Christians. And by God's works and the grace of the most pure Virgin, and thanks to the prayers of the new miracleworkers of the great Russian tsarstvo – Peter and Aleksei and Iona – and through your Church's request to God, according to your imperial counsel, this great deed is fulfilled.[74]

For the only time in an official document, whether ecclesiastical or temporal, the Third Rome formulation appears. Prior and subsequent to this decree, it appears only in unofficial, non-documentary sources, unless one considers the *Velikie chet'i-minei*, which contains Filofei's letter to Misiur' Munekhin, to be an official document. Indeed, Gol'dberg has pointed out that the above-quoted passage in the *Decree of 1589* derives from the "Third Rome" passage in that very letter to Misiur' Munekhin.[75]

The statement of Third Rome in the decree cannot have been pleasing to Patriarch Jeremiah. Although he was under a great deal of pressure to do things Moscow's way, he was no passive assenter to all their demands.[76] Again, one notes that the phrase "Moscow the Third Rome" does not appear in the *Decree*. Instead, the reference is to "your great Russian tsarstvo." While there is no doubt that, in the document, Moscow is being designated as both the political and the spiritual

---

[73] Normally, when a prelate was made patriarch, he was merely installed in the position. Gudziak, "Crisis and Reform," p. 291 and fn. 85.

[74] "Ulozhennaia gramota 1589 goda," *SGGD*, vol. 2, no. 59, p. 97.

[75] Gol'dberg, "Tri 'poslaniia Filofeia,'" p. 86.

[76] See Gudziak's description of the difficulties Jeremiah encountered in Moscow during the course of his sojourn there 1588–1589 and the concerns the Moscow hierarchy had about what he would do or not do in approving Iov as patriarch. Gudziak, "Crisis and Reform," pp. 252–303.

capital, the distinction between "Russia" and "Moscow" is an important one. *Rossiiskii* had, at this time, a religious connotation that "Moskovskii" did not have, and Iov was designated the patriarch not only of Moscow but of all Rus' as well.

Reference to Third Rome does show up in the 1653 edition of the *Kormchaia kniga*, where, in the Russian text of Patriarch Jeremiah's address of 1589 to Tsar Fedor, the above-quoted passage is included.[77] One can legitimately doubt the reliability of this reference. The detailed account in the *Posol'skaia kniga* regarding the negotiations between, on the one side, Jeremiah and Eastern Church prelates and, on the other, the Muscovites makes no mention of Third Rome by either side at any time either before or after the establishment of the patriarchate.[78] In addition, Jeremiah makes no mention of Third Rome in his letter of May 1590 to Tsar Fedor confirming the establishment of the patriarchate.[79] Either Patriarch Jeremiah thought better of his own agreement of Third Rome theory by eliminating it for his Greek-reading audience or the reference was added in the middle of the seventeenth century in the *Kormchaia* version. It is more likely that the *Kormchaia* version is a misrepresentation of what Jeremiah said. Except for the *Decree of 1589*, which Jeremiah was about to sign under duress, he would not have known of Filofei's formulation, so he could not have included it in his address to Fedor.

The answer to the question of why Jeremiah signed the *Decree* with references to Third Rome in it without raising any objection may have been answered by Pseudo-Dorotheos, who provides his own account of the establishment of the Moscow patriarchate. Pseudo-Dorotheos was most likely the Metropolitan of Monemvasia Hierotheos who accompanied the entourage of Jeremiah to Moscow, so he would have had an insider's viewpoint. He describes what happened when the *Decree* was presented to the Greeks for signing:

And they brought a large, exceedingly wide parchment document written in Bulgarian letters. And the Patriarch signed it. But the Metropolitan of Monemvasia asked: "What is written here? [When you tell me] then I will sign." And the first one, Andrei Tzalkanos [Shchelkalov] by name, answered: "It is

---

[77] Taken from the 1787 *Kormchaia kniga* (a republication of the 1653 edition), pt. 1, p. 15, as trans. in *A Source Book for Russian History from Early Times to 1917*, 3 vols., vol. 1: *Early Times to the Late Seventeenth Century*, comp. Sergei Pushkarev, ed. George Vernadsky, Ralph T. Fisher, Jr., Alan D. Ferguson, and Andrew Lossky, New Haven, CT, Yale University Press, 1972, p. 176.

[78] *Posol'skaia kniga po sviaziam Rossii s Gretsiei (pravoslavnymi ierarkhami i monastyriami) 1588–1594 gg.*, ed. M. P. Lukichev and N. M. Rogozhin, Moscow, Institut istorii SSSR AN SSSR, 1988, pp. 11–170.

[79] See *Analecta byzantino-russica*, ed. W. [V. E.] Regal, St. Petersburg, Imperatorskaia Akademiia nauk, 1891, pp. 85–91.

written how you installed the patriarch and how you came here." And the Metropolitan of Monemvasia said: "It should have been written in Greek, not in Russian." But they did not listen to him. The Patriarch's hieromonks signed as well, as did the Archbishop of Elasson [Arsenios]. But the Metropolitan of Monemvasia was completely against this, lest the Church should be divided and another head and a great schism be created. He was in danger of being thrown into the river, until the Patriarch took an oath that the Metropolitan of Monemvasia had said nothing.[80]

In other words, Jeremiah and the other Greek prelates signed the document without being able to read it and without learning the specifics of what it said. In his own letter, written in 1590, to Tsar Fedor confirming the establishment of the patriarchate, Jeremiah does not refer to "Third Rome."

Isolated references and allusions to "Third Rome" continue to appear in other works after that time. There is an allusion in the letter of Meletios Pegas, Patriarch of Alexandria, to Tsar Fedor in 1593 to the effect that the Muscovite *basileus* was carrying on the traditions and duties of the *basileus* in Rome and in Constantinople.[81] But Pegas does not explicitly cite the Third Rome formula. In the seventeenth century, in a letter to the False Dmitrii, Protopop Terentii borrowed the Third Rome passage from the *Letter About the Sign of the Cross*.[82] In a psalter from 1594 of the boyar D. I. Godunov, an inscription refers to "the imperial city Moscow, the Third Rome."[83] Patriarch Filaret mentions Third Rome in a characterization of Semen Shaklovskoi's *Book About the Chasuble (Kniga o rize)* in 1625.[84] The *Tale of the Founding of Moscow (Povest' o zachale Moskvy)* makes a reference to Third Rome.[85] The nature of the reference led Salmina to point out its similarity to the formulation in Filofei's letter to Munekhin.[86] Although some scholars have tried to push the date of

[80] Konstantinos N. Sathas, *Viographikon schediasma peri tou Patriarchou Ieremiou II (1572–1594)*, Athens, 1870; reprinted Thessalonika, 1979, *Parathema*, Appendix, p. 22. Translation taken from Gudziak, "Crisis and Reform," p. 293; reproduced in Boris Gudziak, "The Sixteenth-Century Muscovite Church and Patriarch Jeremiah II's Journey to Muscovy, 1588–1589: Some Comments Concerning the Historiographical Sources," *Kamen" kraeug"l'n"*, p. 223.

[81] See *Analecta byzantino-russica*, p. 100.

[82] RNB, Pogod. 1622, fol. 12, as reported in Gol'dberg, "Tri 'poslaniia Filofeia,'" p. 85; and A. L. Gol'dberg, "Istoriko-politicheskie idei russkoi knizhnosti XV–XVII vekov," *Istoriia SSSR*, 1975, no. 4, p. 72.

[83] *Opisanie rukopisei Solovetskogo monastyria, nakhodiashchikhsia v biblioteke Kazanskoi dukhovnoi akademii*, 3 parts, Kazan', Tipografiia Imperatorskogo universiteta, 1881–1898, pt. 1, p. 23 (RNB, Solov. 15/748, fol. 5).

[84] RNB, Kolob. 515, fol. 136ᵛ as reported in Gol'dberg, "Istoriko-politicheskie idei," p. 72.

[85] M. A. Salmina, *Povesti o nachale Moskvy*, Moscow and Leningrad, Nauka, 1964, pp. 173–174.

[86] Salmina, *Povesti o nachale Moskvy*, p. 77. Gol'dberg placed it closest to the wording in

composition of the *Tale of the Founding of Moscow* back to the sixteenth century,[87] others have placed it more toward the middle of the seventeenth century.[88] I have to agree with those who place its composition near the middle of the seventeenth century, because its presentation of the Third Rome formulation is so different from any of its sixteenth-century incarnations. For the first time in extant literature, we find Third Rome associated explicitly with Moscow rather than with the Russian tsarstvo: "Then our Third Rome, the Moscow state, was built not without blood but by the spilling and shedding of much blood."[89] But the *Tale of the Founding of Moscow* appears to have been intended for a popular audience and had no official status.

Likewise, the *Kazanskaia istoriia* refers to Moscow specifically not only "as a second Kiev" but also "as a third new great Rome."[90] As with the *Tale of the Founding of Moscow*, some scholars have attempted to date the composition of the *Kazanskaia istoriia* to the second half of the sixteenth century, more specifically, the 1560s.[91] But such an early dating has been challenged and a seventeenth-century time of composition, specifically the 1650s, suggested.[92] The form of the reference to Moscow as Third Rome speaks in favor of the seventeenth-century proposed date of composition.

Soon after the *Tale of the Founding of Moscow* and the *Kazanskaia istoriia* were being written, the Church Council of 1666–1667 denounced the *Tale About the Novgorodian White Cowl* as "apocryphal and false" and stated that its author "wrote it from his own imaginings" (отъ вътра главы своея).[93] This decision would seem to indicate an explicit renunciation of Third Rome by the established Church and of those who sought to make it Church doctrine. Such a renunciation

the MS. RNB, Q.XVII.254 of that letter. Gol'dberg, "Tri 'poslaniia Filofeia,'" pp. 78–79 and fn. 31.

[87] M. N. Tikhomirov, "Skazanie o nachale Moskvy," *Istoricheskie zapiski*, no. 32, 1950, p. 241 (second half of the sixteenth century); L. N. Pushkarev, "Povest' o zachale Moskvy," *Materialy po istorii SSSR*, vol. 2, pp. 226–228 (sixteenth century).

[88] S. K. Shambinago, "Povesti o nachale Moskvy," *TODRL*, vol. 3, 1936, p. 76 ("not earlier" than the second half of the seventeenth century); and Salmina, *Povesti o nachale Moskvy*, p. 81 (second quarter of the seventeenth century).

[89] Salmina, *Povesti o nachale Moskvy*, p. 174.

[90] *Kazanskaia istoriia*, 1954, p. 57; *PSRL*, vol. 19, cols. 9, 204.

[91] K. G. Kuntsevich, *Istoriia o Kazanskom tsarstve ili Kazanskii letopisets. Opyt istoriko-literaturnogo issledovaniia*, St. Petersburg, I. N. Skorokhodov, 1905, pp. 176–178; G. N. Moiseeva, "[Introduction]," *Kazanskaia istoriia*, pp. 21–22.

[92] Pelenski's suggestion, who then rejected it as "most unlikely." Pelenski, *Russia and Kazan*, pp. 115–116. Cf. Edward L. Keenan, "Coming to Grips with the Kazanskaya istoriya: Some Observations on Old Answers and New Questions," *Annals of the Ukrainian Academy of Arts and Sciences in the U.S.*, vol. 9, 1964–1968, pp. 143–183.

[93] *Dopolneniia k aktam istoricheskim*, 12 vols., St. Petersburg, Arkheograficheskaia kommissiia, 1846–1872, vol. 5, no. 102, p. 472, art. 21.

makes sense if we understand the *Tale About the White Cowl* as an anti-Muscovite and pro-Novgorodian document. Nikon, too, was admonished by the Council of 1666–1667, and he had been metropolitan in Novgorod before becoming patriarch in Moscow. Gol'dberg suggested that Nikon had tried to make Third Rome official doctrine.[94] But Gol'dberg's evidence for this suggestion is slight – the interpolation in the 1653-printed *Kormchaia kniga* of Patriarch Jeremiah's address to Tsar Fedor in 1589, discussed above.

Thus, Third Rome, as initially formulated in the sixteenth century had an explicitly anti-Muscovite resonance. As a result, we must consider it a cultural artifact of the sixteenth-century clash between Novgorod and Moscow. The original intent, as indicated in the *Letter Against Astrologers*, was to upbraid the agent of the Muscovite ruler in Pskov and warn him against going beyond his secular limits. The two subsequent compositions, *Letter About the Sign of the Cross* and *Work About the Offenses*, attempted to focus the secular ruler's attention on protecting Church lands and upholding ecclesiastical discipline. Filofei and whoever the authors of the other texts might be hoped to remind the secular authorities that the duties allowed them in the external Church sphere were the result of co-responsibility with the spiritual ruler, in this case, the Archbishop of Novgorod.

The Third Rome formulation was based entirely on Eastern Church sources and owed nothing to the Apocalypse of Ezra, a work predominantly associated with the Western Church. With the exception of the *Decree of 1589*, the leaders of the Muscovite Church throughout the sixteenth and seventeenth centuries generally rejected the Third Rome formulation. Only in the middle of the seventeenth century, when the words "Moscow state" were substituted in the historical fiction of the time for the earlier designations, "Roman tsarstvo," "your tsarstvo," "your Christian tsarstvo," and "your Russian tsarstvo," did the Third Rome idea become associated with the Muscovite State instead of the Rus' Church. And only in the nineteenth century did some writers associate it with Russian imperial expansion. Yet, the fact remains that we have no reliable evidence that it was used at any time in the decision making or as a justification for Russian governmental policy or action.

---

[94] Gol'dberg, "Istoriko-politicheskie idei," p. 73.

11   The myth of the "Tatar yoke"

By the end of the sixteenth century, all the elements of the Church's anti-Mongol ideology were in place. The Mongols were depicted as evil, and they had to be resisted. They had caused great destruction and hardship among the Russian people. They were said to have tried to convert Christians to Islam by force. Muscovy was said to have acquired very little, if anything, of value from the Tatars. One exception to this is the Church's frequent citation of the forged *iarlyk* to Metropolitan Peter, which the Church used to defend its right to landowning. Otherwise, anything of value that may have come from the Tatars, such as the tsar's crown, was provided a Byzantine provenance.

By the middle of the sixteenth century, this virtual past of the period of Mongol hegemony was fully articulated in the term "Tatar yoke." According to Halperin, the term "Tatar yoke" first appears in an interpolation in the 1660s in one of the copies of the *Skazanie o Mamaevom poboishche*.[1] L. A. Dmitriev attributed this interpolation to Feodosii Safanovich, hegumen of the Kievan Mikhailo-Zlatoverskii Monastery.[2] This interpolation was subsequently picked up by the author of the *Synopsis* published in 1674.[3] From there, it entered the mainstream of Russian historiography. Both Halperin and Dmitriev, however, overlooked an earlier use of the term "Tatar yoke" in Muscovy. It appears almost 100 years earlier in Latin, as *jugo Tartarico*,

---

[1] Charles J. Halperin, "The Tatar Yoke and Tatar Oppression," *Russia Mediaevalis*, vol. 5, 1984, pp. 25–26.

[2] L. A. Dmitriev, "Kniga o poboishchi Mamaia, tsaria tatarskogo, ot kniazia Vladimirskogo i Moskovskogo Dmitriia," *TODRL*, vol. 34, 1979, pp. 70, 71.

[3] On the authorship of the *Synopsis*, possibly by Innokentii Gizel', hegumen of the Kievan Caves Monastery, see Hans Rothe, ed., *Sinopsis, Kiev 1681: Facsimile mit einer Einleitung*, Cologne and Vienna, 1983 (= Bausteine zur Geschichte der Literatur bei den Slaven, vol. 17), pp. 42–64. Cf. Frank E. Sysyn, "The Cultural, Social and Political Context of Ukrainian History-Writing: 1620–1690," *Europa Orientalis*, vol. 5, 1986, p. 307, and Frank E. Sysyn, "Concepts of Nationhood in Ukrainian History Writing, 1620–1690," *Harvard Ukrainian Studies*, vol. 10, 1986, p. 402. See also P. N. Miliukov, *Glavnyia techeniia russkoi istoricheskoi mysli*, 3rd edn, St. Petersburg, M. V. Aver'ianov, 1913, pp. 7–15.

in Daniel Prinz's account of his diplomatic mission to Moscow in 1575.[4] This means that the term was already in use in Muscovy in the second half of the sixteenth century.

The historian Miliukov pointed out the overwhelming influence Muscovite Church bookmen have had in forming our view of the history of Muscovy:

> In the last century, when Russian historical scholarship began gradually to uncover its sources, these sources came into the hands of historians with their own ready-made view evolved over the centuries. It is not surprising that the ready-made ideology presented in sources led the student of history along well-worn paths, ordering historical facts for him as they were seen and understood by contemporary writers. The student imagined that he was discovering and giving meaning to history when in reality he was simply riding on the shoulders of fifteenth- and sixteenth-century philosophers.[5]

The negative views of the Mongols that we read in our history books can be traced back to these Muscovite Church bookmen (Miliukov's "philosophers"), who devised an anti-Tatar ideology to divert the Muscovite ruling class from a pro-Tatar orientation. That ideology, like other pre-modern ideologies, included three functional components. The political component stated that the grand prince ruled by the Grace of God. The social component stated that, as long as the ruler followed the laws of God, the people were to obey silently, but when the ruler transgressed the laws of God, then the wise advisers were to speak up. The virtual-past component stated that the Rus' princes had been trying to free Rus' from Tatar domination since the thirteenth century. An implicit economic component, it might be argued, attempted to keep Russians from trading with Tatars, but that was not made explicit in the literature of the time.

Alternatives to this anti-Tatar ideology were possible but do not appear in our extant sources. For example, those who formulated the virtual past could have argued in favor of a positive impact for the Tatar hegemony in that it helped to prevent Lithuanian absorption of Muscovy in the fourteenth and fifteenth centuries, but they did not argue that. None of the elements of the ideology can be dated earlier than the middle of the fifteenth century. Although the phrase "Grace of

[4] Prinz [Printz], *Moscoviae ortus, et progressus*, p. 203, as reprinted in *Scriptores Rerum Livonicarum*, vol. 2, p. 721. Prinz [Prints], "Nachalo i vozvyshenie Moskovii," p. 58. The term "Tatar yoke" appears in both Rockhill's and Jackson's translations of a passage in William of Rubruck in regard to the Moxel, a Mordvinian people, who were fleeing the Mongols. But the phrase being translated is *a servitute Tartarorum*, not *jugo Tartarico*. Rubruck, *Journey* (Rockhill), p. 99; Rubruck, *Mission* (Jackson), p. 111; Rubruck, *Itinerarium*, ch. 14, para. 1, p. 199.
[5] Miliukov, *Glavnyia techeniia*, p. 177.

God" had begun to be used regularly by 1433, it appears as part of the grand-princely title only in 1449. Beginning in 1447, the term *gosudar'* (sovereign) was used as part of the title on coins. The metropolitan began to use the term *samoderzhets* to apply to the grand prince in 1492, but the grand-princely chanceries did not adopt it until the 1590s. They did use the term *tsar'* to apply to the grand prince by 1474, but it was not an official part of the title until 1547. The Augustan ancestry of the Muscovite grand prince and the Monomakh legend can be dated no earlier than the 1510s. And the Third Rome theory, which dates no earlier than the 1520s, reached its peak in the decree establishing the patriarchate in 1589, but never again appeared in an official document, secular or ecclesiastical.

My hypothesis in this book is that the secular administration was heavily Mongol influenced and the ecclesiastical administration was heavily Byzantine influenced. The two influences clashed, to a certain degree, both with each other and with the indigenous East Slavic culture in Muscovy. To my mind, this helps to explain why our sources tend to contradict one another, and why historians come to such diametrically opposed positions on the nature of Muscovite political culture. Mongol influences were strongest in the fourteenth century as the Muscovite grand princes borrowed political institutions and practices directly from the Qipchaq Khanate (Ulus of Jochi), which they visited frequently. To establish what those institutions and practices are, I had to look at our evidence for what was going on at the time in Yuan China and the Ilkhanate of Persia.

As we move from the fourteenth through the sixteenth centuries, the Byzantine-based written Church culture gains more and more influence on the secular administration. The Church bookmen directly combat the residual Mongol influence by formulating an anti-Tatar ideology. They can do so freely after 1448, when the Rus' Church begins choosing its own prelates and thus does not have to follow Eastern Church policy as defined by Constantinople. The policy of the Byzantine Empire was one of accommodation with the Qipchaq Khanate, which is reflected in the un-interpolated Rus' chronicles. After 1448, interpolations of a definite anti-Tatar content appear in the chronicles. The highwater mark for Church (Byzantine) influence was the establishment of the Moscow patriarchate in 1589, where I end the book. By that time, both the Byzantine Empire and the Qipchaq Khanate had ceased to be independent political entities. The Patriarch of Constantinople invoked his authority to establish a patriarch in Moscow, but no longer had the power to enforce Eastern Church policies on the Muscovite Church.

Yet, the Muscovite secular rulers continued to "face east" as they forged ahead with the conquest of Siberia, the Caucasus, and then Inner Asia. And the Church was in harmony with this orientation, as is clear, for example, in the decree establishing the patriarchate. Along with the promotion of the metropolitan of Moscow to partriarchal status, the decree created four new metropolitanates. The archiepiscopal see of Novgorod, the second highest position in the Rus' Church, became a metropolitanate, as did the archiepiscopal see of Rostov. The archiepiscopal see of Kazan' and Astrakhan', which had been created in the 1550s, also became a metropolitanate. The promotion of the three archbishops to metropolitans was to be expected. What was unexpected was the promotion of the bishop of Sarai to metropolitan status, who thus leapfrogged over six other bishops: of Suzdal', Smolensk, Vologda, Riazan', Tver', and Kolomna.[6] Creation of the metropolitanates of Kazan' and of Sarai in Tatar territory is evidence of the Church's acknowledgment of the importance of these areas to the secular authority and secular ruler's adoption, from a steppe perspective, of the title *tsar'*.

By the middle of the sixteenth century, owing to the efforts of Rus' Churchmen, foremost among whom was Metropolitan Makarii, all the elements of the Muscovite Church's ideology were already taking shape. By the end of the seventeenth century, that ideology had entered the mainstream of history writing. The Church's propaganda attacks against the Tatars in the late fifteenth and sixteenth centuries still control historians' interpretations of the period of Mongol hegemony over Rus'.

The main question of this book has been why Muscovite secular rulers seemed to be acting in ways that were inexplicable in terms of Church-based views. In other words, why do the sources present such contradictory evidence about what was going on in early and middle Muscovy? My answer has been that the ecclesiastical and secular establishments were affected by two different outside influences – Byzantium and the Qipchaq Khanate, respectively. The traditions, practices, doctrines, and values of the Byzantine Empire drew on those of the Christian Roman Empire (the largest empire in the West in the ancient world), developed them, and transmitted them through the Church to Muscovy. The traditions, practices, doctrines, and values of the Qipchaq Khanate drew on those of the Mongol Empire (the largest land empire in world history), developed them, and transmitted them through the governmental apparatus to Muscovy.

Church sources attempted to explain the actions of the secular government within a Byzantine frame of reference, while secular govern-

---

[6] "Ulozhennaia gramota 1589 goda," pp. 98, 102. Cf. Stroev, *Spiski ierarkov*, cols. 287–288, 1035.

ment sources present actions taken within a Mongol frame of reference. Both societies that provided these competing frames of reference disappeared as independent entities within fifty years of each other. The Ottoman Turks took Constantinople in 1453 and the *uluses* and *ordu* of the Qipchaq Khanate submitted to the Crimean Tatar Khan Mengli Giray in 1502.[7] These two events, however, did not end the influence on Muscovy from these cultures. The book culture of Byzantium began to revive in new forms in Muscovy in the latter half of the fifteenth century. And émigré Tatars from the successor khanates brought with them to Muscovy a renewal of steppe practices. I see these outside influences in a strained relationship during the course of the sixteenth century culminating in the somewhat bizarre behavior of Ivan IV, who through his actions was attempting, however crudely, to work out his own synthesis of these two influences.

In the end, the Byzantine book culture showed greater vitality. Works like the *Velikie chet'i-minei*, the *Stepennaia kniga*, saints' lives, narrative tales, and chronicle entries and interpolations carried an ideology, whose central component was a myth of a pious, holy, and Christian liberation from the perfidious, cruel, and godless Tatars. By the seventeenth century, the education of tsars was entirely church based. Aleksei Mikhailovich's education, for example, included study of a reader designed by his grandfather Patriarch Filaret, as well as the Book of Hours, Psalter, Acts of the Apostles, *Oktoikh*, and Holy Week chants.

At the same time as the Church was developing its anti-Tatar ideology, the myth of the Tatar yoke, and the Rus' princes leading the liberation against it, the Rus' grand princes and tsars were assimilating Tatars into the military and administration in large numbers. Policies, such as the establishment of *pomest'e*, based on Islamic *iqṭā'*, were borrowed to administer the newly acquired territory and to accommodate the influx of Tatar princes and service men. Nonetheless, Church ideology proved effective in determining subsequent historical interpretations and our understanding of Muscovy. Only now, with a better understanding of the evidence, can we historians come out from under the oppressive myth of the Tatar yoke.

---

[7] Leslie Collins, "On the Alleged 'Destruction' of the Great Horde in 1502," *Manzikert to Lepanto: the Byzantine World and the Turks 1071–1571*, ed. Anthony Bryer and Michael Ursinus (= *Byzantinische Forschungen*, vol. 16), Amsterdam, Adolf M. Hakkert, 1991, pp. 361–399.

Addendum: types of cross-cultural influences

In discussing possible influences on Russia in the early nineteenth century, Peter K. Christoff suggested a typology of the twelve "most familiar types of historical influences." These include:

1. Complete and sudden impact of one culture upon another on the broadest possible front, as the Mongol conquest of Russia and the Ottoman conquest of the Balkans.
2. Negative and positive influences, particularly from this type of influence flow.
3. Peaceful, gradual, and scattered influence flow, either conscious or unconscious, through trade and commerce where the carriers of merchandise (and ideas) are individuals or small groups.
4. Influence flow as a result, at least in part, of a dramatic act such as the opening up of Japan in the mid-nineteenth century.
5. Historical influences that are the result of efforts at deliberate amalgamation of two or more cultures.
6. The "wedge" type of influence, which enters one area (as romanticism seems to have appeared in English horticulture) and eventually fans out into art, literature, music, painting, philosophy, and ideology.
7. The influence of a major discovery in one sphere of knowledge (science) upon human relations, like Darwinism and Social Darwinism, or of human relations (organic theory), which as Huizinga has shown, was reflected in some of the sciences.
8. The influence of one individual or a small group upon other individuals or groups as in the establishing of a new religion, philosophy, or ideology, or of a school in music, painting, architecture, literature, science, etc.
9. The steady absorption of ideas descended from the anonymous originators of folk forms in art, literature, and other areas of creative endeavor.
10. The flow of ideas and influences, negative as well as positive, initiated by individuals or small groups of students studying abroad and returning to their native countries. Travel, movies, television, radio, printed matter of all sorts would fall in this category of recent, powerful means of influence transmission.
11. The influence of modern advertising and propaganda—closely related to the preceding form of influence—which depends upon modern means of communication, transportation, and indoctrination.
12. The influence of one or several cultures upon "underdeveloped" societies

when members of such societies, few in number but determined and dedicated, consciously seek a solution to the basic or "hub" problems of their respective societies or countries.[1]

These twelve types of influence can be re-categorized into three sets of opposing features: imposition by the source culture (target culture is passive) vs. borrowing by the target culture (target culture is active); imposition or borrowing along a broad front vs. imposition or borrowing initially as a wedge or along a narrow front, which might then expand to a broader influence; and sudden, immediate change vs. gradual, long-term change. The primary influence of one culture on another can be imposed on a broad front very suddenly, such as the Hyksos conquest of ancient Egypt. Or it can be borrowed by the host culture on a broad front relatively gradually, such as Japanese borrowing of Western methods of industrialization in the late nineteenth and twentieth centuries. I have constructed a table (see Table A1) that uses these three sets of features as criteria in which to place examples of core culture influences. The placement of my examples is extremely tentative and open to suggestions for rearrangement, but the categories themselves are I think fairly solid.

Table A1. *A typology of cross-cultural influence*

		sudden	gradual
Imposed	broad	Hyksos on Egypt	Europeans on Amerindians
	narrow	Islam on Europe	England on India
Borrowed	broad	Mongols on Muscovy	China on Japan
	narrow	Japan on English Romanticism	Byzantium on Muscovy

Christoff placed Mongol influence into his first and second types of influence, both of which imply imposition of ideas, practices, and customs by the source culture. But, as we know, the khan at Sarai tended to adopt a *laissez-faire* attitude toward Rus', as long as the tax money continued flowing in an uninterrupted manner. The khan intervened in most cases only at the behest of his agent, the grand prince. Instead of imposition as a basis of cultural influence, I would place Mongol influence under Christoff's twelfth type of influence. That is, certain members of Muscovite society, "few in number but determined and dedicated," sought solutions to the "hub" problems of their society. Churchmen tended to adopt institutions and practices from Byzantium. Secular leaders tended to adopt institutions and practices from the Qipchaq Khanate.

[1] Peter K. Christoff, *The Third Heart: Some Intellectual-Ideological Currents and Cross Currents in Russia 1800–1830*, The Hague, Mouton, 1970, pp. 14–15.

Glossary

bāsqāq	Turkic term for a military commander, who acted as governor in areas that needed to be pacified.
Council of Florence	Held partly in Florence and partly in Ferrara, Italy, from 1437 to 1439. Out of it came a decision to reunify the Eastern and Western Churches. The Muscovite grand prince and the Rus' Church rejected that decision, which rejection contributed to the *de facto* autonomous status of the Rus' Church.
daruγači	A governor within the civilian administration of the Mongol Empire.
d'iak	A scribe, but in certain contexts can mean a state secretary, as in *dumnyi d'iak*.
iarlyk	A decree by a khan.
iqṭāʿ	A military land grant. Prominent in areas ruled by Islamic administration. From it a cavalryman derived maintenance for his horses, equipment, weapons, and himself and family. He also collected taxes and passed them on to the central authority. In return, he provided administrative and judicial functions to the peasants on the estate.
kormlenie	Literally, "feeding." System by which local administrators, such as *namestniki* and *volosteli*, were paid by contributions from the populace in lieu of salaries. It was phased out in the sixteenth century.
namestnik	Literally, "lieutenant." The name given to a local administrator in early and middle Muscovy of regions and towns.
oprichnina	Originally that portion of an estate, either *vot-*

	china or *pomest'e*, that was set aside for the use of the widow of the servitor. From 1565 to 1572, it was applied to the separate "state within a state" that Ivan IV set up, in contrast to the Zemshchina.
pomest'e	A military land grant. Prominent in areas ruled by Muscovite administration. From it a cavalryman derived maintenance for his horses, equipment, weapons, and himself and family. He also collected taxes and passed them on to the central authority. In return, he provided administrative and judicial functions to the peasants on the estate (see *iqṭāʿ*).
Qipchaq Khanate	The name used in this book for the *ulus* of Jochi, that is the area of the Mongol Empire that was apportioned to Jochi, the son of Chingiz Khan. Traditionally, historians have called this polity "the Golden Horde," but that term is anachronistic and incorrect.
quriltai	An assembly of Mongol notables whose function it was to advise the reigning khan or select the successor to a deceased one.
seclusion of women	During the middle and late Muscovite periods, our sources tell us that the wives and daughters of the Muscovite elite lived in separate rooms from their husbands and fathers. Women of the elite were also not supposed to be seen in the streets of the city or town. When they did go out, they were veiled and traveled in closed carriages.
tammači	Mongol term for a military commander, who acted as governor in areas that needed to be pacified (see *bāsqāq*).
uezd	A county.
ulus	Partitions of the Mongol Empire.
voevoda	A military governor.
volostel'	Chief administrator of a district, called *volost'*, in early and middle Muscovy. Replaced in the seventeenth century by *voevody*, or military governors.
votchina	An estate that was "in the family," that is, not granted by the grand prince or tsar.

yām (iam)	A system of posts.
Zemshchina	The part of Muscovy that was not part of the Oprichnina of Ivan IV.
zemskii sobor	Council of the representatives of the land, first called in 1549 to advise the tsar.
zhitie	Written "life" or *vita* of a saint.

Chronology to 1589

Entries in bold represent years in which a change occurred in who was grand prince of Rus'.

1147   First mention of Moscow in chronicles
1156   Moscow surrounded with wooden walls
1206   *quriltai*; Chingiz Khan declared leader of tribal confederation
1211   *quriltai*; Mongols begin conquest of northern China
1215   Chingiz Khan and Khwarezm Shah open hostilities
1218   Chingiz Khan conquers Qara-Khitan Empire
1223   Vladimir Riurikovich becomes Grand Prince of Kiev; battle on Kalka River; Mongols defeat combined Polovtsian–Rus' army
1227   Chingiz Khan dies
1229   Ögödei becomes great khan (qagan)
1236   Mikhail Vsevolodovich becomes Grand Prince of Kiev; Mongols annihilate Bulgars on Volga; Novgorodians under their prince, Alexander Iaroslavich, defeat Swedes on Neva River
1237   Mongols invade Rus'; Riazan' sacked
1238   Moscow and Vladimir sacked; forces of Iurii Vsevolodovich, Prince of Vladimir, routed by Mongols on Sit River; Prince Iurii killed (March 4); Iaroslav Vsevolodovich becomes Prince of Vladimir
1239   Mongols take Pereiaslavl' and Chernigov
1240   Kiev sacked by Mongols; Aleksandr Iaroslavich (Nevskii) defeats Swedes at Neva River
1241   Great Khan Ögödei dies; battles of Liegnitz and Brataslava
1242   Kirill (Cyril) becomes metropolitan; Batu becomes Khan of the Ulus of Jochi; Aleksandr Nevskii defeats Teutonic knights at Lake Peipus

1243	Batu confirms Iaroslav Vsevolodich as Prince of Vladimir
1245	John of Plano Carpini, papal envoy, begins his journey to Qaraqorum; Batu confirms Daniil Romanovich as Prince of Galicia and Volynia
1246	Batu executes Mikhail Vsevolodovich, Grand Prince of Kiev; Güyük becomes great khan; Iaroslav Vsevolodovich, Prince of Vladimir, dies
1247	Aleksandr Nevskii and Novgorod yield up tribute to Tatars; John of Plano Carpini returns from Qaraqorum; Sviatoslav Vsevolodovich becomes Prince of Vladimir
1248	Great Khan Güyük dies
1250	Church of the Archangel Michael built in Moscow's kremlin
1251	Möngke becomes great khan
1252	Sviatoslav Vsevolodovich, Prince of Vladimir dies; Andrei of Suzdal' is made Grand Prince, then relieved of grand-princely patent; Aleksandr Iaroslavich (Nevskii) made Grand Prince of Vladimir
1253	William of Rubruck, papal envoy, begins his journey to Qaraqorum
1255	William of Rubruck returns from Qaraqorum; Khan Batu dies
1256	Sartaq becomes khan of the Qipchaq Khanate
1257	Mongols begin census of Rus' lands; Khan Sartaq dies; Ulaγči becomes khan of the Qipchaq Khanate; Khan Ulaγči dies; Berke becomes khan of the Qipchaq Khanate
1259	Great Khan Möngke dies; Aleksandr Nevskii enforces Mongol census in Novgorod
1260	Battle of 'Ayn-Jālūt; one *quriltai* chooses Qubilai as great khan; another *quriltai* chooses Ariγ-böke as great khan; civil war between the forces of Qubilai and the forces of Ariγ-böke
1261	archiepiscopal see established in Sarai
1262	uprisings in Rus' towns against tax collectors
1263	Grand Prince Alexander Nevskii dies in Gorodets returning from Qaraqorum; Daniil Aleksandrovich appointed Prince of Moscow
1263–64	Berke defeats Hülegü
1264	Iaroslav Iaroslavich of Tver' becomes Grand Prince of Vladimir; Qubilai defeats Ariγ-böke; Qubilai decides to

	establish capital of Mongol Empire at Dadu (Khan-baliq, Beijing) rather than Qaraqorum
1267	Khan Berke dies; Möngke Temür becomes khan of the Qipchaq Khanate; Möngke Temür issues *iarlyk* to Metropolitan Kirill
c. 1270	Möngke-Temür issues decree to Grand Prince Iaroslav Iaroslavich guaranteeing freedom of passage for merchants
1271	Grand Prince Iaroslav Iaroslavich dies
1272	Vasilii Iaroslavich of Kostroma becomes Grand Prince of Vladimir; Danilov Monastery church built in Moscow
1276	Grand Prince Vasilii Iaroslavich dies
1277	Dmitrii Aleksandrovich becomes Grand Prince of Vladimir
1279	Rus' princes join with Tatars against Lithuanians
1280	Khan Möngke Temür dies; Töde Möngke becomes khan of the Qipchaq Khanate; Metropolitan Kirill dies
1282	Maksim becomes metropolitan
1287	Khan Töde Möngke resigns; Töle-Buqa becomes khan of the Qipchaq Khanate
1290	Khan Töle-Buqa dies; Toqta becomes khan of the Qipchaq Khanate
1291	Mamlūks evict Crusaders from Syria
1293	Tatars sack Vladimir, Moscow, and other towns in northeast Rus'
1294	Grand Prince Dmitrii Aleksandrovich dies; Andrei Aleksandrovich becomes Grand Prince of Vladimir; Great Khan Qubilai dies; Timur becomes great khan
1297	Council of Vladimir decides Pereiaslavl' belongs to Ivan Dmitrievich instead of Grand Prince Andrei; Toqta becomes khan of Qipchaq Khanate
1298	Tatars sack Moscow
1299	Steppe war between Nogai and Toqta; Metropolitan Maksim leaves Kiev and takes up residence in Vladimir-on-the-Kliazma
1300	Nogai killed; Toqta dies
1301	Council of Dmitrov concerning Pereiaslavl'
1303	Daniil Aleksandrovich, Prince of Moscow, dies
1304	Grand Prince Andrei Aleksandrovich dies; Mikhail Iaroslavich of Tver' becomes Grand Prince of Vladimir; Iurii Daniilovich becomes Prince of Moscow

1305	Metropolitan Maksim dies
1308	Peter becomes metropolitan
1312	Khan Toqta dies
1313	Özbeg becomes khan of the Qipchaq Khanate
1315	Iurii summoned to Sarai, remains there two years, marries Konchaka (Agrafa), sister of Khan Özbeg; Novgorod sends 50,000 grivna of silver to Grand Prince Mikhail
1317	Iurii marches against Tver'; Mikhail of Tver' defeats Iurii; Agrafa captured, dies a prisoner in Tver'
1318	Grand Prince Mikhail Iaroslavich executed by Khan Özbeg; Iurii Daniilovich of Moscow made Grand Prince of Vladimir
1320–1322	Rostov uprising
1322	Khan Özbeg deprives Iurii Daniilovich of grand-princely patent and makes Dmitrii Mikhailovich of Tver' Grand Prince of Vladimir
1325	Grand Prince Dmitrii kills Prince Iurii of Moscow; Ivan Daniilovich becomes Prince of Moscow
1326	Aleksandr Mikhailovich becomes Grand Prince of Vladimir; Khan Özbeg orders execution of Grand Prince Dmitrii Mikhailovich in Sarai for murder of Iurii; Cathedral of the Assumption founded in Moscow; Metropolitan Peter dies
1327	Aleksandr Mikhailovich relieved of grand-princely patent; uprising in Tver'; grand prince takes over duties of *baskaks* in certain areas of Rus'
1328	Ivan Daniilovich of Moscow becomes Grand Prince of Vladimir; Feognost becomes metropolitan of Rus'
1330	Savior of the Forest Church constructed in Moscow
1332	Stone Church of the Archangel Michael replaces wooden one in Moscow kremlin; stone Church of St. John Climachus built in Moscow kremlin; Grand Prince Ivan travels to Sarai
1333	Grand Prince Ivan travels to Sarai; Metropolitan Feognost travels to Sarai; Ibn Baṭṭūta visits Sarai; Vychegoda and Pechora begin paying tribute to Moscow
1336	Grand Prince Ivan travels to Sarai
1338	Grand Prince Ivan travels to Sarai
1339	Grand Prince Ivan travels to Sarai
1340	Prince Semen travels to Sarai; all Rus' princes gather in Sarai

1341	Grand Prince Ivan I (Kalita) dies; Semen Ivanovich becomes grand prince; Khan Özbeg dies; Tinibeg becomes khan of the Qipchaq Khanate
1342	Khan Tinibeg dies; Janibeg becomes khan of the Qipchaq Khanate; Metropolitan Feognost travels to Sarai; Grand Prince Semen travels to Sarai
1344	Grand Prince Semen travels to Sarai; some chronicles report that all Rus' princes gather in Sarai
1347	Grand Prince Semen travels to Sarai; Semen sends money to Constantinople for repair of Hagia Sophia Cathedral; Semen supports request of Metropolitan Feognost for abolishment of the metropolitanate of Galicia; Taydula, Khan Janibeg's wife, issues *iarlyk* to Metropolitan "Ioann" (Feognost?)
1350	Grand Prince Semen travels to Sarai
1353	Grand Prince Semen's sons die of the plague; Grand Prince Semen (the Proud) dies of the plague; Ivan Ivanovich, the younger brother of Semen, becomes grand prince; Metropolitan Feognost dies
1354	All Rus' princes gather in Sarai; Taydula issues *iarlyk* to metropolitan-designate Aleksei for passage to Constantinople; Aleksei becomes metropolitan
1357	A. P. Khvost, *tysiatskii* of Muscovy, murdered; Aleksei travels to Sarai where he cures Khatun Taydula; Khan Janibeg dies; Berdibeg becomes khan of the Qipchaq Khanate; Khan Berdibeg issues *iarlyk* to Metropolitan Aleksei
1359	Grand Prince Ivan II (the Meek) dies; Dmitrii Konstantinovich of Suzdal' appointed grand prince; Khan Berdibeg dies; Qulpa becomes khan of the Qipchaq Khanate; Metropolitan Aleksei becomes regent for Dmitrii of Moscow
1360	Khan Qulpa dies; civil wars until 1374 follow in Qipchaq Khanate, during which time Nevruz, Mürid, Ordu Melik, 'Abd Ullāh, 'Azīz, Meḥmed Būlāq, and others rule as khan for brief periods of time
1363	Khan Mürid appoints Dmitrii of Moscow as grand prince, then changes mind, because Emir Mamai supports Dmitrii, and reappoints Dmitrii of Suzdal' instead
1364	Rostov, Ustiug, and Ustiug's possessions in Velikaia Perm' begin paying tribute to Moscow
1365	Riazan' defeats Tatar raiding force

1367	Palad driven off from Nizhnii-Novgorod; stone replaces wood in fortification of the Moscow kremlin; Velikaia Perm', Pechora, Mezen', and Kegrola begin paying tribute to Moscow
1368	Algirdas (Olgerd), Grand Duke of Lithuania besieges Moscow
1370	Algirdas besieges Moscow again
1372	Tver'–Moscow war begins
1373	Mamai lays waste Riazan'
1374	Mamai's envoys and 1500 Tatars killed at Nizhnii-Novgorod; Vasilii Vel'iaminov dies in Moscow – last *tysiatskii*; Urus becomes khan of the Qipchaq Khanate
1375	Nizhnii-Novgorod devastated; treaty between Dmitrii of Moscow and Mikhail of Tver'
1376	Dmitrii compels Kazan' to pay him to raise the siege; first Toqtaqyia, then Temur Melik becomes khan of the Qipchaq Khanate
1377	Rus' force routed on the Piana; Grand Duke of Lithuania Algirdas dies; Jagiełło (Jagailo) becomes Grand Duke of Lithuania; Tokhtamish becomes khan of the Qipchaq Khanate
1378	Tatars burn Nizhnii; Dmitrii wins on the Vozha; Metropolitan Aleksei dies
1379	Pimen becomes metropolitan
1380	Battle of Kulikovo Field; Dmitrii imprisons Metropolitan Pimen
1381	Tokhtamish defeats Mamai at the Kalka River; Kiprian becomes metropolitan
1382	Tokhtamish sacks Moscow
1385	Metropolitan Kiprian travels to Sarai
1386	Novgorod placed under tribute by Dmitrii of Moscow; Jagiełło marries Jadwiga, uniting Lithuania with Poland
1387	Conflict between Tokhtamish and Timur
1388	Metropolitan Theognostus of Trebizond travels to Moscow seeking donations
1389	Grand Prince Dmitrii (Donskoi) dies; Vasilii I becomes grand prince; Metropolitan Pimen dies; Kiprian (Cyprian) becomes metropolitan of Rus'
1390	Vasilii I marries Sofiia, daughter of Vytautus (Vitovt) of Lithuania
1391	Timur Qutlug defeats Tokhtamish at Kondurcha River
1392	Sergei of Radonezh dies

1393	Vytautus becomes grand duke of Lithuania; Patriarch of Constantinople Antonios writes letter upbraiding Vasilii I
1395	Timur Qutlug sacks Sarai, becomes Khan of the Qipchaq Khanate; Tokhtamish defeated by Timur Qutlug at Terek River
1398	Vasilii I sends money to Constantinople to help in the defense against the Ottoman Turks
1399	Battle on River Vorskla; Vytautus defeated by Timur Qutlug
1401	Sadi Beg becomes khan of the Qipchaq Khanate
1405	Timur Qutlug dies
1406	Metropolitan Kiprian dies
1407	Pulad Han becomes khan of the Qipchaq Khanate
1408	Treaty with Lithuania; Edigei's expedition against Moscow; Fotii (Photius) becomes metropolitan of Rus'
1410	Battle of Tannenberg; Teutonic knights defeat Vytautus; Temur becomes khan of the Qipchaq Khanate
1411	Emir Edigei overthrown
1412	Gelāl ed-Dīn becomes khan of the Qipchaq Khanate; Kerīm Berdī becomes khan of the Qipchaq Khanate
1414	Kibak becomes khan of the Qipchaq Khanate
1417	Jeremferden becomes khan of the Qipchaq Khanate
1419	Ulug Mehmed becomes khan of the Qipchaq Khanate, which is contested by Devlet Berdi until 1424
1422	Barāq claims to be khan of the Qipchaq Khanate (until 1427)
1425	Vasilii I dies; Vasilii II becomes grand prince
1430	Vytautus, Grand Duke of Lithuania, dies
1431	Iurii, brother of Vasilii I, claims throne from Vasilii II; Metropolitan Fotii dies; Iurii and Vasilii travel to Sarai to have Khan Ulug Mehmed decide the succession.
1432	Ulug Mehmed decides in favor of Vasilii, who is installed in Moscow as grand prince by a Jochid
1433	Iurii gives up claim but reconsiders; Sajjid Ahmed claims to be Khan of the Qipchaq Khanate (until 1465)
1434	Iurii dies after defeating Vasilii II in battle
1435	Küčük Mehmed claims to be khan of the Qipchaq Khanate by ousting Ulug Mehmed
1436	Vasilii II orders the blinding of Vasilii Kosoi, his cousin;

	Isidore becomes metropolitan; Josef Barbaro visits Riazan' and Kolomna
1437	Council of Florence begins
1438	Ulug Meḥmed defeats Rus' at Belev, founds Kazan' Khanate
1439	Council of Florence ends; Ulug Meḥmed besieges Moscow
1440	Casimir becomes Grand Duke of Lithuania
1441	Metropolitan Isidore returns to Moscow; after conducting church service in Catholic manner, he is forced to flee from Moscow
1445	Ulug Meḥmed captures Vasilii II at Battle of Suzdal'; Mahmeduk, Ulug Meḥmed's son, captures Kazan' from Qipchaq Khanate; Crimean Khanate breaks away from Qipchaq Khanate; Moscow burns
1446	Ulug Meḥmed allows Vasilii II to return to Rus' after taking a ransom of 200,000 rubles; Dmitrii Iur'evich Shemiaka siezes throne, blinds Vasilii II
1447	Vasilii II ousts Shemiaka from Moscow, resumes rule; Mahmeduk driven off from Moscow; Casimir IV becomes King of Poland
1448	Council of bishops elects Iona as metropolitan
1449	Vasilii II declares his son Ivan co-ruler; Casimir IV signs treaties with Vasilii II and Boris Aleksandrovich of Tver'
1450	Shemiaka driven off from attack on Moscow, seeks refuge in Novgorod
1451	Sajjid Aḥmed driven off from attack on Moscow
1452	Khanate of Kasimov established; Tatars accept Rus' suzerainty over Kasimov; Vasilii II writes to Byzantine Emperor Constantine XI
1453	April 9: Moscow and the entire kremlin burn; May 29: Constantinople falls to Ottoman Turks; Dmitrii Shemiaka dies in Novgorod
1456	Vasilii II imposes fine and treaty on Novgorod limiting the *veche*
1459	Vasilii II conquers Viatka, but Viatka reasserts independence
1461	Metropolitan Iona writes letter to Khan Maḥmud of Kazan'; Metropolitan Iona dies; Feodosii becomes metropolitan
1462	Vasilii II dies; Ivan III becomes grand prince
1463	Ivan III obtains submission of Iaroslavl'

1464	Ivan's daughter Anna marries Prince of Riazan'; Metropolitan Feodosii resigns; Filipp becomes metropolitan
1465	Tatar punitive expedition stopped in border area; Aḥmed becomes khan of the Qipchaq Khanate
1467	Ivan III sends army to help friendly khan at Kasimov, but fails
1468	Ivan III refuses Pskov a separate bishop; Ivan III presents Great Zion to Assumption Cathedral
1469	Ivan III sends army against Kazan'; fails twice to take Kazan'
1470	Novgorod turns to Casimir IV, for help
1471	Ivan III advances on Novgorod; battle on Shelon River; treaty between Moscow and Novgorod.
1472	Ivan III captures Perm'; Ivan marries Zoe (Sophia); Ivan inherits Dmitrov
1473	Metropolitan Filipp dies; Gerontii becomes metropolitan
1474	Ivan III obtains Rostov
1475	Ivan III comes to Novgorod; Aristotle Fioroventi arrives in Moscow; Crimean khan recognizes suzerainty of Ottoman sultan
1476	Ambrogio Contarini, Venetian ambassador, visits Moscow; Ivan III enters Novgorod to take action against plague
1478	Great bell of Novgorod taken to Moscow
1480	Ivan III encounters Khan Aḥmed at Ugra River; Andrei and Boris come to terms
1481	Andrei of Vologda bequeaths estate to Ivan III; Khan Aḥmed is killed; Murtezā and his brother Sajjid Aḥmed II, and their half-brother Šaih Aḥmed all claim to be khans of the Qipchaq Khanate
1483	Mikhail of Tver' declares himself "younger brother" of Ivan III; Ivan begins confiscations of lands in Novgorod
1485	Ivan III captures Tver'; Prince Mikhail flees to Lithuania
1487	Ivan III sends army against Kazan', installs Mehmed Amīn as khan of Kazan'
1489	Viatka submits to Moscow; Metropolitan Gerontii dies; Nicholaus Poppel meets with Ivan III; new Cathedral of Annunciation in the Moscow kremlin is completed
1490	Ivan III makes agreement with Holy Roman Emperor against Poland; Ivan Molodoi, son of Ivan III, dies;

	Zosima becomes metropolitan; Church Council investigates charges of heresy
1491	Ivan III and Crimean Tatars crush Sarai Tatars
1492	Casimir IV dies; Muscovite–Lithuanian hostilities; Metropolitan Zosima begins to refer to Ivan III as *samoderzhets*
1493	Uglich absorbed; Ivan assumes title Sovereign (gosudar) over Novgorod; Russo–Danish alliance
1494	Muscovite campaign against Lithuania; Zosima resigns as metropolitan; Ivan III closes off Novgorod to Hansa
1495	Grand Duke of Lithuania Alexander marries Ivan's daughter Elena; Simon becomes metropolitan
1496	War with Swedes; Muscovy sends ambassador to Ottoman Empire
1497	*Sudebnik* (Law Code) issued; truce with Swedes
1498	Dmitrii, grandson of Ivan III, installed as co-ruler
1499	Aḥmed becomes khan of the Qipchaq Khanate; Ivan III names his son Vasilii Grand Prince of Novgorod and Pskov
1500	Campaign against Lithuania; Battle of Vedrosha River
1501	Rus' forces subdue Livonians at Helmed
1502	the *uluses* and *ordu* of the Qipchaq Khanate (Great Horde) submit to the Crimean Tatar Khan Mengli Giray in 1502; Ivan III arrests his grandson and co-ruler Dmitrii
1503	Treaties with Lithuania and Livonia; Church Council concerning widower priests and simony
1504	Novgorod–Moscow heretics punished
1505	Ivan III dies; Vasilii III becomes grand prince; Vasilii III marries Solomoniia Saburova; new stone Church of the Archangel Michael constructed in Moscow's kremlin; Tsarevich Kudai Kul converts to Christianity adopting the name Peter
1506	Kudai Kul/Peter marries Evdokhiia Ivanovna, sister of Vasilii III
1508	Nil Sorskii dies
1510	Vasilii III takes over Pskov
1511	Metropolitan Simon resigns; Varlaam becomes metropolitan
1512	War with Lithuania resumes
1514	Vasilii III captures Smolensk
1515	Iosif of Volokolamsk dies

1517	Vasilii III acquires Riazan'
1518	Maksim Grek arrives in Moscow; Patriarch Theoleptos of Constantinople refers to Vasilii III as *tsar'*
1521	Varlaam resigns as metropolitan; Muscovy incorporates Riazan'; Crimean Tatars besiege Moscow
1522	Daniil becomes metropolitan
1523	Treaty with Lithuania confirming Muscovite gains in 1514
1525	Trial of Maksim Grek for heresy; marriage of Vasilii III and Solomoniia annulled
1526	Vasilii III marries Elena Glinskaia
1533	Vasilii III dies; his three-year-old son Ivan becomes grand prince under the regency of Elena Glinskaia and the Boyar Council
1538	Elena Glinskaia dies; Vasilii Shuiskii becomes regent
1539	Metropolitan Daniil is deposed; Ioasaf becomes metropolitan; Ivan Bel'skii becomes regent
1542	Metropolitan Ioasaf is deposed; Makarii becomes metropolitan
1547	Ivan IV marries Anastasia Romanova; Ivan crowned Tsar; great fire in Moscow; Iurii Glinskii killed by mob
1549	Zemskii sobor convenes
1550	*Sudebnik* (Law Code) issued
1551	Stoglav (100 chapter) Church Council meets
1552	Muscovy takes over Kazan'
1553	English explorer Richard Chancellor reaches Moscow; Ivan gains oath from boyars
1554	Khan Bekbulat sends letter in which he refers to Ivan IV as a Chingizid
1555	Chancellor returns as ambassador of Queen Mary
1556	Regulations for military service of gentry; Astrakhan' taken; embassy from Ivan IV to Sigismund II justifies Ivan's adoption of the title *tsar'*
1558	Beginning of Livonian War
1561	Ivan IV marries Mariia (Kochenei) Temriukovna
1563	Polotsk captured; Metropolitan Makarii dies
1564	Afanasii becomes metropolitan; Ivan leaves Moscow for Aleksandrova Sloboda; Andrei Kurbskii defects; Ivan Fedorov prints first book in Moscow
1565	Ivan IV establishes Oprichnina
1566	Zemskii sobor meets; Metropolitan Afanasii resigns;

	German becomes metropolitan for two days before being ousted; Filipp becomes metropolitan
1568	Synod deposes Metropolitan Filipp; Kirill becomes metropolitan
1569	Union of Lublin; Filipp, former metropolitan, murdered; Ottoman Empire attempts to capture Astrakhan'
1570	Oprichnina ravages of Novgorod; Ivan's proposition to Elizabeth of England
1571	Bride-show for Ivan IV; Crimean Tatars under Devlet Girei sack Moscow
1572	Ivan IV abolishes Oprichnina; Ivan appoints Mikhail Kaibulich to head a recombined Boyar Council; Sigismund Augustus dies; Metropolitan Kirill dies; Antonii becomes metropolitan
1573	Crimean Tatars stopped at Lopasnia River
1575	War with Swedes over Estonia; Stefan Batory elected to Polish throne; Ivan IV "appoints" Simeon Bekbulatovich as grand prince of all Rus'; Daniel Prinz visits Moscow as ambassador of the Holy Roman Emperor
1576	Ivan IV "takes back" his position and sends Simeon to Tver'
1578	Swedes defeat Muscovite forces at Wenden
1579	Loss of Polotsk and Velikie Luki
1580	Monasteries prohibited from inheriting lands
1581	Ostrov lost; Poles under Stefan Bathory march as far as Pskov; Ivan kills his son Ivan, the heir to the throne; Metropolitan Antonii dies; Dionisii becomes metropolitan
1582	Truce with Poland; Antonio Possevino visits Moscow as ambassador of Pope Gregory XIII; Ermak defeats Khan of Sibir'
1583	Truce with the Swedes; Ermak presents western Siberia to Ivan IV; Livonian War ends
1584	Ivan IV dies; Fedor begins rule as tsar
1586	Stefan Batory dies; Fedor's unsuccessful bid to become King of Poland; Metropolitan Dionisii deposed; Iov becomes metropolitan
1588	Boris Godunov becomes effective ruler
1589	Patriarchate of Moscow established; Iov becomes first Patriarch of Moscow and All Rus'

Bibliography

SOURCES

1100 Jahre österreichische und europäische Geschichte, ed. Leo Santifaller, Vienna, Druck und Kommissionsverlag der Österreichischen Staatsdruckerei, 1949.

Acta et diplomata graeca medii aevi sacra et profana, ed. Fr[anz von Ritter] Miklosich and Ios[if] Müller, 6 vols., Vienna, Karl Gerold, 1860–1890.

Akty istoricheskie, sobrannye i izdannye Arkheograficheskoi komissiei, 5 vols., St. Petersburg, 1841–1842.

Akty, otnosiashchiesia k istorii iuzhnoi i zapadnoi Rossii, 15 vols., St. Petersburg, Tipografiia brat. Panteleevykh, 1863–1892.

Akty, sobrannye v bibliotekakh i arkhivakh Rossiiskoi imperii Arkheograficheskoi ekspeditsiei imperatorskoi Akademii nauk, 4 vols., St. Petersburg, 1836.

Analecta byzantino-russica, ed. [W.] V. E. Regal, St. Petersburg, Imperatorskaia Akademiia nauk, 1891.

Ancient Near Eastern Texts, ed. James B. Pritchard, Princeton University Press, 1950.

Attaleiates, Michael, *Historia*, ed. Immanuel Bekker, Bonn, 1853.

Bank, A. V., *Vizantiiskoe iskusstvo v sobraniiakh Sovetskogo Soiuza*, Leningrad, Sovetskii khudoznik, 1966.

Bank, [A. V.] Alice, *Byzantine Art in the Collections of Soviet Museums*, trans. Inna Sorokina, Leningrad, Aurora Art, 1977.

Barbaro, Josafa, and Ambrogio Contarini, *Travels to Tana and Persia*, London, Hakluyt Society, 1873.

Barbaro, Iosaphat, "Viaggio alla Tana," in *Barbaro i Kontarini o Rossii*, pp. 113–136.

Barbaro i Kontarini o Rossii. K istorii italo-russkikh sviazei v XV v., ed. E. Ch. Skrzhinskaia, Leningrad, Nauka, 1971.

Barker, Ernest, *Social and Political Thought in Byzantium: From Justinian I to the Last Palaeologus*, Oxford, Clarendon Press, 1957.

Barsov, E. V., "Drevne-russkie pamiatniki sviashchennogo venchaniia tsarei na tsarstvo," *ChOIDR*, 1883, bk. 1, pp. I–XXXV, 1–160.

Baṭṭūṭa, Ibn, *The Travels of Ibn Baṭṭūṭa AD 1325–1354*, 4 vols., vols. 1–3 trans. H. A. R. Gibb, vol. 4, trans. C. F. Beckingham, Cambridge University Press, 1958–1994.

Baṭṭūṭa, Ibn, *Ibn Battuta in Black Africa*, trans. Said Hamdun and Noël King, Princeton, NJ, Markus Wiener, 1994.

Beccaria, Cesare, *On Crimes and Punishments*, trans. David Young, Indianapolis, Hackett, 1986.

Belinskii, V. G., *Polnoe sobranie sochinenii*, ed. S. A. Vengerov, 12 vols., St. Petersburg, Tipografiia Tovarishchestva "Obshchestvennaia pol'za," 1903.

Bodde, Derk, *Statesman, Patriot, and General in Ancient China: Three Shih Chi Biographies of the Ch'in Dynasty (255–206 BC)*, New Haven, CT, American Oriental Society, 1940.

Bodin, Jean, *Les six livres de la République*, Paris, 1576.

[Carpini, John of Plano] Iohannes de Plano Carpini, "Ystoria Mongalorum," in *Sinica Franciscana*, vol. 1, pp. 27–130.

Carpini, John of Plano, "History of the Mongols," in *The Mongol Mission*, pp. 3–72.

Castiglione, Baldesar, *The Book of the Courtier*, rev. edn, trans. George Bull, London, Penguin, 1974.

Chancellor, Richard, "The First Voyage to Russia," in *Rude & Barbarous Kingdom*, pp. 9–41.

Choniatēs, Niketas, *Historia*, ed. Immanuel Bekker (CSHB, vol. 22), Bonn, E. Weber, 1835.

Clavijo: Embassy to Tamerlane 1403–1406, trans. Guy Le Strange, ed. E. Denison Ross and Eileen Power, London, George Routledge and Sons, 1928.

Collins, Samuel, *The Present State of Russia*, London, John Winter, 1671.

Contarini, Ambrogio, "Viaggio in Persia," in *Barbaro i Kontarini o Rossii*, pp. 188–210.

Cronica fratris Salimbene de Adam Ordinis minorum, ed. O. Holder-Egger, *Monumenta Germaniae historica. Scriptorum*, vol. 32, Hanover and Leipzig, Impensis Bibiopolii Hahniani, 1905–1913.

D'Aguilers, Raymond, *Historia Francorum qui ceperunt Jerusalem* in *Recueil des historiens des Croisades. Historiens occidentaux*, 5 vols., Paris, Imprimerie Royale, 1844–1895.

Dances with Wolves, dir. Kevin Costner, with Kevin Costner, Mary McDonnell, Graham Greene, Rodney A. Grant, Floyd Red Crow Westerman, Tantoo Cardinal et al., Panavision, 1990.

Dashkova, Ekaterina, *The Memoirs of Princess Dashkova*, trans. Kyril Fitzlyon, Durham, NC, Duke University Press, 1995.

Diakonos, Leo, *Historia*, ed. Karl Benedict Hase (CSHB, vol. 5), Bonn, E. Weber, 1828.

Dmitrieva, R. P., *Skazanie o kniaz'iakh vladimirskikh*, Moscow and Leningrad, Akademiia nauk SSSR, 1955.

Dmytryshyn, Basil, *Medieval Russia: a Source Book, 850–1700*, 3rd edn, Fort Worth TX, Holt, Rinehart, and Winston, 1990.

"Dokumenti koji se tichu odnosa izmeću srpske tsrkve i Rusije u XVI veku," ed. M. Dimitrijević, in *Spomenik*, vol. 39, 1903, pp. 16–42.

Dopolneniia k aktam istoricheskim, 12 vols., St. Petersburg, Arkheograficheskaia kommissiia, 1846–1872.

Dukhovnye i dogovornyie gramoty velikikh i udel'nykh kniazei XIV–XVI vv., ed. L. V. Cherepnin, Moscow and Leningrad, Akademiia nauk SSSR, 1950.

Fiedler, Joseph, "Die Allianz zwischen Kaiser Maximilian I. and Vasilji Ivanovič, Grossfürsten von Russland, von dem jahre 1514," *Sitzungsberichte der*

Kaiserlichen Akademie der Wissenschaften. Philosophisch-historische Classe, vol. 43, no. 2, 1863, pp. 183–289.

Fletcher, Giles, "Of the Russe Commonwealth," in *Rude & Barbarous Kingdom*, pp. 109–246.

Gabrieli, Francesco, *Arab Historians of the Crusades*, trans. E. J. Costello, London, Routledge & Kegan Paul, 1969.

Geanakoplos, Deno John, *Byzantium: Church, Society, and Civilization Seen Through Contemporary Eyes*, University of Chicago Press, 1984.

General History and Collection of Voyages and Travels, 18 vols., ed. Robert Kerr and F. A. S. Edin, Edinburgh, George Ramsay, 1811.

Geschichte Wassaf's, ed. and trans. [Joseph von] Hammer-Purgstall, Vienna, Kaiserlich-königlichen Hof- und Staatsdruckerei, 1856.

Goar, R. P. Jacobi, *Euchologion sive rituale Græcorum*, 2nd edn, Venice, Ex Typographia Bartholomæi Javarina, 1730.

Golokhvastov, D. P., and Archimandrite Leonid, "Blagoveshchenskii ierei Sil'vestr i ego poslaniia," *ChOIDR*, no. 88, 1874, bk. 1, pp. 69–87.

Gramoty velikogo Novgoroda i Pskova, ed. S. N. Valk, Moscow, Akademiia nauk SSSR, 1949.

Gregoras, Nicephorus, *Historiae Byzantinae*, 3 vols. ed. Ludwig Schopen and Immanuel Bekker (CSHB, vols. 6–7, 48), Bonn, E. Weber, 1829–1855.

Gregory of Tours, *History of the Franks*, trans. E. Bréhaut, New York, W. W. Norton, 1969.

Grigor of Akner [Akancʻ], "History of the Nation of the Archers (The Mongols)," ed. and trans. Robert P. Blake and Richard N. Frye, *Harvard Journal of Asiatic Studies*, vol. 12, 1949, pp. 284–383.

Heng, Liang, and Judith Shapiro, *Son of the Revolution*, New York, Vintage, 1984.

Herberstein, Sigismund von, *Notes upon Russia*, 2 vols., trans. R. H. Major, New York, Burt Franklin, 1851–1852.

[Herberstein, Sigismund von] Sigizmund Gerbershtein, *Zapiski o Moskovii*, ed. V. L. Ianin, A. V. Nazarenko, A. I. Pliguzov, and A. L. Khoroshkevich, Izdatel'stvo Moskovskogo universiteta, 1988.

Horsey, Jerome, "Travels," in *Rude & Barbarous Kingdom*, pp. 262–369.

Ioasafovskaia letopis', ed. A. A. Zimin, Moscow, Akademiia nauk SSSR, 1957.

Istoricheskiia pesni XIII–XVI vekov, ed. B. N. Putilov and B. M. Dobrovol'skii, Moscow and Leningrad, Akademiia nauk SSSR, 1960.

Istoriia russkogo iskusstva, 13 vols., Moscow, Nauka, 1954–1964.

"Itinerary of Pegoletti Between Asof and China, in 1355," in *General History and Collection of Voyages and Travels*, vol. 1, Edinburgh, George Ramsay, 1811, pp. 435–437.

Jenkinson, Anthony, "A Voyage to Russia in 1557," in *Rude & Barbarous Kingdom*, pp. 43–58.

Jus graeco-romanum, ed. K. E. Zachariae von Lingenthal, 4 vols., Leipzig, T. O. Wiegel, 1856–1865.

Jus graecoromanum, ed. J Zepos and P. Zepos, 8 vols., Darmstadt, Scientia Aalen, 1962 (reprint of 1931 edn).

Juvaini [Juwaynī], ʻAla-ad-Din ʻAta-Malik, *The History of the World-Conqueror*, trans. John Andrew Boyle, Cambridge, MA, 2 vols., Harvard University Press, 1958.

Jūzjānī, Minhāj al-Dīn, *Tabakāt-i-Nāṣirī: a General History of the Muhammadan Dynasties of Asia*, trans. M. G. Raverty, 2 vols., London, Gilbert and Rivington, 1881.

Kadlubovskii, A., "Zhitie Pafnutiia Borovskogo, pisannoe Vassianom Saninym," *Sbornik Istoriko-filologicheskogo obshchestva pri Institute kniazia Bezborodko v Nezhine*, vol. 2, Nezhin, M. V. Glezer, 1899, pp. 98–199.

Kantakouzenos, John, *Historiae*, 3 vols., ed. Ludwig Schopen (CSHB, vols. 2–4), Bonn, E. Weber, 1828–1832.

Kazanskaia istoriia, ed. G. N. Moiseeva, Moscow and Leningrad, Akademiia nauk SSSR, 1954.

Komnenē, Anna, *Alexiades*, ed. Ludwig Schopen, 2 vols. (CSHB, vols. 37, 49), Bonn, E. Weber, 1839, 1878.

[Komnenē] Comnena, Anna, *Alexiade*, ed. Bernard Leib and P. Gautier, 4 vols., Paris, Les belles lettres, 1967–1976.

Kotoshikhin, Grigorii, *O Rossii v tsarstvovanii Alekseia Mikhailovicha*, 4th edn, St. Petersburg, Glavnoe upravlenie udelov, 1906.

Kurz, Eduard, "Zwei griechische Texte über die Hl. Theophano, die Gemahlin Kaisers Leo VI," *Zapiski Imperatorskoi Akademii nauk*, series 8, *Po istoriko-filologicheskomu otdeleniiu*, vol. 3, no. 2, 1898.

The Laws of the Salian Franks, trans. Katherine Fischer Drew, Philadelphia, University of Pennsylvania Press, 1991.

Malinin, V., *Starets Eleazarova monastyria Filofei i ego poslanie. Istoriko-literaturnoe issledovanie*, Kiev, Tipografiia Kievo-Pecherskoi Uspenskoi Lavry, 1901, Appendix.

Markos Eugenikos, Metropolitan of Ephesus, "Marci Ephesii epistola ad Theophanem Sacardotem in Euboea insula," ed. Louis Petit, *Patrologia orientalis*, vol. 17, fasc. 2, 1923, pp. 480–482.

Martinez, A. P., "The Third Portion of the History of Ġāzān Xān in Rašidu 'd-Dīn's Taʾrīx-e Mobārak-e Ġāzānī," *Archivum Eurasiae Medii Aevi*, vol. 6, 1986[1988], pp. 41–127.

Medieval Russia's Epics, Chronicles and Tales, rev. and enlarged, ed. Serge A. Zenkovsky, New York, E. P. Dutton, 1974.

Mongγol-un niuča tobča'an, in Igor de Rachewiltz, *Index to the Secret History of the Mongols*, Indiana University Publications, Uralic and Altaic Studies, vol. 121, Bloomington, Indiana University Press, 1972.

The Mongol Hordes: Storm from the East, 4 parts, *World Conquerors*, produced and directed by Robert Marshall, NHK and BBC, 1992.

The Mongol Mission: Narratives and Letters of the Franciscan Missionaries in Mongolia and China in the Thirteenth and Fourteenth Centuries, ed. Christopher Dawson, London, Sheed and Ward, 1955; reprinted as *Mission to Asia*, New York, Harper Torchbooks, 1966.

The Mongol Onslaught 850–1500, "World TV History," BBC Production, 1985.

Montagu, Lady Mary Wortley, *The Letters and Works of Lady Mary Wortley Montagu*, ed. Lord Wharncliffe, London, Henry G. Bohn, 1861.

Montesquieu, Charles-Louis de Secondat de, *The Persian Letters* (originally published in 1721).

Monumenta Germaniae Historica, ed. G. H. Pertz, T. Mommsen et al., Hanover, 1826.

Moschus, John, *Patrum spirituale*, in *PG*, vol. 87, pt. 3, cols. 2851–3112.

Munkuev, N. Ts., *Kitaiskii istochnik o pervykh mongol'skikh khanakh. Nadgrob-naia nadpis' na mogile Eliui Chu-tsaia. Perevod i issledovanie*, Moscow, Nauka, 1965.

[Munkuev] Münküyev, N. Ts., "A New Mongolian P'ai-Tzŭ from Simferopol," *Acta Orientalia Academiae Scientarium Hungaricae*, vol. 31, 1977, pp. 185–215.

The Muscovia of Antonio Possevino, S. J., trans. Hugh F. Graham, Pittsburgh, University Center for International Studies, University of Pittsburgh, 1977.

Nasawī, Sikhab ad-Din: Muḥammad an-, *Histoire du sultan Djelal ed-din Mankobirti*, 2 vols., trans. O. Houdas (= *Publications de l'école des langues orientales vivantes*, 3rd series, vols. 9–10), Paris, 1891–1895.

Nasawī, Sikhab ad-Din: Muḥammad an-, *Zhizneopisanie sultana Dzhalal ad-Dina Mankburny*, ed. and trans. Z. M. Buniiatov, Baku, Elm, 1973.

"Nicephori Gregorae epistola ad Praefectum mensae seu Russiae principem," ed. and annot. Fr. Xav[ier] Berger, in *Beyträge zur Geschichte und Literatur*, ed. Johann Christoph von Aretin, 9 vols., Munich, Kommission der Schererschen Kunst- und Buchhandlung, 1803–1807, vol. 4, 1805, pp. 609–619.

Nicephori Gregorae epistulae, ed. [Pietro Luigi] Petrus Aloisius Leone, 2 vols., Matino, Tipografia di matino, 1983.

The Nikonian Chronicle, trans. Serge A. Zenkovsky, 5 vols., Princeton, NJ, Kingston Press, Darwin Press, 1984–1989.

Novgorodskaia pervaia letopis'. Starshego i mladshego izvodov (NPL), ed. M. N. Tikhomirov, Moscow and Leningrad, Akademiia nauk SSSR, 1950.

Onasch, Konrad, *Ikonen*, Berlin, Gütersloher Verlagshaus, 1961.

Opisanie rukopisei Solovetskogo monastyria, nakhodiashchikhsia v biblioteke Ka-zanskoi dukhovnoi akademii, 3 parts, Kazan', Tipografiia Imperatorskogo universiteta, 1881–1898.

Palmer, William, *The Patriarch and the Tsar*, 6 vols., London, Trübner, 1871–1876.

Pamiatniki diplomaticheskikh snoshenii drevnei Rossii s derzhavami inostrannymi, 10 vols., St. Petersburg, 1851–1871.

Pamiatniki literatury drevnei Rusi, 11 vols., Moscow, Khudozhestvennaia litera-tura, 1978–1987.

Pamiatniki russkogo prava, 8 vols., Moscow, Gosudarstvennoe izdatel'stvo iuridicheskoi literatury, 1952–1961, vol. 1: *Pamiatniki prava kievskogo gosudarstva. X–XII vv.*, ed. A. A. Zimin; vol. 3: *Pamiatniki prava perioda obrazovaniia russkogo tsentralizovannogo gosudarstva XIV–XV vv.*, ed. L. V. Cherepnin, vol. 8: *Zakonodatel'nye akty Petra I. Pervaia chetvert' XVIII v.*, ed. K. A. Sofronenko.

Pamiatniki starinnoi russkoi literatury (Pam SRL), ed. N. I. Kostomarov, comp. Grigorii Kushelev-Bezborodko, vol. 1: *Skazaniia, legendy, povesti, skazki i pritchi*, St. Petersburg, 1860.

Patrologiae cursus completus. Series Graeco-Latina (PG), ed. Jacques-Paul Migne, 161 vols., Paris, Migne, 1857–1866.

Patrologiae cursus completus. Series Latina (PL), ed. Jacques-Paul Migne, 221 vols., Paris, Migne, 1844–55.

Perepiska Ivan Groznogo s Andreem Kurbskim, ed. Ia. S. Lur'e and Iu. D. Rykov, Moscow, Nauka, 1981.

Pervyia sorok snoshenii mezhdu Rossieiu i Angleeiu 1553–1593, ed. Iurii Tolstoi, St. Petersburg, A. Transhel', 1875.

Petukhov, E. V., *Serapion Vladimirskii. Russkii propovednik XIII veka*, Pribavlenie, St. Petersburg, Imperatorskaia Akademiia nauk, 1888.

Pitirim, Arkhiepiskop, "O Volokolamskom paterike," *Bogoslovskie trudy*, vol. 10, 1973, pp. 175–222.

Pizan, Christine de, *The Book of the City of Ladies*, trans. Earl Jeffrey Richards, New York, Persea, 1982.

Pobedova, O. I., *Moskovskaia shkola zhivopisi pri Ivane IV. Raboty v Moskovskoi kremle 40-kh–70-kh godov XVI v.*, Moscow, Nauka, 1972, appendix by K. K. Lopialo.

Polnoe sobranie russkikh letopisei, 40 vols., St. Petersburg/Petrograd/Leningrad and Moscow, Arkheograficheskaia komissiia, Nauka, and Arkheograficheskii tsentr, 1843–1995.

Polnoe sobranie zakonov Rossiiskoi Imperii, s 1649, 1st series, 46 vols., St Petersburg, Tipografiia II Otdeleniia Sobstvennoi Ego Imperatorskogo Velichestva Kantseliarii, 1830.

Polo, Marco, *The Book of Ser Marco Polo the Venetian Concerning the Kingdoms and Marvels of the East*, 2 vols., trans. and annot. Henry Yule, 3rd edn, rev. Henri Cordier, London, John Murray, 1903; reprinted as *The Travels of Marco Polo*, New York, Dover, 1993.

Polo, Marco, *The Travels*, trans. Ronald Latham, London, Penguin, 1958.

Polybius, *The Rise of the Roman Empire*, trans. Ian Scott-Kilvert, Harmondsworth, Penguin, 1979.

Porphyrogenitus, Constantine, *De Administrando Imperio*, 2 vols., ed. Gy. Moravcsik and R. J. H. Jenkins, Budapest, Pazmany Peter Tudomamyegyetemi Gorog Filologiai Intezet, 1949–1962.

"Poslanie Ioganna Taube i Elerta Kruze," ed. Iu. V. Got'e, in *Russkii istoricheskii zhurnal*, vol. 8, 1922, pp. 8–59.

Poslanie Iosifa Volotskogo, ed. A. A. Zimin and Ia. S. Lur'e, Moscow and Leningrad, Akademiia nauk SSSR, 1959.

Posol'skaia kniga po sviaziam Rossii s Gretsiei (pravoslavnymi ierarkhami i monastyriami) 1588–1594 gg., ed. M. P. Lukichev and N. M. Rogozhin, Moscow, Institut istorii SSSR AN SSSR, 1988.

Pravda Russkaia, ed. B. D. Grekov, 3 vols., Moscow and Leningrad, Akademiia nauk SSSR, 1940–1963.

Primary Sources Supplement to Accompany World History, ed. Donald Ostrowski, Minneapolis/St. Paul, West, 1995.

Prince A. M. Kurbsky's History of Ivan IV, ed. and trans. J. L. I. Fennell, Cambridge University Press, 1965.

[Printz] Prinz, Daniel, *Moscoviae ortus, et progressus*, Gubenae, Christophor Gruber, 1681, as reprinted in *Scriptores rerum Livonicarum*, 2 vols., Riga and Leipzig, Eduard Franken, 1853, vol. 2, pp. 687–728.

[Printz, Daniel] Daniil Prints, "Nachalo i vozvyshenie Moskovii," trans. I. A. Tikhomirov, *ChOIDR*, 1876, no. 3, pp. 1–46; no. 4, pp. 47–75.

Priselkov, M. D., *Troitskaia letopis'. Rekonstruktsiia teksta*, Moscow and Leningrad, Akademiia nauk SSSR, 1950.

Prodolzhenie Drevnei Rossiiskoi vivliofiki, 11 vols., St. Petersburg, 1786–1801.

Pskovskie letopisi, 2 vols., ed. A. N. Nasonov, Moscow and Leningrad, Akademiia nauk SSSR, 1941, 1955.

Rachewiltz, Igor de "The *Hsi-yu lu* by Yeh-Lü Ch'u Ts'ai," *Monumenta Serica*, vol. 21, 1962, pp. 1–128.

Rashīd al-Dīn, *Jāmi' al-Tawārīkh*, ed. I. N. Berezin, *Trudy Vostochnogo otdeleniia Rossiiskogo arkheologicheskogo obshchestva*, vol. 7, 1861; vol. 13, 1868; and vol. 15, 1888.

Rashīd al-Dīn, *Djami el-Tevarikh*, ed. Edgar B. Blochet, E. J. W. Gibb Memorial Series, vol. 18, Leiden, E. J. Brill, 1911.

Rashīd al-Dīn, *Sbornik letopisei* (Russian trans. of *Jami' al-Tawārīkh*), 3 vols., Moscow and Leningrad, Akademiia nauk SSSR, 1946–1960, vol. 1, pt. 1, trans. L. A. Khetagurov, ed. A. A. Semenov; vol. 1, pt. 2, trans. O. I. Smirnova, ed. A. A. Semenov; vol. 2, trans. Iu. P. Verkhovskii, ed. I. P. Petrushevskii; vol. 3, trans. A. K. Arends, ed. A. A. Romaskevich, E. È. Bertel's, and A. Iu. Iakubovskii.

Rashīd al-Dīn, *Jāmi' al-Tawārīkh*, ed. Abdul-kerim Ali Ogly Ali-zade, vol. 3, Baku, Akademiia nauk Azerbaidzhanskoi SSR, 1957.

Rashīd al-Dīn, *The Successors of Genghis Khan*, trans. John Andrew Boyle, New York, Columbia University Press, 1971.

Razriadnaia kniga 1475–1598 gg., ed. V. I. Buganov, Moscow, Nauka, 1966.

Razriadnaia kniga 1475–1605 gg., 3 vols., ed. N. G. Savich and L. F. Kuz'mina, Moscow, Akademiia nauk SSSR, 1977–1985.

Reinterpreting Russian History: Readings 860–1860s, ed. Daniel H. Kaiser and Gary Marker, New York, Oxford University Press, 1994.

Ricci, Matteo, *China in the Sixteenth Century: the Journals of Matthew Ricci, 1583–1610*, trans. Louis J. Gallagher, New York, Random House, 1953.

"Rodoslovnaia kniga . . ." *Vremennik Imperatorskogo Moskovskogo obshchestva istorii i drevnostei rossiiskikh*, vol. 10, 1851, pp. 176–181.

Rossiiskoe zakonodatel'stvo X–XX vekov, 9 vols., ed. O. I. Chistiakov, Moscow, Iuridicheskaia literatura, 1984–1994, vol. 1: *Zakonodatel'stvo Drevnei Rusi*, ed. V. L. Ianin.

[Rubruck, William of] Guilliame de Rubruquis, "*Itinerarium*," in *Sinica Franciscana*, vol. 1, pp. 164–332.

Rubruck, William of, *The Journey of William of Rubruck to the Eastern Parts of the World 1253–55*, trans. William Woodville Rockhill, London, Hakluyt Society, 1900.

Rubruck, William of, *The Mission of Friar William of Rubruck: His Journey to the Court of the Great Khan Möngke 1253–1255*, trans. Peter J. Jackson, London, Hakluyt Society, 1990.

Rude & Barbarous Kingdom: Russia in the Accounts of Sixteenth-Century English Voyagers, ed. Lloyd E. Berry and Robert O. Crummey, Madison, University of Wisconsin Press, 1968.

Russkaia istoricheskaia biblioteka, 39 vols., St. Petersburg/Petrograd/Leningrad, 1872–1927.

Russkie povesti XV–XVI vekov, ed. M. O. Skripil', Moscow and Leningrad, Akademiia nauk SSSR, 1958.

Russkii feodal'nyi arkhiv. XIV-pervoi treti XVI veka, 5 vols., Moscow, Akademiia nauk SSSR, Institut istorii SSSR, 1986-1992.

Salimbene de Parma, *The Chronicle of Salimbene de Adam*, trans. Joseph L. Baird, Binghamton, NY, Medieval and Renaissance Texts and Studies, no. 40, 1986.

Salmina, M. A., *Povesti o nachale Moskvy*, Moscow and Leningrad, Nauka, 1964.

Sathas, Konstantinos N., *Viographikon schediasma peri tou Patriarchou Ieremiou II (1572-1594)*, Athens, 1870; reprinted, Thessalonika, 1979, *Parathema*, Appendix, pp. 3-218.

Sbornik Imperatorskogo Russkogo istoricheskogo obshchestva (*SRIO*), 148 vols., St. Petersburg, 1867-1916.

Scriptores rerum Prussicarum: die Geschichtsquellen der Preussischen Vorzeit bis zum Untergange der Ordensherrschaft, 6 vols., ed. Theodor Hirsch, Max Toppen, and Ernst Strehlke, Leipzig, S. Hirzel (Breitkopf & Hartel), 1861-1874, reprinted Frankfurt, Minerva, 1965.

The Secret History of the Mongols, trans. and ed. Francis Woodman Cleaves, Cambridge, MA, Harvard University Press, 1982.

"The Secret History of the Mongols," trans. Igor de Rachewiltz, *Papers on Far Eastern History* (*PFEH*), vol. 4, 1971, pp. 115-163; vol. 5, 1972, pp. 149-175; vol. 10, 1974, pp. 55-82; vol. 13, 1976, pp. 41-75; vol. 16, 1977, pp. 27-65; vol. 18, 1978, pp. 43-80; vol. 21, 1980, pp. 17-57; vol. 23, 1981, pp. 111-146; vol. 26, 1982, pp. 39-84; vol. 30, 1984, pp. 81-160; vol. 31, 1985, pp. 21-93; vol. 33, 1986, pp. 129-137.

Semenov, Viktor, "Drevniaia russkaia Pchela po pergamennomu spisku," *Sbornik Otdeleniia russkogo iazyka i slovesnosti Imperatorskoi Akademii nauk*, vol. 54, no. 4, 1893.

Shchapov, Ia. N., *Drevnerusskie kniazheskie ustavy XI–XV vv.*, Moscow, Nauka, 1976.

Sinica Franciscana, vol. 1, *Itinera et relationes fratrum minorum saeculi XIII et XIV*, ed. P. Anastasius van den Wyngaert, Florence, Apud Collegium S. Bonaventure, 1929.

Sinopsis, Kiev 1681: Facsimile mit einer Einleitung, ed. Hans Rothe, Cologne and Vienna, 1983 (= *Bausteine zur Geschichte der Literatur bei den Slaven*, vol. 17).

Skazaniia i povesti o Kulikovskoi bitve, ed. L. A. Dmitriev and O. P. Likhacheva, Leningrad, Nauka, 1982.

Snimki drevnikh russkikh pechatei, 2 vols., Moscow, Komissiia pechatnaia gosudarstvennykh gramot i dogorov, 1880.

Sobornaia gramota dukhovenstva pravoslavnoi vostochnoi tserkvi, utverzhdaiush-chaia san tsaria za velikim kniazem Ioannom IV Vasil'evichem, 1561 goda, ed. M. A. Obolenskii, Moscow, Sinodal'naia tipografiia, 1850.

Sobornoe ulozhenie 1649 goda. Tekst. Kommentarii, ed. L. I. Ivina, commentary by G. V. Abramovich, A. G. Man'kov, B. N. Mironov, and V. M. Paneiakh, Leningrad, Nauka, 1987.

Sobranie gosudarstvennykh gramot i dogovorov khraniashchikhsia v gosudarstvennoi kollegii inostrannykh del (*SGGD*), 5 vols., St. Petersburg, N. S. Vsevolozhskii, 1813–1894.

A Source Book for Russian History from Early Times to 1917, 3 vols., comp. Sergei Pushkarev, ed. George Vernadsky, Ralph T. Fisher, Jr., Alan D. Ferguson, and Andrew Lossky, New Haven, CT, Yale University Press, 1972.

Sources of Chinese Tradition, 2 vols., comp. Wm. Theodore de Bary, Wing-tsit Chan, Chester Tan, and Burton Watson, New York, Columbia University Press, 1964.

Staden, Heinrich von, *Aufzeichungen über den Moskauer Staat*, ed. Fritz T. Epstein, Hamburg, Cram, de Gruyter, 1964.

Staden, Heinrich von, *The Land and Government of Muscovy*, trans. Thomas Esper, Stanford University Press, 1967.

"Starinnoe Mongol'skoe skazanie o Chingiskhane," trans. Archimandrite Palladii, *Trudy chlenov Rossiiskoi dukhovnoi missii v Pekine*, vol. 4, 1866, pp. 3–258.

Stoglav, ed. I. M. Dobrotvorskii, 2nd edn, Kazan', Tipografiia Imperatorskogo universiteta, 1887.

Sudebniki XV–XVI vekov, ed. B. D. Grekov, Moscow and Leningrad, Akademiia nauk SSSR, 1952.

Sudnye spiski Maksima Greka i Isaka Sobaki, ed. N. N. Pokrovskii, Moscow, Glavnoe arkhivnoe upravlenie pri Sovete ministrov SSSR, 1971.

Syntagma ton Theion kai hieron xanonon ton te hagion kai paneuphemon Apostolon, ed. G. A. Rhalles and M. Potles, 6 vols., Athens, G. Chartophylakos, 1852–1859.

The Testaments of the Grand Princes of Moscow, trans. and ed., with commentary, Robert Craig Howes, Ithaca, NY, Cornell University Press, 1967.

Theophanes, *Chronographia*, ed. Karl de Boor, 2 vols., Leipzig, 1883–1885.

[Tiesenhausen], Tizengauzen, V. G. *Sbornik materialov otnosiashchikhsia k istorii Zolotoi Ordy*, 2 vols., St. Petersburg, S. G. Stroganov, 1884; Moscow and Leningrad, Akademiia nauk SSSR, 1941.

Travels of an Alchemist, trans. Arthur Waley, London, George Routledge and Sons, 1931.

"Travels of Josaphat Barbaro, Ambassador from Venice to Tanna, Now Called Asof, in 1436," in *General History and Collection of Voyages and Travels*, vol. 1, pp. 501–512.

The Travels of Olearius in Seventeenth-Century Russia, trans. and ed. Samuel H. Baron, Stanford University Press, 1967.

Velikie minei chetii, sobrannye vserossiiskim Mitropolitom Makariem, 22 vols., St. Petersburg, Arkheograficheskaia kommissiia, 1868–1917.

Volotskii, Iosif, *Prosvetitel'*, ed. A. Volkov, 3rd edn, Kazan', Tipografia Imperatorskoi universiteta, 1896.

Vremennik Ivana Timofeeva, ed. O. A. Derzhavina, Moscow and Leningrad, Akademiia nauk SSSR, 1951.

Zabelin, I. and V. Shchepkin, *Tron ili Tsarskoe mesto Groznogo v Moskovskom Uspenskom sobore*, Moscow, Sinodal'naia tipografiia, 1909.

Zakon sudnyj ljudem (Court Law for the People), trans. H[orace] W. Dewey and A[nn] M. Kleimola, Michigan Slavic Materials, no. 14, Ann Arbor, MI, Department of Slavic Languages and Literatures, 1977.

STUDIES

Abramzon, I. Ia., and M. V. Gorelik, "Nauchania rekonstruktsiia kompleksa vooruzeniia russkogo voina XIV v. i ego ispol'zovanie v muzeinykh ekspositsiiakh," in *Kulikovskaia bitva. V istorii i kul'ture nashei Rodiny*, pp. 238–244.

Abu-Lughod, Janet L., *Before European Hegemony: the World System* AD *1250–1350*, New York, Oxford University Press, 1989.

Ahmed, Leila, *Women and Gender in Islam: Historical Roots of a Modern Debate*, New Haven, CT, Yale University Press, 1992.

Alef, Gustave, "The Political Significance of the Inscriptions on Muscovite Coinage in the Reign of Vasili II," *Speculum*, vol. 34, 1959, pp. 1–19; reprinted in Alef, *Rulers and Nobles*, item 1.

Alef, Gustave, "The Adoption of the Muscovite Two-Headed Eagle: a Discordant View," *Speculum*, vol. 41, 1966, pp. 1–21; reprinted in Alef, *Rulers and Nobles*, item 9.

Alef, Gustave, "The Origin and Early Development of the Muscovite Postal Service," *Jahrbücher für Geschichte Osteuropas*, vol. 15, 1967, pp. 1–15; reprinted in Alef, *Rulers and Nobles*, item 8.

Alef, Gustave, "The Crisis of the Muscovite Autocracy: a Factor in the Growth of Monarchical Power," *Forschungen zur osteuropäischen Geschichte*, vol. 15, 1970, pp. 15–58; reprinted in Alef, *Rulers and Nobles*, item 5.

Alef, Gustave, "The Battle of Suzdal' in 1445: an Episode in the Muscovite War of Succession," *Forschungen zur osteuropäischen Geschichte*, vol. 25, 1978, pp. 11–20; reprinted in Alef, *Rulers and Nobles*, item 2.

Alef, Gustave, "Aristocratic Politics and Royal Policy in Muscovy in the Late Fifteenth and Early Sixteenth Centuries," *Forschungen zur osteuropäischen Geschichte*, vol. 27, 1980, pp. 77–109; reprinted in Alef, *Rulers and Nobles*, item 10.

Alef, Gustave, *Rulers and Nobles in Fifteenth-Century Muscovy*, London, Variorum, 1983.

Alef, Gustave, "The Origins of Muscovite Autocracy: the Age of Ivan III," *Forschungen zur osteuropäischen Geschichte*, vol. 39, 1986, pp. 7–362.

Alekseev, Iu. G., and A. I Kopanev, "Razvitie pomestnoi sistemy v XVI v.," in *Dvorianstvo i krepostnoi stroi Rossii XVI–XVIII vv. Sbornik statei, posviash-chennyi pamiati Alekseia Andreevicha Novosel'skogo*, ed. N. I. Pavlenko, I. A. Bulygin, E. I. Indova, A. A. Preobrazhenskii, and S. M. Troitskii, Moscow, Nauka, 1975, pp. 57–69.

Allport, Susan, *Sermons in Stone: the Stone Walls of New England and New York*, New York, W. W. Norton, 1990.

Allsen, Thomas T., "The Yüan Dynasty and the Uighurs of Turfan in the 13th Century," in *China Among Equals: the Middle Kingdom and Its Neighbors, 10th–14th Centuries*, ed. Morris Rossabi, Berkeley, University of California Press, 1983, pp. 243–280.

Allsen, Thomas T., "Guard and Government in the Reign of the Grand Qan Möngke, 1251–59," *Harvard Journal of Asiatic Studies*, vol. 46, 1986, pp. 495–521.

Allsen, Thomas T., *Mongol Imperialism: the Policies of the Grand Qan Möngke in*

China, Russia, and the Islamic Lands, 1251–1259, Berkeley, University of California Press, 1987.

Allsen, Thomas T., "Mongolian Princes and Their Merchant Partners, 1200–1260," *Asia Major*, 3rd series, vol. 2, 1989, pp. 83–126.

L'Analyse de l'idéologie, 2 vols., ed. Gérard Duprat, Paris, Galilée, 1980–1983.

Andreeva, M. A., "Priem tatarskikh poslov pri Nikeiskom dvore," in *Sbornik statei, posviashchennykh pamiati N. P. Kondakova. Arkheologiia. Istoriia iskusstva. Vizantinovedenie*, Prague, Seminarium Kondakovianum, 1926, pp. 187–200.

Andreyev, N[ikolay] E., "Filofey and His Epistle to Ivan Vasil'yevich," *Slavonic and East European Review*, vol. 38, 1959, pp. 1–31; reprinted in Nikolay Andreyev, *Studies in Muscovy: Western Influences and Byzantine Inheritance*, London, Variorum, 1970, item 2.

Andreyev, Nikolay [E.], review of The *"Chosen Council"*, *Slavic Review*, vol. 30, 1971, pp. 136–137.

Armstrong, Karen, *A History of God: the 4000-Year Quest of Judaism, Christianity and Islam*, New York, Alfred A. Knopf, 1993.

Ashtor, E[liahu], *A Social and Economic History of the Near East in the Middle Ages*, Berkeley, University of California Press, 1976.

Aspects of Altaic Civilization III. Proceedings of the XXX PIAC, Bloomington, ed. Denis Sinor, Bloomington, Asian Studies Research Institute, Indiana University, 1990.

Atkinson, Dorothy, "Society and the Sexes in the Russian Past," in *Women in Russia*, ed. Dorothy Atkinson, Alexander Dallin, and Gail Warshofsky Lapidus, Stanford University Press, 1977, pp. 3–38.

Attman, Artur, *The Russian and Polish Markets in International Trade 1500–1650*, trans. Eva Green and Allan Green, Göteborg, Kungsbacka, 1973.

Attman, Artur, *The Bullion Flow Between Europe and the East 1000–1750*, trans. Eva Green and Allan Green, Göteborg: Kungl. Vetenskaps- och Vitterhets-Samhället, 1981.

Ayalon, David, "The Great *Yāsa* of Chingiz Khān: a Reexamination," *Studia Islamica*, vol. 33, 1971, 97–140; vol. 34, 1971, pp. 151–180; vol. 36, 1972, pp. 113–158; vol. 38, 1973, pp. 107–156.

Bačić, Jacques, *Red Sea – Black Russia: Prolegomena to the History of North Central Eurasia in Antiquity and the Middle Ages*, New York, East European Monographs, no. 171, 1995.

Baker, Keith Michael, "Introduction," in *French Revolution and the Creation of Modern Political Culture*, 4 vols., ed. Keith Michael Baker and Colin Lucas, Oxford, Pergamon, 1987–1991, vol. 1: *The Political Culture of the Old Regime*, pp. xi–xxiv.

Bakhrushin, S. V., *Ivan Groznyi*, Moscow, OGIZ, 1945.

Bakhrushin, S. V., *Nauchnye trudy*, 4 vols. in 5 pts., Moscow, Akademiia nauk SSSR, 1954–1959.

Balazs, Etienne, *Chinese Civilization and Bureaucracy: Variations on a Theme*, trans. H. M. Wright, ed. Arthur F. Wright, New Haven, CT, Yale University Press, 1964.

Balodis, Frances, "Alt-Serai und Neu-Serai, die Hauptstädte der Goldenen

Horde," *Latvijas Universitates Raksti. Acta Universitatis Latviensis*, vol. 13, 1926, pp. 3–82.

Barbieri, Gino, *Milano e Mosca. Nella politica del Rinasciemento. Storia delle relazioni diplomatiche tra la Russia e il Ducato di Milano nell'epoca sforzesca*, Bari, Adriatica editrice, 1957.

Barfield, Thomas J., "The Hsiung-nu Imperial Confederation: Organization and Foreign Policy," *Journal of Asiatic Studies*, vol. 41, 1981, pp. 46–61.

Barker, John W., *Manuel II Palaeologus (1391–1425): a Study in Late Byzantine Statemanship*, New Brunswick, NJ, Rutgers University Press, 1969.

Baron, Samuel, "Marx and Herberstein: Notes on a Possible Affinity," in *Kamen" kraeug"l'n"*, pp. 66–79.

Barthold, W., "Bukhara," *Encyclopedia of Islam*, 1st edn, vol. 2, pp. 776–783.

Barthold, W., *Turkestan down to the Mongol Invasion*, 3rd edn, London, Luzac, 1968.

Barthold, W., *An Historical Geography of Iran*, trans. Svat Souchek, ed. C. E. Bosworth, Princeton University Press, 1984.

Barthold, W., and Richard N. Frye, "Bukhara," *Encyclopedia of Islam*, new edn, vol. 1, pt. 2, pp. 1293–1296.

Baskakov, N. A., "Russkie familii tiurskogo proiskhozhdeniia," in *Onomastika*, Moscow, Nauka, 1969, pp. 5–26.

Bate, Walter Jackson, *The Burden of the Past and the English Poet*, Cambridge, MA, Belknap Press, 1970.

Bauer, N., "Die Silber- und Goldbarren des russischen Mittalters," *Numismatische Zeitschrift*, n.s., vol. 22, 1929, pp. 77–120 [1–44], vol. 24, 1931, pp. 61–100 [45–84].

Bazilevich, K. V., *Gorodski vosstaniia v Moskovskom gosudarstve XVII v. Sbornik dokumentov*, Moscow and Leningrad, Gosudarstvennoe Sotsial'no-ekonomicheskoe izdatel'stvo, 1936.

Bazilevich, K. V., *Vneshnaia politika russkogo tsentralizovannogo gosudarstva. Vtoraia polovina XV veka*, Izdatel'stvo Moskovskogo universiteta, 1952.

Beck, Hans Georg, *Das byzantinische Jahrtausend*, Munich, Beck, 1978.

Beletskii, L. T., "Literaturnaia istoriia povesti o Merkurii Smolenskom. Issledovaniia i teksty," *Sbornik Otdeleniia russkogo iazyka i slovesnosti*, vol. 99, no. 8, 1922.

Beliakova, E. V., "K istorii uchrezhdeniia avtokefalii russkoi tserkvi," in *Rossiia na putiakh tsentralizatsii*, ed. V. T. Pashuto et al., Moscow, Nauka, 1982, pp. 152–156.

Berezin, I. N., *Vnutrennoe ustroistvo Zolotoi Ordy*, St. Petersburg, 1850.

Berezin, I. N., "Ocherk vnutrennego ustroistva Ulusa Dzhuchieva," *Trudy Vostochnogo otdeleniia Russkogo arkheologicheskogo obshchestva*, vol. 8, 1864, pp. 385–494.

Berman, Harold, *Justice in Russia*, Cambridge, MA, Harvard University Press, 1950.

Berman, Harold, *Justice in the USSR*, Cambridge, MA, Harvard University Press, 1963.

Bielenstein, Hans, *The Bureaucracy of Han Times*, Cambridge University Press, 1980.

Billington, James H., *The Icon and the Axe: an Interpretive History of Russian Culture*, New York, Vintage, 1970.

Blake, Robert P., "The Circulation of Silver in the Moslem East down to the Mongol Epoch," *Harvard Journal of Asiatic Studies*, vol. 2, 1937, pp. 291–328.

Bloom, Harold, *The Anxiety of Influence*, New York, Oxford University Press, 1973.

Bloom, Harold, *A Map of Misreading*, New Haven, CT, Yale University Press, 1975.

Bloom, Harold, *Poetry and Repression*, New Haven, CT, Yale University Press, 1976.

Blunden, Caroline, and Mark Elvin, *The Cultural Atlas of the World: China*, Alexandra, VA, Stonehenge, 1991.

Bobrick, Benson, *Fearful Majesty: the Life and Reign of Ivan the Terrible*, New York, G. P. Putnam's Sons, 1987.

Bochkov, V. N., "'Legenda' o vyezde dvorianskikh rodov," in *Arkheograficheskii ezhegodnik za 1969 g.*, Moscow, Nauka, 1971, pp. 73–93.

Bodde, Derk, *China's First Unifier: a Study of the Ch'in Dynasty as Seen in the Life of Li Ssü (280?–208 BC)*, Leiden, E. J. Brill, 1938.

Boltin, I. N., *Primechaniia na istoriiu gospodina Leklerka*, 2 vols., St. Petersburg, Gornoe uchilishche, 1788.

Boltin, I. N., *Otvet General-Maiora Boltina na pis'mo Kniazia Shcherbatova*, 2nd edn, St. Petersburg, Imperatorskaia tipografiia, 1793.

Boodberg, Peter A., "Turk, Aryan and Chinese in Ancient Asia," in *Selected Works of Peter A. Boodberg*, comp. Alvin P. Cohen, Berkeley, University of California Press, 1979, pp. 1–21.

Boudon, Raymond, *The Analysis of Ideology*, trans. Malcolm Slater, Cambridge, Polity, 1980.

Bowman, Steven B., *The Jews of Byzantium, 1204–1453*, Birmingham, University of Alabama Press, 1985.

Box, G. H., trans., *The Ezra-Apocalypse: Being Chapters 3–14 of the Book Commonly Known as 4 Ezra (or II Esdras)*, trans. G. H. Box, London, Sir Isaac Pitman, 1912.

Bretschneider, E., *Mediaeval Researches from Eastern Asiatic Sources*, 2 vols., London, Trübner, 1888; reprint: London, Kegan Paul, Trench, Trübner, 1910.

Brown, Peter, "Early Modern Russian Bureaucracy: the Evolution of the Chancery System from Ivan III to Peter the Great, 1478–1717," Ph.D. Dissertation, University of Chicago, 1978.

Brumfield, William Craft, *A History of Russian Architecture*, Cambridge University Press, 1993.

Buell, Paul D., "Sino-Khitan Administration in Mongol Bukhara," *Journal of Asian History*, vol. 13, 1979, pp. 121–151.

Buell, Paul D., "Kalmyk Tanggaci People: Thoughts on the Mechanics and Impact of Mongol Expansion," *Mongolian Studies*, vol. 6, 1980, pp. 41–59.

Buganov, V. I., *Razriadnye knigi. Poslednei chetverti XV–nachala XVII v.*, Moscow, Akademiia nauk SSSR, 1962.

[Bühler, Baron Théodore de] Fedor Biuler, "Préface," and "Predislovie," in

Snimki drevnikh russkikh pechatei, vol. 1, Moscow, Komissiia pechatnaia gosudarstvennykh gramot i dogorov, 1880, pp. I–IX and XI–XIX.

Bury, J. B., *The Imperial Administrative System in the Ninth Century*, London, H. Frowde, 1911.

Bury, J. B., *History of the Later Roman Empire from the Death of Theodosius I to the Death of Justinian (AD 395 to AD 565)*, 2 vols., New York, Macmillan, 1923.

Bushkovitch, Paul, "The Life of Saint Filipp: Tsar and Metropolitan in the Late Sixteenth Century," *Medieval Russian Culture*, vol. 2, pp. 29–46.

Butterfield, Herbert, "Universal History and the Comparative Study of Civilization," in *Sir Herbert Butterfield, Cho Yun Hsu, and William H. McNeill on Chinese and World History*, ed. Noah Edward Fehl, Chinese University of Hong Kong, 1971, pp. 17–29.

Bychkova, M. E., *Rodoslovnye knigi XVI–XVII vv. kak istoricheskii istochnik*, Moscow, Nauka, 1975.

Bychkova, M. E., "Obshchie traditsii rodoslovnykh legend praviashchikh domov Vostochnoi Evropy," in *Kul'turnye sviazi narodov Vostochnoi Evropy v XVI v.*, Moscow, Nauka, 1976, pp. 292–303.

Byzantium: an Introduction to East Roman Civilization, ed. N. H. Baynes and H. St. L. B. Moss, Oxford, Clarendon Press, 1953.

Cahen, Claude, "L'évolution de l'iqṭaʿ du IXe au XIIIe siècle: Contribution à une histoire comparée des sociétés médiévales," *Annales: Économies, Sociétés, Civilisations*, vol. 8, 1953, pp. 25–52.

Cahen, Claude, "Dayʿa," *Encyclopedia of Islam*, new edn, vol. 2, pp. 187–188.

Cahen, Claude, "Ikṭaʿ," *Encyclopedia of Islam*, new edn, vol. 3, pp. 1088–1091.

Chaev, N. S., "'Moskva – tretii Rim' v politicheskoi praktike moskovskogo pravitel'stva XVI veka," *Istoricheskie zapiski*, no. 17, 1945, pp. 3–23.

Chekin, Leonid S., "The Godless Ishmaelites: the Image of the Steppe in Eleventh–Thirteenth-Century Rus'," *Russian History*, vol. 19, 1992, pp. 9–28.

Cherepnin, L. V., *Zemskie sobory Russkogo gosudarstva v XVI–XVII vv.*, Moscow, Nauka, 1978.

Cherniavsky, Michael, "Khan or Basileus: an Aspect of Russian Mediaeval Political Theory," *Journal of the History of Ideas*, vol. 20, 1959, pp. 459–476; reprinted in *Structure of Russian History*, pp. 65–79.

Cherniavsky, Michael, "Ivan the Terrible as Renaissance Prince," *Slavic Review*, vol. 27, 1968, pp. 195–211.

Ch'ing-yüan, Chü, "Government Artisans of the Yüan Dynasty," in *Chinese Social History: Translations of the Selected Studies*, trans. and ed. E-tu Zen Sun and John de Frances, New York, Octagon Books, 1966, pp. 234–246.

Christoff, Peter K., *The Third Heart: Some Intellectual-Ideological Currents and Cross Currents in Russia 1800–1830*, The Hague, Mouton, 1970.

Ch'u, T'ung-tsu, *Local Government in China Under the Ch'ing*, Stanford University Press, 1969.

Cipolla, Carlo M., *Between Two Cultures: an Introduction to Economic History*, trans. Christopher Woodall, New York, W. W. Norton, 1991.

Collins, Leslie, "On the Alleged 'Destruction' of the Great Horde in 1502," *Manzikert to Lepanto: the Byzantine World and the Turks 1071–1571*, ed.

Anthony Bryer and Michael Ursinus (= *Byzantinische Forschungen*, vol. 16), Amsterdam, Adolf M. Hakkert, 1991, pp. 361–399.

Consent and Coercion to Sex and Marriage in Ancient and Medieval Societies, ed. Angeliki E. Laiou, Washington, DC, Dumbarton Oaks Research Library and Collection, 1993.

Cracraft, James, "Did Feofan Prokopovich Really Write *Pravda Voli Monarshei?*" *Slavic Review*, vol. 40, 1981, pp. 173–193.

Creel, Herrlee G., *Chinese Thought: From Confucius to Mao Tse-Tung*, University of Chicago Press, 1953.

Crespigny, Rafe de, *Official Titles of the Former Han Dynasty*, trans. H. H. Dubs, Canberra, Australian National University Press, 1967.

Croce, Benedetto, *Teoria e storia della storiografia*, Bari, Laterza, 1917.

Croskey, Robert M., *Muscovite Diplomatic Practice in the Reign of Ivan III*, New York, Garland, 1987.

Croskey, Robert M., and E. C. Ronquist, "George Trakhaniot's Description of Russia in 1486," *Russian History*, vol. 17, 1990, pp. 55–64.

Croutier, Alev Lytle, *Harem: the World Behind the Veil*, New York, Abbeville Press, 1989.

Crummey, Robert O., *Aristocrats and Servitors: the Boyar Elite in Russia, 1613–1689*, Princeton University Press, 1983.

Crummey, Robert O., *The Formation of Muscovy, 1304–1613*, London, Longman, 1987.

Dalai, Chuluuny, *Mongoliia v XIII–XIV vekakh*, Moscow, Nauka, 1983.

Dantsig, B. M., "Iz istorii russkikh puteshestvii i izucheniia blizhnego Vostoka v dopetrovskoi Rusi," in *Ocherki po istorii russkogo vostokovedeniia*, 6 vols., Moscow, Akademiia nauk SSSR, 1953.

Dardess, John W., "From Mongol Empire to Yüan Dynasty: Changing Forms of Imperial Rule in Mongolia and Central Asia," *Monumenta Serica*, vol. 30, 1972–1973, pp. 117–165.

Degtiarev, A. Ia., "O mobilizatsii pomestnykh zemel' v XVI v," in *Iz istorii feodal'noi Rossii. Stat'i i ocherki k 70-letiiu so dnia rozhdeniia prof. V. V. Mavrodina*, ed. A. Ia. Degtiarev, V. A. Ezhov, V. A. Petrova, I. Ia. Froianov, and A. L. Shapiro, Izdatel'stvo Leningradskogo universiteta, 1978, pp. 85–91.

Demkova, N. S., *Zhitie protopopa Avvakuma*, Izdatel'stvo Leningradskogo universiteta, 1974.

The Development of the USSR: an Exchange of Views, ed. Donald W. Treadgold, Seattle, University of Washington Press, 1964.

DeWeese, Devin, *Islamization and Native Religion in the Golden Horde: Baba Tükles and Conversion to Islam in Historical and Epic Tradition*, University Park, Pennsylvania State University Press, 1994.

Dewey, Horace W., "Political *Poruka* in Muscovite Rus'," *Russian Review*, vol. 46, 1987, pp. 117–133.

Dewey, Horace W., "Russia's Debt to the Mongols in Suretyship and Collective Responsibility," *Comparative Studies in Society and History*, vol. 30, 1988, pp. 249–270.

Dewey, Horace W., and Ann M. Kleimola, "Coercion by Righter (*Pravezh*) in

Old Russian Administration," *Canadian–American Slavic Studies*, vol. 9, 1975, pp. 156–167.

D'iakonov, M. A., *Vlast' moskovskikh gosudarei. Ocherk iz istorii politicheskikh idei drevnei Rusi do kontsa XVI veka*, St. Petersburg, I. N. Skorokhodov, 1889.

Dictionary of Russian Historical Terms from the Eleventh Century to 1917, comp. Sergei G. Pushkarev, ed. George Vernadsky and Ralph T. Fisher, Jr., New Haven, CT, Yale University Press, 1970.

Dimnik, Martin, *Mikhail, Prince of Chernigov and Grand Prince of Kiev, 1224–1246*, Toronto, Pontifical Institute of Medieval Studies, 1981.

Dmitriev, L. A., "Kniga o poboishchi Mamaia, tsaria tatarskogo, ot kniazia Vladimirskogo i Moskovskogo Dmitriia," *TODRL*, vol. 34, 1979, pp. 61–71.

Dmitriev, L. A., "Zhitie Feodora Iaroslavskogo," *Slovar' knizhnikov i knizhnosti drevnei Rusi. XI–pervaia polovina XIV v.*, ed. D. S. Likhachev, Leningrad, Nauka, 1987, pp. 179–181.

Dmitrieva, R. P., "K istorii sozdaniia 'Skazaniia o kniaz'iakh vladimirskikh,'" *TODRL*, vol. 17, 1961, pp. 342–347.

Dmitrieva, R. P., "O tekstologicheskikh zavisimosti mezhdu raznymi vidami rasskaza o potomkakh Avgusta i o darakh Monomakha," *TODRL*, vol. 30, 1976, pp. 217–230.

Doerfer, Gerhard, *Türkische und mongolische Elemente im Neupersischen*, 3 vols., Wiesbaden, Franz Steiner, 1963–1967.

Dölger, Franz, "Rom in der Gedankenwelt der Byzantiner," *Zeitschrift für Kirchengeschichte*, vol. 56, 1937, pp. 1–42; reprinted in Dölger, *Byzanz und die europäische Staatenwelt*, Ettal, Buch-Kunstverlag, 1953, pp. 70–115, and Darmstadt, Wissenschaftliche Buchgesellschaft 1976, pp. 34–69.

Dölger, Franz, "Die 'Familie der Könige' im Mitteralter," *Historisches Jahrbuch*, vol. 60, 1940, pp. 397–420; reprinted in Dölger, *Byzanz und die europäische Staatenwelt*, pp. 34–69.

Dölger, Franz, *Byzanz und die europäische Staatenwelt*, Ettal, Buch-Kunstverlag, 1953, and Darmstadt, Wissenschaftliche Buchgesellschaft, 1976.

Doronin, P., "Dokumenty po istorii Komi," *Istoriko-filologicheskii sbornik Komi filiala AN SSSR* (Syktyvkar), vol. 4, 1958, pp. 241–271.

Doroshenko, Dmytro, *A Survey of Ukrainian History*, ed. and updated by Oleh W. Gerus, Winnipeg, Trident Press, 1975.

Dreyer, Edward L., *Early Ming China: a Political History 1355–1435*, Stanford University Press, 1982.

Duffy, Christopher, *Russia's Military Way to the West: Origins and Nature of Russian Military Power 1700–1800*, London, Routledge & Kegan Paul, 1981.

Dunn, Ross E., *The Adventures of Ibn Battuta*, Berkeley, University of California Press, 1986.

Dūrī, 'Abd al-'Azīz, "Landlord and Peasant in Early Islam: a Critical Study," *Der Islam*, vol. 56, 1979, pp. 97–105.

Dvornik, Francis, "Byzantine Political Ideas in Kievan Russia," *Dumbarton Oaks Papers*, vol. 9/10, 1956, pp. 73–121.

Dvornik, Francis, *The Slavs in European History and Civilization*, New Brunswick, NJ, Rutgers University Press, 1962.

Dvornik, Francis, "Byzantium, Muscovite Autocracy and the Church," in *Re-Discovering Eastern Christendom: Essays in Commemoration of Dom Bede Winslow*, ed. A. H. Armstrong and E. J. B. Fry, London, Darton Longman & Todd, 1963, pp. 106–118.

Egorov, V. L., *Istoricheskaia geografiia Zolotoi Ordy v XIII–XIV vv.*, Moscow, Nauka, 1985.

Eisenstadt, S. N., *The Political Systems of Empires*, Glencoe, IL, Free Press, 1963.

Encyclopedia of Islam, 1st edn, 9 vols., Leiden, E. J. Brill, 1913–1936.

Encyclopedia of Islam, new edn, 8 vols. + suppl. + index, Leiden, E. J. Brill, 1954–1996.

Endicott-West, Elizabeth, *Mongolian Rule in China: Local Administration in the Yuan Dynasty*, Cambridge, MA, Harvard University Press, 1989.

Ensslin, Wilhelm, "The Emperor and the Imperial Administration," in *Byzantium: an Introduction to East Roman Civilization*, ed. N. H. Baynes and H. St. L. B. Moss, Oxford, Clarendon Press, 1949, pp. 268–307.

Esler, Anthony, *The Human Venture: a World History from Prehistory to the Present*, 2nd edn, Englewood Cliffs, NJ, Prentice Hall, 1992.

Fedorov, G. B., "Moskovskie den'gi Ivana III i Vasiliia III," *Kratkie soobshcheniia o dokladakh i polevykh issledovaniiakh Instituta istorii material'noi kul'tury AN SSSR*, vol. 30, 1949, pp. 70–81.

Fedorov-Davydov, G. A., *Obshchestvennyi stroi Zolotoi Ordy*, Izdatel'stvo Moskovskogo universiteta, 1973.

[Fedorov-Davydov] Fyodorov-Davydov, G. A., *The Culture of the Golden Horde Cities*, trans. H. Bartlett Wells, Oxford, BAR International Series, 1984.

Fedotov, G[eorge] P., *The Russian Religious Mind*, 2 vols., vol. 2, ed. John Meyendorff, Cambridge, MA, Harvard University Press, 1946, 1966.

Fedotov, George P., *St. Filipp Metropolitan of Moscow: Encounter with Ivan the Terrible*, trans. Richard Haugh and Nickolas Lupinin (= vol. 1 of *The Collected Works* of George P. Fedotov), Belmont, MA, Nordland, 1978.

Fennell, J. L. I., *Ivan the Great of Moscow*, London, Macmillan, 1961.

Fennell, J. L. I., "The Tver' Uprising of 1327: a Study of the Sources," *Jahrbücher für Geschichte Osteuropas*, vol. 15, 1967, pp. 161–179.

Fennell, J. L. I., "The Ideological Role of the Russian Church in the First Half of the Fourteenth Century," in *Gorski vijen: a Garland of Essays Offered to Professor Elizabeth Hill*, ed. R. Auty, L. R. Lewitter, and A. P. Vlasto, Cambridge, Modern Humanities Research Association, 1970, pp. 105–111.

Fennell, [J. L. I.] John, *The Crises of Medieval Russia 1200–1304*, London, Longman, 1983.

Fennell, [J. L. I.] John, *A History of the Russian Church to 1448*, London, Longman, 1995.

Fisher, Alan W., "Muscovite–Ottoman Relations in the Sixteenth and Seventeenth Centuries," *Humaniora Islamica*, vol. 1, 1973, pp. 207–217.

Fleischhacker, Hedwig, *Russland zwischen zwei Dynastien (1598–1613). Ein Untersuchung über die Krise in der obersten Gewalt*, Vienna, Rudolf M. Rohrer, 1933.

Fletcher, Joseph, "Integrative History: Parallels and Interconnections in the

Early Modern Period, 1500–1800," *Journal of Turkish Studies*, vol. 9, 1985, pp. 37–57.

Fletcher, Richard, *The Quest for El Cid*, New York, Alfred A. Knopf, 1990.

Flier, Michael, "The Throne of Monomakh: Cathedra Ex Cathedra," paper delivered at the 27th AAASS Convention in Washington, DC, October 29, 1995.

Florinskii, Timofei [Dmitrievich], *Pamiatniki zakonodatel'noi deiatel'nosti Dushana Tsaria Serbov i Grekov. Khrisovuly. Serbskii Zakonnik. Sborniki vizantiiskikh zakonov*, Kiev, Tipografiia Imperatorskogo universiteta Sv. Vladimira, 1888.

Franke, Herbert, *From Tribal Chieftain to Universal Emperor and God: the Legitimation of the Yüan Dynasty*, Munich, Bayerische Akademie der Wissenschaften, 1978.

Franck, Irene M., and David M. Brownstone, *The Silk Road: a History*, New York, Facts on File, 1986.

French, R. A., "The Urban Network of Later Medieval Russia," *Geographical Studies on the Soviet Union: Essays in Honor of Chauncey D. Harris*, ed. George J. Demko and Roland J. Fuchs, University of Chicago Department of Geography, 1984, pp. 29–51.

Frye, Richard N., "Balkh," *Encyclopedia of Islam*, new edn, vol. 1, pt. 2, Leiden, E. J. Brill, 1954–1996, pp. 1000–1002.

Fuhrmann, Joseph T., "Metropolitan Cyril II (1242–1281) and the Politics of Accommodation," *Jahrbücher für Geschichte Osteuropas*, vol. 24, 1976, pp. 161–172.

Garlake, Peter S., *Great Zimbabwe*, London, Thames & Hudson, 1973.

Gaunt, G. D., and Ann M. Gaunt, "Mongol Archers of the Thirteenth Century," *Journal of the Society of Archer-Antiquaries*, vol. 16, 1973, pp. 18–22.

Geanakoplos, Deno J., *Byzantine East and Latin West: Two Worlds of Christendom in Middle Ages and Renaissance. Studies in Ecclesiastical and Church History*, Oxford, Basil Blackwell, 1966.

Geertz, Clifford, "Ideology as a Cultural System," in *Ideology and Discontent*, ed. David Apteher, New York, Free Press, 1964, pp. 47–76; reprinted in Clifford Geertz, *The Interpretation of Culture*, New York, Basic Books, 1973. pp. 193–229.

Genet, Jacques, *Daily Life in China: On the Eve of the Mongol Invasion 1250–1276*, New York, Macmillan, 1962.

The Genius That Was China, 4 parts, PBS, 1990.

Gol'dberg, A. L., "Tri 'poslaniia Filofeia' (Opyt tekstologicheskogo analiza)," *TODRL*, vol. 29, 1974, pp. 68–97.

Gol'dberg, A. L., "Istoriko-politicheskie idei russkoi knizhnosti XV–XVII vekov," *Istoriia SSSR*, 1975, no. 4, pp. 60–77.

Gol'dberg, A. L., "K istorii rasskaza o potomkakh Avgusta i o darakh Monomakha," *TODRL*, vol. 30, 1976, pp. 204–216.

Gol'dberg, A. L., "Ideia 'Moskva – Tretii Rim' v sochineniiakh pervoi poloviny XVI v.," *TODRL*, vol. 37, 1983, pp. 139–149.

Goldblatt, Harvey, "On 'rusьskymi pismeny' in the *Vita Constantini* and Rus'ian

Religious Patriotism," in *Studia Slavica Mediaevalia et Humanistica. Riccardo Picchio dictata*, ed. M. Colucci, G. Dell'Agata, and H. Goldblatt, Rome, Edizioni Dell'ateneo, 1986, pp. 311–328.

Goldblatt, Harvey, "History and Hagiography: Recent Studies on the Text and Textual Tradition of the *Vita Constantini*," in *Kamen" kraeug"l'n"*, pp. 158–179.

Golden, Peter B., "Turkic Calques in Medieval Eastern Slavic," *Journal of Turkish Studies*, vol. 8, 1984, pp. 103–111.

Goldfrank, David, "Old and New Perspectives on Iosif Volotsky's Monastic Rules," *Slavic Review*, vol. 24, 1975, pp. 279–301.

Goldfrank, David, "Third Rome," in *MERSH*, vol. 23, pp. 118–121.

Goldfrank, David, *The Monastic Rule of Iosif Volotsky*, Kalamazoo, Cistercian, 1983.

Goldfrank, David, "Theocratic Imperatives, the Transcendent, the Worldly, and Political Justice in Russia's Early Inquisitions," in *Religious and Secular Forces in Late Tsarist Russia: Essays in Honor of Donald W. Treadgold*, ed. Charles E. Timberlake, Seattle, University of Washington Press, 1992, pp. 30–47, 287–297.

Gorelik, M. V., "Oruzhie i dospekh russkikh i mongolo-tatarskikh voinov kontsa XIV v.," *Vestnik Akademii nauk SSSR*, 1980, no. 8, pp. 102–103.

Gorelik, M. V., "Mongolo-tatarskoe oboronitel'noe vooruzhenie vtoroi poloviny XIV–nachala XV v.," in *Kulikovskaia bitva. V istorii i kul'ture nashei Rodiny*, pp. 244–269.

Got'e, Iu. V., "Zamoskovnyi krai v XVII veke. Opyt issledovanie po istorii ekonomicheskogo byta Moskovskoi Rusi," *Uchenye zapiski Imperatorskogo Moskovskogo universiteta. Otdel istoriko-filologicheskii*, vol. 36, 1906, pp. 1–602.

Grekov, B. D., and A. Iu. Iakubovskii, *Zolotaia Orda i ee padenie*, Moscow and Leningrad, Akademiia nauk SSSR, 1950.

Grey, Ian, *Ivan the Terrible*, London, Hodder & Stoughton, 1964.

Grigor'ev, A. P., "Ofitsial'nyi iazyk Zolotoi Ordy XIII–XIV vv.," *Tiurkologicheskii sbornik 1977*, Moscow, 1981, pp. 81–89.

Grobovsky, Antony, *The "Chosen Council" of Ivan IV: a Reinterpretation*, Brooklyn, Theo Gaus' Sons, 1969.

Grousset, René, *The Empire of the Steppes: a History of Central Asia*, trans. Naomi Walford, New Brunswick, NJ, Rutgers University Press, 1970.

Gudziak, Boris, "Crisis and Reform: the Kievan Metropolitanate, the Patriarchate of Constantinople, and the Genesis of the Union of Brest," Ph.D. Dissertation, Harvard University, 1992.

Gudziak, Boris, "The Sixteenth-Century Muscovite Church and Patriarch Jeremiah II's Journey to Muscovy, 1588–1589: Some Comments Concerning the Historiographical Sources," *Kamen" kraeug"l'n"*, pp. 200–225.

Guerdan, René, *Byzantium: Its Triumphs and Tragedy*, trans. D. L. B. Hartley, New York, Capricorn, 1962.

Guilland, R., *Correspondance de Nicéphore Grégoras*, Paris, Société Française d'Imprimerie d'Angers, 1927.

Gukovskii, M. A., "Soobshchenie o Rossii moskovskogo posla v Milane (1486 g.)," *Voprosy istoriografii i istochnikovedeniia istorii SSSR. Sbornik statei*, ed. S. N. Valk, "Trudy Leningradskogo otdeleniia Instituta istorii," vol. 5, 1963, pp. 648–655.

Gumilev, L. N., *Drevniaia Rus' i velikaia step'*, Moscow, Mysl', 1989.

Gurliand, I. Ia., *Iamskaia gon'ba v Moskovskom gosudarstve do kontsa XVII veka*, Iaroslavl', Tipografiia Gubernskogo pravleniia, 1900.

Hackel, Sergei, "Under Pressure from the Pagans? – The Mongols and the Russian Church," in *The Legacy of St. Vladimir: Byzantium, Russia, America*, ed. J. Breck, J. Meyendorff, and E. Silk, Crestwood, NY, St. Vladimir's Seminary Press, 1990, pp. 47–56.

Halperin, Charles J. [Jerome], "The Russian Land and the Russian Tsar: the Emergence of Muscovite Ideology, 1380–1408," *Forschungen zur osteuropäischen Geschichte*, vol. 23, 1976, pp. 7–103.

Halperin, Charles J., "'Know Thy Enemy': Medieval Russian Familiarity with the Mongols of the Golden Horde," *Jahrbücher für Geschichte Osteuropas*, vol. 30, 1982, pp. 161–175.

Halperin, Charles J., "Soviet Historiography on Russia and the Mongols," *Russian Review*, vol. 41, 1982, pp. 306–322.

Halperin, Charles J., "The Defeat and Death of Batu," *Russian History*, vol. 10, 1983, pp. 50–65.

Halperin, Charles J., "The Ideology of Silence: Prejudice and Pragmatism on the Medieval Religious Frontier," *Comparative Studies in Society and History*, vol. 26, 1984, pp. 442–466.

Halperin, Charles J., "The Tatar Yoke and Tatar Oppression," *Russia Mediaevalis*, vol. 5, 1984, pp. 20–39.

Halperin, Charles J., *Russia and the Golden Horde: the Mongol Impact on Medieval Russian History*, Bloomington, Indiana University Press, 1985.

Halperin, Charles J., "Russia and the Steppe: George Vernadsky and Eurasianism," *Forschungen zur Osteuropäischen Geschichte*, vol. 36, 1985, pp. 55–194.

Halperin, Charles J., *The Tatar Yoke*, Columbus, OH, Slavica, 1986.

Haney, Jack V. A., "Moscow – Second Constantinople, Third Rome, or Second Kiev? (The Tale of the Princes of Vladimir)," *Canadian Slavic Studies*, vol. 3, 1968, pp. 354–367.

Harris, Nigel, *Beliefs in Society: the Problem of Ideology*, Harmondsworth, Penguin, 1971.

Hartmann, R., "Balkh," *Encyclopedia of Islam*, 1st edn, vol. 2, pp. 622–623.

Hartog, Leo de, "The Army of Genghis Khan," *Army Quarterly and Defence Journal*, vol. 109, 1979, pp. 476–485.

Hartwell, Robert M., "Demographic, Political, and Social Transformations of China, 750–1550," *Harvard Journal of Asiatic Studies*, vol. 42, 1982, pp. 365–442.

Haupt, Herman, "Neue Beiträge zu den Fragmenten des Dio Cassius," *Hermes*, vol. 14, 1879, pp. 431–446.

Hayden, Brian, *Archaeology: the Science of Once and Future Things*, New York, W. H. Freeman, 1993.

Hellie, Richard, *Enserfment and Military Change in Muscovy*, University of Chicago Press, 1971.

Hellie, Richard, "In Search of Ivan the Terrible," in S. F. Platonov, *Ivan the Terrible*, ed. and trans. Joseph L. Wieczynski, Gulf Breeze, FL, Academic International Press, 1974, pp. x–xxxiv.

Hellie, Richard, "Recent Soviet Historiography on Medieval and Early Modern Russian Slavery," *Russian Review*, vol. 35, 1976, pp. 1–32.

Hellie, Richard, "What Happened? How Did He Get Away with It?: Ivan Groznyi's Paranoia and the Problem of Institutional Restraints," *Russian History*, vol. 14, 1987, p. 199–224.

Hellie, Richard, "Zemskii sobor," *MERSH*, vol. 45, pp. 226–234.

Henthorn, W. E., *Korea: the Mongol Invasions*, Leiden, E. J. Brill, 1963.

Herrin, Judith, "In Search of Byzantine Women: Three Avenues of Approach," in *Images of Women in Antiquity*, ed. Averil Cameron and Amélie Kuhrt, Detroit, Wayne State University Press, 1983, pp. 167–189.

Herrmann, Albert, *Historical and Commercial Atlas of China*, Cambridge, MA, Harvard University Press, 1935.

Hilton, R. H., and R. E. F. Smith, "Introduction," in Smith, *Enserfment of the Russian Peasantry*, pp. 1–27.

A History of Private Life, 5 vols., ed. Philippe Ariès and Georges Duby, Cambridge, MA, Belknap Press, 1987–1991.

Howes, Robert Craig, "Survey of the Testaments," in *The Testaments of the Grand Princes of Moscow*, trans. and ed. with commentary by R. C. Howes, Ithaca, NY, Cornell University Press, 1967, pp. 1–109.

[Howlett, Jana] Ia. R. Khoulett, "Svidetel'stvo arkhiepiskopa Gennadiia o eresi 'novgorodskikh eretikov zhidovskaia mudr"stvuiushchikh'," *TODRL*, vol. 46, 1993, pp. 51–73.

Hsiao, Ch'i-ch'ing, *The Military Establishment of the Yuan Dynasty*, Cambridge, MA, Council on East Asian Studies, 1978.

Hucker, Charles O., "Yung-lo," *The New Encyclopaedia Britannica*, 30 vols., 15th edn, Chicago, Encyclopaedia Britannica, 1974, vol. 12, pp. 876–878.

Hung, Chin-fu, "China and the Nomads: Misconceptions in Western Historiography on Inner Asia," *Harvard Journal of Asiatic Studies*, vol. 41, 1981, pp. 597–628.

Hussey, J. M., *The Orthodox Church in the Byzantine Empire*, Oxford, Clarendon Press, 1986.

Iakubovskii, A. Iu., and C. E. Bosworth, "Marw al-Shāhidjān," *Encyclopedia of Islam*, new edn, vol. 6, pp. 618–621.

Ilieva, Iskra I., "Vladetel'skii titul Moskovskikh velikikh kniazei (s serediny XV–do pervoi chetverti XVI veka)," *Bulgarian Historical Review*, vol. 12, 1984, pp. 75–87.

Il'inskij, N., *Sobranie po alfavitnomu poriadku vsekh predmetov, sovderzhash-chikhsia v sviashchennykh i bozhestvennykh kanonakh, sostavlennoe i obrabo-tannoe smirenneishim ieromonakhom Matfeem, ili Alfavitnaia sintagma M. Vlastaria*, Simferopol', 1892.

Inalcik, Halil, "Power Relationships Between Russia, the Crimea and the Ottoman Empire as Reflected in Titulature," in *Turco-Tatar Past Soviet Present: Studies Presented to Alexandre Bennigsen*, eds. Ch. Lemercier-Quelquejay, G. Veinstein, and S. E. Wimbush, Paris, Éditions de l'École des Hautes Etudes en Sciences Sociales, 1986, pp. 175–211.

Jackson, Peter, and David Morgan, "Introduction," in William of Rubruck, *The Mission of Friar William of Rubruck*, trans. Peter J. Jackson, London, Hakluyt Society, 1990, pp. 1–55.

Jagchid, Sechin, "Patterns of Trade and Conflict Between China and the Nomads of Mongolia," *Zentralasiatische Studien*, vol. 11, 1977, pp. 177–204.

Jagchid, Sechin, and Paul Hyer, *Mongolia's Culture and Society*, Boulder, CO, Westview Press, 1979.

Jagchid, Sechin, and Van Jay Symons, *Peace, War and Trade Along the Great Wall: Nomadic–Chinese Interaction Through Ten Millennia*, Bloomington, Indiana University Press, 1989.

Jervis, Robert, *Perception and Misperception in International Affairs*, Princeton University Press, 1976.

Just, Roger, *Women in Athenian Law and Life*, London, Routledge, 1989.

Kagan, M. D., "'Povest' o dvukh posol'stvakh' – legendarno-politicheskoe proizvedenie nachala XVII veka," *TODRL*, vol. 11, 1955, pp. 218–254.

Kagan, M. D., "Legendarnaia perepiska Ivana IV s turetskim sultanom kak literaturnyi pamiatnik pervoi chetverti XVII v.," *TODRL*, vol. 13, 1957, pp. 247–272.

Kagan, M. D., "Legendarnyi tsikl gramot turetskogo sultana k evropeiskim gosudariam – publitsisticheskoe proizvedenie vtoroi poloviny XVII v.," *TODRL*, vol. 15, 1958, pp. 225–250.

Kaiser, Daniel, *The Growth of the Law in Medieval Russia*, Princeton University Press, 1980.

Kaiser, Daniel, "Naming Cultures in Early Modern Russia," in *Kamen" kraeug"l'n"*, pp. 271–291.

Kalinin, V. A., "Monety Ivana III s russko-tatarskimi legendami," *Trudy Gosudarstvennogo Ermitazha*, vol. 21, *Numismatika*, vol. 5, 1981, pp. 112–116.

Kamen" kraeug"l'n": Rhetoric of the Medieval Slavic World. Essays Presented to Edward L. Keenan on His Sixtieth Birthday by His Colleagues and Students, ed. Nancy Shields Kollmann, Donald Ostrowski, Andrei Plizugov, and Daniel Rowland, Cambridge, MA, Harvard Ukrainian Studies, vol. 19, 1995.

Kamentseva, E. I., and N. V. Ustiugov, *Russkaia sfragistika i geral'dika*, Moscow, Vysshaia shkola, 1963.

Kämpfer, Frank, "Beobachtungen zu den Sendschreiben Filofejs," *Jahrbücher für Geschichte Osteuropas*, vol. 18, 1970, pp. 1–46.

Kämpfer, Frank, "Russland an der Schwelle zur Neuzeit Kunst, Ideologie und historishces Bewusstein unter Ivan Groznyj," *Jahrbücher für Geschichte Osteuropas*, vol. 23, 1975, pp. 504–524.

Kantorowicz, Ernst H., "'Feudalism' in the Byzantine Empire," in *Feudalism in History*, ed. Rushton Coulborn, Princeton University Press, 1956, pp. 151–166.

Karamzin, N. M., *Zapiska o drevnei i novoi Rossii*, ed. V. V. Sipovskii, St. Petersburg, M. N. Tolstoi, 1914.

Karamzin, N. M., *Istoriia gosudarstva Rossiiskogo*, 5th edn, 12 vols. in 3 books, St. Petersburg, Eduard Prats, 1842–1843, reprint: Moscow, Kniga, 1989.

Karamzin, Nikolai, *Notes on Ancient and Modern Russia*, ed. and trans. Richard Pipes, Cambridge, MA, Harvard University Press, 1959.

Kashtanov, S. M., "O vnutrennei politike Ivana Groznogo v period 'velikogo kniazheniia' Simeona Bekbulatovicha," *Trudy Moskovskogo gosudarstvennogo istoriko-arkhivnogo instituta*, vol. 16, 1961, pp. 427–462.

Kashtanov, S. M., "Finansovaia problema v period provedeniia Ivanom Froznym politiki 'udela'," *Istoricheskie zapiski*, no. 82, 1968, pp. 243–272.

Kashtanov, S. M., "The Centralised State and Feudal Immunities in Russia," *Slavonic and East European Review*, vol. 49, 1971, pp. 235–254.

Kashtanov, S. M., "Finansovye ustroitsvo moskovskogo khiazhestva v seredine XIV v. po dannym dukhovnykh gramot," in *Issledovaniia po istorii i istoriografii feodalizma. K 100-letiiu so dnia rozhdeniia akademika B. D. Grekova*, ed. V. T. Pashuto et al., Moscow, Nauka, 1982, pp. 173–189.

Kavelin, K. D., *Sobranie sochinenii*, 4 vols., St. Petersburg, M. M. Stasiulevich, 1897, vol. 1.

Kazakova, N. A., *Vassian Patrikeev i ego sochineniia*, Moscow and Leningrad, Akademiia nauk SSSR, 1960.

Kazakova, N. A., and Ia. S. Lur'e, *Antifeodal'nye ereticheskie dvizheniia na Rusi XIV–nachala XVI veka*, Moscow and Leningrad, Akademiia nauk SSSR, 1955.

Kazhdan, Alexander P., "The Concept of Freedom (*eleutheria*) and Slavery (*duleia*) in Byzantium," in *La notion de liberté au Moyen Age: Islam, Byzance, Occident*, ed. George Makdisi, Dominique Sourdel, and Janine Sourdel-Thomine, Paris, Société d'Edition Les Belles Lettres, 1985, pp. 215–226.

Kazhdan, Alexander P., and Simon Franklin, *Studies on Byzantine Literature of the Eleventh and Twelfth Centuries*, New York, Cambridge University Press, 1984.

Keddie, Nikki, and Lois Beck, "Introduction," in *Women in the Muslim World*, pp. 1–34.

Keegan, John, *A History of Warfare*, New York, Alfred A. Knopf, 1994.

Keenan, Edward L., "Muscovy and Kazan, 1445–1552: a Study in Steppe Politics," Ph.D. Dissertation, Harvard University, 1965.

Keenan, Edward L., "Muscovy and Kazan: Some Introductory Remarks on the Patterns of Steppe Diplomacy," *Slavic Review*, vol. 26, 1967, pp. 548–558.

Keenan, Edward L., "Coming to Grips with the Kazanskaya istoriia: Some Observations on Old Answers and New Questions," *Annals of the Ukrainian Academy of Arts and Sciences in the U.S.*, vol. 9, 1964–1968, pp. 143–183.

Keenan, Edward L., "The *Jarlyk* of Axmed-Xan to Ivan III: a New Reading," *International Journal of Slavic Linguistics and Poetics*, vol. 12, 1969, pp. 33–47.

Keenan, Edward L., *The Kurbskii–Groznyi Apocrypha: the Seventeenth-Century Genesis of the "Correspondence" Attributed to Prince A. M. Kurbskii and Tsar Ivan IV*, Cambridge, MA, Harvard University Press, 1971.

Keenan, Edward L., "Ivan Vasil'evich, Terrible Czar: 1530–1584," *Harvard Magazine*, January–February, 1978, pp. 48–49.

Keenan, Edward L., "Ivan the Terrible and His Women: the Grammar of

Politics in the Kremlin," unpublished paper given as lecture at Wellesley College, Newton, Massachusetts, February 1981.

Keenan, Edward L., "Ivan the Terrible and His Women II: Dowagers, Nannies, and Brides," unpublished paper given as lecture at Wellesley College, Newton, Massachusetts, February 1981.

Keenan, Edward L., "Ivan the Terrible: The Man," lecture given at Harvard University, November 16, 1981, typescript notes by Jack E. Kollmann, pp. 108–113.

Keenan, Edward L., "Muscovite Political Folkways," *Russian Review*, vol. 45, 1986, pp. 115–181.

Keenan, Edward L., "On Certain Mythical Beliefs and Russian Behaviors," in *The Legacy of History in Russia and the New States of Eurasia*, ed. S. Frederick Starr, Armonk, NY, M. E. Sharpe, 1994, pp. 19–40.

Kennedy, Craig Gayen, "The Juchids of Muscovy: a Study of Personal Ties between Émigré Tatar Dynasts and the Muscovite Grand Princes in the Fifteenth and Sixteenth Centuries," Ph.D. Dissertation, Harvard University, 1994.

Kennedy, Craig [Gayen], "Fathers, Sons and Brothers: Ties of Metaphorical Kinship Between the Muscovite Grand Princes and the Tatar Elite," *Kamen" kraeug"l'n"*, pp. 292–301.

Keuls, Eva C., *The Reign of the Phallus: Sexual Politics in Ancient Athens*, New York, Harper & Row, 1985.

Khaldûn, Ibn, *The Muqaddimah: an Introduction to History*, trans. Franz Rosenthal, ed. N. J. Dawood, Princeton University Press, Bollingen Series, 1969.

Khazanov, A[natoly] M., *Nomads and the Outside World* (Cambridge Studies in Social Anthropology, no. 44), Cambridge University Press, 1984.

Khazanov, Anatoly M., "Muhammad and Jenghiz Khan Compared: the Religious Factor in World Empire Building," *Comparative Studies in Society and History*, vol. 35, 1993, pp. 461–479.

Khodarkovsky, Michael, *Where Two Worlds Met: the Russian State and the Kalmyk Nomads, 1600–1771*, Ithaca, NY, Cornell University Press, 1992.

Khoroshkevich, A. L., "Ob odnom iz epizodov dinasticheskoi bor'by v Rossii v kontse XV veka," *Istoriia SSSR*, 1974, no. 5, pp. 129–139.

Khoroshkevich, A. L., *Russkoe gosudarstvo v sisteme mezhdunarodnykh otnoshenii kontsa XV–nachala XVI v.*, Moscow, Nauka, 1980.

Khoroshkevich, A. L., and A. I. Pliguzov, "Rus' XIII stoletiia v knige Dzh. Fennela," in Dzhon Fennel [John Fennell], *Krizis srednevekovoi Rusi 1200–1304*, ed. and trans. A. L. Khoroshkevich and A. I. Pliguzov, Moscow, Progress, 1989, pp. 5–32.

Kirchner, Walther, *Commercial Relations Between Russia and Europe 1400–1800*, Bloomington, Indiana University Press, 1966.

Kirpichnikov, A. N., "Fakty, gipotezy i zabluzhdeniia v izuchenii russkoi voennoi istorii XIII–XV vv.," *Drevneishie gosudarstva na territorii SSSR. Materialy i issledovaniia 1984 god*, Moscow, Nauka, 1985, pp. 229–243.

Kishlansky, Mark, Patrick Geary, and Patricia O'Brien, *Civilization in the West*, New York, HarperCollins, 1991.

Kivelson, Valerie, "The Devil Stole His Mind: the Tsar and the 1648 Moscow Uprising," *American Historical Review*, vol. 98, 1993, pp. 733–756.

Kleimola, Ann M., "Boris Godunov and the Politics of Mestnichestvo," *Slavonic and East European Review*, vol. 53, 1975, pp. 355–369.

Kleimola, Ann M., "Justice in Medieval Russia: Muscovite Judgment Charters (*Pravye gramoty*) of the Fifteenth and Sixteenth Centuries," *Transactions of the American Philosophical Society*, n.s. vol. 65, pt. 6, 1975, pp. 3–93.

Kliuchevskii, V. O., *Drevnerusskie zhitiia sviatykh kak istoricheskii istochnik*, Moscow, K. Soldatenkov, 1871.

[Kliuchevskii] Kluchevsky, V. O., *A History of Russia*, trans. C. J. Hogarth, 5 vols., London, J. M. Dent, New York, E. P. Dutton, 1911–1931.

Kloss, B. M., "Determining the Authorship of the Trinity Chronicle," *Medieval Russian Culture*, vol. 2, pp. 57–72.

Kobrin, V. B., "Sostav oprichnogo dvora Ivan Groznogo," *Arkheologicheskii ezhegodnik za 1959 god*, Moscow, 1960, pp. 16–91.

Kobrin, V. B., "Genealogiia i antroponimika (po russkim materialam XV–XVI vv.)," *Istoriia i genealogiia. S. B. Veselovskii i problemy istoriko-genealogicheskikh issledovanii*, ed. N. I. Pavlenko et al., Moscow, Nauka, 1977, pp. 80–115.

Kobrin, V. B., "Stanovlenie pomestnoi sistemy," *Istoricheskie zapiski*, no. 105, 1980, pp. 150–195.

Kobrin, V. B., *Vlast' i sobstvennost' v srednevekovoi Rossii (XV–XVI vv.)*, Moscow, Mysl', 1985.

Kolchin, B. A., "Remeslo," in *Ocherki russkoi kul'tury XIII–XV vekov*, part 1: *Materic 'naia kul'tura*, ed. A. V. Artsikhovskii et al., Izdatel'stvo Moskovskogo universiteta, 1969, pp. 156–230.

Kolchir, G. E., *Sel'skoe khoziaistvo na Rusi v period obrazovaniia Russkogo ' entralizovannogo gosudarstva: kontsa XIII–nachala XVI v.*, Moscow and Leningrad, Nauka, 1965.

Kollmann, Nancy Shields, "The Boyar Clan and Court Politics: the Founding of the Muscovite Political System," *Cahiers du monde russe et soviètique*, vol. 23, 1982, pp. 5–31.

Kollmann, Nancy Shields, "The Seclusion of Elite Muscovite Women," *Russian History*, vol. 10, 1983, pp. 170–187.

Kollmann, Nancy Shields, *Kinship and Politics: the Making of the Muscovite Political System, 1345–1547*, Stanford University Press, 1987.

Kollmann, Nancy Shields, "Women's Honor in Early Modern Russia," in *Russia's Women: Accommodation, Resistance, Transformation*, ed. Barbara Evans Clements, Barbara Alpern Engel, and Christine D. Worobec, Berkeley, University of California Press, 1991, pp. 60–73.

Koo, Madame Wellington, with Isabella Tares, *No Feast Lasts Forever*, New York, Quadrangle, 1975.

Köprülü, Mehmed Fuad, "La proibizione di versare il sangue nell'esecuzione d'un membro della dinastia presso i Turchi ed i Mongoli," *Annali dell'Istituto Universitario Orientale di Napoli*, new series, vol. 1, 1940, pp. 15–23.

Köpstein, Helga, *Zur Slaverei im ausgehenden Byzanz. Philologisch-historische Untersuchung*, Berlin, Akademie-Verlag, 1966.

Koretskii, V. I., "Mongol Yoke in Russia," in *MERSH*, vol. 23, pp. 45–48.

Koretskii, V. I., "Oprichnina," *Sovetskaia istoricheskaia entsiklopediia*, vol. 10, 1967, pp. 565–567.

Kostomarov, N. I., *Russkaia istoriia v zhizneopisaniiakh ee glavneishikh deiatelei*, 4th edn, 2 vols., St. Petersburg, M. M. Stasiulevich, 1895–1896.

Kracke, E. A., Jr., *Civil Service in Early Sung China 960–1067: With Particular Emphasis on the Development of Controlled Sponsorship to Foster Administrative Responsibility*, Cambridge, MA, Harvard University Press, 1953, 1968.

Krader, Lawrence, "Qan-Qayan and the Beginnings of Mongol Kingship," *Central Asiatic Journal*, vol. 1, 1955, pp. 17–35.

Krader, Lawrence, "Feudalism and the Tatar Polity of the Middle Ages," *Comparative Studies in Society and History*, vol. 1, 1958, pp. 76–99.

Kuchkin, V. A., "Pobeda na Kulikovom pole," *Voprosy istorii*, 1980, no. 8, pp. 3–21.

Kulikovskaia bitva. V istorii i kul'ture nashei Rodiny, ed. B. A. Rybakov et al., Izdatel'stvo Moskovskogo universiteta, 1983.

Kunik [K.], A. A., "Pochemu Vizantiia donyne ostaetsia zagadkoi vo vsemirnoi istorii?" *Uchenie zapiski Imp. Akademii nauk po pervomu i tret'emu otdeleniiam*, vol. 2, pt. 3, 1853, pp. 423–444.

Kuntsevich, K. G., *Istoriia o Kazanskom tsarstve ili Kazanskii letopisets. Opyt istoriko-literaturnogo issledovaniia*, St. Petersburg, I. N. Skorokhodov, 1905.

Kwanten, Luc, *Imperial Nomads: a History of Central Asia, 500–1500*, Philadelphia, University of Pennsylvania Press, 1979.

Kyzlasov, L. R., "Pamiatnik musul'manskogo srednevekov'ia v Tuve," *Sovetskaia arkheologiia*, 1963, no. 2, pp. 203–210.

Kyzlasov, L. R., *Istoriia Tuvy v srednie veka*, Izdatel'stvo Moskovskogo universiteta, 1969.

Labunka, Miroslav, "The Legend of the Novgorodian White Cowl: the Study of Its 'Prologue' and 'Epilogue,'" Ph.D. Dissertation, Columbia University, 1978.

Laiou, Angeliki E., "The Role of Women in Byzantine Society," *Jahrbuch der österreichischen Byzantinistik*, vol. 31, 1981, pp. 233–260.

Laiou, Angeliki E., "Sex, Consent, and Coercion in Byzantium,' in *Consent and Coercion*, pp. 109–221.

Lamberg-Karlovsky, C. C., and Jeremy A. Sabloff, *Ancient Civilizations: the Near East and Mesoamerica*, Menlo Park, CA, Benjamin/Cummings, 1979.

Lambton, Ann K. S., "Reflections on the *Iqtā'*," in *Arabic and Islamic Studies in Honor of Hamilton A. R. Gibb*, ed. George Makdisi, Cambridge, MA, Harvard University Press, pp. 358–376.

Langer, Lawrence N., "The Medieval Russian Town," in *The City in Russian History*, ed. Michael F. Hamm, Lexington, KY, University Press of Kentucky, 1976, pp. 11–33.

Langer, Lawrence N., "The End of Mongol Rule in Medieval Rus'," unpublished article, part of which presented as a paper at the 28th AAASS Convention in Boston, Massachusetts, November 15, 1996.

Lattimore, Owen, "The Geography of Chingis Khan," *Geographical Journal*, vol. 129, 1963, pp. 1–7.

Laurent, V., *Les "Mémoires" du Grand Ecclésiarque de l'Église de Constantinople*

Sylvestre Syropoulos sur le concile de Florence, Rome, *Concilium Florentinum documenta et scriptores*, Series B, vol. 9, 1971.

LeDonne, John P., "Ruling Families in the Russian Political Order 1689–1825," *Cahiers du Monde russe et soviétique*, vol. 28, 1987, pp. 233–322.

LeDonne, John P., *Absolutism and the Ruling Class: the Formation of the Russian Political Order, 1700–1825*, Oxford University Press, 1991.

LeDonne, John P., "The Geopolitical Context of Russian Foreign Policy, 1700–1917," *Acta Slavica Iaponica*, vol. 12, 1994, pp. 1–23.

LeDonne, John P., *The Russian Empire and the World 1700–1917: the Geopolitics of Expansion and Containment*, New York, Oxford University Press, 1997.

Ledyard, Gari, "The Establishment of Mongolian Military Governors in Korea in 1231," *Phi Theta Papers*, vol. 6, May 1961, pp. 1–17.

Lefkowitz, Mary R., "Seduction and Rape in Greek Myth," in *Consent and Coercion*, pp. 17–37.

Lenhoff, Gail, *Early Russian Hagiography: the Lives of Prince Fedor the Black*, Berlin, Veroffentlichungen der Abteilung für slavische Sprachen und Literaturen des Osteurop-Instituts (Slavisches Seminar) an der Freien Universitat Berlin, 1997.

Leontovich, F. I., "K istorii prava russkikh inorodtsev drevnii mongolo-kalmytskii ili oiratskii ustav vzyskanii (Tsaadzhin-Bichik)," *Zapiski Imperatorskogo Novorossiiskogo universiteta*, vol. 28, Odessa, 1879.

Lerner, Gerda, *The Creation of Patriarchy*, New York, Oxford University Press, 1986.

Levathes, Louise, *When China Ruled the Seas: the Treasure Fleet of the Dragon Throne 1405–1433*, New York, Simon & Schuster, 1994.

Levin, Eve, *Sex and Society in the World of the Orthodox Slavs, 900–1700*, Ithaca, NY, Cornell University Press, 1989.

Levin, Lawrence Meyer, *The Political Doctrine of Montesquieu's* Esprit des lois: *Its Classical Background*, New York, Columbia University Press, 1936.

Levy, Sandra, "Women and the Control of Property in Sixteenth-Century Muscovy," *Russian History*, vol. 10, 1983, pp. 201–212.

Lewis, Archibald R., *Nomads and Crusaders AD 1000–1368*, Bloomington, Indiana University Press, 1988.

Lewis, Bernard, *The Arabs in History*, rev. edn, New York, Harper, 1966.

Lewis, Bernard, "The Mongols, the Turks and the Muslim Polity," *Transactions of the Royal Historical Society*, 5th ser., vol. 18, 1968, pp. 49–68; reprinted in Bernard Lewis, *Islam in History: Ideas, Men and Events in the Middle East*, 2nd edn, Chicago, Open Court, 1993, pp. 189–207.

Li, Dun J., *The Ageless Chinese: a History*, 3rd edn, New York, Charles Scribner's Sons, 1978.

[Liashchenko] Lyashchenko, Peter I., *History of the National Economy of Russia to the 1917 Revolution*, trans. L. M. Herman, New York, Macmillan, 1949.

Likhachev, D. S., *Russkie letopisi i ikh kul'turno-istoricheskoe znachenie*, Moscow and Leningrad, Akademiia nauk SSSR, 1947.

Likhachev, D. S., "Literaturnaia sud'ba 'Povesti o razorenii Riazani Batyem' v pervoi chetverti XV veka," in *Issledovaniia i materialy po drevnerusskoi literatury*, 6 vols., Moscow, Akademiia nauk SSSR, 1961–1980, vol. 1, ed. V. D. Kuz'mina, pp. 9–22.

Likhachev, D. S., "K istorii slozheniia 'Povesti o razorenii Riazani Batyem,'"
Arkheograficheskii ezhegodnik za 1962 god, Moscow, 1963, pp. 48–51.

Likhachev, D. S., "'Kanon' i 'Molitva' Angelu Groznomu voevode Parfeniia
Urodivogo (Ivana Groznogo)," in *Rukopisnoe nasledie drevnei Rusi. Po
materialam Pushkinskogo doma*, ed. A. M. Panchenko, Leningrad, Nauka,
1972, pp. 10–27.

Likhachev, D. S., "Sochineniia Tsaria Ivana Vasil'evicha Groznogo," in D. S.
Likhachev, *Velikoe nasledie*, Moscow, Sovremennik, 1975, pp. 265–288.

Likhachev, D. S., "'Zadonshchina' i 'Povest' o razorenii Riazani Batyem,'" in
Drevniaia Rus' i slaviane, ed. T. V. Nikolaeva, Moscow, Nauka, 1978, pp.
366–370.

Lindner, Rudi Paul, "What Was a Nomadic Tribe?" *Comparative Studies in
Society and History*, vol. 24, 1982, pp. 689–711.

Lo, Winston W., *An Introduction to the Civil Service of Sung China: With
Emphasis on Its Personnel Administration*, Honolulu, University of Hawaii
Press, 1987.

Loewe, Michael, *Records of Han Administration*, 2 vols., Cambridge University
Press, 1967.

Løkkegaard, Frede, *Islamic Taxation in the Classic Period: With Special Reference
to Circumstances in Iraq*, Copenhagen, Brunner and Korch, 1950.

Lur'e, Ia. S., "Zametki k istorii publitsisticheskoi literatury kontsa XV–pervoi
poloviny XVI v.," *TODRL*, vol. 16, 1960, pp. 457–465.

Lur'e, Ia. S., "Novonaidennyi rasskaz o 'stoianii na Ugre,'" *TODRL*, vol. 18,
1962, pp. 289–293.

[Lur'e, Ia. S.] J. Luria, "Problems of Source Criticism (with Reference to
Medieval Russian Documents)," *Slavic Review*, vol. 27, 1968, pp. 1–22.

Lur'e, Ia. S., "K probleme svoda 1448 g.," *TODRL*, vol. 24, 1969, pp.
142–146.

Lur'e, Ia. S., "O nekotorykh printsipakh kritiki istochnikov," in *Istochnikovedenie
otechestvennoi istorii. Sbornik statei*, vol. 1, ed. N. I. Pavlenko et al., Moscow,
Nauka, 1973, pp. 78–100.

Lur'e, Ia. S., *Obshcherusskie letopisi XIV–XV vv.*, Leningrad, Nauka, 1976

[Lur'e, Ia. S.] Jakov S. Luria, "Unresolved Issues in the History of the
Ideological Movements of the Late Fifteenth Century," in *Medieval Russian
Culture*, [vol. 1], pp. 150–171.

Lur'e, Ia. S., "Iz nabliudenii nad letopisaniem pervoi poloviny XV v.," *TODRL*,
vol. 39, 1985, p. 294–304.

Lur'e, Ia. S., "O putiiakh dokazatel'stva pri analize istochnikov," *Voprosy istorii*,
1985, no. 5, pp. 64–65.

Lur'e, Ia. S., "Kak ustanovilas' avtokefaliia russkoi tserkvi v XV v.," *Vspomogatel'nye istoricheskie distsipliny*, vol. 23, 1991, pp. 181–198.

Lur'e, Ia. S., *Dve istorii Rusi XV veka. Rannie i pozdnie, nezavisimye i ofitsial'nye
letopisi ob obrazovanii Moskovskogo gosudarstva*, St. Petersburg, Dmitrii
Bulanin, 1994.

[Lur'e, Ia. S.] Jakov S. Luria, "Fifteenth-Century Chronicles as a Source for the
History of the Formation of the Muscovite State," in *Medieval Russian
Culture*, vol. 2, pp. 47–56.

Lyon, B., "What Made a Medieval King Constitutional?" in *Essays in Medieval*

History Presented to Bertie Wilson, ed. T. A. Sandquist and M. R. Powicke, University of Toronto Press, 1969, pp. 157–175.

Mahdi, Muhsin, *Ibn Khaldûn's Philosophy of History: a Study in the Philosophic Foundation of the Science of Culture*, University of Chicago Press, 1964.

Majeska, George P., "The Moscow Coronation of 1498 Reconsidered," *Jahrbücher für Geschichte Osteuropas*, vol. 26, 1978, pp. 353–361.

Majeska, George P., *Russian Travelers to Constantinople in the Fourteenth and Fifteenth Centuries*, (Dumbarton Oaks Studies, vol. 19), Washington, DC, Dumbarton Oaks Research Library and Collection, 1984.

Major Problems in Early Modern Russian History, ed. Nancy Shields Kollmann, New York, Garland, 1992.

Mango, Cyril, *Byzantium: the Empire of New Rome*, New York, Charles Scribner's Sons, 1980.

Mangold, Gunther, *Das Militärwesen in China unter der Mongolen-Herrschaft*, Bamberg, Fotodruck, 1971.

Manz, Beatrice Forbes, "The Office of *Darugha* Under Tamerlane," *Journal of Turkish Studies* (= *An Anniversary Volume in Honor of Francis Woodman Cleaves*), vol. 9, 1985, pp. 59–69.

Martin, H. Desmond, *The Rise of Chingis Khan and His Conquest of North China*, Baltimore, MD, Johns Hopkins University Press, 1950.

Martin, Janet, "The Land of Darkness and the Golden Horde: the Fur Trade Under the Mongols XIII–XIVth Centuries," *Cahiers du monde russe et soviétique*, vol. 19, 1978, pp. 401–421.

Martin, Janet, "Muscovy's Northeastern Expansion: the Context and a Cause," *Cahiers du monde russe et soviétique*, vol. 24, 1983, pp. 459–470.

Martin, Janet, "Muscovite Relations with the Khanate of Kazan' and the Crimea (1460s to 1521)," *Canadian–American Slavic Studies*, vol. 17, 1983, pp. 435–453.

Martin, Janet, "Muscovite Travelling Merchants: the Trade with the Muslim East (15th and 16th Centuries)," *Central Asian Survey*, vol. 4, no. 3, 1985, pp. 21–38.

Martin, Janet, *Treasures of the Land of Darkness: the Fur Trade and Its Significance for Medieval Russia*, Cambridge University Press, 1986.

Martin, Janet, *Medieval Russia, 980–1584*, Cambridge University Press, 1995.

Martin, Janet, "Widows, Welfare, and the *Pomest'e* System in the Sixteenth Century," in *Kamen" kraeug"l'n"*, pp. 375–388.

Martin, Russell E., "Royal Weddings and Crimean Diplomacy: New Sources on Muscovite Chancellery Practice During the Reign of Vasilii III," in *Kamen" kraeug"l'n"*, pp. 389–427.

Maslennikova, N. N., "K istorii sozdaniia teorii 'Moskva – tretii Rim,'" *TODRL*, vol. 18, 1962, pp. 569–581.

Matons, José Grosdidier de, "La Femme dans l'empire byzantin," in *Histoire mondiale de la femme*, 4 vols., ed. Pierre Grimal, Paris, Nouvelle Librairie de France, 1965–1967, vol. 3, pp. 11–43.

McKay, John P., Bennett D. Hill, and John Buckler, *A History of World Societies*, 3rd edn, Boston, Houghton Mifflin, 1992.

McNeill, William, *Mythistory and Other Essays*, University of Chicago Press, 1986.

Medieval Russian Culture, [vol. 1] ed. Henrik Birnbaum and Michael S. Flier, Berkeley, University of California Press, 1984.

Medieval Russian Culture, vol. 2, ed. Michael S. Flier and Daniel Rowland, Berkeley, University of California Press, 1994.

Medlin, William-Kenneth, *Moscow and East Rome: a Political Study of the Relations of Church and State in Muscovite Russia*, Geneva, E. Droz, 1952.

Mellinger, George, "The Mongols' Main Interest – Trade," transcript of remarks at the AAASS Convention in Miami, FL, November 1991.

Meyendorff, John, "The Byzantine Impact on Russian Civilization," in *Windows on the Russian Past: Essays on Soviet Historiography Since Stalin*, ed. Samuel H. Baron and Nancy W. Heer, Columbus, OH, American Association for the Advancement of Slavic Studies, 1977, pp. 45–56.

Meyendorff, John, *Byzantine Theology: Historical Trends and Doctrinal Themes*, 2nd edn, New York, Fordham University Press, 1979.

Meyendorff, John, *Byzantium and the Rise of Russia: a Study of Byzantino-Russian Relations in the Fourteenth Century*, Cambridge University Press 1981.

Meyendorff, John, *Imperial Unity and Christian Divisions: the Church 450–680 AD*, Crestwood, NY, St. Vladimir's Seminary Press, 1989.

Meyendorff, John, "Was There Ever a 'Third Rome'? Remarks on the Byzantine Legacy in Russia," in *The Byzantine Tradition After the Fall of Constantinople*, ed. John J. Yiannias, Charlottesville, University Press of Virginia, 1991, pp. 45–60.

Miliukov, Paul, "The Religious Tradition," in Paul Miliukov, *Russia and Its Crisis*, University of Chicago Press, 1906, pp. 65–130.

Miliukov, P. N., *Glavniya techeniia russkoi istoricheskoi mysli*, 3rd edn, St. Petersburg, M. V. Aver'ianov, 1913.

Miliutin, Vladimir, "O nedvizhimykh imushchestvakh dukhovenstva v Rossii," *ChOIDR*, 1859, bk. 4, pp. 1–118.

Miller, David B., "The Coronation of Ivan IV of Moscow," *Jahrbücher für Geschichte Osteuropas*, vol. 15, 1967, pp. 559–574.

Miller, David B., "The Velikie Minei Cheti and the Stepennaia Kniga of Metropolitan Makarii and the Origins of Russian National Consciousness," *Forschungen zur Osteuropäischen Geschichte*, vol. 26, 1979, pp. 263–382.

Miller, David B., "Monumental Building as an Indicator of Economic Trends in Northern Rus' in the Late Kievan and Mongol Periods, 1138–1462," *American Historical Review*, vol. 94, 1989, pp. 360–390.

Miller, David B., "Monumental Building and Its Patrons as Indicators of Economic and Political Trends in Rus', 900–1262," *Jahrbücher für Geschichte Osteuropas*, vol. 38, 1990, pp. 321–355.

Miller, David B., "Creating Legitimacy: Ritual, Ideology, and Power in Sixteenth-Century Russia," *Russian History*, vol. 21, 1994, pp. 289–315.

Miller, David B., "How the Mother of God Saved Moscow from Timur the Lame's Invasion in 1395: the Development of a Legend and the Invention of a National Identity," *Forschungen zur osteuropäischen Geschichte*, vol. 50, 1995, pp. 247–265.

Modern Encyclopedia of Russian and Soviet History, 58 vols., ed. Joseph L. Wieczynski, Gulf Breeze, FL, Academic International Press, 1976–1994.

Morgan, D[avid] O., "The Mongol Armies in Persia," *Der Islam*, vol. 56, 1979, pp. 81–96.

Morgan, D[avid] O., "Who Ran the Mongol Empire?" *Journal of the Royal Asiatic Society*, 1982, no. 2, pp. 124–136.

Morgan, D[avid] O., "The 'Great Yāsā of Chingiz Khān' and Mongol Law in the Īlkhānate," *Bulletin of the School of Oriental and African Studies*, vol. 49, 1986, pp. 163–176.

Morgan, David [O.], *The Mongols*, Oxford, Blackwell, 1986.

Morgan, David [O.], "The Mongols and the Eastern Mediterranean," *Mediterranean Historical Review*, vol. 4, 1989, pp. 198–211.

Mote, F. W., and L. Carrington Goodrich, "Chu Ti," *Dictionary of Ming Biography 1368–1644*, ed. L. Carrington Goodrich and Chaoying Fang, New York, Columbia University Press, 1976, pp. 355–365.

Mottahedeh, Roy P., *Loyalty and Leadership in an Early Islamic Society*, Princeton University Press, 1980.

Müller, Ludolf, *Die Kritik des Protestantismus in der russischen Theologie vom 16. bis zum 18. Jahrhundert*, Wiesbaden, Akademie der Wissenschaften und der Literatur in Mainz, in Komm. bei F. Steiner Verlag, 1951.

Nasonov, A. N., *Mongoly i Rus' (Istoriia tatarskoi politiki na Rusi)*, Moscow and Leningrad, Akademiia nauk SSSR, 1940.

Nazarevs'kyj, O. [A. A. Nazarevskii], "Otchet o zaniatii v Voronezhskom gubernskom muzee," *Universitetskie izvestiia*, Kiev, 1912, no. 8, pp. 36–40.

Nazarevs'kyi, O., "Znadoby do istorii davn'oi povisty," *Zapysky Istorychno-filolohichnoho viddilu Vseukrains'koi akademii nauk*, vol. 25, 1929, pp. 315–335.

Needham, Joseph, et al., *Science and Civilisation in China*, 6 vols. in 16 pts., Cambridge University Press, 1954–1988.

Needham, Joseph, *Clerks and Craftsmen in China and the West: Lectures and Addresses on the History of Science and Technology*, Cambridge University Press, 1970.

Nicolle, David, *The Mongol Warlords: Genghis Khan, Kublai Khan, Hülegü, Tamerlane*, Poole, Dorset, Firebird Books, 1990.

Noonan, Thomas S., "Russia's Eastern Trade, 1150–1350: the Archaeological Evidence," *Archivum Eurasiae Medii Aevi*, vol. 3, 1983, pp. 201–264.

Novaković, Stojan, *Matije Vlastara Sintagmat, azbuchni zbornik vizantijskikh crkvenikh drzhavnikh zakona i pravila*, Belgrad, Štampano u Državnoj štampariji, 1907.

Obolensky, Dimitri, "Byzantium, Kiev and Moscow: a Study in Ecclesiastical Relations," *Dumbarton Oaks Papers*, vol. 11, 1957, pp. 23–78.

Obolensky, Dimitri, "The Relations Between Byzantium and Russia (Eleventh to Fifteenth Century)," *XIII International Congress of Historical Sciences. Moscow, August 16–23, 1970*, Moscow, Nauka, 1970, pp. 1–13.

Obolensky, Dimitri, "Some Notes Concerning a Byzantine Portrait of John VIII Palaeologus," *Eastern Churches Review*, vol. 4, 1972, pp. 141–146.

Obolensky, Dimitri, "A Byzantine Grand Embassy to Russia in 1400," *Byzantine and Modern Greek Studies*, vol. 4, 1978, pp. 123–132.

Ocherki istorii SSSR, 9 vols., Moscow, Akademii nauk SSSR, 1953–1958, *Period feodalizma konets XV v.–nachalo XVII v.*, ed. A. N. Nasonov, L. V. Cherepnin, and A. A. Zimin.

Oderborn, Paul, *Ioannis Basilidi Magni Moscoviae Ducis vita*, Görlitz, Heinrich Räteln zu Sagan, 1589.

Oesterly, W. O. E., *The Books of the Apocrypha: Their Origin, Teaching, and Contents*, London, Robert Scott, 1914.

Ohridski, Kliment, *S"brani s"chineniia*, ed. B. St. Angelov, K. M. Kuev, and Kh. Kodov, 3 vols., Sofiia, Bulgarska akademiia na naukite, 1970–1973.

Olbricht, P., *Das Postwesen in China unter der Mongolenherrschaft im 13. und 14. Jahrhundert*, Wiesbaden, Otto Harrassowitz, 1954.

Oreshnikov, A., *Russkie monety do 1547 g.*, Moscow, Tipografiia A. I. Mamontova, 1896.

Ostrogorsky, George, "Avtokrator i Samodržac," *Glas Srpska Kral'jevski Akademije*, no. 164, Belgrade, 1935, pp. 95–187.

Ostrogorsky, Georg, "Die byzantinische Staatenhierarchie," *Seminarium Kondakovianum*, vol. 8, 1936, pp. 41–61; reprinted in George Ostrogorsky, *Zur byzantinischen Geschichte. Ausgewählte kleine Schriften*, Darmstadt, Wissenschaftliche Buchgesellschaft, 1973, pp. 119–141.

Ostrogorsky, Georg, "The Byzantine Emperor and the Hierarchical World Order," *Slavonic and East European Review*, vol. 35, 1956–1957, pp. 1–14.

Ostrogorsky, Georg[e], *History of the Byzantine State*, trans. Joan Hussey, New Brunswick, NJ, Rutgers University Press, 1969.

Ostrowski, Donald, "A 'Fontological' Investigation of the Muscovite Church Council of 1503," Ph.D. Dissertation, Pennsylvania State University, 1977.

Ostrowski, Donald, "Church Polemics and Monastic Land Acquisition in Sixteenth-Century Muscovy," *Slavonic and East European Review*, vol. 64, 1986, pp. 355–379; reprinted in *Major Problems in Early Modern Russian History*, pp. 129–153.

Ostrowski, Donald, "The Historian and the Virtual Past," *The Historian: a Journal of History*, vol. 51, 1989, pp. 201–220.

Ostrowski, Donald, "A Metahistorical Analysis: Hayden White and Four Narratives of 'Russian' History," *Clio*, vol. 19, 1990, pp. 215–236.

Ostrowski, Donald, "The Mongol Origins of Muscovite Political Institutions," *Slavic Review*, vol. 49, 1990, pp. 525–542.

Ostrowski, Donald, "What Makes a Translation Bad? Gripes of an End User," *Harvard Ukrainian Studies*, vol. 14, 1990, pp. 429–446, and "Errata," *Harvard Ukrainian Studies*, vol. 16, 1992, p. 237.

Ostrowski, Donald, "The Military Land Grant Along the Muslim–Christian Frontier," *Russian History*, vol. 19, 1992, pp. 327–359, and "Errata," *Russian History*, vol. 21, 1994, pp. 249–250.

Ostrowski, Donald, "Why Did the Metropolitan Move from Kiev to Vladimir in the Thirteenth Century?" *California Slavic Studies*, vol. 16, 1993, pp. 83–101.

Ostrowski, Donald, "The *Tamma* and the Dual-Administrative Structure of the Mongol Empire," *Bulletin of the School of Oriental and African Studies*, vol. 61, 1998 (forthcoming).

Oxford Dictionary of Byzantium, 3 vols., ed. Alexander P. Kazhdan, New York, Oxford University Press, 1991.

Paszkiewicz, Henryk, *The Rise of Moscow's Power*, trans. P. S. Falla, Boulder, CO, East European Monographs, 1983.

Pateman, Carole, *The Sexual Contract*, Stanford University Press, 1988.

Paterson, W. F., "The Archers of Islam," *Journal of the Economic and Social History of the Orient*, vol. 9, 1966, pp. 69–87.

Patlagean, Evelyne, "Byzantium in the Tenth and Eleventh Centuries," in *A History of Private Life*, 5 vols., ed. Philippe Ariès and Georges Duby, Cambridge, MA, Belknap Press, 1987–1991, vol. 1: *From Pagan Rome to Byzantium*, pp. 553–641.

Pavlov, A. S., "Vopros o eresi zhidovstvuiushchikh na VI Arkheologicheskom s"ezde," *Sovremennye izvestiia*, Odessa, 1884, no. 266.

Payne, Robert, and Nikita Romanov, *Ivan the Terrible*, New York, Thomas Y. Crowell, 1975.

Pelenski, Jaroslaw, "Muscovite Imperial Claims to the Kazan' Khanate," *Slavic Review*, vol. 26, 1967, pp. 559–576.

Pelenski, Jaroslaw, *Russia and Kazan: Conquest and Imperial Ideology (1438–1560s)*, The Hague, Mouton, 1974.

Pelenski, Jaroslaw, "The Origins of the Official Muscovite Claims to the 'Kievan Inheritance,'" *Harvard Ukrainian Studies*, vol. 1, 1977, pp. 29–52.

Pelenski, Jaroslaw, "The Sack of Kiev of 1482 in Contemporary Muscovite Chronicle Writing," *Harvard Ukrainian Studies*, vol. 3/4, 1979–80, pp. 638–649.

Pelenski, Jaroslaw, "State and Society in Muscovite Russia and the Mongol-Turkic System in the Sixteenth Century," in *Mutual Effects of the Islamic and Judeo-Christian Worlds: the East European Pattern*, ed. Abraham Ascher, Tibor Halasi-Kun, and Béla K. Király, Brooklyn College Press, 1979, pp. 93–109; reprinted in *Forschungen zur osteuropäischen Geschichte*, vol. 27, 1980, pp. 156–167.

Pelenski, Jaroslaw, "The Contest Between Lithuania-Rus' and the Golden Horde in the Fourteenth Century for Supremacy over Eastern Europe," *Archivum Eurasiae Medii Aevi*, vol. 2, 1982, pp. 303–320.

Pelenski, Jaroslaw, "The Emergence of the Muscovite Claims to the Byzantine-Kievan 'Imperial Inheritance,'" *Harvard Ukrainian Studies* (= *Okeanos: Essays Presented to Ihor Ševčenko on His Sixtieth Birthday by His Colleagues and Students*), vol. 7, 1983, pp. 520–531.

Pelenski, Jaroslaw, "The Sack of Kiev of 1169: Its Significance for the Succession to Kievan Rus'," *Harvard Ukrainian Studies*, vol. 11, 1987, pp. 303–316.

Pelliot, Paul, "Les Mongols et la Papauté," *Revue de l'Orient chrétien*, vol. 23, 1922, pp. 4–30; vol. 24, 1924, pp. 225–335; vol. 28, 1931–32, pp. 3–84.

Pelliot, Paul, *Notes on Marco Polo. Ouvrage posthume*, 3 vols., Paris, Imprimerie nationale. Librairie Adrien-Maisonneuve, 1959–1973.

Penzer, N. M., *The Ḥarēm: an Account of the Institution as It Existed in the Palace of the Turkish Sultan*, London, Spring Books, 1965.

Peters, Emrys, "The Proliferation of Segments in the Lineage of the Bedouin of Cyrenaica," *Journal of the Royal Anthropological Institute*, vol. 90, 1960, pp. 29–53.

Peters, Emrys, "Some Structural Aspects of the Feud Among the Camel-Herding Bedouin of Cyrenaica," *Africa*, vol. 37, 1967, pp. 261–282.

Peterson, Claes, *Peter the Great's Administrative and Judicial Reforms: Swedish Antecedents and the Process of Reception*, trans. Michael F. Metcalf, Stockholm, A.-B. Nordska, 1979.

Petrushevskii, I. P., *Zemledelie i agrarnye otnosheniia v Irane XIII–XIV vekov*, Moscow and Leningrad, Akademiia nauk SSSR, 1960.

Peyrefitte, Alain, *The Collison of Two Civilizations: the British Expedition to China, 1792–4*, trans. Jon Rothschild, London, Harvill, 1992.

Phillips, E. D., *The Mongols*, London, Thames & Hudson, 1969.

Piltz, Elisabeth, *Trois sakkoi byzantins. Analyse iconographique*, Stockholm, Almqvist & Wiksell, 1976.

Pipes, Richard, *Russia under the Old Regime*, New York, Charles Scribner's Sons, 1974.

Platonov, S. F., *Lektsii po russkoi istorii*, 3 vols., St. Petersburg, Stolichnaia staropechatnia, 1899.

Platonov, S. F., *Ivan Groznyi*, St. Petersburg, Brokgauz-Efron, 1923.

Platonov, S. F., *History of Russia*, trans. E. Aronsberg, New York, Macmillan, 1925.

Platonov, S. F., *Moskva i zapad*, Berlin, Obelisk, 1926.

Platonov, S. F., *Ocherki po istorii smuty v Moskovskom gosudarstve XVI–XVII vv.*, Moscow, Sotsekgiz, 1937.

Plavsic, Borivoj, "Seventeenth-Century Chanceries and Their Staffs," in *Russian Officialdom: the Bureaucratization of Russian Society, from the Seventeenth to the Twentieth Century*, ed. Walter McKenzie Pintner and Don Karl Rowney, Chapel Hill, NC, University of North Carolina Press, 1980, pp. 19–45; reprinted in *Major Problems in Early Modern Russian History*, pp. 155–181.

Pliguzov, A. I., "Drevneishii spisok kratkogo sobraniia iarlykov, dannykh ordynskimi khanami russkim mitropolitam," in *RFA*, vol. 3, 1987, pp. 571–594.

Pliguzov, A. I., "Bitva na Kulikovom pole v svidetel'stvakh sovremennikov i v pamiati potomkov," in *Zhivaia voda Nepriadvy*, Moscow, Molodaia gvardiia, 1988, pp. 389–634.

Pliguzov, A.I. [Andrei], "On the Title 'Metropolitan of Kiev and All Rus','" *Harvard Ukrainian Studies*, vol. 15, 1991, pp. 340–353.

Pliguzov, A. I., "'Otvet' Mitropolita Makariia Tsariu Ivanu IV," *RFA*, vol. 4, 1988, pp. 717–748.

Pliguzov, A. I., "O titule 'Mitropolit Kievskii i vseia Rusi,'" *RFA*, vol. 5, 1992, pp. 1034–1042.

Pliguzov, A. I. [Andrei], "Tikhon of Rostov, or Russian Political Games in 1489," *Russian History*, vol. 22, 1995, pp. 309–320.

Pliguzov, A. I., and I. A. Tikhoniuk, "Poslanie Dmitriia Trakhaniota novgorodskomu arkhiepiskopu Gennadiiu Gonzovu o sedmerichnosti schisleniia let," in *Estestvennonauchnye predstavleniia Drevnei Rusi*, ed. R. A. Simonov, Moscow, Nauka, 1988, pp. 51–71.

Poe, Marshall, "'Russian Despotism': the Origins and Dissemination of an

Early Modern Commonplace," Ph.D. Dissertation, University of California, Berkeley, 1993.

Poe, Marshall, "What Did Muscovites Mean When They Called Themselves 'Slaves of the Tsar'?" *Slavic Review* (forthcoming).

Pokrovskii, M. N., *History of Russia: From the Earliest Times to the Rise of Commercial Capitalism*, trans. and ed. Jesse D. Clarkson and M. R. M. Griffiths, Bloomington, IN, University Prints and Reprints, 1966 [1928].

Poluboiarinova, M. D., *Russkie liudi v Zolotoi Orde*, Moscow, Nauka, 1978.

Pomeroy, Sarah B., *Goddesses, Whores, Wives and Slaves*, New York, Schoken Books, 1975.

Pope, Richard W. F., "Bulgaria: the Third Christian Kingdom in the *Razumnik-Ukaz*," *Slavia*, vol. 43, 1974, pp. 141–153.

Pope, Richard W. F., "A Possible South Slavic Source for the Doctrine: Moscow the Third Rome," *Slavia*, vol. 44, 1975, pp. 246–253.

Prawdin, Michael, *The Mongol Empire: Its Rise and Legacy*, London, George Allen and Unwin, 1940.

Presniakov, A. E., *Obrazovanie velikorusskogo gosudarstva. Ocherki po istorii XII–XV stoletii*, Petrograd, Ia. Bashmakov, 1918.

Presniakov, A. E., *The Formation of the Great Russian State*, trans. A. E. Moorhouse, Chicago, Quadrangle Books, 1970.

Priselkov, M. D., *Khanskie iarlyki russkim mitropolitam*, St. Petersburg, Nauchnoe delo, 1916.

Pritsak, Omeljan, "Moscow, the Golden Horde, and the Kazan Khanate from a Polycultural Point of View," *Slavic Review*, vol. 26, 1967, pp. 577–583.

Pritsak, Omeljan, *The Origin of Rus'*, vol. 1: *Old Scandinavian Sources Other than the Sagas*, Cambridge, MA, Harvard University Press, 1981.

Pritsak, Omeljan and Anthony Cutter, "Mongols," in *Oxford Dictionary of Byzantium*, p. 1395.

Pushkarev, L. N., "Povest' o zachale Moskvy," *Materialy po istorii SSSR*, 7 vols., Moscow and Leningrad, Akademiia nauk SSSR, 1955–1959, vol. 2: *Dokumenty po istorii XV–XVII vv.*, pp. 211–246.

Putnam, Robert D., "Studying Elite Political Culture: the Case of 'Ideology,'" *American Political Science Review*, vol. 65, 1971, pp. 651–681.

Raba, Joel, review of The *"Chosen Council"*, *Canadian–American Slavic Studies*, vol. 6, 1972, p. 497.

Rachewiltz, Igor de, "Yeh-lü Ch'u-ts'ai (1189–1243): Buddhist Idealist and Confucian Statesman," in *Confucian Personalities*, ed. A. F. Wright and D. Twichett, Stanford University Press, 1962, pp. 189–216, 361–367.

Rachewiltz, Igor de, "Personnel and Personalities in North China in the Early Mongol Period," *Journal of the Economic and Social History of the Orient*, vol. 9, 1966, pp. 88–144.

Rachewiltz, Igor de, *Papal Envoys to the Great Khans*, Stanford University Press, 1971.

Rachewiltz, Igor de, "Some Remarks on the Ideological Foundation of Chinggis Khan's Empire," *Papers on Far Eastern History*, vol. 7, 1973, pp. 21–36.

Raeff, Marc, "An Early Theorist of Absolutism: Joseph of Volokolamsk," *American Slavic and East European Review*, vol. 8, 1949, pp. 77–89, reprinted without footnotes in *Readings in Russian History*, vol. 1, pp. 177–187.

Rasmussen, Knud, "On the Information Level of the Muscovite Posol'skij Prikaz in the Sixteenth Century," *Forschungen für osteuropäischen Geschichte*, vol. 24, 1978, pp. 87–99.

Ratchnevsky, Paul, "La condition de la femme mongole au 12e/13e siècle," in *Tractata Altaica Denis Sinor*, ed. Walter Heissig, John R. Krueger, Felix J. Oinas, and Edmund Schültz, Wiesbaden, Otto Harrasowitz, 1976, pp. 509–530.

Ratchnevsky, Paul, *Genghis Khan: His Life and Legacy*, trans. and ed. Thomas Nivison Haining, Oxford, Blackwell, 1991.

Readings in Russian History, ed. Sidney Harcave, 2 vols., New York, Thomas Y. Crowell, 1962.

Les regestes des actes du Patriarcat de Constantinople, vol. 1: *Les actes des patriarches*, 7 fascs., ed. J. Darrouzès, Paris, Institut Français d'études byzantines, 1972–1979.

Reid, Robert W., "Mongolian Weaponry in *The Secret History of the Mongols*," *Mongolian Studies*, vol. 15, 1992, pp. 85–95.

Reischauer, Edwin O., and John K. Fairbank, *East Asia: the Great Tradition*, Boston, Houghton Mifflin, 1960.

Rémusat, Jean Pierre Abel, *Nouveaux mélanges asiatiques*, 2 vols., Paris, Schubert et Heideloff, 1829.

Riasanovsky, Nicholas, "'Oriental Despotism' and Russia," *Slavic Review*, vol. 22, 1963, pp. 644–649; reprinted in *Development of the USSR*, pp. 340–345.

Riasanovsky, Nicholas, *A History of Russia*, 4th edn, New York, Oxford University Press, 1984.

Riasanovsky, V. A., "The Influence of Ancient Mongol Culture and Law on Russian Culture and Law," *Chinese Social and Political Science Review*, vol. 20, 1937, pp. 499–530.

Riasanovsky, V. A., *Fundamental Principles of Mongol Law*, Tientsin, 1937.

Richard, J., "La conversion de Berke et les débuts de l'islamisation de la Horde d'Or," *Revue des études islamiques*, 1967, pp. 173–184.

Richter, Melvin, "Despotism," *Dictionary of the History of Ideas: Studies of Selected Pivotal Ideas*, 5 vols., ed. Philip P. Wiener, New York, Charles Scribner's Sons, 1973, vol. 2, pp. 1–18.

Rikman, E. A., "Obsledovanie gorodov Tverskogo kniazhestva," *Kratkie soobshcheniia o dokladakh i polevykh issledovaniiakh Instituta istorii materi-al'noi kul'tury AN SSSR*, vol. 41, 1951, pp. 71–84.

Rossabi, Morris, "Khubilai Khan and the Women in His Family," in *Studia Sino–Mongolica: Festschrift für Herbert Franke*, ed. Wolfgang Bauer, Wiesbaden, Franz Steiner, Verlag, 1979, pp. 153–180.

Rossabi, Morris, "The Muslims in the Early Yüan Dynasty," in *China Under Mongol Rule*, ed. John D. Langlois, Jr., Princeton University Press, 1981, pp. 257–295.

Rowland, Daniel, "The Problem of Advice in Muscovite Tales About the Time of Troubles," *Russian History*, vol. 6, 1979, pp. 259–283.

Rowland, Daniel, "Towards an Understanding of the Political Ideas in Ivan Timofeev's *Vremennik*," *Slavonic and East European Review*, vol. 62, 1984, pp. 371–399.

Rowland, Daniel, "Shchelkalov, Vasilii Iakovlevich," in *MERSH*, vol. 31, pp. 180–182.

Rowland, Daniel, "Did Muscovite Literary Ideology Place Limits on the Power of the Tsar (1540s–1660s)?" *Russian Review*, vol. 49, 1990, pp. 125–155.

Rowland, Daniel, "The Political Messages of the Golden Palace," paper delivered at the 27th AAASS Convention in Washington, DC, October 29, 1995.

Rowland, Daniel, "Moscow – The Third Rome or the New Israel?" *Russian Review*, vol. 55, 1996, pp. 591–614.

Rozov, N. N., "Povest' o novgorodskom belom klobuke kak pamiatnik obshcherusskoi publitsistiki XV veka," *TODRL*, vol. 9, 1953, pp. 178–219.

Ruggiero, Guido, *The Boundaries of Eros: Sex Crime and Sexuality in Renaissance Venice*, Oxford University Press, 1985.

Runciman, Steven, *The Emperor Romanus Lecapenus and His Reign*, Cambridge University Press, 1929.

Runciman, Steven, *A History of the Crusades*, 3 vols., Cambridge University Press, 1951–1954.

Runciman, Steven, "The Greek Church Under the Ottoman Turks," *Studies in Church History*, vol. 2, 1957, pp. 38–53.

Runciman, Steven, "Some Notes on the Role of the Empress," *Eastern Churches Review*, vol. 4, 1972, pp. 119–124.

Runciman, Steven, "Patriarch Jeremias II and the Patriarchate of Moscow," *Aksum Thyateira: a Festschrift for Archbishop Methodios of Thyateira and Great Britain*, ed. George Dion. Dragos, London, Thyateira House, 1985, pp. 235–240.

Rybakov, B. A., *Remeslo drevnei Rusi*, Moscow, Akademiia nauk SSSR, 1948.

Rybakov, B. A., *Drevniaia Rus'. Skazaniia. Byliny. Letopisi*, Moscow, Akademiia nauk SSSR, 1963.

Rygdylon, E. R., "O mongol'skom termine *ongu-bogol*," *Filologiia i istoriia mongol'skikh narodov. Pamiati Akademika Borisa Iakovlevicha Vladimirtsova*, Moscow, Vostochnaia literatura, 1958, pp. 166–172.

Sadikov, P. A., *Ocherki po istorii oprichniny*, Moscow and Leningrad, Akademiia nauk SSSR, 1950.

Sakharov, A. M., "Rus' and Its Culture, Thirteenth to Fifteenth Centuries," *Soviet Studies in History*, vol. 18, no. 3, 1979–1980, pp. 26–32.

Salisbury, Harrison E., *War Between Russia and China*, New York, Norton, 1969.

Salmina, M. A., "Letopisnaia povest' o Kulikovskoi bitve i 'Zadonshchina,'" in *Slovo o polku Igoreve i pamiatniki Kulikovskogo tsikla. K voprosu o vremeni napisaniia 'Slova'*, ed. D. S. Likhachev and L. A. Dmitriev, Moscow and Leningrad, Nauka, 1966, pp. 344–384.

Salmina, M. A., "'Slovo o zhitii i o prestavlenii velikogo kniaza Dmitriia Ivanovicha, tsaria Rus'skago,'" *TODRL*, vol. 25, 1970, pp. 81–104.

Salmina, M. A., "K voprosu o datirovke 'Skazanie o Mamaevom poboishche,'" *TODRL*, vol. 29, 1974, pp. 98–124.

Salmina, M. A., "Eshche raz o datirovke 'Letopisnoi povesti' o Kulikovskoi bitve," *TODRL*, vol. 32, 1977, pp. 3–39.

Salzman, Philip Carl, "Introduction: Process of Sedentarization as Adaptation and Response," in *When Nomads Settle: Processes of Sedenterization as Adaptation and Response*, ed. Philip Carl Salzman, New York, Praeger, 1980, pp. 1–19.

Sansom, G. B., *Japan in World History*, Tokyo, Kenkyusha Press, 1951.

Saunders, J. J., *A History of Medieval Islam*, London, Routledge & Kegan Paul, 1965.

Saunders, J. J., *History of the Mongol Conquests*, London, Routledge & Kegan Paul, 1971.

Savva, V., *Moskovskie tsari i vizantiiskie vasilevsy k voprosu o vliianii Vizantii na obrazovanie idei tsarskoi vlasti moskovskikh gosudarei*, Khar'kov, M. Zil'berberg, 1901.

Schaeder, Hildegard, *Moskau des dritte Rom. Studien zur Geschichte der politischen Theorien in der slavischen Welt* (= *Osteuropäische Studien*, vol. 1), Hamburg, Friederichsen, de Gruyter, 1929; 2nd edn, Darmstadt, 1957.

Schamiloglu, Uli, "The *Qaraçï* Beys of the Later Golden Horde: Notes on the Organization of the Mongol World Empire," *Archivum Eurasiae Medii Aevi*, vol. 4, 1984, pp. 283–297.

Schamiloglu, Uli, "Tribal Politics and Social Organization in the Golden Horde," Ph.D. Dissertation, Columbia University, 1986.

Schamiloglu, Uli, "Reinterpreting the Nomad–Sedentary Relationship in the Golden Horde (13th–14th Centuries)," paper presented at the Conference on the Role of the Frontier in Rus'/Russian History, the Eighth through the Eighteenth Centuries, Chicago, May 29–31, 1992.

Schamiloglu, Uli, *The Golden Horde: Economy, Society and Civilization in Western Eurasia, 13th and 14th Centuries* (unpublished).

Scharf, J., "Photius und die Epanagoge," *Byzantinische Zeitschrift*, vol. 49, 1956, pp. 385–400.

Schreiner, P., "Hochzeit und Krönung Kaiser Manuels II im Jahre 1392," *Byzantinishce Zeitschrift*, vol. 60, 1967, pp. 70–85.

Schurmann, H[erbert] F[ranz], "Mongolian Tributary Practices of the Thirteenth Century," *Harvard Journal of Asiatic Studies*, vol. 19, 1956, pp. 304–389.

Schurmann, Herbert Franz, *Economic Structure of the Yüan Dynasty*, Harvard Yenching Institute Studies, no. 16, Cambridge, MA, Harvard University Press, 1967.

Schuyler, Eugene, *Peter the Great Emperor of Russia: a Study of Historical Biography*, 2 vols., New York, Charles Scribner's Sons, 1884.

Serebrianskii, N[ikolai], *Drevne-russkie kniazheskie zhitiia. (Obzor redaktsii i teksty)*, Moscow, Sinodal'naia tipografiia, 1915.

Serruys, Henry, "*Pei-lou fong-sou. Les coutumes des esclaves septertrionaux de Hsiao Ta-heng*," *Monumenta Serica*, vol. 10, 1945, pp. 117–164; reprinted in Henry Serruys, *The Mongols and Ming China: Customs and History*, ed. Francoise Aubin, London, Variorum, 1987, item 1.

Ševčenko, Ihor, "Notes on Stephen the Novgorodian Pilgrim to Constantinople in the XIV Century," *Südost-Forschungen*, vol. 12, 1953, pp. 165–175; reprinted in Ševčenko, *Society and Intellectual Life*, item XV.

Ševčenko, Ihor, review of *Podil iedynoi Khrystovoi tserkvy* by Mytropolyt Ilarion, in *Südost-Forschungen*, vol. 13, 1954, pp. 387–389; review reprinted in Ševčenko, *Byzantium and the Slavs*, pp. 89–91.

Ševčenko, Ihor, "A Neglected Byzantine Source of Muscovite Political Ideology," *Harvard Slavic Studies*, vol. 2, 1954, pp. 141–179; reprinted in *Structure of Russian History*, pp. 80–105, and in Ševčenko, *Byzantium and the Slavs*, pp. 49–87.

Ševčenko, Ihor, "Some Autographs of Nicephorus Gregoras," *Mélanges Georges Ostrogorsky II. Zbornik Radova Vizantoloshkog Instituta*, vol. 8, 1964, p. 448; reprinted in Ševčenko, *Society and Intellectual Life*, item XII.

Ševčenko, Ihor, "Muscovy's Conquest of Kazan: Two Views Reconciled," *Slavic Review*, vol. 26, 1967, pp. 541–547.

Ševčenko, Ihor, "Agapetus East and West: Fate of a Byzantine 'Mirror of Princes,'" *Revue des études sud-est Européennes*, vol. 16, 1978, pp. 1–44.

Ševčenko, Ihor, "Byzantium and the Eastern Slavs After 1453," *Harvard Ukrainian Studies*, vol. 2, 1978, pp. 5–25.

Ševčenko, Ihor, *Society and Intellectual Life in Late Byzantium*, London, Variorum, 1981.

Ševčenko, Ihor, *Byzantium and the Slavs: In Letters and Culture*, Cambridge, MA, Harvard Ukrainian Research Institute, 1991.

Ševčenko, Ihor, "A New Greek Source Concerning the Nikon Affair: Sixty-One Answers by Paisios Ligarides Given to Tsar Aleksej Mikhajlovič," unpublished paper read at Early Slavicists Luncheon, Russian Research Center, March 19, 1996.

Severin, Tim, *In Search of Genghis Khan*, London, Hutchinson, 1991.

Shakhmatov, A. A., "Puteshestvie M. G. Misiuria Munekhina na Vostok i Khronograf redaktsii 1512 g.," *Izvestiia Otdeleniia russkogo iazyka i slovesnosti*, vol. 4, 1899, pp. 200–222.

Shakhmatov, A. A., *Otzyv o sochinenii S. K. Shambinago "Povesti o Mamaevom poboishche"*, St. Petersburg, 1910.

Shakhmatov, A. A., *Obozrenie russkikh letopisnykh svodov XIV–XVI vv.*, Moscow and Leningrad, Akademiia nauk SSSR, 1938.

Shambinago, S. K., "Povesti o Mamaevom poboishche," in *Sbornik Otdeleniia russkogo iazyka i slovesnosti*, vol. 81, 1906, no. 7.

Shambinago, S. K., "Povesti o nachale Moskvy," *TODRL*, vol. 3, 1936, pp. 59–98.

Shapiro, A. L., "Ob absoliutizme v Rossii," *Istorii SSSR*, 1968, no. 5, pp. 69–82.

Shapiro, A. L., *Problemy sotsial'no-ekonomicheskoi istorii Rusi XIV–XVI vv.*, Izdatel'stvo Leningradskogo universiteta, 1977.

Shchapov, Ia. N., *Vostochnoslavianskie i iuzhnoslavianskie rukopisnye knigi v sobraniiakh Polskoi narodnoi respubliki*, 2 vols., Moscow, Institut istorii SSSR, 1976.

Shcherbatov, M. M., *Istoriia rossiiskaia*, 7 vols., St. Petersburg, M. M. Stasiulevich, 1901–1904 [originally published 1770–1791].

Sheviakov, V. N., "K voprosu ob oprichnine pri Ivan IV," *Voprosy istorii*, 1956, no. 9, pp. 71–77.

[Shmurlo, Evgenii] *Rossiia i Italiia. Sbornik istoricheskikh materialov i issledovanii*, 4 vols., St. Petersburg, Imperatorskaia Akademiia nauk, 1907–1911, Leningrad, Akademiia nauk SSSR, 1927.

Sinor, Denis, "On Mongol Strategy," *Proceedings of the Fourth East Asian Altaistic Conference*, December 26–31, 1971, Taipei, China, ed. Ch'en Chieh-hsien, Department of History, National Ch'engkung University, Tainan, Taiwan, ROC, n.d., pp. 238–249.

Skrynnikov, R. G., *Nachalo oprichniny*, Izdatel'stvo Leningradskogo universiteta, 1966.

Skrynnikov, R. G., *Oprichnyi terror*, Izdatel'stvo Leningradskogo universiteta, 1969.

Skrynnikov, R. G., *Ivan Groznyi*, Moscow, Nauka, 1975.

Skrynnikov, R. G., *Rossiia posle oprichniny*, Izdatel'stvo Leningradskogo universiteta, 1975.

Skrynnikov, R. G., *Boris Godunov*, Moscow, Nauka, 1978.

Skrynnikov, Ruslan G., *Ivan the Terrible*, ed. and trans. Hugh F. Graham, Gulf Breeze, FL, Academic International Press, 1981.

Skrynnikov, R. G., "An Overview of the Reign of Ivan IV: What Was the Oprichnina?" *Soviet Studies in History*, vol. 24, 1985, pp. 62–82.

Skrynnikov, R. G., "Obzor pravleniia Ivana IV," *Russian History*, vol. 14, 1987, pp. 361–376.

Skrynnikov, R. G., *Gosudarstvo i tserkov' na Rusi XIV–XVI vv. Podvizhniki russkoi tserkvi*, Novosibirsk, Nauka Sibirskoe otdelenie, 1991.

Skrynnikov, R. G., *Tretii Rim*, St. Petersburg, Dmitrii Bulanin, 1994.

Smirnov, I. I., "Sudebnik 1550 goda," *Istoricheskie zapiski*, vol. 24, 1947, pp. 267–352.

Smirnov, I. I., "Vostochnaia politika Vasiliia III," *Istoricheskie zapiski*, no. 27, 1948, pp. 18–66.

Smirnov, I. I., *Ocherki politicheskoi istorii russkogo gosudarstva 30–50^{kh} godov XVI veka*, Moscow and Leningrad, Akademiia nauk SSSR, 1958.

Smirnov, P. P., "Obrazovanie russkogo tsentralizovannogo gosudarstva v XIV–XVI vv.," *Voprosy istorii*, 1946, pts. 2–3, pp. 55–90.

Smith, John Masson, Jr., "Mongol and Nomadic Taxation," *Harvard Journal of Asiatic Studies*, vol. 30, 1970, pp. 46–85.

Smith, R. E. F., *The Enserfment of the Russian Peasantry*, Cambridge University Press, 1968.

Smith, R. E. F., *Peasant Farming in Muscovy*, Cambridge University Press, 1977.

Smolitsch, Igor, *Russisches Mönchtum. Entstehung, Entwicklung und Wesen, 988–1917* (Das östliche Christentum, N.S. no. 10–11), Wurzburg, Augustinus, 1953.

Sobolevskii, A. I., *Perevodnaia literatura Moskovskoi Rusi XIV–XVII vekov. Bibliograficheskie materialy*, in *Sbornik Otdeleniia russkogo iazyka i slovesnosti Imperatroskoi Akademii nauk*, vol. 74, no. 1, St. Petersburg, 1903.

Sokolov, P. P., "Podlozhnyi iarlyk khana Uzbeka mitropolitu Petru," *Russkii istoricheskii zhurnal*, no. 5, 1918, pp. 70–85.

Sokolov, P[laton], *Russkii arkhierei iz Vizantii i pravo ego naznacheniia do nachala XV veka*, Kiev, 1913.

Solov'ev, S. M., *Istoriia otnoshenii mezhdu kniaz'iami Riurika domu*, Moscow, 1847.

Solov'ev, S. M., *Istoriia Rossii s drevneishikh vremen*, 15 vols., Moscow, Sotsial'naia-ekonomicheskaia literatura, 1960–1966.

Soloviev, A. V., "Zu den Metropolitensiegeln des kiewer Rußlands," in *Byzantinische Zeitschrift*, vol. 56, 1963, pp. 317–320; reprinted in A. V. Soloviev, *Byzance et la formation de l'etat russe*, London, Variorum, 1979, item IXb.

Sovetskaia istoricheskaia entsiklopediia, 16 vols., ed. E. M. Zhukov, Moscow, Sovetskaia entsiklopediia, 1961–1976.

Spassky, I. G., *The Russian Monetary System: a Historico-Numismatic Survey*, trans. Z. I. Gorishina and L. S. Forrer, rev. edn, Amsterdam, Jacques Schuman N. V., 1967.

Špidlíak, Tomaš, *Joseph de Volokolamsk: Un chapitre de la spirtualité russe*, in *Orientalia Christiana Analecta*, vol. 146, 1956.

Spinka, Matthew, "Patriarch Nikon and the Subjection of the Russian Church to the State," *Church History*, vol. 10, 1941, pp. 347–366.

Spitsyn, A. A., "K voprosu o Monomakhovoi shapke," *Zapiski Russkogo arkheologicheskogo obshchestva. Otdelenie russkoi i slavianskoi arkheologii*, vol. 7, pt. 1, 1906, pp. 144–184.

Spuler, Bertold, *Die goldene Horde. Die Mongolen in Rußland*, Leipzig, Otto Harrassowitz, 1943.

Spuler, Bertold, "Russia and Islam," *Slavic Review*, vol. 22, 1963, pp. 650–655. Reprinted in *Development of the USSR*, pp. 346–351.

Stanton, Michael, "The Things That Are God's: the Rus' Church in the Fourteenth Century," unpublished paper.

Stone, Lawrence, *The Crisis of the Aristocracy, 1558–1641*, Oxford, Clarendon Press, 1965.

Strémooukhoff, Dmitri, "Moscow the Third Rome: Sources of the Doctrine," *Speculum*, vol. 28, 1953, pp. 91–101; reprinted in *Structure of Russian History*, pp. 108–125.

Stroev, Pavel, *Spiski ierarkhov i nastoiatelei rossiiskie tserkvi*, St. Petersburg, V. S. Balashev, 1877.

The Structure of Russian History: Interpretive Essays, ed. Michael Cherniavsky, New York, Random House, 1970.

Subbotin, N. [S – n], "Kak izdaiutsia u nas knizhki o raskole," *Russkii vestnik*, vol. 10, 1862, pp. 363–365.

Sumner, B. H., *A Short History of Russia*, New York, Harcourt, 1949,

Syroechkovskii, V. E., "Puti i usloviia snoshenii Moskvy s Krymom na rubezhe XVI veka," *Izvestiia Akademii nauk SSSR. Otdelenie obshchestvennykh nauk*, 1932, no. 3, pp. 193–237 + map.

Sysyn, Frank E., "The Cultural, Social and Political Context of Ukrainian History-Writing: 1620–1690," *Europa Orientalis*, vol. 5, 1986, pp. 285–310.

Sysyn, Frank E., "Concepts of Nationhood in Ukrainian History Writing, 1620–1690," *Harvard Ukrainian Studies*, vol. 10, 1986, pp. 393–423.

Szamuely, Tibor, *The Russian Tradition*, London, Secker & Warburg, 1974.

Szczesniak, Boleslaw, "A Note on the Character of the Tatar Impact upon the

Russian State and Church," *Études Slaves et Est-Européens*, vol. 17, 1972, pp. 92–97.

Szeftel, Marc, "The Form of Government of the Russian Empire Prior to the Constitutional Reforms of 1905–06," in *Essays in Russian and Soviet History: In Honor of Geroid Tanquary Robinson*, ed. John Shelton Curtiss, Leiden, E. J. Brill, 1963, pp. 105–119.

Szeftel, Marc, "Joseph Volotsky's Political Ideas in a New Political Perspective," *Jahrbücher für Geschichte Osteuropas*, vol. 13, 1965, pp. 19–29; reprinted in Marc Szeftel, *Russian Institutions and Culture Up to Peter the Great*, London, Variorum, 1975, item 7.

Szeftel, Marc, "The Title of the Muscovite Monarch Up to the End of the Seventeenth Century," *Canadian–American Slavic Studies*, vol. 13, 1979, pp. 59–81.

Tachiaos, Anthony-Emil N., "The Testament of Photius Monembasiotes, Metropolitan of Russia (1408–1431): Byzantine Ideology in XVth-Century Muscovy," *Cyrillo-methodianum*, vol. 8/9, 1984–85, pp. 77–109.

Tatishchev, V. N., *Istoriia Rossiiskaia*, 7 vols., Moscow and Leningrad, Akademiia nauk SSSR, 1962–1968.

Taube, Moshe, "The Kievan Jew Zacharia and the Astronomical Work of the Judaizers," in *Jews and Slavs*, ed. Wolf Moskovich, Samuel Schwarzband, and Anatoly Alekseev, 3 vols., Jerusalem, Israel Academy of Sciences and Humanities; Hebrew University of Jerusalem, Dept of Russian and Slavic Studies, Center for the Study of Slavic Languages and Literature; St. Petersburg, Slavonic Bible Foundation, Russian Academy of Sciences, 1993–1995, vol. 3: *Ioudaikh arxaiologia: In Honour of Professor Moshe Altbauer*, pp. 168–198.

Temple, Robert, *The Genius of China: 3,000 Years of Science, Discovery and Invention*, New York, Simon & Schuster, 1986.

Thompson, J. M., *The French Revolution*, New York, Oxford University Press, 1945.

Thomson, Francis J., "The Nature of the Reception of Christian Byzantine Culture in Russia in the Tenth to Thirteenth Centuries and Its Implications for Russian Culture," *Slavica Gandensia*, vol. 5, 1978, pp. 107–139.

Tikhomirov, M. N., "Skazanie o nachale Moskvy," *Istoricheskie zapiski*, no. 32, 1950, pp. 233–241.

Tikhomirov, M. N., "Maloizvestnye letopisnye pamiatniki XVI v.," *Istoricheskii arkhiv*, vol. 7, 1951, pp. 207–253.

Tikhomirov, N. Ia., and V. I. Ivanov, *Moskovskii kreml'. Istoriia arkhitektury*, Moscow, Stroiizdat, 1966.

Tikhoniuk, I. A., "'Izlozhenie paskhalii' Moskovskogo mitropolita Zosimy," *Issledovaniia po istochnikovedeniiu istorii SSSR XIII–XVIII vv. Sbornik statei*, ed. V. I. Buganov, V. A. Kuchkin, and V. G. Litvak, Moscow, Akademiia nauk SSSR, 1986, pp. 45–57.

Tikhoniuk, I. A., "Chin postavleniia Dmitriia-vnuka," *RFA*, vol. 3, pp. 604–607.

Timofeev, A. G., *Istoriia telesnykh nakazanii v russkom prave*, 2nd edn, St. Petersburg, V. Bezobrazov, 1904.

Toumanoff, Cyril, "Moscow the Third Rome: Genesis and Significance of a

Politico-Religious Idea," *Catholic Historical Review*, vol. 40, 1954/55, pp. 411–447.

Trigger, Bruce G., "Monumental Architecture: a Thermodynamic Explanation of Symbolic Behavior," *World Archaeology*, vol. 22, 1990, pp. 119–132.

Troyat, Henri, *Ivan the Terrible*, trans. Joan Pinkham, New York, E. P. Dutton, 1984.

Trubetskoi, Nicholas [I. R.], *Nasledie Chingiskhana. Vzgliad na russkuiu istoriiu ne s Zapada, a s Vostka*, Berlin, Evraziiskoe izdatel'stvo, 1925.

Tumins, Valerie A., *Tsar Ivan IV's Reply to Jan Rokyta*, The Hague, Mouton, 1971.

Turan, Osman, "The Ideal of World Domination Among the Medieval Turks," *Studia Islamica*, vol. 4, 1955, pp. 77–90.

'Umarī, Ibn Fadl al-, *Das Mongolische Weltreich. Al-'Umarī's Darstellung der mongolischen Reiche in seinem Werk Masālik al-absār fī mamālik al-amsār*, paraphrase and commentary by Klaus Lech, Wiesbaden, Otto Harrassowitz, 1968.

Usmanov, M. A., "Etapy islamizatsii Dzuchieva ulusa i musul'manskoe dukhovenstvo v tatarskikh khanstvakh XIII–XVI vekov," in *Dukhovenstvo i politicheskaia zhizn' na Blizhnem i Srednem Vostoke v period feodalisma*, ed. G. F. Kim, G. F. Girs, and E. A. Davidovich, Moscow, Nauka, 1985, pp. 177–185.

Utechin, S. V., *Russian Political Thought: a Concise History*, New York, Frederick A. Praeger, 1963.

Vaglieri, Laura Veccia, "The Patriarchal and Umayyad Caliphates," in *The Cambridge History of Islam*, 2 vols., ed. P. M. Holt, Ann K. S. Lambton, and Bernard Lewis, Cambridge University Press, 1970, vol. 1A: *The Central Islamic Lands from Pre-Islamic Times to the First World War*, pp. 57–103.

Val'denberg, V. E. [Vladimir], *Drevnerusskie uchenie o predelakh tsarskoi vlasti. Ocherki russkoi politicheskoi literatury ot Vladimira Sviatogo do kontsa XVII veka*, Petrograd, A. Benke, 1916.

Val'denberg, V. E., "Poniatie o tiranne v drevnerusskoi literature v sravnenii s zapadnoi," *Izvestiia po russkomu iazyku i slovesnosti*, vol. 2, bk. 1, 1929, pp. 214–236.

Vásáry, Istvan, "The Golden Horde *Daruga* and Its Survival in Russia," *Acta Orientalia Academiae Scientiarium Hungaricae*, vol. 30, 1976, pp. 187–197.

Vásáry, Istvan, "The Origin of the Institution of *Basqaqs*," *Acta Orientalia Academiae Scientiarum Hungaricae*, vol. 32, 1978, pp. 201–206.

Vásáry, István, "History and Legend in Berke Khan's Conversion to Islam," *Aspects of Altaic Civilization III, Proceedings of the XXX PIAC, Bloomington*, ed. Denis Sinor, Bloomington, Asian Studies Research Institute, Indiana University, 1990, pp. 230–252.

Vasiliev, A. A., "Was Old Russia a Vassal State of Byzantium?" *Speculum*, vol. 7, 1932, pp. 350–360.

Vasmer [Fasmer], Max, *Etimologicheskii slovar' russkogo iazyka*, 2nd edn, 4 vols., trans. O. N. Trubachev, Moscow, Progress, 1986.

Vernadsky, George, "The Scope and Contents of Chingiz Khan's *Yasa*," *Harvard Journal of Asiatic Studies*, vol. 3, 1938, pp. 337–360.

Vernadsky, George, *A History of Russia*, 5 vols., New Haven, CT, Yale University Press, 1943–1969, vol. 1: *Ancient Russia*; vol. 3: *The Mongols and Russia*; vol. 4: *Russia at the Dawn of the Modern Age*; vol. 5: *The Tsardom of Muscovy 1547–1682*.

Veselovskii, N. I., *Khan iz temnikov Zolotoi Ordy Nogai i ego vremia*, Petrograd, Rossiiskaia akademiia nauk, 1922.

Veselovskii, S. B., "Uchrezhdenie oprichnogo dvora v 1565 g. i otmena ego v 1572 godu," *Voprosy istorii*, 1946, no. 1, pp. 86–104.

Veselovskii, S. B., *Issledovaniia po istorii oprichniny*, Moscow, Akademiia nauk SSSR, 1963.

Veselovskii, S. B., *Issledovaniia po istorii klassa sluzhilykh zemlevladel'tsev*, Moscow, Nauka, 1969.

Vilinbakhov, G. V., "Vsadnik russkogo gerba," *Trudy Gosudarstvennogo Ermitazha*, vol. 21, *Numismatika*, vol. 5, Leningrad, 1981, pp. 117–122.

Vipper [Wipper], R. Iu., *Ivan Grozny*, trans. J. Fineberg, Moscow, Foreign Languages Publishing House, 1947.

Vladimirskii-Budanov, M. F., *Obzor istorii russkogo prava*, 3rd edn, Kiev, N. Ia. Ogloblin, 1900.

Vladimirtsov, B. Ia., *Obshchestvennyi stroi Mongolov. Mongol'skii kochevoi feodalizm*, Leningrad, Akademiia nauk SSSR, 1934.

Vodoff, Wladimir, "Remarques sur la valeur du term 'tsar' appliqué aux princes russes avant le milieu du XVᵉ siècle," *Oxford Slavonic Papers*, vol. 11, 1978, pp. 1–41; reprinted in *Princes et principautés russes*, item 3.

Vodoff, Wladimir, "La titulature princière en Russie du XIᵉ au début du XVIᵉ siècle: Questions de critique des sources," *Jahrbücher für Geschichte Osteuropas*, vol. 35, 1987, pp. 1–35; reprinted in *Princes et principautés russes*, item 1.

Vodoff, Wladimir, *Princes et principautés russes (Xᵉ–XVIIᵉ siècles)*, Northampton, Variorum, 1989.

Vodoff, Wladimir, "Le titre *tsar'* dans la Russie du nord-est vers 1440–1460 et la tradition littéraire vieux-russe," *Studia Slavic-Byzantina et Mediaevalia Europensia*, vol. 1, 1989, pp. 54–60.

Vodovozov, N. V., "Povest' o razorenii Riazanii Batyem," *Uchenye zapiski Moskovskogo gorodskogo pedagogicheskogo instituta imeni V. P. Potemkina. Kafedra russkoi literatury*, vol. 18, no. 5, 1956, pp. 3–37.

Vogelin, Eric, "The Mongol Orders of Submission to European Powers, 1245–1255," *Byzantion*, vol. 15, 1940–1941, pp. 378–413.

Voronin, N. N. *Zodchestva severo-vostochnoi Rusi XII–XV vekov*, 2 vols., Moscow, Akademiia nauk SSSR, 1961–1962.

Vryonis, Speros, Jr., *The Decline of Medieval Hellenism in Asia Minor and the Process of Islamization from the Eleventh Through the Fifteenth Century*, Berkeley, University of California Press, 1971.

Waugh, Daniel Clarke, *The Great Turkes' Defiance: On the History of the Apocryphal Correspondence of the Ottoman Sultan in Its Muscovite and Russian Variants*, Columbus, OH, Slavica, 1978.

Weinstein, Fred, *History and Theory After the Fall*, University of Chicago Press, 1990.

Westwood, J. N., *Endurance and Endeavor: Russian History 1812–1980*, 2nd edn, Oxford University Press, 1981.

White, Lynn, [Jr.], "Technology and Invention in the Middle Ages," *Speculum*, vol. 15, 1940, pp. 141–159; reprinted (without "A Note on the Sources") in Lynn White, Jr., *Medieval Religion and Technology*, Berkeley, University of California Press, 1978, pp. 1–22.

Wieczynski, Joseph L., "Archbishop Gennadius and the West: the Impact of Catholic Ideas upon the Church of Novgorod," *Canadian–American Slavic Studies*, vol. 6, 1972, pp. 374–389.

Wittfogel, Karl A., "Russia and the East: a Comparison and Contrast," *Slavic Review*, vol. 22, 1963, pp. 627–642; reprinted in *Development of the USSR*, pp. 323–339.

Wittfogel, Karl A., "Reply," *Slavic Review*, vol. 22, 1963, pp. 656–662. Reprinted in *Development of the USSR*, pp. 352–358.

Wittfogel, Karl, *Oriental Despotism: a Comparative Study of Total Power*, New York, Vintage, 1981.

Women in the Muslim World, ed. Nikki Keddie and Lois Beck, Cambridge, MA, Harvard University Press, 1978.

Yanov, Alexander, *The Origins of Autocracy: Ivan the Terrible in Russian History*, Berkeley, University of California Press, 1981.

Zdan, Michael B., "The Dependence of Halych-Volyn' Rus' on the Golden Horde," *Slavonic and East European Review*, vol. 35, 1956/57, pp. 505–522.

Zelenin, D. K., *Russkaia sokha. Ee istoriia i vidy*, Viatka, 1907.

Zenkovsky, Serge A., "Introduction," in *The Nikonian Chronicle*, 5 vols., trans. Serge A. Zenkovsky, Princeton, NJ, Kingston Press, Darwin Press, 1984–1989, vol. 1, pp. xiii–lxxxi.

Zhmakin, V., "Odin iz literaturnykh pamiatnikov XVI veka," *Zhurnal Ministerstva narodnogo prosveshcheniia*, part 221, 1882, June, Otdel nauk, pp. 235–248.

Zimin, A. A., "Narodnye dvizheniia 20-kh godov XIV veka i likvidatsiia sistemy baskachestva v severo-vostochnoi Rusi," *Izvestiia Akademii nauk SSSR. Seriia istorii i filosofii*, vol. 9, 1952, pp. 61–65.

Zimin, A. A., "O politicheskoi doktrine Iosifa Volotskogo," *TODRL*, vol. 9, 1953, pp. 159–177.

Zimin, A. A., review of R. P. Dmitrieva, *Skazanie o kniaz'iakh vladimirskikh*, in *Istoricheskii arkhiv*, 1956, no. 3, pp. 235–238.

Zimin, A. A., *I. S. Peresvetov i ego sovremenniki*, Moscow, Akademiia nauk SSSR, 1958.

Zimin, A. A., *Oprichnina Ivan Groznogo*, Moscow, Mysl', 1964.

Zimin, A. A., "'Skazanie o Mamaevom poboishche' i 'Zadonshchina'," *Arkheograficheskii ezhegodnik za 1967 g.*, Moscow, Nauka, 1969, pp. 41–58.

Zimin, A. A., "Ivan Groznyi i Simeon Bekbulatovich v 1575 g.," *Uchenye zapiski Kazanskogo gosudarstvennogo pedagogicheskogo universiteta*, vyp. 80: *Iz istorii Tatarii*, vol. 4, 1970, pp. 141–163.

Zimin, A. A., "Antichnye motivy v russkoi publitsistike kontsa XV v.," *Feodal'naia Rossiia vo vsemirno-istoricheskom protsesse. Sbornik statei, posviashchennyi L'vy Vladimirovichu Cherepninu*, ed. V. T. Pashuto et al.,

Moscow, Nauka, 1972, pp. 128–138; parts reprinted in Zimin, *Rossiia na rubezhe XV–XVI stoletii*, pp. 152–159.

Zimin, A. A., *Rossiia na rubezhe XV–XVI stoletii (Ocherk sotsial'no-politicheskoi istorii)*, Moscow, Nauka, 1982.

Zimin, A. A., "V bor'be za Moskvu (vtoraia chetvert' XV stoletiia)," *Voprosy istorii*, 1982, no. 12, pp. 75–90.

Žužek, P. Ivan, *Kormčaja kniga: Studies on the Chief Code of Russian Canon Law*, in *Orientalia Christiana Analecta*, no. 168, Rome, 1964.

Zyzykin, M. V., *Patriarch Nikon. Ego gosudarstvennye i kanonicheskie idei*, 3 vols., Warsaw, Sinodal'naia tipografiia, 1931–1938.

Index